WESTMAR COLLEGE

W9-BKE-386

LAWRENCE HENRY GIPSON

AUTHOR

JARED INGERSOLL: A STUDY OF AMERICAN LOYALISM IN RELATION TO BRITISH COLONIAL GOVERNMENT

STUDIES IN CONNECTICUT COLONIAL TAXATION

THE MORAVIAN INDIAN MISSION ON WHITE RIVER

LEWIS EVANS

THE COMING OF THE REVOLUTION, 1763–1775

THE BRITISH EMPIRE BEFORE THE AMERICAN REVOLUTION

VOLUME I. THE BRITISH ISLES AND THE AMERICAN COLONIES: GREAT BRITAIN AND IRELAND, 1748–1754 (revised and reset, 1958)

VOLUME II. THE BRITISH ISLES AND THE AMERICAN COLONIES: THE SOUTHERN PLANTATIONS, 1748–1754 (revised and reset, 1960)

VOLUME III. THE BRITISH ISLES AND THE AMERICAN COLONIES: THE NORTHERN PLANTATIONS, 1748–1754 (revised and reset, 1960)

VOLUME IV. ZONES OF INTERNATIONAL FRICTION: NORTH AMERICA, SOUTH OF THE GREAT LAKES REGION, 1748–1754

VOLUME V. ZONES OF INTERNATIONAL FRICTION: THE GREAT LAKES FRONTIER, CANADA, THE WEST INDIES, INDIA, 1748–1754

VOLUME VI. THE GREAT WAR FOR THE EMPIRE: THE YEARS OF DEFEAT, 1754–1757

VOLUME VII. THE GREAT WAR FOR THE EMPIRE: THE VICTORIOUS YEARS, 1758–1760

VOLUME VIII. THE GREAT WAR FOR THE EMPIRE: THE CULMINATION, 1760–1763

VOLUME IX. THE TRIUMPHANT EMPIRE: NEW RESPONSIBILITIES WITHIN THE ENLARGED EMPIRE, 1763–1766

VOLUME X. THE TRIUMPHANT EMPIRE: THUNDER CLOUDS ON THE AMERICAN HORIZON, 1763–1766 (in preparation)

"Every considerable library on American and British history will require Mr. Gipson's volumes as an indispensable work of reference, and most readers will be so captivated by the lively reports of this intelligent and humane historical surveyor as to look forward with impatience to future volumes."

SAMUEL ELIOT MORISON

THE BRITISH EMPIRE

BEFORE THE AMERICAN REVOLUTION

VOLUME III

THE BRITISH ISLES AND THE AMERICAN COLONIES:

THE NORTHERN PLANTATIONS

1748–1754

THE BRITISH EMPIRE
BEFORE THE AMERICAN REVOLUTION
VOLUME III

THE BRITISH ISLES

AND

THE AMERICAN COLONIES

THE NORTHERN PLANTATIONS
1748–1754

BY

LAWRENCE HENRY GIPSON

MCMLX
ALFRED A. KNOPF
NEW YORK

942.072
G449
v.3

DA
500
.G5

L. C. catalog card number: 58–9670

© *Alfred A. Knopf, Inc., 1960*

THIS IS A BORZOI BOOK,
PUBLISHED BY ALFRED A. KNOPF, INC.

COPYRIGHT 1936, 1960 BY ALFRED A. KNOPF, INC.
All rights reserved. No part of this book may be reproduced in any form without permission in writing from the publisher, except by a reviewer who may quote brief passages and reproduce not more than three illustrations in a review to be printed in a magazine or newspaper. Manufactured in the United States of America. Published simultaneously in Canada by McClelland & Stewart, Ltd.

FIRST BORZOI EDITION

Originally published in 1936 by The Caxton Printers, Ltd., Caldwell, Idaho.

This edition completely revised, reset, and printed from new plates.

65054

TO THE MEMORY *of* ALBERT EUGENE GIPSON *and Lina Maria West Gipson, my parents, who helped in the building of the West as did their ancestors in the building of colonial New England.*

Preface

As was indicated in the prefaces of the revised edition of Volume I of this series, published in 1958, and of the revised edition of Volume II, published earlier in 1960, the first edition of all three volumes, including the present one, appeared simultaneously in 1936 under the general title *Provincial Characteristics and Sectional Tendencies in the Era Preceding the American Crisis, 1748–1754*, as the first book in my work *The British Empire before the American Revolution*. Not only have the new editions of these three volumes been printed separately, but the book title to cover them has been changed to *The British Isles and the American Colonies, 1748–1754*, as one more clearly descriptive of their contents.

In Volume I chief attention was given to a description of civilization in the British Isles during the 1740's and early 1750's, with emphasis upon the more important constitutional, political, economic, and social aspects of the period. In Volume II colonial developments during these same years in the more southern colonies, as well as in the British West Indies, the Bermudas, and the Bahamas, are stressed, supplemented by chapters on the tobacco trade, the sugar trade, and the slave trade. These southern colonies had certain things in common. One was that the use of slave labour, or at least of white indentured labour, was characteristic of their agricultural economy and was considered to be essential to it. Again, the economy was of the plantation type, at least in the earlier tidewater area. Finally, outside of the Bermudas, the colonies gave their chief attention to the production of some one staple export. Exceptions to these generalizations were to be found, especially in the case of the less densely populated back-country areas of all the southern colonies, where the emphasis was on general farming and stock-raising in addition to the Indian trade in deerskins.

The present volume is concerned with the older northern continental colonies. It therefore does not include Nova Scotia, a colony demanding particular consideration in a later volume of the series, but does comprehend Newfoundland and the Hudson Bay country, although the latter was not considered to be a colony in the technical sense in which this term was used during the period under consideration. Among the northern colonies — excluding Newfoundland, where at this period the cultivation of the land had little, if any, significance — general farming, rather than the plantation system, for the production of a variety of export staples, was the occupation of most of the inhabitants living outside the larger towns. In this northern area great stress was also placed on the processing of commodities grown on the farms: the milling of wheat and corn, the making of ship biscuits from the flour, and the barrelling of beef and pork, or on the processing of imported commodities, such as the distillation of rum from molasses.

From the year 1750 the production of iron and steel and the fabrication of many articles from these metals had become a major interest in a number of colonies, particularly in Pennsylvania. Of equal importance was shipbuilding, an activity centred in New England. As barrel staves and headings, furniture, and domestic appliances were made of wood, lumbering gave employment to thousands of people; so also did the fisheries and the carrying trade. With production limited to one or two export staples, uniformity had become the keynote of the economy of the southern continental colonies and of the British West Indies. By contrast, diversity of occupations typified the northern colonies. These aspects of the Northern Plantations, together with some that are cultural and political, will be considered in this volume. It should be noted that no attention has been given to Indian relations in this volume or the one that precedes it. By reason of their vast importance and the exent to which they involved foreign policy, it seemed best to reserve treatment of Indian matters to Volumes IV and V of the series, which deal with the frontiers of the Empire during the same period, 1748-1754. Two additions have been made to the contents of this revised edition of Volume III: the inclusion of a chapter on the Lower Counties on the Delaware and a concluding chapter on the British Colonial System in the middle of the eighteenth century. As was true of Volume II, no effort has been made to present all institutional aspects of every colony. Rather than overburden the reader with details, I have emphasized only the more pertinent aspects best suited to illuminate the history of the period in each.

The material for writing the original volume and for making this revision has been gathered from numerous depositories, among which are: the London Public Record Office, the British Museum, the Library of Congress, the Clements Library at Ann Arbor, the Huntington Library at San Marino, California, the Sterling Library at Yale, the Widener Library at Harvard, the John Carter Brown Library at Brown University, the Boston Public Library, the library of the New Hampshire Historical Society at Concord, the Connecticut State Library and the library of the Connecticut Historical Society at Hartford, the New York State Library and Archives at Albany, the library of the New York Historical Society, the Columbia University Library and the Public Library in New York, the library of the Historical Society of Pennsylvania and the Library Company in Philadelphia, the Pennsylvania Archives and the State Library at Harrisburg, and, finally, the transcripts on deposit at Memorial University, St. John's, Newfoundland, made from the original documents relating to Newfoundland, in the Public Record Office. In this connection I must mention the aid that I have received through the Hudson's Bay Record Society publications, under the editorship of Professor E. E. Rich, Master of St. Catherine's College, Cambridge.

For financial aid in the preparation of the original edition of this volume and the present revised edition I am indebted to the American Council of Learned Societies, the American Social Science Research Council, the Rockefeller Foundation, the Lehigh Institute of Research, and Lehigh University. Lehigh University has also generously provided me with the facilities for carrying on my activities at the Library since my retirement as an active member of the staff in 1952. In this connection I desire particularly to express my appreciation to President Martin D. Whitaker, Provost Harvey A. Neville, and Librarian James D. Mack for exerting much effort in behalf of my project. My labours have been greatly lightened by Mrs. Jere Knight, my full-time Research Assistant, and by the many years of valuable service of my Secretary, Mrs. Geraldine E. Scudner. In checking data and in a variety of other ways, the part-time work of the following Lehigh University graduate students has been of considerable value: Michael H. Banks, Geraint N. D. Evans, Ernest B. Fricke, and James R. Smith. To my brother, James H. Gipson, president of the Caxton Printers, which brought out the first edition of this volume, and to Alfred A. Knopf, my present publisher, as well as to Jeannette Reed Gipson, my wife, who has done so much to improve the quality of the series, I must express my gratitude.

A final word of explanation should be given. On the recommendation of Mr. Knopf, who took over the publication of the series in 1939, I changed to the English accepted usage in spelling, rather than the American. In the revised editions of the first three volumes this difference will be found, therefore, upon comparison with the first editions.

LAWRENCE HENRY GIPSON

The Library
Lehigh University
Bethlehem, Pennsylvania
April 12, 1960

Contents

Chapter I

THE HEART OF NEW ENGLAND

The Northern Colonies characterized in contrast with the British
colonies to the South   3
Agricultural aspects   3
Diversified farming rather than production of plantation staples   4
Industrial aspects   4
Domestic manufactures in the north threaten the British mer-
cantilist system of trade   4

Massachusetts Bay — the heart of New England   4
Boston as the commercial metropolis of North America in 1750   4
Contemporary descriptions and social aspects of the town   4
The town as a seaport and shipbuilding centre   6
Commerce of the port   6
Multifarious activities of its merchants, typified   7
The balance of trade   8
Value of exports and imports compared to other colonies   9
Boston as an entrepôt for a vast area   10

The province's financial reorganization in 1750   10
Required by the inflation of the 1730's   11
Need for a sound money system   11
The land-bank scheme, 1739   11
Colonial acceptance of parliamentary regulation   11
Thomas Hutchinson's plan for redemption of bills of credit   12
The province becomes a hard-money colony   13

The economy of the province at mid-century   14
Population estimates, 1750   14
Chief occupations   14
Occupational distribution figures   15
Need to import subsistence food staples for seafaring and
urban population   15

Regional areas of agricultural production   15
Chief industrial products   16
    Relative importance of iron and ironwares   16
    Importance of the rum industry   16

Rum as the foundation of prosperity in 1750   16
    Importance of the product to the labourers in lumbering, ship-
        building, and the fisheries   16
    The product used as the basis for commerce with other colonies
        and other parts of the Empire   16
    Its use in the Indian and slave trades   16
    The sale of "refuse" fish in the West Indies to obtain molasses 16

The fisheries   17
    Absorption of the fishing grounds of the Gulf of Maine   17
    The Canso fisheries   17
    Growth in importance of the cod and mackerel fisheries by 1750   17
        Activities of Peter Faneuil   18
    Increased interest in Nova Scotia and Newfoundland fishing
        grounds   18
    Whale-fishing activities   18

Characteristics of the men of Massachusetts Bay   18
    Aggressiveness of the seamen   18
    Pioneering instincts of the landmen   18
        Creation of new settlements   18
        Threats to the boundaries of neighbouring colonies   19

Land policy of the province   19
    Early policy of the provincial government   19
        Grants limited to organized groups   19
    Modifications by 1750   19
        Permit individual grants   19
        Land speculation results   19
        Community solidarity diminishes   19
    Town-building processes exemplified in Penacook   20

The Congregational Establishment in 1750   21
    Comparison with its position in 1650   21
    Influences of the expanding frontier and other forces   21
    The earlier concessions of the Halfway Covenant, 1657 and 1662   21
        Modifications and innovations of individual pastors   22
    The Charter of 1691 and the Establishment   22
    Rationalistic aftermath of 1692 witchcraft terror   22

Exemptions gained by the Anglicans, Quakers, and Baptists 22
Legal compulsions for other nonconformists remain 22
Additional weakening forces of latitudinarianism and Arminianism 23
Efforts of the Church to restore its prestige 23
   Jonathan Edwards and the Great Awakening 23
   Ultimate effects of the revival 25

The press in Massachusetts Bay 26
Developments of newspapers, 1690–1750 26
Its secular tendencies 26
   Its influence destined to rival the pulpit 26

Higher education in the province 27
   The influence of Harvard College 27
   Spread of the humanistic enlightenment 28

The provincial government 28
Withdrawal of the original charter and the Andros regime 28
The Charter of 1691 28
   The territorial limits of the province after 1691 29
Governor, Lieutenant Governor, and Secretary as Crown
     appointees 29
Council of twenty-eight assistants 29
The Great and General Court of Assembly 29
   Powers of the Assembly 29
   The royal Governor's control of legislation 30
A normal royal-colony type of government 31
   Legislation submitted to the Privy Council 31
   Governor acts under commission and royal instructions 31
   Exception in the selection of the twenty-eight councillors by
     the Assembly 31
Protection of the province's white pine provided in the charter 31
Town representation 31
   Characteristics of the House of Representatives 31
   Leadership by an élite 32
   Discriminatory statutes in 1750 32

The administration of Governor William Shirley 33
Shirley's early years in the province 33
   Concern for Nova Scotia and the Canso fisheries, 1744 33
   Relations with the northern Indians 34
   Advocate of the reduction of Louisbourg 34
   Plans for overthrow of French power in Canada 34
   His efforts rewarded by knighthood 34

Appointed a member of the Anglo-French Commission   34
Excellent relationship between the Governor and the people of
    the province   35
Shirley seeks a new appointment in 1750   35
Lieutenant Governor Spencer Phips in temporary control in 1750 35
    Complaints of the Board of Trade regarding his laxity   35

The relationship of Massachusetts Bay to the Crown in 1750   35
Its degree of loyalty   36
Pride in its able and popular royal Governor   36
Growing understanding of British religious attitudes   36
Its devotion to the King expressed by the Assembly   36
Extent of self-sufficiency attained by 1750   37
    Pride in the superiority of the province   37

CHAPTER II

IN THE WHITE-PINE BELT

White pine—New Hampshire's chief resource   39
Its production in the early part of the eighteenth century   39
    The wastefulness of lumbering methods   39
    Great demand by England for ship timbers   40
Regulations governing its preservation and utilization   41
    Appointment and functions of the Surveyor General of the
        King's Woods   41
    Parliamentary legislation under Queen Anne and her successors 41
    Restrictions and penalties for preservation of the trees   41
    Bounties granted to ensure exportation to England   42
    Provincial legislation   42

Decline in importance of New Hampshire's lumber industry   43
Governor Belcher's report in 1737   43
Other regions offer better facilities   43
Relationship of the Wentworth family to the masting trade   43
Apprehensions of leaders in the lumber industry for the future 44
    Link between prosperity and the masting trade   44

The disputed boundaries of New Hampshire   44
Governor Belcher's report on the reputed boundaries   44
    The lack of boundary delimitation in the Governor's com-
        mission   45
    The Governor's desire for a union with Massachusetts Bay   45

The dispute is referred to a commission, 1737   45
  The commission's report on the eastern limits of the province   45
The problem of the southern boundary   45
  The power of the Wentworths and the London agent   45
The Privy Council's decision, 1741   45
  In favour of New Hampshire   46

The question of the support of Fort Dummer   46
  The earlier purpose of the fort in the defence of Massachusetts
    Bay frontiers   46
Reluctance of New Hampshiremen to support the garrison   46
  Massachusetts Bay's interim garrisoning of the fort   46

The problem of ownership of unappropriated lands, 1750   46
  Questioned validity of early proprietorial claims   47
    Captain John Mason's charters validated in 1675   47
  Massachusetts Bay assumes responsibility for protecting in-
    habitants   47
New Hampshire's establishment as a royal colony, 1678   47
Continued disputes, rivalries, and complications over land owner-
    ship   47
Summary of claims to ungranted lands, 1750   47
  Heritage of confusion in land titles   48

Governor Benning Wentworth's administration of New Hampshire   48
  His attitude toward the newly acquired region   48
    Favours assuming responsibility for defence of the western
      frontier   48
    Supports representation in the Assembly of the western un-
      privileged towns   48
    Assembly opposes Governor's usurpation of its rights   48
    Wentworth's appeal to the Crown wins a favourable decision,
      1748   48
    Continued opposition by the Assembly   48
  Harmony restored within the provincial government   49
    Realization of the value of the western lands produces new
      attitudes   49
    New members seated by 1752   49
    New Hampshire troops posted at Fort Dummer and Keene   49

Wentworth's project for exploitation of the upper Connecticut
    Valley   49
  His steps toward this end   49
    Secures Crown commission to grant lands on a quit-rent basis,

1748   49
  Claims lands to the westward of the Connecticut River, 1749   50
  Makes grants in territory claimed by New York, 1751   50
  Reserves land acreage for himself in lieu of fees   50
Aggressiveness of New Hampshire under Wentworth alarms
  New York   50

New Hampshire at mid-century   51
  Population figures   51
  Occupational and religious trends   51
    Commercial and farming activities   51
    The influence of Whitefield's preaching   51

The dominant position of the Wentworth family in New Hamp-
  shire affairs   51
  Heritable traits of money-making and power   51
  Political nepotism and the government of the province   51
    The regime of Lieutenant Governor John Wentworth   51
    Government posts held by Benning Wentworth's relatives   52
    Futile attempts to displace Wentworth in the 1740's   52
  The influence of the Wentworths on the rise of Portsmouth   52

Importance of Portsmouth as a seaport, 1750   52
  An entrepôt for lumber commerce   52
    Hub of the masting trade   52
  Importance as a ship-building centre   53
  Social distinctions in the town resulting from opulence   53

CHAPTER III

A LIBERTARIAN COMMONWEALTH

Rhode Island's characteristics   54
  Its religious background   54
    Seventeenth-century origins   54
  Principle of soul liberty, except for Catholics   55
    Legal origins of the exception   55
  Tradition of toleration   55
    Contrasted with Massachusetts Bay and Connecticut   56
    Position of the Jews of Newport   56

Natural resources of the colony   56
  Agricultural production   56
    Export of food surpluses   56

Land units in the rural areas 57
  Small farms with diversified products 57
  The modified plantation system of the Narragansett Bay area 57
  Dairies and animal husbandry, the rule 57
  Utilization of slave labour 57
  Rapid increase of population in the middle of the century 57
  An indication of favourable conditions 57

Rhode Island's expanding foreign trade, 1750 58
  Great increase of shipping in the early part of the century 58
  Results of the enterprise of the men of Newport and Providence 58
  The colony's ports as entrepôts for interior Massachusetts Bay
    products 58
  The great commercial families 58
  Newport's merchant princes 58
  The Browns of Providence 58
  The sugar-and-molasses trade 59
  Vastness of the traffic with the West Indies 59
  Protests of the British West India planters against French com-
    petition 59

The Sugar Act of 1733 and the contraband trade 59
  Objections to the high duties imposed by the Act 59
  The illicit trading with the French sugar islands 59
  Jamaicans protest the commerce of Rhode Island with foreign
    sugar islands 60
  Smuggling activities become widespread 60
  The case of the sloop *Jupiter* 60
  The trading towns oppose compliance with the Act 61
  Government efforts to end smuggling 62

The trade pattern of Rhode Island commerce, 1750 62
  Importation of molasses from the West Indies 62
  Distillation of rum from molasses 62
  Exportation of rum to Africa 63
  Carrying of slaves from Africa to the West Indies 63

Rhode Island as the leading slaving colony 63
  Large number of vessels engaged in the slave trade 63
  Examples of Rhode Island slaver activities 64
  Disposal of slaves in the British or Spanish West Indies 65
  Use of proceeds to purchase French sugar-island products 65

Newport as a leading eighteenth-century seaport 66

Extent of its commercial activities   66
    Andrew Burnaby's description   66
    A New England cultural centre   66
    A summer resort for southern planters   67

Political sectionalism in the colony   67
    Newport's commercial interests supported by the region of the
        aristocratic Narragansett planters   67
    The northern agricultural population supports the interests of the
        Providence merchants   67

Government of Rhode Island   67
    Based upon the Charter of 1663   67
    Control exercised by freemen   67
        Election of deputies to the General Assembly   67
        Annual election court   67
    The appointment of officeholders by the Assembly   67
    Changes in qualifications for freemanship   68
        Restrictions on the franchise, 1724, 1730, and 1746   68
        Inflation as a cause of change   68
        Preferential treatment of privileged individuals   68

Government loans or "banks," 1715–1750   68
    Granting of loans on real estate   68
    Allocation of loans to the towns   68
        An important barrier to acquiring freemanship   68
        Results in virtual government financing of private industry   68
        Percentage of freemen "voters" against total population   69

The New England currency problems at mid-century   69
    Rhode Island typical of the confusion involved   69
    Failure to redeem the "bank" loans, 1728–1750   69
        Extension of repayment dates   69
    Bills of credit replace taxation, 1710–1747   70
        Volume of unredeemed bills creates depreciation   70
    Board of Trade queries the dangers of Rhode Island's monetary
        practices   71
    Governor Ward's defence of the system   71
    Dangers become apparent too late   71
    Comparison between paper-money policies of the colony and
        those of the Massachusetts Bay and Connecticut   71
    Effects of depreciation upon Rhode Island commerce   71
        Petition of the leading merchants, 1750   71
        Repercussions from British merchants trading with the colony   72

Board of Trade intervention through the colonial agent in London 72
Threat of no reimbursement of war expenses 72
The Rhode Island Assembly is not intimidated 72

Parliament takes a hand in the New England currency problem 72
The passing of the Currency Act of 1751 72
Restricts the issuance of bills of credit 72
Directed primarily against Rhode Island 72

CHAPTER IV

A PURITAN STRONGHOLD

Characteristics of the government of Connecticut 74
Most democratically constituted of all British colonies 74
A corporate colony with an unaltered charter 74
Liberal franchise provisions 74
Governor possesses little power 74
Privy Council assent not required on its laws 74
Without a fixed governmental centre 74
Lacks important direct commerce with Britain 74
No quit-rents levied 75
No ungranted lands remain after 1737 75
Widespread urban settlements 75
Equal distribution of wealth 75

Economic and social structure of Connecticut, 1750 75
Population distribution and increase 75
Farming and stockraising, the chief occupations 75
Agriculture as a mainstay leads to search for new lands 76
Creation of the Susquehanna Company, 1753 76
Production of export staples 76
Intercolonial demands 76
Nature of trade with the West Indies 76
Shipping of the colony 76
Illicit commerce 77
Industrial developments 77
Iron and steel interests 77

Regionalism within the colony 77
Geographical division by the Connecticut River 77
Eastern Connecticut's commercial and cultural affiliations with
Massachusetts Bay 77

Western Connecticut's commercial outlet through New York 77
Common ties between the entire colony and Massachusetts Bay 78

The last of the Puritan commonwealths 78
Puritanism as a small-town movement 78
Common religious ties 78
Social solidarity produces a conservative élite 78
Uniformity of thought and action expressed in legal regulations 79
Organs of social solidarity 79
The town meeting house as a centre for religious and secular activity 79
Congregational Church establishment 79
The church communion as the town's conscience 79
Limitations upon membership in the communion 79
The disrupting effect of the Great Awakening 79
Persecution of the Separatists in the 1740's 80
The ecclesiastical society 80
Disappearance of its all-inclusiveness after 1746 81
The freeman's meetings 81
Qualifications for freemanship 81
Political privileges and responsibilities 82
The freemen, a minority in the towns 82

Machinery of government 82
The election by freemen of deputies to the Assembly 83
The balloting for the Governor and other colonial offices 83
The conservatism of the freemen as a group 83
Their influence as a propertied element 83
The town proprietors as a distinct group 84
The Law of 1703 distinguishing between town proprietors and other inhabitants 84
The town meeting 85
Its scope 85
Limitations on inhabitants according to the law of 1750 85
Qualifications for participation in town meeting 86
Religious nonconformity not a disqualification 86
The filling of the multiplicity of town offices 86
The infinite variety of local interests considered 87
Its value as a political school 88
A stronghold of conservative influence 88
Train bands 88
A factor in the political life of the colony 88

Exemption of the more responsible classes from this military
    service   88
The solidarity of enrolled men and their self-appointed officers   88
Control of the bands by nonfreemen elements   89
The strong inclination toward radicalism among the men   89

The central government   89
  The Governor and his Assistants   89
  The deputies to the General Assembly   89
    Representation by township   89
  Terms of office and other conditions of public service   89

Units of local government larger than towns   89
  The probate districts   89
    A probate court in each   89
  The counties   89
    Appointment of their officials   89
    Jurisdiction of the county courts   90
  The superior courts of judicature   90

The laws of Connecticut   90
  Comparison between the codes of 1650 and 1750   90
    Laws providing capital offences in 1650   91
    Changes in punishments in the 1750 code   91
    The persistence of Sabbitarianism   92
  Reflection in the laws of deep solicitude for moral and spiritual
    welfare   93
  They demonstrate interdependence of the people and a sense
    of collective responsibility for individual welfare   93

Evidence of a transition from rigid Puritanism   94
  The controversies between the Old Lights and New Lights   94
  Effects of eighteenth-century wars upon the colony's religious
    viewpoints   95
  Influence of the press   95
  Comparison between the code of 1750 and that of 1784   95
    Disappearance of many old capital laws   95
  Waning universality of the Congregational Establishment in the
    colony   95

Relationship of Connecticut to the mother country   96
  Effects of the preservation of its charter   96
  Its jealousy toward any encroachment by Crown or Parliament   96

Connecticut's London agency   96
    Its history from 1690   96
    The colony's effective use of the agency   96
        Leading agents and their accomplishments   96
        The crowning achievement of the agency: the preservation of
            the charter   100
    The freedom of the colony to act according to its own light   100
        Lack of hindrance from the mother country   100
        The colony characterized, 1750   101

CHAPTER V

IN THE REGION OF THE OLD PATROONSHIPS

The land system of New York   102
    The great patents and manors in 1750   102
        To the east of the Hudson   102
        Along the New Jersey border   103
        The Hardenburgh patent   103
    History of the land grants   103
        The patroonships   103
        The grants under Fletcher, Nanfan, and Cornbury   104
        Vague terms of the grants   105

Boundary disputes   105
    The New Hampshire claims   105
        Privy Council decides in favour of New York   106
        The bitterness of the dispute   106
    The Massachusetts Bay claims   106
        Massachusetts Bay people intrude into the Livingston Manor   106
        Incidents ensue between the two colonies, 1750–1755   107
        The dispute typifies the struggle between two different land-
            holding systems   107
    The New Jersey conflicting claims   108
        Exorbitant nature of the New York patents in Orange County   108
        The home government takes steps to improve the situation,
            1753   109

Political and social life of the province   109
    Influential position of the great landholders and merchants   109
        Lords of the manors constitute an aristocracy   109
        Political control by great landowners aided through the plural
            voting system   109

Factions within the aristocratic élite 110
 The de Lancey faction 110
 The Livingston faction 110
Reasons for political control by the élite despite internecine differences 110
Franchise qualifications 111
 Assembly elections 111
Effects of aristocratic policies upon settlement and utilization of land 112
 Movement of poor farmers out of the province 112
 The Palatine German trek into Pennsylvania 113
 Attitude of other colonials toward New York's land policies 113
Slow growth of the population at mid-century 113
Exploitation of the manors 114
 Tenantry system the rule 114
 Use of slave or indentured labour on some 114

New York City in the 1750's 115
 The capital, and social and commercial centre of the province 115
 Peter Kalm's description 115
 Importance as a seaport 115
 Distribution centre for western Connecticut and eastern New Jersey 116

Economic life of the province 116
 Low value of goods imported from Great Britain 116
 Small number of vessels owned by provincial maritime interests 116
 Dependency upon mother country in commercial relations 117
 Slow development of industry 117
 Beginnings of various industries 117

The Indian fur trade 118
 Comparatively few white men engaged in the trade 118
 Rivalry of the New York traders with those from Pennsylvania 118
 Albany as a great fur-trading centre 118
 Description of the town in 1750 118
 Oswego, the English fur outpost 119
 Dutch trading methods 119
 Peter Kalm's indictment of the Albany traders 119

The government of the province in 1750 120
 The administration of Governor George Clinton 120
 Early influence of James de Lancey upon Clinton 120

Clinton's concessions to the Assembly and surrender of control of public finances — 120

The Assembly's administration of the province — 121

Maintains its own London agent — 121

Exercises control in many phases of government — 121

Clinton's repudiation of de Lancey in favour of Cadwallader Colden — 122

Colden as a distinguished colonial — 122

Colden and the Assembly — 122

Tries to intervene in the conspiracy against the Governor — 122

Defends the Governor's position — 123

Clinton fails to win the Lieutenant Governorship for Colden — 123

He is forced by the hostile Assembly to yield under financial pressure — 124

Clinton's struggle with the Assembly finally results in action by the Board of Trade — 124

Provisions made in the instructions for the new Governor — 124

Sir Danvers Osborn is appointed to succeed Clinton — 125

His death by suicide — 125

The triumph of de Lancey — 125

CHAPTER VI

PLOUGHMEN OF THE JERSEYS

New Jersey characterized at mid-century — 126

Population and economic interests — 126

Importance of diversified farming and lumbering — 126

Nature of the land dictates population distribution — 127

Export commodities — 127

Lack of direct commerce with mother country — 127

Governor Belcher on the province's trade — 127

Differentiation between East and West New Jersey — 127

Role of New York and Philadelphia as respective entrepôts — 127

Distinctive money standards of each — 128

Favourable living conditions within the province in the middle of the century — 128

Absence of menace by foreign foes or hostile Indians — 128

Lack of taxation to support the government — 128

No taxes raised since 1732 — 128

High yield of bills of credit put out on loan — 128

Soundness of public finance   128

New Jersey and the legal-tender issue   128
  Early history of the province's system of finance   129
  Growing opposition in England to provincial paper money   129
    Board of Trade's instructions to colonial governors   130
  The currency bill of 1742   131
    Opposition of Governor Morris and his Council to the bill   131
    Attempt of the representatives to bribe the Governor   132

Governor Belcher and the province finances   132
  His determination to work harmoniously with the Assembly   132
  Signs the paper-money bill in 1748   133
    The bill before the Board of Trade in 1749   133
    Struggle between creditor and debtor groups   133
    The stand of the province's London agents on the bill   133
    Board of Trade recommends disallowance of the bill   134
  Anarchic political conditions in the province in 1753   134
    Demands of New Jersey lower house for bills of credit persist
      until 1757   135
    Involvement in war changes the situation   135
  New instructions on money bills upon Governor Bernard's suc-
      cession to the administration of the province   135
    Issuance of paper money permitted as a war measure   136
  Summarization of the New Jersey paper-money problem   136

Lack of provincial solidarity in New Jersey   136
  Survival of the old divisions of East and West New Jersey   136
    New England influences in East New Jersey   137
    The Scots and Presbyterianism in the East   137
    The religious and political influence of the Quakers in West
      New Jersey   137
  No provincial capital possible   137
    Alternate meeting places of the General Assembly   138
    The balance of county representation in each section   138
  Powerful individualism stems from religious influences   138
  The breakdown of political authority does not prevent economic
      prosperity   138

The New Jersey Proprietors and the ungranted lands   138
  The coming of the Ulster Scots   139
    Their tendency to squat upon ungranted lands   139
    The securing of Indian deeds and resistance to the proprietorial
      claims by them   139

The decade of violence against the Proprietors after 1745   139
Rioting in Essex County in resistance to proprietorial claims   139
  Sympathy of tenants with the squatters   139
  Interrelatedness of the disaffected   140
  Impossibility of enforcing legal rights   140
The spread of disorder into other parts of the province   140
  Refusal to recognize rights of landlords   141
  Looting of timber-lands   141
The rioters organize to protect their "rights"   141
  The appeal to the natural rights of man on behalf of squatters   141
Appeal to Connecticut by rioters   142
  Connecticut refuses to interfere   142
The threat of British regulars in the midst of the war, 1755   142
  Fear of retribution for lawlessness stabilizes conditions   142

Boundary conflicts with New York   142
  Long-standing aspects of the dispute   143
  New York's objections to the 1719 line   143
New Jersey's law for running the line *ex parte*, 1748   144
  Fails to secure royal approval   144
New York settlers appeal to Connecticut's Assembly, 1751   144
  Organization of the Delaware Company   144
Creation of Sussex County by New Jersey   144
Privy Council fails to terminate the controversy, 1754   145
Boundary commission appointed in 1764   145
  Decision of 1769 protects occupants and upholds New Jersey
    claims   145

Disagreement between executive and legislative branches of the
    province's government   145
Tradition of hostility of inhabitants toward their executives   146
  Unpopularity of itinerant Governors   146
  Assembly promises to support a resident Governor   146
Appointment of Lewis Morris   146
  Qualifications for office   146
  Aristocratic tendencies   146
  Strained relations with the legislature   146
Governor Belcher's delicate position   147
  Fruitless attempts to pacify the Assembly   147
  Inability to obtain concerted action at the time of the land riots   147
  Helplessness in the face of a hostile Council and an empty
    treasury   147

Seeks the favour of the anti-proprietorial group 148
His reprimand by the Board of Trade 148

CHAPTER VII

THE NEW WORLD PARADISE OF THE SECTS

Pennsylvania as the haven for Europe's persecuted sects 149
  The multiplicity of sects in 1750 149
    Mittelberger's description of religious conditions and characterization of the province 149
  The proportion of Germans to the total population, 1755 150
  Population divisions by religious groups 150
  The position of the Quakers, 1755 150

The Pennsylvania Germans 151
  The German emigration 151
    Volume of German immigrants 152
    Dissatisfaction with conditions in Germany 152
  The orderly migration of the persecuted Moravians 152
  The activities of the Newlanders 153
  The horrors of the passage to America 153
    The Rhine-boat trip 153
    The delay in Holland 154
    The tragedies of the immigrant ships 154
    Cost of the passage 155
  Betrayal of the redemptioners 155
    Their sale as white slaves 155
    Working conditions of indentured labour 156
  The voluntary indentured servants 156
  The industry and prosperity of the free and settled Germans 156
    Their tendency to acquire lands along the frontier 156

The indentured-labour supply 157
  Chief source stemming at first from the British Isles 157
    Preponderance of Ulster Scots, 1729 157
  Preponderance of Germans by 1750 157
    These more highly esteemed as servants than the Ulster Scots 157
  Hardiness of the Ulster Scots on the frontier and as colonizers 157
    Establishment of their communities in Pennsylvania and Delaware 158
    Lack of respect for law and order of the Ulstermen 158

Political influence and population distribution of national and religious groups   158
In the older counties   158
The waning Quaker control   158
The emerging Anglican influence   158
In the newer counties   158
The numerical preponderance of Germans   158
The position of the Ulstermen and the English   159
The slow growth of political consciousness among the Germans   159
The emerging strength of the German electorate after 1750   159
Effects of naturalization laws and rights of affirmation   159
The Quaker-German political alliance   160
Common pacifist principles   160
Common support of humane measures   160
Reaction against the Quakers and their German supporters after 1754   161
German rights to naturalization are challenged   161
Composition of the Assembly in 1752 and 1756   161
The over-representation of the eastern Quaker counties   162
The Quakers and the shaping of legislative policy   162

Pennsylvania's criminal codes   163
The Duke of York laws reflect Puritan conceptions of statecraft, 1676   163
Quaker humane sentiments reflected in Penn's "Great Law," 1682   163
Lawlessness produces harsher laws   164
The code of 1700 and statute of 1718   164
The severity of Pennsylvania criminal law after 1722   165

The happy and prosperous state of the province in 1750   166
Agricultural assets   166
Favourable factors of climate, soil, and transportation   166
Great surplus of food and other commodities   166
Generosity of spirit among the people   166
Production of staple crops, livestock, and export products   166
The growth of commerce   167
The production of export commodities   167
The Indian trade   167
Shipbuilding supports the growing commerce   167
Import-trade and carrying-trade activities   168

Philadelphia, the metropolis of the middle colonies   168
Importance as a town and a seaport   168

Characterized by Peter Kalm 169
Description in 1749 169
Architecture of the homes 170
Multiplicity of churches and meeting houses 170
Importance as a cultural centre 170
Its libraries, college, hospital, printing establishments, and
learned societies 170
Benjamin Franklin and James Logan 171
Evidences of prosperity and aristocratic leanings 171

Social attitudes of the people 172
Social divisions and racial pride 172
Slavery as a manifestation of provincial aristocracy 172

The people and their government 173
Benefits of financial aid to farmers through the loan office 173
Absence of serious public burdens in 1750 173
No military-service law 173
No system of direct taxation 173
The financing of the provincial government 174
Interest upon public loans 174
Excise on the sale of spirits 174
Income of the province, 1752 174
Governor Morris on the healthy state of finances, 1755 174

Pennsylvania as a proprietary, 1750 174
The background of the charter and subsequent parliamentary
limitation of prerogatives of the Proprietors 175
William Penn's early experimentations in government 175
The Body of Liberties of 1701 175
Government by the Proprietor and a representative unicameral
Assembly 175
Governor's Council not part of the legislature 175
Aggressiveness of the Assembly 176
Competition between Governor and Assembly 176
Extraordinary powers exercised by the Assembly 176
The submission of laws to the Privy Council for approval 176
Assembly's evasions of this restriction 176
The issue of 1746 over the approval of laws 177
The province questions the King's right to interfere in its gov-
ernment 177
The Queries of the Board of Trade in 1752 177
The weakness of the government at mid-century 178

Laid to Assembly control of all public money 178
Governor Morris asserts his inability to defend the colony, 1755 178

The Proprietors of Pennsylvania 179
Thomas and Richard Penn at mid-century 179
Their rights of succession 179
The Proprietors characterized 179
Their inheritance of debts 180
The problem of collecting quit-rents 180
Increased opposition to the land system by 1750 181
A well-regulated system, according to Lewis Evans, 1753 181
Increased revenue by 1774 182
Thomas and Richard Penn and Quakerism 182
Richard's early defection to the Anglican church 182
Thomas remains a Quaker until 1751 182
Thomas Penn and plans for the proprietary 182
His desire to become the Governor 182
His stand in favour of military defence, 1743 182
Renunciation of plans to live in the province, 1755 183
His good relationship with Governor Hamilton 183

The civilization of the province characterized at mid-century 183

Chapter VIII

A NONDESCRIPT COLONY ON THE DELAWARE

Background to the unusual position of Three Lower Counties on
the Delaware at mid-century 184
Rival claims of the Penn and Baltimore families to the "Territories" 184
Earlier history of the area 184
Origins of the rival claims 185
Penn's deeds and leases from the Duke of York, 1682 185
Penn's efforts to unite the Lower Colonies to Pennsylvania 186
Difficulties in plans for a permanent political union 186

Divergencies between the Province and the "Territories" 186
Needs of the Lower Counties for adequate defensive measures
versus the pacifistic status quo of Pennsylvania 186
Contrasting national and religious origins of early settlers 187
Territorial delimitations compared 187
Commercial rivalry between the seaports of Pennsylvania and
Lower Counties 187

The issue of union or separation in the beginning of the century 187
  Problems arising from Delaware representation in a united As-
    sembly 187
  William Penn's efforts to promote union, 1699–1700 187
    Early separatist movements, 1701–1703 188
  Permanent political separation of the Lower Counties 189
    First Assembly of Lower Counties meets in 1704 189

Unique aspects of Delaware by 1750 189
  A colony without official name or recognized type of government 189
  The lack of a legal constitution 189
  The Governor receives no specific commission or instructions
    applying to the colony 190
  Problems arising from defects in the proprietorial claims of the
    Penn family 190
    The Earl of Sutherland's proprietorial aspirations become a
      threat, 1717 190
  Attempts of Lower Counties at reunion with Pennsylvania 190
  Pennsylvania's negative attitude 190
  Unfavourable report of the Crown lawyers on the Penn family
    claims 190

Further anomalous situation of Delaware in 1750 191
  Existence as colony not recognized in London 191
  Rights of inhabitants undefined 191
    Inherent rights of Englishmen claimed, but land titles not
      secure 191
  The issue of a royal charter for New Castle's incorporation 191
  Reasons for Delaware inhabitants clinging to Penn connection 192
    Fears created by revival of Sutherland family application for
      proprietorship, 1715 192
  Additional fears resulting from the Baltimore petition of 1737 192
  The position of the Board of Trade 192
  The stand of the Privy Council 193

Delaware's well-rounded government in 1750 193
  Harmony between Governor and Assembly 193
  Composition of the legislature 193
  Codification of its laws in 1741 193
    Inclusive nature of laws 193
  Laws characterized 193
    The example of the comprehensive statute of 1742 194
  Freedom of legislation compared to Pennsylvania 194

Not required to submit laws for approval by Privy Council   194
Ability to legislate against importation of convicts   194
Administrative divisions of government   195
    The hundreds   195
Similarities to Pennsylvania's governmental system   195
    Unicameral Assembly   195
    Qualifications of electors   195
Dissimilarities to Pennsylvania's system of government   195
    Compulsory voting after 1734   195
    Rights of affirmation denied to members of the Assembly   195
    Special declarations required of Assembly members   196
    Militia acts passed in the Lower Counties   196
    Delaware supports the Spanish War   196

Delaware's status within the framework of imperial administration   197
Participation in war brings rewards   197
Reimbursement by Parliament   197
    Payment through Delaware's London agent   197
Encouragement and support by the mother country   197
    Government rejects Baltimore claims in delimiting New Castle
    County   197

Decision of Lord Chancellor Hardwicke in favour of Pennsylvania
    claims, 1750   198
Relationship of Delaware to Penn family defined   198
Result of small profit to the Penns   199
    Land titles remain defective   199
Non-payment of quit-rents continues throughout the colonial
    period   199

Financial system of the Lower Counties in 1750   199
Issuance of bills of credit begun in 1723   199
    Loan office established in each county   199
    Prudent administrative methods evolved   199
    Effective liquidation plans   199
Soundness of Delaware finances   200
    Little depreciation in loans   200
    Small portion of bills of credit in circulation by 1750   200
    Minimal need for taxes   200

Delaware as an agricultural colony   200
Piloting at Lewes as an exception   200
Burnaby's description   201
Elsewhere diversified farming and stockraising obtain   201

Philadelphia the chief market for Delaware farmers   201
Comparative sizes of Philadelphia and New Castle   201
Relative unimportance of New Castle by 1754   201
Growing importance of Wilmington   201
   As shipping centre, location for iron forges, and for saw and
    grist mills   202
Shipbuilding begun there in 1740   202

Characteristics of inhabitants of the Lower Counties in 1750   202
Assimilation of nationalistic groups   202
   Prevalence of Quakers in New Castle county   203
   Prevalence of Anglicans in Kent and Sussex counties   204
Population estimates   204
A median standard of living among whites   205
Lack of intense local pride or self-awareness at mid-century   205
   Security ties link them to the Empire   205
Evidence of growth in homogeneity by 1750   205

CHAPTER IX

THE IRON MEN

Production and manufacture of iron in the British Empire   206
   The Iron Act of 1750   206
     Imposes severe restrictions on the colonies   206
     As an example of British mercantile policy   206

Importance of the iron industry to England in 1750   206
   Threat of the growth of American iron-production   206
   Birmingham as a typical iron centre of industrial England   207
   The widespread distribution of ironworks   207

English methods for producing cast and wrought iron   208
   Early direct process   208
   The blast-furnace process   208
   Qualities of the various domestic ore supplies   208
    Location and utilization of each type of ore   208

The essential factors for iron-production at mid-century   208
   Accessibility to supplies of ore, wood, coal, water power, labour,
    and means of transportation   208
    Importance of water power to operation of the blast furnace,
     forges, and mills   208
    Limited use of coal and coke in smelting by 1750   209

The problem of wood wastage in iron- and steel-production   209
  Earlier shortages controlled by legislation   209
  Shortage in wood resources causes shift of smelting locations   209
  Stabilized charcoal supply and stabilized iron-manufacture in the
    early part of the century   210
    The continued need to import Swedish and Russian iron   210
  Use of coal in production of bar iron   210
    Contributes to rise of iron-manufacture in Worcestershire   210
    The seventeenth-century utilization of pit-coal in the manufac-
    turing process   211

Growing demands of the iron trade   211
  Supply of bar iron inadequate to manufacturers' demand by 1700   211
  Growing dependence upon iron secured abroad   211
  Encouragements to iron-production in Ireland under William III   211
  Iron requirements of the trade in 1736   211
    Percentage of bar iron secured abroad   211
  Disadvantages of dependence upon foreign iron   211
  Reasons for inadequacy of furnacemen to meet the demands   212
    Wood supply the key factor   212
    Rising cost of production based on scarcity of wood   212
  The dilemma of the landowner seeking profit from woodland   212
    Competition of other products for the landowner's acres   212
    Increased value of trees withheld from the market   212
    Presence of ironworks stimulates production of wood in Lan-
    cashire   212
  Existence of potential wood supply sufficient for manufacturing
    needs   213
    Limitations upon the furnacemen in meeting the price of wood   213
    Foreign competition as the deciding factor   213

Reasons for lack of legislation barring foreign competition in iron   213
  Need for foreign markets for the hardware trade   213
  Violation of mercantilistic principles and employment policies   213
  Fear of the power of foreign nations to flood the market   214
  Concern over the decline in demand by American markets for
    English iron products   214

The rise of the American iron industry   214
  Effects first felt in England in the 1730's   214
    Falling off of orders   214
    Growing idleness of English forges and furnaces   214
    Unemployment at Stourbridge and Wolverhampton   214

Miserable conditions in Dudley, Birmingham, and Worcestershire   215
Parliamentary attempts at restrictions on colonial iron   215
  The abortive bill of 1719   215
  The removal of export duties on British iron, 1721   215
Iron-smelting in Virginia and Maryland   216
  Spotswood's ironworks in Virginia and the Principio Works in Maryland   216
  Large production of pig iron by mid-century   216
  Virginia offers inducements to ironworkers   216
Iron industry in New England   217
  Well established by 1718 in Massachusetts Bay   217
  Massachusetts Bay bounties encourages ironware-production   217
  Importation of bar steel from England   217
  New England furnaces produce hardware for export to the Southern colonies in competition with England   217
Iron industry in the middle colonies   218
  Relative unimportance in New York   218
  Growth in New Jersey and Pennsylvania in the 1730's 218

Pennsylvania as the most important iron-producing colony, 1750   218
  Number of iron-producing centres by 1750   218
  Vast acreage included in the typical "iron plantation"   218
  Description of a Pennsylvania ironworks   218
  Location of the mills, plants, and furnaces   219
  The excellent quality of American ironware   219
  Local demand for domestic tools   219

Renewed agitation for the relief of the British iron trade   219
  Petitions to Parliament begun in 1736   219
    Demand for a bounty to encourage importation of American crude iron   220
    Demand that colonials be restrained from manufacturing iron   221
    Economic and social implications of decline in the English iron industry   221
    Arguments concerning comparative merits of American iron and foreign iron   221
  Petitions referred to a Parliamentary Committee   222
  Arguments continue on the relative importance of colonial markets   222

The Parliamentary Bill of 1738   222
  Chief features of the measure   223

Failure to become law 223

The need for imperial solidarity with the outbreak of the Anglo-Spanish war 223

The Iron Act of 1750 223

Bill proposed in 1749 to encourage importation of American iron 223

Designed to obviate dependence upon Swedish iron 223

Implications of potential unemployment of English iron-workers 224

The justifications for restrictions upon and concessions to the American trade 224

Petition of the Bristol Merchant Venturers in 1749 224

Enactment of the bill and its provisions 225

Protection of English forge-operators 225

Encouragement for the restricted importation of colonial pig and bar iron 225

Erection of new colonial iron- and steel-manufacturing plants prohibited 225

Colonial governors called upon to enforce the measure 226

Reactions of colonials to the Iron Act 226

Failure of bill to meet its supporters' expectations 226

Figures on importation of American iron, 1750–1757, analyzed 226

No check on American iron-manufacturing results 227

Favours English ironmasters rather than the manufacturers 228

The Iron Act of 1757 228

Bar-iron importation freely admitted into England 228

Colonial exports to England increase 228

Manufacturers complain against insufficient quantity and poor quality of American bar iron 228

Subsequent efforts to secure a bounty on American iron and high duties on foreign iron 228

Opposition to duties on Swedish iron is based an criticisms of the quality of American iron 228

The effects of parliamentary legislation upon the American iron industry 228

Prohibits neither iron-production nor its manufacture into hard-ware 228

Results in a kind of monopoly of existing mills and plants by prohibiting erection of new ones 229

Production of colonial iron triples by 1775 229

Economic sectionalism renders ineffectual the parliamentary attempts to control complex economic forces   229

CHAPTER X

HUDSON BAY BEAVER

The British North American fur trade   230
  The Hudson's Bay Company holds no monopoly   230
    Open competition in all markets   230

The Hudson's Bay Company in 1750   230
  Strategic geographical location   230
    Failure to provide a northwest passage not a serious liability   230
    Profitable for the beaver trade   230
  Charter of the company   231
    Grants exclusive fur exploitation rights in the area   231

The Hudson Bay region   231
  Its isolation and forbidding climate   231
  The lack of settlements within the granted area   231

Hudson's Bay Company trading posts   231
  Forts and factories on the Bay and contiguous rivers   231
    Those on or near the western shore   231
    The northern fort on the Churchill   231
    The two small forts on the eastern shore   232
    The southernmost forts   232
  York Factory in 1750   232
    Most important of the Company's trading posts   232
    Description of this post   232

Activities of the Hudson's Bay Company   233
  Shipping engaged in the trade   233
  Imports and exports of the Bay stations   233
    Value of exported articles in 1748   233
    Cost of maintaining the posts, 1741 and 1745   233
  Regulation of the Indian trade   234
    Restrictions on the Indians   234
    Regulations on the use of spirits   234
  Influence of French competition   234
    Difference in prices of barter goods at the several forts   234
    Activities of the French *coureurs*   235

Vast region exploited by the Company   235
  Indians most involved in the fur trade   235
    The Crees and Assiniboines   235
  Company's agents confine trade mainly to the posts on the Bay 235
    Henry Kelsey, a seventeenth-century exception   235
    Travels of Anthony Henday to the Blackfoot country 235
  Indians come to the posts from far-flung regions   235
    Lack of continuity in the trade   235
  The Company makes no efforts to civilize the Indians or colonize
    the area   235
  Undetermined limits of its wilderness possessions   236
    Boundary claims according to a memorial laid before the
    Board of Trade in 1750   236

The Company as a business enterprise   236
  Capital stock in 1749   236
    Its distribution among stockholders   236
  Company headquarters at Beaver House in London   236
    Centre for auction sales of skins and pelts   237
    Competition of buyers   237

Hudson Bay beaver and the English hat industry   237
  History of the English beaver-hat industry   237
    Origins of the craft   237
    Opulence of the master hatters in 1701   237
    Effects of French control of the Bay area, 1701–1711   238
  Growth of the French beaver-hat industry   238
    Its capture of English continental markets   238
    Its protection by the French government   238
  Decline of the English industry   238
    Exodus of English hatters to France   238
    Superiority of the French product   238
    Efforts to bring relief by legislation, 1722   238
    Further threat of competition from the American colonies   239
    English hatters protest colonial underselling practices   239

The Hat Act of 1732   239
  The motivation in protecting an established craft   239
    Colonial industry must not destroy one in the mother country   239
  Compromise aspects of the act   240
    Prohibits export of colonial product but permits its local
    manufacture and sale   240
  Continuation of colonial hat-manufacture   240

The act fails to restore the British industry   240
    Foreign markets not regained   240
    Inability to meet French competition prevails   240
    Attempts to prohibit the export of beaver felt   240

Reassessment of the English hat-trade situation, 1764   241
    The flood of petitions and memorials to Parliament   241
    The compromise legislation of 1764   242
        Lowering of the import duty on beaver skins   242
        Elimination of the drawback and other export benefits   242
    Act fails to limit export of beaver to the Continent   242
        Rise of exports in beaver pelts and wool to 1775   242
        Decline in export of English hats to 1775   242
        English hats priced out of the market   242

Attempts to break down the Company monopoly   242
    Great profits involved in the fur trade   242
        Upon annual stock in trade   243
    Arthur Dobbs's challenge to the monopoly   243
        His earlier interests in discovering a northwest passage, 1735   243
        Continued attempts to find a northwest passage, 1742 and 1746   243
        His attack on the legality of the Company charter   244
    Dobbs appeals to the Privy Council and Parliament   244
        His efforts to throw open the trade of the Bay   244
        Wide support given by English merchants and others   245
        Appointment of a committee of investigation   245
    The *Report* of the parliamentary committee   245
        Tendency to confirm Dobbs's stand   245
    The Company's petition   245
        Defends its conduct in carrying out its objectives   245
        Produces conclusive arguments in its own favour   245

The Company weathers the storm   245
    Defeat of the powerful opposition in 1749   245
    Its continued survival   245
    French rivalry in 1750   246
        French establishments about Lake Winnipeg   246
        Obstacles to easy access to their trading posts   246
    The Hudson's Bay Company remains ascendant   247

Chapter XI

BANKERS AND SACKMEN: THE PROVINCE OF AVALON

Newfoundland in the eighteenth century 248

The importance of the Banks as international fishing grounds 248

Cod fisheries and the European fishing interests 248

Slow movement of permanent settlers to the Island 249

Anglo-French rivalry in Newfoundland 249

The Treaty of Utrecht confirming British territorial claims 249

The French retain coastal fishing privileges 249

French superiority in the cod trade in 1750 250

Advantages of location at Cape Breton and on the coasts of the Island 250

Their production of a better commodity 250

The Avalon Peninsula in 1750 250

Centre of the English activity 250

Importance of St. John's as chief town and port 250

Defences of the peninsula 250

The Placentia garrison 250

Locations of other garrisons 251

Population at mid-century 251

Permanent inhabitants and seasonal fishing itinerants 251

The role of the Boston merchant in the life of the Island 251

Traders supply the stores in the fishing communities 251

Fish accepted in payment of debts 251

Methods of disposing of prime and refuse fish 251

Occupations of the permanent dwellers 252

Their employments and mode of living 252

Inactivity of the winter months 252

Activities in the cod-fishing season 252

Animation of vessels and people 253

English methods of catching and curing cod 253

Marketing the cod 254

Value of the annual catch in 1749 254

Other products of the Island 255

Train oil, furs and pelts, salmon 255

Value of total exports and imports of the Island 255

Relative unimportance of the commerce with Great Britain 255

British regulation of the fisheries   256
  Governmental concern with the decline of the British cod fisheries   256
    Instructions to Governor Rodney in 1749 on curing cod   256
    Efforts to protect Newfoundland as an outlet market for British
      woollens   256
  The Banks and maritime power   256
    Desire to maintain the fisheries as a school for seamanship   256
    Governor's instructions to foster British seamanship and the
      home mercantile marine   257
  Earlier opposition to permanent settlements to prevent absorp-
    tion of the fisheries by inhabitants   257
  Restrictions placed upon the inhabitants   258
    Protection of the fishery conveniences out of season   258
  Appointment of harbour admirals limited to English shipmasters   258
  Attempts to control the New England shipping activities about
    the Banks   258
    Instructions to Newfoundland Governors on supervision of
      colonial vessels   258

The government of Newfoundland in 1750   258
  Its rudimentary nature   258
  Early opposition to recognition of the Island as a colonial entity   259
  The administration of the first Governor, Captain Henry Osborn,
    1729   259
    The Governor takes over military defence and judicial control
      of the Island   259
    Divides the Island into administrative districts   259
    Conflict develops between the Governor and the harbour
      admirals   259
  Brief tenure in office of the Governor   259
    Governors as commodores of the sack-ship convoys   259
    List of Governors between 1748 and 1750   259
  Varied responsibilities of the Governor's office   260
    Instructions to Rodney in 1749   260
    Inability of the Governors to fulfill multiplicity of duties   261
    Necessity of relying upon subordinate officials   261
  The justices of the peace   261
    Friction between them and the harbour admirals   261
    Their inability to control the inhabitants   262
  The harbour admirals   262
    Their neglect of civic duty in favour of fishing activity   262
  The problem of maintaining order on the Island   262

Rodney's report on the hostility of the Irish Catholics to the
King's authority   262
Report of the military commander on the failure of justice   262
Necessity of sending criminals to England for trial   263
Efforts of the Crown to strengthen local government   263
Powers of the Governor extended to take cognizance of capi-
tal crimes on the spot   263
Grant of commissions of oyer and terminer   263
Restrictions on executions maintained   264
Continued opposition of the English cod-fishing ports to at-
tempts to stabilize the Newfoundland government   264
The turbulent state of the population in 1765   264

Revival of the Baltimore claims to the Peninsula of Avalon, 1755   265
The early relations of the Calverts to Newfoundland   265
The letters patent of 1623   265
The establishment of Ferryland by George Calvert   266
Appointment of deputies by the first two Calverts   266
Rival claims by the Marquess of Hamilton denied by the Crown   266
Baltimore's appointment of Governors, 1661–1674   267
Parliament's granting of free trade and fishing rights, 1699   267
The Baltimore line of succession down to Frederick in 1751   267
Baltimore pleads lack of continuous proprietorial activity as
due to religious discrimination and war   267
Frederick seeks to establish a government for Avalon, 1753   268
His petition based on rights granted under the letters patent of
1623   268
Board of Trade refers the petition to the Attorney General and
the Solicitor General   268
The "objections and answers" prepared by Baltimore's legal
adviser   269
The opinion of the Attorney General, Sir Robert Henley   270

The decision of the Crown against the Baltimore claims   271
The weighty considerations of public policy dictating the decision   271
Board of Trade hostility to proprietorial and corporate colonial
charters   272
The threat to English maritime power, a factor   272

CHAPTER XII

THE BRITISH COLONIAL SYSTEM IN 1750

SUMMARIZATION

Government of the British colonies 273
Based upon well-established principles 273
Contrasted with other colonial empires 273

The role of Parliament 273
Decline of old prerogative powers of the King 273
Superseded by combined authority of King and Parliament 273
Evolution of the British constitution 274
Privy Council continues as chief administrative agency for co-
lonial affairs by permission of Parliament 274
The sovereignty of Parliament in matters of state 274
Comprehensive statute of 1696 in force in 1750 274
Subordination of colonial law to parliamentary power 274
Supplementary laws binding on colonies 274
Lack of colonial challenge to parliamentary supremacy 275

Constitutions of the British colonies 275
Parliament creates no rigid pattern of colonial governmental
machinery 275
Basis of colonial constitutions 276
Letters patent 276
Commissions and instructions to royal Governors 276
Fundamental colonial laws approved by the Privy Council 276
Acts of Parliament restricting colonial legislative competence 276
Wide latitude of colonial powers under their constitutions 276
Similarities of most colonial constitutions 277
Certain common duties assigned to all royal Governors 277
Flexibility of constitutions to meet new needs 277
Provisions for changes in commissions and instructions 277

The colonial Assembly 278
A common feature of colonial government 278
Election of members by freemen or freeholders 278
Its legislative powers and powers of the purse 278
Relationship of the Assembly to the Governor 278
Political awareness of colonial inhabitants 278

Increasing prestige of colonial Assemblies in the eighteenth
    century   278
Corresponding weakening of executive authority   278
Precarious position of the colonial Governor   278
    Governor's power of veto balanced by Assembly's control over
        funds   278
    Need for mutual understanding between Governor and As-
        sembly   278

Processing of colonial legislation   279
    Submission to the Privy Council for approval required of most
        colonies   279
Right of appeal to Privy Council from highest colonial courts   279

Currency legislation   279
    Tendency of the local Assemblies to support legislation running
        counter to royal instructions   279
Need for a medium of exchange   279
    The creation of bills of credit   279
    Inflation of paper money defrauds the creditors and leads to
        parliamentary legislation   279
New England Currency Act, 1751   279
Controversies between Governors and Assemblies over legal-
    tender acts   280

The dynamic quality of colonial civilization and the vitality of its
    institutions   280
Contrasted with other imperial powers   280
Stems from degree of personal freedom in colonial life   280
Religious and economic encouragements attract a multitude of
    immigrants   280
    Contributions of the immigrants of various nationalities   280
Stability of the British colonials   281
    Hard core of conservatism retains the best of traditional herit-
        age   281
Preference for the English judicial and governmental systems   281

Religion and the colonial system   282
Contrasted with other imperial powers   282
    Characterized by tolerance in 1750   282
The two so-called established churches in the colonies   282
    The Anglican Establishment   282
    The Congregational Establishment   282

Presence of other Christian denominations and sects 282
Discrimination against Catholics and Jews in 1750 282
  Prevailing attitude of tolerance despite legal discrimination 283
  Their status in specific colonies 283

Importance of institution of slavery in 1750 284
  A legally established common factor in all colonies 284
  Economic importance of slavery varies with individual colonial
    needs 284
    Importance of Negro slaves to staple-producing colonies 284
    Relative importance of slavery in tobacco-producing colonies 284
    The holding of slaves as a symbol of wealth in Northern col-
      onies and the Bermudas 284
  Factors determining the severity of slave codes 285
    Concentration of Negro population 285
    Degree of fierceness of the type of slave 285
    Fear of insurrection 285
  The practice of manumission 285
  Miscegenation in the West Indies 285
    Jamaica's extension of unusual legal rights to Negro women
      and their mulatto children 285

Intercolonial boundary disputes 286
  Westward expansion of colonies claiming sea-to-sea grants based
    on early letters patent provokes disputes 286
  Clashes arising from disputed territorial limits in colonies with-
    out sea-to-sea grants 286
  Final determination of boundary issues by colonial commissions 286

Economic Sectionalism 287
  Question of trade policy in 1750 287
    Extent of proper confinement of British colonial trade 287
    Divergencies of interest between the British West Indies and
      the Northern colonies 287
  The problem of competition between the French and British
    sugar islands 287
    Advantages of the French islands and their provision of cheap
      molasses for the North American rum trade 288
    Parliamentary attempts to protect the British islands by legis-
      lating in their favour against the Northern colonies 288
  The Molasses Act of 1733 fails of its purpose 288
    Lack of governmental machinery to enforce this and earlier
      legislation 289

British planter interests fail to secure additional legislation to stem the flow of French-produced molasses to North America at mid-century 289

Predominant influence in Parliament of the continental colonies in 1750 289

The trade-and-navigation system 289

The complex body of laws regulating economic activity within the Empire 289

Abercromby's "Examination" of the acts 289

Lack of opposition in Great Britain before 1775 to trade restraints 290

Duties on colonial commerce to be called for as a source of national income in the 1760's and 1770's 290

Large expenditures involved in maintaining imperial defence measures 290

The size of the national debt in 1759 290

Obligation upon colonials to help support measures beneficial to themselves under terms of the trade acts 290

Restrictions imposed by the system on colonial industry and commerce 291

Duties on certain foreign-produced commodities carried in the colonial trade require certification 291

The "enumerated commodities" list and other parliamentary legislation restrict colonial exportation 291

Certain tariffs, duties, and requirements designed to protect British merchants and maritime power 291

Benefits of government regulation to colonial commerce 291

Government bounties encourage certain colonial products 292

Benefits of the system to the colonial shipbuilding and carrying trade 292

Lack of enforcement of the restraining acts 292

Prevalence of law-violation in the Northern colonies 292

Laxity of law-enforcement machinery 292

Venality of the government law-enforcement agents 293

The healthy state of the Empire's economy in 1750 293

Extent of realization of the objective of economic self-containment 293

Multifarious activities of trade and commerce everywhere 294

The satisfaction of British North Americans with their lot 294

Index *follows page* 294

Maps

I. A portion of the Western Hemisphere showing British possessions. (From "A Map of the World, on Mercator's
Projection," *Gentleman's Magazine,* 1755)   Facing page   6

II. The northern colonies. (From *A Complete Atlas* by Emanuel
Bowen, 1752)   Facing page   7

III. The eastern part of the Province of Massachusetts Bay, later
to become the State of Maine. (From "A Map of the
Most Inhabited part of New England . . . Divided into
Counties and Townships. . . ." Printed for Carrington
Bowles, 1771, based on Thomas Jefferys's "Map of New
England," 1755)   Facing page   30

IV. The main part of the Province of Massachusetts Bay. (From
the Bowles map of New England, 1771)   Facing page   31

V. The Province of New Hampshire, with the new townships
laid out west of the settled area. (From the Bowles map
of New England, 1771)   Facing page   46

VI. A map showing the area of the boundary dispute between
New Hampshire and New York, later to become the
State of Vermont. (From "A Map of the Province of New
York" by Claude Joseph Sauthier, 1776)   Facing page   47

VII. The Colony of Rhode Island. (From "The Plan of the British
Dominions of New England in North America" by William Douglass, 1753 [?])   Facing page   70

VIII. The Colony of Connecticut. (From the Jefferys map of New
England, 1755)   Facing page   71

IX. A portion of the Province of New York. (From Sauthier's "A
Chorographical Map of the Province of New York in
North America . . . ," 1779)   Facing page   118

X. The Province of New Jersey. (From "A Map of Pensilvania,
New Jersey, New York, and the Three Delaware Counties" by Lewis Evans, 1749)   Facing page   119

XI. "A Map of the Province of Pensilvania Drawn from the Best Authorities" by Thomas Kitchin, 1756.   Facing page 174

XII. The eastern portion of the Province of Pennsylvania and the Three Lower Counties on the Delaware. (From the second edition of the Lewis Evans map, 1752)   Facing page 175

XIII. A portion of "A New Map of Hudson's Bay and Labrador" (From *A Complete Atlas* by Emanuel Bowen, 1752) (Canadian Archives, Map Division)   Facing page 238

XIV. The Island of Newfoundland. (From *A Complete Atlas* by Emanuel Bowen, 1752)   Facing page 239

THE BRITISH EMPIRE

BEFORE THE AMERICAN REVOLUTION

VOLUME III

THE BRITISH ISLES AND THE AMERICAN COLONIES:

THE NORTHERN PLANTATIONS

1748–1754

CHAPTER I

The Heart of New England

"THERE is not one of our settlements which can be compared, in the abundance of people, the number of considerable and trading towns, and the manufactures that are carried on in them, to New England," declared the authors of *An Account of the European Settlements in America.* They then affirmed: "The most populous and flourishing parts of the mother country hardly make a better appearance. Our provinces to the southward on this continent are recommendable for the generous warmth of the climate, and a luxuriance of soil which naturally throws up a vast variety of beautiful and rich vegetable productions; but New England is the first in America, for cultivation, for the number of people, and for the order which results from both." These words, imputed to William and Edmund Burke,[1] aptly place the northern colonies in relation to that portion of Britain's overseas empire largely dependent upon slave labour and utilizing a so-called plantation system of agriculture.

From Pennsylvania to the borders of Maine, the farm rather than the plantation was the characteristic land unit.[2] The term "farm," as employed in the eighteenth century, basically implied diversification in production rather than dependence upon a single staple.

---

[1] (William Burke and Edmund Burke [?], 1st edn., 1757; 6th edn., 2 vols., London, 1777), II, 171-2.

[2] Neither in the South, as we have seen in the preceding volume, nor in the North, as will be developed later in this volume, was agriculture exclusively plantation or farm. Farms were found in the South beyond the Tidewater, and something approximating the plantation system was evolved in such regions as the old King's Province in Rhode Island.

It implied also a unit of land sufficiently small to be developed by the personal efforts of the freeholder and his immediate family, aided by the labour of hired hands or of those bound by indenture; it implied, further, the existence of no such social distinctions as were almost universally manifested in connection with the plantation system.

However, farming instead of planting was only one of the characteristics that set the colonial North apart from both the tidewater South and the British West Indies. Already great strides had been taken in the development of handicrafts,[3] in the production of flour, in the manufacture of rum and iron, in shipbuilding, and in the exploitation of the North Atlantic fisheries. In the South these activities were rudimentary or sporadic, with the exception of the production of flour and crude iron in Maryland and Virginia. But in the North by 1750 development along some of these lines, at least, had proceeded so far as to arouse the apprehension of Englishmen who found themselves faced with threatening competition and who consequently could not feel that this region was properly adjusted to the mercantilistic conception of the part that colonies should play in supplementing the efforts of the mother country.

The oldest of the northern colonies, Massachusetts Bay, was in some respects the most dangerous rival in America of England's vital economic interests, owing to its strategic position, its considerable population, its thriving fisheries, and its success in shipbuilding and in the manufacture of iron and rum. Both historically and economically, as the result of its early settlement and the dynamic power of its leadership, this colony was the heart of old New England in 1750, as in 1650.

The Province of Massachusetts Bay at this period possessed in the town of Boston the greatest commercial and shipping centre in the Empire beyond the British Isles. Situated on a peninsula in the security of the Bay, protected by the frowning batteries of Castle William, the buildings of the town rose gradually from Long Wharf and extended southward for about two miles. The traveller Daniel West, who visited the town in 1720, was so impressed with the polite quality of the conversation of the merchants and the evidence of their prosperity as to declare, "that a gentleman from London

---

[3] See Carl Bridenbaugh: *The Colonial Craftsman* (New York & London, 1950).

would almost think himself at home at Boston, when he observes the number of people, their houses, their furniture, their tables, their dress and conversation, which perhaps is as splendid and showy as that of the most considerable tradesmen in London."[4] Another English traveller in 1740 stated that the houses and streets were only a little inferior to some of the best in London.[5] In 1750 Captain Goelet of New York recorded in his diary, on the occasion of a visit to the New England seaport, that of its three thousand houses two thirds were of wood, the remainder of brick, "much better and Stronger Built, more after the Modern Taste all Sashd and Prety well Ornamented haveing Yards and Gardens Adjoyning Also." The better buildings, he stated, were very spacious, two and three stories in height, and, together with the gardens that surrounded them, covered a good deal of ground.[6] In fact, in the course of a century the town had become a real centre of wealth and aristocracy. The Tramount,[7] the exclusive residential section of that period, possessed some of the finest houses to be found in any part of North America, such as the Bromfield Mansion, the Ewing Mansion, and that of Peter Faneuil. Over the paved streets of the town rolled the coaches of the leading families. Many of these equipages were drawn by four spirited horses and accompanied by blacks in livery. Indeed, taking all things together, one traveller was led to assert that "considering the bulk of the place they outdo London!"[8] As a further proof of the aristocratic spirit in evidence

---

[4] *The Memorial History of Boston . . . 1630–1880* (ed. J. Winsor, 4 vols., Boston, 1880–1), II, 440–1.

[5] *Ibid.*

[6] "Extracts from Capt. Francis Goelet's Journal," *The New England Historical and Genealogical Register* (Boston, 1870), XXIV, 62. The student interested in the growth of Boston should consult the important new book by W. M. Whitehill: *Boston: A Topographical History* (Cambridge, 1959), particularly Chap. 2, "The Eighteenth Century."

Lord Adam Gordon of the 66th Regiment — during a leisurely tour of British North America covering the years 1764 and 1765 — noted in his journal that Boston had "2100 houses, many of which are better, more Spacious and more Commodious, than those I saw either at Philadelphia or New York — they all have Gardens, . . . the number of inhabitants are supposed to be 23,000. . . . This is more like an English old Town than any in America, — the Language and manners of the People, very much resemble the old country . . ." ("Journal of an Officer . . .," B.M., King's Mss., 213:67); see also Gordon's itinerary as published by Sir Keith W. Murray: *Genealogist,* new ser., XIV.

[7] First called Trimontaine, the word is now Tremont.

[8] *Memorial History of Boston,* II, 441.

within the town in the early 1750's, Boston could boast almost a thousand slaves.[9]

From this seaport at least a thousand vessels sailed each year. It appears that most of the ships not only were owned by the local mercantile interests but also had been built in the various shipyards of the province.[10] Even early in the eighteenth century these yards were launching annually from 140 to 150 vessels, large and small; among the leading types were the three-masted ships, sloops, snows, and brigs. Later the schooners appeared.[11] Many of the vessels, after picking up a cargo for the maiden voyage across the Atlantic, were sold by their owners upon arrival to London, Liverpool, or Bristol merchants and thus lost their identity with Massachusetts Bay, as did many others built upon order of British firms.[12] For it

---

[9] The number of slaves in Boston in 1754 was 989 and in Suffolk County, 1,270. See Massachusetts Historical Society *Collections*, 2nd ser., III, 95–7.

[10] Without taking into account vessels engaged in the New England coasting trade and in the fisheries in 1753, the number that entered and cleared the port of Boston, according to the Naval Office lists for that year, was 459. Of this total, 351 carried a Boston registration, while 9 others were registered from some other Massachusetts Bay port; vessels with an English registration were but 14. The total tonnage of the Massachusetts Bay vessels was 21,129 tons, as against a total tonnage of the English vessels of 1,961 tons. See the tables in an article by M. G. Lawson: "The Boston Merchant Fleet of 1753," *American Neptune*, IX, 205–15. Figures for the year from Christmas of 1747 to that of 1748 were given as 500 vessels clearing out for foreign trade and 450 entered inward. See [William and Edmund Burke]: *op. cit.*, II, 173. For the shipbuilding and commercial activities of William Pepperell at Kittery see Byron Fairchild: *Messrs. William Pepperell: Merchants at Piscataqua* (Ithaca, 1954).

[11] Boston, it appears, declined as a shipbuilding centre in the eighteenth century. In 1738 some 41 vessels of 6,324 tonnage were constructed there; in 1749 but 15 vessels of 2,450 tonnage. William Douglass: *A Summary, Historical and Political of the . . . Present State of the British Settlements in North America* (2 vols., Boston, 1747–51 [1760 London edn. used throughout this Vol.]), I, 540; see also A. P. Usher's chapter "Colonial Business and Transportation" in the *Commonwealth History of Massachusetts* (5 vols., New York, 1927–30), II, 399–400, and especially Paul Huffington and J. N. Clifford: "Evolution of Shipbuilding in Southwestern Massachusetts," *Economic Geography*, XV, 362–78, for a discussion of shipbuilding in Massachusetts. It was asserted that between the years 1769 and 1771, inclusive, Massachusetts Bay built 441 ocean-going vessels, or 35 per cent of all vessels constructed in the colonies. See Carl Bridenbaugh: *op. cit.*, p. 92.

[12] Ever since the days of the navigation legislation, beginning with the law of 1660, the sale of New England vessels to England had been a factor of great significance in the economic relations of the two portions of the Empire. In 1715 it was estimated that from 40 to 50 ships were purchased by the mercantile interests of the mother country and that the total value of all vessels sold was over £90,000. See V. S. Clark: *History of Manufacturing in the United States, 1607–1860* (3 vols., Washington, 1929), I, 95; see also W. A. Fairburn: *Merchant Sail* (6 vols., Center Lovell, Me., 1945–55), I, 235–6.

A portion of the Western Hemisphere showing British possessions.
(From "A Map of the World, on Mercator's Projection," *Gentleman's Magazine*, 1755)

The Northern Colonies.

(From *A Complete Atlas* by Emanuel Bowen, 1752)

was found that the cost of ship-construction was less in New England than in any other part of the Empire.[13] The importance of Boston as a commercial centre is also indicated by the fact that in the early 1740's over 166 warehouses were needed to hold the great supplies of commodities brought to Massachusetts from foreign parts for distribution and also to house the export produce of this colony and other American plantations.[14] In these warehouses were stored bales of broadcloth, flannel, and baize; haberdashery, ironware, canvas, twine, and cordage, with East India goods and numerous other articles from England as well as certificated and also uncertificated goods from Europe. There were hogsheads of rum, molasses, and sugar, with logwood from the West Indies and Honduras Bay, wines from the Madeiras and the Canary Islands, countless barrels of cod, mackerel, alewives, and other cured fish — the latter the product of the Bay and also of the Straits of Canso and of Newfoundland — together with oil and bone brought by the whalers, and, lastly, the products of the New England forest, such as timber, deals, tar, and turpentine.[15]

The multifarious activities of the Boston merchants are well illustrated in the dealings of Thomas Hancock. Starting his career as a bookbinder, this versatile man turned to foreign trade, engaging in it extensively in partnership with other local men. He shipped rum, fish, oil, flour, and other goods to Newfoundland, the West Indies, and Europe, loading his ships for the return voyage with the products of these places. Business correspondents in London and at many other seaports enabled him to buy and sell successfully in those places. In addition to this wholesale and retail business he acted as a banker, selling and purchasing bills of exchange and

---

[13] According to figures presented by Usher (*op. cit.*), a vessel could be built in Massachusetts for £8 per ton; in the middle colonies it cost £8.10; in the Carolinas, £10.10; in England, from £15.5 to £16.5.

[14] William Douglass; *op. cit.*, I, 531. For Boston's trade with the outside world during the period under review see M. G. Lawson: "The Routes of Boston Trade, 1752–1765," Colonial Society of Massachusetts *Publications*, XXXVIII, *Transactions*, 1947–1951, pp. 81–120. The importance of shipbuilding and shipping to Boston in the early eighteenth century is emphasized by Bernard and Lotte Bailyn in their *Massachusetts Shipping, 1697–1714* (Cambridge, 1959).

[15] "The Answer of the Governor of Massachusetts to several Queries," March 2, 1736/7. Shelburne Papers, 45:187–91, Clements Library. The port of Salem, including Marblehead, however, was perhaps the greatest fish-exporting town of New England and of North America.

profiting by war contracts. It must be added that in building up his family fortune he was apparently none too scrupulous about observing the customs laws, but rather frequently dealt in illegal traffic in foreign wares.[16] The career of Hancock is a typical one of many of the most successful colonial merchants not only of Boston but also of Newport, New York, and Philadelphia.

The busy and energetic people of the colony, taken as a group, seem to have maintained a high standard of living during this period. This was also true of the more settled parts of the rest of New England, as the following description by the author of *American Husbandry* indicates:

"There is in many respects a great resemblance between New England and Great Britain. In the best cultivated parts of it, you would not, in travelling through the country, know, from its appearances that you were from home. The face of the country has in general a cultivated, inclosed, and chearful prospect; the farmhouses are well and substantially built, and stand thick; gentlemen's houses appear every where, and have an air of a wealthy and contented people. Poor, strolling, and ragged beggars are scarcely ever to be seen; all the inhabitants of the country appear to be well fed, cloathed, and lodged, nor is any where a greater degree of independency and liberty to be met with; nor is that distinction of ranks and classes to be found which we see in Britain, but which is infinitely more apparent in France and other arbitrary countries."[17]

It was asserted that to discharge the heavy annual trade balances against the people of Massachusetts Bay resulting from their large importations, "all the produce of their cod fish at the markets in Spain and Portugal — all the oil they catch — all the ships they build — all the freights they make — all the money they get by

---

[16] See Edward Edelman: "Thomas Hancock, Colonial Merchant," *Journal of Economic and Business History*, I, 77–104, and especially W. T. Baxter: *The House of Hancock* (Cambridge, Mass., 1945), pp. 84–5, *passim*.

[17] *American Husbandry . . . By An American* (2 vols., London, 1775, reissued and edited by H. J. Carman, New York, 1939), p. 46.

That the well-being of the inhabitants was affected by diseases from time to time is made clear in J. B. Blake's new book (*Public Health in the Town of Boston* [*Harvard Historical Studies*, LXXII], Cambridge, Mass., 1959), in which he describes the smallpox epidemic in Boston in 1751 (Chaps. 5 and 6) and other diseases brought into the ports of Massachusetts Bay; see also John Duffy: *Epidemics in Colonial America* (Baton Rouge, 1953), pp. 56–7.

specie or bills of exchange — and all the profits from every branch of their trade . . ." centred in Great Britain. This evidence would seem to indicate the prevailing nature of their commercial activities with the outside world, but it is not the whole story by any means.[18]

According to Robert Dinwiddie, acting at the time as a surveyor general of customs, the total value of the commodities shipped from Great Britain (directly or through the Guinea trade or otherwise) to the plantations in 1743 was estimated to be £3,635,000; almost one sixth of this amount, or a total of £600,000 worth of goods, came to Massachusetts Bay. These imports, Dinwiddie claimed, carried a higher value than all the goods shipped directly to the combined colonies of North Carolina, Pennsylvania, New Jersey, New York, Connecticut, Rhode Island, New Hampshire, and Nova Scotia.[19] Impressive as this is, the total value of exports of the province to all places — including ships for sale, oil, fish, deer skins, ironware, naval stores, bricks, horses, cattle, earthenware, and furs — amounted in the same year to not less than £800,000 out of a total export of commodities valued, according to these estimates, at

---

[18] See G. R. Minot's *Continuation of the History of the Province of Massachusetts Bay* . . . (2 vols., Boston, 1798–1803), I, 155–61, for a discussion of the above topic.

[19] This amount included British manufactures, East India goods, German linens, the Guinea and the Madeira trade. Robert Dinwiddie's report is embodied in James Abercromby's "Examination, 1752," Shelburne Papers, 47:35–9. Dinwiddie gives the following estimates for other colonies: North Carolina, £50,000; Pennsylvania, £250,000; New Jersey, £40,000; New York, £150,000; Rhode Island, £30,000; Connecticut, £30,000; and Nova Scotia (before the establishment of Halifax in 1748), £10,000.

These figures differ remarkably from those returned by the Governor of Massachusetts Bay. For example, in an account sent by Belcher in 1736–7 to the Board of Trade the total value of British manufactures and India goods imported into the province was placed at the modest sum of £120,000. The natural produce was rated at £100,000. For his report see the Shelburne Papers, 45:187–91. According to "authentic documents," the average annual value of imports into New England between 1738 and 1748 was £181,289 sterling. See G. R. Minot: *op. cit.,* I, 162, for tables. The official figures for colonial imports and exports are of course notoriously defective.

The predominance of New England in trade relations with England in the early part of the century is indicated by the fact that between 1716 and 1719 there sailed from London to that region 101 vessels, while only 19 sailed to New York, 25 to Pennsylvania, 26 to South Carolina; during the same period 123 sailed from New England to London while from New York there were 44, from Pennsylvania 8, from South Carolina 91. This is taken from a "List of ships trading with the colonies from the port of London"; see C. P. Nettels: *The Money Supply of the American Colonies before 1720* (Madison, 1934), p. 101 n.

£5,036,000 sent out from all the plantations. In other words, the value of its exports in 1743 almost equalled the combined exports of Pennsylvania, New York, Connecticut, Rhode Island, New Hampshire, and Nova Scotia.[20]

It is clear, if the above estimates have the slightest validity, that Massachusetts Bay importations from the mother country were far beyond its own requirements. The great mercantile houses of Boston had made that town the entrepôt for a vast territory embracing much more than New England; in fact, it dominated Nova Scotia and Newfoundland to the north and even North Carolina to the far south. Building its own ships, using them as the carriers of its own commerce and much of that of its neighbours, Boston levied financial tribute in the form of freights, commission services, insurance policies, and credit and other facilities from all those communities which it habitually served. For over a century, indeed, it had been the undisputed commercial metropolis of the English possessions in North America. The challenge to this supremacy was to come from Pennsylvania only after 1750.

In spite of the commercial prominence and general affluence of the province at this period, the trade of Boston was much disturbed by the reorganization of the colony's financial system. This reorganization, which was to give Massachusetts the distinction of becoming the only "hard money" colony in America, was due to the receipt of funds from Great Britain, amounting to £183,649 sterling, as reimbursement for the expense involved in the Louisbourg expedition during King George's War.

In 1748, according to William Douglass, the debt of the province, in the form of depreciated bills of credit, stood at £2,405,000 old tenor.[21] Between 1703 and 1749 bills of credit to the amount of

---

[20] Dinwiddie's estimates for the above colonies are as follows: Pennsylvania, £300,000; New York, £250,000; Connecticut, £90,000; Rhode Island, £90,000; New Hampshire, £96,000; Nova Scotia, £10,000. Abercromby's "Examination," Shelburne Papers 47:28–9.

[21] As in other New England colonies, the issue of paper currency in Massachusetts Bay, which began in 1690, led to rapid depreciation; in the course of years, as a result of a series of emissions, we find various denominations of these bills of credit: beginning with old tenor, then the middle tenor, then new tenor first, and new tenor second. All, according to Douglass, passed at the same value in 1748, which was £1,100 as the equivalent of £100 of British sterling. In contrast, Virginia currency in terms of treasurer's certificates, had a value only slightly less than sterling, so that £125 in Virginia money was the equivalent of £100 sterling; in Barbados

£3,259,708 had been issued, of which only £1,218,598 had been called in.[22] By the end of the 1730's it became clear that the problem of inflation was seriously affecting the economic life of the province and that it was a matter of vital necessity that a sound money system should be provided. John Colman, a merchant with numerous supporters, brought forward in 1739 a plan for a land bank with power to issue notes on land security to the amount of £150,000. When in the June 1740 session of the General Court the House of Representatives refused to forbid this venture and many towns began to take the notes, Colman and his partners went ahead despite the stormy opposition of Governor Belcher and the Council.[23] The land-bank project now came before the Privy Council in England on petition of London merchants. The Council, after a hearing, ordered that the Governor be instructed to discountenance such a scheme by proclamation and by a public address to the General Court.[24]

What is more, continuing to assert its supremacy even in the internal affairs of the American colonies, just as it had done in 1696, Parliament in 1741 passed "An Act restraining and preventing several unwarrantable Schemes and Undertakings in his Majesty's Colonies and Plantations in America,"[25] thus extending to the colo-

---

it was £130 to £100 sterling; in Jamaica it was £140 to £100 sterling; in St. Chistopher it was £160 to £100 sterling; in Pennsylvania and in West New Jersey it was £180 to £100 sterling; in East New Jersey and New York it was £190. See William Douglass: *op. cit.*, I, 493–4, 509, n.; see also A. M. Davis: *Currency and Banking in the Province of the Massachusetts-Bay* (American Economic Association *Publications*, 3rd ser., 2 vols., New York, 1901–1), I, 168, and his "Provincial Banks: Land and Silver," Colonial Society of Massachusetts *Transactions*, III (1895–7), 2–40.

[22] J. B. Felt: *An Historical Account of Massachusetts Currency* (Boston, 1939), p. 251. The author of *A Brief Account of the Rise, Progress, and Present State of the Paper Currency of New-England. And of Measures taken by Massachusetts Province, for establishing a Silver Currency for the Future* (Boston, 1749, p. 5, n.) points out the sensible steps that should have been taken to prevent the great depreciation of the bills of credit.

[23] *Journals of the House of Representatives of Massachusetts* (1740–41), XVIII, 47–8, 131–2, and A. M. Davis: *Currency and Banking*, I, 131. In this connection the student should consult the important article by Theodore Thayer: "The Land-Bank System in the American Colonies," *Journal of Economic History*, XIII, 145–59, and also G. A. Billias: *The Massachusetts Land Bankers of 1740* (University of Maine *Studies*, 2nd ser., No. 74, Orono, Me., 1959).

[24] *Acts of the Privy Council, Col. Ser., 1720–1745*, p. 684.

[25] 14 Geo. II, c. 37, *Statutes at Large* . . . (10 vols., printed by Eyre & Strahan, London, 1786); this edition is used for all Acts of Parliament cited hereafter.

nies the restrictions of the so-called "Bubble Act" of 1718 (6 Geo. I, c. 18). This statute was aimed directly at the land bank. Not only was there no protest on the part of the House of Representatives over this interference by Parliament in this important matter, but in 1743, tacitly accepting the binding power of parliamentary legislation, it joined with the Council in legislation that would put an end to the bank.[26]

It was during this period of controversy over the land-bank scheme that Thomas Hutchinson laid down a plan for establishing a sound currency through the redemption of the depreciated bills of credit. Upon the receipt of the reimbursement funds from England and after some hesitation, the proposed law with a few alterations was approved by the General Court in 1748.[27] It carried the title "An Act for drawing in the Bills of Credit of the several Denominations . . . issued by this Government and . . . still outstanding, and for ascertaining the Rate of coin'd Silver in this Province for the future."[28] The statute, providing among other things for the exchange of silver for the depreciated old-tenor bills of credit upon the basis of ten pounds in these to one pound sterling, was thereupon — in conformity with the charter requirements — submitted to His Majesty in Council. In June of that year a Board of Trade representation favouring its confirmation was accepted.[29] The Lords Commissioners referred to the fact that the plan of redemption "may appear at the first View to be in some Degree a Breach of the public Faith of the Province and an Injustice to the possessors of the said Bills," but then went on, in referring to the bills of credit,

---

[26] *Acts and Laws of Massachusetts-Bay* (Boston, 1762), pp. 345–8, 353–4. For a detailed history of the land bank see A. M. Davis: *Currency and Banking*, II, 130–61. As Mr. Davis pointed out (p. 260): "At a later date this practical approval of the act of parliament by local legislation, proved a stumbling block for some of the politicians of the revolutionary party, in the discussions concerning parliamentary supremacy."

[27] Malcolm Freiberg: "Thomas Hutchinson and the Province Currency," *New England Quarterly*, XXX, 190–208; A. M. Davis: *op. cit.*, I, 214–52.

[28] *Acts and Laws of Massachusetts-Bay* (Boston, 1762), pp. 381–6; this was explained by an act in 1749 (pp. 391–2), and still further explained by an act of 1750 (pp. 395–6). For the delay in receiving the funds from England see A. M. Davis: *Currency and Banking*, I, Chap. 11.

[29] The language employed by the Board on this occasion should be of interest to the economist and political scientist of today, in light of the important decision of the United States Supreme Court in 1935 on the fulfilment of promises to pay in gold.

to emphasize the fact "that by far the greatest part thereof have passed from hand to hand and been received by the present possessors at even a lower Rate than is set upon them by this Act." As to redemption at face value, they declared that since "the first possessors never did or could receive near that Nominal Value so it would be unreasonable that the present possessors should avail themselves of a Benefit which they have never purchased and cannot in Equity be entituled to."[30]

Massachusetts Bay now attained the status of a silver-money colony. The law provided that all Spanish-milled pieces of eight of full weight should be valued at the rate of six shillings for the discharge of every contract entered into after March 31, 1750, with a penalty of £50 to be levied upon any person taking or paying a higher rate. Again, the raising of a tax of £75,000 in the year 1749, in terms of the middle- or new-tenor money, was voted. Further, to prevent the depreciated bills of credit of the other New England colonies circulating within the province, severe penalties were provided for anyone attempting to circulate them during a period of four years, beginning with March 1750.[31]

The sterling money received — that is, £183,649 — was equal to £244,866 in the new "lawful money" of the province. This was sufficient to retire £1,836,495 of the old depreciated currency reduced to old-tenor rates of exchange. The old, badly depreciated bills of credit were thereupon called in. Yet it appears that it was not at the rate signified in the law but at the higher rate of seven and one half to one, and Spanish pieces of eight were paid to the holders.[32] This ultimately was most advantageous, for the people were at last furnished with a stable hard money, something they had not had

---

[30] *Acts of the Privy Council, Col. Ser., 1745–1766*, pp. 85–9.

[31] *Ibid.* After the passage of the act under consideration a petition signed by merchants and other inhabitants of Boston was submitted to His Majesty praying that he would compel the governments of New Hampshire, Connecticut, and Rhode Island to redeem their bills at the rate which Massachusetts Bay had covenanted to observe and to refrain from issuing any additional paper money. *Ibid.*, pp. 81–2.

[32] That is, payment was made upon the basis of 50 shillings to the ounce of silver, instead of 55 shillings as was first proposed. Thomas Hutchinson: *History of the Colony and Province of Massachusetts-Bay* (ed. L. S. Mayo, 3 vols., Cambridge, 1936), II, 335–6. Boston Correspondence, *Pennsylvania Journal*, June 14, 1750. For a discussion of this see C. H. J. Douglas: *Financial History of Massachusetts from the Organization of the Colony to the American Revolution* (Columbia University *Studies*, I, New York, 1892); J. B. Felt: *op cit.;* and, especially, A. M. Davis, *op. cit.*, I, Chap 12.

since the gradual disappearance of their old Pine Tree shillings, which — first struck in the middle of the preceding century — had not been minted since 1686.[33]

But conditions in 1750, due to the dislocation of business resulting from a rather sudden resumption of specie payments, were, temporarily, chaotic. One gentleman, writing from Boston in June, declared that "Trade is quite dead" and that "the Town is as dull and still as on Sunday." Although it was full of goods, there was no money with which to buy: there was less Massachusetts Bay current money "by five hundred thousand pounds," and that of the other colonial governments, which previously had circulated there freely, was no longer a tender. "All countenances are dull; we curse one another; especially those are cursed that were for the Act. As soon as the dollars come out they are shipped to London, New York, Philadelphia, or Hispaniola or are laid up to worship. . . . *What a deplorable picture is here.*"[34]

In spite of the extent of the territory of Massachusetts Bay, the inhabitants, including those living in Maine, numbered only 220,-000, according to an estimate made in 1755.[35] They were employed chiefly in farming, in the fisheries, in navigation, and in the building of ships as well as in providing materials for their construction.[36]

---

[33] For the fate of the Pine Tree shilling see C. P. Nettels: *op. cit.,* pp. 171–5.

[34] See a letter in the *Pennsylvania Journal,* June 7, 1750. See also a letter from Boston in the August 2 issue of the *Pennsylvania Journal:* "You can't possibly imagine what an alteration there is in our affairs for want of a medium there being scarce any money of any sort to be seen except a few coppers, and they seem to diminish; all trade seems to be stagnated, and little else goes on but drinking." "The effect was frightful. Ruin stalked in every home; the people could not pay their taxes; and were obliged to see their property seized by the sheriff," Alexander Del Mar asserted with some exaggeration in his *The History of Money in America* (New York, 1899, p. 83), referring to Boston of this period.

The refusal of the government of the province to accept the bills of credit of other colonies led "a poor Journeyman Tradesman" on December 8, 1749, to complain bitterly for himself "and ten thousand others in like Circumstance" that the money he had laid aside for his taxes, 121 bills of other colonies, could not be used for that purpose. In this connection he emphasized that it was impossible for him to lay his hands on any of the bills of Massachusetts Bay. See the *Boston Evening Post,* December 18, 1749.

[35] New Hampshire Historical Society *Collections,* V, 230; E. B. Green and Virginia D. Harrington: *American Population before . . . 1790* (New York, 1932), pp. 5–6.

[36] G. R. Minot: *Continuation of the History . . . of Massachusetts Bay,* I, 155–61.

The comparative value of the exports of farm produce and of wealth derived from the sea by Massachusetts Bay in 1715 was, according to Captain Thomas Banister, £113,000 and £491,000, respectively. See "Essay on the Trade of New

So busy, in fact, were the people in the pursuit of these particular interests and so unsatisfactory was the cultivation of wheat, owing to the barberry rust, that it was necessary to import annually from North Carolina, Virginia, Maryland, and other southward points, large quantities of flour and bread, together with corn and pork, in order to subsist the great seafaring, as well as the town-dwelling, population.

That the province was, nevertheless, peopled largely by agriculturalists is indicated by the rating of the counties in 1751. Out of the ratable polls numbering 41,126, Essex County stood first with 7,622, then followed Suffolk with 6,518, and Middlesex with 6,488. The total number of dwelling houses was placed at 23,463, with Essex again first with 4,778, followed by Middlesex with 4,175, Worcester with 2,696, Plymouth with 2,416 and Suffolk with 2,400. The grist mills numbered 814, with Middlesex leading with 129, followed by Essex and Worcester with 115 each, and Plymouth with 107. There were 22,161 horses and mares, with Middlesex holding first place, after which came Essex, Worcester, Hampshire, Suffolk, and Bristol; oxen were more numerous than horses, totalling 37,429, with the counties rated in the following order: Middlesex, Essex, Worcester, Plymouth, Bristol, and Suffolk; cows far surpassed oxen in the enumeration, for a total of 79,614, with Middlesex well in the lead and Essex in second place, after which came Worcester, Suffolk, Plymouth, Bristol, and York. However, in sheep, which numbered 233,-502, Essex took first place; then came Middlesex, Worcester, and Plymouth. When it came to grain[37] and flax, and to orchards and the production of cider, Middlesex in each instance again stood first,[38]

England" (1715), C.O. 5:866, no. 67, quoted by C. P. Nettels in his *The Money Supply of the American Colonies before 1720*, p. 100.

[37] Wheat was not an important crop in Massachusetts Bay. In 1660 the black stem-rust made its appearance and remained a serious menace to this cereal. Indian corn or maize, rye, barley, and oats were grown successfully and corn and rye bread became staple articles of food. See P. W. Bidwell and J. I. Falconer: *History of Agriculture in the Northern United States, 1620–1860* (Washington, 1925), pp. 13–14. Jared Eliot, writing in 1748 from his home in Connecticut, speaks of raising 60 or 70 bushels of Indian corn from his land. See *Essays upon Field Husbandry in New England and Other Papers by Jared Eliot* (eds. H. J. Carman and R. G. Tugwell, Columbia University, *Studies in Agriculture*, New York, 1934), pp. 15, 29, and 58. Eliot attributed the lack of wheat harvests to the failure of farmers to dress their lands properly.

[38] "Valuation of the Severall Counties in the Prov^ce of Mass. Bay," 1751, Massachusetts Historical Society, Miscellaneous Mss. XII, 1749–1760.

as it did in slaves fit to labour. Out of a total of 1,941 listed, it accounted for 503; Essex was credited with 405, Suffolk with 285, Bristol with 189, Plymouth with 172, York with 129, Hampshire with 88, Barnstaple with 80, Worcester with 69, Dukes with 16, and, finally, Nantucket with 5.[39]

In the field of industry the province, while not a leading producer of iron and ironware, had a total of fifty bloomeries and forges in operation in 1751, almost half of which were located in Plymouth County, with Barnstaple and Suffolk accounting for most of the rest.[40] Much more important than iron products was rum, distilled from molasses. At this period some sixty-three distilleries were in operation, producing annually over 15,000 hogsheads of this heady beverage, or not far from two million gallons.[41]

According to the opinion of traders of the period, rum was the foundation of all the happy prosperity and material welfare evidenced by the inhabitants of the province. It was called "the great support of all their trade and fishery, without which they can no longer subsist,"[42] for it was the common beverage of practically all their labourers: their loggers, timber men, sailors, and fishermen. Men asserted that they could not endure the hardships of their employment or the rigours of the seasons without it. The precious article was the basis of the trade with the southern continental colonies, with the Indians for furs, with Newfoundland for prize fish, and with the Guinea Coast for gold and slaves. To obtain the molasses from which it was distilled, an immense quantity of "refuse"

---

[39] *Ibid.* See also the enumeration of Negro slaves at the end of 1754, Massachusetts Historical Society *Collections*, 2nd ser., III, 95–7. L. J. Greene: *The Negro in Colonial New England, 1620–1776* (New York, 1942) gives a broad scholarly treatment of New England slavery.

[40] Massachusetts Historical Society, Miscellaneous Mss. XII, 1749–1760.

[41] G. R. Minot: *op. cit.*, I, 155–61; Charles W. Taussig: *Rum, Romance and Rebellion* (New York, 1928), p. 16.

[42] The above observations are from the brief drawn up by the traders of Massachusetts Bay in the face of the efforts of the British West India planters in 1748 to prohibit trade to the foreign sugar islands. See G. R. Minot: *op. cit.*, I, 155–61. Out of a total of some 15,000 hogsheads of rum exported by the province, 9,000 went to the Newfoundland fisheries, 3,000 to the southern colonies, 1,300 to the Straits of Canso and other adjacent places, and 1,700 to Africa. See Colonial Society of Massachusetts *Publications*, XIX, 386–7. It is asserted that a gallon of molasses would make almost a gallon of rum. Witt Bowden: *The Industrial History of the United States* (New York, 1930), p. 86.

or "Jamaica" fish was carried to the West Indies. The profitable disposal of this inferior article was indeed a vital matter, for it constituted between one fourth and one half of the total catch of the cod fishermen and made up a large proportion of the cargoes brought from Newfoundland. Happily, the British sugar-planters were eager to receive the fish for their slaves and generally agreed to pay for it in specie. As the planters on the French sugar islands were usually faced with a great surplus of molasses which they were naturally anxious to sell, it was highly advantageous for the Massachusetts Bay skippers to approach them with this specie, by means of which they drove excellent bargains with the Frenchmen. At the same time, it is undoubtedly true that much of the abundant supply of molasses thus purchased for the Boston distillers found its way into Massachusetts Bay without the payment of the duties provided for by the Molasses Act of 1733.[43]

The inhabitants of the colony from the very beginning had shown an interest in the development of the fisheries. In the course of the seventeenth century they succeeded in appropriating the great cod and mackerel beds of the waters now known as the Gulf of Maine,[44] and in the eighteenth century the equally valuable beds to the south of the Strait of Canso which lie between Nova Scotia and Cape Breton Island. By 1731 over 5,000 New England men were engaged in the fisheries and were catching approximately 230,000 quintals of fish, which yielded some £700,000 local currency; by 1750 some 400 vessels were employed in the cod fisheries — principally in the Gulf of Maine and about Nova Scotia and Newfoundland — while 200 sought the mackerel and other small fish about the

---

[43] From 1733 to 1749 total duties to the amount of £1,043 were received by the customs officials at the Massachusetts Bay ports of entry on foreign rum, molasses, and sugar. New York, a port of much less importance, paid duties on these articles during the same period amounting to £2,002. See G. R. Minot: *op. cit.*, I, 163 for tables.

[44] It seems that no codfish of finer quality was cured within the Empire than in New England, where, according to the testimony of Governor Bellomont in 1700, it was caught and cured during the period of cold weather and was therefore considered so superior that it brought in the markets of Portugal one piece of eight more per quintal than the Newfoundland fish. His letter to the Board of Trade of November 28 is quoted by C. P. Nettels: *The Money Supply of the American Colonies before 1720*, p. 78; see also William Douglass: *op. cit.*, I, 301, and Raymond McFarland: *A History of New England Fisheries* (New York, 1911), pp. 69 and 86.

inshore grounds of the coast in that year.[45] These activities laid the fortunes of such men as Peter Faneuil of Boston, who showed his munificence to his own town by erecting the famous market building that bears his name. Moreover, as will be stressed in a later chapter of this volume, the interest of the men of Massachusetts Bay in Newfoundland developed to such a point that it became a matter of public concern in England. For it was frankly viewed with apprehension by those who looked to the annual sailing of the fleets from the fishing towns of the mother country as one of the principal guarantees of the maintenance of English naval supremacy. They feared that, just as other fisheries had been monopolized by New Englanders, so might those of the Banks — resulting in the decay of English shipping and the western seaports.

In addition to cod- and mackerel-fishing interests, Massachusetts Bay men were deeply involved in whaling. From the towns of the Bay, such as Gloucester — with New Bedford and Nantucket soon to assume first importance — a hundred whalers, carrying hardy, adventurous crews, sailed into the subarctic regions and especially into the Gulf of St. Lawrence in pursuit of sperm oil, head material, and whalebone.[46] They seldom returned without an annual supply.

The foregoing developments indicate the extreme aggressiveness of the Massachusetts Bay seamen. The same could be said of her landmen. They had dotted with townships the whole region from the Merrimac on the north to the neighbourhood of Narragansett Bay on the south, from Cape Cod on the east to the Connecticut

---

[45] W. B. Weeden: *Economic and Social History of New England, 1620–1789* (2 vols., Boston and New York, 1890), II, 641; see also Raymond McFarland: *op. cit.*, Chap. 1. In 1762 the Massachusetts Bay fisheries, it was estimated, brought in £ 164,466 sterling, with the cod shipped to Europe selling for 12 shillings per quintal and that to the West Indies for 9 shillings per quintal. For this data and facts relating to these fisheries in general see "State of the Trade," 1763, in the Colonial Society of Massachusetts *Transactions*, XIX, 383–90.

[46] W. B. Weeden: *op. cit.*, II, 644. In 1771 there were 665 Massachusetts Bay ships engaged in the cod fisheries, 304 in whaling, and 90 in catching mackerel and other fish. See *The Commonwealth History of Massachusetts* (ed. A. B. Hart, 5 vols., New York, 1927–30), II, 404, for these and other figures. For whaling see G. F. Dow: *Whale Ships and Whaling* (Marine Research Society, Salem, 1925), pp. 3–40; W. S. Tower: *A History of the American Whale Fishery* (Philadelphia, 1907), p. 45; Alexander Starbuck: *The History of Nantucket* (Boston, 1924), p. 176; Raymond McFarland: *op. cit.*, p. 86; and Obed Macy: *The History of Nantucket* (Boston, 1835), p. 54.

and beyond to the west.[47] In the course of the seventeenth century they had swallowed up the Province of Maine and the Colony of Plymouth and had threatened with extinction, by reason of their extravagant boundary claims, New Hampshire to the northward and Rhode Island to the southward. By 1750, pushed by an insatiable land hunger, they were crowding along the western border and beyond the settled portions of York County, Maine, and were about to challenge the rights of those great land magnates of the Province of New York established to the east of the Hudson. For Massachusetts still held to the ancient limits from sea to sea laid down by royal patent in the Charter of 1629.[48]

In the seventeenth century and the early part of the eighteenth, vacant lands had been granted by the government to church congregations or other groups desiring a change of location. But this method of land settlement — with the growing influence of the secular in government as against the clerical, and of individualism as against the old Puritan conception of social solidarity — had been sufficiently modified by 1750 so that it was possible for an individual interested in land speculation to secure a very considerable grant, frequently in payment for military services. This in turn he disposed of in small allotments to actual settlers,[49] which resulted in an in-

[47] The expansion along the frontiers of Massachusetts Bay is indicated by the creation of towns between 1750 and 1765. In 1750 there were 156 towns, and by 1765 there were 206 — including, of course, those within the old Province of Maine. The county with the largest number of towns in 1750 was Middlesex, with 32, and it increased the number to 37 by 1765; Suffolk had 18 in 1750 and the same number in 1765; but Worcester had 22 in 1750 and 35 by 1765, and Hampshire had 17 in 1750 and 29 in 1765. Further, Berkshire, the westernmost county, was in existence by 1765 with 6 towns; likewise, in Maine, in addition to York County, there were now the two new counties of Cumberland with 7 towns and Lincoln with 6, although the subdivision of York County left it with but 7 towns instead of 11 as in 1750. See the *Journals of the House of Representatives of Massachusetts* (1749–1750), XXVI, 4, and the "Census of 1765," *The Commonwealth History of Massachusetts,* II, 112; and also the map, *ibid.,* II, opposite p. 102, indicating the new settlements created in Massachusetts Bay proper between 1740 and 1765.

[48] The Governor of Massachusetts Bay to the Board of Trade, March 2, 1736/7, Shelburne Papers, 45:187–91.

[49] See Colonial Society of Massachusetts *Publications,* XVIII, 69; also the petition in 1753 of Samuel Waldo and Windham Beawes, attorneys for Robert Mackey and John Corner of London, Merchants, praying for a grant of land. *Journal of the Commissioners for Trade and Plantations from . . . 1704 to . . . 1782, preserved in the Public Record Office* (14 vols., London, 1920–38), *1749–1753,* pp. 411, 412 (to be referred to hereafter as the Board of Trade *Journal*). For a discussion of land speculation in New England see R. H. Akagi: *The Town Proprietors of the New England Colonies, 1620–1770* (Philadelphia, 1924).

creased tendency for individuals to seek isolated farms rather than to unite with others in establishing community centres in the wilderness.

Nevertheless, the conditions under which Penacook[50] to the west of the upper Merrimac River was settled may be accepted as characteristic of the processes of Massachusetts Bay colonization down to 1750. In the beginning of the year 1725, upon petition of a group of intended settlers — mostly of Haverhill, it appears — the government created a township of seven square miles in the region of the projected settlement. This was granted to the petitioners under certain specified conditions, among which were these: that the tract should be divided into 103 equal shares or lots; that 100 families should settle thereon within the space of three years; that each settler should build a good dwelling house and break up and fence six acres of land within the time aforesaid; that the houses should be erected within twenty rods of each other on the home lots and "in a regular and defensible manner"; that a convenient house for the public worship of God should be completely finished within the time first mentioned; and, finally, that each settler should pay the province £5 for his right. As soon as the hundred families were admitted as settlers, they were empowered to hold proprietary meetings to care for their common interests. Of the three remaining rights (out of the 103 lots) one was reserved for the first settled minister, one for a parsonage, and one for "the use of the church forever."[51] In 1726 a committee of the grantees proceeded to lay out the lots, and the following year the required number of settlers was approved under the terms laid down and thereupon proceeded to the Penacook area. By 1730 a church was built and a minister ordained, and three years later the community was incorporated as

---

[50] Penacook was the name of a tribe of Indians once settled near the upper waters of the Merrimac River. From 1733 to 1765 the new town held the name Rumford, and in the latter year it was incorporated as the town of Concord, which later became the capital of New Hampshire.

[51] New Hampshire Historical Society *Collections*, I, 154–218. For a study of the early land system of Massachusetts Bay see Melville Egleston: "Land System of the New England Colonies," Johns Hopkins University *Studies*, 4th ser., XI, pp. 1–56; R. H. Akagi: *Town Proprietors of the New England Colonies;* H. E. Osgood: *American Colonies in the Seventeenth Century* (4 vols., New York, 1924), I, Chap. 11.

a township by act of the Massachusetts Bay General Court under the name Rumford.[52]

The century of pioneering by the descendants of those who crowded into Massachusetts Bay during the days of the Great Migration had had the result, taken together with other influences exerted from across the Atlantic, of profoundly modifying the character and general outlook on life of the majority of people. The Congregational Church, in spite of its powerfully entrenched position in 1750, was no such force within the colony as it had been in 1650. At the earlier date the local church had directly or indirectly exercised a very great influence over the lives of individuals. Through its influence upon the government of the colony, all the people, whether members or non-members, were subject to minute regulations, extending to the most private interests.[53] The members were those in fellowship who not only had received baptism but also had qualified (by open confession) to participate in the church communion and were consequently designated as being of the communion. It was this group which had looked after the ecclesiastical functions of the town and in addition had controlled its civil interests. The pastor of the congregation, alone of the group, had been considered competent to unlock the mysteries of the word of God. He had ruled without a serious rival. However, the expanding frontier and the exigencies that grew out of it, together with other forces almost equally as potent, had in the course of a century brought about certain changes profoundly affecting the Congregational Establishment.

In 1657 and 1662 synods of the church significantly made concessions by establishing the halfway covenant. This required baptism as the only condition for the enjoyment of the civil privileges of church membership, although not for participation in the sacra-

---

[52] *Acts of the Privy Council, Col. Ser., 1745–1766*, pp. 239–43.

[53] See Perry Miller: *Orthodoxy in Massachusetts, 1630–1750: A Genetic Study* (Cambridge, 1933); H. M. Dexter: *Congregationalism of the Last Three Hundred Years* (New York, 1880); Williston Walker: *The Creeds and Platforms of Congregationalism* (New York, 1893); Champlin Burrage: *Early English Dissenters in Light of Recent Research, 1550–1641* (2 vols., Cambridge, 1912); S. E. Morison: *Builders of the Bay Colony* (Boston and New York, 1930); J. T. Adams: *The Founding of New England* (Boston, 1921).

ment of the Lord's Supper, which presupposed testimony of conversion. Subsequently Solomon Stoddard, pastor of the Northampton church, persuaded the Reforming Synod of 1679 "to make a mere profession of faith and repentance and not a relation of a personal experience of grace the requisite for church membership." Moreover, the new charter granted to the colony in 1691 struck squarely at the Church Establishment, although it is true that the provincial government continued to pass measures aimed at maintaining the old and still cherished ecclesiastical system.[54] In 1692 came the witchcraft terror, the rationalistic aftermath of which was not conducive to the continued great influence of the church. Further, the Anglicans and especially the Quakers, always in opposition, gradually became most formidable enemies of the Establishment.[55] These groups, together with the Baptists, in the course of the first half of the eighteenth century succeeded in gaining special exemptions[56] that freed them from the necessity of attending the religious services of the Congregational Church and also of contributing financial support to it. All others of course remained under the same compulsions, legally at least, as had existed in the seventeenth century.[57]

---

[54] For an excellent statement regarding this point see the "Opinion of Messrs. Yorke & Talbot respecting certain grievances complained of by the Church of England Clergy in the Massachusetts Bay," submitted in 1732 to the Board of Trade, *Historical Collections Relating to the American Colonial Church* (ed. W. S. Perry, 5 vols., Hartford [Conn.], 1870), III, 274–88.

[55] This topic has been carefully treated by Susan M. Reed in her "Church and State in Massachusetts, 1691–1740," University of Illinois *Studies in Social Science*, III, No. 4. See also J. C. Meyer: *Church and State in Massachusetts Bay, 1740–1833* (Cleveland, 1930).

[56] In 1728 the Baptists and Quakers were exempted by temporary laws from poll taxes for the support of the Congregational Establishment. But this did not exempt them from having their estates taxed. For the law and comments upon it see Isaac Backus: *A Church History of New England . . .* (3 vols., Boston and Providence, 1777–96), II, 86–7. Members of the Church of England also obtained this exemption and in addition a permanent law in their favour in 1742 (16 Geo. II, c. 8). See *Acts and Laws of Massachusetts Bay*, pp. 331–2; see also "A List of Acts passed in the Massachusetts Bay . . . [1752]," Shelburne Papers, 49:63–98.

[57] The following brief description of Boston in 1751 shows the divisions along denominational lines: "The three Episcopal Congregations of this Town are large, and tho' mine is not so well situated for services, yet is increasing. The independent congregations are 10 large ones, and two small ones, owing to and leaven'd with Methodism. We have two small Anabaptist Congregations, one sprung from Methodism. Papists are among us not a few, but how many or whether increasing I cannot find" (Mr. Cutler to the Secretary [of the Venerable Society], Boston, New England, December 26, 1751, W. S. Perry: *op. cit.*, III, 440–1).

In the eighteenth century the Establishment was weakened by still other forces. First, there had taken place a dispersion of the sons of its earlier supporters. Many of them, leaving their ancestral abodes, went to live on the outskirts of new townships and consequently far from the church's ministrations and discipline. Again, in the region of the old seated towns and especially in Boston the press undoubtedly introduced factors that struck at ecclesiastical authority. Further, the prevailing latitudinarianism in England at this period was undoubtedly exerting its influence even in Massachusetts Bay. There was also an acknowledged weakening of the old religious ardor with the growth of the doctrines of Arminius in New England which struck at the Calvinistic foundations of the church.[58]

In 1731 young Jonathan Edwards — who had succeeded his grandfather, the Rev. Mr. Stoddard, and was destined to become New England's leading theologian and preacher — started a powerful drive against the prevalent New England religious drift in his Boston public lecture on "God Glorified in Man's Dependence."[59] His preaching, together with that of George Whitefield, Gilbert Tennent, and others, gradually stirred up the most astonishing religious revival in all American history. Known as the Great Awakening,[60] it might better be described as the coming of the Great Fear.

---

[58] See H. B. Parkes: "New England in the Seventeen-thirties," *New England Quarterly,* III, 397–419.

[59] For a revealing background of conditions within the Congregational Church in Massachusetts Bay in 1731, the student should consult Perry Miller's *Jonathan Edwards,* in the *American Men of Letters Series* (New York, 1949), Chap. 1. For Edwards's early life and ancestry see especially Ola E. Winslow's *Jonathan Edwards, 1707–1758* (New York, 1940).

[60] The latest study having to do with the New England phase of the great religious revival is by E. S. Gaustad: *The Great Awakening in New England* (New York, 1957). Gaustad also presents an extended bibliography of sources (pp. 160–8) relating to the New England aspect of this movement; see also Ola E. Winslow: *op. cit.,* pp. 373–93, for a still more extended bibliography of the Great Awakening. An earlier important work, on account of its presentation of New England source materials, is Joseph Tracy: *The Great Awakening: A History of the Revival of Religion in the Time of Edwards and Whitefield* (Boston, 1842); see also L. W. Labaree: "The Conservative Attitude toward the Great Awakening," *William and Mary Quarterly,* 3rd ser., I, 331–52.

Subject of continuous debate in the Massachusetts Bay colony, the preachings of George Whitefield received constant attention in the *Boston Evening-Post* during 1745–7. In contrast to the serious thought given to the Great Awakening movement, the following letter in the January 14, 1745, issue may be of interest:

"Sir,

"I am one of the unhappy Men that are plagued with a *Gospel gossip*. Lectures

To Edwards, God was the embodiment of supreme love and also of supreme and stern justice. To quote from one of his sermons:

"Though he will know that you cannot bear the weight of omnipotence treading upon you, yet will he not regard that, but he will crush you under his feet without mercy; he will crush out your blood, and make it fly, and it will be sprinkled on his garments so as to stain all his raiment. He will not only hate you, but he will have you in the utmost contempt."[61]

The sinner once condemned was beyond all hope of salvation and redemption in face of the inflexible will of God, and only a few out of each generation would escape this terrible fate. Nor were those of tender age free from the "wrath of God of infinite love":

"As innocent as young children seem to be to us, yet, if they are out of Christ, they are not so in God's sight, but are young vipers, and infinitely more hateful than vipers . . . ."[62]

The titles of Edwards's sermons are sufficiently indicative of the development of his theological conceptions. Examples of these are: "The Eternity of Hell Torments," "Sinners in the Hands of an Angry God," and "The Justice of God in the Damnation of Sinners." The immediate effect of this sort of preaching upon the simple-hearted, receptive people who gathered to hear the great Northampton theologian and his followers is quite beyond description. They wailed, they wrung their hands, they fell to the floor in emotional fits.[63]

In spite of this, Edwards was by no means the typical revivalist and was far removed from such a ranter as his contemporary James

---

in the *Morning*, Church meetings at Noon, and Preparation Sermons at Night take up so much of her Time, 'tis very rare she knows what we have for Dinner, unless when the Preacher is to be at it. With him comes a Tribe, all *Brothers* and *Sisters* it seems; while others, *really such*, are deemed no Relations. If at any Time I have her Company alone she is a meer Sermon Pop gun, repeating and discharging Tests, Proofs, and Application so perpetually, that however I may go to Bed, the Noise in my Head will not let me sleep till towards Morning. . . ."

[61] *Life and Works of Jonathan Edwards* (ed. S. E. Dwight, 8 vols., Leeds, 1806–11), IV, 320.

[62] See Professor A. V. G. Allen: *Jonathan Edwards* (Boston and New York, 1891), p. 191.

[63] See *ibid.*, pp. 177–218, and Joseph Tracy: *The Great Awakening* . . . (Boston, 1842), pp. 215–16.

Davenport. A man of extraordinary intellect, he spoke in a quiet, well-modulated voice as he sought to illuminate the ways of God. His sermons dealt with what most people today would regard as some of the unfathomable mysteries of life.[64]

Many of the pastors of Congregational churches enthusiastically promoted the revival, welcoming the itinerant evangelists who now appeared in every town and village to further the work. Others saw in this tremendous excitement an enemy of true religion and of an orderly church. Started as a movement to restore the old fervour of Congregationalism and its ministry in New England, the revival was having other consequences. By the middle of the century sober men had become convinced that the revival was shattering the Establishment. For in practically every town of importance the more ardent supporters of the new movement had led secessions from the community congregation to set up a rival organization, generally known as the New Light Congregational Church. The Baptists also received many accessions to their membership. The conservative reaction was equally pronounced. Even Edwards became a victim of it. He not only opposed the halfway covenant approved by his own congregation, but also alienated himself further by openly denouncing those who were reading such popular novels as Samuel Richardson's *Pamela*. Thus, by a vote of the Northampton town meeting in 1749, he was forbidden the use of the pulpit from which he had preached with almost unprecedented power for over twenty years. Indeed, once the revival had died down, theology was never again the all-absorbing interest it had been so long in New England.[65]

There was something really prophetic in the decision made by young Samuel Adams in 1743 to base his master's thesis at Harvard upon politics in discussing the query "Whether it be Lawful to resist the Supreme Magistrate, if the Commonwealth cannot otherwise be preserved." Nevertheless, it would be quite untrue to take the posi-

---

[64] The two most recent biographies of Edwards cited above by Ola E. Winslow and Perry Miller, both stress the greatness of the man. To Miller he is "intellectually the most modern man of his age" (*op. cit.*, p. 305). This position has been challenged by Vincent Tomas in his "The Modernity of Jonathan Edwards," *New England Quarterly*, XXV, 60–84.

[65] T. H. Billings: "The Great Awakening," Essex Institute Historical *Collections*, LXV, 89–104.

tion that the Great Awakening was barren of good results. It caused men to re-examine seriously the basis of their own religious beliefs and also those of others. It promoted piety among many whose lives had been abandoned. And, in the end, as a reaction to the narrowness of its objectives, it led to greater breadth of religious outlook and to wider sympathy toward those of kindred faiths. This was especially true as the revival penetrated into frontier areas among pioneering groups whose members had differing backgrounds, yet shared a desire for spiritual uplift.

The gradual change in the attitude of many people toward the ecclesiastical system is well illustrated by the appearance in 1721 of *The New-England Courant* under the editorship of James Franklin, the elder brother of the later distinguished Benjamin. In it were to be found fiery and coarse attacks upon the clergy and the prevailing social order. That the paper was able to survive until 1727 indicates that it supported the point of view of a respectable number of people — although they may not have been considered by their contemporaries a number of respectable people.

The press, in fact, was destined to usurp in a great measure the place of the pulpit in Massachusetts. The first news sheet printed in America had made its appearance in the colony in 1690 under the title *Public Occurrences, both Foreign and Domestic.*[66] But the printer, Richard Pierce, had not the temerity to put forth more than one issue in view of the denunciations by the authorities. Nevertheless, in 1704 John Campbell, postmaster, founded *The Boston News-Letter,* which, under different editors and names, exerted considerable influence and appeared continuously until it ceased publication during the War for American Independence. In 1719 *The Boston*

---

[66] For a treatment of the press in Boston see D. A. Goddard: "The Press and Literature of the Provincial Period," *Memorial History of Boston,* II, Chap. 15; see also C. S. Brigham: *History and Bibliography of American Newspapers, 1690–1820* (2 vols., Worcester, Mass., 1947), and G. E. Littlefield: *The Early Massachusetts Press, 1638–1711* (2 vols., Boston, 1907). The year 1690 also saw the beginnings of papermaking in the colonies, when William Rittenhouse and his son Nicholas constructed the first paper mill, located near Germantown in Pennsylvania. New Jersey had the second paper mill, established in 1726, and Massachusetts Bay was third, but not until 1744 (in which year Virginia also acquired a paper mill). The press in America was thus largely freed from the necessity of relying upon the importation of printing paper. See Dard Hunter: *Paper Making in Pioneer America* (Philadelphia, 1952). For "Government Printing in Massachusetts-Bay, 1700–1750" by R. G. Silver see American Antiquarian Society *Proceedings,* LXVIII, 135–62.

Gazette was established by Postmaster William Brooker and printed by James Franklin, but it passed to four successive postmasters before its absorption in 1741 by the publishers of *The New-England Weekly Journal,* which, in turn, had come into existence shortly after the disappearance in 1727 of *The New-England Courant.* Published between October 1741 and 1752 as the *Boston Gazette and Weekly Journal,* it then reverted to the name *Boston Gazette,* and under the editorship of Edes and Gill it was to become perhaps the most extremely anti-British of the New England papers. Next came *The Weekly Rehearsal* in 1731, to remain literary in character as long as it was published by Jeremiah Gridley. Thomas Fleet became the proprietor in 1733 and continued to publish it and its successor, *The Boston Weekly Post,* which was virtually the same paper under a different name, but with an evening rather than a morning printing. Two years later it became known as the *Boston Evening-Post* and as such survived until April 1775.

Meanwhile, in 1734 Ellis Huske, upon succeeding to the postmastership, started *The Boston Weekly Post-Boy,* destined to appear regularly under his ownership for twenty years, echoing news from the London journals. Revived later as *The Boston Weekly Advertiser,* it continued until 1775. Finally, during the period before 1750, the short-lived *Independent Advertiser* was launched in 1748 and had an impact on public opinion for two years through its publication of political essays by writers such as Samuel Adams.

The influence of the press was supplemented by the growing influence of Harvard and Yale, where, it is asserted, there were five times as many students attending college in 1740 as there had been in all New England in 1680,[67] in spite of the decline in the number of grammar schools with their stress upon classical, college-preparatory studies.[68] For these institutions of higher education, by the

---

[67] Yale was, of course, not founded until 1701. For Harvard College in the eighteenth century see S. E. Morison: *Three Centuries of Harvard, 1636–1936* (Cambridge, Mass., 1936), Chap. 7; see also C. K. Shipton: *Biographical Sketches of those who attended Harvard College, Sibley's Harvard Graduates,* Vols. VIII and IX (Boston, 1951 and 1956). For the early years of Yale College see Edwin Oviatt: *Beginnings of Yale (1701–1726)* (New Haven, 1916), *Documentary History of Yale University . . . 1701–1745* (ed. F. B. Dexter, New Haven, 1916), and Thomas Clap: *The Annals . . . of Yale-College . . . 1700–1766* (New Haven, 1766).

[68] C. K. Shipton: "Secondary Education in the Puritan Colonies," *New England Quarterly,* VII, 646–61. For the decline of the secondary schools in Massachusetts

middle of the eighteenth century, had become cultural centres where were trained men of the calibre of Thomas Hutchinson, Jared Ingersoll, and William Samuel Johnson, with their broad-minded approach to issues of public importance. It would also seem that many whom these institutions prepared for the ministry at this period entered upon their pastoral duties carrying with them a growing spirit of catholicity and comprehensiveness evidenced particularly by Harvard, which, for example, led its graduates into sharp opposition to the fanaticism involved in the Great Awakening.[69] Indeed, one may question whether in any other portion of the Empire a greater proportion of the population was influenced by what may be called the new humanism than in Massachusetts Bay. And, in the spreading of this enlightenment, certain of the clergy apparently were among the most effective agents.[70]

Massachusetts Bay was one of the three corporate colonies surviving within the old British Empire. Due to its extraordinary aggressiveness and self-sufficiency in the course of the seventeenth century, its original charter had been voided in the Court of Chancery in 1684. Two years later the government of this plantation was embodied in the so-called Dominion of New England, which was ruled by Edmund Andros as Governor,[71] with the assistance of a Council, from 1686 until 1689, when his regime collapsed as the result of the

Bay see M. W. Jernegan's important study in the *School Review*, Vol. XXVII; see also E. D. Grizzell: *Origin of the High School in New England before 1865* (New York, 1923), Chap. 1; J. T. Adams: *Provincial Society, 1690–1763: A History of American Life* (New York, 1927), pp. 132–4; and Charles Angoff: *A Literary History of the American People* (2 vols. in one, New York, 1935), I, 64.

[69] Many Harvard graduates of course supported the Great Awakening. For example, among those graduated in the classes of 1726 to 1730, twenty-two favoured the movement, while thirty-one came out against it. *Sibley's Harvard Graduates*, VIII.

[70] For the development of this theme see C. K. Shipton: "A Plea for Puritanism," *American Historical Review*, XL, 460–7. The growth of scientific activity in New England and elsewhere in America during the last half of the eighteenth century is dealt with in Brooke Hindle's *The Pursuit of Science in Revolutionary America, 1735–1789* (Chapel Hill, N.C., 1956); see also W. J. Bell, Jr.: *Early American Science . . .* (Williamsburg, 1955); Theodore Hornberger: *Scientific Thought in American Colleges* (Austin, 1945); and F. G. Kilgour: "Rise of Scientific Activity in Colonial New England," *Yale Journal of Biology and Medicine*, XXII, 123. For scientific relations between Europe and America see Michael Kraus: *The Atlantic Civilization: Eighteenth-Century Origins* (New York, 1949), Chap. VII.

[71] For Andros's commission see *Rhode Island Colonial Records*, III, 212–18; see also the *Andros Tracts*, III, 1868–74, and Viola F. Barnes: *The Dominion of New England* (New Haven, 1923).

Revolution in England. In 1691 a new charter was granted by William and Mary.[72] This has been well described as "the nearest approach to the creation of a constitution for a royal province by means of a single document that we have before the passage of the Quebec Act in 1774."[73]

Under the terms of the charter, all of the lands within the recognized boundaries of the colony under the first patent, together with the "Colony of New-Plymouth, the Province of Main, the Territory called Accadia, or Nova-Scotia; and all that Tract of Land lying between the said Territories of Nova-Scotia, and the said Province of Main, [were to] be erected, united and incorporated . . . into one Real Province by the Name of Our Province of the Massachusetts Bay in New-England."[74] By this same instrument the freedom of action of the colony was greatly restricted by the provision that the Governor, the Lieutenant or Deputy Governor, and the Secretary should be royal appointees. The Great and General Court of Assembly, consisting of the Governor, a Council of twenty-eight assistants,[75] and the deputies of the freeholders of the various towns,[76]

---

[72] For the text of the charter see *The Charter granted by their Majesties King William and Queen Mary to the Inhabitants of the Province of the Massachusetts-Bay in New-England* (Boston, 1742), or *Acts and Resolves of the Province of Massachusetts Bay*, I, 1–20, or *The Federal and State Constitutions, Colonial Charters, and other organic laws* . . . (ed. F. N. Thorpe, 7 vols., Washington [D.C.], 1909), III, 1880–6.

[73] L. W. Labaree: *Royal Government in America* (*Yale University Publications* VI, New Haven, 1930), pp. 7–8.

[74] *The Charter granted by their Majesties King William and Queen Mary* (Boston, 1742). After the Treaty of Utrecht of 1713, Nova Scotia was placed under a separate administration when Francis Nicholson was appointed Governor on April 15 of that year.

[75] For lists of active assistants in 1754, see "Council Records, 1747–1755" (Massachusetts Archives), pp. 330, 333, 334.

[76] To vote, one had to possess either a forty-shilling freehold or other estate to the value of £40 sterling. A town with 100 families was allowed to send two deputies; a town with 40 families, one. Boston was given four. See the Governor of Massachusetts Bay to the Board of Trade, March 2, 1736/7, Shelburne Papers, 45:187–91.

That the responsibilities involved in the sending of deputies were not infrequently considered irksome, especially when no crisis confronted the province and public affairs were running smoothly, is indicated by the fact that in 1753 fifteen towns were fined, in amounts ranging from £5 against both Sunderland and Dudley to £26 against Plymouth, for failure to send any representative for that year. Forty-three other towns failed to be represented, but were not fined. Of the towns entitled to send two deputies, only three sent more than one. See *Journals of the House of Representatives of Massachusetts Bay* (1753–1754), XXX, pp. 4 and 13. In 1765 at least 132 towns had over 100 families. See E. B. Green and V. D. Harrington: *American Population before* . . . *1790*, pp. 21–30.

was empowered to make laws, create courts of judicature, grant lands except to the east of the Sagadahoc River [the Kennebec], erect towns, and appoint and settle all civil officers not holding patents from the Crown. However, the power of law-making did not extend to the denial of religious freedom except to Roman Catholics, or to the erection of any vice-admiralty jurisdiction, or to the restriction of freedom of fishing rights granted to all subjects of England.

This charter gave the Governor the power of controlling the course of legislation, possessing as he did an absolute veto on all bills and elections.[77] As a further check upon the colony, it was provided that all laws were to be transmitted home by the first opportunity after engrossment, and, upon being presented to His Majesty in Council, could be rejected within a period of three years.

It would seem to be abundantly clear that the provisions of the new charter had the effect of making the legislature of the province — distinguished in the seventeenth century for its recalcitrancy — much more solicitous in the course of the eighteenth to frame measures in harmony with the spirit of the imperial conceptions of government.[78] Out of 304 acts passed between the years 1703 and 1753 which were referred to England for approval, only six were reported for disallowance and two for repeal.[79] As a further safeguard against

---

[77] In the early part of the eighteenth century an issue arose as to the power of the Governor to negative the choice of a Speaker of the House of Representatives. In 1725 an explanatory charter issued by the Crown upheld the authority of the chief magistrate. *Acts of the Privy Council, Col. Ser., 1720–1745*, pp. 94–5, 103. For "The Explanatory Charter granted by His Majesty King George" in 1725 see *The Charter granted by their Majesties King William and Queen Mary* . . . (Boston, 1742), pp. 13–14.

[78] However, between 1695 and 1701 some thirty-three acts were disallowed. *Acts of the Privy Council, Col. Ser., 1680–1720*, pp. 841–4.

[79] Two of the acts disallowed were passed in 1718: one related to imposts and tonnage; the other regulated the culling of fish. Another, passed in 1723, was for apportioning and assessing a tax; a fourth, of the year 1731, was for ascertaining the number of representatives; the fifth, for granting imposts and tonnage for one year, was passed in each of the years 1731, 1732, and 1733 and led to the issuing of an additional instruction to Governor Belcher forbidding any future import duty on Negroes and felons; and the sixth, passed in 1750, granted to His Majesty an excise upon sundry articles. Of the acts reported for repeal, one was passed in 1733 to prevent the currency issued by a New Hampshire society from circulating in Massachusetts; the other, of the year 1742, sought to take off the entail from certain lands in Ipswich belonging to the estate of John Wainwright. See "A List of Acts passed in the Massachusetts Bay, as have been reported on between the year 1703 & the present time [1753]," Shelburne Papers, 49:63–98.

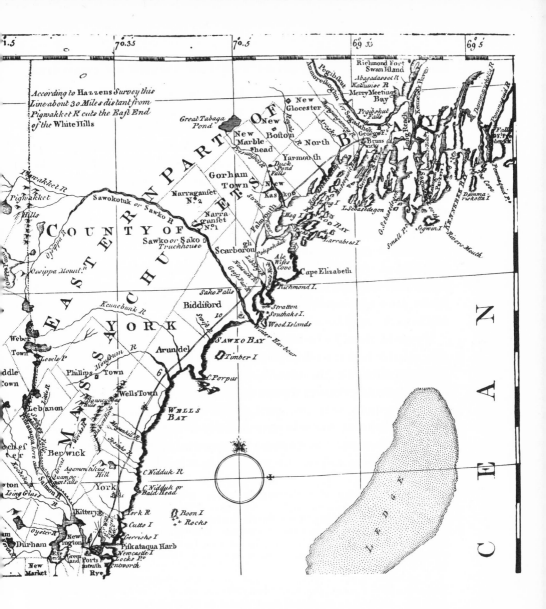

The Eastern Part of the Province of Massachusetts Bay,
later to become the State of Maine.
(From "A Map of the Most Inhabited part of New England...
Divided into Counties and Townships..." Printed for Carington Bowles,
1771, based on Thomas Jefferys's "Map of New England," 1755)

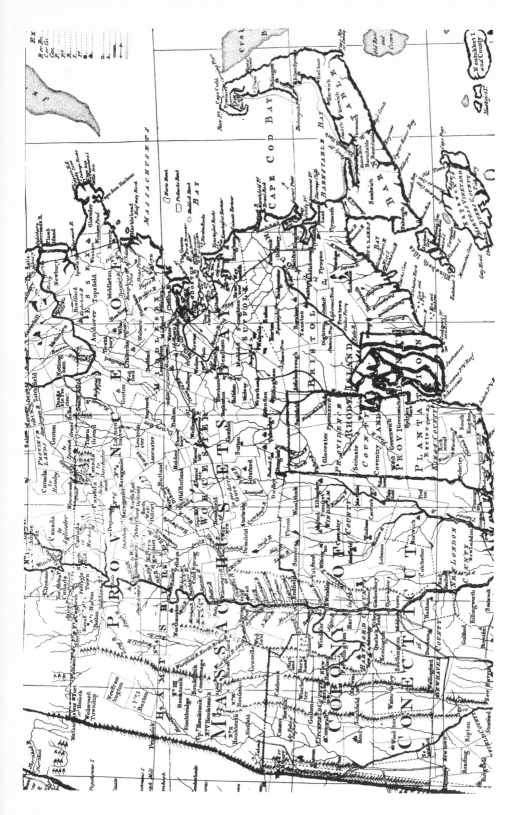

The main part of the Province of Massachusetts Bay.
(From the Bowles map of New England, 1771)

the spirit of independence on the part of the Assembly, the Governor was given the power to adjourn, prorogue, and dissolve that body. In the above respects — with the exception of the existence of a charter that preserved the power of the Assembly over the lands as well as over certain provincial appointments — the government of Massachusetts Bay differed little from that of a normal royal colony, with the Governor in each case receiving his commission under the Great Seal and acting under royal instructions.[80] In the selection of the twenty-eight Councillors of the province, however, there was a fundamental difference. Under the Massachusetts Bay charter this was not by Crown appointment but by action of the General Assembly. These men served in the capacity of an upper chamber of the Assembly. In addition, seven of them with the Governor could constitute an executive council for directing the affairs of the province; among other duties, this executive council was authorized to appoint judges and other officers for the courts of justice.

Finally, the charter, anticipating subsequent parliamentary regulation of the King's woods in North America, placed the people of the province under special restrictions by providing a penalty of £100 sterling for the destruction of any white-pine tree growing within the colony reserved by the Crown for the royal navy.[81]

Massachusetts Bay, as a recent writer has clearly demonstrated in his broadly based study, was what one might properly call a "middle-class democracy."[82] Representation of the towns was widely and fairly extended, and the requirements for exercising the franchise could easily be met by those permanently established in an organized township. Nor is there any indication of development in the middle of the eighteenth century of a system of ruling families characteristic of aristocracies. A study of the House of Representatives rolls shows that considerable changes took place from year to year in its membership. Nevertheless, in the actual work of

---

[80] L. W. Labaree: *Royal Government in America,* pp. 195–6.

[81] For an interesting analysis by James Abercromby of the Massachusetts Bay charter in the year 1752 see the Shelburne Papers, 47:26–31.

[82] Robert E. Brown: *Middle-Class Democracy and the Revolution in Massachusetts, 1691–1780* (Ithaca, N.Y., 1955). On the use of the term "democracy" in eighteenth-century America see the illuminating article by R. N. Lokken: "The Concept of Democracy in Colonial Political Thought," *William and Mary Quarterly,* 3rd ser., XVI, 568–80.

the House, certain men were repeatedly appointed to key committees that went far to determine the character of the laws and resolves. Those men were predominently from the eastern towns and
in the middle of the eighteenth century included such persons as
the great merchant Thomas Hubbard, James Allen, Esq., James
Bowdoin, and Samuel Welles, Esq., all of Boston; James Otis, Esq.,
of Barnstable; Colonel John Choate of Ipswich in Essex County;
Colonel Joseph Heath of Roxbury in Suffolk County; and Thomas
Foster of Plymouth. In other words, there is little doubt that in matters of legislation a fairly small group of eastern Massachusetts Bay
men in the House — merchants and lawyers — gave it guidance and
shaped specific measures. To this extent they constituted what may
not inaccurately be called an *élite*, without reference to the role
played by members of the Council, who at this period formed a
rather conservative group. These leaders in the House of Representatives upheld, it can be inferred, their middle-class constituents' eighteenth-century point of view — some aspects of which would in
twentieth-century Massachusetts be considered both undemocratic
and discriminatory.

There still remained on the statute books of the province in 1750
such laws as the following: a law that a person who dwelt in a town
and was obliged to pay its rates did not thereby acquire the rights
and privileges of a so-called "inhabitant" of the town;[83] a law that
forbad any keeper of an inn to serve any manner of drink to any
servant, apprentice, or Negro;[84] a law that made it illegal to free any
slave unless the owner was in a position to furnish security that the
town would not be liable for the maintenance of these former slaves
in case of sickness, lameness, or otherwise;[85] a law that provided as
a penalty a severe whipping in case a Negro or mulatto should strike
a white person, but not *vice versa*;[86] a law that compelled the sale

---

[83] 13 Geo. II, c.1, par. 1, *Acts and Laws of Massachusetts Bay*, pp. 318–19. This
act in its first paragraph provides that even when the assessors shall rate a person living in the town who is not an inhabitant, this will not in itself constitute the basis for
requiring the town to support him.

[84] 10 Wm. III, c. 8, *ibid.*, p. 94.

[85] 2 Anne, c. 2, *ibid.*, p. 157.

[86] 4 Anne, c. 5, *ibid.*, p. 167.

outside the province of any Negro or mulatto man or woman who should have illicit intercourse with a white person;[87] and, finally, a law prohibiting marriage between a white person and a Negro or a mulatto, with a heavy penalty for any one solemnizing such a marriage.[88]

Although the House of Representatives was destined to become the most powerful organ of the provincial government of Massachusetts Bay after the middle of the eighteenth century,[89] the colony in 1750 possessed an energetic, capable, and popular Governor in the person of William Shirley.[90] He was the son of a London merchant and had made something of a reputation in the law in England, but had come to America in 1731, accepting thereupon the office of Surveyor of the King's Woods; in 1734 he was appointed Advocate General of the Court of Vice-Admiralty. Later he was selected by the Massachusetts Assembly to serve on the boundary commission to settle the disputed line separating the province from Rhode Island and in general was favourably regarded, especially as he was known not to be in sympathy with Belcher, who was Governor jointly of Massachusetts Bay and New Hampshire and was by no means popular in either. Upon the recall of Belcher, who was later transferred to New Jersey, the way was opened up for Shirley. In 1741 he was given a commission limited to Massachusetts Bay, over which he acted as Governor for a period of some fifteen years.[91]

A man of tremendous energy and enthusiasm, Shirley set himself to promote the interests of the commonwealth. He was especially concerned with the situation in Nova Scotia when in 1744 news ar-

---

[87] *Ibid.*

[88] *Ibid.*

[89] See M. L. Cole: "The Rise of the Legislative Assembly in Provincial Massachusetts," *Abstracts in History*, IV (University of Iowa, 1941), 91–102.

[90] For an account of the administration of Shirley see G. A. Wood: *William Shirley, Governor of Massachusetts, 1741–1756: A History*, Columbia University *Studies* (2 vols., New York, 1920), Vol. I. This biography leaves off with the year 1749; see also *The Correspondence of William Shirley . . . 1731–1760* (ed. C. H. Lincoln, 2 vols., New York, 1912) and John A. Schutz: "Imperialism in Massachusetts during the Governorship of William Shirley, 1741–1756," *Huntington Library Quarterly*, XXIII, 217–36.

[91] For Shirley's commission, dated June 25, 1741, see P.R.O., C.O. 5:199, pp. 111–20; for his instructions, dated September 10, 1741, see C.O. 5:199, pp. 127–68.

rived of the British declaration of war against the French King.[92] The great Canso fisheries, which had been under the control of the fishermen of his own province, had already fallen to the French with the capture of Canso. Annapolis Royal, the only English stronghold in the northern province, was also menaced. Moreover, the Indians along the border of Maine, an integral part of Massachusetts Bay, began to assume a threatening attitude, as they were much under the influence of French missionaries. The Governor now succeeded in making treaties with these Indians. In the same year he raised a force for the relief of Annapolis. Early the following year he recommended to the Assembly the reduction of the great fortress of Louisbourg, which guarded the mouth of the St. Lawrence and directly threatened Nova Scotia. His advice was acted upon, and, with the assistance of the other New England colonies, an expedition under the leadership of William Pepperrell and Admiral Sir Peter Warren brought about its capture. He subsequently formulated plans for the overthrow of the French power in Canada. These were approved in England, and some eight thousand troops were assembled for that purpose. The plans were abandoned, however, as the result of a change in the conduct of the war by those in general charge at home. Indeed, in the subsequent peace of Aix-la-Chapelle, much to the Governor's despair, even Louisbourg was returned to the French under an agreement providing for a *status quo ante bellum*. Nevertheless, the ministry did not let Shirley's notable achievement pass unrewarded. He and Pepperrell were knighted by the King, and the colonies that had participated in the Cape Breton adventure were voted compensation by Parliament for their expenses.

Shirley was now at the height of his power and influence in public life. His distinguished achievements in North America and his knowledge of the respective rights and claims of the English and French in the regions south of the St. Lawrence and including the Peninsula of Acadia led to his appointment as one of the two English commissioners to meet in Paris with the representatives of the French government to settle all outstanding issues between the two nations — especially those arising out of conflicting claims in North

---

[92] See J. B. Brebner: *New England's Outpost* (New York, 1927) for an extended treatment of the Massachusetts Bay fishing interests off the coast of Nova Scotia.

America and the West Indies.[93] Leaving for England in the latter part of 1749, he carried with him striking proof of the confidence of the people of Massachusetts Bay, embodied in the answer of the two houses of the General Assembly to his address notifying them of his intended departure for a year's absence. "And when we reflect," they declared, "on your knowledge of the present Circumstances of the Province and the great ability to set the same in a true light, our expectations are justly raised, that you will in every Respect consult and by all proper Methods in your Power promote the real Interest of his Majesty's good Subjects . . . under your charge."[94]

Well might Shirley declare to the Duke of Newcastle upon arriving in London, "that throughout my whole Administration a perfect Harmony has ever subsisted between me and the Assembly . . . and that I left 'em in perfect tranquility and well affected to his Majesty's Government; whilst some of the Neighbouring Colonies are involved in Factions and the utmost Confusion."[95] In view of this pleasant relationship, it may be considered surprising that Shirley during his leave of absence, which was extended to 1753, sought a change of post. Not only did he solicit Newcastle in 1750 for an appointment to the governorship of New York, should it fall vacant, but in 1752 he wanted the same office for the Leeward Islands.[96]

During the Governor's absence from the province the control of administration was entrusted to Lieutenant Governor Spencer Phips. The latter was apparently so remiss in communicating with the Board of Trade and in keeping it in touch with the state of affairs in Massachusetts Bay — notably, he failed to answer its heads of inquiry — that in May 1751 it rebuked him, pointing out that "Their Lordships consider this neglect as a great mark of disrespect and disregard to His Majesty's Service and a Breach of the Trust." Phips, in reply, sought to excuse himself by stating that he was unable to find among the public papers addressed to Shirley the docu-

---

[93] For an extended treatment of the above topic see Chap. 10 of Volume V of this series.

[94] A copy of this answer is printed in the *Pennsylvania Journal,* August 31, 1749.

[95] *Correspondence of William Shirley,* I, 494.

[96] *Ibid.,* I, 508–9; II, 1–4.

ment in question. The Board forwarded a copy, admonishing him not to fail to send a full answer to the heads every six months.[97]

Massachusetts Bay at this period was quite free from dangerous agitation and designs against imperial unity. The colony was proud of its able and popular royal Governor and gave such appearance of growing understanding of the point of view of the mother country in things religious that a proposal was actually made in the year 1750 by the English humanitarian Thomas Coram for the erection in Cambridge in the vicinity of Harvard College of "a college for University Learning according to ye Church of England. . . ."[98] Its devotion to the Crown was expressed in almost extravagant terms early in the same year when the General Court in an address to His Majesty denounced the disloyal tendencies of the French-speaking inhabitants of Nova Scotia and petitioned the King either to compel "such uncertain and precarious subjects" to leave his dominion or to reduce them to a more perfect obedience. It ends with these words:

> "It is the high sense we have of the Happiness we enjoy as . . . the subjects of the Crown of Great Britain, and the Dread which proceeds even from the most distant prospect of being ever subjected to the Yoke, and Tyranny of the French, that induces us to this our humble Address to your Majesty and it is our Constant and devout Prayer to almighty God, that your Majesty may long continue to Reign over us, and that our Posterity may remain the faithful subjects of your Royal House to the end of time."[99]

Further, in the year 1754, an address was voted by the two chambers returning "their humble thanks to His Majesty for His Paternal Goodness to His Subjects in that Province."[100] Here, surely, one might have thought, was a colony committed irrevocably to sentiments of devotion to the King of England! Yet not many years were to pass before the faintest expression of such loyalty to the Crown on the

---

[97] C.O. 5:918, pp. 257–62.

[98] Thomas Coram to George Onslow, May 12, 1750. "Alfred Morrison Papers," *Historical Manuscript Commission*, 9th Report, Part II, Appendix, p. 478.

[99] This was signed January 31, 1750, by Lieutenant Governor Phips, as well as by Josiah Williams for the Council and by Speaker Thomas Hubbard, "in the name and by Order of the House of Representatives." P.R.O. A. 40, Nova Scotia, 1751, 63:189.

[100] *Acts of the Privy Council, Col. Ser., 1745–1766*, p. 203.

part of any inhabitant would lead to his denunciation by the deputies of the towns and to threats and even acts of terrorism against him by his fellow townsmen.

In fact, by the middle of the eighteenth century — in common with the rest of New England, which it dominated in many respects — the province had developed, both as a centre of population and wealth and in political experience, to the point that it possessed an attitude of almost complete self-sufficiency — despite all formal testimony of loyalty to the King and to the imperial ideal. The successful capture by New England volunteers of the great French fortress of Louisbourg, the most conspicuous stroke on the part of the British in King George's War, did not fail to reinforce this attitude.[101] It was also doubtless based upon the conviction that New England had become the seat of a peculiar and superior civilization. John Adams later gave forcible expression to this concept and at the same time set forth why, in his opinion, this portion of the Empire had an advantage over "every other colony in America, and indeed, of every other part of the world that I know anything of." His illuminating statement set forth a point of view that may well have been widespread among the inhabitants of the commonwealth at the period under consideration. He found the following five causes for the superiority of the Province of Massachusetts Bay:

"1. The people are purer English blood; less mixed with Scotch, Irish, Dutch, French, Danish, Swedish, etc., than any other; and descended from Englishmen, too, who left Europe in purer times than the present, and less tainted with corruption than those they left behind them.

"2. The institutions in New England for the support of religion, morals, and decency exceed any other; obliging every parish to have a minister, and every person to go to meeting, etc.

"3. The public institutions in New England for the education of youth, supporting colleges at the public expense, and obliging towns to maintain grammar schools, are not equaled, and never were, in any part of the world.

---

[101] The *Boston Evening Post* for the years 1745–7 devotes a great deal of attention to the Cape Breton expedition in terms of pride in the part taken by men from Massachusetts Bay in this military effort of intercolonial defence and of anticipation of rewards from the mother country for services rendered.

"4. The division of our territory, that is, our counties, into townships; empowering towns to assemble, choose officers, make laws, mend roads, and twenty other things, gives every man an opportunity of showing and improving that education which he received at college or at school, and makes knowledge and dexterity at public business common.

"5. Our law for the distribution of intestate estates occasions a frequent division of landed property, and prevents monopolies of land."[102]

---

[102] *Familiar Letters of John Adams and His Wife Abigail Adams, during the Revolution* (ed. C. F. Adams, New York, 1876), pp. 120–1.

CHAPTER II

In the White-Pine Belt

WEDGED between the geographical divisions of Massachusetts Bay, which after the year 1677 included the former Province of Maine, lay the Province of New Hampshire. The colony's chief source of wealth was its forests, for in the eighteenth century there extended from Nova Scotia southward into New Jersey a broad belt of white pine. With reason was this tree called "the prince of the American forest," owing to "its size, age and majesty of appearance." One may well picture the slopes of the mountains and hills and the stretches of valley in this region covered here and there with these splendid trees, many of them towering above the sky line, with their lower branches at least a hundred feet from the ground. It is recorded that one of them had a trunk measuring over seven feet in diameter at the base.[1] These giant conifers when sound were highly prized. They were valued not only for the lumber they yielded but especially for their availability as ship timber; for from them were fashioned the great masts as well as the bowsprits and yards. There was, however, considerable waste in the harvesting of these huge trees. A contemporary observed that among "trees of the largest size, fit to make 34 to 38-inch masts, 48 out of 50 may

---

[1] "An[no] 1736, near Merimack river a little above Dunstable, was cut a white pine strait and sound, seven feet eight inches diameter at the butt-end . . ." (William Douglass: *A Summary, Historical and Political, of the . . . British Settlements in North-America* [2 vols., London, 1760], II, 53).

happen to be defective, although while standing they appear to be perfectly sound. . . ." He further added: "Some very good trees are broke in falling, nor is it possible to prevent it. Trees of 45 or 50 yards long, and from 4 to 6 feet in diameter, are of such immense weight it is almost beyond the power of man to use any secure management in lowering them. Much is done by bedding with bushes and small trees to help secure them, but notwithstanding there still remains a very great risque."[2] Furthermore, once the limbs and branches had been removed, there was the problem of getting the trunk safely to the edge of the water. A straight road had to be prepared and all obstructions of trees and rocks eliminated. Burnaby was told that the largest pine trees were cut only in times of deep snow. "When the trees are fallen," he wrote, "they yoke seventy or eighty pair of oxen, and drag them along the snow. It is exceedingly difficult to put them first into motion, which they call raising them; and when they have once effected this, they never stop upon any account whatever till they arrive at the water's side."[3] The "sticks," as the trunks were called, were then floated downstream — for example, down the Piscataqua River to Portsmouth at its mouth. There they were dressed by expert ship-timber workers. Only then were they ready for export.

In spite of the difficulties involved, many of the ships of the royal navy required masts that could be provided only from trees of very large size, and these had to be secured from some source, whatever the expense or hazard. Further, there was a great demand for masts for ships of the vast merchant marine.[4] England therefore turned to New Hampshire.

The existence of this growth of virgin white-pine forest in America

---

[2] John Wentworth to the Earl of Hillsborough, December 4, 1771, "Wentworth Letter Books," New Hampshire Archives, Concord; see also L. S. Mayo's "The King's Woods," Massachusetts Historical Society *Proceedings*, LIV, 53.

[3] Andrew Burnaby: *Travels Through the Middle Settlements in North-America in the Years 1759 and 1760* (London, 1775), pp. 87–8. Among the rivers used for floating masting logs was the Merrimac. In Manchester a road still called the Mast Road is located on this river.

[4] For example, in one year Portsmouth sent ten mast cargoes to England, only two or three of which were to fulfil navy contracts. A mast ship of 400 tons or over would carry from 40 to 100 masts. See R. G. Albion: *Forests and Sea Power: The Timber Problem of the Royal Navy, 1652–1862* (Cambridge, Mass., 1926), pp. 237–8; see also W. R. Carlton: "New England Masts and the King's Navy," *New England Quarterly*, XII, 4–18.

had been known to the people of England for over a century and was held to be a matter of first importance. While their oak trees provided superb material for the hulls of ships, they had for centuries been dependent upon the forests of Scandinavia and Russia for masting materials.[5] This was considered highly undesirable. As early as 1692 the first steps were taken by the government in the direction of the proper preservation and utilization of this imperial asset when a Surveyor General of His Majesty's Woods in North America was appointed in the person of the famous Edward Randolph.[6] His successor, Jahleel Brenton, was followed by John Bridger; then came in turn Charles Burniston, Charles Armstrong, and David Dunbar, the latter serving until 1744.[7]

The task assigned to the Surveyor General was by no means trifling. Not only was he to protect for the King's use the best of the white pine standing in the unappropriated forest regions, but he was expected also to encourage the production of various naval stores by the settlers. Under Queen Anne and her immediate successors, legislation was passed in Parliament which strictly forbad, without special licence, the cutting of any white pine whose diameter twelve inches from the base was two feet or more, within the entire region of the growth of these trees, except on land that then was private.[8] All lands were subsequently granted under limitation providing for the reserve of these trees;[9] there was also the requirement that no white pine of any description should be felled without express licence from the Surveyor General.[10] The King's broad arrow was to be placed upon these reserved trees by the Surveyor General or his deputies, and violators of the regulations

---

[5] See R. G. Albion: *op. cit.*, pp. 139–99.

[6] *Calendar of State Papers, Colonial Series, America and West Indies, 1689–1692,* Par. 1830.

[7] P.R.O., C.O. 391:51, p. 52. For this topic see Eleanor L. Lord: *Industrial Experiments in the British Colonies of North America* (Baltimore, 1896), pp. 89–100.

[8] 3 and 4 Anne, c. 10, Sec. 6; 9 Anne, c. 17; 8 George I, c. 12; 2 George II, c. 35.

[9] It would appear that in some stands of white pine all the trees were of such dimension as to lead to the reserve of the tract. For example, in George Mitchell's "A Plan of His Majesty's Province of New-Hampshire," 1755, two areas about Lake Winnepesaukee carry the following legend: "The King's Wood of White Pine Preserved for The Use of the Royal Navy." For this map and other illustrations having to do with the white-pine belt see H. N. Andrews, Jr.: "The Royal Pines of New Hampshire," *Appalachia*, XXVII, 186–98.

[10] L. S. Mayo: *op. cit.*, pp. 53–4.

were by act of Parliament subject to trial in a vice-admiralty court[11] — an extraordinary extension of the authority of this tribunal and an indication of the degree of importance attached to this imperial resource by the British government.

On the other hand, to bring about the legitimate production of ship timber from these trees and its exportation to the mother country, Parliament provided that those who transported masts, bowsprits, and yards from the plantations to England should be entitled to a premium of £1 sterling per ton.[12] That this bounty was a decided encouragement may be appreciated, particularly as a good mast twenty-four inches in diameter at its base would bring, on contract with the royal navy, something over £13 sterling, and a thirty-four-inch one as high as £90. Bowsprits ran in value from £2.10 to over £52, and yards from £6.10 to some £32, according to the accounts of the contractor of the royal navy.[13]

So greatly were these contracts for ship timber prized that those interested, it appears, brought about the passage of a provincial law laying a fine of £100 sterling upon any one cutting down one of these masting trees without licence.[14] Nevertheless, there were

---

[11] 8 Geo. I, c. 12.

[12] 2 Geo. II, c. 35, Par. 3; 25 Geo. II, c. 35; 32 Geo. II, c. 23.

[13] The largest mast desired by the navy was one not exceeding 36 inches at the butt end. Colonel William Partridge, who in 1696 became Lieutenant Governor of New Hampshire, had for ten years a mast contract with these restrictions. Nevertheless, he sent to England some masts of 38 inches and two of 42 inches. See William Douglass: *op. cit.*, II, 53 n. During the two decades before the American Revolution the contract was in the hands of Mark Hunking Wentworth, brother of Governor Benning Wentworth. According to his papers, he sent masts ranging from 25 inches to 34 inches in diameter at the base. The value of the smallest mast was £13.8, that of the largest, £90. See Jeremy Belknap: *The History of New-Hampshire* . . . (3 vols., 2nd edn., Boston, 1813), III, 80 n. The length of a mast could be determined exactly by the diameter of the butt end. It was one yard for each inch of diameter. One, for example, of 34 inches would be 34 yards or 102 feet in length. See R. G. Albion: *op. cit.*, p. 28. In 1769 the value of the masts sent to England was placed at £7,819 before exportation. G. L. Beer: *Commercial Policy of England Toward the American Colonies* (New York, 1948), p. 99.

[14] 5 Anne, c. 17, Par. 1, *Laws of New Hampshire* (10 vols., Manchester, Concord & Bristol, 1904–22), II, 82–3. See also *Provincial Papers: Documents and Records Relating to the Province of New Hampshire* (7 vols., ed. N. Bouton, Concord, 1867–73), V, 19–20; these volumes form part of what is now the 40-volume series of *Provincial and State Papers*, [1623–1800] (Concord, 1867–1941), cited hereafter as *New Hampshire Provincial Papers*.

In tracing the history of the supply of New England masts to the navy of the mother country upon contract, one finds that during the years 1689–96 Samuel Allen

signs of the gradual lessening of New Hampshire's importance as a lumbering centre. As early as 1727 Colonel Westbrook, contractor for the royal navy, transferred many important contracts for timber to the lumbering interests of Maine; in 1737 Governor Belcher, in his report on the state of the Province of New Hampshire, declared that within the past decade the trade in pine lumber had decreased by three quarters and that the trees growing on private property near the seashore had all but disappeared.[15] It was necessary to go some distance from the water, even well up the Piscataqua, for suitable ship timber, especially for masts. This entailed additional labour, expense, and time.

It is therefore probably true that by 1750 there existed in Maine and on the upper Connecticut River bodies of white pine suitable for the needs of the royal navy which could be tapped more economically than the timber growing in New Hampshire. However, the agent of the chief contractor for the royal navy, Mark Hunking Wentworth, was one of a powerful group of New Hampshire capitalists and a brother of the Governor. He seems to have been responsible for the exploitation of the colony's resources, with the result that he favoured his provincial associates with lucrative contracts.[16] Indeed, the deep personal interest of the Wentworth group in the masting trade could hardly be questioned, even if there existed no other evidence, in light of the fact that Governor Wentworth was furnished £2,000 by interested New Hampshire parties to buy the relinquishment of the post of Surveyor General of His Majesty's Woods in 1744 from the incumbent, David Dunbar, al-

---

agreed to furnish a shipload annually; he was followed by Isaac Taylor, who supplied as many as four annually; then a Francis Collins, between 1708 and 1713, furnished three annually. See C. P. Nettels: *The Money Supply of the American Colonies before 1720*, p. 74 n.

[15] Jonathan Belcher to the Board of Trade, April 4, 1737, "Answers to Queries," Shelburne Papers, 45:150–2. The author of *A Letter from a Merchant of the City of London* (London, 1757) indicates that the white-pine act passed in 1729 (2 Geo. II, c. 35), which permitted the cutting of white-pine trees less than 24 inches in diameter 20 inches from the ground, while prohibiting the cutting of those of greater size, had proved very detrimental to the growth of these trees to a size fit for masts. In this connection he writes: ". . . as Experience, Sir, has convinced us of the bad Consequence resulting . . . from this Clause, I and many more Merchants of this City . . . entertain hopes of seeing this Bar to the growth of Pines of proper Dimensions . . . soon removed."

[16] Eleanor L. Lord: *op. cit., p. 99.*

though the stipend attached to it was only £200 a year.[17] There is abundant proof that this great power of the Wentworth family was used freely to protect the Portsmouth lumbering interests.[18]

In spite of the success of the New Hampshire lumbering group in maintaining temporary control of the ship-timber contracts, evidence is not lacking that the leaders looked to the future of the province with concern. Since its most conveniently located timber had been largely cut away, the time was not far distant when the cost of lumbering within its borders would become prohibitive, especially that carried on for obtaining ship timber. Yet it seemed that without a continuation of this industry the colony could hardly fail to sink to insignificance. To ensure, therefore, the continued prosperity of New Hampshire through the maintenance of the mast trade became indubitably the mainspring of much of Benning Wentworth's activity during the period of his governorship, which lasted from 1741 to 1767.[19] Most intimately related to this problem was the boundary dispute involving the exact geographical limits of the province.

When Governor Jonathan Belcher, Wentworth's predecessor, reported on the New Hampshire boundaries to the Board of Trade in 1737, he stated that although the reputed southern boundary was a line "three miles to the northward of the Merrimac River and

---

[17] At the time of Wentworth's appointment as Governor, his friend, John Thomlinson, London agent of New Hampshire, wrote regarding him: "I have good hopes of having something more done for him that will put him into a capacity soon to discharge all obligations of this sort" (John Thomlinson to Theodore Atkinson, May 9, 1741, *New Hampshire Provincial Papers*, V, 930). This "something" was the office of Surveyor General of the King's Woods.

[18] For a discussion of this see the author's *Jared Ingersoll: A Study of American Loyalism in Relation to British Colonial Government* (New Haven and London, 1920), Chap. 4.

[19] For Wentworth's commission as Governor of New Hampshire, dated June 25, 1741, see P.R.O., C.O. 5:199, pp. 1–17. This commission is all but identical with that given to him dated April 4, 1760, which is printed in *New Hampshire Provincial Papers*, X, 908–13. For his instructions, dated September 10, 1741, see C.O. 5:941, pp. 30–102. The Wentworth commission and instructions are printed in *The Laws of New Hampshire . . .* (eds. A. S. Batchellor, H. H. Metcalf, and E. Bean, 10 vols., Manchester, Concord, Bristol, 1904–22), II, 600–55, and III, 241–37.

In order to protect the masting trees in British North America, Wentworth in 1763 recommended to the Board of Trade the appointment of a judge of vice-admiralty for all America with special jurisdiction over the white-pine forest. See Board of Trade *Journal, 1759–1763*, p. 420. For an excellent brief account of the life of Benning Wentworth by Clifford K. Shipton, see Volume VI of *Sibley's Harvard Graduates* (Boston, 1942), pp. 113–33.

every part thereof," dividing New Hampshire from Massachusetts Bay proper, and that to the east was the county of York in Maine, these limits were in dispute. Indeed, even the most moderate claims of her powerful neighbour, he judged, would leave the province narrowly restricted and almost surrounded by the lands of the other. In his commission as the province's Governor, no boundaries were given, and in none of the earlier commissions, he declared, was any mention made of any, except "at the head or at the sea."[20] In fact, as he saw it, the Province of New Hampshire was "but a small strip of Land, no more than fifteen Miles wide by the Sea, and not so big by the half as some counties of Massachusetts."[21] It is, however, well known that he was prejudiced and was actively seeking the union of the two colonies of New Hampshire and Massachusetts Bay, over both of which he was serving as Governor.[22]

In the very year that Belcher's report was made, an order in Council referred the disputed boundaries to a commission drawn from the Governors' Councils of New York, Rhode Island, and Nova Scotia. Ultimately the commission made a report on the eastern limits which vindicated the New Hampshire contentions, but it experienced difficulty in coming to a satisfactory conclusion regarding the southern limits, owing to the peculiar wording of the charter of Massachusetts Bay. Nevertheless, in 1741, largely by reason of the powerful influence of the Wentworths and those intimately associated with them — especially the London provincial agent, John Thomlinson — an order in Council was secured establishing this boundary along a curved line starting from a point three miles north of the Merrimack River and "ending at a Point

---

[20] For Belcher's commission, dated December 16, 1729, see C.O. 5:192, pp. 251–64.

[21] J. Belcher to the Board of Trade, April 4, 1737, "Answers to Queries," Shelburne Papers, 45:150–2. According to a memorandum drawn up by the Board of Trade in 1721, New Hampshire included "all that part of the main land in New England lying upon the Sea Coast, beginning from the middle part of Merrimack River and from thence to proceed Northwards along the Sea Coast to Pescattaway River & so forewards up within the said River and to the furthest head thereof, and from thence north westward untill 60 Miles be finished . . . and from thence to cross overland to the 60 Miles accounted from Piscattaway River, together with all Islands, & Isletts within 5 Leagues distance of the Premises, and abutting upon any part of parcell thereof" (Memorandum relating to State of the . . . Colonies . . . ," September 8, 1721, Shelburne Papers, 45:101–2).

[22] W. H. Fry: New Hampshire as a Royal Province (Columbia University Studies, XXIX, New York & London, 1908), pp. 256–7.

Due north of . . . Pawtucket falls and a strait line drawn from thence due west cross s^d river till it meets with his Majesties other Governments. . . ."[23] The decision quadrupled the hitherto supposedly restricted limits of New Hampshire and actually went far beyond the most sanguine expectations of the inhabitants of the colony. In fact, so liberal was this decision at the expense of Massachusetts Bay that the New Hampshire government was temporarily embarrassed when it was found that the new limits included Fort Dummer on the upper Connecticut, a spot far removed from the most western of the settled townships.

Fort Dummer had been built by Massachusetts Bay, as a result of a vote of the House of Representatives in 1723, to protect its outlying western settlements. As the fort was located not more than three or four days' march distant from the powerful French stronghold at Crown Point, its strategic importance was not to be questioned. From the time of its construction, Massachusetts Bay had supported it, keeping it garrisoned and in a fair state of repair. Now the question arose: which province should pay the cost of its maintenance, the one requiring its protection or the one within whose territory it stood? The people of New Hampshire, as a group, felt that it was unjust to expect them to defend the frontiers of Massachusetts Bay, especially as along the line of their own settlements there were nine posts that had to be maintained in time of hostilities as a barrier to the French and their Indian allies.[24] The deputies took this position strongly in the General Assembly in 1745, but the dispute continued for years, with Massachusetts reluctantly garrisoning the fort during the interim.[25]

New Hampshire was unlike other New England colonies in that the ownership of its unappropriated lands was in dispute in 1750. There was, in fact, a series of claimants, each one basing a claim

---

[23] See the instructions to Governor Wentworth, *New Hampshire Provincial Papers*, V, 595–6; see also *Acts of the Privy Council, Col. Ser., 1720–1745*, pp. 594–600.

[24] These posts were Rochester, Barrington, Nottingham, Chester, Londonderry, Jun Cook, Penny Cook, Contucook, and Canterbury. See the statement of John Thomlinson, London agent of New Hampshire, before the Board of Trade, March 2, 1748/9, Board of Trade *Journal, 1741–1749*, pp. 388–9. For an excellent account of the progress of this dispute see the testimony of the agents of the two provinces before the Board at the session of February 17, 1748/9, *ibid.*, pp. 382–4. For fuller details see the "Thomlinson Papers," *New Hampshire Provincial Papers*, V, 921–31.

[25] *Ibid.*, VI, 2–3.

The Province of New Hampshire, with the new townships
laid out west of the settled area.
(From the Bowles map of New England, 1771)

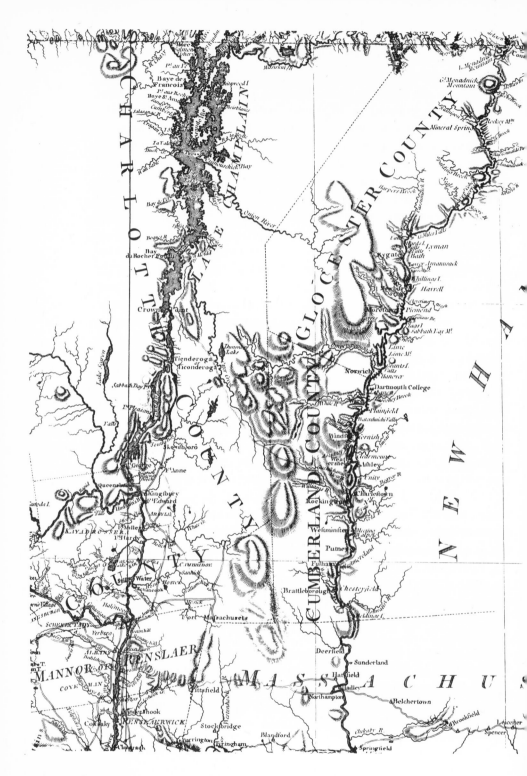

A map showing the area of the boundary dispute
between New Hampshire and New York,
later to become the State of Vermont.
(From "A Map of the Province of New-York"
by Claude Joseph Sauthier, 1776)

upon some prior right. The confusion followed the questioning of the validity of Captain John Mason's proprietorial claim based upon charters granted in 1622 and 1629 by the Council for New England — the first of these providing for grant of all lands between the Merrimac and Sagadahock rivers to Sir Ferdinando Gorges and Mason, and the second confirming to Mason all the lands between the Merrimac and Piscataqua rivers, under the name New Hampshire. Although Mason did nothing effective in the way of planting his colony and provided no government, his claim was held to be valid in 1675 when his grandson, Robert Tufton Mason, secured an opinion from one of Charles II's legal advisers, Sir William Jones. Meanwhile the inhabitants of the region had been taken under the protection of the government of Massachusetts Bay in time of war. This status was maintained until on September 18, 1678, a commission was issued under the Great Seal setting up New Hampshire as a royal province. But the lands within the colony were apparently still regarded by the Crown as the property of the heirs of Mason. Then, on April 27, 1691, for the consideration of £2,750 sterling, they granted their rights to Colonel Samuel Allen of London, who was commissioned Governor of the province the following year. In attempting to take over his proprietorship in person he met with such great obstructions on the part of the people that he returned to England and appealed to the Crown, but he died before anything was settled. In 1706 his heir, Thomas Allen, it was asserted, conveyed one half of the lands to a Sir Charles Hobby. To complicate things still further, in 1738, John Tufton Mason, a descendant of Captain John Mason, the original Proprietor, revived the Mason claim to all ungranted New Hampshire land upon the basis that the conveyance of 1691 to Allen was defective. On April 6, 1746, he entered into an agreement with a small group of powerful men, closely connected with Governor Wentworth, to transfer to them his New Hampshire rights for £1,500 current money of New Hampshire.

Thus, while in 1750 New Hampshire was administered as a royal province, there were the following claimants to all its ungranted lands: first of all, the claim of the Crown, upon the ground that Mason and his heirs had never complied with the conditions upon which the original grant to John Mason rested; secondly, the New

Hampshire group to whom in 1746 John Tufton Mason had transferred his rights; thirdly, John Hobby, grandson and heir of Sir Charles Hobby, who had received in 1706 one half of the Allen New Hampshire claims, and who had associated with a (but not "the") John Adams of Boston; fourthly, the so-called "million" land purchased from the Indians by one Jonathan Tyng in 1683 which was conveyed subsequently in tracts to certain persons and confirmed by Robert Tufton Mason in 1686 and by Joseph Dudley of the New England Council. The confusion in land titles was destined to remain until New Hampshire became established as a state independent of Great Britain.[26]

But — to return to the western extension of the New Hampshire boundary — the far-seeing plans of Governor Wentworth comprehended the newly acquired region. He brought constant pressure upon the representatives of the people to undertake the responsibility of defending the western frontier. In this connection he summoned to the Assembly, by writ directed to the sheriffs, representatives from the unprivileged western towns of Chester, Haverhill, South Hampton, Rumford,[27] Methuen, and Dracut in order to gather needed support in that body. These, however, were denied the right to seats by the older towns.[28] Wentworth now carried the issue to His Majesty in Council, who in 1748 ordered an instruction to be prepared empowering certain New Hampshire towns and districts to send deputies to the House of Representatives.[29] Even in the face of this royal authorization and the sending of the King's writ to the sheriffs, the representatives up until the year 1752 stoutly stood by what they considered to be an inherent right of determining, without interference from the executive, all questions involving the

---

[26] See *ibid.*, I, 373, *passim;* II, 544, *passim;* III, 153, *passim;* V, 823–5; XXIX, 143, *passim*. See also William Douglass: *A Summary, Historical and Political, of the . . . British Settlements in North America* (II, 22–33) for the situation of the dispute over land titles in 1750, and likewise the *Boston Weekly Post-Boy*, November 9, 1749. For a comprehensive study of the problem see W. F. Fry: *op. cit.*, pp. 209–320.

[27] Rumford, as was brought out in the preceding chapter, had been established by Massachusetts Bay people to the west of the Merrimac and, much against the desire of the inhabitants, had been included in the lands received by New Hampshire in the settlement of the boundary.

[28] "Journal of the House of Representatives," January 24, 1744/5, *New Hampshire Provincial Papers*, V, 260–1; W. H. Fry: *op. cit.*, pp. 156–61.

[29] *Acts of the Privy Council, Col. Ser., 1745–1766*, pp. 30–3, and Board of Trade *Journal, 1741–1749*, p. 292.

right of the towns to be therein represented.[30] Wentworth, in turn, resorted to repeated prorogations of the Assembly.

Nevertheless, a change was slowly taking place in the attitude of the public toward the larger issue, involving as it did the support of the Governor's policy in western New Hampshire. This seems to have been particularly true after the return of Major Goffe and Matthew Patten, who had gone into the region of the upper Connecticut to view Fort Dummer in 1749.[31] The information gradually spread that the new acquisition lying adjacent to the river was not only "the Garden of New England,"[32] but also afforded an abundant supply of white-pine trees and was therefore an asset of vast importance, the benefit of which might be generally shared by the people. This appears to have had the desired effect. At least, late in the year 1752 Wentworth was able to write to the Board of Trade that harmony within the provincial government had been restored and that the new members had been seated.[33] Soon after this, detachments of New Hampshire troops were posted on the upper Connecticut both at Fort Dummer and at Keene. The Governor now found himself possessed of the necessary support for the ambitious project he had long been evolving.

This project involved the immediate exploitation of the lands of the upper Connecticut Valley. As the first step in this direction, Wentworth had secured in 1748 a special commission from the Crown to make grants within the province upon a quit-rent basis of one shilling sterling for each one hundred acres.[34] Late in 1749,

---

[30] Address of the General Assembly, April 7, 1749, *New Hampshire Provincial Papers*, VI, 89–93; see also L. W. Labaree: *Royal Government in America* (Yale University *Studies*, VI, New Haven, 1930), pp. 180–3.

[31] *New Hampshire Provincial Papers*, VI, 581.

[32] See Grant Powers: *Historical Sketches of . . . the Coos Country . . . 1754– 1785* (Haverhill, N.H., 1841), pp. 10-17, for valuable source material covering the period under consideration.

[33] Wentworth to the Board of Trade, November 18, 1752, Board of Trade *Journal, 1749–1753*, pp. 379–80. In *Sibley's Harvard Graduates* (VI, 125), C. K. Shipton writes of Wentworth's success: "It has been said, with reason, that this was the most important political victory in the prerogative field in the history of the colonies. Had there been more royal governors with Wentworth's political courage, American history would have been different."

[34] In 1741, in preparing Wentworth's instructions, the Privy Council determined that the royal quit-rent on each 100 acres of land should be one shilling proclamation money. *Acts of the Privy Council, Col. Ser., 1720–1745*, pp. 696–7; for the instruction of 1748 see P.R.O., C.O. 5:941, pp. 207–45; see also B. W. Bond, Jr.: *The Quit-Rent System in the American Colonies* (New Haven & London, 1919), p. 60.

in communicating with Governor Clinton of New York, he announced, in the name of his own colony, a claim to lands a considerable distance to the westward of the Connecticut River.[35] Two years
later came the first of a series of grants of townships, each six miles
square, which ultimately extended sixty miles along the Connecticut
and westward to a point not many miles from Albany. This was
done in the face of continued protests by the government of New
York, which claimed that the lands were under its jurisdiction. It
further alleged that settlers were attracted by Wentworth's invitation to take out New Hampshire patents rather than those of New
York because the quit-rent asked was but one shilling per hundred
acres instead of the two shillings and sixpence charged by the latter
under terms of the royal instructions.[36]

In all, some 140, if not more, townships were allotted by the
Governor of New Hampshire to favoured parties. At the same time
Wentworth reserved for himself, in lieu of a fee for affixing the seal,
five hundred acres for each grant — a total of some 70,000 acres of
land, undoubtedly selected for its potential white-pine harvest.[37]

Now, instead of struggling for existence in the face of the intense
pressure of Massachusetts Bay, as had been the case from the
beginning of its history until the year 1741, New Hampshire was
relieved of this pressure. In fact, the province became so extraordinarily aggressive by the middle of the eighteenth century under

---

[35] Wentworth took the position that, as both Massachusetts Bay and Connecticut
claimed lands west of the Connecticut River, "New Hampshire had an equal right to
claim the same extent of western boundaries [eastward of the Hudson River] with
these Charter Governments . . ." (Wentworth to Governor George Clinton, April 25,
1750, New Hampshire Provincial Papers, X, 201–2).

[36] For a history of the New Hampshire-New York boundary dispute up to the
beginning of 1764, as viewed by New York authorities, see Lieutenant Governor
Colden to the Board of Trade, January 20, 1761, Documents Relative to the Colonial
History of the State of New York (ed. E. B. O'Callaghan, 15 vols., Albany, 1853–87),
VII, 595–8; for the controversy as viewed by New Hampshire authorities, see New
Hampshire Provincial Papers, X, 199–221; see also W. H. Fry: op. cit., pp. 265–74.

[37] Although in 1749 Wentworth granted a township six miles square lying to the
west of Connecticut and only twenty-four miles east of Albany, most of his grants
before 1761 were in the area to the east of the Connecticut River. However, in 1761
sixty grants were made of townships on either side of this river; in 1762 ten grants
were made, in 1763 there were thirty-nine grants, and in 1764 eleven grants, six of
which were individual grants to officers. Counting regrants, some 131 grants were
made up to 1765. For a list of Wentworth grants to 1765, see New Hampshire Provincial Papers, X, 204–7.

the leadership of its powerful Governor as to thoroughly alarm the Province of New York.

New Hampshire's population in 1750 can be estimated roughly at between 30,000 and 50,000 people,[38] and the majority of the inhabitants seem to have been engaged in general farming. In religion they were inclined strongly toward Congregationalism[39] and came so much under the influence of the preaching of White-field that upon the banners of the New Hampshire forces furnished for the reduction of Louisbourg was placed his motto, *"nil desperandum Christo duce."*

It cannot be over-emphasized how much the rise to importance of the Province of New Hampshire had been bound up with the Wentworth family's rise to a dominant position in its affairs. This family, typical of the ruling colonial *élite*, was of Lincolnshire origin and was represented among the early settlers of Exeter, where a William Wentworth was a selectman of the town, an elder in the church, and an extensive landowner. The father of Benning and Mark Hunking was John Wentworth, who was Lieutenant Governor of the province between 1717 and 1730 and who made the family the first in importance in New Hampshire, both in political life and in the field of commercial undertaking.[40] His sons inherited his

---

[38] In 1737 the population, according to Governor Belcher (who, because of his desire to annex New Hampshire to Massachusetts, was doubtless anxious to play down the number of inhabitants), was 11,000 whites and about 200 blacks; in 1755 it was given as 30,000. See "Account of the Several Provinces in North-America," from *Ames' Almanack* for 1756, New Hampshire Historical Society *Collections*, V, 228–30. Governor Wentworth, in answering the queries of the Board of Trade in 1754 (and undoubtedly eager to show the importance of the province), gave the total population as 80,000, of which some 550 were blacks. For these and other estimates see Greene and Harrington: *American Population before . . . 1790* (New York, 1932), p. 72.

[39] See C. B. Kinney, Jr.: *Church and State: The Struggle for Separation in New Hampshire, 1630–1900* (New York, 1955), pp. 1–82; see also the New Hampshire Historical Society *Collections*, I, 150–2. The Rev. Andrew Burnaby declared that there were only two missionaries of the Church of England within the province and that one of them had applied to be removed to Rhode Island. *Travels Through the Middle Settlements . . .* , p. 87.

[40] For the New Hampshire Wentworth family, distantly related to the seventeenth-century Thomas Wentworth, Earl of Strafford, and to the eighteenth-century Charles Watson Wentworth, Marquess of Rockingham, see John Wentworth: *The Wentworth Genealogy: English and American* (3 vols., Boston, 1878), I, 5, 71, 286–9. For a genealogical table of the Wentworth family see the authoritative one-volume edition of Belknap's *History of New Hampshire* edited by John Farmer (Dover, N.H., 1831), p. 253.

instinct for money-making and power, and each of them (in spite of Benning's financial reverses before he attained the governorship) became exceedingly wealthy. The degree to which the government of New Hampshire during the governorship of Benning Wentworth was a family arrangement could probably not be duplicated in any other part of the old British Empire. George Jaffrey, who had earlier married Benning's sister, was not only the President of the Council but also the provincial Treasurer; the Chief Justice of the Supreme Court, Theodore Atkinson, another brother-in-law, was likewise in the Council; Jotham Odiorne, also a councillor and second judge, was related in marriage to Mark Hunking Wentworth, Benning's brother; Henry Sherburne, a cousin, was a councillor; while Samuel Solley, another councillor, was married to Jaffrey's daughter; and Thomas Packer, Benning's brother-in-law, was High Sheriff.[41]

Out at Little Harbour, not far from Portsmouth, was the Wentworth mansion, where the owner, living in semi-regal fashion, dealt with public affairs. This spacious residence, at one time containing some fifty-two rooms, could be approached by land or water. It was prepared for defence with an armoury off the hallway and with underground quarters for the horses in times of dangers. A great chamber was set apart for the meetings of the Provincial Council, and the amusement room had billiard tables and an inviting buffet.

Benning Wentworth was so powerfully entrenched in the government that for years he was quite safe from the attacks of his enemies. It is true that in the 1740's Richard Waldron, whom he had dismissed from the Council, headed a movement to displace him, and became Speaker in the Assembly. But the Wentworth influence in England could not be overcome, and the contest only added to Benning's strength.[42] Moreover, as a result of his political influence, together with contracts for masting and other business ventures flowing from his activities and from those of his family circle, Portsmouth had become by 1750 one of the most flourishing seaports in North America. As the entrepôt for the province's thriving lumber commerce, it was to grow to be second only to Boston as a

---

[41] See John Wentworth: *The Wentworth Genealogy*, I, 287; New Hampshire Historical Society *Collections*, V, 232–3.

[42] *New Hampshire Provincial Papers*, VI, 39–61. Waldron was a brother-in-law of former Governor Belcher.

shipbuilding centre[43] and to achieve real importance in the manufacture of other articles of wood, such as house frames, desks, chests
of drawers and other furniture — which were carried southward to
Virginia and the Carolinas[44] — as well as of many luxury goods.[45]

The opulence of the town at this period was reflected in the
tendency of the wealthier people to imitate the fashions and
splendid living of the socially privileged class in the mother country.
One contemporary asserted that there "were more private carriages
and livery servants in Portsmouth in proportion to the number of
inhabitants, than in any other place in New England."[46] Robert
Hale, a Harvard graduate, was greatly impressed with the exclusive-
ness of the upper crust of Portsmouth society in the 1740's. "Their
Manner of Living here," he wrote in his journal, "is very different
from many other places. The Gentlemen treat at their own houses
& seldom go to the Taverns. Their treats are Splendid, they drink
Excessively all Sorts of Wine & Punch — their Women come not into
Company, not so much as at Dinner."[47]

Such were New Hampshire and Portsmouth in the days of Governor Benning Wentworth.

---

[43] During the war years, 1754–63, shipbuilding at Portsmouth was greatly stimulated. Between 1760 and 1775 some of the merchants there built yearly as many as a
dozen ocean-going vessels of between 200 and 300 tons burden. Of vessels that were
built between 1769 and 1771, Massachusetts Bay produced 34 per cent of the total
colonial tonnage, according to one authority, with New Hampshire building 17 per
cent, or 147 vessels of the larger categories as against 411 for Massachusetts Bay. For
this and an account of the rise of other crafts in New Hampshire see Carl Bridenbaugh: *The Colonial Craftsman* (New York & London, 1950), pp. 92–3 and 108–12.

[44] Shelburne Papers, 45:313–18.

[45] See Carl Bridenbaugh: *op. cit.*

[46] Quoted by Alfred Gooding: *Portsmouth in the Eighteenth Century* (Portsmouth
[1923?], pp. 10–11. For the population of Portsmouth in 1744, given as 4,590, see
Carl Bridenbaugh: *op. cit.*, p. 109.

[47] See *Sibley's Harvard Graduates*, VI, 114, for the above excerpt from Hale's
Journal, which is in the Library of the American Antiquarian Society.

CHAPTER III

A Libertarian Commonwealth

SOUTH of Massachusetts Bay and even more narrowly confined than was New Hampshire before 1740, the corporate colony of Rhode Island and Providence Plantations lay mostly to the westward of Narragansett Bay, although fringing its northern and eastern shores. "Rhode Island, with a portion of the adjacent Continent under the same Government," declared the Rev. George Berkeley in 1731/2 in a sermon before the Society for the Propagation of the Gospel in Foreign Parts, "is inhabited by an English Colony, consisting chiefly of sectaries of many different denominations, who seem to have worn off part of that prejudice which they inherited from their ancesters against the national Church of this land; though it must be acknowledged at the same time, that too many of them have worn off a serious sense of all religion."[1] The colony came into existence in the fourth decade of the seventeenth century as the result of the efforts of religious refugees who had fled from Massachusetts Bay's iron rod of church discipline. By the middle of the eighteenth century most of the inhabitants were comprehended within four religious denominations, of which the strongest and most articulate was the Baptists, followed by the Quakers, the Congregationalists, and the Episcopalians, in order of numerical strength

---

[1] *The Works of George Berkeley, D.D.* . . . (ed. A. C. Fraser, 4 vols., Oxford, 1871), III, 242–3.

and influence.[2] However, with the Great Awakening, which came upon the colony with dramatic force, other sects had made their appearance, largely on account of secessions from the older groups. Thus, in the Rhode Island colony of 1750 much of the spirit of the seventeenth-century religious zealots still survived, especially outside the towns.

Since the days of Roger Williams, Anne Hutchinson, and Samuel Gorton, the colony had stood for liberty of soul as against religious restraints, and for the separation of the affairs of church and state. In spite of this, a much-disputed religious clause had crept into the Rhode Island code of laws by a process not entirely clear. Apparently it was one of the results of the sharp reaction throughout the British Empire to the attempts of the Old Pretender, a devout Catholic, to gain the throne of England in 1715. This clause, which denied all political rights of citizenship, including the franchise, not only to non-Christians but also to Roman Catholics, first appeared in the digest of the laws of the year 1719 and was reprinted in those of 1730 and 1745 and reads as follows:

> ". . . and that all rights and privileges granted to this Colony by his Majesties Charter be entirely kept and preserved to all his Majesties subjects residing in or belonging to the same; and that all men professing Christianity and of competent estates and of civil conversation, who acknowledge and are obedient to the civil magistrates, though of different judgements in Religious Affairs (Roman Catholics only excepted) shall be admitted Freemen and shall have liberty to choose and be chosen officers in the Colony both military and civil."[3]

Despite the presence of this legal restriction, Rhode Island in practice set a worthy example of religious tolerance to her neigh-

---

[2] In 1739 the little colony possessed thirty-three church edifices, of which twelve were Baptist, ten were Quaker, six were Congregational (called Presbyterian), and five were Anglican. Frederic Denison: *Westerly (Rhode Island) and its Witnesses . . .* (Providence, 1878) p. 88.

[3] *Acts and Laws of His Majesty's Colony of Rhode Island and Province-Plantations in America* (Boston, 1719), p. 3. For an extensive treatment of this law see Sidney S. Rider: *An Inquiry Concerning the Origin of the Clause in the Laws of Rhode Island (1719–1783) Disfranchising Roman Catholics, Rhode Island Historical Tracts* (Providence, 1899), 2nd ser., I, 1–72.

bours and by 1750 had attained an attitude toward religious matters that might be characterized as broad and secular. While earlier in the century Baptist preachers in Massachusetts Bay and Connecticut were visited with sharp persecution and were not exempt from bodily violence,[4] it appears that in Rhode Island no one was molested in the pursuit of his religious principles. In the face of political issues, the Baptists willingly maintained their Quaker friends in office. Even the Sabbatarian or Seventh Day Baptist centre in the township of Westerly showed a spirit of generosity toward other sects.[5] One is therefore not surprised to find Jewish merchants in Newport playing a leading role in the life of the colony. Nevertheless, the Jews who had settled in Rhode Island, despite their influence in promoting trade, were regarded as aliens during most of the eighteenth century.[6]

Rhode Island does not abound in natural resources. The soil in most places is just tolerably good, composed of boulder clay or hard pan. Yet it possesses the quality of endurance and — after being cleared of the glacial surface rocks and smaller stones, frequently a very arduous task — is capable of yielding under careful management fairly abundant crops of cereals as well as other produce. From this stony soil apparently came a surplus of food beyond local needs in the middle of the eighteenth century. At least there were considerable quantities of beef, pork, butter, cheese, Indian corn, horses,

---

[4] See Isaac Backus: *A History of New England; with Particular Reference to . . . Baptists* (3 vols., Boston, 1777–96), II, 68, 88, 191.

[5] Frederic Denison: *op. cit.*, p. 89.

[6] For the importance of the Jews in the commercial life of Rhode Island see M. J. Kohler: "The Jews of Newport," *American Jewish Historical Publications*, No. 6 (Baltimore, 1893), and S. Broches: *Jews in New England*, Vol. II, *Jewish Merchants in Colonial Rhode Island* (New York, 1942). It appears that the first Jew to obtain naturalization papers was James Lucena in 1760, but that when the great merchants Aaron Lopez and Isaac Elizer sought the same privilege the following year they were refused. The number of Jews at Newport at the outbreak of the War for American Independence seems to have been about 200 and in the Thirteen Colonies about 1,000. See A. V. Goodman: *American Overture: Jewish Rights in Colonial Times* (Philadelphia, 1947). The first synagogue to be built in America was constructed in Newport in 1759 by Sephardic Jews. Contributions to this project came not only from Jews in New York but also from those living in London, Jamaica, Curaçao and Surinam. See Carl Bridenbaugh: *Peter Harrison: First American Architect* (Chapel Hill, N.C., 1949), pp. 98–104. For American Jewish communities before the War for American Independence see J. R. Marcus: *American Jewry: Documents, Eighteenth Century* (Cincinnati, 1959).

and sheep available, whether obtained locally or from neighbouring colonies, for export each year from the colony. If one were to assume that this surplus was produced locally, it could have been obtained only by the sustained and intelligent efforts of the agricultural population, which was made up mainly of small farmers whose individual holdings probably did not average beyond one hundred acres. In general, the conditions confronting the dwellers in rural Rhode Island were not favourable to aristocratic tendencies and the operation of large land units. Nevertheless, the leading people in South Kingstown, within the region of old South County, possessed large bodies of land and rather numerous slaves, and had developed a modified plantation system — with dairies, flocks of sheep, and herds of that splendid breed of horse, the Narragansett pacer — all of which had survived from the days when this region, known as King's Province, was the object of dispute between Rhode Island and Connecticut.[7] Elsewhere, as a rule, all labour on the land was supplied by the farmers and their sons. These men, strongly independent and individualistic, bore the reputation of thinking for themselves to a surprising extent.

During the period under consideration the population of Rhode Island was increasing perhaps more rapidly than at any other similar period of years in the eighteenth century. According to an estimate in 1730, there were 17,935 people; by 1755 the number had mounted to 40,636. The increase after this was slow; by 1783 there were only 51,869 people and by 1790 but 68,825.[8] This would seem to imply that conditions during the middle of the century were particularly favourable for a natural increase in the number of in-

[7] See W. D. Miller: "The Narragansett Planters," *American Antiquarian Society Proceedings*, n. ser., XLIII (1935), pp. 49–115, and Edward Channing: "The Narragansett Planters: A Study of Causes," *Johns Hopkins University Studies in Historical and Political Science* (ed. H. B. Adams, 4th ser., No. III, Baltimore, 1886), pp. 12–16. William Douglass, in his *A Summary, Historical and Political, of the . . . British Settlements in North-America* (2 vols., London, 1760, II, 100), writes of a Narragansett dairy farm where 110 cows were milked, 200 loads of hay were cut each season, and 13,000 hundredweight of cheese was produced, besides butter. The planters of South Kingston in 1758 are said to have had some 4,668 slaves, although in 1774 there were 1,000 fewer.

[8] See E. B. Greene and V. D. Harrington: *American Population before . . . 1790,* (New York, 1932), pp. 63–4; see also K. B. Mayer: *Economic Development and Population Growth in Rhode Island* (Providence, 1953), pp. 11–21.

habitants and for attracting immigrants. At least the colony sustained its agricultural population in a state of self-respect and comfort.

By 1750 Rhode Island had acquired real importance and very considerable wealth in the field of its expanding foreign trade. According to a report sent to the Board of Trade in 1708, 29 vessels were accredited to the people of the colony,[9] representing a sixfold increase over the amount of shipping owned locally twenty years earlier. By 1721 there were 60 vessels; by 1740 the number had amounted to 120;[10] and by 1750 there were reported to be some 300, made up largely of sloops, brigantines, and other small craft engaged in foreign as well as the coasting trade.[11] The twofold explanation of this increase lies in the enterprise of the men of Newport[12] and later those of Providence and in the favourable location of the colony in relation to the interior of the Province of Massachusetts Bay, which seems to have become increasingly dependent commercially upon the ports of Narragansett Bay in the course of the eighteenth century.[13]

The leaders of this expanding commercial life in Rhode Island were such men as those of the Wanton family, Abraham Redwood, Joseph Whipple, Godfrey Malbone, Moses and Aaron Lopez,[14] Stephen Ayrault, Daniel Ayrault, Nathan Angel, William Vernon, Philip Wilkinson, and Stephen Hopkins, as well as the Browns of Providence. The vessels of these and other merchants haunted all the ports of the West Indies, carrying on a vast traffic, especially in molasses and sugar secured in the French islands. The general course of this West India trade may well be illustrated by articles

---

[9] Governor Cranston to the Board of Trade, December 5, 1708, *Records of the Colony of Rhode Island and Providence Plantations in New England* [1636–1792] (10 vols., Providence, 1856–65), IV, 55–9. Hereafter cited as *Rhode Island Colonial Records*.

[10] Governor Richard Ward to the Board of Trade, January 9, 1740, *ibid.*, V, 12.

[11] W. F. Crawford: "The Commerce of Rhode Island with the Southern Continental Colonies in the Eighteenth Century," Rhode Island Historical Society *Collections*, XIV, 99–110, 124–30.

[12] S. G. Arnold in his *History of the State of Rhode Island and Providence Plantations* [1636–1790] (2 vols., New York and London, 1859, 1860), II, 300, points out that by 1769 Newport had some 200 vessels employed in foreign commerce and between 300 and 400 in the domestic trade.

[13] H. C. Dorr: *Planting and Growth of Providence* (Rhode Island Historical Tracts, No. 15, Providence, 1882), pp. 172 and 207.

[14] For the activities of Aaron Lopez see B. M. Biglow: "Aaron Lopez: Colonial Merchant of Newport," *New England Quarterly*, IV, 757–76.

of agreement which Philip Wilkinson and Company, owners of the *Charming Polly*, entered into with its captain, one Richard Penmure, in 1752. According to this document, after the master had loaded his ship at Newport with suitable goods, he was to sail to the Windward Islands and, if possible, dispose of these articles at St. Vincent; otherwise he was to sail to Dominica, and, should there still be any portion of the cargo left, he was to proceed to the Dutch island of St. Eustatius, where the residue should be sold. With all of his goods thus converted into money, he was then to sail with the greatest dispatch to the French island of St. Domingue (Hispaniola) and purchase molasses, muscovado sugar, and indigo, with which cargo he was to return to Rhode Island.[15]

This type of activity, in which scores of the colony's vessels were engaged, assumed such importance as to lead the British West India planter interests in 1750 to protest to the Board of Trade that the commerce between Rhode Island and St. Domingue was no casual traffic, but part of a well-formed plan conceived by the court of France for the destruction of the British interests in the Caribbean. These planter interests, as has been noted in the preceding volume of this series, called upon the officials of the mother country for protection from such competition, and asked for an investigation of the extent of the enforcement of the Sugar Act of 1733, which had placed a series of high duties upon foreign-produced sugar, molasses, and rum brought into the English plantations.[16] Well they might. For there is no evidence that at this period the local collector of the customs made any effort to secure the duties on these articles.[17] In fact, in 1749 when the Deputy Collector of Customs at

15 This agreement is printed in *Commerce of Rhode Island, 1726–1800* (Mass. Hist. Soc. *Coll.*, 7th ser., 2 vols., Boston, 1914–15), I, 60–1. For the commercial activities of the Browns of Providence—James, who died in 1749, and his brothers, Nicholas, Joseph, John, and Moses—in the period under consideration see the recent study by J. B. Hedges: *The Browns of Providence Plantations: Colonial Years* (Cambridge, Mass., 1952), especially Chapters 1 and 2; see also *The Letter Book of James Browne* [Brown] *of Providence, Merchant, 1735–1738* (ed. G. P. Krapp and J. C. Brown Woods, Providence, 1929).

16 C. O. 137:25, p. 112. See also Chap. 9, "The Struggle for the Muscovado Markets" in Volume II of this series.

17 In "An Account of all the duties collected under the Molasses Act in each of the Northern Colonies from 1733 to 1750 . . . ," the British Custom House report has opposite Rhode Island the following notation: "N.B. No Accots received since Mich[aelma]s 1744." For a printed copy of this see F. W. Pitman: *Development of the British West Indies, 1700–1763* (New Haven & London 1917), p. 275.

Newport, Joseph Wanton, seized a cargo of molasses belonging to John Banister, the latter, filled with indignation at this unprecedented occurrence, wrote:

> "What Mr. Wanton means by this Extraordinary Proceedings, I am at a loss to Judge—few in the Government has carried on a Greater Illicit Trade than the Deputy Collector."[18]

The records of the local court of vice-admiralty are concerned with many types of cases, such as prize, salvage, and wage issues, but except for one case — involving an English vessel seeking to run a cargo of wine into Newport in 1740 — it is silent about violations of the trade and navigation acts.[19]

Many circumstances favoured the activities of the smuggler. He would customarily appear at his port of entry with his ship in ballast. Should a complaint be lodged against him, he could boldly produce a certificate of having sailed from some British West India island also in ballast and would thereby be acquitted. For in approaching the colony with his dutiable cargo, he could easily slip into a secluded cove and there discharge his sugar and molasses, perhaps under cover of darkness. Admiral Knowles asserted in 1752 that "nothing could be a stronger proof of this Practice than their Sailing . . . in Ballast all the winter Season, when it was Certain no Vessels in the world in a set of Ballast only could Encounter the Weather on their Coasts."[20]

A Jamaica vice-admiralty-court case of the year 1751 will illustrate how deeply the Jamaican authorities felt regarding the commerce of Rhode Island with the foreign sugar islands; it also demonstrates the evenhanded justice that all colonials might expect of His Majesty's Privy Council. This case involved the sloop *Jupiter* owned by Gideon Cornell of Newport. The vessel was loaded in 1750 with lumber and horses furnished by a number of Rhode Island merchants for sale at St. Domingue (Hispaniola) and carried orders to return with a lading of articles from that island. After

---

18 See *Records of the Vice-Admiralty Court of Rhode Island, 1716–1752* (ed. Dorothy S. Towle with Introduction by C. M. Andrews, Washington, 1936), p. 97.
19 *Ibid.*
20 Governor Knowles to the Board of Trade, November 10, 1752, Library of Congress accessions, No. 2413.

disposing of his cargo, the master, a Frenchman naturalized in Ireland named Bontin, took on board a partial credit load of French sugar and molasses for a M. de Pond and other residents of St. Domingue. Because of desertions by his crew, he also had to take on a sufficient number of French mariners to man the sloop for the return voyage. Unfortunately, the vessel ran into a hard gale and broke her boom, with the result that she made for the nearest anchorage for repairs — Port Royal, Jamaica. While there the vessel, together with the cargo, was seized by the Receiver General of Customs, Benjamin Hume, for not operating according to navigation laws, and was thereupon libelled and condemned in the local vice-admiralty court on multiple charges of bringing into the island foreign sugar and molasses, of failure to have the proper complement of British seamen, and of irregular registration.

Bontin immediately appealed to His Majesty in Council. However, upon petition of the advocate of the vice-admiralty court of Jamaica, James Innes, and of Hume, his appeal was dismissed in 1753 for non-prosecution, with an assessment of £80 additional costs. Cornell, the owner of the vessel, the following year petitioned that the order dismissing the appeal be discharged, alleging that Bontin had died bankrupt. This was finally done, after the payment of costs by Cornell and the furnishing of proper security by himself and the Rhode Island London agent, Richard Partridge. Finally, in the summer of 1758 the Lords of the Committee on Appeals reversed the sentence after the case was heard *ex parte,* restoring the ship and cargo to the owner with interest and levying upon the respondent £100 costs.[21]

One may perhaps conclude that when the *Jupiter* finally returned to Newport there was no effort to smuggle her cargo of French sugar and molasses into the colony, little as the owners may previously have expected or been inclined to pay the high duties levied thereon. If this were so, it must have been in the nature of an exceptional gesture in the direction of good citizenship and loyalty, for the whole spirit of the people of the trading towns was in direct opposition to compliance with the law.[22] This tendency to lawless-

---

[21] *Acts of the Privy Council, Col. Ser., 1745–1766,* pp. 191–4.
[22] The Rev. Andrew Burnaby, who visited Rhode Island in 1760, was unhappily impressed with the spirit of lawlessness of the people of Newport, despite the kindness

ness is illustrated by an incident in 1764, the year of the passage of the Sugar Act lowering the duties on foreign-produced sugar and molasses.

The British government had at last determined to make an effort to end smuggling into the continental colonies. Toward this end His Majesty's cutter the *St. John* was dispatched to Narragansett Bay and its commander, Lieutenant Hill, was placed in charge of the custom-house. The Lieutenant, attempting to perform his duty, found himself confronted by overpowering opposition in June of that year when a mob forced the governor at Fort George on Goat Island to fire upon the cutter, wounding several men in the customs service; they also threatened to burn the vessel should the keeper of the customs not desist in his activities.[23]

A profitable pattern of trade was being developed by Rhode Island in 1750 of which the West India commerce was but one of the features. The molasses thus brought from the Caribbean area was distilled into rum in the colony. The quantity produced at this period can perhaps be judged by an assertion made in 1764 by the merchants of Rhode Island that 14,000 hogsheads of molasses were imported annually and that all the British West India islands together could not supply the demands of the local distilleries.[24] At this period molasses cost from thirteen to fourteen pence a gallon. To distill it in one of the twenty-two distilleries cost fivepence two farthings a gallon, according to one Newport writer who affirmed that: "good distillers were expected to turn out gallon for gallon, but the average was about ninety-six gallons of rum for every hundred gallons of molasses."[25] These distilleries, we are informed, were kept

shown to him while ill in that town. "The private people," he wrote, "are cunning, deceitful and selfish: they live almost entirely by unfair and illicit trading. Their magistrates are partial and corrupt: and it is folly to expect justice in their Courts of Judicature: for he, who has the greatest influence, is generally found to have the fairest cause" (*Travels Through the Middle Settlements in North-America* . . . *1759 and 1760* [London, 1775], p. 73–5).

[23] *Acts of the Privy Council, Col. Ser., 1745–1766*, pp. 690–2.

[24] Rhode Island Assembly to the Board of Trade, January 24, 1764, *Rhode Island Colonial Records*, VI, 379–80; H. W. Preston: *Rhode Island's Historic Background* . . . (Providence, 1930), p. 24.

[25] G. C. Mason: "The African Slave Trade in Colonial Times," *American Historical Record* (ed. B. J. Lossing, Philadelphia, 1872), I, 311–19. The importance of Mason's article lies in the fact that it was based on a study of many "original papers . . . which, for more than a century, had been hid away in garrets, under the eaves of old houses and in strange out-of-the-way places. . . ." See also *ibid.*, 338–45.

running continuously and demanded so much of the enormous quantity of molasses imported that in the middle of the eighteenth century it was difficult for outsiders to secure any amount at Newport. A Boston merchant seeking this article in 1752 was informed that all the molasses there found its way into the stills, in order to send vessels loaded with rum to the African coast.[26]

If Rhode Island had to take second place in the continental colonies to Massachusetts Bay as a distiller of rum, this was not true of slaving. It appears that Rhode Island had the unenviable reputation of sending almost as many ships to the African coast as all other North American colonies combined. It has been stated that in 1750 as many as 170 of its vessels, large and small, were involved in slaving and that before the outbreak of the War for American Independence at least 150 of them were engaged in this traffic.[27] Most of these vessels were small, some of as little as forty tons burden and the majority of less than eighty tons. The crews were correspondingly small, rarely exceeding eighteen men.[28] The ships set sail for Africa each loaded with perhaps as many as 130 hogsheads of rum, (containing about 14,000 gallons)[29] and little else, except subsistence for the crew and also for the slaves to be purchased and then carried to the New World. Most of the rum, in fact, not consumed domestically or sold in neighbouring colonies was transported to the Guinea Coast to be traded for African slaves. For

---

[26] *Ibid.*, I, 316. For the importance of the manufacture of rum to Massachusetts Bay see G. R. Minot's *History of the Province of Massachusetts Bay* (Boston, 1798, I, 155–8), in which he states (pp. 157–8): "The rum carried from Massachusetts Bay, and other northern colonies, to the coast of Guinea, is exchanged for gold and slaves. The gold is sent to London, to help to pay for their annual supplies; and the slaves are carried to the English sugar Colonies, and exchanged for their commodities, or sold for bills of exchange on Great-Britain." This would certainly seem to imply that Rhode Island, as well as other northern colonies, was engaged in the triangular trade of rum, slaves, and molasses.

[27] J. S. Tilley: *The Coming of the Glory* (New York, 1949); Arnold Whitridge: "The American Slave Trade," *History Today*, VIII, 465; Board of Trade *Journal, 1749–1753*, p. 23.

[28] G. C. Mason: *op. cit.*, I, 314; L. J. Greene: *The Negro in Colonial New England* (New York, 1942), p. 26; Elizabeth Donnan: *Documents Illustrative of the History of the Slave Trade to America* (4 vols., Washington, 1930–5), III, 51, 183, 337–40.

[29] For example, the *Success*, owned by the Newport merchant William Ellery, carried to Africa in 1749 as cargo 130 hogsheads of rum (14,147 gallons). On the other hand, the *Sierra Leone* (also called the *Siraloone* and *Siralone*), owned by Philip Wilkinson & Co., carried but 34 hogsheads, 10 tierces, 8 barrels, and 6 half-barrels of rum. See *ibid.*, III, 143, 147.

at this period the Rhode Islanders were unquestionably the great American slavers. For example, in 1755 with 6,313⅔ gallons of rum Caleb Godfrey, master of Samuel and William Vernon's sloop *Hare*, procured 28 Negro men, 25 women, 12 girls, and 7 boys.[30] A contract signed in Africa in 1756 in behalf of William Vernon and Jonas and William Redwood, by Captain Taylor of their *Cassada Garden*, called for delivery of 4,353 gallons of rum to be exchanged for slaves at the rate of 115 gallons for a good man and 95 gallons for a good woman.[31]

While large profits were undoubtedly made from these voyages, serious difficulties sometimes arose. David Lindsay of Newport, riding in his rum ship off the great slave mart of Anamabo on the Gold Coast,[32] gives a vivid description of the problems presented to those who came to trade with the expectation of quick profits. His letter to the Newport owners of the ship, dated February 20, 1752, reads as follows:

> "Gentlemen,
> "This third of mine to you, and now I am to let you Know my proceed'gs Since my Last Daited 3th Jan.ʸ; . . . I have Gott on bord 61 Slaves and upards of thirty ounces of Goold, and have Gott 13 or 14 hhd.ˢ of Rum yet Left on bord, and God noes when I shall Gett Cleare of it[;] ye trade is so very Dull it is actuly a noof to make a man Creasey[;] my Cheef mate after making foor or five Trips in the boat was taken Sick and Remains very bad yett[;] then I sent Mr. Taylor and he got not well and three more of my men has sick. James Dixson is not well now, and wors, then I have wore out my Small Cable, also ockam, and have ben oblige to buy one heare; for I thought the conciquance of yr Intrust on bord this vessel was Two great to Rusk with bot a cable to trust to. Therefor I begg you not Blam me in so doeing. I should be Glad I coold Com Rite home with My slaves, for my vesiel will not Last to proceed farr[;] we can See Day Lite al Roond her bow under Deck[.] however I hope She will carry me Safe home once more. I need not inlarge. heare Lyes Captains hamlet, James, Jepson, Carpenter, Butler, Lindsay; Gardner is Due; Ferguson has Gone to

[30] *Ibid.*, III, 151.
[31] *Ibid.*, III, 166–7.
[32] For the importance of Anamabo see Volume II, Chap. 10, of this series.

Leward[;] all these is Rum ships. Butler is in a brig with 150 hhds from Barbados belong to Cape Coast Castle. Ivve sent a small boye to my Wife. I conclude with my best Endevors for intrust, Gentlemen, your faithful Servant at Command.

"DAVID LINDSAY.

"N.B. on the whole I never had so much trouble in all my voiges[.] I shall Write to barbadoes in a few days."[33]

Once the cargo of the Rhode Island slaver was completed, the ship was usually dispatched to the English sugar islands,[34] stopping at either Barbados or St. Christopher; then, if the cargo had not been disposed of, it was often carried to Jamaica, where, owing to the contraband sale of Negroes to the Spaniards of the Main, as well as to the legal sale under the *cedules,* and to the steady demand by the local sugar-planters, a sale was sure to be consummated, at least for all healthy blacks.[35] With this ready money the ship was again stored with French sugar-island products before returning home. The owners were thereupon ready to start the process over again.

---

[33] *Commerce of Rhode Island, 1726–1800,* I, 59–60. In 1736 Captain John Cahoone in a letter to the owner of his ship, which also stood in the roadway of Anamabo, writes in a similar vein. On October 27 he declared that there never was so much rum on the coast at one time before "Nor the like of French shipen — never seen before for no. for the hole Coast is full of them." He declared that he had purchased but twenty-seven slaves and there had been as many as nineteen ships at one time in the road; that with his own vessel at the time of writing there were seven rum ships and that they were "Ready to Devour one another; for our Case is Despart . . . Cap. Hammond hath ben heair six months and has but 60 Slaves on Bord . . ." (*Ibid.,* I, 46–7).

[34] Not all Rhode Island vessels succeeded in reaching the New World with their slaves. In 1730, George Scott, master of the brig *Little George* (or *Charming Betty*), owned by Godfrey Malbone of Newport, after taking on board 96 Negroes on the Coast of Guinea was faced by a revolt after putting out to sea. After killing some of the crew, the slaves got control of the brig, which then drifted ashore, where the slaves escaped. Elizabeth Donnan: *op cit.,* III, 118–21, and Kenneth Scott: "George Scott, Slave Trader of Newport," *American Neptune,* XII, 222–8.

[35] See the instructions to Captain David Lindsay of the schooner *Sierra Leone* by its owners, Philip Wilkinson and Danil [Daniel] Ayrault, *Commerce of Rhode Island, 1726–1800,* I, 64.

Professor Lawrence A. Harper, who has been engaged in a detailed study of colonial trade, takes the position, based upon a study of the figures of clearances from Rhode Island and other northern ports, that the so-called triangular trade involving molasses, rum, and slaves has been much exaggerated in certain historical studies, although he "in no way contends that the colonists did not have lawless moments when it came to the importation of molasses." He calls attention to G. M. Ostrander's "The Colonial Molasses Trade," *Agricultural History,* XXX, 77–84.

In the middle of the eighteenth century Newport was a commercial and business centre equal if not superior to New York in importance.[36] Besides numerous distilleries the town possessed sugar-refineries and a number of establishments for producing spermaceti candles. In addition, it was deeply interested in shipbuilding and the production of iron nails,[37] while in the warehouses of its merchant princes were large assortments of European and East India commodities. Burnaby thus succinctly described the commercial activities in 1759 of the canny traders of Rhode Island:

> "Their mode of commerce is this; they trade to Great Britain, Holland, Africa, the West Indies, and the neighbouring colonies; from each of which they import the following articles: from Great Britain, dry goods; from Holland, money; from Africa, slaves; from the West Indies, sugar, coffee and molasses; and from the neighbouring colonies, lumber and provisions; and with that they purchase in one place they make their returns in another. Thus with the money they get in Holland, they pay their merchants in London; the sugar they procure in the West Indies, they carry to Holland; the slaves, they fetch from Africa they send to the West Indies, together with lumber and provisions, which they get from the neighbouring colonies; the rum that they distill they export to Africa; and with the dry goods, which they purchase in London, they traffick in the neighbouring colonies. By this Kind of circular commerce they subsist and grow rich."[38]

Newport, moreover, was the cultural centre of that region economically dependent upon it and from which it drew much wealth. Such families as the Callendars, Ellerys, Wards, Honeymans, Cheekleys, Updikes, and Johnstons strove to maintain the traditions established as the result of the sojourn of the great Bishop Berkeley in the town.[39] It was here also that the accomplished Dr. Ezra Stiles

---

[36] For a view of Newport in 1740 see *Rhode Island Historical Society Collections,* XVIII, 91–3.

[37] There were, however, at least according to the Governor's report to the Board of Trade, no forges or furnaces for making steel within the colony in 1750. *Rhode Island Colonial Records,* V, 313–15. For Rhode Island ironworkers in 1766 see A. C. Bining: *British Regulation of the Colonial Iron Industry* (Philadelphia, 1933), p. 14.

[38] Andrew Burnaby: *op. cit.,* pp. 93–4.

[39] *Newport Historical Magazine,* II, 174–5. For various cultural aspects of colonial life at this period see L. B. Wright: *The Cultural Life of the American Colonies, 1607–1763* (New York, 1957).

resided for many years preceding his acceptance of the presidency of Yale College. Here, too, came many people from South Carolina and the West Indies seeking to escape oppressive summer weather and to relax.[40]

The flourishing community was involved at this period in a sharp political struggle over issues destined to affect its prosperity, as will be shown later in this chapter. These issues had the effect of dividing Rhode Island into two sectional zones, with a so-to-speak southern area, encompassing the aristocratic Narragansett planters and supporting the immediate objectives of the Newport commercial interests, arrayed against the agricultural population living in the northern area and supported by merchants of Providence, the rival town to Newport.[41]

The government of Rhode Island was based upon the charter of the year 1663, giving title to the "Governor and Company of the English Collonie of Rhode Island and Providence Plantations in New England, in America." This instrument placed the actual control of the government in the hands of the freemen of the Company. It was these freemen who, meeting in Newport each May and October, voted in person or by proxy for the deputies of the towns to the General Assembly. Together, they then formed a court of election at the May meeting for the purpose of selecting a governor, a deputy governor, ten assistants, a secretary, and a treasurer for the ensuing year.[42] Upon the General Assembly there had further devolved the task of choosing some three hundred local officials — the colony judges, the judges of the county courts, the sheriffs, the justices of the peace, the field officers and those of the regimental companies, the grand committees on the bills of credit, and others — a task that consumed most of the month of May. With

---

[40] Carl Bridenbaugh: *Cities in the Wilderness* (New York, 1955), p. 443, and "Charlestonians at Newport, 1767–1775," *South Carolina Historical and Genealogical Magazine*, XLI, 43–7.

[41] For an excellent analysis of the basis of the struggle, largely personal in nature, between the Ward and Hopkins factions of Rhode Island see the recent study by D. S. Lovejoy: *Rhode Island Politics and the American Revolution* (Providence, 1958), Chap. 1.

[42] *Rhode Island Colonial Records*, II, 3–21. This system, originating with the beginning of the charter government, survived until 1760. *Ibid.*, VI, 256–7; W. E. Foster: *Town Government in Rhode Island* (Johns Hopkins University *Studies*, 4th ser., No. II, Baltimore, 1886), p. 26.

the growth in importance of these offices and of the work of the Assembly there ensued a gradual increase in the qualifications for freemanship. In 1724 the right to vote was limited by an act restricting the franchise to white men owning land valued at £100; in 1730 this qualification was increased to £200; and in 1746 to £400.[43]

The increase in the qualifications for those entitled to exercise the franchise was doubtless an effort to keep pace with the rapid depreciation of the colony's currency. The effect on the franchise seems to have been to limit it drastically. In fact, one can detect a new attitude on the part of the voting population of Rhode Island toward their government. Up until the second decade of the eighteenth century they had looked to political organization simply to regulate and guard certain common interests. Thereafter the government began to assume a new position. It became the dispenser of valuable favours with the creation of a series of so-called "banks" which were, in effect, government loans to privileged private individuals. The first of these banks, provided for by act of the Assembly in 1715, came into existence when £40,000 in bills of credit were emitted[44] and thereupon distributed to those who offered security in land double the value of the ten-year loan. To provide an equitable allocation of these funds among the inhabitants, £11,511 was assigned to Newport, £6,500 to Providence, £5,993 to Portsmouth, and £2,363 to Warwick; the remainder was in like manner allotted to the towns South Kingstown, Westerly, Greenwich, Jamestown, and New Shoreham.[45] Here apparently is a cause even more important than that of inflation for the progressive raising of barriers against acquiring freemanship within the colony. For who but freemen, under the circumstances, stood the slightest prospect of securing a loan? Moreover, the fewer the freemen, obviously the

---

[43] For other aspects of these laws see A. E. McKinley: *The Suffrage Franchise in the Thirteen English Colonies in America* (Philadelphia, 1905), pp. 453–9.

[44] *Rhode Island Colonial Records*, IV, 201; *Acts and Laws of . . . Rhode Island and Providence Plantations* (Newport, 1730), pp. 78–83.

[45] See E. R. Potter and S. S. Rider: *Some Account of the Bills of Credit or Paper Money of Rhode Island* (*Rhode Island Historical Tracts*, No. 8, Providence, 1880), pp. 11–16. See also C. P. Nettels: *The Money Supply of the American Colonies before 1720* (Madison, 1934), Chap. 10.

better would be the opportunity for each one with more land than ready money to obtain financial assistance for extending his enterprises.[46] For example, in 1748 Newport with 5,335 white inhabitants had but 96 freemen "voters," Providence with 3,177 had but 32, South Kingstown with 1,405 had but 21, and Gloucester with 1,194 but 11. Other towns made a better showing. Tiverton with 842 white inhabitants had 102 freemen voters, and little Compton with 1,004 had 107. Nevertheless, with a white population estimated at 28,439, in that year there were only 888 freemen "voters" in the entire colony. Earlier in the eighteenth century, when the qualifications for freemanship were low, the number of voters never exceeded 1,300. In 1730 the census returned 15,302 whites.[47]

How this program of government financing of private ventures worked out in Rhode Island is part of the confused currency problem in New England at mid-century.

When the ten years had passed in the life of the first bank, the final period of repayment was extended to 1728, at which time it was arranged that this loan should be liquidated by a series of partial payments to be completed by 1738.[48] Meanwhile, in 1721 the second bank was established, with the same relative allotments to the towns, when £40,000 was loaned for five years. The time of repayment was lengthened in 1728, at the same time as the period for the repayment of the first bank was extended. In that year the third bank was provided for, with £40,000. In 1731 came a fourth bank with £60,000; in 1733, a fifth bank with £100,000; in 1738, a sixth with £100,000; in 1740, a seventh with £20,000 (now of so-

---

[46] On this subject W. A. Greene, in *The Providence Plantations for Two Hundred and Fifty Years* (Providence, 1886, p. 53), writes: "The fact that the large landowners were the ones who received the benefit of the banks so frequently issued may explain this increased restriction."

[47] For a table giving the number of freemen "voters" or proxies in 1748 together with the population (whites, Negroes, and Indians) of each town see William Douglass: *op. cit.*, II, 88–9; see also *Rhode Island Colonial Records*, V, 270, which reproduces the Douglass table. D. S. Lovejoy, in his *Rhode Island Politics and the American Revolution* (pp. 16–17), indicates that in 1757 — on the basis of the ratemakers' report for that year — about 79 per cent of those with ratable polls in five towns owned enough real property to permit them to vote. The student should also refer to Lovejoy's note on ratable polls on pages 197–8 of his work.

[48] See Governor Richard Ward to the Board of Trade, January 9, 1740, *Rhode Island Colonial Records*, V, 8–14.

called new tenor);[49] in 1743–4, an eighth bank with £40,000 (also of new tenor, loaned for ten years at four per cent); and finally in 1750, a ninth bank with £25,000.[50] It is needless to suggest that in the intoxication of this easy method of acquiring wealth the money began to depreciate in value. Between 1710 and 1747 there was issued, in addition to these banks, £312,300 in bills of credit for the supply of the colony's treasury, of which sum £135,335 was unredeemed in 1749, making a total of £525,335 outstanding. By 1752 the bills of credit of the older issues that had first circulated at a value not far removed from the proclamation or lawful value established by Queen Anne — namely, of six shillings to the Spanish-milled dollar — had sunk to a ratio of fifty-six to one.[51]

For a period of thirty years — that is, from 1714 to 1744 — there no longer seemed to be a need to levy taxes, and none were raised. The use of the printing press proved to be a magic way to relieve people of their public responsibilities and at the same time permit them to use their resources for the expansion of individual enterprises. It was a period of exhilaration or intoxication such as never had been known in the colony. "The landed interests gained additional importance in political life when nearly every land owner, and hence every voter, in the colony got into debt to the government." With "no earnest effort to redeem . . . [paper money] issues, . . . dishonesty and repudiation everywhere attended the attempt of the people to enrich themselves by getting into debt."[52]

---

49 *Ibid.*, for a history of the above paper-money emissions during 1715–40. One pound of the new tenor was worth four of the old bills-of-credit issues at this juncture.

50 Report of the Committee on Bills of Credit, February 27, 1749, *ibid.*, V, 282–4, 321. For the apportionment to the various towns of bills of credit emitted in 1750 see *ibid.*, V, 321. The *Boston Evening Post* for September 10, 1750, contains the following letter to the editor from Newport, dated August 28, 1750: "The election of General Officers in this Colony for the current Year was carried on (as is reported) by the detach'd Partisans of the two contending Parties for the Government by promising the People a Bank in lieu of their Votes, at the General Choice. It is but just to mention this, that as both Parties were culpable, each should have a share in the Consequences."

51 *Rhode Island Colonial Records*, V, 312, 343; see also Henry Phillips, Jr.: *Historical Sketches of the Paper Currency of the American Colonies* (Roxbury, Mass., 1865), p. 111, and A. M. Davis: *Currency and Banking in the Province of Massachusetts-Bay* (2 vols., New York, 1900–1), I, 354–6.

52 H. K. Stokes: *Finances and Administration of Providence* (Baltimore, 1903), p. 122.

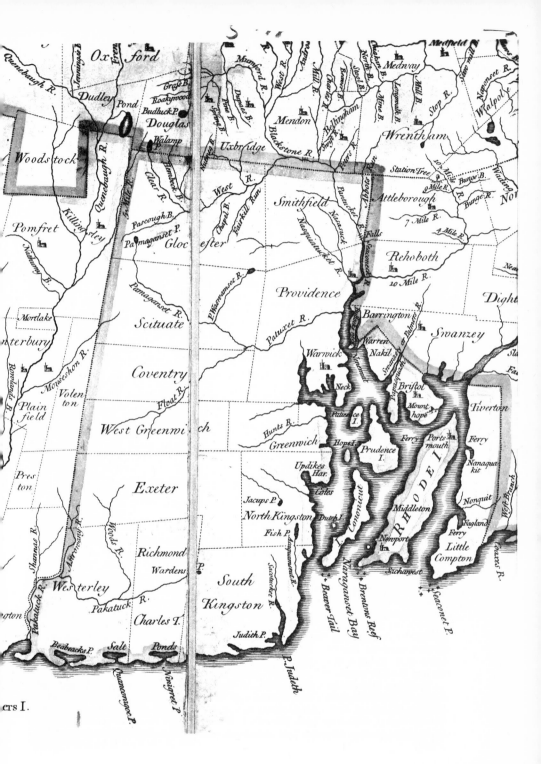

The Colony of Rhode Island.
(From "The Plan of the British Dominions of
New England in North America"
by William Douglas, 1753 [?])

The Colony of Connecticut.
(From the Jefferys map of New England, 1755)

The dangers of this situation, however, were too long ignored. Governor Richard Ward, in a letter to the Board of Trade sent early in 1740, replied to their request for an account of the issue of bills of credit and strongly defended the soundness of the policy. "In short," he declared, "if this colony be in any respect happy and flourishing, it is paper money, and a right application of it, that hath rendered us so." His argument was "that navigation is one main pillar on which this government is supported at present; and we never should have enjoyed this advantage had not the government emitted bills of credit to supply the merchants with a medium of exchange, always proportioned to the increase of their commerce."[53] Nevertheless, in the course of the decade following this defence, advocates of paper money found their colony involved in deep difficulty. Although Massachusetts Bay had also been guilty of issuing great quantities of paper money, she emerged in 1750 with a hard-money program, having previously forbidden the circulation after 1742 of the paper money of Rhode Island issue.[54] Connecticut also, in the early 1750's, forbad the circulation of all Rhode Island bills of credit. The trading interests, now belatedly seeing the danger, petitioned the British government against the orgy of money bills.

In this petition, signed by seventy-two persons, many of them leading merchants, and sent in the fall of 1750, it was declared that during the past seven years the currency had depreciated by one half of its value, "whereby all the creditors of the colony, have been greatly defrauded. . . ." It was further asserted that the land-

---

[53] Richard Ward to the Board of Trade, January 9, 1740, *Rhode Island Colonial Records*, V, 12. The traditional views on the harmful effects of the Rhode Island bills of credit as expounded by E. R. Potter and S. S. Rider in their study of the colony's paper currency — a work already cited — have been challenged by two students. Bruce Bigelow, in his unpublished doctoral dissertation at Brown University on "Rhode Island Trade in the Eighteenth Century," reached the conclusion that Rhode Island trade attained its greatest prosperity in the 1730's and 1770's. John McInnis, in his unpublished dissertation also prepared at Brown, on "Rhode Island Currency in the Eighteenth Century," has sought to demonstrate that the paper money issued by the colony was an instrument by means of which Rhode Island captured much of the trade of Massachusetts Bay and that only when these issues of bills of credit got out of hand did the merchants complain; further, that, all in all, they were not too seriously affected by the circulation of these depreciated bills of credit.

[54] *Acts and Laws of the Province of Massachusetts-Bay* (Boston, 1742), p. 314.

holders of the colony, "having generally mortgaged their farms or plantations, as a security for the bills of credit they have taken upon loan, have found it to their interest to multiply such bills, that they may depreciate and lessen in value, and which they have recourse to, as a legal expedient of wiping away their debts without labour."[55] This situation struck a deadly blow at the business interests of the colony and manifestly had a most adverse effect upon the British merchants dealing with Rhode Island.

To check this financial irresponsibility the Board of Trade two years earlier had intimated to the agent of the colony, Richard Partridge, that Rhode Island, among other New England colonies, need not look to reimbursement of the expense incurred during the war, then just concluded, unless it would take steps to call in depreciated bills of credit.[56]

The Rhode Island Assembly, dominated by inflationists, was in nowise deterred by the threat. It went ahead with its plans for the establishment of an additional bank and, in 1750, voted to call upon the Governor to instruct Partridge to oppose strenuously any bill that might be brought into Parliament for regulating colonial paper money.[57] In the face of the determination of the debtor agricultural elements to continue the process of repudiation, Parliament the following year passed its famous act narrowly restricting further issues of bills of credit by the governments of New England. Evidence that the "Act to regulate and restrain Paper Bills of Credit in his Majesty's Colonies or Plantations of Rhode Island and Providence Plantations, Connecticut, The Massachusetts Bay, and New Hampshire in America; and to prevent the same being legal Tenders in Payment of Money"[58] was primarily directed against Rhode Island is indicated in the following resolution passed by the House of Commons on March 12, 1750/1:

---

[55] Petition to the King, Newport, September 4, 1750, *Rhode Island Colonial Records*, V, 311–13.

[56] Partridge to Governor Greene, December 17, 1748, *The Correspondence of the Colonial Governors of Rhode Island, 1723–1775* (ed. Gertrude S. Kimball, 2 vols., Boston & New York, 1902–3), II, 88.

[57] Governor Greene to Richard Partridge, December 4, 1750, *Rhode Island Colonial Records*, V, 315–16. This was a reply to the petition of 72 signers against the bills of credit.

[58] See 24 Geo. II, c. 53.

"That in the great Rise in the Value of Silver and in the Exchange, occasioned by the repeated Emissions of Paper Bills of Credit particularly in Rhode Island hath been the means of defrauding the Creditors in all the four Governments of a great Part of their Property and by introducing Confusion into Dealings, hath proved a great Discouragement to the Trade of these Kingdoms."[59]

---

[59] The House of Commons in a further resolution referred to the "Contempt and Defiance of the Authority of His Majesty and this House" by the Act of the Rhode Island Assembly in 1750 for issuing £50,000 in bills of credit. See E. R. Potter and S. S. Rider: *op. cit.*, pp. 84–8, for these resolutions and for a full discussion of the background and terms of the New England currency act of 1751. While defending the issuing of bills of credit by the American colonies, E. J. Ferguson ("Currency Finance: An Interpretation of Colonial Monetary Practices," *William and Mary Quarterly*, 3rd ser., X, 153–80) makes an exception of Rhode Island and North Carolina. "The depreciation in New England," he writes, "was mainly the fault of Rhode Island, whose emissions flooded the unitary economy of that area and undermined the currency of her neighbors. Elsewhere, North Carolina was the leading offender."

CHAPTER IV

A Puritan Stronghold

AMONG all the British plantations in North America and the West Indies, Connecticut in 1750 was organized on the most democratic constitutional basis. It and Rhode Island were the only colonies that were fully corporate and that had retained unaltered seventeenth-century charters; but in Connecticut alone the freemen voted directly and locally for their governors. Its provisions for the exercise of the franchise were also more liberal than those of its eastern neighbour. With the exception of Rhode Island, it was the only colony with an assembly in which the governor did not possess an absolute veto upon the measures of that body;[1] and, excepting Rhode Island, Delaware, and Maryland, it was the only colony not required to send its laws to England for confirmation by the King's Council. In common with New Jersey and North Carolina in 1750, it had no fixed governmental centre, the Assembly meeting alternately at Hartford and New Haven; in common with these two provinces and Delaware, it had neither a chief city[2] nor any impor-

---

[1] Georgia was, of course, a trusteeship at this period and was about to pass under royal control. William Stephens was the President of the Georgia Board under the Trustees. See Volume II, Chap. 6, of this series.

[2] In the year 1756 Middletown had 5,446 white inhabitants; Norwich, 5,317; New Haven, 5,085; Wallingford, 3,713; New London, 3,171; and Hartford, 2,926; in 1774 New Haven stood first, with 8,022 whites; then came Norwich, with 7,032; New London, with 5,366; Hartford, with 4,881; Wallingford, with 4,777; and Middletown, with 4,680. See *The Public Records of the Colony of Connecticut [1636–1776]* (15 vols., Hartford, 1850–90), subsequently cited as *Connecticut Colonial Records*, XIV, 483–92.

tant direct commercial intercourse with the mother country.[3] Again, as was also true of Massachusetts Bay and Rhode Island, no quit-rents were ever levied on lands within the then generally accepted boundaries of Connecticut. Similar to Rhode Island, in the middle of the century Connecticut had no public lands within these bound-aries — other than those belonging to the township corporations — since the Assembly had taken steps in 1737 to dispose of the re-maining ungranted lands lying in the northwestern part of the colony and had erected seven townships in them.[4] At the same time, for its limited size Connecticut was perhaps the most "urban" of all the colonies in terms of the number of towns with a population over 4,000. Wealth, moreover, was neither in the hands of a privi-leged few, nor was it concentrated geographically.[5]

Possessed of neither a first-class port nor a town with as many as 6,000 inhabitants before the last of the intercolonial wars, by 1756 Connecticut had a population of over 125,000 people[6] primarily interested in farming and stock-raising. Since the population had

---

[3] Between 1749 and 1755 the firm of Williams, Trumbull, and Pitkin, with es-tablishments at Lebanon, Norwich, Wethersfield, and East Haddam, developed some commercial relations with England, the continent of Europe, the West Indies, and Halifax. Likewise, the McAulays of New Haven in the early 1760's sent their little schooners to Lisbon for salt and wine. See Glenn Weaver: *Jonathan Trumbull: Connecticut's Merchant Magistrate* (Hartford, 1956), pp. 41–72; I. W. Stuart's *Life of Jonathan Trumbull* (Boston, 1859), pp. 67–70; T. F. Trowbridge: "Commerce, Foreign and Domestic" in the *History of the City of New Haven* (ed. E. E. Atwater, New York, 1887), p. 484.

[4] See *Connecticut Colonial Records*, VIII, 134–7, and William Douglass: *A Sum-mary, Historical and Political* . . . (2 vols., Boston, 1760), I, 244 n; see also Dorothy Deming: *The Settlement of Litchfield County* (New Haven, 1933), and C. S. Grant: "Land Speculation and the Settlement of Kent [in Litchfield County]," *New England Quarterly*, XXVIII, 51–71. For the creation of towns in Connecticut see Dorothy Deming: *The Settlement of Connecticut Towns* (New Haven, 1933), a Tercentenary Commission publication, as is her study of Litchfield County.

[5] The following was the rating for taxation in 1750 of the six towns standing highest on the list: New Haven, rated at £54,448; Norwich, at £51,881; Middle-town, at £48,456; Fairfield, at £47,561; Windsor, at £38,597; Farmington, at £38,396. In 1770 the six towns standing highest on the list were Norwich, rated at £63,870; New Haven, at £63,335; Farmington, at £60,727; Woodbury, at £54,099; Stratford, at £49,210; and Fairfield, at £49,008. It will be noticed that neither Hart-ford nor New London appears in these lists, which indicates that the wealth of the colony was largely agricultural in character. *Connecticut Colonial Records*, IX, 563; for the valuation of the towns in 1770 see *ibid.*, XIII, 368.

[6] For the census of 1756 see *ibid.*, X, 617–18; see also A. L. Olson: *Agricultural Economy and the Population in Eighteenth-Century Connecticut* (New Haven, 1935), p. 11, and Greene and Harrington: *American Population before . . . 1790* (New York, 1932), pp. 49–50, for other figures.

doubled in the twenty-five years preceding 1750, men were eagerly searching for good, new farm lands. Lying to the east of New York, south of Massachusetts Bay, and west of Rhode Island, the colony seemed to be hemmed in, with no more room for expansion. At this juncture certain individuals began to study again the seventeenth-century charter and arrived at the conclusion that, since this instrument was still valid, so was the rather vague sea-to-sea grant that it contained. As a result, a movement developed in eastern Connecticut for laying claim to the northern part of what after 1680/1 had become by royal grant the Province of Pennsylvania. In 1753 the Susquehanna Company was formed to colonize the Wyoming Valley, and two years later the project received the endorsement of the Assembly. This led to the movement of Connecticut settlers into the region and the outbreak of the so-called Pennamite War.[7]

Although agriculture was the mainstay of the people of Connecticut and land expansion therefore followed, the importance of commerce was growing. The export staples were chiefly beef and pork; together with ship timber, wheat and other cereals, flax, potashes, and horses, these brought in a return of some £130,000 sterling, which in turn was largely spent in the purchase of European commodities.[8] While most of the produce of its farms went to Boston and New York, there was a ready demand for Connecticut beef, pork, flour, horses, and lumber in the West Indies, in return for which rum, sugar, molasses, and salt, together with bills of exchange, were received. The shipping of the colony at this period was composed of some seventy-five sloops, brigantines, schooners, and snows, the largest of which possessed a capacity of merely ninety tons and carried a ten-man crew.[9] However, it appears that these diminutive ships built in Connecticut yards were adequate to meet the modest commercial needs of the people. During the year

---

[7] See *The Susquehanna Company Papers* (ed. J. P. Boyd, 4 vols., Wilkes-Barre, 1930–3), and L. H. Gipson: *Jared Ingersoll: A Study of American Loyalism in Relation to British Colonial Government* (New Haven & London, 1920), Chap. 11.

[8] *Connecticut Colonial Records*, X, 622–3.

[9] *Ibid.*, X, 625; see also Glenn Weaver: *op. cit.*, pp. 5, 17 et seq.; A. E. Van Dusen: "Colonial Connecticut's Trade with the West Indies," New England Social Studies *Bulletin*, March 1956; Margaret E. Martin: "Merchants and Trade in the Connecticut River Valley, 1750–1820," *Smith College Studies in History*, XXIV (1938–9), 21 et seq.; and Oscar Zeichner: *Connecticut's Years of Controversy, 1750–1776* (Chapel Hill, N.C., 1949), p. 82 et seq.

1749 only 37 vessels entered the principal port of the colony, New London, but 62 cleared outwards.[10] As all but a few of these vessels were of Connecticut registration, it must be inferred that a large proportion of them on the return voyage were never legally entered; it may likewise be inferred that there was good reason why the owners avoided entry. As was true of Rhode Island, the Connecticut customs records are silent on the subject of the importation into the colony of dutiable West Indies merchandise, which in the case of New York, for example, amounted to £2,003 in the years 1733–50.[11]

In spite of its major emphasis upon agriculture and its commercial backwardness at least with respect to European trade, Connecticut was far ahead of its western neighbour in the production and manufacture of iron. While New York had in operation only one pig-iron furnace and no forge in the year 1750, Connecticut could boast a steel furnace, built at Killingsworth in 1744, and some eight forges with tilt hammers, three of which had been erected in 1732, the remainder during the period from 1742 to 1748. It is noteworthy that all of these ironworks were in eastern Connecticut within the counties of New London and Windham.[12] In fact, the great Connecticut River, winding its way southward through the heart of the colony, divided it into two rather distinct regions or sections that had somewhat different interests and on occasions manifested opposing points of view, particularly during the decade preceding the outbreak of the War for American Independence. Eastern Connecticut tended to look in the direction of Boston, western Connecticut in the direction of New York. This was true culturally as well as commercially.[13]

For example, in the 1750's most of the commercial dealings between New Haven and any other part of North America were centred in New York. As a result of the influences flowing from New

---

[10] William Douglass: *A Summary, Political and Historical, . . . of the British Settlements in North-America* (2 vols., London, 1760), II, 2.

[11] See "An Account of all Duties Collected in each of the Northern Colonies from 1733 to 1750," P.R.O., C.O. 5:38.

[12] The existence of iron furnaces and forges and a steel furnace was ignored in the reply to the query of the Board of Trade in 1748 respecting the manufactures of the colony. This was also true in 1756. See *Connecticut Colonial Records,* IX, 595–6, and X, 623.

[13] See the author's *Jared Ingersoll,* p. 198 n.

York, an Anglican church was organized in New Haven in 1752. By this year at least twenty-five churches of that communion were in existence to the west of the Connecticut River, the first of which came into existence in 1707 at Stratford.[14] In fact the church at this place by 1750 had become something of an Episcopalian centre, and furnished, in the person of Dr. Samuel Johnson, the first president for the newly created King's College in New York. On the other hand, to the east of the Connecticut the trade contacts were largely with Boston; moreover, the towns of this region were deeply interested in whatever issues agitated the citizens of that seaport and were generally among the first to espouse their radical ideas.[15]

Despite the existence of this regionalism within the colony, it may be suggested that western Connecticut had more in common with Massachusetts Bay than with New York, and that a fundamental solidarity existed between the two sections. For the organized life of the colony embodied a political and social system that could have evolved in its fullness only in New England, and that was preserved more faithfully in Connecticut perhaps than in any of the other New England plantations. As William Douglass, an acute observer, pointed out in writing his famous *Summary . . . of the . . . Present State of the British Settlements in North-America*, first printed in 1750 and reissued in 1760: ". . . in all their elections of governor, counsellors, representatives, judges, and other publick officers, by custom, they generally prefer the most worthy."[16] Connecticut may truthfully be called the last of the Puritan commonwealths. For this reason certain aspects of its government, both local and central, bear closer scrutiny.

New England Puritanism took the form of a community or small-town movement based upon adherence to certain common religious principles and practices. What these principles and practices should be was, however, determined by an *élite* made up of ministers, members of old families, leading merchants, landowners, and professional people. The location of their pews in the church and their

---

[14] Glenn Weaver: "Anglican-Congregationalist Tensions in Pre-Revolutionary Connecticut," *Historical Magazine of the Protestant Episcopal Church*, XXVI, 269–85, and Maud O'Neil: "A Struggle for Religious Liberty: An Analysis of the Work of the S.P.G. in Connecticut," *ibid.*, XX, 173–89.

[15] L. H. Gipson: *Jared Ingersoll*, pp. 176 and 268.

[16] William Douglass: *A Summary . . .* (London, 1760), II, 158.

dress were visible distinguishing marks of this superiority — a situation comparable to that in most parish churches in England. In their views on community affairs they were strongly conservative in outlook — an outlook that had its foundation in the seventeenth-century puritanical conception of social solidarity in all matters that touched the common town life, demanding as it did a certain uniformity of thought and action.[17] This social solidarity expressed itself through certain distinct avenues regulated by law, such as the church communion, the ecclesiastical society, the proprietors' meetings, the freemen's meetings, and the town meetings. Symbolic of all this was the town meeting house, a centre of the religious and secular activity of the town.[18]

The Congregational Church communion was limited to those in full Christian fellowship who, before admittance, had subscribed to the church covenant and who — in most instances — had publicly testified to their conversion. Leading the group of communicants in any new local church erected according to the old New Haven Colony rule were the so-called seven "pillars" or organizers. The communion seems to have embraced most of the consecrated Christians of the community, unless these were dissenters from the established Congregational Church. The communicants gave a vitality and, in a sense, a spiritual validity to the work of the ecclesiastical society of which they formed the inner circle. From its membership also were chosen, almost without exception, those to whom important powers within the community were delegated. When the inhabitants acted on issues of first importance bearing on the religious life of their community, they doubtless were guided by the communicants, the heart and conscience of the town.

The Great Awakening of the 1740's, which in its New England phase has already been considered, brought with it a breaking-down of the old solidarity of the communion in many Connecticut towns, with the division of the church fellowship into the Old Lights and the New Lights. As a result, there was generally a secession of the

---

[17] R. S. Osterweis: *Three Centuries of New Haven, 1638–1938* (New Haven, 1953), pp. 106–8. For town life in colonial New England see Carl Bridenbaugh: "The New England Town: A Way of Life," American Antiquarian Society *Proceedings*, LVI, Part I, 19–48.
[18] See Noah Porter: *The New England Meeting House* (New Haven, 1933, reprinted from the *New Englander* for May 1883).

latter from the parent body for the purpose of establishing a separate communion. In most places this was apparently accomplished only after considerable agitation in which bitterness and intolerance were much in evidence. Especially was this true in eastern Connecticut, where in 1744 at Saybrook, for example, fourteen Separatists were arrested and fined for "holding a meeting contrary to law on God's holy Sabbath day" and, upon refusal to make payment, were driven through the mud to New London, twenty-five miles distant, and there thrown into prison without fire, food, or beds.[19]

This deplorable and unneighbourly treatment of men and women whose only crime was loyalty to religious conviction can be explained only in the light of the long history of religious persecution. In almost every case there was felt to be at stake the precious causes of conformity and solidarity, with all the blessings these have in store for mankind in an ordered existence. And so the hostility of the Connecticut ecclesiastical authorities was particularly directed against these secessionists from the Establishment. Even as late as 1777 a writer bitterly complained of the plight of the Separatists: "They have been persecuted, oppressed, and most cruelly treated, their property has most unjustly been taken from them to support ministers that in conscience they would not hear preach; and at the same time, they have had ministers of their own to support; they have been imprisoned for not paying the rates to the clergy and fined for not attending public worship with the standing churches."[20]

The ecclesiastical society previous to 1746 legally comprehended all those living within the bounds of the town. This seems to have been the case in spite of the act of the General Assembly in 1727

---

[19] See Maria L. Greene: *Development of Religious Liberty in Connecticut* (Boston and New York, 1905), pp. 276–7. This book is especially excellent in its treatment of the breakdown of religious conformity in Connecticut as the result of the Great Awakening. See also Joseph Tracey: *The Great Awakening* . . . (Boston, 1842), and Mary H. Mitchell: *The Great Awakening and Other Revivals in the Religious Life of Connecticut* (New Haven, 1934).

[20] *The Connecticut Journal*, March 26, 1777. A penalty of ten shillings was to be levied against any person assisting in forming a "separate company for worship in a private House." *Acts and Laws of His Majesty's English Colony of Connecticut* . . . (New London, 1750), p. 139, subsequently cited as *Acts and Laws of Connecticut*. Unitarians and deists were struck at by a statute which declared that anyone convicted of denying "any of the persons of the Holy Trinity to be God," or denying that the Scriptures were of divine authority, should be incapable of enjoying any office, ecclesiastical, court, or military. *Ibid.*, p. 69. See M. L. Greene: *op. cit.*, pp. 234 and 239.

exempting from church attendance and the payment of local church rates, under certain conditions, those who were communicants of the Church of England and the acts of the year 1729 extending these immunities, under similar terms, to Quakers and Baptists.[21] After 1746 the law provided that groups which had been expressly exempt by law from the payment of the ecclesiastical-society dues should be debarred from further participation in the activities of the society.[22] This legislation marked the disappearance of the all-inclusiveness of the local societies. Within them still remained the membership of the communion, those who had never taken the covenant nor made any profession of faith, and those who belonged to religious bodies other than the Anglican, Quaker, and Baptist denominations. Unless prevented by bodily infirmity, all under the jurisdiction of the local society were expected, on pain of fine, to attend its church services and while there to conduct themselves in a seemly fashion. They were also permitted, if they were adult males possessed of a freehold within the society limits rated at fifty shillings or were rated at £40 or more in the common list, to be present at the business meetings of the society and to participate in the choice of a pastor, in the selection of society officers, in decisions regarding church rates, and in the regulation of the parish school.[23]

While every effort was made to include in the activities of the ecclesiastical society everyone living within its limits, there was no corresponding solicitude to see that all men should share in the privileges and responsibilities of freemanship. For only freemen could vote to fill the colony's offices or could be entitled to occupy them. A freeman had to be male, twenty-one years of age, in possession either of a freehold estate to the value of forty shillings per annum or of £40 personal estate in the general assessment list for that year, and to be "of a quiet and peaceable Behaviour and Civil Conversation." In addition, he was required to secure a certifi-

21 *Connecticut Colonial Records*, VII, 106, 237, and 257. For the Act of 1708 giving freedom of worship in order to conform to the English act of toleration (1 Wm. and Mary, c. 18) see *ibid.*, V, 50. However, those tolerated were expected to pay the church rates.

22 *Ibid.*, IX, 218–19.

23 *Acts and Laws of Connecticut* (1750), pp. 165–8. For the "Act directing how Persons shall be qualified to Vote in Society Meetings" passed in 1728 see *Connecticut Colonial Records*, VII, 211.

cate of endorsement from a majority of the selectmen of the town, and in a freeman's meeting to take the prescribed oath.[24] Once having attained this privilege, a man apparently remained in the enjoyment of it, irrespective of the vicissitudes of fortune, except when, upon judgment of the superior court that he had been guilty of "walking scandalously," he was penalized by being disfranchised.[25]

Exactly what proportion of the adult male population exercised freemen's privileges in colonial Connecticut in the middle of the eighteenth century is difficult to estimate with accuracy. However, it is likely that not more than one third of the adult males were qualified voters in 1750. At least, this seems to have been the case in New Haven.[26]

The semi-annual freemen's meetings were held regularly on the Monday following the first Tuesday in April[27] and the second or

---

[24] This oath is given in *Acts and Laws of Connecticut* (1750), p. 175. By it the applicant was obliged to swear that he would be true and faithful to the King and his successors and to the government of the colony and act according to conscience "without Respect of Persons, or Favor of any Man."

[25] *Ibid.* This law struck Francis Fane, legal adviser of the Board of Trade, as deserving of disallowance, since "walking scandalously" was too vague a phrase for disfranchisement. See Charles M. Andrews: *Fane's Reports on the Laws of Connecticut,* Acorn Club *Publications* (New Haven, 1915), pp. 44–5.

[26] A. E. McKinley, in his *The Suffrage Franchise in the Thirteen English Colonies in America* (Philadelphia, 1905), arrived at the conclusion that there was one voter in twelve of the adult male population in Connecticut (pp. 419–20); Alfred C. Bates of the Connecticut Historical Society was inclined to take the position that about one adult male in eight enjoyed the right of franchise in Connecticut in 1754. See his Introduction as editor of *The Wolcott Papers . . . 1750–1754* (Connecticut Historical Society *Collections,* XVI, Hartford, 1916), p. xxv. These figures seem too low. Although the number of votes cast in 1754 in the election was 2,564 (*ibid.,* xxxi), the number of qualified freemen was doubtless much greater in that year. According to William Douglass (*op. cit.,* II, 89), 4,000 freemen voted in a heated election for governor in 1740. In 1766 John Tully of Saybrook put the number of freemen at between 7,000 and 8,000, and in 1767 Dr. Ezra Stiles calculated that their number was about 12,000, out of which a total of 8,322 cast votes in that year. See C. M. Andrew's review of *The Wolcott Papers* in the *American Historical Review,* XXIII, 402–3. In the election of 1766 in New Haven concerning very important matters a total of 274 "voters" were present. With a population in that year of apparently over 6,000, this would mean that out of the adult males less than one out of four voted. See L. H. Gipson: *Jared Ingersoll,* p. 19. On the general problem of interpreting franchise statistics in Connecticut an article relating to the seventeenth century has value. See David Fowler: "Connecticut Freemen: The First Forty Years," *William and Mary Quarterly,* 3rd ser., XV, 312–33.

[27] Down to 1740 the freemen met the last Tuesday in April. *Connecticut Colonial Records,* VIII, 297.

third Tuesday in September in all the towns of the colony.[28] At the last-named meeting, deputies were elected to represent the towns in the October session of the Assembly, and each freeman gave his vote by written ballot for twenty persons whom he judged qualified "to stand in nomination for election in the month of May following." These ballots were forwarded to the General Assembly by the town clerk, and counted. The twenty freemen receiving the greatest number of votes were thereupon declared to be nominated to stand as the candidates at the spring election, when all the elective offices of the colony were filled. At the April meeting of the freemen, after the deputies to the May meeting of the Assembly had been chosen, they then proceeded to ballot for the Governor, the Deputy Governor, the Treasurer, and the Secretary of the colony, as well as for the twelve assistants who acted both as a Governor's Council and as an upper house of the General Assembly.[29] Once again the ballots were sent to the General Assembly, where the final results were declared.

The freemen, representing the propertied element in each community, were inclined toward conservatism in action. They, rather than the non-propertied inhabitants, naturally determined the political tone of the little commonwealth. In the words of Albert C. Bates, a life-long student of eighteenth-century Connecticut: "Among the freemen themselves the higher offices were closely held to a large degree by a small coterie of prominent families and individuals, who may be considered as the true aristocracy of the colony. . . . In the century following the Andros interregnum, 1689–1788, there were but eleven persons elected to the governorship, thirteen to the deputy governorship, and ninety-seven to the . . . House of Assistants, which was composed of twelve members. . . . This small aristocracy was for the most part made up of de-

---

[28] The freemen in New Haven, Hartford, and Fairfield counties were to meet the third Tuesday, while those of New London and Windham counties met the second Tuesday in September. *Acts and Laws of Connecticut* (1750), pp. 45–7.

[29] Although it was necessary to select the assistants and the Treasurer and Secretary from the list of twenty nominees, the Connecticut code of 1750 stated that "the Free-men shall have Liberty to choose the Governor and Deputy-Governor, where they see cause, of all, or any of the Free-men within this Colony" (*ibid.*, pp. 45–6). From 1670 to 1750 a freeman might go to Hartford to cast his vote for colonial officers or do so at his local freemen's meetings. The code of 1750 did away with personal attendance. *Ibid.*, p. 46. See A. E. McKinley: *op. cit.*, pp. 416–17.

scendants of families of the earliest settlers who were men of prominence, education and ability, many of whom were persons of
wealth. . . ."[30]

It was not until the approach of the Revolution that the non-
freeman elements, who constituted an overwhelming majority of
the people, through violent and terroristic means wrenched political
control, for the moment at least, from the hands of the more cautious and legal-minded freemen.[31]

In eighteenth-century colonial Connecticut one might be both
an inhabitant of a town and a freeman without being a town
proprietor. Prior to 1685 there seems to have been no clear-cut
differentiation between the proprietors of the unoccupied lands
within the limits of the towns and the rest of the settled population.
The general town meetings from time to time granted lands to individuals on petition.[32] In that year, however, the General Court
authorized a confirmation to the so-called proprietors and settled
inhabitants of the titles to the common and undivided lands in
twenty-eight of the towns.[33] This legislation was brought about as
the result of disputes between the old established families and
newcomers as to which were entitled to share in the periodic land
divisions. The law was so ambiguous that it only added to the keen-
ness of the struggle between the two groups. As a result, in 1703
the Assembly specifically confined the proprietorial rights within
the towns to those who had been considered proprietors in 1685,
and their children.[34] From this time on, a sharp distinction was
drawn between the proprietors and other inhabitants, and all matters having to do with the township lands were cared for in distinct
meetings attended only by property-owners. At any regularly called
meeting, taxes might be levied upon those with proprietorial rights

---

[30] *The Wolcott Papers*, Introduction, pp. xxv–xxvi; see also Oscar Zeichner:
op. cit., pp. 9–10.

[31] For example, Thomas Darling and Joshua Chandler, ultra-conservatives, were
repeatedly sent by the New Haven freemen to the General Assembly even as late as
1774. In opposition within that town were members of the train band, sailors, and
those who made up the mobs in times of excitement. See L. H. Gipson: *op. cit.*, pp.
20, 31.

[32] See, for example, the action of the New Haven town meeting of April 29, 1684.
New Haven Town Records, 4: 2–3.

[33] *Connecticut Colonial Records*, III, 177–8; IV, 432–3.

[34] *Ibid.*

for the purpose of making fences, gates, and bridges. According to the law, on the first Monday in March a special meeting was to be held for the purpose of choosing a committee to care for the common lands during the year to follow. This committee was empowered to select fence-viewers and haywards and to make other necessary arrangements regarding the lands.[35]

Proprietors' meetings, those of the freemen, and those of the members of the ecclesiastical societies were merely offshoots of the parent gathering. The town meeting was by all odds the most comprehensive of all the local assemblages both in scope of action and in the number of inhabitants admitted to its privileges.

It should be made clear that a man might be a dweller in a New England colonial town and yet technically be not an inhabitant. Three classes of individuals — transients or "single persons newly come," indentured servants, and slaves — were not entitled to such recognition.[36] The code of 1750 declared that, "Whereas several Persons of Ungoverned Conversation, thrust themselves into the Towns in this Colony and by some under-hand Way, as upon pretence of being Hired Servants, or of Hiring Lands, or Houses; or by purchasing the same, Endeavour to become Inhabitants in such Towns," it should be understood that no newcomers would thereafter be admitted as such except those of "honest conversation." The law further stated that strangers might not even abide in any town without consent of the selectmen or the major part of the town, and that those who had been warned out of town were liable to a penalty of ten shillings a week or to be whipped ten stripes if they did not leave.[37]

But not even all adult male inhabitants were qualified to partici-

---

[35] Acts and Laws of Connecticut (1750), pp. 61–8.

[36] At a New Haven town meeting held January 18, 1702, it was laid down that the above classes "never were or are inhabitants in the Town" (New Haven Town Records, 4:133). See also Mary H. Mitchell: "Slavery in Connecticut and Especially in New Haven," New Haven Colony Historical Society Papers, X, 286–312.

[37] Acts and Laws of Connecticut (1750), pp. 99–100. The law of 1750 also provided that "the Setled and Approved Inhabitants . . . Qualified and having Estate . . . shall have Power . . . Provided they . . . be of a Prudential Nature, and that their Penalties exceed not 20s. for One Offence" . . . (ibid., p. 240). See in this connection J. H. Benton: Warning Out in New England (Boston, 1911), pp. 67–70. For a broad treatment of the care of the unfortunate see E. W. Capen: The Historical Development of the Poor Law in Connecticut (Columbia University Studies in History . . . , XXII, New York, 1905).

pate in the proceedings of the town meetings. One not only had to be a lawful inhabitant twenty-one years of age but in addition a householder in possession either of a freehold estate rated at fifty shillings on the tax lists, or of personal estate valued at £40. There was, however, one exception: no one could be debarred from voting in the town meeting who had established himself as a freeman.[38] It will be noticed that there was no provision of the law, as it stood in the middle of the eighteenth century, disqualifying anyone, by reason of religious nonconformity, from taking part in the activities of the town meeting,[39] although deists and Unitarians were debarred from holding any civil, ecclesiastical, or military office within the colony.

One of the most important functions performed by the town meeting was the annual selection of the host of local officials required to carry out the manifold activities of the community. For few matters, even in the middle of the eighteenth century, were considered to be so personal in nature as not to be subject to the inquisitorial scrutiny of individuals delegated for that purpose. Selectmen, some seven in number, were elected to have general oversight of local affairs when the town meeting was not in session; a clerk, to keep the town records; a treasurer, to guard and disburse the funds of the town; a varying number of constables, to watch over the peace and quiet of the community; and tithingmen, to maintain the ecclesiastical regulations by watching over the moral welfare of the inhabitants on week days, and on the Sabbath by preserving order in the meeting house during the sermons, with authority, in the words of the old formula, "to smite such as are

---

[38] *Acts and Laws of Connecticut* (1750), p. 241.

[39] This was denied by Edward Channing (*History of the United States* [6 vols., New York, 1905–36], II, 439), who gives as his authority the act of 1728, which he asserts was in force in 1760. The act is entitled "An Act directing how Persons shall be qualified to Vote in Society Meetings," *Connecticut Colonial Records*, VII, 211–12. This law does not refer to the town meetings, which at that period occasionally dealt with church matters, but is carefully worded so as to limit its application to the periodic meetings of the local ecclesiastical society. Further, it did not debar nonconformists from voting even in these meetings, provided that they had established a residence within the bounds of the society and were rated at fifty shillings or £40 in the common list. Not until 1746 were Episcopalians, Baptists, and Quakers, who had previously been exempt from financially supporting the ecclesiastical society, finally debarred from the privilege of voting at its meetings. *Ibid.*, IX, 218–19; *Acts and Laws* (1750), pp. 231–3.

unruly or of uncomely behaviour in the meeting." Many other officials were chosen whose work was scarcely of less importance: key-keepers, to impound stray animals; branders, to place the town brand on all the horses;[40] highway-surveyors, to care for the miserable township roads and in this connection to see that each man not exempt did his required two days' work; fence-viewers, to supervise the maintenance of fences and other boundaries of the community; haywards, to carry out the work of fence repairs and to secure animals that were straying;[41] gaugers and packers, to supervise the packing of beef, pork, and fish in casks for export; sealers of leather, of measures, and of weights; excise masters, to collect locally the colonial excise on rum, brandy, and other distilled liquors; listers, to prepare the assessment rolls; and, finally, tax-collectors.

In other words, it was necessary in many Connecticut towns to find men qualified to fill over a hundred public posts. That public service was not infrequently considered a burden is indicated by the code of 1750, which provided for a fine of twenty-six shillings from any person who refused to exercise the office to which he was elected unless he could show that he was "Oppressed by such Choice; and that Others are unjustly Exempted."[42]

The town meetings, beyond those given over to holding courts of election, were concerned with an infinite variety of local interests. The killing of crows, the straying of geese, the yoking and ringing of pigs allowed to run at large, the hiring of bulls and boars for the town commons, and the eradication of the barberry bushes were objects of deliberation and action at this period. As trivial as many of these matters may now appear to be, they were then among the things that bulked largest in the eyes of the average man at town

---

[40] Each town in the colony had its own brand. The town branders were required to keep a record and description of every animal branded and also of all sales of the same. All branding was to be done at one of the town pounds, under heavy penalties. This applied only to horses. The brands of cattle, sheep, and swine were to be placed by the owners, but the marks were to be registered.

[41] The term "hayward" is used also to designate one who keeps cows. See G. E. Howard: *Local Constitutional History of the United States* (Johns Hopkins University *Studies*, IV, Baltimore, 1889), p. 221. Toward the middle of the century the hayward is no longer found in many communities. For example, in 1727 twelve haywards were chosen in New Haven, but after 1740 the office disappears. This seems to have resulted from the erection of more permanent fences.

[42] *Acts and Laws* (1750), p. 240.

meetings, for they really conditioned his immediate welfare far more than most of the weightiest imperial legislation. Indeed, these meetings dealing with matters of vital personal importance were excellent schools in which to gather political experience, and no colony produced politicians shrewder than those Connecticut men who had had their training at them. Controlled largely by the same elements that directed ecclesiastical societies, the freemen's meetings, and those of the proprietors, the town meetings, while considered to be centres of radicalism by the home authorities, were generally the strongholds of conservative influence during the decades preceding the Revolution. This was especially so in western Connecticut. The controlling element stood for maintaining the old order of things and discountenanced change and the extreme policies of the radical group.

Against these influences, which could be counted on to oppose hasty and radical political action within the community, stood the train bands. Under the law all males between sixteen and fifty years of age — except those holding posts under the colonial government, those connected with Yale College, Masters of Arts, justices of the peace, physicians, surgeons, schoolmasters, attorneys at law, one miller to a gristmill, constant herdsmen, mariners and ferrymen, as well as lame and otherwise disabled persons, Negroes, and Indians — were required to attend musters and to engage in military exercises.[43]

The train bands, under the terms of the law, were not required to meet more frequently than four days annually for training. This, however, had little bearing on the degree of solidarity that existed within the ranks of these military units or on the extent of the influence they exercised in times of crisis. While the regimental officers were appointed by the colonial authorities, the officers of the train bands from captain downward were selected by the enrolled men. As a result of the exemption from military service of the more

---

[43] *Ibid.*, p. 157. Each band had the following complement: a captain, a lieutenant, an ensign, four sergeants, and as many as sixty-four privates. While the smaller towns would support but one train band, larger towns would have six or seven. Every listed soldier and, indeed, every householder was required by law to possess a well-regulated firelock whose barrel was not less than three and one half feet long, a good sword or cutlass, a trimming-wire fit for his gun, a cartridge box, a pound of powder, four pounds of bullets, and twelve flints. *Ibid.*, pp. 155–9.

responsible men of the communities, the election of officers was quite under the control of the radical and on occasion more irresponsible elements, who naturally supported those who sympathized with their point of view. These popular officers — many of them adventurous characters, such as Benedict Arnold of New Haven and John Durkee of Bean Hill in eastern Connecticut — at times exercised a degree of authority in the affairs of the colony which resulted in the brushing aside of any and all opposition to their objectives.[44]

The central government of Connecticut consisted of the Governor and the General Assembly — constituted of the Governor's assistants or Council and Deputies of the towns. The older townships during the period under consideration sent two representatives each to the Assembly, while two sent one each and eighteen "new or poor townships [that] pay no colony rates . . . consequently send no representatives. . . ."[45] Members of the Assembly, numbering 101 in 1751, were paid for their services out of the colonial treasury. The Governor, elected for but one year as were other officers, had little power. Only in case the members of the Council were tied over some issue could he give a casting vote; nor could he either dissolve or prorogue the Assembly, which alone enjoyed these powers. This body also selected all judges and justices and all higher officers in the train bands. Needless to say, a good deal of time was given to the performance of these strictly administrative functions. Yet the government of the colony functioned smoothly and thriftily as a rule. The units of local government larger than the Connecticut towns were the probate districts — thirteen in number — in each of which a court of probate was erected to care for matters relating to wills, letters of administration, and guardianship.[46] Above these were the counties, the officials of which were not elected by the people but appointed by the General Assembly or by the Governor and Council or in some cases by the county courts. In 1698 a law was passed providing that in each county at least four of the most able freemen should be appointed justices of the peace, three of

---

[44] This influence was to be manifested during the periods of crisis connected with the Stamp Act and the preliminaries of the Revolution.

[45] For a list of the townships in 1751 that sent no deputies to the Assembly see William Douglass: *op. cit.*, II, 166-7.

[46] *Acts and Laws* (1750), p. 33.

whom, a quorum, with a judge to preside, were empowered to hold court.[47] At first these appointments were during pleasure, but subsequently they were made annually.[48] The five county courts were authorized by the code of 1750 to try all civil cases and those criminal cases not extending to life, limb, banishment, or to divorce, and also to levy taxes for paying the debts of the county.[49] They were empowered to appoint a king's attorney to prosecute all criminal offenders "and to doe all other things necessary or convenient . . . to suppresse vice and imorallitie."[50] Twice a year a superior court of judicature met at the county seats with power to try by jury or otherwise all pleas of the Crown.[51] The county sheriffs, appointed by the Governor and Council of the colony, brought offenders before the lower and higher courts and subsequently carried out the judicial mandates.[52]

The laws applied by these courts were binding upon the people in the middle of the eighteenth century. Examination of them gives an indication of the colony's development and shows that, although still influenced to a degree by the religious conceptions of the previous century, they were being modified by the new forces assaulting even this, the chief stronghold of Puritanism in the Old British Empire.

A comparison between the Connecticut codes of 1650 and 1750 indicates the nature of the changes that had taken place. The code of 1650 was based upon the "Body of Libertys" adopted in Massachusetts Bay in 1641 with its twelve capital laws supplemented soon afterwards by three additional laws.[53]

---

[47] *Connecticut Colonial Records*, IV, 235–6.

[48] *Acts and Laws* (1750), pp. 105–6.

[49] Taxes were raised for the payment of county officials, for the upkeep and building of gaols, and for the other limited county activities.

[50] The above office came into existence in 1704. *Connecticut Colonial Records*, IV, 468. Virginia alone of the other American colonies seems to have made use of this title to designate the office of county prosecuting attorney. For a discussion of the history of this office see the author's *Jared Ingersoll*, pp. 42–54.

[51] *Acts and Laws* (1750), pp. 30–2.

[52] *Ibid.*, pp. 221–4. The sheriff in Connecticut was expected to serve and execute all lawful writs, to have the power of a water bailiff to search vessels, to command assistance when necessary, and, with the advice of an assistant or a justice of the peace, to raise the militia.

[53] These appear in the Massachusetts Bay Code of 1648. For an illuminating study of the early Massachusetts Bay laws and their relationship to English law see G. L. Haskins: *Law and Authority in Early Massachusetts . . .* (New York, 1960).

These capital offences were: worshipping a strange god, witch-craft, blasphemy, wilful murder, slaying another through guile, bestiality, sodomy, adultery, rape, kidnapping, false testimony, and rebellion against the colony, and were supplemented by two other capital offences: the cursing of parents by a child over sixteen years of age and "stubbornness" on the part of a child over sixteen years. The penalty for the third offence of burglary or of robbery was also capital.

Among other penalties, branding, mutilation, whipping, the pillory, the stocks, imprisonment, and fining were employed in 1650. For example, the punishment of burglary or robbery for the first offence was branding on the forehead with the letter "B," for the second, another branding and a whipping, for the third, death as an incorrigible;[54] for drinking more than one half-pint of wine at one time or for tippling for more than half an hour or after nine o'clock at night, a fine of five shillings — with whippings and the stocks for excessive drinking. For the use of tobacco by those under twenty years of age or not already addicted, and for using it publicly, the punishment was a fine of sixpence; for keeping bachelor house alone, a fine of twenty shillings for every week; for staying away from church services, five shillings; and for the first offence of behaving contemptuously toward the Word of God or messengers thereof, open reproval by the magistrate, for the second offence, either a fine of £5 or the humiliation of standing two hours upon a four-foot block on lecture day, bearing a placard reading: "An open and obstinate Contemner of God's Holy Ordinances."

In the code of 1750, under the heading of "Capital and other Felonies," seven offences are enumerated. Among the old fifteen capital laws of 1650 blasphemy in the name of God the Father, Son, and Holy Ghost, bestiality, sodomy, and false testifying still find a place.[55] On the other hand, the old laws against worshipping a strange god, witchcraft, wilful murder,[56] slaying another through guile, adultery, rape, kidnapping, rebellion against the colony, the cursing of parents by a child, and stubbornness on the part of a

---

[54] For the code of 1650, see *Connecticut Colonial Records*, I, 77–8 and 509–63. See also the author's study entitled "The Criminal Codes of Connecticut," *Journal of the American Institute of Criminal Law and Criminology*, VI, 177–89.

[55] *Acts and Laws* (1750), pp. 68–9.

[56] Still punishable by death.

child have either disappeared from the category of capital crimes in favour of other laws or, if still capital, are not classified with the capital felonies. Further, among capital laws not found in the code of 1650 but given a place of first importance in the later code is that relating to conspiracy against the colony, which takes the place of the old law against worshipping a strange god.[57] Then there was the law against the crime of arson and that against mayhem when the victim thereby is deprived of his tongue, an eye, or a private organ.[58] Other crimes in the code of 1750 not found in the earlier code which were punished capitally were counterfeiting the King's seal, levying war against him, and compassing his death. Counterfeiting of money, another crime not mentioned in 1650, was not capital, but was very severely punished by the later eighteenth-century code: the offender was not only branded, but also lost his right ear, was debarred from all trade, was deprived of his estate, and was committed to the workhouse for life. The crime of adultery, a capital offence in 1650, in the later code was punished by means of whipping, branding, and the wearing of a halter about the neck outside the garments of the guilty party.

While the above changes would seem to indicate some slackening in the severity of the capital laws, the keeping of the Sabbath as a holy day was as vigorously enjoined in the middle of the eighteenth century as earlier. The law declared that on the Sabbath all persons were to apply themselves to private and public duties of religion. For working or playing on the Lord's Day or day of public fasting or thanksgiving there was a penalty of ten shillings; for convening in companies on the evenings preceding or following the Lord's Day a penalty of three shillings or not over two hours in the stocks; for drinking in taverns on these evenings, five shillings; for standing outside a meeting house and talking during worship, three shillings; for going on the Lord's Day from house to house, other than to church or on some work of necessity or mercy, five shill-

---

[57] This, of course, is closely related to the old law punishing rebellion against the colony and to the law of 1750 punishing the levying of war against the King.

[58] In the earlier part of the century a man convicted of mayhem was punished according to the principles of the *lex talionis*, and the court passed sentence of *"membrum pro membro"* — in this case, castration. See *Connecticut Colonial Records*, VIII, 578–9. See also the article by Simeon Baldwin in the *Yale Law Journal*, VIII, 381 *et seq.*

ings; for travelling on that day, twenty shillings; and for rude or profane behaviour on the Sabbath, forty shillings.[59]

All officers were to restrain people from unnecessarily walking in streets or fields, swimming, keeping open their shops or following their secular occupations or recreations the evening preceding the Lord's Day or that following. Those convicted of profaning the Holy Day itself and refusing to pay their fines were to be publicly whipped not over twenty stripes.[60]

The deep solicitude of the lawmakers for the moral and spiritual welfare of the Connecticut people is further evidenced by the law requiring all parents and masters to teach the children under their care to read the English tongue well and to know by heart the laws against capital offenders. If this were not possible, the boy or girl was to be taught some short orthodox catechism without the Book.[61] Selectmen were especially enjoined to enquire to what extent the householders were furnished with Bibles and also with catechisms and other good books, according to the number of persons capable of using them; while constables, grand jurymen, and tithingmen, in the suppression of vice and in promotion of Christian knowledge, were charged with making diligent search after all breaches of the laws that related to their office; and the two first-named groups were, moreover, expected to walk the streets on evenings before and after the Lord's Day and duly to search places harbouring people contrary to law.

The underlying feature in this form of community organization was that of interdependence and collective responsibility for individual welfare. The demand above all things was that men should be their brothers' keepers; if possible, keeping one another from falling by the removal of temptations and opportunity for sin and crime through constant scrutiny of the actions of one another and through the severe punishment of breaches of the code. This will explain why for over one hundred years there remained in the Connecticut code the law forbidding an unmarried man to keep bachelor house without consent of the town authorities[62] and why

---

[59] *Acts and Laws* (1750), pp. 139–40.
[60] *Ibid.*, p. 142.
[61] *Ibid.*, pp. 20–1.
[62] *Connecticut Colonial Records*, I, 538–9.

in the eighteenth century no tavern-keeper was allowed to demoralize his customers through the possession of dice, cards, tables, bowls, shuffle-boards, billiards, quoits, or other games of amusement.[63]

These concerns and regulations undoubtedly had the effect of producing men of great soberness and a certain rugged severity of character who were scarcely tolerant of the weaknesses of others. Speaking of the Connecticut "body of laws lately revised and published anno 1750," William Douglass called its provisions "the most natural, equitable, plain and concise laws for plantations, hitherto extant."[64] It will at least bear comparison with any eighteenth-century code. One may, even today, approve the enlightened language of the enacting clause:

> "Be it Enacted and Declared . . . ; That no Man's Life shall be taken away; no Man's Honour or Good Name shall be Stained; no Man's Person shall be Arrested, Restrained, Banished, Dismembered, nor any ways Punished; No Man shall be deprived of his Wife or Children, no Man's Goods or Estate shall be taken away from him, nor any ways Indamaged under the colour of Law, or countenance of Authority; Unless it be by Virtue or Equity of some express Law of this Colony Warranting the same, Established by the General Court, and sufficiently Published: or in case of Defect of such Law in any particular Case, by some clear and plain Rule Warranted by the Word of God."

From the foregoing comparison of the codes of 1650 and 1750 the impression is gained that Connecticut at the latter date was in the midst of a great transition, although still powerfully bound by older modes of thought. Attempting to hold fast to its seventeenth-century Puritan heritage, the colony was slowly, probably inevitably, repudiating much of the more rigid part of it. The bitter controversies between the Old Lights and New Lights — an aftermath of the Great Awakening — undoubtedly had important effects in this direction, as did the progress of the Anglicans in western Connecticut and the growing importance of the Baptists in eastern Connecticut. Moreover, the ecclesiastical system and the

---

[63] *Acts and Laws* (1750), p. 81.
[64] *Op. cit.*, II, 158, 193–203.

peculiar ecclesiastical outlook on life which had for a century characterized Connecticut Puritanism were unquestionably most adversely affected by the participation of many thousand men of the
colony in the wars of the eighteenth century. For they were brought
into intimate touch with views that were quite out of harmony
with those presented from the pulpits of their local churches.[65]

Indeed, it is not without significance that during the French and
Indian war there appeared in 1755 the first local newspaper, the
Connecticut Gazette, with its emphasis upon secular interests, to be
followed by the *Connecticut Journal,* the *Connecticut Courant,* published at Hartford, and the *New London Gazette.*

The influence of the press and the many other forces in under-
mining certain aspects of Puritanism is clearly indicated if one
looks ahead to the Connecticut code of 1784. The old capital laws
against blasphemy, false testimony, bestiality, and sodomy which
survived in the code of 1750 disappeared from that of 1784. These
offences against individual decency and integrity were otherwise
dealt with. The keeping of bachelor house, the entertaining of a
young man, and the settlement of strangers within the town without leave were no longer proscribed; nor were the drinking of
more than one half-pint of wine at one time, the imbibing of liquors
after nine o'clock in the evening, and the use of tobacco. Further,
one was no longer liable to a fine, as in 1750, for attending a separate
church without licence nor in danger of the loss of civic rights for
maintaining deistic or Unitarian ideas.[66] By the beginning of the
new century, so far had the Congregational Church lost ground
that it was estimated by one scholar that not more than one third of
the total population of Connecticut was in any way identified with
it,[67] whereas a century earlier an overwhelming majority of the
people of this colony were on its church rolls. Nevertheless, the
Congregational Establishment continued in force until the adoption of the Constitution of 1818.

---

[65] See R. J. Purcell's illuminating study, *Connecticut in Transition, 1775–1818*
(Washington & London, 1918), pp. 5–14.

[66] See *Acts and Laws* (1784), pp. 206–10.

[67] R. J. Purcell: *Connecticut in Transition,* p. 45. Purcell does not make his meaning quite clear. There were, as has previously been emphasized, the actual members
of the church fellowship, as well as those who were merely identified as members of
the congregation or society. By 1784 active church members of the Establishment
probably constituted less than one tenth of the total population of the state.

Connecticut succeeded in preserving its Congregational Establishment throughout the colonial period largely because it was able to retain its prized charter. Behind this bulwark the colony was able to lead an existence little disturbed by outside interference. It sought its own counsel and followed an established policy of reticence in its relations with the mother country. Only in the face of attack or other pressing causes did it become really articulate, and then, after the occasion had passed, it sank back into silence. It had small sympathy with the type of government which prevailed in England in the eighteenth century, and its best efforts were always given to warding off any encroachments by Crown or Parliament. To this end it employed with extraordinary effectiveness its so-called London agency. In fact, no colony used this instrumentality of government with greater results.

Perhaps no better way of illustrating the effective functioning of the London agency in protecting the essential interests of Connecticut can be found than in surveying briefly the relations of this colony with the mother country during the first half of the eighteenth century.

The permanent London agency of Connecticut came into existence at the time of the English Revolution.[68] When the results of the proceedings of the Convention Parliament became known in the colony, Colonel Robert Treat, the Governor, and the assistants, under the newly restored charter government, "saw the necessity of doing something to preserve or [our] standing," and proceeded to draw up an address to the King, which was sent, together with £50 borrowed for the occasion, to James Porter, a London merchant, who was besought to present the address and otherwise to act as the Connecticut agent.[69] Porter, however, was unwilling to assume the responsibility, so in 1693 Major-General Fitz-John Winthrop was sent over. The latter exerted himself to secure a confirmation of the charter. He opposed vigorously not only the commission of Governor Fletcher of New York which gave him command of the Connecticut militia, but also Randolph's scheme for

---

[68] See Volume I, Revised, Chap. 1, of this series for a general account of the London agency, pp. 10–13.

[69] "Foreign Correspondence," Connecticut Archives 1: 39a; 2: 19–21, 22, 23. The colony seemed to have been ignorant of the fact that Mary was queen regnant.

appointing Crown attorney generals in all the colonies. He sought, in addition, to secure for the colony the Narragansett country so long in dispute between it, Rhode Island, and Massachusetts Bay.[70] Upon his return to America his place was taken by the Massachusetts agent, Sir Henry Ashurst, a member of Parliament, a Whig, and a leading dissenter, who, with all of his self-importance, proved to be one of the most efficient representatives ever accredited by a colony to the government of the mother country. Ashurst did much to block the very serious attempts made at this period to place royal governors over all the colonies; he also exerted himself in behalf of Connecticut in connection with the Mohegan Indian land controversy which Captain John Mason, supporting the Indians, had referred to the King for settlement.[71] In 1710 he was assisted in his post by the Governor of the colony, Gurdon Saltonstall, who had been sent over by the General Assembly to care for Connecticut interests concerning the military problems arising out of the attempted invasion of Canada in 1709.[72] Upon Ashurst's death the following year, the learned but unfortunately rather dissolute Jeremiah Dummer, an expatriated New England man, took up the agency and held it for almost twenty years. Despite his masterly *Defense of the New England Charters* written in 1715 and published in 1721, Dummer gradually grew in disfavour with the colonial authorities, especially after surrendering to Bolingbroke's influence and by reason of his failure to guard Connecticut interests in the Winthrop appeal, so that in 1730, when obliged to go into the country for his health, he was rather summarily dismissed from his post.[73]

---

[70] Connecticut Archives 2: 64; *Connecticut Colonial Records,* IV, 102, 234, 238; "Winthrop Papers," Massachusetts Historical Society *Collections,* 5th ser., VIII, 327–43; *Letters from the English Kings and Queens to the Governors of . . . Connecticut together with the Answers . . . 1635–1749* (ed. R. R. Hinman, Hartford, 1836), pp. 195–203.

[71] *Letters from the English Kings and Queens . . . ,* pp. 279–80.

[72] *Connecticut Colonial Records,* V, 122, 140. The cause of the Saltonstall visit related to the unfortunate situation that arose in 1709 when the Queen ordered an expedition against Canada. The Connecticut and New York troops were assembled at Wood Creek, where many died of sickness, and toward winter they buried their stores and returned home.

[73] *Connecticut Colonial Records,* V, 188, 190, 300, 303, 305, 362; VI, 133, 226, 318; VII, 307; *Sewall's Letter Book,* Massachusetts Historical Society *Collections,* 6th ser., (2 vols., Boston, 1886), I, 305 n.

The famous Winthrop appeal to the King in Council against the Connecticut intestacy law, opposed as it was to the English principle of primogeniture brought a decision unfavourable to the colony in 1728.[74] When the news reached the colony that the case had gone against it, steps were taken to send over as agent Jonathan Belcher of Boston, the most successful and influential advocate in New England, with instructions to use every exertion to secure a reversal of the decision, involving as this did the validity of innumerable land titles.[75] Hardly had he settled down to work when the intelligence was received in London of the death of Governor Burnet of Massachusetts Bay. Belcher thereupon succeeded in securing an appointment to the governorship not only of this province but also of New Hampshire.[76] Before his return to America, however, he had been authorized to transfer the work of the agency into the hands of Francis Wilks, another New England man by birth, who had become an influential London merchant and was a member of the East India Company.[77] Wilks was already the Massachusetts Bay agent and possessed such "a great and growing interest at court" that he was retained until his death in 1742. Although he failed to secure the repeal of the decision in the Winthrop case involving the intestacy law, "in subsequent cases this colony had no regard to the declaration."[78] Wilks was followed in the agency by Eliakim Palmer, Esq., of London.[79] While Palmer was agent, the General Assembly voted in 1745 "that for the purpose

[74] *Acts of the Privy Council, Col. Ser., 1720–1745*, pp. 112, 208; C. M. Andrews: "The Connecticut Intestacy Law," *Select Essays in Anglo-American Legal History* . . . (3 vols., Boston, 1907), I, No. XIII. John Winthrop, who made the appeal, was the only son and heir of Major-General Wait Winthrop of Boston; he was also the nephew and heir of Fitz-John Winthrop, who had been Governor of Connecticut; in addition, he was the heir of his grandfather John Winthrop, Jr. He appealed from two decisions of the Superior Court in favour of Thomas and Anne Lechmere, involving the estates left him by his ancestors. For by these decisions the administrator, Thomas Lechmere, was empowered to dispose of them.

[75] Jonathan Law had first been approved, but refused to go to England. *Connecticut Colonial Records*, VII, 185, 218–19. The *Talcott Papers*, Connecticut Historical Society *Collections*, IV and V (ed. Mary K. Talcott, 2 vols., Hartford, 1892–6), are especially valuable for the light they throw upon the affairs of the Connecticut agency of this period.

[76] *Connecticut Colonial Records*, VII, 282.

[77] *Ibid.*, VII, 308; *Talcott Papers*, I, 199, 253.

[78] William Douglass: *op. cit.*, II, 174.

[79] *Connecticut Colonial Records*, VIII, 361, 440, 506, 517, 578.

of getting reimbursement in the Cape Breton Expedition," either Thomas Fitch of Norwalk or Colonel John Bulkley, both of them members of the Governor's Council, should go over to support his efforts.[80] Neither of these men was in position to go. Nor was their presence needed in England in view of the effective work of the regular agent. Palmer died in 1749, and the General Assembly selected for his post the distinguished publicist and Unitarian Dr. Benjamin Avery, who was then Chairman of the Committee of English Dissenters.[81] But Avery could not see his way clear to undertaking this work, and upon his refusal the colony turned, surprisingly enough in light of its historic attitude toward the Society of Friends, to the London Quaker Richard Partridge, the veteran agent for Rhode Island and New Jersey.[82]

To ward off the serious attempt — made at this time in connection with the New England currency bill — to compel Connecticut, Rhode Island, and Maryland to follow the practice of the other colonies and submit all laws to the Crown for approval or rejection, Partridge was reenforced in 1750 by a Connecticut man of the highest intellectual attainments, Colonel Elisha Williams.[83] Despite the regulation of the New England currency, the threat to freedom of legislation of the three colonies subsided.

Again, in 1756 and also in 1758, Jonathan Trumbull — later to become Connecticut's Revolutionary War Governor — was asked by the General Assembly to go to England in behalf of the colony

---

[80] *Ibid.*, IX, 185, 217, 264, 418.

[81] *Wolcott Papers*, XVI, pp. 40 *et seq.*, for letters to and from Avery. Although refusing to accept the agency, he nevertheless agreed to take care of the money received by the colony as reimbursement for the Cape Breton expedition. *Connecticut Colonial Records*, IX, 471, 472, 511; X, 14, 103.

[82] *Ibid.*, IX, 509, 512; X, 14, 17, 61, 214, 484, 566; *Wolcott Papers*, pp. 516–17, for Partridge's appointment and letter of agency. The *Papers* also contain a large number of letters to and from Partridge.

[83] *Connecticut Colonial Records*, IX, 512–13; *Wolcott Papers*, 50, 376, 421. Elisha Williams had a distinguished career. After the dismissal of the Rev. Timothy Cutler from the rectorship of Yale College for his change to Anglicanism, Williams was elected to this office, which he retained from 1726 to 1739. Although he met with great success, ill health forced him to resign this work. He later acted as deputy for Wethersfield in the General Assembly, was a chaplain with the Cape Breton expedition, and in 1746 was appointed colonel in connection with the expedition launched against Canada. See Francis Parsons: "Elisha Williams, Minister, Soldier, President of Yale," in the New Haven Colonial Historical Society *Papers*, VII, No. 8.

65054

in order to deal with the important financial problems arising out of the military operations in North America in the course of the Great War for the Empire.[84] After his second refusal to undertake the work, the task was turned over to Jared Ingersoll, the most distinguished among the Connecticut lawyers, who gradually gained a great influence with the home government.[85] Ingersoll was followed in 1760 by Richard Jackson. Known as "Omniscient Jackson" because of his extraordinary knowledge, this agent in 1762 became a member of Parliament, highly esteemed by his contemporaries both in Great Britain and in America.[86]

It may be noticed in this survey of the Connecticut London agency that only a serious crisis led to the sending of a representative from America to England to take over the work of this office. The colony appeared to feel that under ordinary circumstances a capable resident of London was able to discharge satisfactorily the often very great responsibilities of the agency. Thus, while Connecticut and other colonies were not technically represented in Parliament, in practice the vital interests of these dependencies were doubtless given almost every protection that might have been expected had these colonies enjoyed representation in the House of Commons, under the given conditions. This situation was made possible through the efficient work of their influential agents, some of them members of Parliament.

The crowning achievement of the Connecticut agency, it goes without saying, was the preservation of the charter and with it the freedom of the colony to act according to its own light — still the light of seventeenth-century Puritanism — with little hindrance from the mother country.[87]

---

[84] *Connecticut Colonial Records*, X, 484; XI, 108.

[85] For an account of Ingersoll's first and second London agency see the writer's *Jared Ingersoll*, pp. 60–78, 126–48.

[86] For an excellent account of the public career of Richard Jackson see Carl Van Doren: *Letters and Papers of Benjamin Franklin and Richard Jackson, 1753–1785* (Philadelphia, 1947), Introduction.

[87] Only two laws affecting Connecticut's fundamental conceptions of social solidarity were disapproved in the eighteenth century: the Act for the Suppression of Heretics, disapproved in 1705, and the Act for the Settlement of Intestate Estates, disapproved in 1728. See C. M. Andrews: *Connecticut and the British Government, with special Reference to the Acts and Laws of the Colony* (reprinted from "Fane's Reports on the Laws of Connecticut," Acorn Club *Publication* (New Haven, 1915), p. 47.

By 1750 the people of the little commonwealth of Connecticut were living a life free from the heavy financial burdens carried by British subjects in the homeland.[88] Under a thrifty, almost parsimonious government, they were able to devote their energies without outside interference to the improvement of their farms, to the rearing of their families, and — not the least important to them by any means — to the pursuit of spiritual values after their own manner of life.

---

[88] For example, the taxes in England in the middle of the eighteenth century amounted in the neighbourhood of a per-capita levy of twenty-one shillings sterling per annum; in Connecticut the annual levy at the same period did not exceed three and three-fourth farthings sterling. See the author's "Connecticut Taxation and Parliamentary Aid Preceding the Revolutionary War," *American Historical Review*, XXXVI, 721–39.

CHAPTER V

In the Region of the Old Patroonships

A LONG the eastern and southern borders of the Province of New York, like the military marks protecting the frontiers of the early medieval German Empire, stretched a series of great grants. For, whereas in the more northern colonies land-holding was, as a rule, on a popular basis — with the towns still in possession of very considerable bodies of land, and with individual estates generally of modest proportions — in New York aristocratic and even monopolistic tendencies had been manifested ever since the days of the Dutch patroons.

Beyond the Hudson River to the east were Philipsborough (Philipsburgh) Manor, Pelham Manor, Scarsdale Manor, Morrisania, Fordham Manor, the Manor of Cortlandt, Philipse's Patent, Rumbout's Patent, Beekman's Patent, the Great Nine Partners' Patent, the Little Nine Partners' Patent, the Manor of Livingston, Rensselaerwyck, and the Manor of Rensselaer.[1] Corresponding to these there lay between the Hudson and the east branch of the Delaware, fac-

---

[1] For a map of the patroonships and manors that came into existence between 1629 and 1704 see that included in Montgomery Schuyler's *Patroons and Lords of Manors of the Hudson* (New York, 1933), p. 108. The Sauthier chorographical map prepared for Governor Tryon and published in 1779 indicates clearly the bounds of most of the manors and patents in existence at this period; see also J. H. French: *Historical and Statistical Gazetteer of New York State* (Syracuse, 1860), pp. 49–52.

ing New Jersey, the patents of Kakiate, Cheesecock (Chesecook), Wawayanda, and Minisink, "enormous Grants of 2 or 300,000 Acres of Land . . . at so small a Quit-Rent as a Beaver Skin, . . ."[2] Furthermore, in the interior of the province, up to the Indian country, much of the land was held by great patentees who in many cases had received 100,000 or even 200,000 acres for a trifling quit-rent of twenty or forty shillings a year. Indeed, some proprietors, such as those controlling the Hardenburgh Patent lying eastward of the Delaware in Ulster County, had claims to great stretches of country containing above "a million of Acres," according to the Surveyor-General.[3]

A number of these vast land tenures came into existence as patroonships, granted by the Dutch West India Company during the period of its control of the New Netherlands to encourage the planting of settlements. At the time the province passed under English control the Dutch patroons were guaranteed the safe possession of their lands. The earlier English governors were fairly cautious in making grants, realizing the evil effects of the Dutch policy. Sir Edmund Andros, who administered the province from 1674 to 1683, was especially careful to see that there was a definite survey before any patent was issued, also that the quit-rent to be paid should be fixed at the time of the grant. Not until after the Revolu-

---

[2] *A Letter from a Gentleman in New York to his Friend in Brunswick* (September 26, 1750, Broadside, New York Historical Society). For a map of the County of Orange, New York, indicating the limits of the above patents see E. M. Ruttenber: *History of the County of Orange* (Newburgh, N.Y., 1875), opposite p. 27; see also *ibid.*, pp. 23–8, for details of these patents. The instructions of Sir Danvers Osborne in 1753 refer to ". . . several exorbitant Grants of Lands . . . within that part of Your Majesty's Province which adjoins to New Jersey. . . ." The Governor was to employ all lawful means to vacate these. For this instruction see *Acts of the Privy Council, Col. Ser., 1745–1766*, p. 210.

[3] Cadwallader Colden to Governor William Shirley, July 25, 1749, *Letters and Papers of Cadwallader Colden, 1748–1754* (New York, 1921), p. 123. It is important for the student to note that the *Colden Papers*, as they will be cited hereafter, are published in nine volumes (1918–1937) in the New York Historical Society *Collections*, but as the *Collections* bear a volume number and the *Colden Papers* bear a different volume number, it is thought best to refer to them by the years covered, as appears on the binding. It is also noteworthy that the *Colden Letter Books* are published in a separately numbered series by the New York Historical Society *Collections* and should not be confused with the *Papers*.

For the Hardenburgh Patent see the Sauthier map. For the workings of the New York land system as actually applied in creating private land titles and the detrimental results of this process to the growth of settlements on the New York frontier see Edith M. Fox: *Land Speculation in the Mohawk Country* (Ithaca, N.Y., 1949).

tion of 1689 was there a marked return to the earlier practice of extravagant allotments. But of Governor Benjamin Fletcher it was said that "the most extraordinary favours of former Gov^{rs} were but petty grants in comparison of his"; for Fletcher gave away parcels containing upwards of 100,000 acres and, to particular favourites, four or five times that quantity,[4] some of which, however, under his successor, the Earl of Bellomont, were vacated by act of Assembly in the year 1699.[5] Unfortunately, the Assembly on this occasion was actuated by party spirit, with the result that several of the most exorbitant of these patents were, so it was charged, ignored, while others that did not fall within this category were recalled. Under Lieutenant-Governor John Nanfan so-called "ambulatory" grants were made by which the patentees had liberty to claim lands now in one part of the province and again in another part. Following Nanfan came Lord Cornbury, whose gifts of large tracts at trifling quit-rents seem to have equalled those of all of his successors put together.[6] Further, in 1702, during his governorship, the Assembly, carried away by the spirit of monopolization, sought to repeal the act of the year 1699. This effort failed only by reason of the disapproval of the Queen in Council.[7]

In 1732 a report was made on the state of the lands by the Surveyor General, Cadwallader Colden. In referring to the large grants of from 50,000 to over 1,000,000 acres lying about the prov-

---

[4] See Cadwallader Colden's "Report on the Lands in the Province of New York" of the year 1732 with addenda of the year 1752. This is printed in E. B. O'Callaghan: *The Documentary History of the State of New York* (4 vols., Albany, 1850–1), I, 249–55.

[5] *The Colonial Laws of New York from . . . 1664 to the Revolution* (5 vols., Albany, 1894–6), I, 412–17; *Acts of the Privy Council, Col. Ser., Unbound Papers,* pp. 59–61.

[6] Among the larger grants made after the Andros administration, Rumbout's Patent came into existence in 1685, the Livingston Manor in 1686, Pelham Manor in 1687 (based upon the patent of 1666), Philipsborough Manor in 1693, Kakiate Patent in 1696, Cortlandt Manor, Morrisania, and the Great Nine Partners' Patent in 1697, Scarsdale Manor in 1701, the Wawayanda and Beekman patents in 1703, the Little Nine Partners' Patent in 1706, Cheesecock's Patent in 1707, and the Hardenburgh Patent in 1708. A list of manors is to be found in Montgomery Schuyler's *Patroons and Lords of Manors of the Hudson;* see also for additional information the *Historical and Statistical Gazetteer of New York State* (1860), p. 258 *et seq.* For Fletcher's grants see the representation of the Board of Trade of July 29, 1707, *Acts of Privy Council, Col. Ser., Unbound Papers,* p. 60.

[7] *The Colonial Laws of New York,* I, 523–5; *Acts of the Privy Council, Col. Ser., 1745–1766,* p. 850; *ibid., Unbound Papers,* pp. 59–64.

ince, most of them uncultivated, Colden stressed the point that in most cases no specified quantity of land or number of acres was mentioned, but rather they were designated as lying within certain limits bounded by natural features, such as streams carrying Indian names, which gave every opportunity to enlarge and explain the patent according to the inclinations of the grantee. Even in cases where the number of acres was specified the tendency, it appears, was to extend it. ". . . I have heard of one instance at least," he asserted, "where the patent Grants 300 acres, and the patentee now claims upwards of sixty thousand acres within the bounds of his Grant."[8]

By 1750 many of these great concessions lying along the eastern and southern borders of the province, as well as unappropriated lands in these regions, were threatened by the movement of people from New Hampshire, Massachusetts Bay, and New Jersey searching for fresh lands. Already in the fall of 1749 Governor Wentworth of New Hampshire (as we have made clear in an earlier chapter) had notified George Clinton, the Governor of New York, of his intention to make certain grants to the west of the Connecticut River. Shortly afterwards he issued his letters patent for the township of Bennington, twenty-four miles to the east of Albany, which Clinton hastened to inform him had previously been granted by his own government. Nevertheless, Wentworth proceeded to run a line as an extension of the New Hampshire southern boundary which brought the territorial claims of that colony within eight or ten miles of Albany and covered lands that, according to the Surveyor General of New York, by this time paid yearly rents to the Crown.[9]

---

[8] *The Documentary History of New York*, I, 252. Some of the great manors east of the Hudson River paid little in the way of quit-rents. Van Cortlandt Manor of 86,000 acres involved but 40 shillings per annum; the Livingston Manor of 150,000 acres, but 28 shillings; the Philipse Manor of 156,000 acres, but £4.12; and Rensselaerwyck of 1,000,000 acres, but 50 bushels of wheat. See Irving Mark: "Agrarian Conflicts in New York and the American Revolution," *Rural Sociology*, VII, 279, and his *Agrarian Conflicts in Colonial New York, 1711–1775* (Columbia University Studies, New York, 1940); E. W. Spaulding: *New York in the Critical Period, 1783–1789* (New York, 1933), pp. 65–6; and B. W. Bond: *The Quit-Rent System* (New Haven, 1919), pp. 25 and 111.

[9] See Governor Wentworth to Governor Clinton, November 17, 1749, and April 25, 1750; Governor Clinton to Governor Wentworth, June 6, 1750; the "Observations" of Surveyor General Colden, October 14, 1751, *Documentary History of New York*, IV, 331–3, 339–40.

Thus was inaugurated one of the bitterest intercolonial controversies of the eighteenth century. Although this one was finally submitted for adjudication to His Majesty in Council, resulting in a decision favourable to the claims of New York, it was by no means terminated by this settlement, but continued until the close of the War for American Independence. During its later phases the controversy especially involved the conflicting claims of the settlers themselves over titles derived from the two provinces.[10]

To the south of this particular region of conflict were those huge grants referred to previously, among them the Manor of Livingston of 160,000 acres over which Robert Livingston was ruling as a proprietor in 1750.[11] It had been granted in 1686 and confirmed by royal authority in 1715 to an ancestor carrying the same name as the incumbent; the successive heads of the family had up to this period enjoyed peace and quiet in undisturbed possession of the great patent. However, early in the 1750's the people of Westenhook, an adjacent township in Massachusetts Bay, began to settle on lands hitherto considered to be within the bounds of the manor. By 1753 the intruders were threatening most of its eastern part. Even a considerable number of the Livingston tenants long settled under leases now showed a disposition to unite with the newcomers in ignoring the right of the proprietor by applying for grants of this same land from the Massachusetts Bay government — thereby hoping to be able to escape the payment of rentals. The movement certainly boded no good for the landed magnates of New York as a group, and it follows quite naturally that fear was expressed that the "Infection will very Soon be general and then no man that has an Estate in this Province or perhaps in North America, will be Safe or able to Call it his owne."[12]

In view of what were felt to be the encroachments of Massachusetts Bay people, the Council of New York on February 28, 1753, in

---

[10] See "Papers Relating to the Difficulties between New York and New Hampshire," *ibid.*, IV, 329–624.

[11] The manor extended eastward from the Hudson some nineteen miles in an area embracing today about seven townships. For a map of the Manor of Livingston as of the year 1714 see *ibid.*, III, opposite p. 414; for the patent of 1686 and that of 1715 see pp. 373–6 and 414–20.

[12] Robert Livingston to William Alexander, March 26, 1753, William Alexander Papers 1:25, New York Historical Society; see also Carl Becker: "Nominations in Colonial New York," *American Historical Review*, VI, 261.

a formal report under the official seal, set forth claims "to the Jurisdiction and soil of the Lands westward of Connecticut river and northward of the Colony of Connecticut as part of this his Majesty's province of New York." The report also called upon the General Court of Massachusetts Bay to inform the New York government "By what Warrant they claim or exercise any right . . . west of the Connecticut River."[13] Without answering this query, the General Court of the Bay colony proposed on April 12 that commissioners of the two provinces should be appointed to settle the common boundary. This was refused by the government of New York. Whereupon on June 12 the Massachusetts Bay General Court decided to proceed in support of its claims to lands west of the Connecticut, and on July 19 officers of their government entered Livingston Manor with the support of disaffected tenants, arrested two New York men under warrant of the Bay province, and carried them off to confinement.[14] This led to the issuing of a proclamation by Governor Clinton on the 28th of that month calling upon the sheriffs of Albany and Dutchess counties to apprehend all persons who should enter upon and take possession of any lands already granted under the seal of the province.[15] The Massachusetts General Court on September 11 reported that the lands in dispute were within the boundary of the County of Hampshire and that the town of Springfield, on the east bank of the Connecticut, had been settled almost 120 years before.[16]

In this contest between the two provinces incident followed incident. Early in 1755 the high sheriff of Albany County, Abraham Yates, attempted to hold in custody a Massachusetts Bay man who had settled in Claverack well within the manor. The settler was rescued by his fellow townsmen, and Yates, in spite of his high office, was placed under arrest and conducted to Sheffield in Massachusetts Bay.[17] Before receiving his liberty he was obliged to give bail for his appearance there at the next sitting of the court of the

---

[13] *Documentary History of New York,* III, 454.

[14] *Ibid.,* III, 455.

[15] For a copy of the proclamation see the "Broadsides" of the New York Historical Society.

[16] For the report of the Massachusetts Bay General Court of September 11, 1753, see *Documentary History of New York,* III, 451–2.

[17] The township of Sheffield was incorporated in 1733; its north parish in 1761 was in turn incorporated as Great Barrington.

quarter session. As a consequence, James de Lancey, now Lieutenant Governor of New York, issued a second proclamation calling for the apprehension of those parties who thus defied the authority of the province.[18] This event was followed by the killing of William Rees, a Massachusetts Bay man, settled on disputed lands, who had resisted arrest. Governor Phips countered with a proclamation ordering the arrest of those who had killed Rees.[19] Ultimately the reprisals went as far as the capture of Livingston's ironworkers and the confining of the sheriff of Albany with others in the Springfield gaol, whence they were at length released only as the result of the intervention of Governor Shirley. The latter, again at the head of the government of Massachusetts Bay, was now primarily interested in securing the harmony of the colonies in the face of the great struggle opening up in North America between the English and the French.[20]

The implications of the struggle between New York and Massachusetts Bay went beyond the issues of a boundary dispute. That it was also a struggle between two different systems of landholding is borne out by the subsequent great land riots that broke out in the 1760's to the southward of Livingston Manor in Dutchess County during which it was necessary to employ British regulars to restore peace and good order.[21]

Along the southern boundary, between the Hudson and the east branch of the Delaware, much the same situation existed. Many of the great patents in Orange County, each of which embraced several hundred thousand acres, overlapped grants made by the Proprietors of East and West New Jersey in what are now Sussex and Passaic counties. Even the home government regarded these vast New York holdings as exorbitant. In preparing the instructions

---

18 Broadside bearing date of April 2, 1755, New York Historical Society.

19 *Documentary History of New York*, III, 471–6.

20 For Shirley's intercession in the Livingston Manor riots in 1755, see his letter to one Benjamin Franklin, involved in the riots, dated Albany, November 16, Redmond Papers, New York Historical Society.

21 See *Correspondence of General Thomas Gage* . . . *1763–1775* (ed. C. E. Carter, *Yale Historical Publications*, XI, 2 vols., New Haven, 1931–4), I, 95, 99, 107–8; *Documents Relative to the Colonial History of the State of New York, procured in Holland, England and France* (ed. E. B. O'Callaghan and B. Fernow, 15 vols., Albany, 1853–87), VII, 879; this will be cited hereafter as *New York Colonial Documents*. For a general study of agrarian problems see Irving Mark: *Agrarian Conflicts in Colonial New York, 1711–1755*, previously cited.

for Sir Danvers Osborne in 1753 the Board of Trade represented that, since the grants had been made without any proper condition attached regarding cultivation and upon trifling and inconsiderable quit-rents — "by which your Majesty's Revenue has been injured and the settling and improving the Province greatly obstructed" — he be directed to inquire into the state of all New York patents and to take every lawful means to vacate those which were defeating the desirable ends of government.[22]

As may be imagined, the great landholders and merchants occupied a position of decisive influence in the political and social life of the Province of New York and were adept in guarding their own interests. Lords of manors were also aided by a certain degree of control they undoubtedly exercised over their tenants. Their powerful position was supported by a system of plural voting which permitted freeholders with estates in several counties to participate in elections in each; it was also upheld by personal support from other men of wealth as well as from lesser freeholders. No man who did not have ample financial means, or could not depend upon others who had, could afford the expense of an election, which invariably included the liberal supply of food and drink at election time and even the payment of money to voters.[23]

The leading aristocratic families of this period, many of whom were intermarried, were the Schuylers, the de Lanceys, the Livingstons, the Philipses, the van Cortlandts, the Bayards, the Heathcotes, the Crugers, the Wattses, the Waltons, the van Rensselaers,

---

[22] C. O. 5:1128, pp. 60–76.

[23] *New York Colonial Documents*, IV, 127–9; VI, 56; C. F. Bishop: *History of Elections in the American Colonies* (New York, 1893), p. 69; A. E. McKinley: *The Suffrage Franchise in the Thirteen English Colonies in America* (Philadelphia, 1905), pp. 215–16. A recent important article by Professor M. M. Klein: "Democracy and Politics in Colonial New York," *New York History*, XL, 221–46, indicates that the tenants of the great manors exercised more freedom in voting than previous writers concerned with the political history of the Province of New York had indicated. The least that tenants expected of the lord of a manor at election time was entertainment on a liberal scale if they were to vote for him or for the man he preferred. Dr. Nicholas Varga of Loyola College kindly permitted the writer to read his unpublished paper "Election Proceedings and Practices in Colonial New York." In this study Professor Varga agrees with Professor Klein as to the independent attitude of the voters, but he also stresses the point that, while the franchise was broad, only a rich man or one who had wealthy supporters could easily bear the cost of an election to the Assembly. He also emphasizes that after 1720 appointments to county offices by the Governor were "cleared" with "some favored Assemblyman."

the Beekmans, the Bluchers, the Barclays, the Joneses, the Jays, the Verplancks, the Harrisons, the Morrises, the Alexanders, and the Smiths — nor must one omit the name of Colonel William Johnson, who exercised a great influence in Albany County. Some of them were deeply involved in commercial activities, but most enjoyed important landholdings, and many controlled immense tracts of land.

Here we have an *élite* who dominated the political life of the province as well as its social and economic aspects. They were in control not only of all the chief administrative offices but also of the Council and the Assembly. In the middle of the eighteenth century this *élite* was divided into two factions, one controlled by Chief Justice James de Lancey,[24] and the other by the young lawyer William Livingston,[25] whose grandfather, Robert Livingston, was the first lord of Livingston Manor. This factional division was apparent in both branches of government. During the period under discussion the Assembly was almost solidly under the control of the de Lancey faction — a faction welded together by a network of intermarriages, personal ties, and business as well as political interests — which took care that only those who favoured its views were put forward as Assemblymen. As William Smith in his *The History of the Late Province of New York* describes the political situation existing in 1753, there is little room to doubt that the membership in the Assembly was hand picked with great deliberation.[26] Today the

24 For the career of de Lancey see *Documentary History of New York*, IV, 627–39.

25 For Livingston see T. Sedgwick, Jr.: *A Memoir of the Life of William Livingston* (New York, 1833); see also M. M. Klein: "The Rise of the New York Bar: The Legal Career of William Livingston," *William and Mary Quarterly*, 3rd ser., XV, 334–58, and Dorothy R. Dillon: *The New York Triumvirate: A Study of the Legal and Political Careers of William Livingston* . . . (Columbia University *Studies*, No. 548, New York, 1949), and L. H. Leder: "Robert Livingston: A New View of New York Politics," *New York History*, XL, 358–67. Dr. Leder's biography of Livingston is due for early publication by the University of North Carolina Press.

26 William Smith: *The History of the Late Province of New York . . . to the Appointment of Governor Colden in 1762*, New York Historical Society *Collections*, V (2 vols., New York, 1829), I, 306–7, II, 142–3. Cadwallader Colden, writing on July 7, 1770, apparently to Lord Hillsborough, has the following to say about the political grouping of provincial New Yorkers: "From the different political and religious Principles of the Inhabitants, opposite Parties have at all Times, and will exist in this Province, which at different times have taken their denominations from some distinguished Person or Family who have appeared at their Head . . ." (*Colden Letter Books*, Vol. II, *1765–1775*, New York Historical Society *Collections*, 1877, X, 223–4). For the importance of William Smith as an historian see the article by R. A. Wines in *New York History*, XL, 3–17.

procedure in which issues were defined and strategy mapped would be called a caucus. Professor R. B. Morris called this a government by "Junto."[27] But only the *élite,* we may be sure, participated in these preliminary political-strategy gatherings. As a result, the landed and commercial aristocracy, even when divided into warring factions, was able to exercise political control. They were undoubtedly aided by the indifference and lack of political experience of the "lower classes," by infrequent and irregular elections to the Assembly, and doubtless by the fact that a comparatively small number of people voted in the country districts.[28]

It is difficult to arrive at any figure on the number of people who exercised the right of franchise in the rural areas. Both freeholders and people holding leases for life enjoyed this right.[29] In New York City the number who could qualify as freeholders or freemen and thus vote was rather impressive. Nevertheless, leadership among these voters seems to have come from the *élite* during the period under consideration. Voting, moreover, was *viva voce* in both county and city.[30] Although five elections were held between 1743 and 1753 as the result of Governor Clinton's repeated dissolutions

---

[27] R. B. Morris: *Studies in the History of American Law* (New York, 1930), pp. 64–5.

[28] Carl Becker: "Nominations in Colonial New York," *op. cit.,* VI, 261–3; see also his *History of Political Parties in the Province of New York, 1760–1776* (Madison, Wis., 1909), in which he states (p. 15): "Candidates were in the phrase of the time 'set up' by private personal agreement among those leaders whose 'interests' were likely to carry the election." For the dominance of the great landlords in the government of New York see also Irving Mark: *op. cit.,* Chap. 3, "Political Power and Landlord Dominance." Professor Varga of Loyola College in his unpublished study, previously cited, takes the position that before candidates for the Assembly were finally agreed upon, there took place "a rather broad canvass among civil and military officers of the county, the local clergy, as well as among the more 'civil-minded' freeholders." Yet he would doubtless agree that in so far as members of these groups were identified with an opposing political faction they would not be consulted.

[29] See again M. M. Klein: "Democracy and Politics in Colonial New York," *New York History,* XL, 235–6.

[30] As Professor Klein makes clear (*ibid.,* pp. 232–7), skilled labourers and mechanics in New York City did not find it difficult to pay the two shillings to secure registration as freemen. In 1735, he discloses, out of 1,465 adult white males 812 were voters and in 1761 of 2,581 adult white males 1,447 were voters. For the position of freemen in New York under the Dongan charter of 1686 and the Montgomerie charter of 1731 see Beverly McAnear: "The Place of the Freeman in Old New York," *New York History,* XXI, 418–30. McAnear indicates that many elected to local offices were artisans such as shoemakers, carpenters, blacksmiths, and painters. That the law limiting local offices to freeholders or freemen was frequently violated is also brought out by McAnear.

of the Assembly, the circumstances of these elections rather intensified the warring of factions headed by powerful men to control the twenty-seven seats in the legislature, the holders of which received *per-diem* pay.[31]

It was unfortunate for New York that comparatively few families tended to monopolize the finest lands of the province up to the Indian country; for, as a rule, they were indisposed to sell any portion of their holdings — except at a price that was considered out of all reason by the prospective freeholder — preferring to exploit them by developing tenancies. Moreover, the adoption of legal principles of primogeniture and entail by New York in 1683 consolidated these holdings.[32] Further, they were held without difficulty in view of the fact that unimproved lands were not subject to taxation in 1750.[33] As a consequence of these practices, the province was not nearly so well cultivated or so populous as other colonies in the hands of the British in 1750, although it had been among the first to be settled by Europeans and although it enjoyed many natural advantages over neighbouring plantations both in its favourable situation for trade and commerce and in the quality of its soil.[34] Indeed, so unfavourable were conditions in the early part of the eighteenth century, especially for the sons of poor people who desired to acquire land and to engage in agriculture as independent small farmers rather than as tenants on the great estates,

[31] For the representation in the New York Assembly and the *per-diem* pay of each member see William Smith: *op. cit.*, I, 306–7. It may be noted that a number of the Assemblymen were farmers. While their patrons might own most of the county, unless they lived within it they themselves could not be candidates. Most of them in fact had their homes in New York City. Irving Mark (in his article in *Rural Sociology*, VII, 282–3) stated that 110 out of 137 persons holding leading posts in the government of provincial New York between 1750 and 1776 were large landholders with at least 1,000 acres, or their relatives. In this connection he writes: "Against the landlords' political dominance small farmers had neither the power to shape laws nor the wealth to sustain the expense of judicial redress." For an expanded treatment of this subject see the same author's *Agrarian Conflicts in Colonial New York, 1711–1755*, pp. 88–94.

[32] See the *Colonial Laws of New York*, I, 114.

[33] For Robert R. Livingston's defence of the practice of not taxing unimproved lands, apparently written in 1752, see Beverly McAnear: "Robert R. Livingston's Reasons against a Land Tax," *Journal of Political Economy*, XLVIII, 63–90.

[34] See William Livingston's "A Brief Consideration of New York With Respect to its Natural Advantages, Its Superiority in Several Instances over the Neighboring Colonies" (1753). This appeared in the *Independent Reflector* of that year, was reprinted in *Heartman's Historical Series*, No. 39, and, more recently, in 1925 (ed. E. G. Swem, Metuchen, N.J.).

that many left the province to establish themselves in near-by colonies, among them a great many Palatine Germans.[35] These, ejected from the lands they had squatted upon in the valleys of the Mohawk and the Schoharie, trekked into Pennsylvania and, incidentally, warned all their fellow Germans seeking homes in the New World to avoid New York.

Doubtless many well-informed colonials who were not residents of the province shared the attitude of Secretary Richard Peters of Pennsylvania toward its land policy. "What misfortune has it been to the province of New York," he declared, "that the Land has been monopolized, and 'till lately not the least encouragement ever given, for the poor industrious to settle there." He then suggested a solution that would hardly have met with any favour on the part of New York Assembly, constituted as it was: "I'm vastly surprised that this monstrous Monopoly has never been taken Notice of when the remedy appears so plain & effectual, nothing more than a Tax upon each 100 Acres of unimproved land wch would render it impracticable for any single man to hold a very large Tract, & wou'd very soon divide these vast bodies into more useful Parts."[36] But this was just the sort of thing landed magnates strongly opposed.

From 1737 to 1746 only 1,152 people were added to the population of the province, which in the latter year reached a total of 61,589 inhabitants — an increase of not more than two per cent. During the same period Pennsylvania was growing at a rate that brought about the doubling of her population in a period of twenty years.[37] In spite of the fact that there was a great increase in the

---

[35] In 1710, 3,000 of these Palatines were sent to New York for the purpose of producing naval stores. Parliament for this purpose made a grant of £ 10,000. After two years of effort Governor Hunter was obliged to give up the enterprise when he had exhausted his own credit. For the Palatines in New York see W. A. Knittle: *Early Eighteenth Century Palatine Emigration* (Philadelphia, 1937); also for many documents relating to them see *New York Colonial Documents,* V, 117 *et seq.*

[36] This comment — made, it appears, about 1755 — was appended to "A Brief Account of Pennsylvania," prepared by Lewis Evans in 1753, a copy of which, with the Peters notations, is in the library of the Historical Society of Pennsylvania. See L. H. Gipson: *Lewis Evans* . . . (Philadelphia, 1939), p. 99, n.

[37] It is true that the period between 1746 and 1776 saw a very rapid increase in the number of inhabitants of New York. This mounted from 61,589 in 1746 to 96,765 in 1756, and by 1771 reached 168,007, which indicates that it doubled itself within twenty years. It also perhaps implies the existence of a somewhat more favourable land policy than during the earlier period. For population statistics see Greene and Harrington: *American Population before* . . . *1790,* (New York, 1932), pp. 90–1, and *Documentary History of New York,* I, 472–3.

settlement of lands, especially after 1750, Governor Tryon reported in 1774 that only one fifth of the acreage of the province was undergoing improvement.[38]

From the foregoing an impression might be gained that the great landowners were attempting personally to exploit much of their vast estates. This, of course, would give an inaccurate picture. While it is true that on Morrisania Manor there were in 1755 some twenty-nine slaves and on Philipsborough Manor some thirty-one, who were doubtless usefully employed,[39] yet the prevailing form of agricultural economy favoured fairly small farm units. As has already been suggested, a system of tenantry had become well established by the middle of the century on most of the large grants, especially those immediately about the Hudson River, to the eastward of it, and on Long Island — many of the tenants having a life interest and paying a fixed rent. Certain reserved lands were, of course, worked by the lord of the manor by means of both slave or indentured labour and hired hands. However, on the reserve the manor house was seldom impressive in appearance since few of the great landowners lived on their estates, preferring instead the stimulating social life of New York City.[40] Besides the estate house, there were generally the quarters for the workers, with barns, granaries, a gristmill and a sawmill, both operated by water power, a small cider mill, a brewery, a smokehouse, and a bakehouse, as well as packing sheds where meat, butter, flour, bread, beer, and cider were placed in containers made by the manor coopers. On Livingston Manor there were, in addition, a furnace and a forge, which at this period — by means of the abundant available supplies of iron ore and wood for the making of charcoal — were turning out very respectable quantities of pig iron and bar iron. Further, the manor

---

[38] "Report on the State of the Province of New York, 1774," *ibid.,* I, 509.

[39] See the Chap. 10, "Social Classes and Customs," by Michael Kraus, in the *History of the State of New York* (ed. A. E. Flick, 10 vols., New York, 1933–7), II, 407, and especially Samuel McKee: *Labor in Colonial New York, 1664–1776* (Columbia University *Studies,* New York, 1935), Chap. 4.

[40] "Gentlemen of estates rarely reside in the country, and hence few or no experiments have been made in agriculture. The farms being large, our husbandmen for that reason, have little recourse to act for . . . improving their lands . . ." (William Smith: *op. cit.,* I, 278).

reserve frequently, if not generally, bordered navigable water.[41] In such cases, there was to be found a wharf for vessels and a warehouse where supplies of necessaries were received and disposed of to the tenants and to others living round about. The successful great landowner of New York was indeed not only a landlord; he was also a miller, a lumberman, a merchant, a banker, a land speculator, a shipowner, and perhaps also an Indian trader and an ironmaster.[42] In addition, if he had manorial rights, he would hold manor courts; not infrequently he also held high provincial office and might be obliged to spend a generous amount of his time in the city of New York on the affairs of the province.

In the middle of the eighteenth century the city of New York was, as it has always been, the social[43] and commercial centre of the province.[44] It was also the capital.[45] To secure itself from attack it was defended not only by a fort but also by palisades and blockhouses that had been constructed in the 1740's to connect the North and East rivers, thus giving it something of the appearance of a frontier town.[46]

Peter Kalm, who visited the city in 1748, found an extremely pleasant place. It seemed quite like a garden to him with the streets shaded by beech, locust, lime, and elm trees. The neatness, the substantial quality, as well as the height of the brick houses impressed

---

[41] "The whole Province is contained in two narrow Oblongs, extending from the City East and North, having Water Carriage from the Extremity . . . of One Hundred and Sixty Miles . . . ; and by the most accurate Calculation, has not, at a Medium, above Twelve Miles of Land Carriage throughout its whole Extent" (William Livingston: *op. cit.*, pp. 3–4).

[42] For a brief but excellent account of the activities of the people of the province, see the chapter on "A Century of Labor" by Samuel McKee, *History of the State of New York*, II, 285, 290–1.

[43] See Esther Singleton: *Social New York under the Georges, 1714–1776* (New York, 1902).

[44] For a detailed account of the business activities of the Beekman family see *The Beekman Mercantile Papers, 1746–1799* (ed. P. L. White, 3 vols., New York, 1956); for biographies of the Beekmans, especially Gerard G. Beekman and James Beekman, see P. L. White: *The Beekmans of New York in Politics and Commerce* (New York, 1956).

[45] See G. W. Edwards: *New York as an Eighteenth Century Municipality, 1731–1776* (New York, 1917).

[46] See the Miller Papers, New York Historical Society, for the notes of the Rev. John H. Abeel describing New York in the middle of the century. For the influence of Dutch Renaissance architecture on the older part of New York City see T. J. Wertenbaker: *The Founding of American Civilization: The Middle Colonies* (New York, 1938), pp. 171–83.

him, and the cosmopolitan character of the population he noted by the presence of places of worship for Anglicans, Dutch Reformed, Presbyterians, German Lutherans, German Reformed, Quakers, and Jews — without counting the sprinkling of Huguenots and Roman Catholics.[47] Although in size it gave place to both Boston and Philadelphia,[48] it was a centre of opulence with a commerce so extensive as to lead Kalm to declare that it "disputed the preference" with the two latter seaports. Hundreds of brigantines, sloops, and schooners annually left this port for England, New England, the West Indies, the southern continental colonies, and other parts of the world.[49] Already it had become the distributing centre of western Connecticut and eastern New Jersey. However, it is of interest to note that in 1752 the annual value of the goods shipped to the province from Great Britain was reported by James Abercromby to be but £150,-000 sterling — just equal to the value of the importations of the little island of Antigua from the mother country and but one half the value of those of Barbados.[50] In 1749 the number of vessels owned by the maritime interests of the province was only 157, with an average registered carrying capacity of little over forty tons. These were manned by crews that averaged merely eight men, which indi-

---

[47] Peter Kalm: *Travels in North America* (ed. A. B. Benson, 2 vols., New York, 1937), I, 131–3. In view of the great importance of the Jews in the life of the City of New York, the student is referred to the best work relating to their earlier activities, H. B. Grinstein: *The Rise of the Jewish Community in New York, 1654–1860* (Philadelphia, 1945). It may be added that Jews as well as Catholics were not permitted to vote. See G. W. Edwards: *op. cit.*, p. 45.

[48] According to the notes of the Rev. John Abeel, there were 2,200 houses and 12,743 inhabitants in 1754. See Miller Papers, *loc. cit.* Lord Adam Gordon, a British officer who came to New York in 1765 after visiting all leading colonial towns in British North America to the southward, writes in his journal: "New York does not measure up to Philadelphia in beauty, regularity, size or the number of inhabitants and houses. Of the last there are 3,000, about 300 slaves, 12 churches and places of worship and perhaps 20,000 inhabitants." He also affirmed that there were more Negroes in the province than in any other northern colony. See "Journal of an Officer . . . ," B.M., King's Mss., 213:39.

[49] Much of this commerce was carried on in the ships of Great Britain and New England. For commercial activity in 1753 see the *New York Mercury* of June 11 and 18 for vessels entering the port of New York from various regions on those days and the departure of vessels with their destinations.

[50] James Abercromby's "Examination," May 22, 1752, Shelburne Papers, 47:37. The above figure on New York imports is perhaps low. A table of imports from Great Britain between 1747 and 1765 gives £194,030 sterling as the value of British imports in 1752. The value of its exports to the mother country was but £40,648 in that year, according to the same table, which is printed in *The History of the State of New York* (ed. A. C. Flick, 10 vols., New York, 1933–7), II, 266.

cates not only that a small proportion of the scanty population of the province was seafaring but also that commercial relations with the mother country continued, as earlier in the century, to be maintained chiefly by British merchants and by British ships.[51]

Industrially, the province was not so advanced as several of the other American plantations. Although there were numerous iron mines, it appears that the only production of crude iron was taking place at Ancram on the Manor of Livingston,[52] which smelted in 1751 some six hundred tons of pig iron, one fourth of which was transformed into bar iron.[53] There was, it is true, in the great patent of Wawayanda in Orange County a "plateing Forge" with a tilt hammer, but this was not in use during the period under discussion.[54] A good deal of weaving of flax and wool was reported, but only in a domestic way for local use; beaver hats also were made, yet the exportation of these after 1732 had been prohibited by act of Parliament.[55] Lamp-black production, however, had assumed some importance,[56] and the baked and refined sugar of the province was marketed not only in other continental colonies but even in the West Indies, while six distilleries manufactured rum and other spirits used domestically and in both the Indian and the Guinea trade. Further, there were produced for export very considerable quantities of flour, together with other foodstuffs from wheat, which had long been one of the great staples of the province.[57] Unfortu-

---

[51] Governor Clinton to Board of Trade, May 23, 1749, Shelburne Papers, 45:91–7; see also *Documentary History of New York*, I, 494–5.

[52] James de Lancey to the Board of Trade, December 1, 1757, *Documentary History of New York*, I, 496.

[53] "An account of Iron Made at Ancram, 1750–1756," *ibid.*, I, 496.

[54] "Governor Clinton's Certificate About Iron Rolling Mills," 1750, *ibid.*, 495. For iron-production in New York see Irene D. Neu: "The Iron Plantations of Colonial New York," *New York History*, XXXIII, 3–24.

[55] 5 George II, c. 22. The manufacture of hats, at least for domestic consumption, was continued on a wide scale. The Board of Trade, in a representation to the Privy Council in 1764, pointed out that the production of hats was carried on extensively in the province. See *Acts of the Privy Council, Col. Ser., 1745–1766*, p. 638.

[56] In 1724 Susanna Parmyter had been granted a monopoly of this commodity for a period of ten years. *Colonial Laws of New York*, II, 242.

[57] The total annual value of the exports of New York between 1763 and 1766 averaged £526,000. Almost one half of this came from the exportation of 250,000 barrels of flour and biscuit, according to figures presented by Alexander Cluny: *American Traveller: or Observations on . . . the British Colonies in America* (London, 1769), p. 75; see also *American Husbandry* (2 vols., London, 1775, and reissued, New York, 1939, ed. H. J. Carman), p. 91.

nately, as the result of the fraudulent exportation of unmerchant-
able flour — especially flour mixed with Indian corn — and the false
taring of bread and flour casks, by 1750 these commodities had lost
their reputation to a great extent in the markets abroad. But leading
merchants of the province were seeking to restore their quality at
this period by suitable legislation.[58]

One of the most profitable commercial activities of the province
in the seventeenth century had been the Indian fur trade, although
it gave direct employment to comparatively few white men. There
had, however, been a falling off in the receipts of fur, due no doubt
largely to the disappearance of beaver in great numbers from the
western part of the colony as the result of continuous trapping, and
to the influences exerted upon the "far Indians" to bring in their
furs which emanated from the French trading posts of Canada,
especially Montreal, and even from the Hudson's Bay Company
posts far to the north. Further, the growing importance of the
Pennsylvania fur trade on the upper waters of the Ohio adversely
affected the New York trade. Nevertheless, Albany was still considered one of the great fur-trading centres of the New World.[59]

The old Dutch town of Albany must have presented a quaint
appearance in 1750. Most of the houses were so constructed that
one of the gable ends faced the street. This end was generally faced
with brick while the three other walls presented to view bare un-
painted planks. The roofs extended far out into the thoroughfare,
and on either side of the street entrance, generally centred, were
benches, upon which in fair weather the people would spend the
day — when the womenfolk were not scrubbing their floors in good
Dutch fashion. One broad street five times the width of the others
served as a market place, and at either end of this was a stone

---

[58] Among the Sterling Papers at the New York Historical Society is a letter written
by William Alexander to John Provost of London, dated November 16, 1750, in which
he refers to the fact that the grand jury had returned several indictments against ex-
porters of bad flour and that a meeting was held soon afterwards by seventy merchants, who called upon the Assembly to retrieve the reputation of New York flour
by legislation similar to that passed in Pennsylvania to protect its quality. It is clear
that by 1763 New York flour was again held in high esteem.

[59] According to a table giving the value of skins exported from the northern part
of North America before 1775, those sent from Canada were valued at £76,000, those
from Pennsylvania at £50,000, those from New York at £35,000, and those from
Hudson Bay at £29,000; see American Husbandry (1939 edn.), p. 493.

A portion of the Province of New York.
(From Sauthier's "A Chorographical Map of
the Province of New York in
North America...," 1779)

The Province of New Jersey.

(From "A Map of Pensilvania, New-Jersey, New-York,
And the Three Delaware Counties" by Lewis Evans, 1749)

church — at the east end the Dutch Reformed, and at the west end the Anglican. It would appear, however, that in 1750 there was little demand for the latter, except on the part of the garrison, as all of the people spoke Dutch and were particularly attached to the Rev. Theodorus Frielinghausen, the minister of the Reformed church.

Within the town were made great quantities of wampum for the Indian trade. Here also were stored supplies of various commodities in the warehouses of the wealthy merchants who lived on their extensive estates in the country round about. For to Albany came the Iroquois and also, less frequently, those tribes in alliance with them. Here also appeared parties of Canadian Indians carrying on a secret trade in beaver skins. Moreover, from the town each spring there left for Oswego, the English outpost on Lake Ontario, representatives of practically every Albany merchant house. At Oswego they spent the summer bargaining with Indians from many distant tribes, who came with their peltries. In 1749, for example, 190 canoes arrived there from eleven far western tribes; in addition, three canoes from the Upper Lakes brought French traders. These together carried over sixteen hundred people with 1,385 packs of furs, which possessed a value ranging from £14 to £20 per pack, or a total value of £21,406.[60]

Limited as it was, the Indian trade was enormously profitable, but by no means carried on at all times with absolute fairness to the Indians. Peter Kalm, who visited Albany in 1749 and 1750, wrote: "Many people have assured me that the Indians are frequently cheated in disposing of their goods, especially when they are drunk; and that sometimes they do not get one half or even one tenth of the value of their goods. I have been a witness to several transactions of this kind. The merchants of Albany glory in these tricks, and are highly pleased when they have given a poor Indian a greater portion of brandy than he can stand, and when they can, after that, get all his goods for mere trifles." It would appear that

---

[60] Report of John Lindsay, Commissary at Oswego, August 20, 1749, *New York Colonial Documents*, VI, 538. A recent writer makes the following interesting assertion: "The pelts exchanged at Oswego in 1749 would today sell for well over $2,000,-000. During the period 1750 to 1755 the fur trade reached its peak, causing the British to consider Oswego one of the most important points on the continent, and the French to think of it as a place to be destroyed at all costs" (F. K. Zercher: "The Port of Oswego," *New York History*, XVI, 310).

the methods employed in this commerce were reflected in the general conduct of the people of this region, for Kalm further declared: "The avarice, selfishness, immeasurable love of money of the inhabitants of Albany are very well known throughout all North America. . . . If a real Jew, who understands the art of getting forward perfectly well should settle amongst them, they would not fail to ruin him."[61] The good man found an intense hatred of these people, especially among New Englanders, who accused them of having encouraged the French Indians to desolate the New England settlements in the late war in order to bring to them the loot, especially plates, spoons, bowls, cups, etc., for which they paid the Indians good prices.[62]

In 1750 George Clinton was acting as royal Governor of the province.[63] A son of the Earl of Lincoln, he had followed the sea without winning distinction as a naval commander before his appointment in 1741, and in 1743 came to his post, so it is asserted, loaded with debts, hoping by this new situation to recoup his fortunes. By all accounts he was generally complaisant, decidely indolent, and always inept in the art of governing. Soon after his arrival he began to lean for guidance in the affairs of state upon James de Lancey, one of the most powerful and astute politicians of the province. Upon de Lancey's advice,[64] it appears, the Governor made, from the point of view of the Crown, the initial fatal mistake of surrendering into the hands of the General Assembly the complete control of public finance, accepting without a serious struggle a reversal of the policy

[61] Peter Kalm: *Travels*, I, 242, 244.

[62] *Ibid.*, I, 245. This charge was also made by Governor Clinton in 1747 in his "Observations on the Representations of the Assembly," C.O. 5:1085 pp. 265–74. "According to the information I have received some of those French Indians were lately trading at Albany, when others of them were at the same time, scalping and Butchering his Majty's subjects on the boarders of New England; which we can not but look upon with the same resentment, as if done to any people of this province; and besides, whatever these Indians Barter these furs for, whether for cloathing, or gunpowder, is so much clear gain to the French, and the strengthening of the hands of his Majty's Enemie" (Governor Clinton to the Assembly of New York, August 23, 1745, *New York Colonial Documents*, VI, 372).

For a sympathetic study of Albany in its relations to the larger problem of imperial expansion see A. H. Buffington: "The Policy of Albany and English Westward Expansion," *Mississippi Valley Historical Review*, VIII, 327–66.

[63] For Clinton commission, dated May 21, 1741, see *New York Colonial Documents*, VI, 187–95; for his instructions see P.R.O., C.O. 5:1126, pp. 144–235.

[64] *New York Colonial Documents*, VI, 614–17.

maintained by his predecessors, Governors Hunter, Burnet, Montgomery, and Cosby, of insisting on establishments based on estimates for a five-year period and the granting "in general" of supplies
for the support of government.[65] He accepted the act of 1744 which
provided for specific appropriations and submitted to the creation
of a group of officials solely dependent upon the Assembly. Moreover, the latter, through its own committees, purchased and distributed munitions of war, raised, employed, provisioned, and paid
the provincial troops, named officers, built fortifications, and supported scouts in the Indian country.[66] Not only did this body employ as its own agent in London Robert Charles, secretary to Sir
Peter Warren, but also it dismissed the Governor's appointee "as
tidewaiter of the colony's imports" and selected one in his place. De
Lancey, appointed by the Governor Chief Justice of the province
during good behaviour[67] and also designated (although not commissioned as yet) as Lieutenant Governor, rode on a wave of popularity while the authority of the King's representative was thus being flouted. For a period of almost three years he shaped affairs
according to his own desires.[68] However, in 1746 Clinton became con-

---

[65] *Ibid.* It should be pointed out that it was in 1737, under Governor Clarke, that
the General Assembly first deviated from the above practice that had been in effect for
a period of twenty-eight years. The Assembly of course since the days of the notorious
Cornbury had been striving to establish an absolute control of the finances. This was
in line with a general movement on the part of the royal colonies. Attorney General
Richard Bradley, writing from New York in 1729, complained: "I doubt not, but Y^r
Grace, is or soon will be convinced that the General Assembly's of these Country's;
Seem to aim at an Arbitrary, and Independent power, by their assuming the sole
appropriation of money raised for the publick Service, Their usual insisting on
passing of bills hurtfull to his Majesty's Prerogative and interest, at the Same time
they pass Money bills, And by refusing to give any Salary, at all, to some officers of
the Crown; and lessening those of Others, when, at the Same time, they Augment the
Salary of such as they appoint; and that without any apparent application for it"
(C.O. 5:1086, folio 13).

[66] See Governor Shirley's "View of the Situation in New York," C.O. 5:1095; see
also *New York Colonial Documents*, VI, 615–16.

[67] As to Clinton's power to appoint by commission under the seal of New York
de Lancey as Chief Justice of the province during good behaviour, the Board of Trade
expressed doubt, and on June 28, 1753, asked the Attorney and Solicitor General, Sir
Dudley Ryder and William Murray, for their opinions. Clinton's instructions on this
point seem to have been contradictory, with the result that in framing his successor's
instructions the one that directed the Governor not to place any limitation of time
on the appointment of judges was dropped and power was expressly given the Governor to remove all judges and justices under certain restrictions. See P.R.O., C.O.
5:1128, pp. 57 and 60–76.

[68] For the great power of de Lancey in the government of New York see William
Smith: *op. cit.*, II, 142–3.

vinced that he had been betrayed and, repudiating this masterful man, turned to the Surveyor General, Cadwallader Colden, for advice.[69]

Colden, a man of means, was a native of Scotland; he had been educated at Edinburgh and in London, and for a time was a Philadelphia merchant; he was certainly one of the most distinguished among British colonials, the friend of many of the world's most famous scientists, a philosopher, a student of botany, astronomy, and physics, a physician, and a historian. He looked with abhorrence upon the recent usurpations of the Assembly and dedicated himself to the task of extricating the Governor from his embarrassing situation. This brought down upon him the hatred of the popular leaders. "We esteem it a great Misfortune to the Country," declared the Assembly in addressing the Governor in October 1747, "that you have fallen into such ill Hands, that the Fate of this Colony should in this Time of eminent Danger, depend solely upon the Advice and Caprice of a Man so obnoxious; who by the whole Course of his Conduct, seems to have only his own Interest in view, without any Regard to the Safety or Welfare of the Colony."[70] But Colden returned their odium with interest. "You know Sr What kind of a Creature an American assembly is," he declared in writing to Governor Shirley in 1749, "& yet you cannot have a sufficient conception of the Ignorance & mean Spirit of the Dutch members here most of them of the lowest rank of Artificers."[71]

Colden's case against the Assembly, and also against a majority of the Governor's Council, was based upon what to him was indubitable proof that the members had been influenced in their opposition to the Governor by a group of powerful men who, for sinister purposes, sought to strip Clinton of his power and to preserve the neutrality of the Province of New York in the war then being waged between England and France. He charged that this conspiracy had taken place in order that, among other advantages to be gained by this neutrality, the French Indians might make Al-

---

[69] For Colden see Alice M. Keys: *Cadwallader Colden: A Representative Eighteenth Century Official* (New York, 1906); see also *supra*, n. 3.

[70] *New York Colonial Documents*, VI, 618.

[71] *Colden Papers, 1748–1754*, p. 120. At this time the Assembly was composed of but twenty-seven members,

bany a rendezvous for the disposal of their plunder, in connection with their savage incursions in New England across the Hudson. It seemed to Colden that de Lancey had largely won his popularity in the promotion of this scheme of neutrality.[72] Further, he defended strongly the conduct of Clinton. To the accusation that the Governor had drawn out public money for private use, he declared:

> "I have been near 30 years in the Council of this Province & longer conversant in the publick affairs of it & in all that time I do not remember that any publick money was drawn by any Gov[r] from the Treasury & applied to any other use than what it was design'd for by the assembly that granted it . . . ."

He then went on to observe:

> "If Gov[r] Clinton had made use of his power in drawing the least sum out of the Treasury contrary to the intent of the granters it cannot be doubted this assembly would have pointed it particularly out but no such thing has so much as been attempted[.] On the Contrary I am perswaded that there has been more of the publick money converted to private use since the Assem[y] assumed the sole power of issueing it than has been don in any shape by all or any of the Governors since I came into this Province[.] I am so much perswaded of the truth of this that I could but [put] the whole contraversy upon this single issue[.]"[73]

Clinton spent the remainder of the period of his administration, after his break with de Lancey, in attempting to strip the latter of influence and to win back the powers that had slipped into the hands of the Assembly. He sought, among other things, to prevent the confirmation of de Lancey's appointment to the office of Lieutenant Governor and exerted himself to secure that honour for Colden, especially in the late 1740's when he saw that his own tenure of office was drawing to a close. The ministry, however, could not be prevailed upon to incur the hostility of this leader of the

---

[72] For the connection of the de Lancey family with the Canada trade see Professor C. H. McIlwain's Introduction to Peter Wraxall's *An Abridgment of the Indian Affairs* . . . (Cambridge, Mass., & London, 1915), p. lxvii, n.4. Respecting the question of neutrality see *The History of the State of New York*, II, 226–7.

[73] Cadwallader Colden to Governor William Shirley, July 25, 1749, *Colden Papers, 1748–1754*, p. 122.

popular group.[74] The Governor also threw down the gauntlet to the Assembly and, for a period of two years after peace was restored, refused to sign bills that made yearly specific appropriations. However, in 1750 he yielded under great financial pressure.[75]

In the course of the struggle between Clinton and the Assembly of New York the issues involved finally came before His Majesty in the form of a report upon the state of that province prepared by the Board of Trade in the spring of 1751.[76] This report was strongly adverse to the Assembly. As a result, when a new Governor was appointed to office in 1753 the 39th article of his instructions called upon him to secure a permanent and fixed revenue for the support of government as a means of restoring peace and tranquillity and preventing encroachments upon His Majesty's authority and prerogative within the province.[77] When this instruction came before the Assembly it was voted that His Majesty should be addressed with the assurance that the imputations contained therein were groundless and had been most falsely and maliciously represented. The address, however, was dismissed, and the Privy Council went on record to the effect that as the result of exigencies of the service in time of war the Assembly had taken to itself not only the disposal of the public money, but had wrested from the Governor "the nomination of all Officers of Government, . . . and in short almost every other executive part of Government, by which unwarrantable Encroachments and Invasions of Your Majestys just and undoubted authority, Order and good Government were subverted, Your Majestys Service obstructed, and the Security of the Province endangered . . ."[78]

---

[74] It seems to be true that Lord Halifax in 1749 expressed the hope that de Lancey would not be allowed to serve as deputy in case Clinton returned. Governor Clinton to Cadwallader Colden, November 6, 1749, *ibid.*, pp. 148–9. De Lancey, however, had powerful friends at court, among them the Archbishop of Canterbury and Vice-Admiral Sir Peter Warren.

[75] For two years Clinton had been without salary because of his insistence that the Assembly provide a revenue for the colony "conformable to the directions of the King's commission and instructions" that all laws for the supply and support of government "be indefinite and without limitation, except the same be for a temporary service . . ." (William Smith: *op. cit.*, II, 124). See also *New York Colonial Documents*, VI, 702.

[76] For this long report see *ibid.*, VI, 639–703.

[77] For Osborn's instructions drawn up July 5, 1753, see P.R.O., C.O. 5:1128, pp. 77–214; for his commission, dated July 23, 1753, see William Smith: *op. cit.*, I, 295–304.

[78] *Acts of the Privy Council, Col. Ser., 1745–1766*, pp. 209, 246–7.

As for Clinton's plan for circumventing de Lancey by securing the appointment of Colden as Lieutenant Governor, this did not materialize.[79] The Board of Trade decided to disappoint both groups by sending over to New York an Englishman of weight. As a result, Sir Danvers Osborn, a kinsman of the Earl of Halifax, was made Governor in place of Clinton. Unfortunately, when he arrived in the colony his mind was greatly disturbed by the realization that he could not carry out his instructions, especially the 39th article, and soon after assuming office he took his own life.[80] Thus de Lancey, who had by now received his commission as Lieutenant Governor, realized his ambition, and in his own person combined that office with those of Chancellor and Chief Justice of the province.[81]

---

[79] In 1761 Colden received the commission as Lieutenant Governor only upon the death of de Lancey. See C.O. 324:1130, pp. 47–8.

[80] For a contemporary account of the death of Osborn see the letter by the New York merchants Robert and Richard Ray, dated October 13, 1753, New York Historical Society *Quarterly*, XXXV, 405–7.

[81] De Lancey was given a commission as Lieutenant Governor under date of October 27, 1747; it is recorded in C.O. 324:50, p. 200. Clinton, however, kept it in his possession, hoping to persuade the home government to rescind it as indicated in the text. When this failed, he reluctantly turned the commission over to de Lancey before returning to England.

CHAPTER VI

Ploughmen of the Jerseys

H ow can he get wisdom that holdeth the plow and that glorieth in the goad, that driveth oxen, and is occupied in their labors and whose talk is of bullocks?"[1] asked rather caustically Governor Lewis Morris[2] of New Jersey. He was replying to the popular branch of the legislature, called the General Assembly, which had in its address to him in the spring of 1745 confessed with an air of mock humility that most its members were farmers and ploughmen.[3]

While farming occupied the attention of the overwhelming majority of the people of the province during the period under consideration, lumbering went hand in hand with agriculture and represented a rather important economic interest. The population, which totalled 61,383 in the year 1747 and 79,000 in 1752,[4] was centred

---

[1] Ecclesiasticus 38:25–6.

[2] Morris was the first to receive a commission as Governor which was limited to New Jersey. From 1702 to 1738 the Governor of New York had also received a commission as Governor of New Jersey. For Morris's commission, dated March 3, 1738, see P.R.O., C.O. 5:197, pp. 165–92; for his instructions see C.O. 5:197, pp. 189–238.

[3] *Papers of Governor Lewis Morris, 1738–1746* (ed. W. A. Whitehead, New York, 1852), pp. 237, 277–8. As William Douglass pointed out in 1751 in his *A Summary, Historical and Political, of the . . . British Settlements in North-America* (2 vols., London, 1760), I, 290, the name "General Assembly," as applied to the lower house of the legislature, was improper.

[4] *Documents relating to the Colonial, Revolutionary and Post-Revolutionary History of the State of New Jersey* (36 vols., Newark, N.J., 1880–1941), 1st ser., VII, 245; this will be referred to hereafter as *New Jersey Archives*. See also Greene and Harrington: *American Population before . . . 1790* (New York, 1932), pp. 106–7.

largely on the rich alluvial soils in the eastern and western parts of the colony. Between these two sections, especially in the north central area — a wide tract of hilly, almost mountainous land, then valued chiefly for its pine and cedar trees — there were comparatively few people in 1750. The Rev. Andrew Burnaby, who traversed the Jerseys from Trenton in the west to Elizabeth in the east in 1759, observed that it was not as flourishing as it might be, on account of its lack of foreign trade. However, he was impressed with the fact that it was "well cultivated, thickly seated and the garden of North America," with hospitable "gentleman farmers" everywhere living on their "estates."[5]

Out of the labour of the ploughmen of the Jerseys came abundant supplies of grain, beef, and pork.[6] The annual surplus of these commodities, together with the timber from the hills — the total valued at £30,000 sterling — was exported to the West Indies, Lisbon, Madeira, Ireland, and England. According to Governor Jonathan Belcher, writing in 1749, the exports were shipped abroad mostly in New Jersey vessels, of which there were but twenty with a total displacement of 1,500 tons.[7] Despite Governor Belcher's claims for New Jersey's foreign trade, the people of the province were supplied with European commodities almost entirely through New York and Pennsylvania. As was true of Connecticut, there was little direct commerce with the mother country. The city of New York continued through the middle of the eighteenth century to be the entrepôt for East New Jersey just as Philadelphia was for West New Jersey.[8] A similar differentiation between East and West New

---

[5] Andrew Burnaby: *Travels through the Middle Settlements of North-America in the Years 1759 and 1760* (London, 1775), pp. 54–60. For Peter Kalm's observations on New Jersey when he passed through it in 1748 see his *Travels in North America* (ed. A. B. Benson, 2 vols., New York, 1937), I, 116–24.

[6] See C. R. Woodward: *The Development of Agriculture in New Jersey, 1640–1880* (New Brunswick, N.J., 1927), and by the same author: "Agricultural Legislation in Colonial New Jersey," *Agricultural History*, III, 15–28, and especially, also by the same author: *Ploughs and Politics: Charles Reed of New Jersey and His Notes on Agriculture, 1715–1774* (New Brunswick, 1941), pp. 229–411.

[7] Governor Belcher to the Board of Trade, April 21, 1749, *New Jersey Archives*, 1st ser., VII, 244. In 1742, according to Governor Morris, there were only three brigantines and four or five sloops belonging to the people of the colony; these traded to the Madeiras and the West Indies. Lewis Morris to the Board of Trade, December 15, 1742, *Papers of Governor Lewis Morris*, p. 156.

[8] The efforts of East New Jersey to assert an economic independence of the port of New York were indicated when, in the surrender of their political powers in 1702,

Jersey was manifested in their respective money standards. That of the East, which was the official standard, conformed to New York currency, that of the West, to the currency of Pennsylvania.[9]

All accounts of this period, official or otherwise, point to the fact that the great majority of New Jersey inhabitants lived comfortably. Indeed, it was stated in 1742 by one who knew them well that they regarded themselves as "the most easie and happy people of any Collony in North America."[10] And well they might congratulate themselves. Conditions were generally favourable. Since no foreign foes or menace from native Americans lurked along their borders, no extensive expenditures were required for fortifications and none to secure the friendship of powerful Indian tribes. In peace men ploughed their fields and went about the pursuit of their personal interests. There was a remarkable absence of public burdens. According to a report sent to the Board of Trade in 1749, "'Tis 17 Years since any Tax was raised on the people for Support of Government,"[11] the expense of which was entirely met by the loan of bills of credit of the colony to the inhabitants for the improvement of their lands, an operation which in the early 1740's yielded some £3,000 in the form of interest. Surprisingly enough, this manner of financing the provincial government apparently was never gravely abused. On the contrary, the history of public finance in colonial New Jersey is in marked contrast to that, for example, in Rhode Island, where the scandal of defaulted payments and consequent inflation had by 1750 given the little New England colony a very unsavoury reputation. Nevertheless, when New Jersey attempted to continue even the fairly conservative practice of issuing money on land security and utilizing the interest thereon to meet the charges of government, an issue of great importance arose.

---

the proprietors reserved the right to retain Perth Amboy as a free port. This was granted, but the Crown insisted that the same duties should be paid on articles entering New Jersey as were paid in entering New York. See Governor Hunter's instructions, December 27, 1709, C.O. 5:995, pp. 53–4.

[9] See *Papers of Governor Lewis Morris*, p. 122. During the period under discussion a Spanish-milled dollar was worth 27 shillings in West Jersey, but only 26 shillings in East Jersey. Board of Trade *Journal, 1741–1749*, p. 439.

[10] Lewis Morris to Peter Collinson, May 24, 1742, *Papers of Governor Lewis Morris*, p. 147.

[11] Governor Belcher to the Board of Trade, April 21, 1749, *New Jersey Archives*, 1st ser. VII, 246.

This issue grew out of the Assembly's practice — a practice by no means limited to New Jersey — of issuing in the course of the eighteenth century bills of credit to circulate for a limited period as legal tender for all debts incurred either "for Sterling Money Silver Money of America or any other Species of Gold Silver or any other quantity of Plate or Gold."[12] Upon this basis £40,000 had been issued for the colony in 1723, £20,000 in 1730, and £40,000 in 1733, all of which had been lent to the inhabitants with interest at five per cent.[13]

When some of the colonies had turned to the use of paper money at the end of the seventeenth century and early in the eighteenth as the result of war-time emergencies, the government of the mother country had been permissive.[14] As time went on, however, the demand in the colonies for paper money had increased, even in peace time, and concurrently the tendency to inflate the colonial currency. Naturally opposition developed in Great Britain against accepting inflated paper money as tender for acquitting debts. As a result, in 1720 an instruction was sent to all royal Governors to restrain them from assenting to any act for striking bills of credit without a clause to prevent its going into effect until approved by the Crown, except in the case of an act designed to secure a revenue for meeting the charges of government.[15] It was under the shadow of this instruction that New Jersey had felt free to erect her system of provincial finance. This was done in spite of the fact that the Lords of Committee of the Privy Council showed their hostility in 1731 to "a Most pernicious practice" on the part of several of the colonies of issuing bills of credit "in lieu of Money in Order to Discharge their publick Debts and for other purposes."[16] In fact, the colony was singled out

---

[12] *Acts of the Privy Council, Col. Ser., 1745–1766*, p. 26. See Volume II of this series for a discussion of the North Carolina legal-tender legislation. For the hostile attitude of the Board of Trade toward the Barbados and New York legal-tender acts of 1706 and 1709, respectively, see also C. P. Nettels: *Money Supply of the American Colonies before 1720* (Madison, Wis., 1934), pp. 269–75.

[13] See *Acts of the Privy Council, Col. Ser., 1745–1766*, p. 25, confirming the issue of bills of credit provided for in the acts of 1723, 1730, and 1733.

[14] By 1715 the use of bills of credit had become quite general, although Virginia, Maryland, Jamaica, Barbados, and the Leeward Islands were not involved. C. P. Nettels: *op. cit.*, p. 275.

[15] *Acts of the Privy Council, Col. Ser., 1720–1745*, pp. 329–30.

[16] *Ibid.*

in 1734 for special commendation by the Board of Trade when a group of Bristol merchants strongly voiced their opposition to the Crown's approving the act of the Assembly of the preceding year providing for the printing of £40,000 in bills of credit. The measure was not only accepted, but, in referring to it, the Lords Commissioners pointed out that there was no essential difference between this and a former New Jersey law that had been executed to good effect and had proved beneficial to the province.[17]

Nevertheless, one can detect a growing opposition in England to colonial paper money, especially to the practice of the New England colonies. For example, in 1736 the Privy Council desired the Board of Trade to lay before it a state of the paper currency in New England, having been informed that bills of credit to a great value had been issued there.[18] The following year, while approving certain supply acts of Massachusetts Bay, it was decided to send the Governor of that province a peremptory instruction not to give his assent in the future to any paper-money bill without a suspending clause.[19] It was therefore not surprising that in April 1740 the House of Commons should resolve:

> "That the creating and Issuing Paper Bills of Credit in the British Colonys and Plantations in America by Virtue of Acts of Assembly there and making it obligatory on all Persons to take such Bills of Credit in payment for Debts Dues and Demands hath frustrated the good intentions of an Act . . . Entituled An Act for ascertaining the Rates of Foreign Coins in Her Majestys Plantations in America and hath been a great Discouragement to the Commerce of this Kingdom by occasioning a Confusion in Dealings and lessening of Credit in those parts."[20]

Close upon the heels of this resolution the Board of Trade prepared two additional instructions for the Governors of those colonies obliged to submit their laws to the King for approval. The first provided for the enforcement of the act of Parliament passed in the sixth year of the reign of Queen Anne for ascertaining the rates of

---

[17] *Ibid.*, p. 424.
[18] *Ibid.*, p. 507.
[19] *Ibid.*, pp. 561–2.
[20] *Ibid.*, *1745–1766*, pp. 24–9.

foreign coins;[21] the second, for the introduction into all laws that provided for the issuing of bills of credit in lieu of money a clause suspending the operation of such laws until the pleasure of His Majesty had been made known. These were approved in July 1740 and forthwith sent to America.[22] As Maryland, Connecticut, and Rhode Island were not obliged to submit their laws, the Lords of the Committee recommended sending them a circular letter containing the address of the House of Commons and directions regarding acts providing for a paper currency, which was so ordered.[23]

In 1742 the New Jersey General Assembly desired Governor Lewis Morris to sign a bill for the printing of £40,000 in bills of credit of the same type as the three that earlier had been approved. In view of his additional instructions of 1740, the Governor was obliged to face the wrath of the popular chamber by refusing to do so unless the bill should carry a clause suspending its operation until approved by His Majesty.[24] He also proceeded to censure the Assembly for resolutions it had entered into when the news had arrived that a bill was about to be introduced into Parliament to regulate the colonial paper currency. This resolution declared "That if the said Bill, or any Bill of that Tendency, should pass into a Law, it would not only be an Encroachment upon the fundamental constitution of this Colony, and the Concessions made to the First Settlers thereof by His Majestys Royal Ancestors, but also Destructive of the Liberties and properties of his Majestys Subjects now Inhabitants of the same."[25]

However, the opposition of Governor Morris was not the only obstacle to enactment of the money bill. The Governor's Council, sitting in its capacity as the upper chamber of the Assembly, was bitterly opposed to the measure and described the emitting of large sums of bills of credit as similar in effect to giving cold water to a

---

[21] 6 Anne, c. 30, *Statutes at Large* (Eyre and Strahan), IV, 311–12.

[22] *Acts of the Privy Council, Col. Ser., 1720–1745*, p. 677.

[23] *Ibid.* Although the Three Lower Counties on the Delaware did not submit their laws either, they were not mentioned in this recommendation, just as they were ignored officially in other instances — a fact pointing up their anomalous status vis-à-vis Pennsylvania and the mother country.

[24] *Ibid., 1745–1766*, pp. 24–5; Morris to the Board of Trade, December 15, 1742, *Papers of Governor Lewis Morris*, pp. 152–6.

[25] *New Jersey Archives*, 1st ser., XV, 396–7.

man in a high fever — "the more is given, still the more is called for. . . ."[26] In rejecting the bill, the Council emphasized the fear of inflation and its attendant evils. The majority of the House of Representatives, however, thought that the attitude of the Council was due to the Governor's influence. They then proceeded on the false assumption that, could the supposed basis for the opposition of Morris be removed, the desired legislation would pass the Council. An unsuccessful attempt was made to bribe Morris both to consent to the passing of the money bill and to try to obtain permission from the Crown to sign the bill without the objectionable reservation. The futile bribe was the promise of suitable financial support for the government. In this the representatives appear to have displayed a remarkable ignorance of the type of man their Governor was.

For Morris was one of several prominent men with large vested interests in both New York and New Jersey. He was not only lord of the manor of Morrisania in New York but also the owner of the estate "Tintern" ("Tinton") in New Jersey. As a man of wealth he could not be easily reached by financial inducements that might have swayed a more impecunious Governor. Furthermore, before assuming his post in New Jersey he had been involved in many bitter political disputes in both colonies, especially in New York, and had learned how to hold his ground with great ability and tenacity. He therefore stubbornly adhered to the letter of his instructions until his death in office on May 21, 1746.

Morris's successor was Jonathan Belcher, another man with much experience in public life. Born in Massachusetts Bay, he served on the Massachusetts Council and as agent in England for the House of Representatives before he was appointed Governor of Massachusetts Bay and New Hampshire in 1730, an office he held until his dismissal in the spring of 1741. Having been restored to the confidence of the home government, he was appointed Governor of New Jersey in the summer of 1746 after the death of Morris.[27] Although he could equal Morris's ability to defend his position vigorously, he determined to work harmoniously with the New Jersey Assembly

---

[26] *Ibid.*, 1st ser., XV, 385–8.

[27] Although Belcher was designated as Governor of New Jersey in 1746, his commission bears the date February 13, 1747. For his commission see P.R.O., C.O. 5:200, pp. 199–211; for his instructions see C.O. 5:200, pp. 385–419.

even though bound by the same limiting instructions that had hampered his predecessor.[28] Therefore in 1748 he signed a bill — carrying the necessary suspending clause — which provided for an issue of paper money, similar in amount to the preceding bill to be current for sixteen years, and he strongly urged His Majesty to give it favourable consideration.[29] The following year it came before the Board of Trade. Richard Partridge, the New Jersey London agent of the Assembly and Belcher's Quaker brother-in-law, also earnestly endorsed its acceptance, while Ferdinand Paris, London agent for the East New Jersey Proprietors, "in behalf of himself and other Creditors . . . of the Province," as heartily opposed it.

The New Jersey agent argued that a further supply of paper currency was absolutely necessary for purposes of trade. He emphasized the fact that all of the bills emitted by the previous acts had been redeemed, with the exception of one half of the last £40,000, which would be called in in 1754. The New Jersey bills, he declared, were more highly esteemed than those issued by any of the other colonies, and were actually considered better than silver or gold by the inhabitants, who were accustomed to demand these rather than specie in all transactions. Indeed, when the time would come to redeem them at the Loan Office the premium, he affirmed, would rise to as much as seven per cent unless there was a new supply of bills. His testimony was supported by that of a Captain Ware who had recently come from the province.[30]

Paris pointed out, on the other hand, that, although the preamble of the act set forth specious pretences, nowhere did the bill authorize the interest arising from the loan of the bills to be applied to the service of government, but rather, left its disposition to the legislature. He further declared that the exchange on the old bills was at 175, that new emissions would lessen their credit, and that the act's direction for *all* contracts already made to be paid in these bills was unjust and unreasonable, as was the clause providing that those accused of counterfeiting the bills, although residing in another prov-

---

[28] The nineteenth article of Belcher's instructions directed him not to give his assent to any act for issuing money bills unless a draft of the bill had previously been submitted to His Majesty for directions or carried a suspending clause. *Acts of the Privy Council, Col. Ser., 1745–1766*, p. 372.

[29] Board of Trade *Journal, 1741–1749*, p. 343.

[30] *Ibid.*, p. 439.

ince, were subject to trial by a jury of two counties in New Jersey. A further argument against the countenancing of additional issues was that they laid a burden upon the poor, who, as the only borrowers, plunged themselves into greater difficulties. Finally, he insisted that the legal-tender feature of the act was contrary to a resolution by the House of Commons passed in 1729.[31]

In recommending that the bill be disallowed the Board of Trade followed Paris's line of argument, making clear that experience had shown the issuing of bills of credit for loan to have the pernicious effect of tempting persons in low and desperate circumstances to borrow beyond their ability. They further objected that the burden of public taxation consequently fell upon the shoulders of these poor people, while the more wealthy "do not contribute in any Degree to the Charges and Support of Government."[32]

Not to be discouraged, in 1753 the New Jersey General Assembly petitioned the King to permit the Governor to sign a bill for making current £60,000 in bills of credit similar to those heretofore emitted by the colony.[33] After mature consideration the Board of Trade prepared a report which was subsequently embodied in a royal instruction. This instruction seemed to accomplish a number of desirable things in the face of the anarchic political conditions within the province and the unwillingness of the popular chamber to support the Governor's efforts to uphold the law and re-establish order. First of all, it made clear that because of the beneficial effect and successful operation of bills of credit formerly issued by New Jersey, a moderate quantity of these bills — based upon good security with a proper fund for redemption within a limited time — might be of advantage in promoting trade and settlement and in offering the least burdensome method of levying money for the support of the government. No objection, therefore, would be raised to the emission of the sum requested by the Assembly, provided that three conditions were satisfied: first, that the bills were not to be declared legal tender; second, that the interest arising from their loan should be definitely

---

[31] *Ibid.*, pp. 438–9. For a detailed account of the activities of Paris and the London agents on the boundary-line issue see E. P. Lilly: *The Colonial Agents of New York and New Jersey* (Washington, 1936), pp. 176–90.

[32] *Acts of the Privy Council, Col. Ser., 1745–1766*, p. 27.

[33] *Ibid.*, p. 227.

appropriated to the services of government and should be issued by warrant from the Governor and Council only; third, that Governor Belcher should not implement any part of the act until all of the older bills of credit had been called in and destroyed.[34]

Although the Board of Trade's stipulations were far from acceptable, the New Jersey lower house persisted in its demand for paper money. In 1755 its draft of a bill for printing £70,000 in bills of credit was presented to the Privy Council for approval, although "drawn contrary in every respect to his Majestys aforementioned Instruction."[35] This was followed in 1757 by still another which was not any more favourably received by the Crown than the previous drafts, although it provided for the issuing of the sum of £79,000 in bills of credit for the use of His Majesty, or, if not needed, for the relief of the colony, and was accompanied by another calling for the printing of an additional sum of £60,000, to be lent out, with a provision that the interest arising thereon should be used to sink the former issue.[36]

Meanwhile the Empire had become involved in war. The demand for immediate action was therefore so great, particularly in the case of the exposed colonies, that at last the Governors of the neighbouring provinces of New York and Pennsylvania — who had also been forbidden by royal instructions from approving bills for the printing of paper money without the suspending clause — felt under necessity to violate both this interdiction and another instruction as to the length of time such paper should be current.[37]

While the people of New Jersey were not considered to be in any immediate danger, in due course of time an appeal was made to them, as well as to the inhabitants of other colonies, to support the war. In view of this altered situation the Privy Council at last decided to change the Governor's instructions to conform to an alteration already made for the Governor of New York. Thus, when Francis Bernard took Belcher's post in 1758, the twenty-second article of his instructions permitted him, in case of emergency in time of war, to assent to bills for the issuing of paper currency under

---

[34] *Ibid.*, pp. 228–9.
[35] *Ibid.*
[36] *Ibid.*, p. 361.
[37] *Ibid.*, pp. 362–3.

the same conditions and regulations as were prescribed by the act of Parliament in 1750 for the New England colonies.[38]

In its essence this struggle over the emission of bills-of-credit acts was between, on the one hand, the creditor English mercantile and New Jersey land-proprietorial groups favouring deflation, and, on the other, the debtor, quit-rent-paying groups supporting inflation. The British government, firmly committed to a policy of enforcing a system of sound public finance throughout the colonies, was therefore strongly arrayed against the inflationists. Nevertheless, it felt impelled as a war measure to make the desired concessions with respect to bills of credit, under the prescribed limitations.

In summarizing this account of paper money in New Jersey, it may be affirmed that, according to the evidence, circulation of bills of credit had only beneficial effects in providing a convenient medium of exchange. For it does not appear that creditors were defrauded or debtors relieved unfairly of their burdens. The same is true of the bills emitted by New York, Pennsylvania, and Delaware during the eighteenth century.[39] In all four colonies prudence in financial management was manifest. Nevertheless, the desire of the people to be allowed to secure loans from the New Jersey land bank — as they had been permitted to do in connection with the issues of bills of credit in 1723, 1730, and 1733 — was denied when bills of credit were once more emitted for war purposes only to the amount of £347,000.[40]

Although there were few people living within the borders of New Jersey who did not employ the English language by 1750 — and in this the colony was in marked contrast to its neighbours, New York and Pennsylvania — no great degree of provincial solidarity existed. The old seventeenth-century political divisions of East New Jersey

---

[38] *Ibid.*, pp. 371–2. For an excellent but brief account of financial history during the years of the French and Indian War see D. L. Kemmerer: *Path of Freedom: The Struggle for Self-Government in Colonial New Jersey, 1703–1776* (Princeton, 1940), pp. 243–55; see also by the same author: "A History of Paper Money in Colonial New Jersey, 1668–1775," New Jersey Historical Society *Proceedings*, LXXIV, 107–44.

[39] R. A. Lester: *Monetary Experiments, Early American and Recent Scandinavian* (Princeton, 1939), pp. 56–141.

[40] See D. L. Kemmerer: "Colonial Loan-Office System in New Jersey," *Journal of Political Economy*, XLVII, 867–74, and Theodore Thayer: "The Land-Bank System in the American Colonies," *Journal of Economic History*, XIII, 145–59.

and West New Jersey were still in evidence. In the former section of the province to the south of the seventeenth-century Dutch settlements in Bergen County on the Hudson were a number of transplanted New England towns such as Newark, Elizabethtown, Woodbridge, Middletown, and Shrewsbury. There the local institutions of New England had been reproduced with greater or lesser degrees of fidelity. There too, doubtless as the result of the influence of such institutions as the "Log College" and Princeton College, by the middle of the eighteenth century the Presbyterian rather than the Congregational Church had apparently become dominant among the many religious organizations.[41] Large numbers of Scots were also to be found in East New Jersey, chiefly concentrated in Somerset, Middlesex, and Monmouth counties, where they had established their Presbyterian kirks.[42]

In West New Jersey, on the other hand, the Quaker influence was the leading factor not only in the religious life but also in governmental matters.[43] It may be added that the Quakers, the Presbyterians, and the Anglicans, the latter especially well represented among the official and proprietorial groups, were the only religious groups that exerted any great influence on the political life of New Jersey in 1750.[44]

Because of its sectional jealousies the province could boast of no

---

[41] See W. A. Whitehead: *East Jersey under the Proprietary Governments . . .* (Newark, N.J., 2nd edn, 1875); E. P. Tanner: *The Province of New Jersey, 1664–1738* (New York, 1908), pp. 25–9; E. J. Fisher: *New Jersey as a Royal Province, 1738–1776* (New York & London, 1911), p. 361; and H. J. Ford: *The Scotch-Irish in America* (Princeton, 1915), pp. 110–14, 413–36. For the founding of Princeton by the Presbyterians see T. J. Wertenbaker: *Princeton, 1746–1896* (Princeton, 1946); see also Beverly McAnear: "College Founding in the American Colonies, 1745–1775," *Mississippi Valley Historical Review*, XLII, 24–44.

[42] See George E. Pryde: "The Scots in East New Jersey," New Jersey Historical Society *Proceedings*, XV, 1–39.

[43] See J. E. Pomfret: "West New Jersey: A Quaker Society, 1675–1775," *William and Mary Quarterly*, 3rd ser., VIII, 493–519, and by the same author: *The Province of West New Jersey, 1609–1702 . . .* (Princeton, 1956), Chap. 12, "The Quakers." There were numerous Quakers also in East New Jersey. In 1745 they numbered 3,557, while in West New Jersey they numbered 6,079. See J. R. Sypher and E. A. Apgar: *History of New Jersey . . .* (Philadelphia, 1871), p. 264.

[44] For the Anglicans see N. R. Burr: *The Anglican Church in New Jersey* (Philadelphia, 1954), pp. 87–115. For the turning of the New Jersey Congregational churches to the Presbyterian form of organization and discipline in the seventeenth and eighteenth centuries and the problems created see T. J. Wertenbaker: *The Founding of American Civilization: The Middle Colonies* (New York, 1938), pp. 171–83.

single capital. The General Assembly met alternately at Perth Amboy on the Eastern Shore and at Burlington on the Delaware. There was, moreover, a balance between the two sections. In each there were five counties and one so-called "city." Each county enjoyed two representatives and each city the same number in the General Assembly of twenty-four members.[45] The influence of ideals maintained by both the Presbyterian and the Quaker groups had resulted in the development of a powerful spirit of individualism among the people. This spirit was heightened by the appearance, especially in northern New Jersey in the 1740's, of large numbers of Ulstermen, who brought their Presbyterianism with them from Ireland along with a certain attitude toward government typical of border peoples.

The history of New Jersey at mid-century illustrates how a people may live in the midst of economic prosperity and yet under political conditions that border on anarchy, with a government powerless to function in the direction of establishing even the semblance of law and order. The explanation lies in the temporary break-down of all political authority when an effort was made to maintain a land policy consistent with strict legal rights in the face of widespread and determined opposition to it.[46]

Although New Jersey had been a royal province since 1702, it was a peculiar one in that all ungranted lands within its borders belonged, not to the Crown, but rather to those who were the Proprietors (or their heirs or assigns), either of East New Jersey or of West New Jersey at the time of the transference of the government.[47] These two proprietary groups and their patentees became

---

[45] In 1750 in East New Jersey there were the city of Perth Amboy and the counties of Bergen, Essex, Middlesex, Somerset, and Monmouth; in West New Jersey there were the city of Burlington and the counties of Hunterdon, Burlington, Gloucester, Salem, and Cape May.

The law of 1705, still in effect in 1750, provided that to exercise the franchise an elector must be a freeholder possessing at least 100 acres of land or £50 value of personal and real estate. This also was interpreted to include "Inhabitant Householders." Representatives in the Assembly were to possess 1,000 acres of land or £500 value in lands and personal property. For the New Jersey law of 1705 see *Statutes of New Jersey* (Bradford edition of 1717), p. 5; see also A. E. McKinley: *The Suffrage Franchise in the Thirteen English Colonies* (Philadelphia, 1905), pp. 254–5, and especially R. C. McCormick: *History of Voting in New Jersey . . . 1664–1911* (New Brunswick, N.J., 1953).

[46] E. J. Fisher: *op. cit.*, pp. 171–206.

[47] *Ibid.*, p. 171.

involved in the most serious difficulties. New Jersey lands had from time to time been surveyed, transferred by patent to others, and subsequently subdivided. Individual proprietors such as James Alexander, the Surveyor General, and Chief Justice Robert Hunter Morris had also received important concessions. The anti-proprietorial groups asserted that the disposal of the land had been done in a manner in East New Jersey that involved many irregularities and led to confusion in land titles and boundaries.[48]

Meanwhile the Ulstermen were pouring into the vacant northern portion of the province, many of them coming without invitation and settling down without invitation. When once they had squatted on land, it was a problem of the greatest difficulty to persuade them to leave. In resisting the claims of the Proprietors of East New Jersey they would frequently secure Indian deeds. The influence of the presence and example of these people upon those already living within the province was indubitably profound. It became the general practice for families to squat upon any favourable body of land in defiance of the legal rights involved and to resist efforts at removal.

The year 1745 saw the beginnings of a decade of violence as the result of efforts of the Proprietors to survey and allot certain of their lands occupied by intruders in the "Van Gesin" and "Horseneck" purchases in upper Essex County not far from Newark.[49] When one of the leaders among the occupiers was placed in the Newark gaol to await trial he was rescued by his fellows, who, after making a breach in the wall of the jail, most thoughtfully mended it again before dispersing.

A large part, if not most, of the settled population of New Jersey, including the townships settled by New England people, were expected to pay rentals for their lands. These people expressed an intense sympathy with the squatters and other intruders openly resisting the proprietorial claims. Apparently they were encouraged in this attitude by many of the local magistrates. In face of the situa-

---

[48] Petition of the General Assembly of October 19, 1749, Board of Trade *Journal, 1749–1753,* p. 69, and *Acts of the Privy Council, Col. Ser., Unbound Papers,* p. 277.

[49] For an account of the activities of the Proprietors of East New Jersey, see D. McGregor: "The Board of Proprietors of East New Jersey," New Jersey Historical Society *Proceedings,* n.s., VII, 177–95.

tion, the arm of the law was paralyzed. The anti-proprietorial elements were described in 1748 as "a Torrent bearing down all before them, & Trampling on all Law, & authority."[50] According to certain depositions made in 1749, about one third of the people of Essex County were rioters and a much larger number were "favourers" of them. With most of the people of the county related either by blood or marriage to at least some one of the disaffected, it was utterly impossible to find a jury that could be depended upon to stand for impartial justice. Among the rioters themselves, three fifths, it was estimated, held their lands by patents and surveys under the Proprietors, one fifth had squatted upon lands and later acquired Indian deeds, while the remaining fifth had no pretence whatsoever to any land and made a living by plundering the timber from the property of others.[51]

All that was needed, apparently, to bring together a New Jersey mob numbered by hundreds was for information to be spread among the resisters to proprietorial claims that one or more of their number was within the clutches of the law. Although none was imprisoned at Perth Amboy, on one occasion a great body of rioters, under the impression that some of their sympathizers were imprisoned there, entered that seaport, broke open the gaol, and loosed all prisoners. Between 1745 and 1748 twenty riots are recorded, and many occurred subsequently.[52]

From Essex County the uprising against the Proprietors spread northward into Bergen, south to Middlesex, and westward to Morris, Somerset, and Hunterdon counties, thus including, finally, all of the northern part of the province. In Hunterdon County, the West Jersey Society, possessed of patents in East New Jersey as well as in West New Jersey, had one tract of 100,000 acres under cultivation as a result of numerous lease assignments. In 1735 the tenants living upon this tract had numbered but one hundred, yet by 1745 there

---

[50] "Journal of the Provincial Council," December 1, 1748, New Jersey Archives, 1st ser., XVI, 15–19.

[51] For the depositions of officials respecting the riots see ibid., 1st ser., XVI, 192–3.

[52] For an extended report of the quit-rent riots see Acts of the Privy Council, Col. Ser., Unbound Papers, pp. 274–5, 277–93, 310, 312, 315; see also B. W. Bond: The Quit-Rent System (New Haven & London, 1919), pp. 105–8, and H. L. Osgood: The American Colonies in the Eighteenth Century (4 vols., New York, 1924), IV, 24–31.

were several times that number. Although previously the lessees had been quiet and attentive to their obligations, they now joined with the Essex County rioters and refused not only the payment of rentals but also any recognition of their landlords. In Morris County the lands belonging to the Penn family were brazenly stripped of valuable timber in spite of everything that the family's representatives could do, including appeals to the local authorities. Hardly less serious was the situation in the other counties just mentioned.

In the course of time the rioters, to protect their interests, finally organized themselves after a fashion, took common oaths to uphold what they chose to call their rights, and appointed committees empowered to levy upon the members and to do all things necessary to defeat the demands of the Proprietors. At first they urged, in defence of their lawless acts, that frauds and abuses had been committed by the Proprietors or their patentees whereby the same lands had been sold to people two or three times, thus imposing upon multitudes of innocent people.[53] The proprietorial groups denied this and challenged their opponents to prove that more than six people had ever been imposed upon since the year 1665 by any wilful or inadvertent duplication of grants, insisting that they had always stood ready to grant compensation to those who had received injury.

In the midst of the struggle over New Jersey land rights, an appeal was made to the natural rights of man to vindicate the claims of the squatters. Declared a correspondent (manifestly a resident of New Jersey) in the June 9, 1746, issue of the *New York Weekly Post-Boy:*

"No man is naturally intitled to a greater Proportion of the Earth than another; but tho' it was made for the equal Use of all, it may nevertheless be appropriated by every Individual. This is done by

---

[53] This argument was used particularly with respect to the Elizabethtown Purchase and the Monmouth Purchase, which had been secured by settlers from Governor Nicolls before he learned of James, Duke of York's deed of lease and release to Berkeley and Carteret. See E. P. Tanner: *The Province of New Jersey, 1664–1738,* pp. 80–95; E. F. Hatfield: *History of Elizabeth, New Jersey . . .* (New York, 1868), p. 372; and E. J. Fisher: *New Jersey as a Royal Province,* pp. 171–209. In defence of the rights of the East New Jersey Proprietors, James Alexander drew up in 1746 a most elaborate bill in chancery directed against the "Elizabeth-Town clinker Lot Right Men," while William Livingston and William Smith, as counsel for Elizabeth, prepared an answer in 1751.

the Improvement of any Part of it lying vacant, which is thereupon distinguished from the great common of Nature, and made the Property of that Man, who bestowed his Labour on it; from whom it cannot afterwards be taken, without breaking thro' the Rules of natural Justice; for thereby he would be actually deprived of the Fruits of his Industry."

Later on in the course of the conflict, it is interesting to note, the claims of Connecticut to the northern portion of New Jersey were actually set up by the anti-proprietorial group when a number of the rioters in Hunterdon County and their sympathizers signed a memorial to the government of this New England colony praying that they and their lands should be taken under its protection and that a Connecticut county be created in those parts.[54] But the people of Connecticut had on foot much more ambitious plans than meddling with a situation that offered few prospects of large gains. Their eyes were turned in the direction of northern Pennsylvania.

It was not until 1755, in the midst of war, that the resisters lost at least some confidence in their ability to make good their pretensions. In that year, with the coming of the British regulars to North America and the subsequent spreading of a rumour that after these troops had finished with the French and Indians they would carry fire and sword into northern New Jersey and thus reduce the country to peace, many rioters threw themselves upon the mercy of the court.[55] It may be added that the judges treated them with unexampled leniency, at most fining them only small sums of money while requiring them to furnish recognizances for their future good behaviour. Others, feeling a greater confidence in their position, banded together to secure a favourable decision from the provincial court of chancery.[56]

Adding to the confusion in New Jersey was the controversy with

---

[54] *New Jersey Archives,* 1st ser., XVI, 545–6, 552–5. It is of interest that Thomas Fitch, who in 1751 was Deputy Governor of Connecticut, had in 1744 been the legal adviser of the Elizabethtown rioters. E. J. Fisher: *op. cit.,* p. 184.

[55] For the use of British regulars to put down land rioters in Dutchess County, New York, in 1766 see *Correspondence of General Thomas Gage, . . . 1763–1775* (ed. C. E. Carter, 2 vols., New Haven & London, 1931–4), I, 96–9, 107–8.

[56] E. J. Fisher: *op. cit.,* pp. 204–9. For an illuminating study on the strong democratic tendencies in eighteenth-century New Jersey see R. B. Morris: "Spotlight on the Plowmen of the Jersies," New Jersey Historical Society *Proceedings,* LXVII, 106–23.

New York over the boundary between the two provinces. While this dispute was of long standing, by the 1740's it had reached an acute stage that led to clashes between settlers of the borderland, each setting forth claims based upon conflicting grants of land. A proper solution of the problem was a matter of the most vital importance to New Jersey; for to admit the claims of Lieutenant Governor de Lancey of New York meant the loss of much of the most valuable land. Under the terms of the New Jersey grant made to Carteret and Berkeley in 1664, it was stated that the northern boundary should be as far as the "northernmost branch of the said Bay or River of Delaware, which is in forty-one degrees and forty minutes of latitude, and crosseth over thence in a strait line to Hudson's River in forty-one degrees of latitude."[57]

What did this grant mean? The New York government emphasized the word "Bay," seeking to ignore the stated latitude, which would carry the line beyond Delaware Bay well up the course of the Delaware River; New Jersey stressed the specific latitude and explained away the previously mentioned term. While a somewhat informal understanding was reached in 1684 by Governor Dongan and Deputy Governor Lawrie, no definite formal solution of the problem was found. In 1719, as the result of an agreement between the two provinces, a line was run which, however, was not accepted by the Council of New York by reason of the opposition of the patentees of some of vast land grants in what was then considered to be parts of Ulster and Orange counties, New York. In vain the Proprietors of East New Jersey, and those who had received allotments from them for lands in this disputed region, sought a settlement of the matter. Apparently owing to the powerful influence exerted in London by the great New York land magnates, especially the de Lancey family, concerned in the "great Minisink Patent" — the grant of which was so worded as to extend far into New Jersey — for many years nothing further was done. This policy of delay was followed in spite of the fact that the Proprietors of East New Jersey stood ready to assume half of the total cost of making a definite survey. At last, in the year 1748, the General Assembly of New

---

[57] For the Carteret-Berkeley grant see Aaron Leaming and Jacob Spicer: *Grants, Concessions, and Original Constitutions of New Jersey* (Somerville, N.J., 1881), pp. 8–11.

Jersey passed a law providing for the running of the line *ex parte* in case New York would not agree to participate. This act was submitted for the sanction of the Crown, but, despite an extended hearing before the Board of Trade, failed to secure the royal approval.[58]

The imperativeness of the situation now demanded an agreement. Hundreds of families were moving into the northwest part of New Jersey and settling upon lands in the very region subject to dispute. This movement brought dismay to those who had established themselves there under the New York patents. Many New Yorkers, losing faith in the ability of their government to protect their interests, now turned to the authorities in Connecticut, as did the Hunterdon County inhabitants of New Jersey. In 1751 a memorial in their behalf came before the Connecticut General Assembly asking for a grant "to Any or All the lands they now have by Virtue of the Royall Charter that Lyeth to the Westward of Hudson's River. . . ."[59] One outcome was the organization of the so-called Delaware Company by Connecticut men to prosecute the westward claims of their colony. While most of the activities of this company were concerned with lands to the westward of the Delaware River, it should be mentioned here that late in 1754 an Indian deed was secured to a great body of land to the eastward of the Delaware — not, however, in Orange County, the boundaries of which were the centre of dispute between New York and New Jersey, but in Ulster County, New York, just south of the great Hardenburgh Patent.[60] Thus, little relief for New Yorkers was obtained by this interesting appeal to Connecticut.

In order to provide the New Jersey people in the disputed region with a local government, there was erected in 1753 out of the older County of Morris, the new County of Sussex, the magistrates of which determined to defend the rights of New Jersey men against the hostile acts of the New York patentees. The following year

---

[58] E. J. Fisher: *op. cit.*, pp. 210–39; *Acts of the Privy Council, Cor. Ser., 1745–1766*, p. 214.

[59] This memorial and the report of the committee of the Assembly upon it are printed in *The Susquehannah Company Papers* (ed. J. P. Boyd, 4 vols., Wilkes-Barre, Pa., 1934), I, 3–5.

[60] For the deed of the Delaware Indians to the Delaware Company see *ibid.*, I, 196–200.

witnessed a series of border disturbances in which the New Yorkers seem to have fared second best.[61]

It then became apparent that the issue must be settled without delay. In 1754 the New York Assembly passed an act calling upon the Privy Council to terminate the controversy. Instead, that body repealed the act the following year, assigning as their reason that the procedure involved was contrary to constant practice. They stated that questions of disputed colonial boundaries had never been determined in the first instance by the Crown, as the bill called for, but by commissions which, of course, reserved the right of appeal to the King in Council. The act was also obnoxious, they ruled, since it sought to determine, to some extent at least, the rights of certain of the New York patentees.[62] In place of the act the Privy Council recommended that a commission be appointed, in line with the wishes of the East New Jersey Proprietors. However, not until 1764 did the Crown approve the acts of the two provincial legislatures providing for such a commission and move to appoint fifteen eminent colonials to it.[63] The decision of the commission was finally announced late in 1769 and was ratified by the agents of the two provinces under the provision that the rights of the occupants of lands on either side of the line should be confirmed.[64] In the main the claims of New Jersey were vindicated.

If anything more than the disputes over lands and boundaries were needed to ensure political chaos in New Jersey in the year 1750, this was supplied by the deadlock between the executive and legislative branches of the provincial government. Underneath the cloak of formal courtesy which usually characterized the relations of the Governor and the Assembly, there had long been a confirmed, if latent, hostility, which occasionally came to the surface in bitter

---

[61] For James Alexander's letter to Governor Belcher, dated February 2, 1754, giving an account of disturbances between the people of New York and New Jersey in the disputed area, see *New Jersey Archives*, 1st ser., XVI, 435–9.

[62] The Act of 1754 was entitled "An Act for submitting the Controversy between the Colonys of New York and New Jersey relating to the Partition between the said Colonys to the final determination of His Majesty." See *Acts of the Privy Council, Col. Ser., 1745–1766*, pp. 301–2.

[63] *Ibid.*, pp. 214, 301, 686–7.

[64] W. A. Whitehead: *Northern Boundary Line: The Circumstances Leading to the Establishment in 1769 of the Northern Boundary Line between New Jersey and New York* (New Jersey Historical Society *Proceedings*, VIII); see also E. J. Fisher: *op. cit.*, pp. 210–39.

denunciations and equally cutting retorts. Much of this friction was doubtless caused by an inherited attitude of the people of New Jersey toward their executives. Previous to 1738, and after the surrender of all political authority by the proprietorial groups in 1702, the Governor of New York had also been commissioned to govern New Jersey. Most of these itinerant executives were intensely unpopular. Consequently, there were repeated and insistent demands for a separate establishment with simultaneous assurances to the home government by the General Assembly that the colony would provide liberal support for a resident Governor.

It had been as a result of these demands that the native-born colonial Lewis Morris had been so commissioned. It was apparently hoped that this would be a happy choice, for, as has been mentioned previously, Morris possessed a great political experience in the affairs of both New Jersey and New York. In the Council of the former he had opposed the notorious Lord Cornbury, and, as the Chief Justice in the latter, he had taken a popular stand in the struggle against Governor Cosby. Morris, distinctly the aristocrat with great landed interests, was confirmed in what might be called the official point of view on all public issues. He was also extremely sceptical of the moral and intellectual capacity of the people among whom he was living to participate in public affairs, although he had no doubts as to the determination of their representatives to control the provincial government. The year after taking over the administration he had felt impelled to declare that there was "much Insincerity and Ignorance among the people . . . with so rooted a Jealousy of their Governours & . . . an Inclination in the meanest of the people (who are the majority & whose votes make the assembly) to have the sole direction of all the affairs of the government. . . ."[65]

The first and only outburst of popularity that Morris enjoyed died away when he indicated his disappointment that the Assembly had provided only half the amount of support he had every reason to anticipate. Before his administration closed with his death in 1746, his relations with the popular branch of the legislature had become so strained — particularly over the problem of the Gover-

---

[65] Governor Morris to Sir Charles Wager, May 10, 1739, *Papers of Governor Lewis Morris*, pp. 40–1.

nor's salary and the previously considered question of the printing of additional bills of credit for loans — that the Assembly refused to appropriate money for his office. Ultimately, at the time of his widow's application that the back salary owing him be paid to her, it even denied that New Jersey was under the slightest obligation to his estate.[66]

As for Governor Jonathan Belcher,[67] he sought to avoid his predecessor's difficulties and to win the confidence and favour of the popular branch of the legislature, by his nominations to the Council, by his attitude toward money bills, and by other means.[68] His position was one of great delicacy. In the midst of the land riots he was impelled to apply to the Assembly for the funds necessary to enlist soldiers who, he felt, could at least be counted upon to guard the jails from the attacks of the mobs. The General Assembly outwardly condemned the violent conduct of the squatters and other disturbers of the peace. At the same time they could not be persuaded to make any appropriation except upon a basis that the upper chamber, dominated by the proprietorial interests, considered to be in plain violation of the Governor's royal instructions concerning the taxation of unprofitable lands. Belcher, although willing to run the risk of approving the Assembly's bill in the emergency, was helpless during this period. In fact, the Council, dominated by James Alexander and Robert Hunter Morris, had grasped the whip hand and, supported by the general attitude of the home government toward New Jersey affairs, continued to exercise an unprecedented influence in the affairs of the colony for some years. As a

---

[66] For the House of Assembly's defence of its conduct see the *New Jersey Archives*, 1st ser., XVI, 149–56. The action of the Assembly in refusing to pay Morris's salary as Governor unless he consented to particular measures not connected with his salary is unique in New Jersey history. According to Professor Labaree, only three similar cases occurred in the American colonies in the eighteenth century. See L. W. Labaree: *Royal Government in America* (New Haven, 1930), pp. 343–4.

[67] Belcher's commission is identical with that given to his predecessor, Morris, outside of the salutation. For the Morris commission see *New Jersey Archives*, 1st ser., VI, 2–15. The Belcher papers covering the period of his administration of New Jersey from 1747 to 1757 are to be found in *ibid.*, 1st ser., Vols. VII and VIII. John Hamilton and John Reading were successively in charge, as President of the Council, before Belcher appeared.

[68] The franchise requirements in New Jersey were liberal. In the counties one had to possess a freehold of 100 acres of land or a personal estate valued at £50; in the towns one had to be an "inhabitant householder." See R. P. McCormick; *The History of Voting in New Jersey* . . . , pp. 40, 60–2.

result of this deadlock, the provincial treasury was destined to remain empty for years and the provincial authority to be held up to mockery.

In the course of this struggle, Governor Belcher was accused of seeking to win favour with the anti-proprietorial group by his recommendation of William Morris of Hunterdon County to a seat in the provincial Council. This Morris, according to Robert Hunter Morris when testifying before the Board of Trade in 1750, was not only identified with the rioters but also had spoken publicly in their favour on several occasions and was connected with a group in the General Assembly which had "endeavoured to pull down or trample upon the authority of the Crown."[69] Later the Governor recommended Samuel Smith, Clerk of the House of Representatives, for another place on the Council. He, too, was accused before the Board of being sympathetic to the resisters and at the same time it was charged that his "family were the most active persons concerned in that faction."[70] As a result, the Lords Commissioners ordered the drafting of a letter reprimanding Belcher for nominating persons of that type for such responsible posts. Further, upon the advice of Morris, Chief Justice of the Supreme Court of the province and perhaps Belcher's most vigorous opponent on the Council, the Board proceeded in 1751 to recommend that mandamuses to seats in the Council be granted to David Ogden and to Lewis Morris Ashfield, grandson of Lewis Morris, the late Governor, both of whom were agreeable to the great proprietorial interests.[71] All this was in the nature of a sharp rebuke to the Governor who, in spite of his extreme reluctance to seat Ashfield, was compelled to do so even after a delay of some two years.[72]

Such were the Jerseys of the ploughmen and their government in the middle of the eighteenth century.

---

[69] *New Jersey Archives*, 1st ser., XVI, 91 and 357; Board of Trade *Journal, 1749–1753*, p. 153.

[70] *Ibid., 1749–1753*, p. 174.

[71] *Acts of the Privy Council, Col. Ser., 1745–1766*, p. 791.

[72] *New Jersey Archives*, 1st ser., XVI, 315–17, 324–7, 346–7, 365, 385, 402.

CHAPTER VII

The New World Paradise
of the Sects

THE proprietary colony of Pennsylvania at this period may be called truly the New World paradise of Europe's persecuted sects. "Coming to speak of Pennsylvania," declared Gottlieb Mittelberger, in describing his journey to the province in the year 1750,

> "that colony possesses great liberties above all other English colonies, inasmuch as all religious sects are tolerated there. We find there Lutherans, Reformed, Catholics, Quakers, Mennonites or Anabaptists, Herrnhuters or Moravian Brethren, Pietists, Seventh Day Baptists, Dunkers, Presbyterians, Newborn, Freemasons, Separatists, Freethinkers, Jews, Mohammedans, Pagans, Negroes and Indians. The Evangelicals and Reformed, however, are in the majority. But there are many hundred unbaptized souls there that do not even wish to be baptized."[1]

---

[1] See his *Journey to Pennsylvania in the year 1750 and Return to Germany in the year 1754* (translated by Carl T. Eben, Philadelphia, 1898), pp. 54–5. Dr. William Smith, in writing to Archbishop Secker on November 27, 1759, gave the relative strength of various religious groups in Pennsylvania. The Presbyterians he credits with 55,000, the Quakers with 50,000, the Lutherans with 40,000, the Reformed and German pietistic groups each with 30,000, the Church of England with 25,000, Roman Catholics, English, Irish, and German with 10,000. See G. S. Klett: *Presbyterians in Colonial Pennsylvania* (Philadelphia & London, 1937), p. 35 n.

Mittelberger then described the trials of a preacher of the gospel in this land of liberty. Most preachers, he asserted, were hired by the year like the cowherds in Germany, and the most exemplary were often "reviled, insulted, and scoffed at like the Jews, by the young and old especially in the country. I would, therefore," he affirmed, "rather perform the meanest herdsman's duties in Germany than be a preacher in Pennsylvania. Such unheard-of rudeness and wickedness spring from the excessive liberties of the land, and from the blind zeal of the many sects. . . . There is a saying in that country: Pennsylvania is the heaven of the farmers, the paradise of the mechanics, and the hell of the officials and preachers."[2]

Out of a population estimated at between 200,000 and 300,000[3] it was asserted in 1755 that one half were Germans and that of the remainder some two fifths were Ulster Presbyterians, two fifths were Quakers, and the rest, except for a few Baptists, were members of the Anglican Church.[4] These figures are remarkable as indicative of the numerical but not the political submergence of the Quaker group, which as late as 1721 still constituted, it was estimated, four fifths of the entire population.[5]

---

[2] Gottlieb Mittelberger: op. cit., p. 63. Mittelberger further illustrates the freedom in religious matters which existed at this period in Pennsylvania. "I was well acquainted with an old German neighbour, who had been a Lutheran, but had rebaptized himself in a running water; some time afterwards he circumcised himself and believed only in the Old Testament; finally, however, shortly before his death, he baptized himself again by sprinkling water upon his head" (ibid., p. 110).

[3] It was given as upwards of 300,000 in 1755 by Governor Morris in a letter to General Braddock. Papers of the Governors, 1747–1759, Pennsylvania Archives, 4th ser. (ed. G. E. Reed, Harrisburg, 1900), II, p. 373. This figure seems too high. See C. A. Herrick: White Servitude in Pennsylvania (Philadelphia, 1926), pp. 179–80, for various estimates; also Greene and Harrington: American Population before . . . 1790 (New York, 1932), p. 115.

[4] William P. Smith, D.D.: A Brief State of the Province of Pennsylvania . . . (2nd edn., London, 1755), p. 4; W. J. Mann: Life and Times of Henry Melchior Muhlenberg (2nd edn., Philadelphia, 1888), Chap. 20.

[5] Representation of the Board of Trade upon the State of His Majesty's Plantations, September 8, 1721. Shelburne Papers, 45:236, Clements Library.

The extraordinary wealth of material available on the numerous religious groups and sects in this period of Pennsylvania history can best be indicated by reference to N. B. Wilkinson's Bibliography of Pennsylvania History (2nd edn., Harrisburg, 1957), pp. 58–89, 127, 641–90. Of the leading religious groups in Pennsylvania in the eighteenth century, for the Quakers see Rufus Jones: The Quakers in the American Colonies (London, 1911) and his Later Periods of Quakerism (2 vols., New York, 1921); for the Anglicans see the articles by Nelson Burr, F. J. Klingberg, and L. C. Washburn in the Historical Magazine of the Protestant Episcopal Church, IV, VII, VIII, XVI; for the Lutherans, Robert Fortenbaugh: Development of . . . the

The inundation of German-speaking peoples, which had its beginning toward the end of the seventeenth century, when the modest stream of immigration widened gradually into a flood, is one of the most notable aspects of American colonial history.[6] While this flood spread itself rather widely, it had its greatest effects upon the civilization of provincial Pennsylvania and was at its height in the period under consideration. The following brief notice in the *Pennsylvania Journal* for December 6, 1750, tells the story:

> "Capt. Hasselwood from Holland arrived since our last [issue], which makes the fourteenth vessel arrived from Holland this year in which we brought over 4317 Germans."[7]

Lutheran Church (Philadelphia, 1926) and C. H. Glatfelter: *The Colonial Pennsylvania German Lutheran and Reformed Clergymen* (Johns Hopkins Doctoral Dissertation, 1952); for the Reformed, J. W. Beardslee: *The Church in Delaware and Pennsylvania* (New York, 1928) and H. M. J. Klein: *History . . . of the Reformed Church* (Lancaster, 1943); for the Evangelicals, R. W. Albright: *History of the Evangelical Church* (New Berlin, Pa., 1942); for the Presbyterians, G. S. Klett: *Presbyterians in Colonial Pennsylvania* (Philadelphia & London, 1937); for the Baptists, R. E. E. Harkness: "Early Relations of Baptists and Quakers," *Church History*, II, 227–42; for the Catholics, Sister Marie Blanche: "The Catholic Church in Colonial Pennsylvania," *Pennsylvania History*, III, 240–58, IV, 32–46; for the Moravians, various *Transactions of the Moravian Historical Society*, especially Vol. V, J. W. Jordan: *Moravian Immigration to Pennsylvania, 1734–1767*, pp. 51–90; and Vol. VI, J. T. Hamilton: *History of . . . the Moravian Church . . .*; for the Jews, Miriam K. Freund: *Jewish Merchants in Colonial America* (New York, 1939), and Edwin Wolf, Jr. and Maxwell Whiteman: *History of the Jews of Philadelphia . . .* (Philadelphia, 1957); for the Mennonites, C. H. Smith: *The Mennonite Immigration . . . in the Eighteenth Century* (Norristown, 1929); for the Amish, C. G. Bachman: *The Older Order Amish . . .* (Norristown, 1942); for the smaller German sects, G. N. Falkenstein: *The German Baptist Brethren or Dunkers . . .*, Pennsylvania German Society *Proceedings*, IV (Lancaster, 1900), J. F. Sachse; *The German Pietists of Provincial Pennsylvania* (Philadelphia, 1895), H. W. Kriebel: *The Schwenkfelders in Pennsylvania* (Lancaster, 1904); and, in general, Lucy F. Bittinger: *German Religious Life in Colonial Times* (Philadelphia, 1906), and I. D. Rupp: "Defunct German Sects in Pennsylvania" in *Notes and Queries . . .* Annual Volume, 1896 (ed. W. H. Egle, Harrisburg, 1897), pp. 166–70, 172–4, 177–9.

[6] In this connection see I. D. Rupp: *Collection of Thirty Thousand Names of Immigrants in Pennsylvania, 1727–1776* (Philadelphia, 1876) and S. B. Strassburger and W. J. Hinke: *Pennsylvania German Pioneers* (Pennsylvania German Society *Proceedings*, XLII–XLIV, Part I), giving the original lists of arrivals in the port of Philadelphia from 1727 to 1775. Also consult Lucy F. Bittinger: *The Germans in Colonial Times* (Philadelphia & London, 1901); A. B. Faust: *The German Element in the United States* (2 vols., Boston & New York, 1909); F. R. Diffenderfer: *The German Immigration into Pennsylvania through the Port of Philadelphia, 1700–1775* (Pennsylvania German Society *Proceedings*, X); and J. F. Sachse: *The German Sectarians of Pennsylvania, 1708–1800* (2 vols., Philadelphia, 1899–1900).

[7] See also Gottlieb Mittelberger: *Journey to Pennsylvania*, p. 37, and E. R. Diffenderfer: *op. cit.*, Part II: *The Redemptioners*, pp. 45, 207.

Indeed, it would appear that for years an average of something over eighteen ships came each autumn to the port of Philadelphia loaded with these precious cargoes.[8] It is asserted that from 1750 to 1754 — that is, in a period of some four years — at least 25,000 Germans were brought to the province, while numbers went directly to other plantations, especially to Maryland, the Carolinas, and Nova Scotia.[9] In view of the indescribable hardships sustained by many of the newcomers in attempting to get a footing in the New World, reports of which inevitably reached Germany, one is impressed with the deep-lying dissatisfaction with conditions at home which led so many, in spite of at least some knowledge of the hazards involved, to risk family, freedom, and even life itself for the prospect of expatriation and existence under new conditions.[10]

In the case of the *Unitas Fratrum* or Moravian Brethren, who in the early 1740's established the town of Bethlehem, it appears that numerous edicts had been launched against them by various authorities in Europe, including the King of Prussia, the Tsarina of Russia, the King of Denmark, the Duke of Gotha, and the city of Basel in Switzerland.[11] Even the Elector of Hanover, who was also the King of England, issued a proclamation against them which declared, among other things: "We therefore Order that all Herrenhutter Books which are already Known as their Hymn Book and the Sermons of the Count Zintzendorff, and all other that for the future may be printed, shall not be tolerated in our Dominions." The people were warned not only to give up their books but also to bear in mind that the Ordinance of 1734 permitting private devotions did not give permission to meet with such as were the Moravians.[12] However, while not tolerated by George, acting as Elector of Han-

---

[8] R. B. Strassberger and W. J. Hinke: *op. cit.*, I, xxix. From 1727 to 1755, 233 of these ships came. *Ibid.*, I, xlvii–lii.

[9] Mittelberger: *op. cit.*, pp. 37–8; see also F. R. Diffenderfer: *op. cit.*, II, 209; Strassberger and Hinke: *op. cit.*, I, 1–676, for lists of German immigrants for the years 1727–54.

[10] For a discussion of conditions that led to German emigration in the eighteenth century see K. F. Geiser: *Redemptioners and Indentured Servants in . . . Pennsylvania* (Supplement to *Yale Review*, X, New Haven, 1901), Chap. 2. See also A. B. Faust: *op. cit.*, I, 53–72; F. R. Diffenderfer: *op. cit.*, II, 14–20; and Daniel Häberle: *Auswanderung und Koloniegründunzen der Pfälzer im 18, Jahrhundert* (Kaiserlautern, 1909).

[11] See the *Pennsylvania Journal* for December 20, 1750.

[12] *Ibid.*

over, this kindly people with pacifistic principles were received with open arms by the same George in his role of King of England. Parliament, in fact, passed a special act at this period which guaranteed the Moravians an asylum,[13] with the result that many of them joyfully seized the opportunity and in coming to America became loyal and valuable subjects whose influence with the Indians was as great as it was wholesome. Sailing to America in ships chartered expressly for them, they came with a full knowledge of what conditions they could anticipate and with the way prepared in advance by their leaders. They therefore suffered comparatively little hardship.[14]

On the other hand, many thousands of distressed Germans, quite ignorant of the risks involved, were lured from their homes by agents of the Dutch "man-stealers," known as Newlanders, without adequate provision for establishing themselves independently. The music master Mittelberger declared that when in 1754 he was about to return to Württemberg (Würtemberg) from Pennsylvania, "many Würtembergers, Durlachers and Palatines, of whom there are a great number there who repent and regret it while they live that they left their native country, implored me with tears and uplifted hands, and even in the name of God, to make this misery and sorrow known in Germany, so that not only the common people, but even princes and lords, might learn how they fared. . . ."[15]

It is hard to realize today how great an effort it took to make the trip from the region of the upper Rhine, where many of those prospective emigrants were living, to the port of Philadelphia. The weary, heartbreaking journey frequently lasted from about the first of May to the end of October. Traveling from Heilbronn to Rotterdam by Rhine boat took from four to six weeks because of the thirty-six custom-houses between those two towns. After arrival in Holland there was a month's or six weeks' delay. In passing from

---

[13] 22 Geo. II, c. 30, "An Act for encouraging People known by the Name of Unitas Fratrum or United Brethren, to settle in his Majesty's Colonies in America." For the history of the passage of the act of 1749 see J. T. Hamilton: *A History of the . . . Moravian Church . . . during the Eighteenth and Nineteenth Centuries, Transactions of the Moravian Historical Society*, VI (Bethlehem, Pa., 1900), pp. 135–7.

[14] *Transactions of the Moravian Historical Society* (Nazareth, Pa., 1876), I, 33–50, 107–24.

[15] Mittelberger: *op. cit.*, p. 16.

Holland to England, if the winds were contrary, another month could be consumed. In addition, two weeks might be spent at some English port, generally at the Isle of Wight, before the ship was examined and the customs duties were paid. Finally the long voyage began, probably to last from six to twelve weeks.

Under modern conditions such a summer's trip, in spite of its length, might be far from unpleasant; but those emigrant ships were the scenes of grim tragedy. On a two-hundred-ton vessel there might be four hundred passengers together with a heavy cargo of household goods and farm implements.[16] Each individual received a place scarcely two feet wide and six feet long for sleeping quarters. There was a total absence of privacy. The drinking water was black, thick, and likely to be full of worms; the ship biscuits were frequently rotten and alive with creatures; there were indescribable stenches. Scurvy and other loathsome diseases accompanied starvation and thirst, and appalling scenes of death followed. Few women in confinement, so it was asserted, escaped with their lives. The crews did not always wait for death. "One day, just as we had a heavy gale," Mittelberger recorded sadly, "a woman in our ship, who was to give birth and could not . . . under the circumstances, was pushed through a loop-hole [port hole] in the ship and dropped into the sea, because she was far in the rear of the ship and could not be brought forward!" He further declared: "Children from 1 to 7 years rarely survive the voyage; . . . I witnessed such misery in no less than 32 children on our ship, all of whom were thrown into the sea."[17] The despair of the disillusioned people caught

---

[16] The average number of passengers on a vessel of 200 tons burden was, according to Diffenderfer, 300. See *German Immigration into Pennsylvania,* p. 49. Not until the year 1750 did the Pennsylvania Assembly act to limit the number of people that could be crowded into an immigrant ship. For the act of 1750 see *Statutes at Large of Pennsylvania from 1682 to 1801* (ed. J. T. Mitchell and H. Flanders, 17 vols., Harrisburg, 1896–1915), V, 94–7; C. A. Herrick: *op. cit.,* pp. 161–3. The act was highly commended by the Board of Trade. See *Acts of the Privy Council, Col. Ser., 1745–1766,* pp. 115–16.

[17] Mittelberger: *op. cit.,* p. 23. For shipboard diseases on emigrant ships see John Duffy: "The Passage to the Colonies," *Mississippi Valley Historical Review,* XXXVIII, 21–38. For the extent to which immigrants of all nationalities brought with them disease and epidemic and the effects of epidemics upon mid-century life in the colonies see, by the same author: *Epidemics in Colonial America* (Baton Rouge, La., 1953).

When Johann Adam Gruber came to Pennsylvania in 1726 the trip from Rotter-

in these death-traps only too frequently beggars description.[18]

The sight of land raised great joy in the hearts of the survivors, accompanied by prayer and singing. But alas! In most cases the private funds of these Germans were too limited to pay the passage, which for adults varied from £6 to £10 and for children was half of that fare.[19] As a result, they were obliged to permit the ship captain to sell their labour to those who would pay their fares and other expenses incurred during the voyage. This meant that they were bound out to service for periods of from 2 to 7 years, if over 15 years of age, and if from 5 to 15 years of age, till they were 21 years old. Consequently, many parents were compelled to "sell and trade away their children like so many head of cattle."[20]

To the port of debarkation came prosperous, land-owning Englishmen, Dutchmen, and Germans, many from great distances, to purchase their labour. The barter proceeded, usually until the cargo was disposed of, with an adult selling at prices ranging from £10 to £14. On occasions those not thus disposed of were led about the country until a purchaser could be found. "It often happens," declared a witness, "that whole families, husband, wife and children are separated by being sold to different purchasers, especially when they have not paid any part of their passage money."[21] And should a husband or wife die at sea when the ship had made more than half the voyage, the survivor was obliged to serve for the deceased as well as for himself or herself.

The character of the service to which these so-called redemptioners were bound depended upon the inclinations of the master and his occupation. As most of the people of means had estates

---

dam lasted twenty-one weeks. He and his wife lost all their children on the voyage. In a letter to his own parents in Germany Gruber stated: "It was primarily because of my children that I went along on this trip, and I have lost them at sea. Moreover, I had to watch them perish, and, so to speak, die of thirst" (D. F. Durnbaugh: "Johann Adam Gruber, Pennsylvania-German Prophet and Poet," *Pennsylvania Magazine of History and Biography*, LXXXIII, 391).

[18] For an account of the sufferings of the passengers on board the *Love and Unity*, which brought Palatines to Philadelphia in 1731, see F. R. Diffenderfer: *op. cit.*, pp. 62–3. Of over 150 passengers more than 100 perished from starvation.

[19] C. H. Herrick: *op. cit.*, p. 186.

[20] *Ibid.*, pp. 176–7; Peter Kalm: *Travels in North America* (ed. A. B. Benson, 2 vols., New York, 1937), I, 16–17; Gottlieb Mittelberger: *op. cit.*, p. 28.

[21] *Ibid.*

and as much of the land was still wild in a native forest,[22] there was great need for labourers to clear the land or, if it had been cut over, to remove stumps of oak and other hardwoods, brush, and rocks. Therefore, most of the bondsmen were purchased to perform this arduous labour and were occasionally forced to work side by side with Negro slaves, who were fairly numerous within the province. Should they attempt to escape, the penalty for each day's absence, according to Mittelberger, was an additional week, for each week, a month, and for a month, half a year.[23]

It is perhaps surprising that there were many German immigrants who, according to Peter Kalm, had means to pay their passage but who voluntarily entered into indentures for the purpose of gaining knowledge of land-cultivation methods peculiar to the New World and also funds for the purchase of a farm when they should have earned their freedom. Once settled, they soon prospered. As the lands in the region of the lower Delaware River were mostly in private hands and held at a high price, those wanting to secure good but cheap allotments were obliged to look westward and northward. Therefore, as a rule, the German redemptioners left the region where they had laboured as bondsmen to acquire homes along the frontier.[24] Their industry and economical methods and the fruitfulness of the lands in this region generally brought them prosperity.[25]

---

[22] Lewis Evans, writing in 1753 about Pennsylvania, has the following to say: "This Country is all a Wood, where not artificially cleared, but the Timber will not answer the expense of bringing many Miles to Philadelphia. . . ." L. H. Gipson: *Lewis Evans, to which is added Evans' A Brief Account of Pennsylvania* . . . (Philadelphia, 1939), p. 103.

[23] Gottlieb Mittelberger: *op. cit.*, p. 29. The law provided that five days' labour could be exacted for each day the servant was absent without permission. *Pennsylvania Statutes at Large*, II, 54–6. For an extended treatment of this see C. A. Herrick: *White Servitude in Pennsylvania*, Chap. 11, and K. F. Geiser: *Redemptioners and Indentured Servants* . . . *in Pennsylvania*, Chap. 8.

[24] Lewis Evans wrote in 1753: "In Pennsylvania the Land is too dear to be engross'd & yet cheap enough to any Body that will improve it. Our Surveys have been very regular almost all adjoining one another. This keeps up good Neighbourhood, and husbands the Proprietaries Interest. The people are thick settled, have easy intercourse, & need not want Mills, Schools, or Churches" (*op. cit.*, pp. 99–100).

[25] Lewis Evans, in referring to the spread of settlements into the interior, declared that "the Economy of the Germans has since taught us the method of bringing their produce to Market, from the remotest part at a small Expence. The Method is this, ev'ry Farmer in our province almost, has a Waggon of his own, for the Service of his Plantation, & likewise horses for Tillage, in the Spring & Fall of the Year (when it is here a Vacation from farming) they load their Waggon & furnish themselves with

While it is clear that the farmers of Pennsylvania in the middle of the eighteenth century looked to German immigration for the principal supply of indentured labour, during the first quarter of the century reliance was placed chiefly upon the arrival of sufficient numbers of servants from Britain and especially Ireland. In 1729 out of some 6,208 immigrants only 243 apparently were Palatines while 276 were English and Welsh, 43 were native Scots, and the remainder were Ulstermen.[26] By 1750 the relative importance of the supply from Ireland and Great Britain had declined so that out of some 5,317 immigrants who arrived in that year scarcely over 1,000 came from the British Isles; the remainder were from Germany.[27] It would appear that the Ulstermen were less highly esteemed as servants than were the Germans. They were combative and not overindustrious, and it is certain that they were much more inclined to run away from their masters.[28] Whatever may have been their defects as servants, they were hardy, adventurous men who courted the vicissitudes and dangers of the western Pennsylvania frontier.

---

beasts, & provender for the Journey. The Waggon is their Bed, their Inn, their every thing. many of them will come one hundred & fifty miles without spending one Shilling. It is pretty to behold our back Settlements, where the barns are large as pallaces, while the Owners live in log hutts; a sign tho' of thriving Farmers" (*ibid.*, pp. 100–1). For an excellent article on the Germans as Pennsylvania farmers see J. G. Gagliardo: "Germans and Agriculture in Colonial Pennsylvania," *Pennsylvania Magazine of History and Biography*, LXXXIII, 192–218; see also L. A. Bressler: "Agriculture among the Germans in Pennsylvania during the Eighteenth Century," *Pennsylvania History*, XXII, 103–33, and Frederick Klees: *The Pennsylvania Dutch* (New York, 1950).

[26] Writers in the eighteenth century did not distinguish between the native Irish and the Ulstermen. The latter contributed most of the emigrants from Ireland during this period. See Volume I, Revised, of this series, especially pp. 226–30. For the Ulster-Scot see W. F. Dunaway: *The Scotch-Irish of Colonial Pennsylvania* (Chapel Hill, N.C., 1944); G. S. Klett: *The Scotch-Irish in Pennsylvania* (Gettysburg, 1948); H. J. Ford: *The Scotch-Irish in America* (Princeton, 1915); C. A. Hanna: *The Scotch-Irish, or the Scot in North Britain, North Ireland, and North America* (New York & London, 1902); and E. R. R. Green: "Scotch-Irish Emigration, an Imperial Problem," *Western Pennsylvania Historical Magazine*, XXXV, 193–209.

[27] William Douglass: *A Summary, Historical and Political, of the . . . British Settlements in North-America* (2 vols., Boston, 1747–51, 1760 edn.), II, p. 326; C. A. Herrick: *White Servitude in Pennsylvania*, p. 165.

[28] *Ibid.*, pp. 166–7. See also Michel Guillaume Jean de Crèvecoeur: *Letters from an American Farmer* (London, 1782), p. 62. Out of every twelve families that came to America respectively from Germany, Scotland, and Ireland, nine from Germany made a success, seven from Scotland, and four from Ireland. For an interesting analysis of the fate of a miscellaneous group of immigrants from Great Britain see Catherine S. Crary: "The Humble Immigrant and the American Dream: Some Case Histories, 1746–1776," *Mississippi Valley Historical Review*, XLVI, 46–66.

In the course of the eighteenth century they succeeded in establishing some 130 communities within the province and the Lower Counties on the Delaware. In the process of this very significant colonization movement they boldly seized and squatted on lands, asserting that it was "against the laws of God and of nature that so much land should remain idle while so many Christians wanted it to labour on." They then defied those who attempted to eject them and doggedly resisted the payment of quit-rents.[29] As a people they demanded aggressive action against hostile Indians and were bitterly opposed to the pacifistic policies of the Quakers and other noncombatant sects.

A map illustrating the location of the various national and religious groups within Pennsylvania in 1756 would show that of the three so-called old counties of Philadelphia, Chester, and Bucks, the first was inhabited largely by Quakers, who also played the leading role in the second two. There, however, Ulster Presbyterians, Welsh Baptists and Presbyterians were to be found in considerable numbers, along with a sprinkling of Germans.

To the west and north of the old counties were the five newer counties of Berks, Lancaster, York, Cumberland, and Northampton.[30] Berks was a fourth county that the Quakers had originally controlled, but Germans, divided into several religious groups, were now massed there; in both Lancaster and York the Germans were predominant, but mixed with them were numerous Ulstermen; Cumberland was settled almost entirely by the latter, whereas Northampton was a mixture of German, English, and Ulstermen. The Anglicans, constituting less than one tenth of the total population, were numerous and influential in the three old counties, especially in the city of Philadelphia and in Berks County. In the

---

[29] For a discussion of the above point as it relates to western Pennsylvania see J. N. Fullerton: "Squatters and Titles to Land in Early Western Pennsylvania," *Western Pennsylvania Historical Magazine*, VI, 165–76. See also W. R. Shepherd: *History of Proprietary Government in Pennsylvania* (New York, 1896), pp. 48–53, 111–12, 547; C. H. Lincoln: *The Revolutionary Movement in Pennsylvania, 1760–1776* (Philadelphia, 1901), p. 33; and W. F. Dunaway: "Pennsylvania as an Early Distributing Center of Population," *Pennsylvania Magazine of History and Biography*, LV, 134–69.

[30] Lancaster County was taken out of Chester in 1729; York County, out of Lancaster in 1749; Cumberland County, out of Lancaster in 1750; Berks County, out of parts of Philadelphia, Chester, and Lancaster counties in 1752; Northampton County, out of the unsettled portions of Bucks County also in 1752. *Pennsylvania Statutes at Large*, IV, 131–4; V, 70–7, 87–94, 133–40, 141–6.

tier of Delaware River counties, inhabited largely by people of British ancestry, the Quakers and Anglicans were busy contending for political supremacy. To the west of this region up to the Susquehanna was planted the great body of the German people. Interspersed among them were the Ulster Scots, who were also settling in many scattered communities along the extreme western frontier; their centre was Carlisle, established west of the Susquehanna in 1751.

The numerical preponderance of the German element might well have placed political control of the province in its hands without the co-operation of any other group. However, a very large proportion of the Germans who had entered Pennsylvania previous to 1750 apparently had not as yet sought naturalization.[31] Only slowly, indeed, did they become politically conscious.

The laws of the province encouraged the change in nationality, as illustrated by the act of the year 1742 which gave foreign Protestants with religious objections to oaths the right to affirm, a right already enjoyed by the Quakers.[32] With the growing realization of the value of participation in government, the Germans — especially those living in the more settled part of the province — increasingly availed themselves of the opportunity to become British subjects. This is made clear in the reports on naturalization sent to the Board of Trade from time to time.[33] As a result of this tendency, the German-speaking electorate was fast becoming by the middle of the century a powerful and active element in political life. It was with this group that the Quakers, now in a numerical minority, were allied in their opposition to the participation of Pennsylvania in warlike activities, an alliance perfectly understandable in view of the principles of public policy espoused by the Mennonites, Dunkards, and Moravians and the powerful influence exerted by Christoph Saur (Sauer, Sower), who at this period was editor of the *Pennsylvanische*

---

[31] An act passed by Parliament in 1740 provided for naturalization of foreign Protestants who had resided seven years or more in any of the American colonies and who would take the prescribed oaths and make a required declaration (13 Geo. II, c. 7). On the subject of naturalization see E. A. Hoyt: "Naturalization under the American Colonies: Signs of a New Community," *Political Science Quarterly*, LXVII, 248–66.

[32] *Pennsylvania Statutes at Large*, IV, 391–4.

[33] For lists of those who were naturalized as Pennsylvanians from 1743 to 1753 see P.R.O., C.O. 5:1271 and 1273.

Berichte, a newspaper that, with some change in title, was in existence from 1739 to 1777.[34] Saur, bitterly opposed to the proprietorial interests, moulded the opinions of many who were not of these pacifistic sects. At the approach of war between the English and the French in 1754 he warned his fellow Germans that there was a design to enslave them, that a military-service law was planned, and that all the miseries they had suffered in Germany and additional aggravations would be their lot.[35] This warning did not fail of its effect, for most of these people were peaceably inclined. In fact, the atmosphere of the province was, in the main, one of good will toward all men.

Considering that numerous religious and racial groups existed side by side in Pennsylvania, there was remarkably little friction. This circumstance obviously appealed to those who had left their ancestral abodes because of intolerance, persecution, and the existence of military despotism.[36] "To speak the truth, one seldom hears or sees a quarrel among them," declared Mittelberger in describing the people of Pennsylvania. "Even strangers trust each other more than acquaintances in Europe. People are far more sincere and generous than in Germany; therefore our Americans live more quietly and peacefully together than the Europeans; and all this is the result of the liberty which they enjoy and which makes them all equal."[37]

The Quakers had laid the foundations of the spirit of good will by their treatment of the Indians. Germans such as Mittelberger, coming from the oppressions of the Old World, attributed this hu-

---

[34] The elder Saur died in 1758, and his son with the same name took his place as editor. See D. F. Durnbaugh: "Christopher Sauer, Pennsylvania-German Printer . . . ," *Pennsylvania Magazine of History and Biography,* LXXXII, 316–40; see also Daniel Miller: *Early German American Newspapers* (Lancaster, 1911), and J. O. Knauss: *Social Conditions among the Pennsylvania Germans in the Eighteenth Century . . .* (Lancaster, 1922), pp. 3–6.

[35] William Smith: *A Brief State of the Province of Pennsylvania,* p. 27. J. O. Knauss: *op. cit.,* pp. 38–9; see also Dietmar Rothermund: "The German Problem of Colonial Pennsylvania," *Pennsylvania Magazine of History and Biography,* LXXXIV, 3–21.

[36] Saur reported a conversation in which a native of Württemberg, on being asked why so many Germans risked the long and dangerous voyage, replied that they had scarcely been able to live in Germany due to governmental oppression. Although Prussia welcomed them, he declared, there they would be slaves and vassals. *Pennsylvanische Berichte,* December 1754, quoted by Knauss: *op. cit.,* pp. 141–2.

[37] *Journey to Pennsylvania,* p. 113.

manity to liberty and to lack of compulsion in measures involving hostile relations of peoples. It is therefore not surprising that those Germans not exposed to the actualities of frontier warfare were strongly inclined to rally to the support of the Quaker political principles and to vote for Quaker candidates to the Assembly. At the same time, in the middle of the eighteenth century there was little demand by the German group to assume the responsibilities of office themselves. Nevertheless, so decisive was the aid that these newcomers were able to bring to the Friends that Dr. William Smith, a political opponent influential enough to have been elected Provost of the new College of Philadelphia in 1755, sought to eliminate them from political life. In an open letter to a friend in England he declared that the only remedy for the evils of the situation facing the commonwealth — then in the midst of war, with French Indians harrying its frontiers — was the suspension of the rights of naturalized Germans to vote for members of the Assembly. He then raised the question: "What can be more absurd and impolitic, than to see a Body of ignorant, proud, stubborn Clowns (who are unacquainted with our Language, our Manners, our Laws, and our Interests) indulged with the Privilege of Returning almost every Member of Assembly?"[38]

In this connection, the three old counties in 1752 each returned 8 members to the Assembly, and the city of Philadelphia 2 members, making 26 out of a total of 36 members; Lancaster returned 4, York and Cumberland 2 each, and Northampton and Berks, created that year, one each.[39] Even up to October 1756 there were still 16

---

[38] William Smith: *op. cit.*, p. 40. For an account of the relations of the Quakers with the Proprietors of Pennsylvania and their attitude toward the defence of the province see Volume VI, pp. 22, 66–8, and Volume VII, pp. 49–57, 299, of this series; see also Theodore Thayer: "The Quaker Party of Pennsylvania, 1755–1765," *Pennsylvania Magazine of History and Biography*, LXXI, 19–43, and especially his *Pennsylvania Politics and the Growth of Democracy, 1740–1776* (Harrisburg, 1953), and F. B. Tolles: *Quakers and the Atlantic Culture* (New York, 1960).

[39] For purposes of the annual election of members of the General Assembly, each county was divided into eight election districts, each district consisting of a number of townships. Each township in September by vote of the freeholders nominated one person as the district inspector for the election, who was thereupon chosen by lot at the county seat from the district nominees. The eight inspectors received by written ballot ("in a piece of Paper rolled up") the votes of all freeholders possessing either at least fifty acres, "well situated," twelve of which were in cultivation, or £50 current money, who had been residing within the province for two years. If the circumstances of the voter were known to the inspector, the ballot was deposited unquestioned in a

Quakers in the Assembly,[40] 11 Anglicans, 6 Ulster Presbyterians, one Lutheran, one Moravian, and one Baptist. This may be taken as a typical display of strength by the various groups in view of the Quaker-German combination. However, as the four Quakers elected for Bucks and Chester counties resigned in that year out of loyalty to the principles of their society — in face of threats from the mother country to require all in the service of the province to take the usual oaths rather than affirmations — the strength of the Anglicans was increased to 14 and the Ulstermen to 7. At last a Quaker control that had been really continuous from the beginning of the life of the colony gave way, at least temporarily, to the militant policies of the other groups.[41]

In the face of this dominating position of the Quakers in the Pennsylvania Assembly down to 1756 and their influence in the shaping of public policy,[42] the question may here be pertinent as to

---

box; otherwise, he was obliged to swear or affirm as to his qualifications. Clerks were present to record the names of voters. With the close of the election, the votes were tabulated by the judges and inspectors, and the names of those elected were proclaimed from the courthouse door. Assemblymen received six shillings a day from the provincial treasury during the session, with mileage from and to their places of residence. For the statutes of 1705/6 and 1727 regulating elections see *Pennsylvania Statutes at Large*, II, 213, and IV, 77–80. For the representatives of Lancaster, York, Cumberland, Northampton, and Berks counties see *ibid.*, IV, 132, V, 72, 88, 132, and 134; see also L. H. Gipson: *Lewis Evans . . .*, p. 130. A. E. McKinley stresses the point that in rural Pennsylvania most people otherwise qualified to vote could meet the freehold requirement but that in the city of Philadelphia few could meet either the freehold or £50-income requirement. See his *Suffrage Franchise in the Thirteen English Colonies in America* (Philadelphia, 1905), pp. 285–99.

[40] For the prominence of Quakers not only in politics but also in business in Pennsylvania see F. B. Tolles: *Meeting House and Counting House: The Quaker Merchants of Colonial Philadelphia, 1682–1763* (Chapel Hill, N.C., 1948).

[41] In a report of October 14, 1756, as to religious composition of the Pennsylvania Assembly, the Church of England is credited with 14 members, Quakers with 8, people called Quakers "but not owned by the Society" with 4, Presbyterians with 7, Baptists, Lutherans, and Moravians with one each, with the election of the last named contested by a Churchman. Newcastle Papers, B.M., Add. Mss. 33029, folio 354. Daniel J. Boorstin, in his recent striking study of colonial America, *The Americans: The Colonial Experience* (New York, 1958), in "Part Two, The Inward Plantation: The Quakers of Pennsylvania," stresses the point that the religious principles of the Quakers so set them apart as a sect that they were peculiarly unfitted to assist in colonial government.

[42] For the history of pacifism in Pennsylvania down to 1756 see G. F. Hershberger: "Pacifism and the State in Colonial Pennsylvania," *Church History*, VIII (1939), 54–74, and, by the same author: "The Pennsylvania Quaker Experiment in Politics, 1682–1756," *Mennonite Quarterly Review*, X, 187–221; see also Rufus Jones: *The Quakers in the American Colonies* (London, 1911), pp. 475–94, and especially Isaac Sharpless: *A Quaker Experiment in Government* (Philadelphia, 1898), pp. 226–76.

how far the public law of the province was an embodiment of the peculiar conceptions of this sect. For here alone in the New World was Quakerism able to develop a sufficient control of legislative processes to give sustained direction to its ideals.[43]

When William Penn took over the lands embraced within the province, the Swedish and Dutch settlers were living under the protection of the so-called Duke of York laws adopted in 1664 at Hempstead on Long Island and extended in 1676 to this district. Based largely upon the New England codes, especially those of Massachusetts Bay and of the former colony of New Haven, these laws reflected the Puritan conceptions of statecraft. Among the capital laws — that is, laws entailing the death penalty — were: the law against the denial of the true God, one against false witnessing, another directed against any child over sixteen years of age guilty of smiting a parent unless under proper provocation, as well as others against unnatural sexual acts, kidnapping, the slaying of a defenceless man with a sword, and the killing of a man while lying in wait. The code provided also for such penalties as branding on the forehead, the boring of the tongue with a red-hot iron, whipping, and other, milder punishments.[44] All this was swept away, at least so far as Pennsylvania was concerned, when on December 10, 1682, at a popular assembly held at Upland, in Chester County, Penn secured the ratification of a body of laws that he and those assisting him had drawn up in England the preceding May. This "Great Law," as the code was designated by contemporaries and by subsequent lawmakers, became the basis of the later provincial law. It fully reflected the Friends' spirit of humanity and toleration and their horror of bloodshed. One crime alone, that of murder, was punishable with death;[45] mutilation quite disappeared; on the other hand, some comparatively mild penalties such as the forfeiture of goods, the wearing of a badge of shame, and gagging were intro-

---

[43] It is, of course, true that in West New Jersey and later in East New Jersey the Quaker influence was also felt and that in the western section the Friends were numerically and politically the dominant group down to the middle of the eighteenth century.

[44] See the writer's "The Criminal Codes of Pennsylvania," *Journal of the American Institute of Criminal Law and Criminology*, VI, 323–5; also his "Crime and Its Punishment in Provincial Pennsylvania," *Pennsylvania History*, II, 3–16.

[45] Under the charter, treason also carried the death penalty. On the "Great Law" see R. M. Jones: *op. cit.*, pp. 472–3.

duced. Like many another great soul, Penn must have been convinced that men would react in harmony with their environment, and that if the social order created by his Holy Experiment dealt with the individual in mercy and kindness, these qualities would be reflected in men's conduct. But as the years passed, he became very much alarmed over reports of confusion and lawlessness which reached him from the province. In a letter directed to the Governor "to be opened only and read in a full Council," held February 9, 1687/8, the Proprietor stated: "The Reports are . . . that there is no place more overrun with wickedness, Sins so very Scandalous, openly committed in defiance of Law and Virtue: facts so foul, I am forbid by Comon modesty to relate y^m."[46] As a result, he journeyed again to his proprietary. There in 1700 the Great Law was profoundly modified by a code drawn up under his direction, ratified at New Castle in the Lower Counties on the Delaware, and reaffirmed in Philadelphia the following year. Mutilations, branding, and whipping once again stand out prominently among other sanctions.[47] This code, when submitted to the Privy Council, was criticized for embodying unusual penalties, with the result that, out of a total of 105 acts, 52 were disallowed.[48]

Although many of the laws thus annulled were repassed in 1705 with the objectionable features eliminated, there seems to have been a growing conviction that the comparative mildness of the New Castle code had the effect of attracting men of lawless tendencies into the province since they ran no risk of serious punishment. Consequently, in 1718 the General Assembly passed "An Act for the Advancement of Justice and More Certain Administration Thereof,"

---

[46] Colonial Records [Pennsylvania Archives] (ed. Samuel Hazard, 16 vols., Harrisburg & Philadelphia, 1838–53), I, 527. That the mildness of the code of law in Pennsylvania was in part responsible for the influx of lawless people, especially through the port of Philadelphia, may be judged by the report to the Council of a special committee appointed to study the Proprietor's letter. They stated that "as this place hath grown more populous, & the people increased, Loossness & vice Hath also Creept in. . . ." The report went on to claim that all proper efforts had been made to control this situation, but recommended that a proclamation be issued "until some wholsome & severer Laws be made. . . ." See ibid., I, 528.

[47] See the Pennsylvania Statutes at Large, II, 1–140. In this code castration was provided for in the case of certain acts violating the moral order of nature. See ibid., II, 8.

[48] Acts of the Privy Council, Col. Ser., 1680–1720, p. 851. For a discussion of the royal disallowance of Pennsylvania laws see W. T. Root: The Relations of Pennsylvania with the British Government, 1695–1765 (Philadelphia, 1912), Chap. 5.

in which it was stated that the unhappy situation confronting the people was due to the fact that the statutes of Parliament did not extend to Pennsylvania. To remedy this difficulty it was thereby expressly declared that certain offences such as arson, burglary, mayhem, petit treason, and misprision of treason were felonies of death punishable according to the laws of Great Britain.[49] As a result, the number of offences involving the death penalty now mounted to twelve, while five offences made those guilty liable to branding on the forehead.[50] Finally, an act passed in 1722 declared that anyone convicted of counterfeiting the money of the province should be placed upon the pillory, have both ears cut off, be whipped thirty-one lashes, and, in default of the payment of damages that his acts might have caused, should be sold into servitude for seven years.[51]

One may assert that the Pennsylvania criminal law after 1722 down to the outbreak of the war for American Independence was one of the harshest bodies of law in North America. Nevertheless, there was a steady growth in the number of crimes of a serious nature. Nor were the severe measures of punishment allowed to remain mere threats on the statute books of the province.[52] The Quakers, confronted by a situation not of their own creating or choosing, had indeed been impelled to rule the province by means other than brotherly love and a merciful spirit. In other words, they were fundamentally British, with many of the practical-minded attitudes of that nation. Faced with the actual responsibilities of government, they felt obliged to make some compromises in applying their conceptions of human relations as they tried to reconcile theory and practice.[53]

---

[49] *Pennsylvania Statutes at Large*, III, 199.

[50] These offences were adultery, burglary, house-breaking, rape, and robbery.

[51] *Ibid.*, III, 331–2.

[52] See the author's "Crime and Its Punishment in Provincial Pennsylvania," *Pennsylvania History*, II, 10–16.

[53] Referring to the government of Pennsylvania in the middle of the eighteenth century, Lewis Evans makes the rather caustic comment: "The present Form is extremely defective; 'tis upon a Supposition that all Mankind are virtuous. Nobody need be told that, that is a Mistake. Tis a Government without Rewards or Punishments, adequate to Merit or Iniquity. The Inhabitants of American Birth are not very eager in Pursuit of Learning except where it be a trade. At this time, nine tenths of the justices of Peace[;] have never read fifty Pages of Law before they had their Com-

Whatever may have been the problems of law-enforcement, the happy material condition of the province cannot be questioned. The climate was temperate and healthful, the soil rich, varying from the light and sandy lands near the rivers to the deep black mould of the interior woodlands. The land was fed by two great rivers, the Delaware and the Susquehanna, which, with their tributaries, afforded excellent means of transportation. With an industrious population labouring under these favourable conditions, there was a surplus of food each year sufficient on an average, it was asserted, to feed at least 100,000 people other than those living within the province.[54] Unquestionably the inhabitants of the rural areas were generous with this abundance. At least one traveller at this period declared: "In Pennsylvania one might travel about a whole year without spending a penny; for it is customary in this country that, when one comes with his horse to a house, the traveller is asked if he wishes to have something to eat, whereupon the stranger is served with a piece of cold meat which has been left over from dinner; in addition to this he is provided with fine bread, butter and cheese, also with plenty to drink. If one wishes to stay over night, he and his horse are harboured free of charge."[55]

Averaging in size from 100 to 400 acres, the farms of provincial Pennsylvania were devoted to raising a variety of field crops and live-stock. The chief agricultural products were wheat, Indian corn, cattle, swine, horses, rye, barley, and oats. Beef and pork were exported in large quantities, as were Indian corn and also wheat, largely in the form of flour and bread.[56] From the hardwood of the

---

missions, tho' they are also Judges of the Court of Common Pleas; but they are mostly trading People, and if they dont understand Law, they do Expediency. There are several who remembers to have seen Men rais'd to Posts, where both natural and acquired Abilities were necessary, whom the World judged to have scarce Wits enough to keep them out of a Well. But who does not now rejoice to see it otherwise?" See L. H. Gipson: *Lewis Evans* . . . , p. 123.

Richard Peters, Secretary of the Province, commenting on the above, says: "Our Author is pretty severe upon our Magistrates, but he is conscious that the Veracity of Assertion will hinder any Contradiction" (*ibid.*).

[54] Governor Morris to General Braddock, March 12, 1755, *Pennsylvania Archives*, 4th ser., II, 373.

[55] Mittelberger: *Journey to Pennsylvania*, p. 97.

[56] In 1751 there were exported from the port of Philadelphia 125,960 barrels of flour, vast quantities of "wheat bisquets" together with wheat, beef, bacon, flax seed, ginseed root, 4,812,943 barrel staves, iron, deerskins, and furs. See Israel Acrelius: *History of New Sweden*, Hist. Soc. of Penna. *Memoirs*, XI (translated from

province large numbers of barrels and other wooden containers were manufactured for export. Pig and bar iron in excess of local needs, produced in local bloomeries, furnaces, and forges, were also sent abroad in quantity. Indian traders brought to Philadelphia a wealth of skins and furs, most of which went to England. Finally, ships, built at Philadelphia and sold in Great Britain, made a considerable return,[57] although it was asserted by Peter Kalm, the Swedish scientist, that hulls made of Pennsylvania oak were not so lasting as those of the oak of New England or Europe.[58] It is of interest that coal had apparently not as yet been discovered in a commonwealth now famed the world over for great anthracite and bituminous deposits, although some of those who went among the Indians higher up in the country claimed to have seen it.[59]

As for importations, during the twenty years preceding 1750 the merchants of the province bought from England commodities valued, according to the custom-house books, at over £1,000,000,

---

the 1759 Swedish edn. by W. M. Reynolds, Philadelphia, 1874), p. 142. An explanation for the vast export of provisions was their excellent quality. This was maintained by a rigid inspection of exports. See A. L. Jensen: "The Inspection of Exports in Colonial Pennsylvania," *Pennsylvania Magazine of History and Biography,* LXXVIII, 275–97. For agriculture in colonial Pennsylvania see S. W. Fletcher: *Pennsylvania Agriculture and Country Life, 1640–1840* (2 vols., Harrisburg, 1950), by far the most complete description. For important contemporary sources see also *American Husbandry . . . By An American* [London, 1775] (ed. H. J. Carman, New York, 1939) and Israel Acrelius: *op. cit.,* Part 3, Chaps. 7 and 8.

[57] Answer of the Lieutenant Governor of Pennsylvania and of the Counties of New Castle, Kent, and Sussex on Delaware to the Queries from the Board of Trade, March 15, 1731. Shelburne Papers 45:205–11.

[58] *Travels in North America* (ed. A. B. Benson, 2 vols., New York, 1937), I, 94–5. A contemporary offers an explanation for the fact that ships built in Pennsylvania were not long-lived: "The Timber used here for Ship building is Oak; . . . that called white Oak is esteemed the best, & is the only sort used for Plank. Our Ship Carpenters never season a Stick, whence you may know the short duration of Ships built here, & indeed Forrest timber is never so durable as that which grows openly in Parks & Fields; New Jersey furnishes us with Pines for the Deck & Masts as well as for all our house building" (L. H. Gipson: *Lewis Evans . . . ,* pp. 102–3).

[59] Kalm: *op. cit.,* I, 47.
Lewis Evans, the surveyor, writing from Philadelphia in 1753, says: "But there is no Sea Coal, Chalk, or Cinnebar yet discovered . . ." (L. H. Gipson: *Lewis Evans . . . ,* p. 106). Nevertheless, Evans in his famous "A General Map of the Middle British Colonies," published in 1755, gives the sites of certain coal deposits in what is now Ohio. For the discovery of coal in western Pennsylvania and in what is now West Virginia and Ohio see H. N. Eavenson: *The First Century and a Quarter of American Coal Industry* (Pittsburgh, 1942), pp. 16–27. For John Pattin's map of 1752 that locates coal deposits in western Pennsylvania see *ibid.,* Map No. 3, p. 6. As early as 1701 coal was discovered in Virginia, and by 1758 its export to other colonies began when 24 tons were shipped to New York, *ibid.,* p. 32.

one fourth of which were foreign-made goods landed in England before trans-shipment by certificate to America. In 1747, goods to the value of £82,404 were received from the mother country; of this total, goods valued at £8,585 were produced abroad. These figures indicate that the imports of that year were more than double the value of imports twenty years earlier.[60] Strikingly different totals also cited from the Philadelphia custom-house accounts showed imports from England for three years, from December 25, 1748, to December 25, 1751, amounting to £647,267.8.9, of which £478,282.5.5 were of British manufacture.[61] These irreconcilable tables perhaps suggest that by 1748 so prosperous was the trade of Philadelphia that imports had doubled in value from one year to the next. To carry this commerce and that of the Lower Counties on the Delaware it was computed that in 1730 170 ships, most of them sloops and small brigantines averaging about sixty tons, cleared from Philadelphia and from New Castle and Lewes in Delaware each year;[62] in 1745 there were over 300,[63] and in 1755, from Philadelphia alone, according to Governor Morris, there sailed some 500 vessels mostly owned by local merchants.[64]

Pennsylvania in 1750 may well be described as among the most prosperous areas within the British Empire. One of its leading men, in fact, called it the most flourishing in North America.[65] By that year Philadelphia had perhaps a larger population than any other

---

[60] For tables of imports for the years 1723–47 inclusive, taken from the London custom-house books, see Kalm: *op. cit.*, I, 29.

[61] Israel Acrelius: *op. cit.*, p. 142. For still other figures see Shelburne Papers, 47:35–9. For a striking profile of the port of Philadelphia, which quotes these import figures, see the Scull and Heap: *East Prospect . . .* print of 1754, commissioned in 1750 by Thomas Penn, who "was undoubtedly familiar with *A South Prospect of Yͤ Flourishing City of New York . . .*, issued around 1720 . . . and . . . A South East View of Yͤ Great Town of Boston . . . , 1723," according to N. B. Wainwright's "Scull and Heap's East Prospects of Philadelphia," *Pennsylvania Magazine*, LXXIII, 16–25.

[62] Answers of the Lieutenant Governor of Pennsylvania to the Queries of the Board, 1730. Shelburne Papers, 45:205–11.

[63] Kalm: *op. cit.*, I, 30.

[64] Governor Morris to General Braddock, March 12, 1755, *Pennsylvania Archives*, 4th ser., II, 373. For Philadelphia mercantile activities see F. B. Tolles: *op. cit.*, and H. B. Berg: "Merchants and Mercantile Life of Colonial Philadelphia," *Abstracts in History*, V (Iowa City, 1943), 91–101. The figures on the insurance of ships, as given in H. E. Gillingham's *Marine Insurance in Philadelphia, 1721–1800* (Philadelphia, 1933), illustrate the importance of Philadelphia as a financial centre.

[65] William Smith: *A Brief State of . . . Pennsylvania*, p. 4.

town in the English settlements of the New World.[66] Peter Kalm
paid tribute to its "grandeur and perfection," declaring that "its
fine appearance, good regulations, agreeable location, natural advantages, trade, riches and power are by no means inferior to those
of any, even of the most ancient, towns in Europe" and that it is
the capital of a province which "now vies with several kingdoms in
Europe in the number of inhabitants."[67] Although ninety miles up
the Delaware, it was a great seaport, and the largest ships sailed
freely to its wharfs, where they rode in five fathoms of fresh
water. In October 1754, for example, it is recorded that there were
117 large sailing vessels in the harbour at the same time.[68] Its
single great disadvantage as a port was that for a period during
the winter the river was apt to freeze over and navigation therefore
be suspended — which did not happen in salt-water ports.[69]

In 1749 the city[70] measured over a mile in length, and in breadth
a half-mile or more, possessing, it seems, something over two thou-

---

[66] The population of American towns in the eighteenth century is difficult to ascer-
tain with accuracy. Richard Peters, comparing New York and Philadelphia in the early
years of the French and Indian War, declared: "The City of New York is much more
advantageously situated than Philadelphia, & yet how surprisingly has the latter risen
to That Superiority, which it at present undoubtedly has, not only over the former, but
over all the Cities in the British colonies" (L. H. Gipson: Lewis Evans . . . , p. 99 n).
Boston, nevertheless, enjoyed a population almost if not quite equal to Philadelphia's.
See E. B. Greene and V. D. Harrington: American Population, pp. 22 and 118.

In 1743 Philadelphia was credited with a population of 13,000, but in 1760 it had
23,750, which made it the largest city in North America. In 1743 New York had
11,000 and in 1760, 18,000. Boston in 1743 had 16,382 and in 1760, 15,631. See Carl
Bridenbaugh: Cities in the Wilderness (2 vols., New York, 1955), II, 5.

[67] Op. cit., I, 33. A British officer, Lord Adam Gordon, after visiting during 1764
and 1765 all other leading towns and cities in British North America and the British
West Indies, declared: "The city of Philadelphia is perhaps one of the wonders of the
World; if you consider its Size, the number of its Inhabitants, the regularity of its
Streets, . . . their spacious publick & private Buildings, Quays & Docks, the mag-
nificence and diversity of places of worship, . . . the plenty of provisions brought to
Market, & the Industry of all its Inhabitants, one will not hesitate to call it the first
Town in America, . . . one that bids fair to rival almost any in Europe" (Journal of
an Officer . . . ," B.M., King's Mss., 261:36–7).

[68] Israel Acrelius: op. cit., p. 142.

[69] The winters two centuries ago appear to have been more severe than today.
Lewis Evans wrote in 1753 respecting the port of Philadelphia: "The River is frozen
over at least two winters in thrice. . . ." He also stated: "It is not safe attempting
this coast in January or February by inward bound ships" (L. H. Gipson: Lewis
Evans . . . , p. 110).

[70] For the incorporation of Philadelphia as a city in 1691, see the Pennsylvania
Magazine of History and Biography, XVIII, 504.

sand dwellings.[71] The streets, running north and south and east and west, were regular and attractive; their width was fifty feet, with the exception of Market Street, which was nearly one hundred. The houses, several storeys in height and generally provided with plate-glass windows and French chimneys, were mostly built of brick[72] and roofed with cedar shingles. This cedar, in the past procurable from trees growing in near-by swamps, was esteemed for its lightness and durability.[73] By the middle of the century its scarcity for roof covering had created a serious problem. It had also proved to be a fire hazard, so that when the time had come for renewal of the roofs it was deemed necessary to change to tile or slate. But the houses had to be provided with stouter walls to carry the additional weight. This in itself entailed the reconstruction of many of the buildings, a task that was then proceeding.

Twelve churches or meeting houses adorned the city — a testimony to the importance of religion in a province that was a haven for those who had suffered persecution for their faith. There were two credited to each of the larger religious denominations — that is, to the Quakers, Presbyterians, German Reformed, and Lutherans; the Anglicans, Baptists, Roman Catholics, and Moravian Brethren each supported one.[74] Vying with Boston as a cultural centre, Philadelphia could boast in 1753 of a fine lending library, a newly founded academy, out of which finally came the University of Pennsylvania,[75] the beginnings of a philosophical society, the first

---

[71] The Maryland Gazette, June 7, 1749. For the architecture of Philadelphia in the eighteenth century see T. J. Wertenbaker: The Founding of American Civilization: The Middle Colonies (New York, 1938), pp. 231–6, 243–9.

[72] "The whole World cannot afford better bricks than our Town is built of, nor is the Lime which is mostly brought from White-Marsh inferior to that wherewith the old Castles in Britain were formerly built" (L. H. Gipson: Lewis Evans . . . , p. 106).

[73] Evans, referring to the white cedar of Pennsylvania, declared that it "is excellent where duration, & not strength is wanting, for which Reason we use it for the Pannels of our wainscotting, Pails, Tubs, Brewers & Distillers Cisterns, Coolers, & Tubs, likewise for shingling Houses and for Fences. The Cultivation of this wood would be the most beneficial of any thing that cou'd be introduced into Europe from America: for they grow very fast, and so close together that there is scarce Room in some places for a Man to squeeze between them, & the Swamps where they grow are the greatest Curiosity in America" (ibid., p. 103).

[74] Peter Kalm: op. cit., I, 20–5.

[75] For the beginnings of "The College, Academy, and Charitable School of Philadelphia," chartered in 1755, see E. P. Cheyney: The History of the University of Pennsylvania, 1740–1940 (Philadelphia, 1940); E. M. Alderfer: "James Logan, Patron

hospital in North America, and two printing establishments, without reference to the *Pennsylvanische Berichte* published in near-by Germantown. Here in the city Benjamin Franklin, editor of the *Pennsylvania Gazette,* was attracting more than local attention with his electrical experiments and with his suggestions as to their significance.[76] Here also at his country place, "Stenton," outside the city bounds, resided James Logan, one of the most cultivated men in the English-speaking world, with his library of some three thousand carefully selected volumes.[77] The chief architectural ornament of the city, one may mention in passing, was a new, impressive town hall where not only the city fathers but also the deputies of the province gathered to deliberate.

One may think perhaps in terms of sober dress as well as sober speech in this centre of Quakerism in 1750. But it is related that the apparel of the men, especially of Englishmen, was very costly, even among the farmers. "Every one wears a wig, the peasant as well as the gentleman," declared Mittelberger. He also found that the women's apparel was "very fine, neat and costly. . . . All wear daily fine white aprons, on their shoes usually large silver buckles, round their throats fine strings of beads, in their ears costly drops

and Philosopher," *Pennsylvania History,* XXIV, 101–20; Benjamin Franklin: *Proposals Relating to the Education of Youth in Pennsylvania* (Philadelphia, 1749); and Bertha S. Fox: "Provost Smith and the Quest for Funds," *Pennsylvania History,* II, 225–38.

[76] Among the many works relating to Franklin see Carl Van Doren: *Benjamin Franklin* (New York, 1938), and by the same writer and others: *Meet Dr. Franklin* (Philadelphia, 1943); see also Carl Becker: *Benjamin Franklin* (Ithaca, N.Y., 1946), and three works by Verner W. Crane: *Benjamin Franklin, Englishman and American* (Providence, 1936), (ed.) *Benjamin Franklin's Letters to the Press, 1758–1775* (Chapel Hill, N.C., 1950), and *Benjamin Franklin and a Rising People* (Boston, 1954). With the publication of *The Papers of Benjamin Franklin,* Vol. I (New Haven, 1959), a definitive edition of Franklin's writings is in process of realization as a joint enterprise of the American Philosophical Society and Yale University, with L. W. Labaree as editor and W. J. Bell, Jr., as associate editor.

For the cultural life of Philadelphia in the eighteenth century see Carl and Jessica Bridenbaugh: *Rebels and Gentlemen: Philadelphia in the Age of Franklin* (New York, 1942); see also Brooke Hindle: *The Pursuit of Science in Revolutionary America, 1735–1789* (Chapel Hill, N.C., 1956), pp. 5, 34 *et seq.* For the extraordinary enterprise of the Philadelphia Quaker merchants in subscribing for and undertaking the management of the first colonial hospital in North America see [Benjamin Franklin]: *Some Account of the Pennsylvania Hospital; from its first Rise, . . . to 1754* (Philadelphia, 1754).

[77] See F. B. Tolles: *James Logan and the Culture of Provincial America* (Boston, 1957); Irma J. Cooper: *The Life and Public Services of James Logan* (New York, 1921); and Edwin Wolf, Jr.: "The Romance of James Logan's Books," *William and Mary Quarterly,* XIII, 342–53.

with fine stones, and on their heads fine white hoods embroidered with flowers and trimmed with lace and streamers." This honest and not unsusceptible man found the English-speaking women ". . . exceedingly handsome, generally gay, friendly, very free, plucky, smart and clever but also very haughty. . . ." Over their shoulders they wore scarlet or blue cloaks when walking and riding and, on their heads, beautifully colored "bonnets" of taffeta, which "serve instead of parasols, but are much prettier."[78] Even the English servant woman, he declared, dressed as elegantly as an aristocratic lady in Germany.

While it may be inferred that there was a degree of political equality among the people of the province — at least among those of Protestant faith who could take the required oaths or affirmations for the purpose of naturalization and for holding office — there were fairly definite social lines and barriers separating English-speaking from non-English-speaking people, freemen from redemptioners, and bondsmen from slaves. A certain racial pride on the part of the English settlers was apparently exhibited too frequently in an objectionable fashion. "In this country there exists, (what we do not find in Old England), among the English settlers, a supreme contempt for the Germans," wrote a German gentleman from Philadelphia in 1747. "This may be owing," he declared, "to the fact, that the former see numbers of lowly and poor German immigrants in comparison with whom they entertain an exalted opinion of themselves."[79]

As for the existence of slavery in Pennsylvania, there was some little sentiment against it in the middle of the eighteenth century, but not so much as one might expect in light of the famous Germantown protest as early as the year 1688. It is true that the number of slaves was not large, at most from two to three thousand, and that not only the Quakers "but also several Christians of other denominations sometimes set their negroes at liberty."[80] Nevertheless, Peter Kalm affirmed in 1749 that, while the Quakers once scrupled to receive slaves, they "are no longer so particular and now they

---

[78] *Journey to Pennsylvania*, pp. 98, 116–17.
[79] *Pennsylvania Magazine of History and Biography*, XVI, 120.
[80] Peter Kalm: *op. cit.*, I, 208.

have as many negroes as other people."[81] Slavery, however, was not a fundamental element in the economy of the colony. Rather, it was an excrescence of provincial aristocracy.

The keynote of eighteenth-century Pennsylvania was fruitful activity among all groups with a consequent abundance of the material things of life. There was, as has been suggested, plenty of good food at low prices, with the farmer and the mechanic comfortably housed and clothed and the merchants prospering as a result of a ready sale of the surplus commodities of the province in the West Indies and in other markets. Doubtless the production of wealth was stimulated by the fact that the government was able to help industrious farmers improve their lands by advancing funds from the loan office created for that purpose, while refraining from placing public burdens on the people at large. For, in addition to the inhabitants of the province not being obliged to render military service, under ordinary circumstances they were quite free from levies on their possessions. "Liberty in Pennsylvania extends so far," observed a contemporary, "that every one is free from all molestation and taxation on his property, business, house and estates. . . . A peculiarity, however, is that unmarried men and women pay from 2 to 5 shillings annually, according to their income, because they have no one but themselves to provide for. In Philadelphia this money is applied to the purchase of the lights which burn every night in the streets of the city."[82]

How then were the charges of government met, if not by direct

---

[81] *Ibid.*, I, 206. For a detailed discussion of slavery in the province see E. R. Turner: *The Negro in Pennsylvania: Slavery-Servitude-Freedom* (Washington, D.C., 1911), especially Chaps. 2, 3, and 4; F. J. Klingberg: "The African Immigrant in Colonial Pennsylvania and Delaware," *Historical Magazine of the Protestant Episcopal Church*, XI, 126–53; and T. E. Drake: *Quakers and Slavery in America* . . . (Yale Historical Publications Miscellany No. 51, New Haven, 1950).

[82] Mittelberger: *op. cit.*, p. 55. Before 1724 the excise on spirits was reduced from eightpence to sixpence a gallon, and in 1733 it was further reduced to fourpence, at which rate it stood in 1750. There was, it is true, an import duty on Negroes which in 1725/6 was placed at £5 lawful money but which in 1729 was lowered to £2. See *Pennsylvania Statutes at Large*, IV, 53, 123, and 239. There were likewise some small local levies such as that in Philadelphia for lighting the streets, referred to in the text, and county levies for the care of the poor and for road maintenance. According to William Douglass, writing in 1750, the assessment of property for this purpose was so low that "a person . . . worth £10,000 is returned upon their [the assessors'] list with from £200 to £300 and to pay two pence on the pound . . ." (*A Summary, Historical and Political, of the . . . British Settlements in North America*, II, 331).

taxation? Lieutenant Governor Patrick Gordon, in reporting to the Board of Trade in 1730 on the provincial revenues, declared that the support of provincial administration came from two sources: the first was from the interest secured on public loans resulting — as we have seen in the case of New Jersey — from the emission of paper currency; secondly, there was a small excise on the sale of spirits. The first source of revenue brought in £3,000 Pennsylvania currency in that year and the latter somewhat less than £1,000 — "a sufficiency to answer all the present exigencies of this Government."[83] By 1752 the income from the excise had mounted to £3,519.6.8, of which £2,224.12.8 came from Philadelphia County, with less than £100 from each of the counties of Northampton, York, and Cumberland, which paid in respectively £77, £54, and £40, in round numbers.[84] In that year it was also calculated that the province was entitled to receive interest amounting to £8,460.-12 on sums advanced on land mortgages by the loan office, with a net revenue, after necessary deductions, of £7,381.1. The happy situation of the province was summed up by Governor Morris in a letter to General Braddock early in 1755: ". . . We are burthened with no Taxes and are not only out of Debt, but have a Revenue of Seven Thousand a Year and Fifteen Thousand Pounds in Bank, all at the Disposal of the House of Assembly."[85]

By 1750 Pennsylvania, Maryland, and, with certain rights remaining reserved to the Crown, Delaware[86] were the surviving proprietary colonies within the British Empire out of all those which came into existence in the seventeenth century. In the two colonies on the Delaware Thomas and Richard Penn, the sons of the first Proprietor, sought jointly to exercise the powers and enjoy

---

[83] Shelburne Papers, 45:205–11.

[84] See statement of excise collected 1752–3, Penna. State Archives (Ms.), Doc. 607. In 1752 there were 120 taverns in Philadelphia with licences and 118 other establishments that were privileged to sell rum and other strong liquors by the quart. See L. H. Gipson: *Lewis Evans* . . . , p. 128. See also R. E. Graham: "The Taverns of Colonial Philadelphia," American Philosophical Society *Transactions*, XLIII, 318–25.

[85] *Pennsylvania Archives*, 4th ser., II, 373. Governor Hamilton, in communicating with the House of Representatives in August 1751, declared that not one shilling was levied on the people for the service of Government (*ibid.*, II, 156) and in 1754 said in a veto message:" You cannot but be sensible, Gentlemen, that the Funds you are now possessed of, which are to continue yet for several Years without Diminution, are greatly more than sufficient for the Support of Government" (*ibid.*, II, 227).

[86] For the peculiar situation of Delaware see the next chapter.

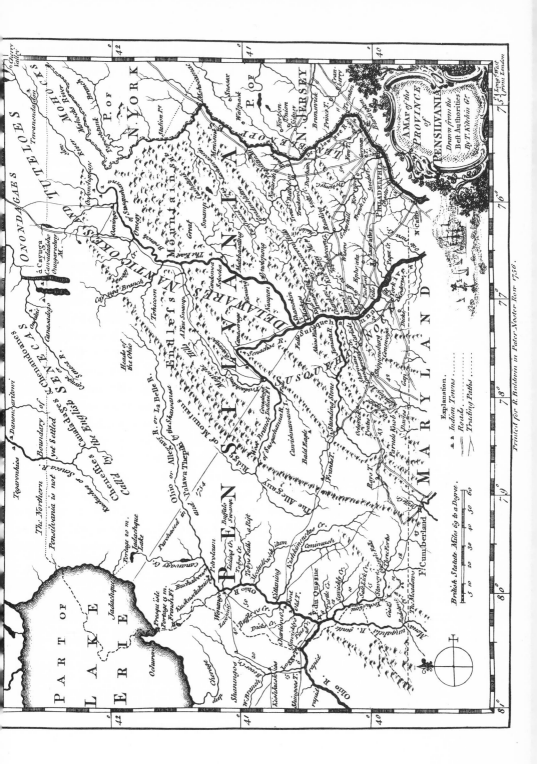

"A Map of the Province of Pensilvania
Drawn from the Best Authorities"
by Thomas Kitchin, 1756.

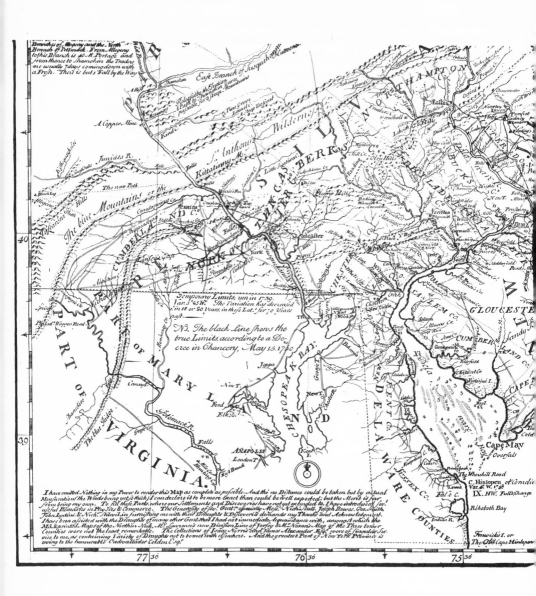

The eastern portion of the Province of Pennsylvania
and the Three Lower Counties on the Delaware.
(From the second edition of the Lewis Evans map, 1752)

the privileges embodied in the royal charter of the year 1681.[87]
These prerogatives had been limited by subsequent parliamentary
enactment — as, for instance, the statute of 1696 requiring royal
approval for proprietary appointments of Governors and the act
placing restrictions on the sale of lands in America to aliens[88] —
and especially by the acts regulating trade and industry which were
binding upon all the plantations. Under the terms of the charter, the
Proprietor, with the assent of the freemen of the province, was empowered to pass measures that would meet the needs of the settlers,
provided that these were in harmony with the laws of England. In
fufilment of this, William Penn, after much experimenting with
idealistic schemes of government and under some compulsion, issued his "Frame" of 1701, known as the Charter of Liberties, which
became the basis of government of Pennsylvania throughout the
remainder of the colonial period. It established a legislature composed of the Governor, appointed by the Proprietor, and the Assembly chosen annually by the freemen.[89] In other words, the
Council of the province was no part of this legislature.[90]

In no other British colony, outside those colonies which were

---

[87] The Delaware Counties came to Penn by a lease and release from James, Duke
of York, after 1681.

[88] 7 and 8 William III, c. 22, Par. 16.

[89] Referring to the difficult position of the Governors of Pennsylvania, Lewis Evans
declared: "If they disobey the Proprietaries they are in danger of losing their places,
and if they disoblige the Assembly they lose their Salaries" (L. H. Gipson: *Lewis
Evans* . . . , p. 127).

[90] William Smith: *Brief State of the Province of Pennsylvania* (1755), p. 5.
The following comment on the Pennsylvania government was made in 1753:
"The Governor for the better execution of his Office has several able and experienced Gentlemen to advise with in an Emergency[,] call'd his Council[,] tho he
nominates & superceds at his pleasure. They are not limited to numbers but generally
consist of 10 or 12[;] they are only his privy Council during his Administration. In
Case of a Lieutenants Death or removal, the oldest Councellor if another is not Chosen,
becomes President of the Council, who with 4 Councellors at least can exercise all
the Powers of a Governor except Legislation. This defect of Power in the President &
Council is one of the greatest in our Constitution. In President Palmers late Administration when our Coast was annoy'd with six or seven Privateers at one time, we had
not power to make an Act for The Public Utility and Safety, tho the whole Province
had been at Stake. . . . Whether this Exception of Legislation was accidental as
some suppose, or design'd as others imagine for the Sake of securing the proprietary
Interst, I cannot tell, But this I venture to say, The Proprietary Interest will Suffer
most, if extremity shou'd oblige the Assembly with the President & Council to pass
acts of Assembly. It is the Opinion of some of the most eminent Lawyers and Statesmen on the Continent that they may pass Laws, tho' an Act of Assembly be expressly
to the contrary" (L. H. Gipson: *Lewis Evans* . . . , pp. 128–9).

corporate, was the deputized power of the people more aggressively employed in the direction of controlling government than in Pennsylvania in the 1750's. The representatives had boldly asserted even their right to sit as a body on their own adjournment, denying thereby the authority of the Governor to prorogue or dissolve them.[91] Since 1723 they had also claimed, upon the basis of legislation passed in that year and assented to by Sir William Keith "in manifest Contempt of all the Instructions of the Proprietary Family," the sole right to dispose of the public money.[92] Further, they had wrested from the Governors the appointment of a number of officers in possession of lucrative posts, such as the provincial treasurer, the trustees of the loan office, the collectors of the excise, the health officer, the brander of flour, and the brander of beef and pork. "The Powers they enjoy," stated a contemporary, "are extraordinary and some of them so repugnant, that they are a Source of greatest Confusion in the Government."[93] Moreover, one unique provision of the charter granted to Penn aided the establishment of a virtual legislative independence from Great Britain. This was the clause allowing the Proprietor five years within which to transmit all acts passed in Pennsylvania to the King's Council for acceptance or rejection, with the provision that rejection must take place within a period of six months after delivery to the Council, otherwise the measures thus transmitted would be considered laws. As a result of this, complained the Board of Trade in 1721, "it frequently happens that several Laws unfit for the Royal Assent continue in force for five years, and after being disallowed by the Crown are enacted again, and by this practice become in a manner perpetual."[94]

---

[91] "But what most distinguishes the Assembly of this Colony from all others in America is to meet on a Set day, and sit upon their own Adjournment & during their own pleasure, without its being in any Bodys Power to disolve or prorogue them. . . . But those Priviledges would not suit any Assembly, who are not elected yearly, on the Expiration of a year is a certain Dissolution" (*ibid.*, p. 131–2).

[92] For the acts of 1723 relating to bills of credit and the laying of an excise on spirits which together gave the Assembly financial control of the public funds see *Pennsylvania Statutes at Large*, III, 389–417.

[93] William Smith: *op. cit.*, pp. 5, 9.

[94] Representation of the Board of Trade, September 8, 1721, Shelburne Papers, 45:111–13. For the reports of the legal advisers of the Board of Trade on the Pennsylvania laws from 1745 to 1753 see C.O. 5:1269, pp. 15, 18, 33; 1273, pp. 58, 59; 1274, pp. 51, 61–3, 67–8, 78, 83, 108–10, 116. For a discussion of this see W. T. Root: *The*

In 1746 an issue arose over the right of the Crown to pass on certain acts that had long been before the Privy Council. The statute directly in question was passed by Pennsylvania in 1742 and was based upon an earlier act, that of the year 1729/30, imposing an import duty of £5 on persons convicted of heinous crimes who were being brought into the colony from the mother country.[95] The earlier act was not called into question, but in September 1746 Francis Fane, the legal counsel for the Board, reported adversely against the act of 1742. This led the Proprietors to petition the King in Council relative to calling into question old acts that had long been before the Commissioners for Trade and Plantations.[96] In spite of this, an order in Council dated December 17, 1746, approved a representation proposing the repeal of the act of 1742 as not warranted by the laws of Great Britain.[97]

Evidence is not lacking that the Crown was concerned by observing a disposition among the people of Pennsylvania to render themselves autonomous and, in the words of a critic, to set up "a pure Republick," as it were. There was much, it is true, not clear in the legal relations between the King and the province, especially as to the degree to which the former could, under the charter, interfere in the government of the latter. For example, in 1752, in response to orders of the Lords of the Committee of the Privy Council, the Board of Trade laid before the Attorney General and the Solicitor General for their opinion certain queries that showed a strong desire on the part of the mother country to exercise a much stricter control over the law-making processes of this plantation. These were: first, Whether, consistent with the charter, the Crown could give to the Governor instructions of any kind, other than such as relate to the laws of trade and navigation; secondly, Whether the Crown could give instructions to the Governor relating to the passing of laws in general; thirdly, Whether the Crown could give instructions to the

---

Relations of Pennsylvania with the British Government, Chap. 5, "The Royal Disallowance."

[95] *Pennsylvania Statutes at Large*, IV, 164–71, 360–70.

[96] P.R.O., C.O. 5:1271, pp. 33, 38. In February 1744/5 the Board took into consideration a body of laws passed in 1725–6 and reported on by Fane in 1727. See *ibid.*, pp. 15–16.

[97] *Ibid.*, p. 44.

Governor not to give his assent to any particular law unless a clause be inserted suspending its execution till His Majesty's pleasure could be determined; fourthly, Whether the Crown could give instructions to the Governor to endeavour to obtain the insertion of a clause in any act suspending its execution until the King's pleasure could be ascertained.[98] The nature of the reply of the legal advisers, if one were sent, has not come to light. However, in a general way the question had arisen previously in the year 1744 — when the law officers of the Crown had been requested by the Board to give an opinion as to what the legislature of Pennsylvania might be obliged to do and what appropriate means were in order to provide for the security of that province — and had elicited the reply that little could be done outside an act of Parliament.[99]

The true state of the government of Pennsylvania in the middle of the eighteenth century is revealed in a letter that Richard Peters, the provincial secretary, addressed to Thomas Penn on February 12, 1753, relating to the weakness of the government of the colony. He attributed this to the fact that the Assembly had the sole disposal of all public money. Its members, he pointed out, "dare not disoblige the People thro fear of losing their seats . . . , and the People knowing their Power insult the Magistrates, contend w^h their Governors, oppose the Proprietaries, influence Courts of Justice, and in short settle Lands without the Proprietaries Consent knowing that the Sheriffs dare not meddle with them."[100] In 1755 Governor Morris, in the midst of war, was obliged to confess to the Governor of Virginia that he could do little to help that province ward off the dangers threatening the frontiers on account of the attitude of the Assembly:

"You are sensible they have been most remarkably indulged, both by the Crown and Proprietaries, and are suffered to enjoy Powers unknown to any other Assembly upon the Continent, and even such

---

[98] See the Board of Trade *Journal, 1749–1753*, pp. 283–4; see also C.O. 5:1273, p. 101.

[99] For the report of D. Ryder and W. Murray, October 19, 1744, see C.O. 5:1271, p. 12. This opinion follows closely that of Attorney General Northey, delivered February 22, 1714. For this see "Edward Northey's Legal Opinions," Library of Congress accessions.

[100] Penn Manuscripts, Official Correspondence, 6:3, 1753–1754, Historical Society of Pennsylvania.

as may render them a very dangerous Body hereafter; but not content with the Privileges granted to them by Charter they [lay] Claim to many more, and among others an absolute Exemption from the Force of Royal and Proprietary Instructions."[101]

Such was Pennsylvania — not only a land of religious sects but a colony where men were aggressively reaching out to grasp all of those powers which they identified with a system of self-government.

Thomas and Richard Penn, the joint Proprietors of Pennsylvania in the middle of the eighteenth century, were the surviving sons of William Penn, the Founder, by his second wife, Hannah. Together with their elder brother, John, they succeeded under the terms of their father's will of 1712, supplemented by one drawn up by their mother six years later, according to which John received one half of the proprietary; the remainder was divided equally between his two younger brothers.[102] After the termination of a suit in chancery which sustained the earlier will and also after a release of the claims of the descendants of William Penn's first wife in 1731, the three sons of Hannah administered their proprietary without interference and with unusual unanimity until the death of John in 1746. His undivided portion, by his own desire, thereupon went to Thomas, who now had rights to three fourths of the total; for, under the terms of a formal agreement executed in 1732, the brothers had determined that the estate should be reserved to their male heirs, under condition that if any one of the three should die without such issue, his estate should go to the surviving brothers or brother as the case might be, "as he might appoint."[103]

What manner of men were these sons of the great Founder? Their father had revealed neither business capacity nor personal ambition. His sole concerns for the proprietary had been to have a colony of contented people and to secure an income sufficient to keep his growing family out of debt. A recent historian has described John and Thomas as not possessed of "an atom of William

---

[101] *Pennsylvania Archives*, 4th ser., II, 352–3.
[102] See *Pennsylvania Colonial and Federal: A History, 1608–1903* (ed. H. M. Jenkins, 3 vols., Philadelphia, 1903), I, 372–3.
[103] *Ibid.*, I, 374.

Penn's goodness of heart or breadth of character. They were sordid, unscrupulous, overbearing and dishonest." As for Thomas, he was "little better than a common blockhead" and "was greedy, stingy and cruel, and withal dull, repellent and morose."[104]

These charges are difficult to sustain unless one is prepared to rely solely upon the opinions of the enemies of these men.[105] For the truth appears to be, as predicated on their correspondence, that John and Thomas were worthy successors to William, although less idealistic than their father. They certainly far surpassed him in common sense and gave the province a businesslike administration, putting an end to a world of confusion — something that the Founder could not do. They were, of course, not unmindful of the potential value of their proprietary in the support of the Penn family and sought to draw the largest possible revenue from it.

However, down to the 1760's Thomas and Richard Penn were so burdened with debts, partly on account of William Penn's negligence and incompetence, that little progress was made in establishing the family fortunes. "People imagine because we are at the head of a large Province we must be rich," declared Thomas in a letter written about 1750, "but . . . I tell you that for fifteen years from 1732 to 1747, I laid by but about one hundred pounds a year."[106] One major problem was the difficulty involved in the proper collection of the quit-rents from the lands. For the quit-rent rolls were in chaotic condition upon the death of the first Proprietor. Even in 1755 Thomas complained that "not one-fifth of our quit-rents are paid."[107] So late as 1764 rents from the appropriated lands of Northampton County amounted to but £161.15.6.[108]

In 1750 the terms for granting lands (as fixed by the Proprietors in 1732) were the payment of £15.10 Pennsylvania currency on each 100 acres and an annual quit-rent payment in addition of a

---

[104] A. C. Buell: *William Penn as Founder of Two Commonwealths* (New York, 1904), p. 348.

[105] The author desires to acknowledge his indebtedness to Muriel Louise Wilson, one of his former Lehigh graduate students, whose unpublished master's thesis, "Thomas Penn, Chief Proprietor of Pennsylvania: A Study of the Proprietorial Activities as Evidenced by the Penn Letter Books," was of great assistance at this point.

[106] Letter Books, Historical Society of Pennsylvania, quoted by Miss Wilson in her "Thomas Penn, Chief Proprietor."

[107] *Ibid.*

[108] *Ibid.*

halfpenny an acre, in place of earlier terms which between 1719 and 1732 had been £10 purchase price and a quit-rent of two shillings per 100 acres. This payment was reduced in 1765 to £5 sterling or £8.10 Pennsylvania currency, but the quit-rent was increased to one penny sterling an acre or eight shillings fourpence per 100 acres.[109] The Pennsylvania land system, although meeting with increased opposition in the 1750's, was apparently fairly well regulated. This at least was the judgement of a careful observer, Lewis Evans.

"What the World has imputed to the Happiness of our Constitution, is with more justice to be ascribed to the happy Management of the Land Offices," he affirmed in 1753. He thereupon described the method employed for the sale of land. The individual desiring a piece of land applied to the provincial Secretary for a survey warrant and at the same time paid £5 for each 100 acres with six months' credit for the payment of the remainder, amounting to £10.10 or a total of £15.10. The warrant was then sent to the Surveyor General. Next the deputy surveyor of the district surveyed the land, and a detailed description was prepared by the Surveyor General, which was returned to the Secretary's office. The patentee, after payment of the sum still due to the Receiver General, then received a patent that passed under the great seal of the province and was recorded in the rolls office. The fees incidental to this for a tract of 200 or 300 acres did not exceed a couple of guineas, "and not a Guinea more on 1,000 Acres."

"The Correct management of the Proprietaries's Affairs," Evans asserted, "has prevented all Disputes, & Law Suits between the Planters, so frequent, in the other Colonies. Every Man is glad of holding immediately under the Chief Lord of the Soil. And if we add to this the great Ease, and Dispatch that Business has been

---

[109] For the variations made by the Penns in the terms upon which lands were granted in the course of the seventeenth and eighteenth centuries see B. W. Bond: *The Quit-Rent System in the American Colonies* (New Haven and London, 1919), p. 134. See also W. R. Shepherd: *History of Proprietary Government in Pennsylvania* (New York, 1896), pp. 17–18, 34. Bond rightly stresses the criticism of the land system which increased from 1755 to the outbreak of the War for American Independence. See B. W. Bond: *op. cit.*, pp. 133–49. For an additional study of the colonial land system see Marshall Harris: *Origin of the Land Tenure System in the United States* (Ames, Iowa, 1953) and especially Chap. 8 and pp. 237–41.

done with in our Offices we need not wonder to see so many Strangers flock thither to partake of our Happiness."[110]

By the year 1774, owing to the most constant attention to the details of business on the part of Thomas,[111] the surviving son of William, the revenue had become large. For example, in June of that year, the Proprietor acknowledged total remittances amounting to £12,700.[112]

The attitude of the Penn family toward the Holy Experiment did not change during the Founder's lifetime. William Penn remained in the Quaker faith until his death. This was also true of his son John, although he was a "fighting" Friend who further believed in compelling settlers suspected of Roman Catholicism to take oaths to clear themselves. However, Richard, early in his manhood, joined the Established Church of England. Thomas remained a member of the Society of Friends until after his marriage in 1751 to Juliana Fermor, daughter of the first Earl of Pomfret. He, however, had had an ambition to act in person as Governor of Pennsylvania. During the years 1732–41 he was in the province giving personal supervision to various matters pertaining to the proprietorial business, and until about 1755 was constantly expecting to have matters so arranged — especially the vexatious boundary dispute with Lord Baltimore — as to permit him to return to spend the rest of his years there.

During the period before the death of John, Thomas Penn might have had the coveted appointment had it not been for the opposition of the Friends in England who insisted that as a Quaker he must not allow himself to take the oaths required of all Governors. This may have influenced him in his decision to break with that sect. By 1743 he had discarded the Quaker garb, due, as he wrote to Governor Thomas, to his stand in favour of the proper defence of the province during the war between Great Britain and Spain, and also,

---

[110] L. H. Gipson: *Lewis Evans* . . . , pp. 135–7.

[111] Thomas Penn died in March 1775.

[112] In 1776, a year after Thomas Penn's death in March 1775, the total proprietorial quit-rents and profits were £10,204.0.7¾, at least on paper. In that year, 1,629,-279 acres called for a penny an acre quit-rent; 1,385,219¼ acres, a halfpenny an acre, and 856,895¼ acres, a shilling per 100 acres. By 1779 there had been paid from 1700 onward a total of over £63,679 sterling in quit-rents, with a balance, however, of over £118,569 still due. See B. W. Bond: *op. cit.*, pp. 134 n. and 161 n.

as he adds, because he might yet become Governor himself. His repudiation of Quakerism in 1751, together with his zeal in promoting the family interests within Pennsylvania, however, brought upon him so much criticism that by 1755 he had decided not to subject his family to the disagreeable treatment sure to follow should he go there to live. As a result, from 1748 to 1754 James Hamilton, a member of a powerful Pennsylvania family and a capable man of good character, was deputized as chief executive. Although he enjoyed the confidence of the Chief Proprietor, he insisted on resigning in 1754 because of continuous disputes with the Assembly and also because he was obliged to neglect his own important business interests while filling a position he did not find particularly profitable.

This was the state of William Penn's Holy Experiment in the middle of the eighteenth century. Writing of the character of civilization in Pennsylvania at this period, Robert Proud refers to the "very remarkable industry, honesty, moderation, and good policy" of the early settlers and their successors, who, enjoying "freedom of thinking, and religious worship, with a just and equal participation of national and civil rights," had turned the wilderness into "a fruitful field."[113]

---

[113] *History of Pennsylvania* (2 vols., Philadelphia, 1798), II, 234.

CHAPTER VIII

A Nondescript Colony on the Delaware

ONLY occasionally referred to as Delaware in the middle of the eighteenth century, the Three Lower Counties on the Delaware held an unusual but undefined position among the North American colonies. Long a bone of contention between the rival claims of the Penn and Baltimore families, the "Territories," as they were frequently called in official *communiqués,* were assumed by William Penn's descendants to be part of their patrimony. A counter claim dating from even earlier was put forward on behalf of the descendants of Cecilius (or Cecil), Lord Baltimore.

The area that is now the state of Delaware was originally explored by the Dutch, colonized by the Swedes[1] and Finns,[2] conquered by the Dutch, and in turn taken over by the English. It was in 1664 that Colonel Richard Nicolls sent Sir Robert Carr to the Delaware, soon after the capture of New Amsterdam, to occupy the region in the name of the Duke of York — not by right of grant, but by right of conquest.[3] This was done. After William Penn obtained

---

[1] For the most authoritative work on the Swedes in Delaware see Amandus Johnson: *The Swedish Settlements on the Delaware* (2 vols., Philadelphia, 1911).

[2] See E. A. Louhi: *The Delaware Finns* (New York, 1925) and J. H. Wuorinen: *The Finns on the Delaware . . .* (New York, 1938).

[3] The Duke of York's royal patent of 1664, while it included what is now New York, a part of what is now Maine, all the lands west of the Connecticut River, and

his patent for Pennsylvania on March 4, 1680/1, he became concerned lest the province should be quite shut off from the Atlantic Ocean by the Baltimore family claims covering the northern boundary of Maryland (which are elaborated later in this chapter). He therefore besought the Duke of York to grant to him the conquered lands lying west of the Delaware River. Although the Duke himself had no royal patent to this territory at the time, he was prevailed upon to execute certain deeds of lease and release in favour of Penn.[4] Despite the fact that the Duke later received a patent for Delaware from Charles II,[5] which gave him a legal title to it, neither as heir apparent to the throne nor later as James II did he ever

---

all of what is now New Jersey, together with Martha's Vineyard and Nantucket, did not extend beyond the west banks of the Delaware River. For the patent of 1664 see *Documents Relative to the Colonial History of the State of New York* (ed. E. B. O'Callaghan, 15 vols., Albany, 1853–87), II, 295–8.

It will be noted that the patent issued on March 22, 1664, to the Duke of York covered those parts of the "maine Land of New England" specified therein. New England, according to the patent given to the Council for New England, dated March 13, 1620, included all lands between "the Degrees of Fourty and Fourty-eight." Although the Council for New England surrendered its patent to the King in 1635, the geographical limits of New England, from the point of view of the patent office, were still held to be the aforesaid degrees. When Virginia became a royal colony at the time the London Company of Virginia lost its charter in 1624, its boundaries likewise remained the same—exclusive of Maryland, which had been granted to Lord Baltimore in 1632.

[4] There were executed on August 24, 1682, two leases and two deeds comprising all the land now a part of the state of Delaware. The originals of three of these documents are in the Delaware State Archives at Dover. In this connection see R. S. Rodney: "Early Relations of Delaware and Pennsylvania," *Pennsylvania Magazine of History and Biography*, LIV, 209–40. For a copy of the Duke's deed of the above date giving to Penn all land twelve miles south of New Castle and extending to Cape Henlopen see *Register of Pennsylvania* (ed. Samuel Hazard, Philadelphia, 1828), I, 429.

[5] The royal patent for Delaware from the King to the Duke bears the date of March 22, 1683. The original also is in the Delaware Public Archives. Although this grant passed through various offices, it apparently never, for reasons that are not clear, received the Great Seal. To this extent it was defective. See C. M. Andrews: *The Colonial Period of American History* (4 vols., New Haven, 1934–8), III, 295 n. Professor Andrews has the following to say about the two land leases that Penn received from the Duke of York: "The very fact that the duke, undoubtedly urged on by Penn himself, tried to obtain a royal confirmation seven months after the leases had been signed, shows that both Penn and the duke had doubts as to the soundness of the title" (*ibid.*, III, 295–6). See also W. R. Shepherd: *History of Proprietary Government in Pennsylvania* (New York, 1896), p. 322, and M. P. Andrews: *The Founding of Maryland* (Baltimore & New York, 1933), pp. 40–1. For Delaware in general at this period see H. C. Reed: *Delaware: A History of the First State* (3 vols., New York, 1947), I, Chaps. 3–4.

make any transfer of the territory to Penn which might validate the latter's title as its Proprietor or even as the grantee of its lands.[6] As a result, *legally* the area became a Crown possession. So it remained *legally* until the War for American Independence.

Nevertheless, Penn proceeded on the assumption that his deeds and leases of 1682 were valid, and upon arriving in the New World later that year he sought to unite firmly the three Delaware counties to the three counties then forming Pennsylvania. An act of union to this effect, petitioned for by representatives of the people, was promulgated by him at Chester or Upland in Pennsylvania on December 7, 1682, "by and with the advice and consent of the deputies of the freemen of the province and counties aforesaid, in Assembly met. . . ."[7] The same body also accepted the idealistic, rather complicated frame of government which Penn had drawn up during the spring of that year while still in England.[8]

Notwithstanding Penn's hopes his attempts to bring the peoples of the two areas to accept political fusion in practice were far from successful. Sharp divergencies soon developed.

The inhabitants of the Lower Counties were in favour of defensive measures — especially in face of the dangers to them from the pirates abounding at the mouth of the Delaware in the latter part of the seventeenth century — and demanded a militia and the construction of adequate forts.[9] The people of the province would have

---

[6] It seems that one of James II's last acts, before his flight from England as a result of the so-called Glorious Revolution, was to order the draft of a grant of Kent and Sussex counties in Delaware to Penn. This was drawn up under date of December 10, 1688, but the King, in his haste to escape, never signed it. For a copy of the draft of the grant see the Appendix of the article by B. A. Konkle: "Delaware: "A Grant Yet Not a Grant," *Pennsylvania Magazine of History and Biography*, LIV, 241–54.

[7] For a copy of "An Act of Union for annexing and uniting of the Counties of Newcastle, James's and Whorekills, Alias Deal, to the Province of Pennsylvania; and of Naturalization of all Foreigners, in the Province and Counties aforesaid," see *Pennsylvania Archives*, 8th ser., I, 328–30.

[8] *Ibid.*, I, 334–41.

[9] For the extent of the threat of pirates and privateers in the Delaware Bay and River areas up to 1748 see W. M. Mervine: "Pirates and Privateers in the Delaware Bay and River," *Pennsylvania Magazine of History and Biography*, XXXII, 459–70, and H. C. Conrad: *History of the State of Delaware* (3 vols., Wilmington, 1908), I, 73–4; see also Leon de Valinger, Jr.: *Colonial Military Organization in Delaware, 1638–1776* (Wilmington, 1938), pp. 27–30, 41–2. For incidents of privateers attacking New Castle in 1747 and the constant threat of their attacks along the Delaware

none of these things. Again, most of those of the Low Counties at the time of the Act of Union were still of Swedish, Finnish, or Dutch extraction and of either Lutheran or Calvinist religious persuasion; most of those of the province were English or Welsh and were predominantly Quaker in religion and pacifistic in outlook. Further, at the time of the union, the territorial limits of the Lower Counties were highly restricted on all sides and were destined to remain so, whereas the three Pennsylvania counties of Chester, Philadelphia, and Bucks were plainly destined to be supplemented from time to time, as the population expanded, by the creation of new counties out of what was still the wilderness of the province. In addition, there was considerable rivalry between New Castle and Philadelphia as centres of commerce and as seaports in 1682. The rapid rise of the city of Brotherly Love, soon overshadowing its competitor, did not fail to create hard feelings, nor were these at all assuaged when the issue arose as to the meeting place of the Assembly. The provincial representatives insisted on Philadelphia and also held that all laws passed at New Castle must be reaffirmed by an Assembly meeting within the limits of Pennsylvania. The colonials of the Lower Counties, facing political and economic submergence in their relations with their more powerful neighbour, became increasingly restless under a yoke that they felt was binding them as unequals. Those of Pennsylvania became equally convinced that they could expect only obstruction in their endeavours to promote the welfare of the province so long as representatives of the Lower Counties remained in the Assembly.[10]

This was the situation when Penn returned to America in 1699. The following year, on October 14, in answer to the general desire for a new frame of government, he assured his petitioners that he

---

River during the summers of 1747 and 1748 see Minutes of the Provincial Council of Pennsylvania, Colonial Records, V, 89–94, 117–19, 245–64, 266–71. As a result of these incidents an embargo was placed upon the Lewes pilots in effect restraining them from their livelihood. This they protested, claiming that the pilots dwelling on the New Jersey side were suffering no such limitations of their activities. See ibid., V, 82, 111–12, 226; see also Pennsylvania Gazette, December 15, 1747, reprinted in the Boston Evening Post, January 18, 1748.

[10] For an extended treatment of the differences between the two areas see R. W. Johannsen: "The Conflict between the Three Lower Counties on the Delaware and the Province of Pennsylvania, 1682–1704," Delaware History, V, 96–150; see also W. R. Shepherd: op. cit., pp. 324–37.

would give them all possible assistance to that end.[11] But during this same session, indications of the future political separation of the Lower Counties became manifest when their representatives proposed:

> "That the Union shall be confirmed on Condition, that at no Time hereafter the Number of Representatives of the People in Legislation in the Province, shall exceed them of the annexed Counties; but if hereafter more Counties shall be made in the Province, and thereby more Representatives be added, that then the Union shall Cease."[12]

This attitude was most distressing to Penn. Early in the fall of 1701, in order to try to persuade both groups to bury differences in point of view, he declared to the general Assembly: "Your Union is what I desire. . . . Yield in Circumstantials to preserve Essentials; and being safe in one another, you will always be so in Esteem with me."[13] But his pleas fell on deaf ears. Thus, when the famous Charter of Liberties of that year was drawn up and approved by Penn — shortly before sailing for England in order to defend his New World territorial limits against both Lord Baltimore's claims and those "Interests" seeking an Act of Parliament that would unite all the proprietary colonies to the Crown — the following statement was included in the closing proviso:

> "If the Representatives of the Province and Territories shall not hereafter agree to Joyn together in Legislation . . . any Time within Three Years . . . the Inhabitants of each County in the Territories shall have as many persons to Represent them in a distinct Assembly for ye Territories as shall be by them Requested. . . ."[14]

When the Assembly met the following year in Philadelphia the representatives of the Province showed their attitude toward a con-

---

[11] Proceedings of the Assembly at New Castle, October 14, 1700, *Pennsylvania Archives*, 8th ser., I, 243.

[12] *Ibid.*, I, 258.

[13] *Ibid.*, I, 311. For Penn's concerns with all the problems of the Lower Counties see *Correspondence between William Penn and James Logan . . . , 1700–1750*, Historical Society of Pennsylvania *Memoirs*, IX–X (Philadelphia, 1870–2).

[14] "Minutes of the Provincial Council of Pennsylvania," *Colonial Records*, II, 60.

tinuing union with the Lower Counties or Territories by affirming to Lieutenant Governor Hamilton that they "had long groaned under the hardship of it [the Union] and now [having] an opportunity . . . to ease ymselves of those troubles they Judged themselves obliged to make use of it for their own Safety & Quiet."[15] As for the representatives of the Lower Counties, they would neither take their seats in the Assembly nor recognize the binding power of the Charter of Liberties over their constituents.[16] They even questioned the legality of Penn's claim to the Three Counties, although willing to accept as their chief executive the Lieutenant Governor appointed by the Proprietor for Pennsylvania. Nevertheless, they were prevailed upon by the Lieutenant Governor in 1704 to elect, under certain specified conditions, members to a joint Assembly. As these conditions involved the question of representation, the Pennsylvania representatives refused to accept them. With a new election called for and held, the representatives of the Lower Counties gathered at New Castle in a distinct Assembly on May 22 of that year. This event marks the permanent political separation of the two areas.[17]

Throughout the period from 1704 to the War for American Independence Delaware was unique in more ways than one among the British colonies. It had no official name; it was legally neither a proprietary nor a recognized royal colony; nor was it a corporate colony as were Connecticut and Rhode Island, nor even a trusteeship in the formal sense that Georgia was during the first twenty years of its existence as a colony. While the laws of Pennsylvania had to be sent to England for approval by the Privy Council, this was never done in the case of the Lower Counties. Although the

---

[15] *Ibid.*, II, 73. According to R. W. Johannsen (*op. cit.*, V, 125), Deputy Governor Hamilton did his utmost to favour the reuniting of the "Territories" and the province, citing among the foremost inconveniences that would result otherwise "the fact that the province would lose the rich tobacco trade which they carried on with England, since all the tobacco was grown in the lower counties." It is worth noting that the growth of excellent-quality tobacco in Delaware, which seems to have had a prominent part in its agriculture in the first quarter of the eighteenth century, had diminished to such a degree by the middle of the century that Israel Acrelius, in his contemporary account (1759), reported: "Tobacco is planted in almost every garden, but not more than for domestic use." See *History of New Sweden*, Pennsylvania Historical Society *Memoirs*, XI, 151.

[16] *Pennsylvania Colonial Records*, II, 75.

[17] For this separation see R. S. Rodney: *op. cit.*, LIV, 236–40.

Lieutenant Governor or Deputy Governor of Pennsylvania also acted in the same capacity for the "Territories" and was nominated by the Penn family and approved for his post by the King with certain rights reserved to the Crown, no distinct commission was ever given to him as the chief executive officer of the Lower Counties. Further, while royal instructions relating specifically to the Province of Pennsylvania were issued to him, he never received any that had special application to the Lower Counties.[18]

Such was the state of uncertainty as to what kind of colony Delaware was that, in addition to questioning the legality of Penn's claim, members of its Assembly meeting at New Castle in 1708 made an effort to secure a royal commission for a Governor of their own.[19] In other words, the people of the three counties wanted to be recognized as a royal colony. However, by 1717 — in view of the attempt of the Earl of Sutherland two years earlier to secure a royal grant of the Lower Counties based upon a claim of £20,000 due from George I for services rendered — the people of Delaware changed their attitude. Thoroughly alarmed lest their land titles might be questioned and a rapacious Proprietor substituted for indulgent supervision, they became more favourably disposed toward Penn. Declaring to Lieutenant Governor Keith in 1717 that their own interests and those of the Proprietor of Pennsylvania were so interwoven that any alteration of this relationship would be disastrous to them, they even sought to be reunited to Pennsylvania in one government. But the Assembly of the Province, once having been freed of the Delaware representatives, was not at all desirous of seeking a reunion.[20]

One result of the Earl of Sutherland's application for a grant of Delaware had been that Crown lawyers were induced to pry deeply into Penn's rights, and the opinions of both the Attorney General and the Solicitor General which ensued were adverse to the Penn family.[21] While the Crown took no steps to assume direct control of

---

[18] See C. M. Andrews: op. cit., III, 324–6.

[19] Pennsylvania Colonial Records, II, 423.

[20] For an abstract of the Earl of Sutherland's memorial, see Secretary Stanhope to the Board of Trade, December 29, 1715, P.R.O., C.O. 5:1265, Q. 110. For the attitude of the Pennsylvania Assembly see W. R. Shepherd: op. cit., p. 349.

[21] See George Chalmers: Opinions of Eminent Lawyers, on various Points of English Jurisprudence . . . (2 vols., London, 1814), I, 40–56.

the little colony, Penn's right to govern it was so clouded that Keith took the precaution on all Delaware documents requiring the use of a seal to utilize one from which Penn's name was omitted,[22] but which contained significantly only the coat of arms of the King of Great Britain.

This was the situation of Delaware before 1750 — a nondescript colony without official name or legal constitution, in the sense that other colonies had one, and without even a separate file of papers in the paper offices in London in recognition of its existence. Its people possessed no clearly defined rights beyond their inherent rights as subjects of the Crown of Great Britain, and the titles to their lands were not above question. When Robert Hunter Morris was appointed Deputy Governor in 1754, the royal approval of his nomination was given only after Thomas and Richard Penn, the sons of William, had signed the following characteristic declaration required of the Penn family since the year 1702:

> "We underwritten do by these Presents declare and promise, that the King's Royal Approbation and Allowance of Robert Hunter Morris, esquire, to be Deputy Governor of Pennsilvania and the Three Lower Counties upon Delaware River, shall not be construed in any Manner, to diminish or set aside the Right claimed by the Crown, to the said Three Lower Countys."[23]

The anomalous situation of Delaware before the War for American Independence may be further illustrated. When the town of New Castle was incorporated as a borough in 1724 with the power to be represented in the Assembly of the Lower Counties, its charter

---

[22] The "Act for Establishing a Great Seal for the Government" stated that "a certain Silver-Seal, now in the Governor's Custody, with the King of *Great-Britain's* Arms cut upon it, and the inscription *Delaware* round it, shall be held and deemed to be the Great Seal of Government in these Counties and Territories" (*Laws of the Government of New Castle, Kent and Sussex upon Delaware* [Philadelphia, 1741], pp. 4–5). Unfortunately, the inscription "Delaware" was spelled "Dellowarre," with the result that by an act passed in 1751 (25 Geo. II, c. 122. a.) a new seal was ordered which also displayed the arms of the King and had an inscription running round the arms which read "Counties on Delaware, 1751." The Assembly in this law provided for the validity of all laws and other acts that carried the defective seal of the colony. See *Laws of the State of Delaware from 1700 . . . to 1797* (2 vols., New-Castle, 1797), I, 299–302.

[23] See P.R.O., C.O. 5:1273, under date June 21, 1754.

was issued not by the Penn family, but in the name of George I.[24] Yet no other steps were taken to implement the King's authority or that of his successors over the Delaware Counties. Meanwhile the people clung to the Penn connection, their fears aroused by the renewal of the 1715 Sutherland application to receive the colony as a proprietary and a later one by his son to this end. Even more did they fear a strongly supported petition presented to the King in 1737 by Charles, Lord Baltimore, the Maryland Proprietor, in which he affirmed "that the Counties are admitted to have been included in the Grant of Maryland" and begged that until the matter had finally been determined "no Deputy Governor for the Three Lower Counties be appointed by commission from the Pennsylvania Proprietors, but only by the Crown."[25]

---

[24] See *New-Castle upon Delaware, May 28, 1724. . . . Sir William Keith . . . caused the King's Charter to be Publish'd for Erecting the Same into a Body Corporate and Politick, . . . by the name of Newcastle; . . . made the following Speech to the Corporation* (Philadelphia, 1724). For a copy of New Castle's charter of 1724 see R. S. Rodney: "Delaware under Governor Keith, 1717–1726," *Delaware History*, III, 26–36.

[25] *Acts of the Privy Council, Col. Ser., Unbound Papers*, p. 244. That Baltimore had the support of the Board of Trade in his position is indicated by its report that came before the Privy Council in 1735. Of the Lower Counties the Lords Commissioners declared: "There is no doubt . . . that the disputed lands were included in Baltimore's patent in 1632. . . . In 1633 and 1638 his right to the whole peninsula was affirmed; in 1683 and 1685 it was denied by the Privy Council. If the right is judged to remain in the Crown, the B[oard] of T[rade] recommend Lord Baltimore's pretensions on the ground of the money spent by his family in colonizing Maryland" (*ibid.*, p. 236).

There seems to be little doubt that the patent for Maryland issued to Lord Baltimore was intended — defective as knowledge was of certain geographical details — to extend from the south bank of the Potomac River up to the fortieth degree of north latitude, where began the possessions of the Council for New England under its grant of 1620. According to the charter, Baltimore was granted lands "in a Country hitherto uncultivated, in Parts of America, and partly occupied by Savages . . ." (see *Laws of Maryland* [ed. Thomas Bacon, Annapolis, 1765], for the patent in both Latin and English, following the Preface but without pagination). If the grant that it contained stopped at the thirty-ninth degree of north latitude, as later urged by Penn, it could not possibly have been interpreted so that its other territorial terms would have any meaning. By it Baltimore received all the land "which lyeth under the Fortieth Degree of North Latitude . . . where New England is terminated, . . . westward by the degree aforesaid unto the true Meridian of the Fountain of the River Pattowmack, then verging to the South unto the further Bank of said River" (*ibid.*). See the study supporting the claims of the Penn family by J. C. Hayes: "Penn vs. Lord Baltimore: A Brief for the Penns," *Pennsylvania History*, VIII, 278–303. For a keen analysis of the basis of the respective territorial claims of Maryland and Pennsylvania, as well as of the Lower Counties on the Delaware, see the letter of Lewis Evans to Governor Horatio Sharpe of October 20, 1753, in my *Lewis Evans . . .* (Philadelphia, 1939), pp. 42–7. Evans supports strongly the validity of Lord Baltimore's claim to all the land from the south bank of the Potomac to the fortieth degree of north latitude.

To the relief of the colonists in the Lower Counties, the Privy Council took no action on the Sutherland memorials or on the Baltimore petition, while the Baltimore-Penn boundary dispute was taken to the High Court of Chancery for final adjudication, as will be stressed subsequently. It is interesting to note that in 1768, in ratifying the agreement made between the Maryland and Pennsylvania Proprietors, the Privy Council still insisted that this should not diminish "his Majesty's claim of right to the Three Lower Counties or the interests of the planters within the same."[26]

In 1750, despite all its handicaps, Delaware had a well-rounded government. The Deputy Governor for the Lower Counties as well as for the Province of Pennsylvania worked quite harmoniously with the House of Assembly, it would appear. The legislature — which met at New Castle during this period — was composed of eighteen members, six of them elected annually by the freemen in each of the counties of New Castle, Kent, and Sussex. In 1741 it had ordered the printing of those laws previously passed and approved by the Deputy Governor which it wished to preserve.[27] They appeared in that same year under the title of *Laws of the Government of New Castle, Kent and Sussex upon Delaware*. Although only seventy-six in number, they are comprehensive in nature and indicate that the machinery for maintaining order and for meeting social and other problems of the age was by no means lacking. These laws, and others passed in the eighteenth century after the colony had separated from Pennsylvania which were not included in the code of 1741, were characterized by a certain circumspection in making innovations and by their moderation, considering the age in which they were passed.[28] The comprehensive statute passed in 1742 (15

---

[26] *Acts of the Privy Council, Col. Ser., Unbound Papers*, p. 469 and *ibid., 1766–1783*, pp. 100–8.

[27] *Minutes of the House of Assembly of the Three Counties on Delaware . . . 1740–1742* (first printed from the manuscript in 1929 by the Public Archives Commission of Delaware), p. 29. The minutes are incomplete and jump from October 25, 1740, to October 1741, leaving off abruptly on March 13, 1741/2.

[28] For the laws of Delaware covering the eighteenth century see *Laws of the State of Delaware from . . . 1700–1797* (ed. George Read, 2 vols., New Castle, 1797). A broad summary of them is given by H. C. Conrad: *History of the State of Delaware*, I, 83–6. Delaware had its county courts of common pleas and criminal courts of quarter sessions. Appeals from these courts ran to a supreme court of three judges, called justices. The justices also had the duty of holding courts of oyer and terminer in each of the Three Counties relating to capital felony cases. For a description of the judicial

Geo. II, c. 90. a.), "An Act for the more effectual preventing and punishing . . . crimes and offences committed within this government,"[29] for example, while strengthening the criminal code, adhered closely — as did the criminal code of Pennsylvania by that year — to the common, as well as statutory, law of England.[30] Yet the fact that no Delaware law was ever submitted to the Privy Council for approval or disapproval permitted legislation to stand which was disallowed in the case of the Pennsylvania Assembly. In 1727 each of the two colonies passed a law having to do with the courts of judicature containing a clause that, in the case of the Pennsylvania law, brought disallowance on the grounds that it was prejudicial to Crown revenues and would encourage illegal trade.[31] Since the Delaware law was not submitted for review, it remained in force;[32] in fact, when in 1760 an act was passed relating to the Supreme Court of the Lower Counties, this feature was retained.[33]

Again, doubtless because Delaware laws were not brought to the attention of the British authorities, the Lower Counties were able to raise a barrier against the importation of people convicted of "Heinous crimes" who had been consigned by the British courts for transportation to some colony to labour there. Such a Delaware law

---

system of Delaware in the middle of the eighteenth century see D. F. Wolcott: "Ryves Holt, of Lewes, Delaware, 1695–1763," *Delaware History*, VIII, 3–50. Holt was commissioned Chief Justice of the Lower Counties in 1745.

[29] *Laws of the State of Delaware* (1797), I, 235–8.

[30] Under terms of the above statute it was provided, for example, that persons convicted of receiving stolen goods other than slaves and live-stock, were to be whipped twenty-one lashes on the back and branded on the forehead with the letter "R," and to make fourfold restitution; if unable to do the latter, the person so convicted was consigned to servitude for a period of seven years; those receiving slaves and live-stock, such as horses, were to suffer the death penalty. In 1741 Parliament had passed a statute (14 Geo. II, c. 6) which provided that anyone who was an accessory to the stealing of sheep was to suffer the death penalty; the following year this was extended to cattle and horses (15 Geo. II, c. 34). In this connection it should be pointed out that a Delaware law passed in 1719, "An Act for the advancement of Justice and more certain administration thereof," provided that for all crimes involving treason and felony of death the common law and statutes of England should be followed. *Laws of the State of Delaware* (1797), I, 64–77.

[31] For the Pennsylvania statute of 1727 see *Charter to William Penn and Laws of the Province of Pennsylvania* . . . (eds. S. George, B. M. Nead, T. MacCamant, Harrisburg, 1879), p. 399.

[32] For the Delaware law of 1727 relating to the judiciary see *Laws of the Government of New Castle, Kent and Sussex upon Delaware* (Philadelphia, 1741), pp. 42–3.

[33] *Laws of the State of Delaware* (1797), I, 376–7. For a discussion of the above point see J. H. Smith: *Appeals to the Privy Council from the American Plantations* (New York, 1951), pp. 249–51.

was passed in 1749 (22 Geo. II, c. 114). It strengthened a statute of the year 1740 and required not only the payment of an import duty of £5 by a shipmaster for every such convicted person brought into the colony but also bound the shipmaster "by good security" to the sum of £50 for the good behaviour of each convict during the following year. Further, any person living within the area governed by the Lower Counties who should purchase one of these convicts was to forfeit £10.[34] As a result, while neighbouring Maryland was flooded with transported criminals, this was not true of Delaware.[35]

For administrative purposes the Lower Counties were divided, not into towns or townships as were Pennsylvania and other colonies to the northward, or into parishes, as were Maryland and colonies to the southward, but into hundreds, in line with the Anglo-Saxon subdivision of the English shires. Yet in some ways the little colony adhered to the pattern of the Pennsylvania government. The Assembly was unicameral like that of the province. The electors of its members could qualify, as they could in Pennsylvania, either by taking the prescribed oaths or by affirmation. But here the similarity ended. In Delaware there was compulsory voting at least after 1734 under terms of a law passed that year for regulating elections.[36] During the administration of Lieutenant Governor Keith (1717–1726) whatever indulgence of affirmation had been permitted earlier was now denied to Assemblymen, with the result that Quakers no longer sat in the Delaware legislative body.[37] For in 1720, during the Keith regime, the Assembly passed "An Act for Regulating Elec-

---

[34] *Laws of the State of Delaware* (1797), I, 166–73, 277–9.

[35] In 1751, presumably influenced by the Delaware statute relating to security bonds for good behaviour, the magistrates of Baltimore and Ann Arundel counties in Maryland attempted to require the posting of £50 for the good conduct of each transported convict, but they were overruled by the provincial court for exceeding their jurisdiction. See A. E. Smith: *Colonists in Bondage . . . 1607–1706* (Chapel Hill, N.C., 1947), pp. 130–1. The attitude of the government of Maryland toward transported convicts is dealt with in Chap. 2 of the preceding volume of this series.

[36] For the law of 1734 see *Laws of the Government of Newcastle, Kent and Sussex upon Delaware . . .* (1741), pp. 76–85; see also H. C. Reed: "The Court Records of the Delaware Valley," *William and Mary Quarterly*, 3rd ser., IV, 198, and his *Delaware: A History*, I, 256.

[37] See R. S. Rodney: "Delaware under Governor Keith, 1717–1726," *Delaware History*, III, 1–36, and W. R. Shepherd: *op. cit.*, p. 349. As the introductory statement of the collection of the laws of 1741 emphasized, the standing of the earlier laws was in doubt.

tions and Ascertaining the Number of Members of Assembly"[38] (7 Geo. II, c. 61. a.) whereby no person could act as a representative unless he were prepared to make certain "Declarations" involving a profession of loyalty to the King, of detestation of the doctrine that the Pope could free a subject of his allegiance, of rejection of the belief in transubstantiation, and, finally, of acknowledgment of belief in the doctrine of the Holy Trinity. Voters, office-holders, and witnesses, on the other hand, could still qualify by affirming.[39]

The contrast between the policies of Pennsylvania and Delaware is likewise reflected in other ways. In 1740 in the midst of the war with Spain, the Assembly of the Lower Counties passed a law providing for the security and defence of the exposed coastal town of Lewes in face of the depredations of privateers and "pirates" in the Delaware Bay (13 Geo. II, c. 68).[40] This law not only gave the Deputy Governor authority to keep a military watch there but also provided that all inhabitants and freemen within the limits of the town should furnish themselves with arms under penalty and that, in case of an alarm, any person who refused to attend the place of rendezvous or muster should forfeit £5, or, if without goods that could be levied upon, should suffer commitment in jail for a period of two months. Significantly, the act provided no exemption for those who had scruples against bearing arms.

Also in 1740 Deputy Governor George Thomas appealed to the Assembly of the Lower Counties in the name of the King to give general military support to Great Britain in the war against Spain. In response the legislature readily voted £1,000 to supply provisions and transportation for the troops that had been recruited in the Lower Counties to participate in the British campaign in the West Indies.[41] The Quaker-dominated Assembly of Pennsylvania, in contrast, refused to place its seal of approval on even so much as

---

[38] *Laws of the Government of New Castle, Kent and Sussex upon Delaware* . . . 1741), pp. 76–85.

[39] See the above law and "An Act for the Advancement of Justice . . . ," *ibid.*, pp. 8–9; see also A. E. McKinley: *The Suffrage Franchise in the Thirteen English Colonies in America* (Philadelphia, 1905), p. 270.

[40] *Laws of the State of Delaware* (1797), I, 175–9. See also footnote 9 above.

[41] It seems that among the troops enlisted were a number of indentured servants. This caused dissatisfaction. Before the funds were voted the members of the Assembly were therefore assured that servants would be discharged from the service. See *Minutes of the House of Assembly of the Three Counties . . . 1740–1742*, pp. 5–8.

defensive measures although the province also was suffering from the depredations of the French upon its shipping and its commerce. As a result the Assembly became involved in a bitter controversy with the Deputy Governor.[42] The following year, while Pennsylvania refused to do so, the Assembly of the Lower Counties passed a general militia law requiring under penalty all freemen between certain ages, unless exempted, to secure arms and appear at military musters.[43] As for the Quakers in the Three Counties, this act relieved them of military service, but only on payment of two shillings sixpence to the poor fund.[44] Later, in the course of the Great War for the Empire between the years 1754 and 1763, the little colony was to participate fully in the military operations, with the result that it received a generous portion of the funds granted by Parliament to certain of the colonies for service during the years 1758, 1759, and 1760. These reimbursements were to help maintain the colony's excellent financial credit.[45] As was true of the other colonies, Delaware had a London agent in the person of David Barclay, and it was he who received and transmitted these reimbursement funds.

The readiness of the government of Delaware to support the mother country in time of war brought even further rewards. When addressing its Assembly in 1740, Deputy Governor Thomas men-

---

[42] For the controversy over the issue of defence see *Pennsylvania Archives*, 8th ser., III, 2529–634.

[43] See *Minutes of the House of Assembly . . . 1740–1742*, pp. 66 and 71. It may be pointed out that all Quakers were not opposed to defensive measures. James Logan, Secretary of Pennsylvania and between 1731 and 1734 Chief Justice of the Supreme Court, was a member of the Society of Friends, but he favoured defensive measures and in 1741 suggested that those of the Society who could not conscientiously vote for such measures should not seek election to the Assembly. For his statement see the *Pennsylvania Magazine of History and Biography*, VI, 402–11. Chief Justice Samuel Chew of Delaware, also a Quaker, in November of that same year, while addressing a grand jury, strongly supported the idea that man has the natural right of self-defence. See *The Speech of Samuel Chew, Esq. . . .* (Philadelphia, 1741).

[44] L. de Valinger, Jr.: *Colonial Military Organization in Delaware, 1638–1776* (Wilmington, 1938), pp. 30–7.

[45] See *Laws of the State of Delaware* (1797), I, 395 and 397, and *Votes and Proceedings of the House of Representatives . . . at an Assembly held in New-Castle . . . 1762* (Wilmington, 1930), p. 7; see also R. S. Rodney: *Colonial Finances in Delaware* (Wilmington, Del., 1928), pp. 37–40. An unsuccessful attempt was made in the Assembly to utilize a part of the funds allotted to Delaware to reimburse those whose servants had been enlisted in the armed forces and had served during the war outside of the colony. Instead it was agreed that this sum be used to sink £7,000 of the bills of credit issued in 1759. *Votes and Proceedings*, pp. 12–13.

tioned that in writing to the Secretary of State for the Southern Department, the Duke of Newcastle, he had more than once represented in the most favourable way the dutiful and loyal behaviour of the people of the colony and added: "I doubt not but it will be hereafter remembered to the advantage of this Government."[46] In other words, from the viewpoint of the imperial administration, Delaware — unimportant as it was in comparison to most of the North American colonies both politically and economically — was considered to be a good colony and worthy of encouragement and support. It received this support in 1750 when Lord Baltimore's claims to it were rejected and a most favourable interpretation of the semicircular limits of New Castle County was rendered at the expense of Maryland in a decision of the High Court of Chancery by Lord Chancellor Hardwicke.[47] The decision of this court also came closer than any previous pronouncement by an authoritative body in Great Britain to defining the relationship of the colony to the Penn family and the Crown. It took the position that the settling of the Lower Counties by William Penn was the equivalent of a valuable purchase of them, that the relation of the Duke of York to Penn was to be likened to that of a trustee for the grantee, and that when the Duke became James II this trusteeship for Penn was conferred on the Crown.[48]

Despite this Chancery decision, the Penn family's title to Delaware remained clouded and defective. Further, the family seems to

---

[46] Deputy Governor Thomas to the Assembly, October 21, 1740, *Minutes of the House of Assembly . . . 1740–1742*, p. 13.

[47] For the Chancery decision of 1750 relative to the Baltimore-Penn dispute see Francis Vesey: *Cases Argued and Determined in the High Court of Chancery . . . from the year 1746/7, to 1755* (2 vols., 3rd edn., London, 1788), I, 452–5; for the breviate in Chancery filed by John Penn, Thomas Penn, and Richard Penn, plaintiffs, in 1735 and amended in 1736, see *The Breviate of the Boundary Dispute between Pennsylvania and Maryland, Pennsylvania Archives*, 2nd ser., XVI (the entire volume); see also *Report on the Resurvey of the Maryland-Pennsylvania Boundary . . . Authorized by the Legislature of Maryland and Pennsylvania* (Harrisburg, 1909), Part III, "History of the Boundary Dispute . . ." by E. B. Mathews, and Part IV, "Manuscripts and Publications Relating to the Mason Dixon Line and other Lines in Pennsylvania, Maryland and the Virginias Involving the Charter Rights of Lord Baltimore and the Penns" by E. L. Burchard, and especially pp. 170–5.

[48] See Dudley Lunt: "Bounds of Delaware," *Delaware History*, II, 1–40 and especially p. 29 for the Hardwicke opinion; see also H. L. Osgood: *The American Colonies in the Eighteenth Century* (4 vols., New York, 1924), IV, 43 n., and W. A. Powell: "Fight of a Century between the Penns and Calverts," *Maryland Historical Magazine*, XXIX, 83–101.

have profited little financially from its claim to the Lower Counties. While quit-rents were expected from the lands, there was so much uncertainty in the minds of even those landowners prepared to pay them — especially in view of the Baltimore family proprietary claims to these same lands — that little if any revenue was received from this source before 1750, with the result that vast theoretical arrears in such rents accumulated.[49] When the decision in 1750 of the High Court of Chancery seemed to have dispelled this uncertainty, these large arrearages, which could be liquidated only with great difficulty and hardship, led the landowners by and large to ignore the obligation. This attitude continued until the War for American Independence settled the matter. The Reverend Acrelius, who had lived for some years among the Delaware people from 1749 onward, stressed that even in the late 1750's, at the time he wrote, there was such confusion over land titles that quit-rents were not paid. He stated:

". . . some have their deeds from the Duke of York, which are safe enough. Another party holds from Penn, another from Lord Baltimore, and some from both. Meanwhile no land-rents have been paid since the year 1715, nor have any been demanded."[50]

Following the example of other colonies to the northward, Delaware in 1723 began the issuing of bills of credit[51] and loaned this paper money through offices set up in each of the Three Counties. Fortunately, the prudent method practiced by Pennsylvania and New Jersey was used in administering these funds. Sums up to £60 would be loaned to landowners who would give first mortgages and would agree to pay interest at five per cent. They were expected to discharge the debt by eight annual payments.[52] As the plan of

---

[49] See B. W. Bond, Jr: *The Quit-Rent System in the American Colonies* (New Haven & London, 1919), pp. 161–73. When the Duke of York, upon receiving a grant of the Lower Counties from Charles II, confirmed the land titles of the Dutch and Swedes, a small quit-rent of a bushel of wheat for each 100 acres of land was specified, as a rule. In the early part of the eighteenth century Penn changed the payment on further grants to a penny an acre.

[50] Israel Acrelius: *A History of New Sweden; or, The Settlements on the River Delaware*, p. 124.

[51] C. P. Keith: *Chronicles of Pennsylvania . . . 1688–1748* (2 vols., Philadelphia, 1917), I, 668.

[52] See the *Pennsylvania Gazette*, February 9, 1730/1.

liquidation of the loan was strictly adhered to, the money remained in good repute throughout the remainder of the colonial period, although from 1729 onward the period until final redemption was increased from eight to sixteen years. That these bills of credit stood high is indicated by the fact that in 1730 it took but £150 in these bills to pay for £100 sterling and in 1739 it took only £134.10 to secure the same amount of sterling; in 1749 it required £159 and in 1761, £172. This was small depreciation indeed when compared to the great depreciation of Rhode Island's bills of credit during the same period.[53] Before 1750 some £67,000 in bills of credit had been issued, but, as much of it had been cancelled, only a portion of this total was in circulation by that year.[54] The interest on these loans was used as the chief source of financing the government of the colony.[55] One may therefore conclude that, as was true of Pennsylvania and New Jersey, public burdens were very light in the Lower Counties in the middle of the eighteenth century. In fact, no taxes seem to have been levied in the Territories at this period, even at the local level.[56]

In summing up the picture of the Three Lower Counties on the Delaware it is clear that the colony was largely occupied with the cultivation of land, although many of the people of Lewes, located just north of Cape Henlopen, had long earned a livelihood as expert pilots for vessels entering the Bay.[57] The Reverend Andrew Burn-

---

[53] Rhode Island bills of credit by 1762 were worth in exchange less than one thirtieth of the English equivalent in pounds and shillings.

[54] In 1739, according to Deputy Governor Thomas, of £35,000 issued by Delaware before that year, only £17,250 was still in circulation. See Governor Thomas to the Board of Trade, December 1739, P.R.O., C.O. 5:1269.

[55] For a fairly comprehensive history of the Delaware bills of credit see R. S. Rodney: *Colonial Finances in Delaware.*

[56] County taxes could be levied to maintain public facilities such as the courts, gaols, and work houses and to pay bounties for the destruction of wolves, crows, and blackbirds. See "An Act for raising county-rates and levies" (16 Geo. II, c. 102, 1743), *Laws of Delaware* (1797), I, 257–67. But since local officials were chiefly paid by fees and since the counties derived a revenue on the loan of bills of credit allocated to each county, the need to pay taxes did not exist in 1750. See M. M. Daugherty: *Early Colonial Taxation in Delaware* (Wilmington, 1938), p. 43.

[57] Israel Acrelius: *op. cit.,* p. 144. See also L. C. Wroth: "Joshua Fisher's 'Chart of Delaware Bay and River,' " *Pennsylvania Magazine of History and Biography,* LXXIV, 90–109, and an earlier outline of this article including a reproduction of the Chart of 1756 on which Lewes is designated as "Pilot's Town": "Some American Contributions to the Art of Navigation, 1519–1802," Massachusetts Historical Society *Proceedings,* LXVIII, 72–113. The 1770 edition of the chart is reproduced on the inside covers of *Delaware: A Pictorial History* by D. B. Tyler (Cambridge, Md., 1955).

aby, in referring to his trip from Newcastle to Philadelphia, declared: "The country . . . bore a different aspect from anything I had hitherto seen in America. It was much better cultivated and beautifully laid out in fields of clover, grain, and flax."[58] In Delaware's fertile but restricted area — which did not include much of rather sterile Sussex County — large crops of cereals, fruits, and vegetables were grown and live-stock flourished in the pastures. The market for these and other products was chiefly Philadelphia.

By 1754, according to Acrelius, New Castle, which had once hoped to rival or even surpass Philadelphia as a trading centre and had been a major port of entry for immigrants, had sunk to comparative unimportance. In 1754 the city of Philadelphia could boast at least 2,300 houses with 117 "large sailing-vessels in the harbour at the same time," whereas the town of New Castle at the same period, although still the capital of the Lower Counties, could claim but 240 houses and was the port of call for few if any large vessels.[59] In fact, Wilmington, its neighbour, called by Burnaby "a very pretty village,"[60] located five miles north at the junction of Brandywine Creek with Christina River and adjacent to the Delaware River, was by 1754 somewhat larger, with 260 houses and with a number of seagoing vessels of its own.[61] It, rather than New Castle, was destined to become the active shipping centre of the Lower Counties and ultimately to assume real importance in America in the field of industry. As early as 1723 an iron forge had been constructed on the so-called Welsh Tract near the Christina, and in 1726 the Abbington Iron Works had been built in this same area at Iron Hill by Pennsylvania ironmasters.[62] Although these ventures had come to an end by about 1736, the water power of the Brandywine and other tributaries of

[58] Andrew Burnaby: *Travels in North America . . . 1759 and 1760* (London, 1775), p. 43.

[59] When Deputy Governor Gordon wrote to the Board of Trade on March 15, 1730/1, in answering its queries, he stated that the town of New Castle was the most considerable one in the Lower Counties and had 100 houses. See Shelburne Papers, 45:205–11, Clements Library. For a popular view of New Castle see B. M. Wootten and Anthony Higgins: *New Castle, Delaware, 1651–1939* (Boston, 1939).

[60] Andrew Burnaby: *op. cit.*, p. 43. In 1744 Dr. Alexander Hamilton found Wilmington compactly built and about the size of Annapolis. See Carl Bridenbaugh: *Gentleman's Progress: The Itinerarium of Dr. Alexander Hamilton* (Chapel Hill, N.C., 1948), p. 15.

[61] Israel Acrelius: *op. cit.*, pp. 142 and 144–5.

[62] See *Forges and Furnaces in the Province of Pennsylvania*, Pennsylvania Society of Colonial Dames of America *Publications*, III (Philadelphia, 1914), p. 42.

the Christina, such as Mill Creek, and the shipping facilities af-forded by the Christina and the Delaware brought about the loca-tion there of saw mills as well as grist mills.[63] In 1740 came the building of the first ocean-going vessel at docks on the Christina where a town had arisen which, first called Willingtown in 1731, was renamed Wilmington eight years later by the Penn family when its inhabitants were given a borough charter.[64]

The original founders of Delaware — the Dutch, Swedes, and Finns — by 1750 were becoming rapidly assimilated into the English pattern of living.[65] For example, the Swedish-speaking Acrelius, who came to Christina Parish in 1749 to take up the ministry in the Swedish Lutheran Church there, found it necessary to make the effort to preach in English, since so many people who came to hear him could not easily understand Swedish.[66] In fact, these people of Dutch, Swedish, and Finnish ancestry found themselves, in the course of the eighteenth century, living in the midst of many others of divergent ancestry who had found their way to the Lower Dela-ware and had established homes and farms: there were English and Welsh Quakers, Ulster-Scot Presbyterians, English Anglicans, and some Irish Roman Catholics, all of them speaking the English lan-guage.[67] That in the 1720's large numbers of people from Ireland

[63] The Gilpin family of Pennsylvania, which in the latter part of the eighteenth century established a paper mill on the Brandywine, in 1745 built there the second flour mill. See Dard Hunter: *Papermaking in Pioneer America* (Philadelphia, 1952), pp. 82–3, and P. C. Welsh: "The Brandywine Mills: A Chronicle of an Industry, 1762–1816," *Delaware History*, VII, 17–36.

[64] Benjamin Ferris: *A History of the Original Settlements on the Delaware . . .* (Wilmington, 1846), pp. 192–232. For the construction of ships at Wilmington see D. B. Tyler: "Shipbuilding in Delaware," *Delaware History*, VII, 207–16; for this development and other activities connected with the growth of Wilmington see also P. C. Welsh: "Merchants, Millers, and Ocean Ships: The Components of an Early American Industrial Town," *ibid.*, VII, 319–30.

[65] The sheriff of New Castle County between 1749 and 1756 was John Van Dyck. Not only had his given name been Anglicized from "Jan" to "John," but it may be seriously doubted if he understood the Dutch language of his forebears.

[66] Israel Acrelius: *op. cit.*, pp. 304–5. By 1786 the Swedish language, employed by clergymen sent from Sweden, could no longer be understood, with the result that all connection with the established church of Sweden ceased. See Benjamin Ferris: *op. cit.*, p. 184.

[67] See R. J. Purcell: "Irish Settlers in Early Delaware," *Pennsylvania History*, XIV, 94–107; Alice A. Johnson: "The Beginnings of Quakerism in Delaware," *Friends in Wilmington, 1738–1938* (Wilmington, 1939 [?]), pp. 13–29; and N. R. Burr: "Welsh Episcopalians of Colonial Pennsylvania and Delaware," *Historical Magazine of the Protestant Episcopal Church*, VIII, 101–22; see also W. A. Powell: *History of Dela-ware* (Boston, 1928), p. 394.

certainly landed at New Castle and Lewes, even if they did not remain within the Lower Counties, is indicated by the statement that between Christmas 1728 and Christmas 1729 there were landed in the "Newcastle Government . . . about 4500 Passengers and Servants, chiefly from Ireland."[68]

The numerical strength of each of the different national groups within the Three Counties is probably impossible to indicate with accuracy. However, according to the listing of family names for the census of 1790, 60 per cent appeared to be of English stock, over 14 per cent of Dutch, Swedish, or French ancestry, 8 per cent of native Scottish, over 6 per cent of Ulster Scottish, over 5 per cent of native Irish, just over one per cent of German, and 4½ per cent unassignable.[69] It seems to be clear that members of the Society of Friends — whose number had been increasing throughout the eighteenth century despite the political disabilities governing their occupation of seats in the House of Assembly — were very numerous in New Castle County by 1770 and especially in Wilmington. The Quaker Joseph Oxley, speaking of Quaker activity in this town, declared in 1770:

> "Attended a very large meeting. The chief part of the inhabitants of this town, which is a very improving one, are under our denomination."[70]

---

[68] *Pennsylvania Gazette,* January 13, 1729/30; see [John Oldmixon:] *The British Empire in America* (2nd edn., 2 vols., London, 1741), I, 321; G. S. Klett: *Presbyterians in Colonial Pennsylvania* (Philadelphia, 1937), p. 32; and C. A. Hanna: *The Scotch-Irish . . .* (2 vols., New York & London, 1902), II, 60 *et seq.;* see also A. E. Smith: *op. cit.,* pp. 317–18, for passengers arriving at New Castle between 1729 and 1735.

[69] See the table prepared by H. F. Barker: "National Stocks in the Population of the United States as Indicated by Surnames in the Census of 1790," *Report of the Committee on Linguistic and National Stocks in the Population of the United States,* American Historical Association *Report, 1931* (Washington, 1932), I, 307.

[70] Quoted by R. M. Jones: *The Quakers in the American Colonies* (London, 1911), p. 524. A wealthy and public-spirited Quaker, William Shipley, was chiefly responsible for the creation of the borough of Wilmington; he also erected the first market building in 1736 and took the leading role in the building of the first ocean-going vessel, *The Wilmington,* which sailed to Jamaica in 1741 loaded with flour, ship bread, barrel staves, barrelled beef, and other commodities. See Benjamin Ferris: *op. cit.,* pp. 210–31. In Shipley's house the first Quaker meetings were held in Wilmington in 1736. See *Friends in Wilmington, 1738–1938,* p. 34, and, in the same volume, the article by Alice A. Johnson: *op. cit.* For Welsh Anglicans and Welsh Baptists in New Castle County see N. R. Burr: *op. cit.,* pp. 117–20.

In Kent and Sussex counties at the same period, it was asserted, "more than half the people were of the Established Church of England." In sparsely settled Kent County in 1743 there were said to be some 1,020 men, among whom were 484 Anglicans, 397 Presbyterians, and 56 Quakers.[71] In 1751 the Reverend Mr. Neill, the Anglican pastor at Dover, county seat of Kent County, declared in a letter to the Secretary of the Society for the Propagation of the Gospel in Foreign Parts that in this county there were 1,320 taxpayers or families and that those who professed themselves of the Church of England were about equal in number to the "Dissenters of all sorts."[72]

The total population of Delaware in 1750 — according to a recent study made by Dr. Stella H. Sutherland, a leading authority on population distribution during the colonial period — was 28,704, of which 1,496 were Negroes, and in 1760 it was 33,250, of which 1,733 were Negroes.[73] Richard Penn, in a petition that he and his brother Thomas jointly addressed to the King in 1734, stated that there were 70,000 inhabitants living within the Three Counties.[74]

---

[71] R. J. Purcell: *op. cit.*, XIV, 102; H. C. Conrad: *op. cit.*, II, 593–5; and W. A. Powell: *op. cit.*, pp. 140 and 360.

[72] *Historical Collections Relating to the American Colonial Church* (ed. W. S. Perry, 5 vols., Hartford, 1870–8), V, 97–8. Volume V of the *Collections* deals entirely with Delaware from 1706 until after the Revolution. However, for the condition of the Anglican churches in Kent County in 1760 see the report by the Rev. Charles Inglis, missionary at Dover for the Society for the Propagation of the Gospel, who reported that besides the church at Dover in the centre of the county — "now handsomely repaired and finished" — there were two other churches at either end of the county, each drawing a great part of its congregation from its neighbouring county. "In this County," his account continues, "there are 5 Presbyterian & 2 Quaker Meeting Houses, all supplied with Teachers & exercising the Discipline of their respective plans of Government whilst the Church of England without a Head or any Discipline, has no support under Providence but what is given by the Honorable and worthy Society." See *ibid.*, II, 312–13.

[73] Dr. Sutherland, author of the standard work *Population Distribution in Colonial America* (New York, 1936), has prepared a table, "Estimated Population, 1610 to 1780," covering all the colonies. The figures for Delaware are included. The table will be embodied in the volume, *Historical Statistics of the United States, Colonial Times to 1957*, to be published in 1960 by the Bureau of the Census. This and other material was kindly placed at the writer's disposal by Professor Lawrence A. Harper of the University of California, who has been assisting the Bureau in preparing this volume for publication.

[74] *Acts of the Privy Council, Col. Ser., Unbound Papers*, p. 234.

Yet, when the first actual census was taken in 1790, there were only 59,096 people, including 8,887 slaves.[75]

Among the white people of Delaware there were apparently no extremes of poverty or wealth in 1750, nor was there to be found among them the degree of intense local pride and loyalty which characterized the inhabitants of some of the other colonies by this time.

With the political status of their colony still shrouded in uncertainty in the middle of the eighteenth century, the people of Delaware were able at least to feel that, whatever permanent political settlement the future had in store for them, as British North Americans they were embraced within the bounds of the Empire and could therefore rest secure. Their geographical location on Delaware Bay was strategic, yet made them highly vulnerable to enemy attack. This fact seems to have coloured their attitude toward supporting the military activities of the mother country. By 1750 a growing homogeneity of thought among the diverse groups within the colony led them not only to favour militia acts but also to maintain a sound financial system and to unite in building a flourishing rural economy. This they achieved, despite the overshadowing of their colony by more powerful neighbours, Pennsylvania and Maryland, and the fact that their lands for so long were the object of the rival claims of the Penn and Baltimore families.

---

[75] See E. B. Greene and Virginia D. Harrington: *American Population before . . . 1790* (New York, 1932), p. 121.

CHAPTER IX

The Iron Men

IN surveying the economic activities of the people of the continental colonies in this and the preceding volume of the present series, one important aspect — the production and manufacture of iron within the British Empire in the eighteenth century — has been reserved to the present for unified treatment. The passing by Parliament in 1750 of the famous Iron Act placed the colonies under severe restrictions in processing iron, an activity then assuming great importance in a number of the colonies north of the Carolinas, with Pennsylvania well in the lead.

The Iron Act has been repeatedly cited as a classic instance of stupidity and selfishness in the relations of the British government with its dependencies. Be that as it may, it does illustrate effectively the motivations of those who were responsible for guiding imperial economic policy and the enormous complexity of the problem involved in attempting to rectify the maladjustments of the mercantile system.

It should be made clear at the outset that many Englishmen in the middle of the eighteenth century were persuaded that they were witnessing, in the astonishingly rapid development of the American iron industry, the beginnings of a rapid decline of their own. Unless this decline were checked, they were convinced, it would inevitably be accompanied by dire economic and social consequences. For already the manufacture of iron had a vast significance in the life of the people of England.[1]

Here is a picture of industrial England left by a traveller in the year 1747. "I forgot to tell you," he declared in a letter to a friend, "that yesterday we saw smoaky Birmingham or (as most people pronounce it Brunigam), on our Left; though the Spires appeared very handsome above those artificial Clouds. I believe the Hardware of this Place travels farther over the World, than any Commodity Britain produces."[2] Ten years earlier Abraham Spooner, an ironmaster of that town, asserted at least 135,000 people living there or within a radius of ten miles of it were dependent upon iron-manufacturing for a living.[3] By 1750 the whole region round about the town was dotted with furnaces, forges, slitting and rolling mills, and the establishments of fabricators of various types of hardware. And what was true of Birmingham was almost equally true of many other places. Indeed, next to the production of woollens, the manufacture of iron employed the largest number of people engaged in industry in England, with ironworks and coppice woods for iron-making to be found in about half the counties of England and Wales.[4]

The working of metals was undoubtedly one of the earliest of the

---

[1] For the English iron industry in the eighteenth century see H. R. Schubert: *History of the British Iron and Steel Industry . . . to A.D. 1775* (London, 1957), pp. 173–335; T. S. Ashton: *Iron and Steel in the Industrial Revolution* (2nd edn., Manchester, 1951), pp. 1–59; and M. W. Flinn: "The Growth of the English Iron Industry, 1660–1760," *Economic History Review*, 2nd ser., XI, 144–54, with a bibliographical note giving a list of the more specialized studies relating to the production of iron before the Industrial Revolution.

[2] *A Tour through Ireland by Two English Gentlemen* (Dublin, 1748), p. 22.

[3] Report of the Committee of the House of Commons, 1738, Penn Manuscripts, Papers Relating to Iron, Peltries, Trade, etc., 1712–1817, p. 45, Historical Society of Pennsylvania. This volume of the Penn family papers includes a large number of manuscripts, pamphlets, and other printed materials, including petitions relating to the iron industry. Reference hereafter to any of these papers will be given consistently as Penn Mss., Papers Relating to Iron. Many of these documents were collected by Ferdinand John Paris, the solicitor for the family, and turned over to Thomas Penn later, in the year 1749.

[4] Testimony of William Rea, an ironmaster of Monmouth, before a Committee of the House of Commons, 1738, *ibid.*, p. 45.

According to one estimate, in 1717 there were 116 forges in England; in 1736 the number had risen to 135; in 1750 the number had dropped to 114. See E. W. Hulme: "Statistical History of the Iron Trade of England and Wales. 1717–1750," the Newcomen Society *Transactions*, IX, 16. For criticism of these figures as defective see M. W. Flinn: *op. cit.*, XI, 145.

skilled occupations established on the island. The cruder direct process of converting the ore into wrought iron had since the fifteenth century been displaced by the indirect method of producing iron through the process of smelting in a blast furnace. This cast iron was subsequently converted at the forge into the wrought iron that supplied the needs of the trade.[5]

Various qualities of iron ore were to be found in England, each adapted to its special purpose. For example, a writer of the period claimed that the Clee Hills iron of Shropshire was the most famous in the world at this period for the making of gun barrels; those produced in Birmingham for the Tower Arsenal were all of this malleable but exceedingly strong iron. The iron from the Forest of Dean in Gloucestershire was, on the other hand, easily converted into highly tempered steel, the same writer asserted, and was used chiefly in making edged articles such as scythes. An iron that was easy to work when hot and could be easily punched and bent but became extraordinarily tough when cold was secured in Shropshire to the west of the Severn and also in larger quantities in Cumberland, where existed a mine of hæmatite ore held to be inexhaustible; from it, according to the same writer, the furnaces of Lancashire, Hampshire, Yorkshire, Cheshire, Staffordshire, Gloucestershire, Worcestershire, and Shropshire were supplied. Ore that produced "cold short iron," excellent for nails, came from deposits east of the Severn in Shropshire and also from the counties of Staffordshire, Yorkshire, Nottinghamshire, Cheshire, and Derbyshire.[6]

Six things were considered essential to the advantageous production of iron in the middle of the eighteenth century: accessibility to an inexhaustible supply of ore, an abundance of wood, coal, water power, and skilled labour, and convenience of transportation. By means of a millrace and water wheel, power was secured for the operation of the great wood-and-leather bellows that forced the blast through the ore and fuel laid in juxtaposition in the "high furnace." This power was also essential for the use of the great hammer at the forge and for both the slitting and rolling mills in the

    [5] See especially H. R. Schubert: *op. cit.*, pp. 157–208.

    [6] For the different types of iron ore see *Some Considerations Showing that the Importation of Iron from America will sooner put a stop to the making of Iron in England than the Importation of Iron from Sweden and Russia*, 1749 (?), Penn Mss., Papers Relating to Iron, p. 83.

later processes. Where power did not exist, the more primitive non-blast or air-furnace method was still extensively employed.

Although in the seventeenth century attempts had been made to use coal in the smelting of iron, and the Dudley Furnace had established the possibilities of this utilization, it was apparently not until the days of Abraham Darby in the early part of the eighteenth century that coke was accepted by any of the furnacemen as a possible suitable substitute for charcoal. But even then the change came very slowly, and in 1750 its use in the iron industry was limited.[7]

One strong argument in favour of the shifting from charcoal to coal was the wastage of the wood resources of England in the processes of iron- and steel-production. This situation had become acute in parts of the kingdom as early as the middle of the sixteenth century, and in 1585 Parliament actually forbad the erection of any additional ironworks in the three southeastern counties, Kent, Surrey, and Sussex.[8] Toward the end of the seventeenth century there were within ten miles of Dudley Castle nearly twenty thousand smiths, and yet, on account of the lack of wood for fuel due to this wastage, many of the ironworks, it is stated, were decayed.[9] Among other reasons, the shortage of this resource finally led to the gradual shifting of iron-smelting, at least from the Midlands, to the valley of the Severn and the forests of Wales.[10] Yet the denuding of the woodlands continued. Malachy Postlethwayt, writing in the 1750's, declared: "Certain it is that the waste and destruction of woods in

---

[7] For the use of coke before 1750 see H. R. Schubert: *op. cit.*, pp. 331–3. The writer of *The State of the Trade and Manufactory of Iron in Great Britain Considered* (London, 1750, p. 2), referring to iron ore, declared: "It is not to be converted with Advantage into good malleable Iron with any other Fire, that we know of, but what is made of Wood, Charkt or Charcoal," Wagner Collection, Yale University. In Staffordshire the use of coke in malt-making had become well established by 1730. See John Pinkerton: *Voyages and Travels* (17 vols., Philadelphia, 1808–14), II. 22.

[8] 27 Eliz. I, c. 19. In the year 1552 it was actually proposed to Parliament that the iron mills be abolished from the realm. In favour of this it was argued that "whereas wood was formerly sold at the stock for one penny a load, by reason of the iron mills it is now at two shillings a load; further, that Spanish iron formerly sold for five marks per ton now there are English iron mills . . . iron is sold at nine pounds per ton" (*Calendar* of the Mss. of the Marquis of Salisbury, Historical Manuscripts Commission *Report*, Part I, p. 164).

[9] Harry Scrivenor: *A Comprehensive History of the Iron Trade* . . . (2nd edn., London, 1854), p. 38.

[10] G. C. Allen: *The Industrial Development of Birmingham and the Black Country* (London, 1929), p. 15, and A. C. Bining: *British Regulation of the Colonial Iron Industry* (Philadelphia, 1933), p. 25.

Warwick, Stafford, Worcester, Hereford, Monmouth, Gloucester, Glamorgan, Pembroke, Shropshire and Sussex, by iron-works is scarce to be imagined."[11] Another writer, using the *nom de plume* "Britannicus," September 27, 1750, dealt with the problem of supplying ironworks with a sufficient amount of wood in his "Thoughts on the Iron Trade." He declared that while in some places there were "considerable quantities of wood, plenty of iron-ore and rivers, suitable for the purpose," yet on examination there did not seem to be enough wood easily available to last more than a few years. This would mean, he went on, that when the suitable wood had been exhausted the furnace would have to stand idle for ten or fifteen years until a new supply had been made available. Special encouragement, he urged, should therefore be given to the owners of land to guarantee a constant supply of wood in the locality of ironworks.[12]

At the same time, evidence exists that the quantity of available charcoal became stabilized by the early part of the century in a fashion that permitted the smelting and forging of a fairly constant amount of iron — some 18,000 tons annually. This still rendered the industry dependent upon the importation of most of its iron supply from Sweden and Russia.[13]

It must not be inferred that coal was not widely used in the iron industry by the middle of the century. On the contrary, the rise of iron-manufacturing in Worcestershire and adjacent counties — due primarily to the presence in this region of inexhaustible supplies of iron ore, the wood from the Forest of Dean, and the Severn River system providing excellent water power and easy transportation of materials — was also made possible by the existence of great deposits of pit-coal.[14] This was commonly used in working the iron after the initial treatment of the crude ore in the charcoal blast. For example, in turning pig iron into bar iron it was customary with each ton of iron to utilize one and a half loads of coal and three

---

[11] *Britain's Commercial Interest Explained and Improved* (2 vols., London, 1757), I, 151.

[12] See *Gentleman's Magazine, 1750*, pp. 444–5.

[13] B. L. C. Johnson: "The Charcoal Iron Industry in the Early Eighteenth Century," *Geographical Journal*, CXVII, 174, and M. W. Flinn: *op. cit.*, XI, 150–1.

[14] See "Humble Petition of the Merchants, Iron Masters & Ironmongers," March 3, 1736, Penn Mss., Papers Relating to Iron, p. 3.

cords of wood. Indeed, the extension of the use of pit-coal in manu-facturing processes in the seventeenth century was doubtless the leading factor in the expansion of iron-fabrication during that period.

In light of the wood shortage it is not surprising that before the beginning of the eighteenth century the demands of the fabricators for bar iron had far outrun the supply of the forges — just as the demands of the forgemen for sows and pigs had far outrun the supply of the furnaces — with the result that producers of English hardware became increasingly dependent upon importations of iron from Sweden, Russia, and Spain. In fact, an act of the reign of William III recognized the scarcity and dearness of bar iron within the Kingdom and, to meet this situation as well as to encourage in-dustry in Ireland, permitted its importation from that island free of duties.[15] It was estimated in 1738 that of a total of 35,000 tons of iron required for the trade at least 23,000 tons had to be secured from abroad each year to meet the demands of the trade.[16] This degree of dependence on a foreign and sometimes hostile power for such an important product in the industrial life of England was so dangerous that it is understandable why Englishmen desired, if possible, to be relieved of it. For example, in 1717 a royal proclama-tion forbad all trade with Sweden. As a result Parliament was del-uged with petitions from iron-fabricators and others about the effects of this interdiction upon thousands of people faced with un-employment.[17] The ban was soon lifted. Again, in 1734 Sweden placed all but prohibitory duties on the importation from England of certain types of goods and prohibited the importation of other types that had helped to pay for the purchase of Swedish iron.[18] But under the existing conditions in iron-production, it was not clear how England could change this disadvantageous situation, especially in time of war.

---

[15] 7 and 8 William III, c. 10, Sec. 17.

[16] Report of the Committee of the House of Commons, 1738, Penn Mss., Papers Relating to Iron, p. 31. The author of *The State of the Trade and Manufactory of Iron* (1750, p. 8), states: "It has been computed and we believe with Fidelity, that within some few years past, there has been produced here of British Materials eight-een thousand Tons per Annum." By 1775 the total amount of iron imported from Sweden, Russia, and other foreign countries was between 45,000 and 50,000 tons a year. See Harry Scrivenor: *op. cit.*, pp. 343–4.

[17] *Journals of the House of Commons*, XVIII, 691, 745–9.

[18] *Ibid.*, XXII, 854.

The explanation of the inability of the furnacemen to produce an adequate supply of pig iron lies of course in the rising cost of its production whenever unusual demands were made upon the proprietors of wood lots. At many furnaces this charcoal represented a very considerable part of the total cost of production.[19] Unlike pitcoal, the charcoal could be secured within the kingdom only in measured quantities, based usually upon the anticipations of those who many years previously had either planted trees toward this end or had preserved their coppices to be harvested after a period of growth of between fifteen and twenty-five years. But the independent landowner was obliged to balance the advantages of utilizing his lands in one or more of several possible ways. He naturally hesitated to devote to coppices acreage that might be more profitably employed during the period involved in the growth of trees. In other words, corn, wool, wood in coppices, and timber, each having its own peculiar economy, were in a sense competing for his fields. The selling price of his cord wood would therefore necessarily be based to a greater or lesser degree upon his estimate of the value of the lands during the years of the slow maturing of the wood for charcoal. This price factor could operate due to the fact that growing trees — not a perishable crop, as is corn for example — could be held indefinitely for a favourable market. In fact, the longer they were held from the market, the more valuable the harvest would be, especially if the trees were oak suitable for ship timber rather than such types as alder, hazel, birch, and beech.

The intimate relationship between the existence of an adequate wood supply and the production of iron is illustrated by the statements of a writer whose "Thoughts on the Iron Trade" was published in *Aris's Birmingham Gazette*. He declared that forty years earlier there was neither an iron furnace nor a refining forge between Lancaster and Cumberland, with the result that many persons grubbed up trees growing even on poor land. About the year 1711 two furnaces and a number of forges were built in this region.

---

[19] B. L. C. Johnson (*op. cit.*, CXVII, 174) indicates that the cost might run as high as 70 per cent to the furnacemen. In support of this position he cites A. Raistrick: "The South Yorkshire Iron Industry," Newcomen Society *Transactions*, XIX, 51–86. This is a rather detailed study of the operations of 10 furnaces, 14 forges, and 5 slitting mills.

During the first twenty years there was not wood sufficient to make 500 tons of bar iron in any year. Nevertheless, due to the encouragement that these and other works built subsequently gave to landowners, there now existed a supply of wood adequate to produce 1,500 tons of iron and it was calculated that in twenty years more there would be wood enough to make 2,000 or even 2,500 tons yearly. "More Endeavours are now used to improve and Enlarge their Woods than ever, several Persons planting Wood on Arable ground, tho' Arable Ground is Scarce, nothing like sufficient to supply them with Bread."[20]

It is true that it was possible to supply almost any quantity of wood to the charcoal-burners or to the furnacemen in various parts of England, to allow them to produce an amount of pig iron adequate for all the needs of the home market. But the price that the furnacemen could pay for their wood was fixed by factors that they themselves could not entirely control.[21] In contrast, in both Sweden and Russia, with low labour costs and an inexhaustible supply of wood and charcoal, iron could be produced at a competitive rate. Further, this foreign-produced metal paid a duty of but forty-eight shillings and sixpence per ton if imported in British ships.[22]

The importation of foreign bar iron could easily have been cut off by prohibitive duties, but that would have resulted in the loss of the important foreign markets won by the hardware trade and in the throwing of thousands of people out of employment — an alternative inconsistent with sound mercantilistic principles. One writer affirmed in 1750 that the cost of producing iron selling at

---

[20] See *Aris's Birmingham Gazette*, November 19, 1750.

[21] Writing on the competition of foreign-produced iron with domestic in England, the author of *The State of the Trade and Manufactory of Iron in Great Britain Considered* (1750, p. 9) also refers to the competition in wood for iron-smelting: "British Timber labours under the same Disadvantages as British Iron it is undersold by Deals and other foreign Woods. Calculate the Value of the Land it shades for a Century or two, and it will by no Means answer to us or our Posterity for the Preservation of it; how much less will it do this, when the Tops and Buts, which now cut into Cord-wood, and are of one third Value of the whole, will then [with the destruction of iron works] become useless and of no Account."

[22] Henry Saxby: *The British Customs containing an Historical and Practical Account of Each Branch of that Revenue* . . . (London, 1757), p. 177. This gives the duty at £2.8.6 per ton, but certain deductions brought the duty down to the figures given above. The duty on pig iron, if produced in the plantations, was three shillings and ninepence per ton. See Report of the Committee of the House of Commons, 1736/7, Penn Mss., Papers Relating to Iron, p. 27.

£17 was made up of the following items: the wood for charcoal, the ore, and the "Rent of Works" not above £4.12, labour per ton at least £10, with the remainder going to the cost of carriage — that is, some £2.8. All other contemporary authorities on iron-production stressed the high price of labour, with English iron priced just under the price of the best Swedish iron; according to the same writer, a very high export duty equivalent to £3.12.6 per ton was paid on the Swedish iron,[23] but this duty might be removed by Sweden at any time, letting in a flood of iron at prices that English iron-producers could not match. Under these circumstances it was felt that the vastly important iron trade of the kingdom was largely at the mercy of foreign powers, as it had been in 1717 when a rupture of relations with Sweden had advanced the price of bar iron from £13 to £22 per ton, at which almost prohibitive price level it had continued during the period of interrupted trade.[24]

The question naturally was raised in the course of the first half of the eighteenth century as to the possibility of securing adequate supplies of iron within the Empire. Other even more pressing questions were raised at this period. For the English ironmasters and ironmongers had been made to realize that something was happening to their former great markets in America. In place of the brisk demand in that quarter for various types of ironware, there was by the 1730's a falling off of orders; stocks were therefore accumulating in warehouses that had previously filled such orders, and many of the weaker, less favourably situated furnaces and forges that had supplied iron for American consumption were obliged to suspend operation. Of the 125 forges scattered through England and Wales at this period, thirty of them, or almost one fourth, were standing idle while the others were running at not more than two-thirds capacity, according to testimony presented before a parliamentary committee.[25] For example, at Stourbridge and Wolverhampton, reported a Richard Keeling, great numbers of artisans previously employed in making nails, scythes, and similar export articles sought

---

[23] *The State of the Trade and Manufactory of Iron,* pp. 8, 10–11.

[24] See a broadside, undated but of this period, entitled *Reasons for Encouraging the Importation of Iron in Bars from his Majesty's Plantations in America,* Penn Mss., Papers Relating to Iron, p. 13.

[25] See testimony of William Rea, ironmaster of Monmouthshire, the Report of the Committee of the House of Commons, 1738, *ibid.,* p. 45.

work in vain, and many in desperation had deserted their families. Further, he testified that at Dudley, another iron centre, the poor-rates mounted from two or three shillings on the pound to the appalling level of twelve or thirteen shillings owing to widespread unemployment.[26] Abraham Spooner, Birmingham ironmaster, declared "that already our manufactures are in a miserable condition occasioned . . . for the want of a demand from the plantations for the several sorts of wrought iron-ware" which formerly he himself had not been able to make fast enough; now he had great quantities of it lying by him. Doubtless one source of the difficulty was that one half of all the iron produced in England and three fourths of that of Staffordshire and Worcestershire was made into nails, "a trade which has decayed," according to Edward Knight, largely as a result of a lessening of the demand in the colonies.[27]

The iron industry in America to the north of the Carolinas was in truth gradually assuming very great importance during the first half of the eighteenth century. Although attempts had been made in the seventeenth century to establish works both in New England and in Virginia, the real development dates from the beginning of the next century.[28] By the end of the second decade sufficient progress had been made in some of the colonies to alarm the English iron-manufacturers. In 1719 a bill was introduced into Parliament which provided that no one in any of the plantations should fabricate any ironware out of sows, pigs, or bars.[29] Nothing came of this attempt at restriction. However, in 1721, to aid in meeting the competition of American ironworks, all export duties on British iron were removed.[30]

---

[26] For the deep interest of English leaders in efforts to combat unemployment and pauperism among the labouring groups as one of the chief goals of eighteenth-century mercantilism, see Charles Wilson: "The Other Face of Mercantilism," *Royal Historical Society Transactions*, 5th ser., IX, 81–101.

[27] For the testimony of Keeling, Spooner, and Knight see Report of the Committee of the House of Commons, 1738, Penn Mss., Papers Relating to Iron, p. 45.

[28] For detailed information on the rise of the iron industry in the British colonies see J. L. Bishop: *A History of American Manufactures from 1608 to 1860* . . . (3rd edn., 3 vols., Philadelphia, 1868), I, 468–617; see also A. C. Bining: *British Regulation of the Colonial Iron Industry*.

[29] See *ibid.*, pp. 42–5; D. Macpherson: *Annals of Commerce, Manufactures, Fisheries and Navigation* . . . (4 vols., London, 1805), III, 72; and G. L. Beer: *The Commercial Policy of England Toward the American Colonies* (Columbia University Studies in History, III, No. 2, New York, 1893), p. 85.

[30] 8 George I, c. 15, Par. 7.

Among the earliest of the American ironmen was former Governor Spotswood of Virginia, who was especially interested in pig-iron production and in the early 1720's was exporting this metal from the Old Dominion to London and Bristol. For example, he sent twenty tons to Bristol in 1723 in the form of ballast in the loaded tobacco ship, the *Greyhound*.[31] Gradually to the north and south of the Potomac there appeared ironworks — such as the Principio works in Maryland in 1715 and the Baltimore ironworks on the Patapsco River in 1731[32] — until by the middle of the century within that province and Virginia there were at least ten blast furnaces making an annual average of 500 tons of pig iron each, for a total of 5,000 tons.

Special inducements, moreover, were offered to colonials to engage in the iron business. For example, to encourage the erection of ironworks, in 1748 Virginia exempted people thus employed from working on the roads other than those necessary for bringing iron ore or iron to some navigable river; they were also exempt from

---

[31] Jefferies Manuscripts, No. 19, Bristol Reference Library. This shipment, perhaps the first iron that Spotswood sent abroad, took place the year after he resigned from his governorship. See Leonidas Dodson: *Alexander Spotswood . . . 1710–1722*, (Philadelphia, 1932), pp. 294–9, for Spotswood's activities as an ironmaster.

Professor Kathleen Bruce in her scholarly study, *Virginia Iron Manufacture in the Slave Era* (New York, 1931), presents (pp. 9–12) a picture of the beginnings of iron-manufacturing in the Chesapeake Bay Region. She suggests that Spotswood began his ironworks as early as 1716 and that by 1732 three blast furnaces and one air furnace were operating, the first three at Germanna and the latter near Fredericksburg. He was undoubtedly the first in Virginia to engage in "the Mystery of Making Iron." She gives 1724 as the date of the actual founding of the Principio Company in Maryland, although a bloomery came into existence in 1715. See her "Introduction," pp. 9–17. For interesting items regarding the ironworks in Stafford County, Virginia, in 1726 see *Tyler's Quarterly Historical and Genealogical Magazine*, October 1934, pp. 89–93.

[32] *A Short Account of Iron, made in the Colonies of Virginia and Maryland only* (without date but after 1746), Penn Mss., Papers Relating to Iron, p. 89.

". . . Here are three Furnaces for melting Iron Ore and one furnace for making Bar Iron, one furnace for casting Iron Posts etc.," wrote Colonel Lee, President of the Virginia Council, to the Board of Trade, September 29, 1750, Shelburne Papers, 45:84–90. For the Principio ironworks see Henry Whitely: "The Principio Company," *Pennsylvania Magazine of History and Biography*, XI, 63–8, 190–8, 288–95; for the Baltimore ironworks see also Keach Johnson: "The Genesis of the Baltimore Iron Works," *The Journal of Modern History*, XIX, 157–79, and by the same author: "The Baltimore Company Seeks English Markets: . . . 1731–1755," *William and Mary Quarterly*, 3rd ser., XVI, 37–60, and also his "The Baltimore Company Seeks English Subsidies for the Colonial Iron Industry," *Maryland Historical Magazine*, XLVI, 27–43.

the requirement of attending muster, were permitted to take timber for building necessary bridges, and for seven years were freed from colonial levies.[33]

Between 1642 and 1674 Massachusetts Bay had made unsuccessful efforts to promote ironworks on the Saugus River.[34] However, by the year 1718 it appears that the colony had laid sure foundations for iron-manufacturing and had people skilled in its production and fabrication. In that year the General Court provided bounties upon various types of ironware produced locally: forty shillings per ton on all bar iron equal in quality to Spanish iron, £5 per ton on rod iron or faggots of a suitable fineness to work into nails, with twentypence per thousand on various sizes of nails and twelve shillings per ton on all Holland ware cast from iron equal in quality to English or Dutch ware.[35] By 1722, as a result of this encouragement, the colony was exporting axes to South Carolina, among other manufactures. By 1733 New England could boast of at least six furnaces and nineteen forges,[36] and by 1758 there were fourteen furnaces and forty-one forges in Massachusetts Bay.[37] So successful were the New England ironmasters in developing a market for their products that they turned to importing considerable quantities of bar steel from England to manufacture into implements, and soon set up furnaces here and there for the production of steel. By 1736 they and the southern ironmasters had succeeded in driving from the American market north of the Carolinas not only English axes but also many other tools, at least according to the testimony of British ironmongers. Moreover, quantities of nails were being turned out from American slitting mills in successful competition with the English product, and Rhode Island was providing herself and

---

[33] *The Statutes at Large; Being a Collection of all the Laws of Virginia, from . . . 1619* (ed. W. W. Hening, 13 vols., Richmond, 1809–23), V, 137–8.

[34] E. N. Hartley: *Ironworks on the Saugus . . .* (Norman, Okla., 1957).

[35] Minutes of the Council of Massachusetts Bay, June 6, 1718, Massachusetts Archives, and *Journals of the House of Representatives of Massachusetts* (32 vols. +, Boston, 1919–57+), II, 6, 18, 20, 26, 41, 66.

[36] See *Considerations on the Bill now Depending before the House of Commons, for Encouraging the Importation of Pig and Bar Iron from America,* 1750 (?), Penn Mss., Papers Relating to Iron, p. 81.

[37] The province also possessed four slitting mills, two plating mills, and one steel furnace, although these were not reported by the Governors. See A. C. Bining: *British Regulation of the Colonial Iron Industry,* p. 14.

neighbouring colonies with anchors.[38] As for Connecticut, ironworks, including a steel furnace, had been erected before 1750 at eight different places.[39] Although New York was slow in developing iron-production and iron-manufacturing and by 1750 had but one furnace in operation and a forge that was idle, New Jersey by the late 1730's had a number of furnaces and forges,[40] as had Pennsylvania. Indeed, the latter province had become the greatest iron-producer of all the British plantations by 1750.

Iron-production began in Pennsylvania in 1716 with the building of a forge by the English Quaker Thomas Rutter near what is now Pottstown. By 1750 there were at least thirty-seven centres for iron-production within the province, and by the year 1775 the number had increased to at least seventy-three.[41] As a rule, these were far removed from towns, as they required a wide enough area to comprehend ore beds, streams for power, and extensive stretches of woodland. For example, Elizabeth Furnace, which came into existence in 1750, included over 10,000 acres. Most of the other ironworks of importance embraced at least 1,000 surrounding acres. On the typical "iron plantation" the mansion house of the iron-master stood on an imposing site. Stretched out below it were the simple cottages of the workers who mined the ore and tended the furnace and the forge, which usually rose beside a stream capable of turning a water wheel. The ironmaster's general store, a grist mill, and a saw mill were likewise characteristic of such isolated ironworks.[42] The most famous and most heavily financed Pennsylvania

---

[38] John Banister's testimony before the Committee of the House of Commons, 1738, Penn Mss., Papers Relating to Iron, p. 45; see also *The State of the Trade and Manufactory of Iron in Great Britain Considered* (1750), p. 11.

[39] Board of Trade Papers, P.R.O., C.O. 5:1273.

[40] See Irene D. Neu: "The Iron Plantations of Colonial New York," *New York History*, XXXIII, 3–24, and C. S. Boyer: *Early Forges & Furnaces in New Jersey* (Philadelphia & London, 1931).

[41] See A. C. Bining: *Pennsylvania Iron Manufacture in the Eighteenth Century* (Harrisburg, 1938); see also *Forges and Furnaces in the Province of Pennsylvania*, Pennsylvania Society of Colonial Dames of America *Publication*, III (Philadelphia, 1914), prepared by the Committee on Historical Research; and J. B. Pearse: *A Concise History of the Iron Manufacture of the American Colonies . . . and of Pennsylvania until the Present Time* (Philadelphia, 1876).

[42] A. C. Bining: "Iron Plantations of Early Pennsylvania," *Pennsylvania Magazine of History and Biography*, LVII, 117–37; see also his *Pennsylvania Iron Manufacture in the Eighteenth Century*, Chap. 2.

ironworks were undoubtedly the Durham Iron Works on the middle Delaware, established in 1727.[43]

Unlike the ore furnaces and forges, the slitting and plating mills as well as the iron-fabricating plants were located in Pennsylvania towns or villages, as were the few small-capacity steel furnaces that began to come into existence in the year 1732.[44] It may be added that, despite the restrictions on the production of steel by the Iron Act of 1750, two steel furnaces were erected in the year 1762 and continued to operate throughout the period of the War for American Independence.[45]

There is little doubt as to the quality of American iron. Jonathan Dickinson, writing from Philadelphia in 1717 after Rutter had begun the production of iron at his bloomery forge, declared that "all the smiths here . . . say that the best of Sweeds' [Swedish] iron doth not exceed it. . . ."[46] American-made tools, especially scythes, were actually preferred by the country people to the best imported article. "The demand for Scythes, which formerly was very large from thence [America], is now come to nothing," complained an English writer in discoursing upon the effects of the erection of ironworks in the colonies and the self-sufficiency of New England in supplying herself and other colonies with "sundry sorts of Iron-wares."[47]

It is not surprising that Parliament was deluged with memorials for the relief of the British iron trade in the early part of the eighteenth century.[48] One petition in 1736 came from the iron-masters and ironmongers of Lancashire, another from the corre-

---

[43] See B. F. Fackenthal: "The Durham Iron Works . . . ," *Bucks County Historical Society Papers*, VII, 59–94, and R. D. Billinger: "Early Ironworks of Pennsylvania: The Durham Furnaces," *Industrial and Engineering Chemistry*, XXX, 428–37. It may be of interest to readers that Hopewell Furnace, built on French Creek by Mark Bird in 1770, has been restored as an example of an eighteenth-century Pennsylvania iron plantation.

[44] A. C. Bining: *Pennsylvania Iron Manufacture in the Eighteenth Century*, p. 51.

[45] *Ibid.*, p. 158.

[46] *Forges and Furnaces in the Province of Pennsylvania*, p. 11.

[47] *Interest of Great Britain in Supplying Herself with Iron Impartially Considered* (London, 1747, 1750), which is cited by A. C. Bining: *British Regulation of the Colonial Iron Industry*, pp. 106–9, as he deals with the growing commerce in iron wares among the colonies and the vigorous but fruitless protests against this by the British manufacturers.

[48] For the efforts in 1719 and 1720 by merchants and forge men to promote the importation of pig iron from the plantations see A. C. Bining: *British Regulation of the Colonial Iron Industry*, pp. 38–44.

sponding groups of Worcestershire, still others came from various Bristol and Staffordshire iron men trading with America. Among the latter was the "Humble Petition of the Merchants, Iron-Masters, & Ironmongers of this Kingdom in behalf of themselves and many others trading to His Majesty's Plantations in America."[49]

This last petition recited that, while premiums had been provided by Parliament for the importation from America of tar, pitch, turpentine, hemp, masts, yards, and bowsprits, no encouragement was given to iron, although this could be produced there in quality equal to the best Swedish iron. It went on to state that several furnaces and forges had already been erected in America, and that by means of these and others to be built, Great Britain could be so adequately supplied with iron as to become independent of any foreign country for this commodity so essential to navigation. It would be necessary, however, to offer encouragement for the importation of American bar iron, pigs, and sows and at the same time to lay restraints on iron-manufacturing in the colonies. The petitioners emphasized the disadvantages of so great a dependence upon Swedish iron. It was well known, they declared, that the government of Sweden had laid high and severe duties upon British manufactures that could be exchanged for bar iron.[50] This commodity, the petition stated, under prevailing conditions had to be purchased abroad "while your own subjects . . . lye unemployed and starving."

The other petitions supported by the furnacemen were in contrast, strongly opposed to giving any encouragement to American iron. They stressed that the erection of forges and slitting mills in the

---

[49] For copies of the above petitions see Penn Mss., Papers Relating to Iron, pp. 5–21; see also *Journals of the House of Commons*, XXII, 772, 810.

[50] On December 11, 1734, the King of Sweden issued an edict prohibiting the importation of certain types of English goods and placing a very high duty, amounting almost to prohibition, upon all other imports, woollen hose and yarn alone excepted. A William Axtell, in testifying before a parliamentary committee at this period, asserted that England was obliged to purchase from that country iron to the value of £150,000 sterling and yet, owing to these prohibitions, was unable to sell goods in return beyond the value of £20,000 or £30,000 at the highest. Report of the Committee of the House of Commons on the Petitions Relating to Iron, 1736/7, Penn Mss., Papers Relating to Iron, p. 27. In 1735, according to the records of the London custom-house, there were exported to Sweden 14,030 pounds of glassware, 3,074 dozen beaver hats, 216 hundredweight of tin, 324 gross of tobacco pipes, 3,320 yards of flannel, 800 pieces of kersies, and 28,732 hundredweight of stuffs. See P.R.O. Treas. 64:273.

plantations within the past few years had already led not only to the making of bar iron and the manufacture of axes, nails, and sundry other things for their own consumption but also to the exportation of great quantities of these articles to many of the other colonies. They expressed the apprehension that, unless the slitting mills were destroyed and some stop put to American manufacturing, the iron trade of England would soon be utterly ruined.[51] The Worcestershire petition emphasized that the iron trade of the region had increased and flourished until lately, but now had greatly declined for want of the usual demands for iron products. This the petitioners ascribed to nothing but the making of iron and ironware in America. The petitioners saw the decline of their industry, especially since many of the artificers and workmen had left of late and, it was feared, had removed themselves to America. Any encouragement to import bar iron from America would not mend matters, they felt, but would increase the evils of which they were complaining.[52]

Nevertheless, it seemed clear to many Englishmen that if America could be induced to give up iron-manufacturing and instead to send its pigs and sows to England, the general situation of the industry in England would be greatly improved, even if this meant nothing more than the substitution of American iron for iron produced abroad. Yet, was it possible to make this substitution?

Certain contemporaries insisted that American iron was of the same composition as the "cold short" of England and quite unlike that of Sweden and Russia. Were this true and were it to be freely imported, would this not, they argued, continually depress the local product without relieving Great Britain's precarious dependence upon the foreign markets for Oregrund[53] and other types of bar iron?[54] This question, with others affecting the iron industry,

---

[51] See, for example, the "Humble Petition of the Merchants, Iron Masters and Ironmongers," March 3, 1736, Penn Mss., Papers Relating to Iron, p. 3.

[52] *Ibid.*

[53] Oregrund, the best quality of Swedish iron, came from Dannemora mines. The Swedish traveller Angerstein, who was in England in 1754, reported the great reputation that Oregrund iron enjoyed in that country. See Alan Birch: "Foreign Observers of the British Iron Industry during the Eighteenth Century," *Journal of Economic History,* XV, 28.

[54] The arguments contained in three pamphlets on the subject are summarized in "Humble Petition of the Merchants, Iron Masters & Ironmongers." The titles of

was referred to a committee of the House of Commons. Joshua Gee, ironmaster of Shrewsbury who had imported Virginia and Maryland pig iron, presented figures to prove that this iron could be produced more cheaply and advantageously in America than in England and warned the committee that if forges and manufacturers were suffered to increase in the colonies, this would eventually drain the kingdom of its workers and would lead to the decline of ironworks of all kinds.[55] Abraham Spooner of Birmingham likewise declared that if America were encouraged to make bar iron, the result would certainly be the destruction of all ironworks in England.[56] According to a custom-house report, in the year 1736 there was shipped to America and the West Indies 43,921 hundredweight of wrought iron. From this report it appeared that Jamaica required a much larger quantity of these exports than the combined demands of Pennsylvania and New York. It indicated, nevertheless, that the iron-producing regions of New England and of the Chesapeake Bay were also important customers — New England purchasing 8,491 hundredweight of wrought iron and Virginia and Maryland 8,983 hundredweight.[57] At the same time one of the ironmasters, William Parkin, asserted before the committee that there should really be a demand for four times the amount of iron now sent to the plantations; that this was not so he attributed only to the quantity of ironware manufactured in America.[58]

As a result of the agitation thus raised there was framed "A Bill for Promoting the Exportation of the Woollen and other Manufactures of this Kingdom and for Encouraging the Importation of Iron from America and for Restraining the Increase of Iron Manufactures there," bearing date of January 31, 1738.[59] The bill provided that

---

these are, *Reasons Against the Making and Manufacturing of Barr Iron in America; Reasons Against the Importation of Sow and Pig Iron from America into Great Britain under the Present low Duty;* and *Some Considerations Showing that the Importations of Iron from America will Sooner put a Stop to the Making of Iron in England than the Importation of Iron from Sweden and Russia,* Penn Mss., Papers Relating to Iron, p. 3.

[55] For Gee's testimony see *Journals of the House of Commons,* XXIII, 113.

[56] Report of the Committee of the House of Commons, 1736/7 (?), Penn Mss., Papers Relating to Iron, p. 45.

[57] P.R.O., Treas. 64:273.

[58] For Parkin's testimony see Penn Mss., Papers Relating to Iron, p. 49.

[59] An annotated copy of this bill is also among the Penn Mss., pp. 35–9.

there might be imported from the plantations, in British and Irish ships, pigs, sows, and bar iron, unwrought and discharged of all poundage, subsidies, and other levies; that in turn for this encouragement after February 1, 1738, no mill or other engine for slitting or rolling iron or any furnace for making steel should be set up in any colony on pain of forfeiting £100 lawful money for each month wherein such mill would operate. It provided further, that after May 1, 1739, all foreign steel exported from Great Britain and Ireland to the plantations should carry a duty of £10 a ton and that after September 1, 1739, it would be unlawful to transport out of any of His Majesty's colonies to any other plantation or to Great Britain or Ireland any iron wrought up there into nails, tools, or other manufactures, under pain of the seizure of the cargo and the payment of £50 for each such offence.[60]

The time proved to be unfavourable for so serious a challenge of the colonies' right to develop their own industrial life; it is true that they already laboured under restrictions on the exportation of their wool and woollen manufactures, on those articles on the enumerated list and also on the making and exporting of hats. War with Spain had appeared on the horizon. This demanded a united front. The war finally became merged with that of the Austrian Succession. It was therefore not until after the Peace of Aix-la-Chapelle in 1749 that the British iron interests again turned to Parliament with appeals for relief. As a result, a bill to encourage the importation of pig and bar iron from America was drafted.

According to one writer, this new bill came most opportunely "when the nation [Sweden] which hitherto chiefly supplied us with Iron is laying farther [export] dutys in order to raise the Price upon us and when our own Iron seems to be falling off and decreasing both in quantity and quality." He then went on to declare: "A few years since it was computed that about two-fifths of all Iron manufactured in Great Britain was first made and produced here; it is believed by those who are most conversant therein that Great Britain does not now Furnish above One Fifth Part of the Quantity

---

[60] On the margin of the manuscript copy of the bill among the Penn Papers, apparently in the hand of Ferdinand John Paris, opposite the last clause is written this comment: "This is an ugly clause in its Consequences." According to the same writer, it might prevent the sending of a ship to Great Britain for sale because it contained American bolts.

here manufactured and a great deal of such fifth is so coarse and bad in quality as not to be fit for nail or small work."[61] Despite this testimony as to the decline of iron-production, probably not less than 600,000 individuals, including women and children, were dependent for a livelihood upon the iron industry in England, according to an estimate of 200,000 workers actually employed in the middle of the century at an average weekly wage of seven shillings.[62] These people had to be kept at work, it was felt. The nation had come out of the just-concluded Austrian Succession War heavily burdened with obligations, with taxes that had mounted to a sum which averaged one guinea for every man, woman, and child within the kingdom. Were half the iron workers thrown upon the parish for relief as the result of unemployment, it was estimated that at the rate of twelvepence per week per individual this would require the raising of an additional £260,000 yearly by the taxpayers, besides bringing about the pauperization of a large percentage of the population.

Many thoughtful Englishmen became convinced that the time had come to attempt to throw off the dependence upon Sweden for iron — as had been done earlier in the century with respect to certain naval stores and ship timber procured from that country and Norway. It was felt with equal earnestness that the plantations should not be allowed to overthrow one of the greatest of the mother country's industries, since such a move would have dire consequences for the labouring classes. Even those interests in England most sensitive to anything that would strike at American prosperity seemed to recognize the justice of placing certain restrictions upon colonial iron-production, so long as concessions corresponding to the new restrictions were provided. The Bristol Merchant Venturers, deeply involved in American trade, doubtless reflected this solicitous attitude when in their petition of March 1749 to the House of Commons they argued in favour of a bill to embody these ideas:

---

[61] "Some Considerations on the Bill to Encourage the Importations of Pig & Bar Iron from America" (March 6, 1749). Penn Mss., Papers Relating to Iron, p. 75.

[62] *Considerations on the Bill now Depending before the Honourable House of Commons, for Encouraging the Importation of Pig and Bar Iron from America* (1750?). Penn Mss., Papers Relating to Iron, p. 81.

"That your Petitioners humbly apprehend that a permission of Importing Pig and Barr Iron into Great Britain from the American Plantations Duty Free will be attended with many valuable Consequences to the Nation in general, as it will greatly promote and encourage our Colonys abroad and thereby our own Manufacturers of various Kinds at Home, will considerably relieve us from the necessity we are now under of being supply'd with these Articles from Foreigners who prohibit many of our Manufactures, receive great sums in specie every year from us & are strictly united with our Rivals in Trade.

"That with regard to our own Manufacturys of Small or fine Iron ware, Your Petitioners are of opinion that there should be a restriction to prevent any Persons abroad [that is, in the colonies] from erecting any Slitting or Rolling Mills, or any Forges for Plating of Iron, whereby that valuable manufactory here will be preserved to us."[63]

The culmination of all this agitation, which had extended over thirty years or more, was the passage of the famous Iron Act of the year 1750.[64] The statute brushed aside the arguments of English furnacemen, but at the same time sought to promote protection of the forge-operators. In doing away with the duty on both pig and bar iron produced by and imported from the plantations, it provided, nevertheless, that bar iron to enjoy this exemption should be carried only to the port of London and should not be conveyed, subsequent to being stamped, more than ten miles from the city limits. The act then declared that in order "that Pig and Bar Iron made in his Majesty's Colonies in America may be further manufactured in this Kingdom, Be it further enacted by the Authority aforesaid, That from and after the twenty-fourth Day of June one thousand seven hundred and fifty, no Mill or other Engine for Slitting or Rolling of Iron, or any Plating Forge to work with a Tilt Hammer, or any Furnace for making Steel, shall be erected, or after such Erection, continue, or cause to be continued, in any of the said Colonies, any such Mill, Engine, Forge or Furnace, every Person or Persons so offending shall . . . forfeit the Sum of two hundred Pounds lawful Money of Great Britain." All Governors or acting

---

[63] Records of the Society of Merchant Venturers of the City of Bristol, Book of Charters, 1749, p. 315.

[64] 23 George II, c. 29, *Statutes at Large* (Eyre and Strahan), VI, 490-2.

Governors were called upon to enforce this measure under penalty of forfeiting £500 lawful money and of being disabled to hold any office of trust.[65]

The reaction of some colonials to the Iron Act is illustrated by the views of the Pennsylvania surveyor and map-maker Lewis Evans in his *A Brief Account of Pennsylvania*, written in 1753:

> "I cannot omit here doing justice to the British Parliament in their Act relating to the Admission of our [Bar] Iron to the port of London only for sale. They knew that thus under a popular appearance, they wou'd effectually damn it. The Vicinity of Sweeden to London will always make the freight & insurance low, and notwithstanding the Duty upon the Iron, it can be afforded cheaper than ours. But freights from Sweeden to Bristol, Liverpool, & other parts of the West coast of Britain, wou'd in War time be nearly as dear as from the british Plantations: and they have taken Care to prevent our enjoying the Consumption of Iron on that Side which is very considerable, by reason of Pontipool, Birmingham, & Sheffield, so that for any benefit Britain may receive in Case of a war with the northern Powers, by being supplied from her own Plantations, the Act had as well never been made, because not a Man in America will set up an Iron Work, for the Sake of the Benefit of it. Supposing our [Bar] Iron cou'd be afforded in London within twenty Shillings as cheap as the Sweedish, we might afford it as cheap as theirs at Bristol in case of a War with France. Oh! the Piety! feed our Enemies."[66]

The Act unhappily did not fulfill any of the rosy expectations of its supporters. Previous to its passage the importation of pig iron from the colonies amounted to something over 2,000 tons. During the year 1750, 2,924 tons of American pig iron and 5 tons of bar iron were imported; in 1751 the amount was 3,220 tons of pig iron and 23 tons of bar iron; in 1755 it reached 3,389 tons of pig iron and 389 tons of bar, but dropped in 1757 to 2,699 tons of pig iron and 69 tons of bar.[67] Virginia and Maryland were the leading ex-

---

[65] See circular letter of May 29, 1750, signed by Thomas Hill, directed to the Governors of His Majesty's Plantations. P.R.O., C.O. 324:13, pp. 244–77.

[66] L. H. Gipson: *Lewis Evans* . . . (Philadelphia, 1939), pp. 101–2.

[67] See Report of the Inspector General of Customs for February 7, 1760, Historical Society of Pennsylvania transcripts; see also B. F. French: *History of the Rise and Progress of the Iron Trade of the United States from 1621 to 1857* (New York, 1858), which gives the figures (p. 8) for the export of pig and bar iron covering the years 1750–5 inclusive.

porters of this iron, with a total for 1750 of 2,508 tons of pig iron, for 1751 of 2,950 tons, and for 1752 of 2,762 tons.[68] The figures indicate that American ironmasters generally found it to their advantage to manufacture the product of their furnaces and forges rather than to ship it to England. "There is indeed a necessity for their manufacturing," wrote the author of *The State of the Trade and Manufactory of Iron in Great-Britain,* published in 1750, "but of a quite different nature from what has been represented. A necessity that will not be removed by the importation of Bar-iron from thence; but will subsist as long as there are Forges there, and increase upon the Erection of more Forges. It is a Necessity of the strongest Nature, arising from Profit and Gain. The *American* manufacturer, by the Cheapness of his Iron, the Profit of manufacturing it at home, and by saving the many Expenses, Disappointments and Damages, that must necessarily attend exporting this Bar-Iron to England, and importing the manufactured Goods back again to *America* will have an Advantage of £45 per Cent."[69]

It was soon apparent, irrespective of the inability of the mother country to enforce the Act of 1750, that little check had been placed upon iron-manufacturing in the plantations.[70] That the government was anxious about this development and any progress in the direction of industrialization, and was seeking every available means of checking it, is indicated by the instructions given to Colonel Hopson, who was sent to Nova Scotia in 1752 to take the place of Governor Cornwallis. He was desired not to give any encouragement to the working of the colliery in that province "which might prevent the clearing of land and is not consistent with the . . . policy observed by this country in relation to its' colonies, as the use of coals in America would furnish the people with the means of carrying on a variety of manufactures, the raw materials of which

---

[68] P.R.O. Treas. 64:274. New England's contribution to these totals for these years was insignificant: 21 tons of pig iron in 1750, 9 tons in 1751, and 41 tons in 1752.

[69] *Op. cit.,* pp. 12–13.

[70] This point is well developed by A. C. Bining: *British Regulation of the Colonial Iron Industry,* Chap. 5. The late H. C. Mercer in his *The Bible in Iron or Pictured Stoves and Stove Plates of the Pennsylvania Germans* (2nd edn. by H. M. Mann, Doylestown, 1941), which is devoted largely to colonial fire-backs, gives (pp. 173–82) a list of furnaces established in the colonies in the course of the eighteenth century with the approximate date of the erection of each.

we now receive from them and afterwards return manufactured."[71]

The Iron Act, some English critics charged, was given its peculiar reading in the interests of the ironmasters as against the manufacturers of iron. "This law," complained a writer, "is of no service to the manufacturer who lives above ten miles from London. Pig iron must go into the hands of the Iron-Masters to be made into Bars which give them an opportunity of setting their own price upon American as well as English bar-iron, and the Swedish Iron, called Orgroon, is monopolized."[72] In 1757 the Bristol Merchant Venturers, disappointed by the results of the Act, again petitioned Parliament to admit freely the importation of bar-iron.[73] This time they were successful,[74] with the result that the amount of iron of this quality exported from the colonies mounted from 69 tons received in that year to 1,059 tons in 1764.[75] The quantity was quite insufficient, with the result that in 1765 the London and Birmingham manufacturers memorialized the Board of Trade in favour of a bounty on all American iron imported, with ten shillings a ton provided for pig iron and forty shillings a ton for bar iron, and with a duty of ten shillings per ton on bar iron imported from Sweden, Russia, and Spain. They were joined in memorials from Wolverhampton and Walsall. Sheffield, however, opposed the duty on Swedish iron, "where it is imagined more steel is made than in the whole Kingdom besides." Its position was that American iron could not be made into anything that deserved the name of steel.[76]

In conclusion it must be emphasized that the Iron Act did not prohibit — nor was it so worded as to prohibit — the production of American iron or its manufacture into hardware. While it was hoped that the inducements of free importation into Great Britain of American pig iron and bar iron would cause these products to be sent over rather than fabricated in the colonies or turned into steel,

---

[71] Board of Trade *Journal, 1749–1753*, p. 302.

[72] See *Reasons for Allowing the Importation of Bar-Iron from America* (without date, but after 1750). Penn Mss., Papers Relating to Iron, p. 77.

[73] Bristol Merchant Venturers, Book of Charters, 1757, p. 339.

[74] 30 Geo. II, c. 16, *Statutes at Large* (Eyre and Strahan), VII, 144. The repeal of the prohibition on the movement of bar iron out of London had the support of the Customs Commissioners. See P.R.O., Treas. 1:441, f. 339.

[75] G. L. Beer: *Commercial Policy of England Toward the American Colonies*, p. 90.

[76] P.R.O., C.O. 323:18. No bounty was granted on iron.

there was a recognition of the utter unfairness of compelling mill-owners operating before the passing of the statute to destroy their property, even with compensation. Therefore, the act tended rather to favour those American ironmasters and steel-producers already in business. As a contemporary pointed out, ". . . it is most certainly true that by prohibiting the future Erection of Slitting Mills, etc., those who had such erected before the Act took place, will enjoy a sort of Monopoly. This was seen very clearly at the time of passing the Act. . . ."[77] By 1775 the colonies were producing three times the amount of iron which had been produced in 1750 at the time of the passing of the Iron Act, according to estimates.[78]

The mother country's unsuccessful attempt to regulate production and sales of colonial iron in the middle of the eighteenth century was not without significance. It served to make clear that — even with the best of motives — it was no easy task to shape by legislation the complex economic forces of the Empire. It also made clear that the government could not guide these forces, as had been hoped, toward realizing the ideals of imperial self-sufficiency and planned economy based on mutual advantages in a way that would supplement — rather than challenge as rivals — the old established English industrial and commercial interests. Economic sectionalism within the Empire, based upon particular and important sectional divergent interests, in the end served to defeat every effort put forth in this direction.

---

[77] "R. Charles of Leicesterfields in England to Thomas Lawrence of Pennsylvania, February 10, 1750," *Pennsylvania Magazine of History and Biography*, VII, 232–3.
[78] See A. C. Bining: *British Regulation of the Colonial Iron Industry*, p. 134.

CHAPTER X

Hudson Bay Beaver

CONTRARY to popular opinion in the mother country in the middle of the eighteenth century, the Hudson's Bay Company had no monopoly of the British North American fur trade. Although it brought the finest-quality beaver from Hudson Bay to the London fur market, it was in open competition in all markets, British and European, with pelts from the English colonies and those produced by French rivals in North America.[1] Nevertheless, its trade, scrupulously carried on within the framework of the navigation acts, was of sufficient importance to Great Britain's commercial system to withstand the pressures of those at home who complained that it had failed of one of its original purposes — the providing of a northwest passage — and their advocacy that the area embraced within its letters patent be opened to further exploration, colonization, and trade. By the 1750's the Company was enjoying the advantages of its strategic geographical location to a degree that enabled it to continue its profitable beaver trade despite challenges of rival claims and rival traders.

Ever since the twenty-second year of the reign of Charles II,

---

[1] See E. E. Rich: *The History of the Hudson's Bay Company, 1670–1870*, Vol. I, *1670–1763* (London, 1958), Chap. 44 and especially p. 658; see also H. A. Innis: *The Fur Trade in Canada: An Introduction to Canadian Economic History* (New Haven & London, 1930). For the fur trade of Pennsylvania see Vol. IV of this series, Chap. 6, and for the trade involving the Six Confederate Nations and the Great Lakes see *ibid.*, V, Chap. 3.

when "The Governor and Company of Adventurers of England trading into Hudson's Bay" were incorporated and granted the lands in the region of Hudson Bay with the sole rights to trade and commerce, England had succeeded, with only brief interruptions as the result of wars, in exploiting the far northern fur trade in America.[2] The region is a forbidding one, with extremely low temperatures in winter. In the eighteenth century is was quite cut off from communication with the mother country for about nine months each year by the blocking of Hudson Strait with impenetrable ice floes and icebergs. Although the Company had been in existence as a corporation for eighty years, in 1750 there was little evidence of development and improvement within the limits of the grant. The area — outside of a scattered Indian population, the Eskimos living northwest of the Bay, and the wild life upon which they preyed — was a vast solitude. Probably not more than 150 Englishmen, all employees of the Company, were living within its confines along the fringes of the great Bay at the various trading posts.[3] These posts were located near the shores of the Bay or on important rivers that emptied their waters into it. On or near the western shore were Moose Fort on the Moose River, Albany Fort and Henley House on the Albany, York Fort on the Hayes, together with Flamborough House, a small post at Flamborough Head built in 1747 on the Nelson, and another, Split Lake Fort on the upper Nelson, likewise constructed in the 1740's.[4] The most northern post, Prince of Wales, where some forty-five of the Company's servants were dwelling, was an unfinished stone fort built in 1734 to replace

---

[2] For the charter of the Hudson's Bay Company, granted May 2, 1670, see *Minutes of the Hudson's Bay Company*, *Publications* of the Hudson's Bay Record Society (London, 1942), Appendix A, pp. 131–53; see also E. E. Rich: *op. cit.*, I, Chap. 6, "The Charter."

[3] According to Andrew Graham's account of the Hudson Bay posts in 1771, not more than 200 Europeans were living in them. See George Bryce: *The Remarkable History of the Hudson's Bay Company* (Toronto, 1900), p. 109.

[4] R. E. Pinkerton: *Hudson's Bay Company* (New York, 1931), p. 86. Not all the smaller posts such as Brunswick House were continually occupied. For a map of the lower Hayes and Nelson rivers in 1747 see Joseph Robson: *An Account of Six Years' Residence in Hudson's Bay* . . . (London, 1752), frontispiece and p. 71. Flamborough House was also described as "Hope post, on Hayes Island . . ."; see E. E. Rich: *op. cit.*, p. 585.

an older wooden structure and was located on the Churchill.[5] On the eastern shore of the Bay were two small posts: East Main House on the Slude and Fort Richmond to the north on the Whale River.[6] Brunswick House on the Moose, the southernmost of these posts, and Henley House, situated 150 miles up the Albany, were especially designed to offset the pressure of the French upon the Indians to the south and southwest of the Bay. York Factory, built of timber in the form of a square with four small bastions, seems to have been by far the most important trading centre possessed by the Company;[7] yet in 1750 only thirty-six men were there, including servants and factors, hardly enough to man the nineteen cannon — twelve-, nine-, and six-pounders — which, with a double palisade, constituted the formal defence. The Company, of course, realized that the chief protection of its possessions lay in their isolation and in the very great difficulties involved in any hostile movement against the Bay. Nevertheless, even this isolation did not preserve the posts from French assaults and capture between 1682 and 1697.[8]

---

[5] James Isham in his "Observations on Hudson's Bay, 1743" gives an extended account of Prince of Wales Fort. It was protected by three batteries of cannon, each battery placed to serve a defensive purpose. The ramparts of stone were 38 feet wide with a stone parapet six feet high with bastions, enclosing an area of 400 yards where was located the main structure; over 100 feet in length and 33 feet in width, it was divided into dwelling quarters and the warehouse; there were also stables for the live-stock, capacious vaults under the bastions for additional stores, a powder magazine, a belfry, and a well. See *The Publications of the Hudson's Bay Record Society: Isham's Observations and Notes, 1743–1749* (ed. E. E. Rich, London, 1949), pp. 173–7. Joseph Robson, who left the Bay in 1747 and who assisted in the construction of the fort, inserted a description of it in the appendix of his *An Account of Six Years' Residence in Hudson's Bay*. For an excellent map of the mouth of the Churchill River see *ibid.*, opposite p. 9, and for a sketch of the fort see *ibid.*, opposite p. 30. Although the weather had caused the walls of the fort to deteriorate by 1750, Beckles Willson called it one of the strongest on the North American continent. See his *The Great Company, 1667–1871* (2 vols., London, 1900), II, 18.

[6] *Ibid.*, II, 18–19.

[7] "This is looked upon to be in all Respect the most valuable of the *Hudson's-Bay* Company's Settlements because the most considerable part of their Trade is carried on here, where it is computed they deal for between forty and fifty thousand rich furs annually" (Henry Ellis: *A Voyage to Hudson's Bay, by the Dobbs Galley and California* . . . [London, 1748], p. 212); see also H. A. Innis: *op. cit.*, p. 143. For a map of the lower courses of the Hayes and Nelson rivers see Joseph Robson: *op. cit.*, opposite the title page; opposite p. 30 is a plan of the fortification of York Fort.

[8] For a chronological account of Anglo-French hostilities in Hudson Bay from 1682 to 1713 see Douglas MacKay: *The Honourable Company: A History of the Hudson's Bay Company* (Indianapolis & New York, 1936), pp. 49–56; for an ex-

In order to prosecute its fur-trading activities, the Company customarily sent out each year from England four ships, which entered Hudson Bay about the middle of July and left, as a rule, before the first of October. These sturdy vessels with powerfully reinforced hulls, built for this hazardous work, were from 120 to 190 tons burden, and on the outward voyage were loaded with stores for the various needs of the posts, together with articles of trade.[9] They returned partly in ballast with furs and other light objects of value.[10] In the Company's report for the fiscal year 1747–8 it is stated that the ships brought back over 52,000 beaver skins, over 8,000 marten, about 1,500 otter, some 1,200 wild cat, together with lesser quantities of bear, fox, wolverine, wolf, elk, deer, and other pelts and such articles as "bed feathers," whale fins, and goose quills to a total value of £30,160.5.11.[11] The cost of carrying on this trade in 1748 was placed at £17,352.4.10, to which was added £5,012.12.3, the

tended account of these hostilities see E. E. Rich: *op. cit.*, I, 116–43, 192–8, 402–15, 482–3.

[9] The Company down through the years sought in vain to be relieved of the expense of sending out large food supplies to the posts. While some vegetables could be grown on the Bay, grain does not often ripen on account of the relatively short growing period. However, Edward Thompson, who appeared before a parliamentary committee in 1749, declared that he saw better barley and oats grown at Moose Fort than in the Orkneys, and Robert Griffin testified in the same hearing that oats grew to perfection at Albany Fort, still farther north than Moose River. See *Report from the Committee Appointed to Inquire into the State and Conditions of . . . Hudson's Bay . . .* ([London], 1749), pp. 25 and 34. James Isham, who for many years served at both York Factory and the Prince of Wales Fort, affirmed that, while vegetables could be grown in those parts, no corn could be raised. See *Isham's Observations and Notes, 1743–1749*, Introduction, p. xxxvii.

[10] The cost of maintaining the posts on the Bay varied, as might be anticipated, from year to year. In 1741 the Company expended £11,757 to purchase trading goods and support the factories; in 1745 this expenditure amounted to £21,701. See H. A. Innis: *op. cit.*, p. 135.

[11] *Reports from Committees of the House of Commons Reprinted by Order of the House*, Vol. II, *Miscellaneous Subjects, 1738–1765* (London, 1803), Appendix, No. X. See also the Shelburne Papers, 112:72–4, Clements Library, for tables showing the imports and exports to and from Hudson Bay. For the year 1748 the imports from the Bay were valued at £12,392.14 and exports to it at £3,651.11.8. The differences between these two sets of figures perhaps represent the difference between the appraised value of these furs at the time of importation and their value when actually sold from the Company's warehouses. See also Shelburne Papers, Vol. 102, for "A Sketch of the Trade to & from England to Hudson's Bay," which gives the total value of the imports from the Bay between Christmas 1751 and Christmas 1752 as £8,092.4.7, of which beaver and other skins were valued at £7,656.17.6; the value of exports to the Bay was placed at £3,380.6.

value of the trading goods, consisting principally of guns, powder, shot, knives, and blankets.[12]

The Company regulations governing the trade with the Indians were exceedingly strict. Not more than two men at a post were entrusted with this responsibility, and all others were forbidden to have any intercourse with the natives.

The Indians arrived at the posts from up the rivers in birch-bark canoes in parties generally numbering about thirty, but sometimes as many as a hundred, and carried their pelts to the Company store. There they remained outside, since all transactions apparently took place at a window or hole in the supply house. As a measure of security, large numbers of Indians were never allowed within the palisades enclosing the post.[13] Moreover, great caution was exercised, it would appear, in supplying the Indians with strong drink. Richard White, a Company factor before 1749, testified in the parliamentary investigation of that year that he had known eleven canoes to leave Fort Albany at one time for want of a present of a bottle of brandy.[14]

The influence of the French was noticeable in the south, and particularly north and west of Lake Superior — especially as a result of the activities of the Sieur de la Vérendrye, who before his death in 1749 had established a number of posts at such places as the mouth of the Winnepeg and the forks of the Saskatchewan. The effect of French competition is indicated by the fact that the Indians who came to the Moose and Albany rivers to trade could get a blanket for six beaver skins and eight knives for one skin, whereas at York Fort, farther removed from French competition, the trader

---

[12] See Beckles Willson: *op. cit.*, II, 8–9. From 1739 to 1748 the Company priced its exports to the Bay at £52,464.5, or a yearly average of £5,246.8; for the same years the average yearly costs of maintaining the posts—beyond the cost of exports in the form of trading goods — were £15,743.5. See E. E. Rich: *op. cit.*, I, 592–3.

[13] Examination of Joseph Robson, *Report from the Committee Appointed to Inquire into . . . Hudson's Bay* (1749), p. 17.

[14] Examination of Richard White, *ibid.*, p. 6. Andrew Graham, who was chief factor at York Fort in 1761 and spent many years in the Bay, has much to say about the deadly effects of strong drink on the Indians. In his "Remarks on Hudson Bay's Trade" he affirmed that the trade in brandy 'is productive of every evil, for it not only degenerates the Natives, loses the Companys Goods, But loses a large Quantity of fine furs yearly, the sooner a stop is put to it by the Company the better it will be" (Huntington Library, Mss., series H.M. 1720:7). However, the practice of giving brandy as pay to Indians who hunted for the people of the fort continued.

demanded seven and four skins respectively for the same bartered items.[15] Even the trade at York and Prince of Wales forts was affected by the activities of the *coureurs* who lived among the Indians.[16]

The fur trade was mostly with the Crees and the Assiniboines, who lived at a distance from the Bay and acted on occasion as the middlemen for the Far West Indians. The Company's agents, as a rule, did not travel to the Indians' abodes to prosecute this trade, although between 1690 and 1692 Henry Kelsey traversed over five hundred miles of wilderness country and reached the Indians of the Plains, to be followed more than sixty years later by Anthony Henday (Hendry), who in 1754 entered the country of the Blackfeet.[17] According to the halfbreed trader Joseph La France, some Indians dwelling in the Far West actually took two years to reach the Company factories, moving along leisurely, inactive during the heat of the day, and hunting for food along the way.[18] In any case, the regions subject to the Company's exploitation must have been very great indeed. But trade was not continuous. At the Prince of Wales factory on the Churchill, for example, the Indians would arrive in July in their birch-bark canoes, only to leave in three weeks' time while the river could still be safely navigated. After Christmas some would return across the ice.

There is no evidence that the Company made any efforts to civilize or Christianize the savages. Indeed, it had very little contact with them beyond that of trade. While a few elderly Indians lived close to the forts, they were seldom employed, except on occasion to secure fresh meat. Neither did the Company put forth any effort

---

[15] See H. A. Innis: *op. cit.*, pp. 145–8, for a careful analysis of this.

[16] For a detailed treatment of the above point see E. E. Rich: *op. cit.*, II, Chap. 38.

[17] For Kelsey's "Journal" see *The Kelsey Papers* (Ottawa, 1929); the *Journal of Anthony Hendry, 1754–1755* has been edited by L. J. Burpee (Royal Society of Canada *Proceedings* and *Transactions*, 3rd ser., I); see also Burpee's *Search for the Western Sea . . .* (2 vols., Toronto, 1908, [revised 1935]). One of the most detailed accounts of the Indians living to the west of Hudson Bay in the 1760's is to be found in "Remarks on Hudson Bay's Trade by Andrew Graham many years Factor at York Fort and Severn House for the perusal of his Employers. 1769" (Huntington Library, San Marino, California). Graham voiced strong opposition to sending traders into the Indian country.

[18] Examination of Joseph La France, *Report from the Committee Appointed to Inquire into . . . Hudson's Bay* (1749), Appendix, II, xxv.

to establish interior posts and settlements. The actual limits of its wilderness possessions were by no means clearly determined. According to a memorial of October 3, 1750, which was laid before the Board of Trade,[19] it was claimed that the boundaries of the grant under the charter were the farthest northern extent of lands down to Cape Perdrix[20] on the Labrador Coast, located in the latitude of fifty-nine and one-half degrees, and from that point to lake Miscosinke (Mistassini) southeast of Hudson Bay and thence to the forty-ninth degree of north latitude and along that meridian westward "to the utmost limits of those lands" — certainly a vast empire! Indeed, had the French acknowledged these limits, they would have been stripped of most of the regions from which they were drawing their wealth in furs.

After all, it was perhaps not vitally important that the boundaries of the grant should be precisely established so long as France made no further hostile thrust in the direction of the British factories about the Bay. The enterprise was not for colonization but for trade and profits to the Company's members. In 1749 the capital stock, amounting to £103,950,[21] was distributed among 103 people, including the minor heirs or administrators of the estates of twenty-six deceased who had been stockholders. The only one among them who seems to have occupied a station in public life of some importance was Mark Thurston, Accountant-General of the Court of Chancery.[22] A great change from the days when the Company met at the lodgings of Prince Rupert in Whitehall!

The headquarters of the Company, where the annual General Court was also held, were located in Fenchurch Street and were known either as Hudson's Bay House or Beaver House. This structure was described in 1683 as "a very elegant brick building, adorned with pilasters and architraves . . . the vast repository of the North-

---

[19] Board of Trade *Journal, 1749–1753*, p. 107; P.R.O., C.O. 323:12, O. 60.

[20] It reads: ". . . at an Island called Grimington's Island in the Latitude of 59½° on the Labrador Coast otherwise Cape Perdrix. . . ."

[21] In 1676 the stock was £10,500; in 1690 it was trebled to £31,500, and in 1720 it was trebled to £94,500. See "Report from the Committee on Hudson Bay" (1749), from *Reports from Committees of the House of Commons, 1738–1765*, Appendix, viii.

[22] See *ibid.*

ern furs of America . . . lodged here till they are sold and exported to various parts of the world, even to the distant China."[23]

The skins and pelts were customarily offered for sale at open auction at Beaver House.[24] At these auctions during the years 1747–8 the Bay beaver brought an average price of seven shillings and sixpence a pound, marten six shillings and eightpence, otter nine shillings, sevenpence and a farthing. Keen competition took place among buyers, for these furs were easily the finest brought out of America and far superior to the pelts secured farther south in the Great Lakes region.[25]

The Bay beaver, as a luxury article, had initially been used largely for making muffs and lining garments. But by the beginning of the seventeenth century the so-called beaver hat had won favour among well-bred men. Its popularity continued until the nineteenth century, when it was finally superseded among people of fashion by the silk hat.[26]

The hat of the eighteenth century – the well-known cocked hat – did not utilize the long outer hair of the beaver skin but only the underneath layer of shorter barbed hair. Once separated from the skin, this short-hair was sold by the pound as a commodity called by the trade "staple fur." Great skill was required to master the art or mystery of making a good beaver hat. It appears that the craft was introduced into England not earlier than the sixteenth century by foreigners who came from Spain and Holland. In the latter part of the seventeenth century Huguenot hatters from France sought refuge in England and helped to bring the art to its perfection.[27] As a result, by the early part of the eighteenth century hats were produced in quantity not only in London but in other English industrial centres. In fact, it was asserted that by 1701 the master hatters had become the most opulent and extensive traders in the kingdom, employing over 20,000 people.[28] But between that year and 1711 the

---

23 Report of the Governor to the General Court of the Hudson's Bay Company held June 26, 1928, Ottawa *Journal*, July 8, 1928.

24 This had been required by law. Should all the furs not be sold at auction, the price of the remainder, if disposed of at private sale, was determined by the last auction price.

25 H. A. Innis: *op. cit.*, pp. 1–2.

26 M. G. Lawson: *Fur: A Study of English Mercantilism* (Toronto, 1943), pp. 1–6.

27 *Ibid.*, pp. 7–8.

28 See their "Memorial" of March 12, 1764, Chatham Manuscripts, Vol. 81, P.R.O.

French, at war with the English, were in temporary control of much of Hudson Bay and its fur trade and used this opportunity to revive the beaver-hat industry that had disappeared with the departure of the Huguenots.[29] Many of the English master hatters soon felt the effects of this. Nor did the restoration of the Bay posts entirely relieve the situation. One traveller in France in 1727 was surprised to find large numbers of English journeymen hatters who had left the stagnating beaver-hat trade in England to seek employment on the Continent.[30] That the French beaver-hat industry was flourishing to an unprecedented degree by 1750 and had outstripped its English competitors was to a considerable extent due to the protection afforded it. No one, under the threat of the severest penalties, was permitted to re-export unmanufactured beaver from France. The manufactured product of beaver was said to "exceed the Value upon Importation in some Cases, ten Fold" and by 1745 to have won most of the markets of Europe and of Spanish America.[31] The other explanation of this would appear to lie in the fact that the French produced a better hat than was made in England. During the war of the Austrian Succession a ship from France, bound for the Spanish West Indies with a consignment of white beaver hats, fell into the hands of the British, who sold a quantity of them in the London market. The hats were considered so far superior to any that the English could produce that one writer affirmed they were "much beyond what they could have imagin'd."[32]

In an effort to bring relief to the English hatters by cutting off large supplies of beaver which were carried from New York and other colonies to Holland and from there went into the hands of French manufacturers, a law was passed in 1722 which, among other things, placed all furs exported from the British plantations in America, Asia, and Africa on the so-called "enumerated" list of colonial products that could be transported only to Great Britain if not carried to some other British colony. By the same act, as a further encouragement to the hat industry, the import duty on

---

[29] *Ibid.*

[30] See *The Present State of British and French Trade to Africa and America* (London, 1745), pp. 7–8.

[31] "Memorial" of March 12, 1764, Chatham Mss., Vol. 81, P.R.O.

[32] *Ibid.*

...ortion of "A New Map of Hudson's Bay
...Labrador" (From *A Complete Atlas*) by Emanuel Bowen, 1752.
...nadian Archives, Map Division)

The Island of Newfoundland.

(From *A Complete Atlas* by Emanuel Bowen, 17

beaver skins was reduced from sixteenpence to sixpence per skin, while the drawback of import duties on furs afterwards exported was reduced from 13¼d to 4⁹⁄₁₀d.[33]

Despite this legislation, the French hat industry continued to flourish while that of the English stagnated. For not only did the English master hatter have to face highly protected French competitors, he also faced competition from the colonies. In both Massachusetts Bay and New York there was considerable activity directed to the making of beaver hats that were then either sold in the local markets in competition with the English product or were exported to Spain, Portugal, and the West Indies — among the chief markets for the sale of English hats.[34] In a memorial to the Board of Trade on January 13, 1731/2, the master hatters of London, on behalf of themselves and all other makers of hats in Great Britain, pointed out that, by reason of the great advantages enjoyed by those engaged in the colonial industry, they were able to offer large rewards to recruit journeymen hatters from the mother country and thereupon sell their hats with a profit at a low rate not only in foreign markets but even in Great Britain. As a result, the London hatters affirmed that "the said trade of hatmaking in Great Britain now does and will daily decline . . . to the great impoverishment of many poor familys whose livelihood depends thereon." They therefore begged that the people of the plantations be "prevented from wearing or vending any hats save what are the manufacture of Great Brittain."[35]

While Parliament was anxious to give some relief to the English hatmakers, it was not prepared to go to any such lengths as this memorial sought. Nevertheless, it was strongly felt that a colonial industry must not be permitted to destroy a well-established and important craft of the mother country — something that, whether rightly or wrongly, no colonizing power in the eighteenth century would have permitted, it goes without saying. The statute enacted in 1732, "An Act to prevent the Exportation of Hats out of any of his

---

[33] 8 Geo. I, c. 15, ser. 24.

[34] According to a representation of the Board of Trade of February 15, 1731/2, to the House of Commons, information had been received that "Great Quantities of hats" made in New England were exported to Spain, Portugal, and the British West Indies. See *Calendar of State Papers, America and West Indies, 1732*, p. 60.

[35] Memorial of the Master Wardens and Assistants of the Company of Feltmakers of London, *ibid.*, pp. 6–7.

Majesty's Colonies . . . and to restrain the Number of Apprentices taken by the Hatmakers in the said Colonies,"[36] represents a compromise between extremes. On the one hand, it prohibited the exportation out of a colony of any hats made of beaver, wool, or other material, as well as the setting up of any manufacture of this article by any one who had not served an apprenticeship of seven years in the art of feltmaking; nor could one so qualified employ a Negro in this craft or more than two white apprentices at any one time, or any apprentice for more than seven years. On the other hand, a colonial properly qualified could legally manufacture hats, could train the members of his immediate family to assist him, could have two apprentices, and could freely offer his products for sale within the colony where he was engaged in his operations.[37] That these restrictions did not prevent the continued manufacture of hats in America is indicated by a representation of the Board of Trade in 1764 to the Privy Council that this manufacture was "now carried on to a great extent, particularly in the Province of New York."[38]

Although the danger to the English manufacturers from the growth in competition of the colonial hatmakers was reduced to some extent, the threat from the Continent remained and was intensified. This led in 1752 to another series of petitions to Parliament for protection. The position taken by those from Manchester and other towns was that since France strictly prohibited the export of beaver, the only market for this fur open to foreigners other than Frenchmen was that of Great Britain; further that, by reason of generous drawbacks and lower wages paid to workers, the Continental hatmakers could pay high prices for the fur and still sell

---

[36] 5 Geo. II, c. 22, *Statutes at Large* (Eyre and Strahan), V, 594–5.

[37] One British colonial official, Archibald Kennedy, a member of the Council of New York and Collector of Customs within this province, in his *Observations on the Importance of the Northern Colonies under Proper Regulations,* published in New York in 1750, wrote (p. 10): ". . . where People are numerous and free, they will push what they think is for their Interest, and all restraining Laws will be thought Oppressive; especially such Laws as according to the Conceptions we have of English Liberty they have had no hand in contriving or making." He then stated: "Give me leave here to mention, some such now in being; . . . Enumerating our Produce [furs went on the enumerated list in 1722, as indicated in the text], and confining it to a single Market is a Solicism in Trade, and the Bane of Industry. Hats, tho' we live almost in the Centre of the Furr Trade, we are prohibited to export, tho' made from those very refuge [refuse?] Furr not fit for a Foreign Market. . . ." These were courageous statements for a British official in 1750.

[38] *Acts of the Privy Council, Col. Ser., 1745–1766,* p. 638.

their hats at lower prices than the English could adopt and continue to remain in business. The petitioners therefore sought either the total prohibition of the export of beaver felt or, if that were not possible, the removal of the drawback when it was purchased to send abroad.[39] No action resulted at that time. In 1759 a bill "for regulating the Company of Feltmakers of London" referred to the fact that "the said Company or Fellowship is of late Years much diminished and decayed."[40] However, not until 1764 was the seriousness of the English hat-trade situation reassessed.[41] By that time the English hatters, or so it was affirmed in a memorial of that year presented to the Board of Trade, had lost to the French their two chief remaining markets in Europe — those of Spain and of Portugal — in addition to those already lost in Germany, Italy, Sweden, Denmark, and other countries.[42] The memorial was partly supported by official figures taken from the register of the export of hats which indicated that in 1736, 30,917 dozen beaver hats had been exported and in 1762 but 8,708 dozens. These figures also indicated that in 1762 the markets in Holland and Portugal were still partly held, although cut in half in the case of Holland and amounting to only a little over one sixth in the case of Portugal as against the earlier year.[43]

The matter finally was taken up by Parliament, where a flood of petitions came before the House of Commons.[44] A bill that embodied the Board of Trade's recommendations[45] was framed and

[39] See *Journals of the House of Commons*, XXVI, 359 and 390; see also *Reports from Committees of the House of Commons* . . . (London, 1803), II, 373–6. The following communication from London, dated September 1, 1750, printed in the *Boston Evening Post* of November 25, 1750, emphasizes the problem that faced the English hatmakers: "We are assured that a very large Quantity of fine hats were lately sent from hence to Portugal, Which were all returned upon the Owner; not for any Objection against Goodness either of the Materials or the Workmanship but merely because the French had stock'd the [Portuguese] Market with goods of the same Qualities at 20 or 25 per cent cheaper than the English could afford them."

[40] See J. H. Hawkins: *History of the Worshipful Company of the Art or Mistery of Feltmakers of London* (London, 1917), p. 157.

[41] See M. G. Lawson: (*op. cit.*, pp. 21–3) for a careful analysis of the situation of the hatmakers between 1732 and 1764.

[42] For the hatters' memorial see *Acts of the Privy Council, Col. Ser., 1745–1766*, pp. 650–1; see also a statement of the plight of the hatmakers in face of the French competition dated March 12, 1764, Chatham Papers, Vol. 81, P.R.O.

[43] *Acts of the Privy Council, Col. Ser., 1745–1766*, pp. 651–2. The East Indies had increased purchases from 521 dozens in 1736 to 2,250 dozens in 1762.

[44] *Journals of the House of Commons*, XXIX, 761, 769, 775, 838.

[45] *Acts of the Privy Council, Col. Ser., 1745–1766*, pp. 638–9.

passed into law. Again a compromise was made between the interested views of the hatters on the one hand and those of the Hudson's Bay Company on the other. The import duty on beaver skins was lowered to become a purely token duty of a penny a skin. Then, instead of prohibiting the exportation of all skins, the drawback was eliminated and an export duty on each skin was placed at sevenpence and on every pound of beaver wool at a shilling and sixpence.[46] Unfortunately for the English hatters, beaver skin and beaver wool still flowed from England to the Continent. In 1750 there were exported 35,403 beaver skins; in 1765 the export figure had jumped to 61,947 skins, and in 1775 it amounted to 80,581. At the same time the export of hats showed a commensurate decline. In 1750, 14,610 dozens beaver hats were exported to Portugal, in 1765 the figure was 1,061 dozens, and in 1775 that country took but 75 dozens; in 1750 the export of them to Spain was 9,144 dozens, in 1765 it was 639 dozens, and in 1775 only 183 dozens.[47] This loss of markets was due not to the fact that people of standing in Europe no longer wore these hats, for they did. But, quality for quality, the English hat, by reason of higher wages paid to workmen, would seem to have been priced out of the market.[48]

It is clear that in the middle of the eighteenth century the Hudson's Bay Company itself was in an enviable position. Unlike the English hatters, it was losing no markets, and its trade in furs was exceedingly profitable. Joseph Robson, a critic of the Company, although a former employee, asserted that members could export from London a quart of English spirits at sixpence, mix it with one-third water, and then exchange it for a beaver skin weighing a pound and a half, for which they could get at auction nine shillings and a penny, making a 2,700-per-cent profit.[49] This of course gives a

---

[46] 4 Geo. III, c. 9.

[47] M. G. Lawson: op. cit., for tables on pp. 93 and 116.

[48] The Board of Trade in 1764 attributed the decrease in the exportation of hats to "the great increase in the price of Labour in this Country," as well as to the fact that inferior hats were sent abroad by many of the manufacturers. See Acts of the Privy Council, Col. Ser., 1745–1766, pp. 637–8.

[49] Joseph Robson: An Account of Six Years' Residence in Hudson's Bay (London, 1752), "Appendix No. I," pp. 49–51. As Glyndwr Williams has recently pointed out in his article "Arthur Dobbs and Joseph Robson: New Light on the Relationship between Two Early Critics of the Hudson's Bay Company," Canadian Historical Review, XL, 132–6, Dobbs carefully edited this appendix.

false impression of the returns from trading operations. It was calculated that the Company realized about 216-per-cent profit upon the annual stock in trade after all expenses had been deducted and about 7⅔-per-cent profit upon their nominal capital of £103,950.[50]

It is not to be wondered at that there were some who sought to break through the monopoly and to secure part of the benefits of this lucrative trade. This challenge came chiefly through the activities of Arthur Dobbs, a native of Ireland, whose later career as Governor of North Carolina has been described in the preceding volume of this series.[51]

In the early 1730's Dobbs became deeply interested in the possibility of discovering a northwest passage to the Pacific ocean. He promoted this project energetically both at the Admiralty Office and at Beaver House. As a result, in 1735 the Company instructed the Governor of the Prince of Wales Fort to send a sloop northward the following year to try to locate a passage. This order was repeated in 1736, with the outcome that in 1737 two small sloops sought to discover such a passage on the northwest shore of the Bay. The venture ended in failure. But Dobbs, who had considerable influence in London as a friend of Robert Walpole, was convinced that the effort had been half-hearted, and that the Company was really out of sympathy with the objective he had so much at heart at the time. He then turned to Sir Charles Wager, First Lord of the Admiralty, for support of a serious attempt to uncover a passage. Toward this project he also enlisted the co-operation of an experienced sea captain, Christopher Middleton, who had been in the service of the Hudson's Bay Company since 1721 and who was at home in waters of the Bay. In 1741 Middleton left the Company's employ, and in June of that year, under Admiralty orders he left London with two vessels, wintered at the Prince of Wales Fort, and in the spring of 1742 sailed as far north as 66°. Finding no passage, he returned to London in the fall of that year.

---

[50] Joseph Robson: *op. cit.*, Appendix, p. 50. Beckles Willson estimates that even in dull times there was a profit of forty per cent on the actual paid-up capital. *The Great Company, 1667–1871*, II, 9. On the other hand, Professor Rich (*op. cit.*, I, 592–3), after careful calculations, places the return at a little over thirty per cent on the outlay of funds.

[51] For a recent excellent life of Dobbs see Desmond Clarke: *Arthur Dobbs, Esquire, 1689–1765, Surveyor-General of Ireland, Prospector and Governor of North Carolina* (Chapel Hill, N.C., 1957).

But Dobbs was not to be persuaded that no northwest passage existed. He charged that the failure was due to the fact that Middleton had been bribed. Middleton vindicated himself, but by this time so great a public interest in uncovering a northwest passage had been aroused that Parliament in 1745 passed an act offering a reward of £20,000 to whoever would discover "a North West Passage through Hudson's Streights to the Western American Ocean."[52]

To provide the means for still another attempt to locate the mythical passage, Dobbs opened a subscription for £10,000, and a committee of prominent men was selected to administer the undertaking. This was known as the "North West Committee." Two ships, the *Dobbs Galley* and the *California*, were purchased, and in the spring of 1746 they left on the mission of discovery. Arriving too late in the season for the exploration of the coast, the crews wintered on the Hayes River near York Fort. But the passage to the Pacific by "Hudson's Streights" could not be found for the simple reason that it did not exist. In the fall of 1747 the survivors of the expedition returned to London.[53]

The redoubtable Dobbs now levelled an attack upon the Hudson's Bay Company, whose charter he challenged as illegal. In this connection he petitioned the King in Council to incorporate the "North West Committee" as a company that would secure all lands that it might discover or settle. When the Privy Council proved reluctant to act against the Company, he petitioned Parliament to throw open the trade of the Bay and to bring into existence a new company — apparently somewhat on the order of the regulated company that the following year was to take the place of the old incorporated Royal African Company.[54] He was supported by a flood

---

[52] See 18 Geo. II, c. 17.

[53] Henry Ellis, who was on the expedition as supercargo on the *Dobbs Galley*, published in London in 1748 *A Voyage to Hudson's Bay by the Dobbs Galley and California, in the Years 1746 and 1747 for Discovering a North West Passage*, which, among other things, was a severe attack on the conduct of the Company's officers, especially those at York Fort, near which he and his companions wintered. See also another interesting work by Ellis: *Considerations of the Advantages which would arise from Discovery of the Northwest Passage* (London, 1750).

[54] For Dobb's activities from 1733 to 1749 see Desmond Clarke: *op. cit.*, pp. 60–70; see also E. E. Rich: *op. cit.*, I, 554–84. For Dobbs's own writings relating to Hudson Bay and the Northwest Passage see *Remarks upon Capt. Middleton's Defense* (London, 1743); *Account of the Countries adjoining the Hudson's Bay in the Northwest part of America* (London, 1744); *Short View of the Countries and Trade*

of petitions in the spring of 1749 from merchants and others from twenty-three towns, boroughs, or cities, including Bristol, Liverpool, London, Chester, Leeds, Whitehaven, Shrewsbury, Coventry, Great Yarmouth, and Wolverhampton.[55] A committee of the House was appointed to consider them. Witnesses both in opposition to the Company and in support of it were called. Their testimony is to be found in *A Report from the Committee Appointed to Inquire into the State and Conditions of the Countries Adjoining the Hudson's Bay, and of the Trade carried on there,* published later the same year.

The *Report,* although presenting many points of view of merchants, shipmasters, and other interested parties, tended to confirm the opinion that throwing open the trade of the Bay would lead to a rapid extension of British influence in the North American interior and the penetration of areas by subjects of Great Britain which only the French *voyageurs* had hitherto entered. Nevertheless, the Company's petition presented on May 1 was a strong defence of its conduct in carrying out the objectives specified in its charter. To find a northwest passage within the Bay was, it affirmed, now clearly impossible; nor would people who were not paid to do so care to live in the barren region as colonizers. As to throwing open the trade of the region, it was pointed out that this would constitute a denial of the rights the Company had long enjoyed and lead to its destruction without benefitting the nation. Added to this was the danger that the trade might pass into the hands of foreigners.[56]

The Company was too powerfully entrenched to be reached by even so powerful an opposition as that presented in 1749. It not only weathered this storm but was destined to survive to our own day, although stripped of many of its eighteenth-century privileges by the terms of the so-called Deed of Surrender, signed in 1869 and confirmed by order in Council the following year.

---

carried on by the Company in Hudson's Bay (London, 1749); and *Short Narrative and Justification of the Proceedings of the Committee appointed by the Adventurers to prosecute the Discovery of the Passage to the Western Ocean of America* (London, 1749).

[55] For these petitions see *Journals of the House of Commons,* XXV, 810–45, 850; see also "The Book of Proceedings of the Bristol Merchant Venturers, 1745–1752," under dates of April 1 and 26, 1749, Merchant Venturers Hall, Bristol.

[56] For the Hudson's Bay Company petition see *Journals of the House of Commons,* XXV, 851–2.

The French rivals of the Company had also been active during this period. By the 1750's they had established, in the neighbourhood of Lake Winnipeg, Fort Dauphin on Lac des Prairies, Fort Bourbon near what is now Cedar Lake, and Fort Paskoyac at the juncture of the Carrot and the Saskatchewan, as well as two other posts, Fort Maurepas at the mouth of the Winnipeg and Fort La Reine on the Assiniboine, already deserted by this period.[57] Further, in 1748 Le Chevalier de la Vérendrye had erected his temporary post at the forks of the Saskatchewan which gave way in 1753 to Fort St. Louis and Fort à la Corne, and in 1751 still another temporary post (Fort La Jouquière) was established on a branch of the south fork of the Saskatchewan within sight of the Rocky Mountains.[58]

These French posts sought to monopolize the trade of the upper Churchill, of Lakes Cumberland and Winnipegosis, and of the Saskatchewan, Assiniboine, and Red rivers. However, they were far removed from Montreal. To reach them involved much laborious portaging and other difficulties. Goods given and received in the course of trade had to be adapted to the exigencies of this situation, for canoes could not be overloaded either in going or returning. As a result, only the lighter, less bulky trading goods could be conveyed to the posts, and only the lighter pelts could be accepted for transfer to Montreal. Therefore, even the Indians trading with the French — in order to secure such articles as guns, ammunition, kettles, iron tools, or even tobacco, and to trade their heavier furs and skins — were obliged to descend the Hayes, Nelson, or Churchill River and resort to the Hudson Bay posts.[59]

In short it may be said that much of the strength of the Hudson's Bay Company's position in 1750 lay in the reluctance of the British government to destroy a company operating lawfully and successfully under a royal charter in North America.[60] But perhaps

---

[57] The two last-named posts, it appears, were unoccupied in 1750 as the result of wars between the Sioux and the Assiniboines which, according to Pierre de la Vérendrye, brought about the ruin of La Reine and the burning of Maurepas. For a discussion of this see H. A. Innis: *op. cit.*, pp. 96–7.

[58] *Ibid.*, p. 97.

[59] *Ibid.*, pp. 98–9.

[60] In *An Account of the European Settlements in America,* attributed to Edmund and William Burke, it was declared (II, 285) that the Hudson's Bay Company acted under their charter "ever since [it was granted] with great benefit to the private men

more of its strength lay in the geographical circumstances of climate and terrain. Both these factors militated against the efforts of rivals in Great Britain to overthrow its charter to promote exploration and colonization of the barren and inhospitable lands about Hudson Bay. They also served as an effective barrier in protecting the lucrative trade of the Company posts — strategically located on the fringes of the Bay — from even the redoubtable wide-ranging French *coureurs*.

---

who compose the company, though comparatively little advantage to Great Britain. It is true, that their trade in beavers and other species of furs is not inconsiderable, and it is a trade in itself of the best kind; its object enters largely into our manufactures, and carries nothing but our manufactures from us to procure it; and thus it has the qualities of the most advantageous kinds of traffic. . . . It is said that the dividends of this company are prodigious; far exceeding what is gained in any of the other great trading bodies. . . ."

CHAPTER XI

Bankers and Sackmen.
The Province of Avalon

O F Newfoundland an eighteenth-century Englishman wrote:

> "The Island is of a triangular Figure, as big as *Ireland,* separate
> from *Canada* or New-*France,* on the Continent, to the *North,* and
> from New-*Scotland* to the *South* . . . It lies . . . in the Course Ships
> usually hold as they return from the *West-Indies;* and the Galleons
> and Flota's from New-*Spain* in a homeward bound Voyage, come
> within 500 Miles of it: 'Tis not above 600 Leagues or 1800 Miles
> distant from the Lands End of *England;* and the *Great Bank* is
> hardly halfway to *Virginia;* it has many commodious Bays along the
> Coast . . . .
> "Some Writers relate that the Fishermen of Biscay frequented the
> Banks of *Newfoundland* and fish'd there for Cod long before
> *Columbus* discovered the *New-World.*"[1]

For almost 250 years Englishmen had sailed to "the Banks" to
fish for cod, as had hardy Breton and Norman fishermen, Basques,
and Portuguese.[2] By 1750 the catching and curing of these fish had

---

[1] [John Oldmixon]: *The British Empire in America* . . . (2 vols., 2nd edn., London, 1741), I, 1–2.
[2] For the best study of early French and Portuguese activities on the Banks of Newfoundland see H. A. Innis: *The Cod Fisheries: The History of an International Economy* (New Haven, 1940), Chap. 2.

become one of the New World's great staple industries and was largely in the hands of the French and English. Even before Sir George Calvert's effort to settle at Ferryland in 1621 and Sir William Vaughan's at Trepassey in 1617, attempts at colonization had been made by Gilbert and his associates in 1583 and by the Newfoundland London and Bristol Company in 1611. However, the Island of Newfoundland, in spite of its important resources, did not attract permanent settlers for the first century after its discovery, although it is true that some small groups of fishermen wintered there.[3]

Nevertheless, the importance of the island was realized and it became a principal prize in the duelling between France and England in the seventeenth and eighteenth centuries. By the Treaty of Utrecht, France resigned all territorial claims to it, at the same time securing the right resort to its coast from Cape Bonavista, on the eastern shore, northward to the farthest point and then southward along the western shore to Cape Riche, which included the peninsula of Petit Nord. This concession, together with the continued French control of Isle Royale or Cape Breton, placed the St. Malo and Cape Breton fishermen in practical control of those parts of Newfoundland most favourable for exploitation of fisheries. In the words of Captain Griffith Williams, who was in the island in the middle of the century:

"This was the Fishery we had then [after the Treaty of Utrecht] cause to lament the Loss of; and, indeed, so we have to this Day; the Fish in those Parts being in greater Abundance, and the Fishery carried on at Half the Expence, the Weather being much better for curing, because the Fogs don't go any farther Northward than the great Bank of Newfoundland . . . ."[4]

---

[3] See *ibid.*, Chap. 4; see also R. G. Lounsbury: *The British Fishery at Newfoundland, 1634–1763* (New Haven, 1934, Chap. 1) for another illuminating account of early English interest in the cod fisheries. The other standard work on Newfoundland is D. W. Prowse's *A History of Newfoundland . . .* (London, 1892, 2nd edn., 1896); even more important than the Prowse book, because more scholarly, is J. D. Rogers's *Newfoundland* (Oxford, 1911), which constitutes Volume V of L. P. Lucas's: *A Historical Geography of the British Colonies* (7 vols., Oxford, 1888–1920).

[4] Griffith Williams: *An Account of the Island of Newfoundland, with the Nature of its Trade* (London, 1765), p. 13. Captain T. Cole, who made proposals to the government in 1761 for excluding the French from the fisheries, also emphasized the above points in declaring that the French were permitted to get their fish to the markets sooner than could the English and to carry it in better condition, "Be-

As a consequence, it was generally conceded that, in spite of the great activity of the English off the Banks and in the inlets of the island, the French had by far the best part of the cod trade. Other reasons can also be assigned for this superiority: French cod was more highly esteemed because it was better cured;[5] it reached the world markets before the English commodity because the Cape Breton fishermen could begin operations before the close of winter; and it sold at a low price. According to Captain Cole, writing in 1761, "The French . . . so far succeeded in that most valuable Branch of Trade, as to get the Preference in most of the *European* markets — which makes a difference to this nation of upward of £2,000,000 per annum." This was, he affirmed, the situation before the outbreak of the Great War for the Empire.[6]

In 1750 the Avalon Peninsula was the centre of the English activity. There was in its chief town, St. John's, according to Captain James Douglas, a population in 1746 of 263 English Protestants fit to bear arms and 311 Irish Catholics who were considered fit neither for this function nor for liberty of conscience.[7] St. John's was not only the port of chief resort for the merchantmen, known as "sackships," destined to load for Portugal, Spain, and Italy, but also for the vessels of the "Bankers," or "West Countrymen," fishermen from the West of England ports. The bankers, soon after their arrival each spring, dispersed along the shore of the island from Bonavista to Placentia bays — south and east of the regions where the French were privileged to dry their catch — to begin the season's operation.[8] Also on the peninsula, at Placentia, was stationed the most important body of troops detached to guard the island. In

---

cause the South Part of this Coast where our People fish, is always covered with Fogs, and Mizzling Rains, which keep the Fish so long in drying, that the Maggots breed in them, and render them of less Value at the European Markets" (*ibid.*, p. 27).

[5] "The Benefit of pure salt is apparent in the cod, as well as in the herring," declared a writer in 1749, adding: "those the Dutch cure are clear and white; those the English cure are brown and dirty. So it is in Newfoundland, where the French fish are much better coloured, and most agreeably tasted" (*Wealth of Great Britain in the Ocean* [London, 1749], p. 54).

[6] Captain Cole's "State of the Fisheries," in Griffith Williams: *op. cit.*, p. 28.

[7] See Douglas's answers to the Board of Trade's Queries, P.R.O., C.O. 194:12, p. 18. For the development of the above point see R. G. Lounsbury: *op. cit.*, pp. 300–4.

[8] Among the English ports most deeply interested in the cod fisheries in the middle of the century were Bideford, Bristol, Dartmouth, Exeter, Poole, Teignmouth, and Topsham. Falmouth, Fowey, Plymouth, Southampton, Truro, and Weymouth also took an important part in these fisheries.

addition, in the middle of the century there were small garrisons at Ferryland, Carbonier, and Trinity.[9]

Various estimates of the population living permanently on the island can be found. It appears that by the middle of the eighteenth century considerably more than 7,000 people were settled within the peninsula. Indeed, in 1753 it was affirmed in a petition to the Crown that, exclusive of those coming for the fisheries and then departing, there were, at the lowest estimate, 12,000 or 13,000, including men, women, and children;[10] while the numbers coming in for the fishing season were placed at 15,420, operating some 1,676 ships and shallops.[11]

By the early part of the century, it appears, the Boston merchants were playing a dominant role in the life of Newfoundland as the result of the importation of various commodities from New England for sale at stores in the fishing communities. These stores were accustomed, after the close of the fishing season and the departure of the ships in the fall, to sell rum and provisions at exorbitant prices and on credit. Many of the inhabitants ran into debt and were compelled to sacrifice the next season's catch.[12] The fish turned over to the New Englanders, if prime, was, as a rule, sold in turn to the English sack-ships for money or bills; if refuse fish, it was carried to the West Indies. This had long been the settled practice of those who came from North America to trade.[13]

---

[9] *Board of Trade Journal, 1749–1753*, p. 37.

[10] See "Case of the Right Honorable Frederick, Lord Baltimore, relating to the Province of Avalon in America . . ." (1754), Calvert Papers, No. 522, Maryland Historical Society. In 1765 the Board of Trade stated that, judging from the best accounts, the number of inhabitants was not less than 15,000, including men, women, and children, the greater part of whom were Roman Catholics. See its representation of April 29, 1765, *Papers Relating to Newfoundland* (London, 1793), p. 5. This document is also to be found in the series *In the Privy Council* (12 vols., London, 1929), IV, 1848–55. According to one writer, there were in 1771 more English than Irish — that is, 3,449 English and 3,348 Irish. See *Diary of Ezra Stiles* (ed. F. B. Dexter, 3 vols., New York, 1901), I, 354.

[11] See "Case of Lord Baltimore" (1754), Calvert Papers, No. 522, p. 3. The official figures for 1751 were 4,359 men who manned the fishing, sack, and trading ships, and 5,429 people in addition, all brought from Ireland. The number of ships resorting to Newfoundland in that year was put at 312 and the number of boats used for fishing at 1,507. See "The State of the Newfoundland Fishing," covering the years 1699 and 1792, *In the Privy Council*, IV, for tables opposite p. 2006.

[12] See "Report of George Larkin on Conditions in Newfoundland," 1701, *In the Privy Council*, IV, 1812.

[13] For example, see the testimony of Captain Norris to the Board of Trade, November 13, 1698, *ibid.*, IV, 1801–6.

From all accounts, most of the permanent dwellers on New-foundland were "by-boatmen," merchants with New England connections, tavern-keepers, men employed at the fish-stages by the Bankers during the season, those engaged in trapping beaver, otter, and other fur-bearing creatures along the streams and in the great swamps of the still little-known interior, together with those who were beginning to cultivate land near the seashore. Most of the habitations were humble. Cattle, sheep, and horses were few in number, and the hardy dwellers were obliged to depend largely upon water transportation, although a breed of powerful dogs was already commonly employed to haul sledges loaded with wood and other necessities.

From early in October to the middle of May little activity was in evidence on the island. Everything wore a deserted aspect — with the long lines of fish-staging and cook houses empty along the shores of the bays, the villages but partly inhabited, and many of the taverns closed. In truth, most of the inhabitants — at least those not occupied in trapping, in building boats, in getting materials from the forests for staging,[14] or in similar activities — all but hibernated between the departure of the sack-ships, the West Country-men, and the New Englanders in the fall and their return in the spring.

One may well imagine with what resignation the settlers waited during the months of gloom, fog, and snow and — as the winter field ice and icebergs melted — with what anticipations must they have looked for the first appearance of the ships from the home ports! For these welcome ships brought news from the outside world, rum, and countless other supplies, buyers of pelts, train oil, and other raw products that had been accumulated for sale, and also, perchance, friends who, to make their way to Newfoundland, had joined the fishing ships. They could do this since the ship masters were required each year to enlist numbers of green men, who only too frequently deserted the ships before the return voyage and thus swelled the ranks of the permanent inhabitants.

In contrast to the apathy of winter were the scenes of animation during the height of the fishing season: the movement of hundreds

---

[14] Griffith Williams: *op. cit.*, (1765), p. 10.

of shallops out of the bays in the early morning hours, propelled by oars and aided by lugsails; the feverish activity of thousands of men at the fish-stages on the beaches, especially in case of rain, when the great piles of fish had to be turned with backs uppermost to be kept from spoiling and then re-turned with the coming of the sun; the swarming of hard-drinking sailors, fishermen, traders, and trappers into the taverns after the labours of the day, with all the wild life associated at that, as at every, period with towns on the fringes of civilization.

By 1750 the Englishmen's methods of catching and curing the cod had become stabilized. The ships of the West Countrymen, instead of remaining on the Banks[15] until a cargo was secured, as had been the custom in the seventeenth century, were usually anchored in the bays; for the main activities were carried on in the "by-boats" or shallops, which generally did not venture more than two leagues from land.[16] There the hardy fishermen cast their lines, returning every evening to the shore to bring in the catch, which was then thrown upon a platform. The fish were immediately dressed by the "cut-throat" and handed to the "carver," who, with a great single-edged knife, split them and passed them to the "salter." But with this the process of curing had just begun. After some days in the salt, the fish were washed and laid out to dry on long but narrow fish-stages and flakes extending for some distance from shallow water back onto the land. They were then alternately piled and aired and piled again in ever larger heaps and sweated until at last they were ready for shipment. This process, covering some

---

[15] This had been an earlier practice of the Portuguese, the Basques, and the Bretons who engaged in the "wet" fishery. The English, who preferred to dry the fish, found the problem of caring for the catch on board ship too great. "Many have been the times," declared Captain Griffith Williams, "when the Masters of Vessels have left the Banks with a fine loading of Fish; and . . . upon opening their Hatches found their Cargo turned to Maggotts" (*ibid.*, p. 12). Yet certain West Countrymen did sail to the Banks for their fish in the eighteenth century and in 1739 they caught some 45,000 quintals of fish as against some 335,000 quintals produced on the eastern and southern coasts. For Captain Taverner's estimates of the inshore and Banks fisheries in 1740 see R. G. Lounsbury: *op. cit.*, pp. 311–12; see also H. A. Innis: *op. cit.*, pp. 150–2.

[16] Captain John Knight to George Brydges Rodney, from Placentia, August 7, 1749, Rodney Papers, P.R.O., G.D. 20:6.

weeks and demanding great watchfulness and experience to secure the best results,[17] was known as inshore fishing.

At the end of the season the cod thus caught and cured was carried by the sack-ships either to southern Europe or to the West Indies. The first-quality fish was disposed of in the seaports of Spain, Portugal, and Italy; the inferior grades were carried to the sugar islands. The ships coming from England to load for southern Europe were apt to bring commodities to the American continental colonies. After discharging their cargoes at various colonial ports they sailed to Newfoundland to load fish for the return trip across the Atlantic to the Iberian peninsula or to Mediterranean ports. The colonial sack-ships brought American continental and West Indian commodities to Newfoundland, which were exchanged usually for the inferior grades of fish, called "Jamaica" fish. This was thereupon carried to the West Indies and sold to the merchants and planters as slave provisions; with the proceeds of the sale, West Indian products, especially sugar and molasses, were bought to be carried home.

As for the value of the fisheries, no accurate statement can be made. Figures for the period under consideration show the most striking divergence. Surveyor General Robert Dinwiddie in the early 1740's estimated that Newfoundland produced annually 800,-000 quintals of cod. The value of this, with some 4,000 tons of oil, he calculated at £400,000.[18] Captain Griffith Williams estimated that the true value of the cod alone before the outbreak of the Great War for the Empire was not less than £1,032,000, with fish selling at an average price of 20 shillings per quintal or hundredweight — certainly a high figure.[19] In contrast to this estimate of over 1,000,-

---

[17] D. Fenning and J. Collyer: A New System of Geography (2 vols., London, 1764–5), II, 631.

[18] See Abercromby's "Examination," 1752, Shelburne Papers, 47:36. In his pamphlet A Letter from a Merchant of the City of London (London, 1757), the author optimistically writes of Newfoundland's fishery (p. 24) that "for the Advantages it produces both to the Trade and Navigation of these Kingdoms, [it] should be prefer'd to the Mines of Peru." He further asserts that "a Ship of 100 Tons, with the Charge only of Victuals and Fishing Tackle for Twenty Hands, will bring to Market in Portugal, Spain or Italy £3,000 worth of Fish, and frequently clear[s] £2,000 for the Proprietors, so that . . . 150 Ships only will clear £300,000. . . ."

[19] See his An Account of the Island of Newfoundland (1765), p. 6. Williams, who engaged in the fisheries in the 1750's, had the utmost contempt for the figures sent from time to time by the Newfoundland Governors on the state of this industry. He declared that the information was secured from merchants at each of the harbours

000 quintals, the official figures for the year 1749 were 506,406 quintals that sold for not 20 shillings per quintal but between 12 and 13 shillings.[20]

However, the cod fisheries do not represent the full value of Newfoundland's financial returns to the mother country.[21] Along the coast were taken great numbers of whales, seals, and porpoises which together yielded thousands of barrels of train oil annually; the forests sheltered the bear, deer, moose, foxes, and wolves sought by trappers; the streams and swamps yielded beaver and otter; lastly, for many years a flourishing salmon fishery had been carried on by merchants of Pool, Southampton, Weymouth, and Lyme in the fresh waters between Cape Bonavista and St. John's.[22] Frederick, Lord Baltimore, in 1754 estimated the total returns from the island, including profits from freight charges, at the conservative figure of £470,547.[23]

Since most of the fish yield was taken southward by the sack-ships, only a small quantity of cod was transported to England. Indeed, the direct commerce between the two islands was unimpressive in light of the total wealth abstracted by fishermen and trappers. For example, in 1752 Newfoundland sent to England raw materials valued at only £41,459.4.7, and of this total £29,666 covered the chief item, train oil; while the island imported from the mother country commodities amounting to but £46,995.2.11, the chief items of which were woollen goods.[24]

---

who were accustomed to fill out the forms at random. To test one report from Harbour Grace as to the total catch along Conception Bay, which has a shoreline of at least seventy miles, Williams visited every cove and creek where boats were kept. Upon the basis of this information he estimated that between 1745 and 1752 the annual catch for the entire island was 1,032,000 quintals. *Ibid.*, p. 5.

[20] See *In the Privy Council*, IV, for tables opposite p. 2006. The value of the English cod fishery was much lower than even the official figures, according to a Captain Smith who prepared his "Newfoundland's Establishment and Output" in 1741. This account set the annual catch at only 366,000 quintals, which, at ten shillings and sixpence per quintal, yielded only £192,465. See Chatham Manuscripts, Vol. 81, P.R.O.

[21] In a petition to the Crown in 1753 Lord Baltimore estimated the total value of the Newfoundland trade, including fish, furs, oil, and freight, at £470,547. See "The Case of Lord Baltimore" (1754), Calvert Papers, No. 522.

[22] See *Atlas Maritimus et Commercialis* (London, 1728), p. 325, and P.R.O., C.O. 5:200, p. 593.

[23] See "Case of Lord Baltimore" (1754), Calvert Papers, No. 522, p. 4.

[24] See "A Sketch of the Trade to and from England to Newfoundland," covering the years 1716–60, Shelburne Papers, Vol. 102. London enjoyed only a small per-

Beginning with the early part of the eighteenth century, if not before, the English dried cod had apparently lost favour in the markets, and the Governors were called upon to correct this situation whenever possible.[25] When George Brydges Rodney was commissioned Governor of Newfoundland in 1749,[26] the sixty-first article of his instructions stressed the vital importance of preventing the sack-ships — between whose commanders there was great rivalry to reach the markets first — from sailing until the fish on board had been properly cured. For by the previous sale of badly cured fish, it was stated, the consumption had been so lessened that there was fear lest the trade be quite lost to the nation.[27] Further, he was to see that the admirals of the harbours were strictly enjoined to take the greatest care that a sufficient quantity of good salt be used in curing the cod, "that the credit thereof may be again recovered and that it may be well received and esteemed in the several places to which it is carried for sale."[28]

Another object of solicitude continually stressed by the government and people of England was that no activity should develop on Newfoundland or in North America which would deprive either the English merchants of a profitable, if limited, market for woollens and similar commodities or the English West Coast fishermen of their ancient interest in the cod fisheries. This, it was feared, would lead to a decline in British manufacturing and in shipping. For the Banks in the eighteenth century, as in the seventeenth, were regarded as a great school for seamanship. Each Governor was in-

centage of this direct commerce, receiving in 1751 commodities valued at £3,589.9.4 and shipping directly commodities valued at £2,603.7.2. *Ibid.*

[25] The Board of Trade in its representation of 1718 referred to reports from British consuls and merchants residing in Spain, Portugal, and Italy that the fish brought to these markets from Newfoundland "for some years past, has been for the most Part so ill cured, that the consumption thereof is greatly abated, and that the Trade is in Danger of being thereby lost." See "Copy of a Representation of the Lords Commissioners for Trade and Plantations to His Majesty relating to the Newfoundland Trade and Fishery," December 19, 1718, *Papers Relating to Newfoundland* (1793), p. 2. Commodore Fitzroy Henry Lee in his report for 1736 stressed this point. See P.R.O., C.O. 194:10, p. 7; see also R. G. Lounsbury: *op. cit.,* p. 318.

[26] For Rodney's commission of May 11, 1749, see C.O. 5:200, pp. 560–4.

[27] The above injunction was also embodied in earlier instructions. It certainly was pertinent to the situation in the middle of the century.

[28] For Rodney's instructions of May 2, 1749, see P.R.O., C.O. 5:200, pp. 568–603, which are identical with those given to his predecessor, C.O. 5:200, pp. 473–502 (except for Articles 63–9, which were new and are to be found in C.O. 195:8, pp. 188–95).

structed to see that, both in the fisheries and on the ships coming to the island, every fifth man was a fresh or green man, as was laid down in the regulations passed under King William.[29] The national sentiment behind these regulations is well expressed by a writer in the middle of the eighteenth century who declared, with reference to the wealth derived from the fisheries, that "all this sum is actually got by our labour, and therefore is of much more service to the Nation by breeding up useful seamen than if so much was to be dug out of the mine, with a thousandths part of the labour."[30]

The desire to foster British seamanship and the home mercantile marine had led to efforts to discourage permanent settlement on the island and to unsuccessful attempts to break up such settlements as began to appear.[31]

Toward the latter part of the seventeenth century it was feared with good reason that, just as the New England fisheries had been earlier engrossed by the people living in the plantations, so would the Newfoundland fisheries, if due care were not taken.[32] Therefore,

---

[29] See "An Act to Encourage the Trade to Newfoundland," 10 and 11 Wm. III, c. 25, sec. 10. This requirement was previously embodied in the so-called New Charter issued January 27, 1675/6. The provisions of this patent are summarized in the representation of the Board of Trade of December 19, 1718, *Papers Relating to Newfoundland* (1793), pp. 8–9; see also *Acts of the Privy Council, Col. Ser., 1613–1680*, pp. 558–63, for the order in Council of 1671, providing for the employment of new or green men.

[30] *Traveller's Magazine*, March 1749.

[31] For example, in 1671 the Lords of the Council of Plantations, in answer to a petition from the fishing towns of western England, issued a series of rules among which was one forbidding settlement within six miles of the seashore; another provided that those already settled on the island should be encouraged to transport themselves to the English West Indies. See *Acts of the Privy Council, Col. Ser., 1613–1680*, pp. 558–65; see also John Reeves: *History of the Government of the Island of Newfoundland . . .* (London, 1793), pp. 12–19, and especially R. G. Lounsbury: *op. cit.*, Chaps. 3 and 4; H. A. Innis: *op. cit.*, Chap. 5; G. L. Beer: *The Old Colonial System, 1660–1754* (2 vols., New York, 1912), II, Part I, Chap. 10; and G. S. Graham's chapter in *Newfoundland: Economic, Diplomatic, and Strategic Studies* (ed. R. A. MacKay, Toronto, 1946), pp. 257–8.

[32] According to the Board of Trade, in 1677 there were 109 fishing ships, with 4,475 seamen and 892 fishing boats belonging to these ships. In that same year it was estimated that 152 "planters" were settled on the island who employed 1,355 servants and 337 boats. In 1682 the number of fishing ships coming from England dropped to 32, the number of seamen to 1,012, and the number of fishing boats to 183, while the inhabitants operated 299 ships and 304 fishing boats. However, as the result of the Act of 1699, "An Act to encourage the Trade to Newfoundland" (10 and 11 Wm. III, c. 25), the fishermen from the mother country were again attracted to the Banks. By 1716 they employed 86 fishing ships, 319 fishing-ship boats, and 184 by-boats, although the settled inhabitants had 408 boats. See the representation of the Board of December 19, 1718, *Papers Relating to Newfoundland* (1793), pp. 9–16.

it was provided by law that neither the permanent inhabitants nor any others should take possession of, or in any way injure, the beaches, stages, cook-rooms, flakes, and other fishery conveniences left behind when the ships returned home in the fall. It was also laid down that the admirals of the harbours should be limited to shipmasters from the mother country arriving earliest each spring in their fishing ships. To them fell the authority of allocating the fishery conveniences for those coming from Great Britain to fish.[33] Also, to prevent the New England ships that came to these waters from bringing in commodities prohibited by the Navigation Act of the fifteenth year of the reign of Charles II (15 Chas. II, c. 7) and from carrying away seamen, mechanics, and workmen, thus defeating one of the prime purposes of the act, each succeeding Governor was expected to watch these ships.[34] This enactment had strictly limited the number of articles that could be transported to the colonies and plantations without being laden at one of the home ports. Indeed, so suspicious was the British government of the activities of the New England shipmasters that the Newfoundland Governors were instructed to oblige all American vessels to leave Newfoundland before the Governors themselves sailed for Europe in the fall of the year.[35]

In light of the vast economic importance of Newfoundland to Great Britain it is perhaps surprising that it had but a rudimentary government in the middle of the eighteenth century.[36] After almost a century of agitation, Captain Henry Osborn had been sent to the Island in 1729 as the first Governor with a formal Crown commis-

---

[33] 10 and 11 Wm. III, c. 25. The so-called Western Charter of February 10, 1633/4, provided "That according to the auncient Custome, every Shipp, or fisher, that first entereth a harbour . . . be Admirall of the said Harbour. . . ." See *Acts of the Privy Council, Col. Ser., 1613–1680*, pp. 193–7. The provisions of this charter, as well as those of the charter of 1675/6, are given in the representations of the Board of Trade of December 19, 1718, *Papers Relating to Newfoundland* (1793), pp. 3–4, 8–9.

[34] The Board of Trade asserted in its representation of December 19, 1718, that in 1716 — according to the testimony of Captain Passenger, commander in chief of the convoy — 1,300 men were carried off by New England vessels. *Ibid.*, p. 18.

[35] For an interesting discussion of the importance of the New England trade to Newfoundland see Ralph G. Lounsbury's "Yankee Trade at Newfoundland," *The New England Quarterly*, III, 607–26.

[36] For the government of Newfoundland in 1730 see Nova Scotia State Papers, Correspondence, Vol. 19, P.R.O.

sion.[37] Under his commission he was authorized to appoint justices of the peace and other officers for the better order of the island. His commission really marks the dividing line between the period when Newfoundland was regarded simply as a British possession, and the recognition of the fact that it was virtually a colony — an event that the fishing towns of England had long sought to prevent.[38]

While Osborn was strictly bound by the Act of 10 and 11 William III not to obstruct the admirals of the harbours or the captains of ships of war,[39] the control of the garrison at Placentia, which had previously been under the Governor of Nova Scotia, was by this commission transferred to him and his successors. In carrying out his instructions, he divided the island into districts, in each of which he appointed justices of the peace and constables from among the inhabitants of the best character. Unhappily, a conflict immediately developed between these new officers, representing the settled inhabitants and supported by the Governor, on the one hand, and the admirals of the harbours, representing the commanders and crews of the English fishing ships, on the other. This conflict was still active in the middle of the eighteenth century and indicates the difficulties faced in regulating the affairs of the island.

As a rule, the Governor held office for only one year and but for the period of the annual voyage. With this office after 1731 went also that of commodore of the convoy for the sack-ships.[40] For example, we have the appointment of Admiral Charles Watson in 1748 to succeed Captain Richard Edwards; thereupon Rodney in 1749 displaced Watson, and Francis William Drake in 1750 displaced Rodney. Drake, however, was recommissioned the following year with much wider powers.[41]

---

[37] For Osborn's commission as Governor, submitted May 14, 1729, see C.O. 195:7, pp. 183–92; for his instructions see C.O. 5:194, pp. 614–48, and 195, pp. 1–11.

[38] As Professor Andrews has made clear, Newfoundland, despite the existence of permanent settlers in the seventeenth century, was not regarded as an English colony, nor indeed was it so regarded even at the time of the Treaty of Utrecht in 1713. See C. M. Andrews: *The Colonial Period of American History* (4 vols., New Haven, 1934–8), IV, 64 and 345.

[39] See John Reeves: *op. cit.*, pp. 71–2.

[40] During the War of the Austrian Succession between 1746 and 1748 no Governor was sent to the island.

[41] For Rodney's commission, dated May 11, 1749, see P.R.O., C.O. 5:200, pp. 560–4; for Drake's commissions, dated January 22, 1750, and May 15, 1751, see *ibid.*, 5:200, pp. 605–8 and 669–75.

An examination of Rodney's instructions of May 2, 1749, which follow closely instructions issued to Watson, will indicate that much was expected of the Newfoundland Governor.[42] Those guilty of capital offences were to be sent to England with witnesses and other sufficient proof of their crimes;[43] the Placentia garrison was not to be permitted to concern itself with the fishery; no engrossment of commodities was to be allowed to the prejudice of the island's chief activity; and the provisions of the navigation acts and the act of the reign of William III for the encouragement of the fisheries were to be strictly enforced. Further, all inhabitants but Papists were to be guaranteed freedom of conscience,[44] although laws governing blasphemy and immorality were to be vigorously enforced by the justices of the peace. Again, steps were to be taken to prevent not only the throwing of ballast into the harbours and the destruction of stages, cook-rooms, and flakes used in the fisheries, but also the appropriation by the harbour admirals of any more of the beaches and flakes than were necessary for their own use. Further, those inhabitants of the island who had engrossed any of these conveniences since the year 1685 to the prejudice of the fishing ships were to be compelled to relinquish them; while masters of vessels, byboat keepers, and inhabitants were to be obliged to employ such numbers of green or new men as the law required.

Among other injunctions, the Governor was directed to protect the woods from unnecessary destruction, and to restrict the use of lumber to the repair of houses, ships, and stages. He was also to make investigations and to report whether or not manufactures from the plantations or from foreign countries were being brought into the Island; whether the inhabitants had enclosed land and erected

---

[42] For Rodney's instructions see C.O. 5:200, pp. 568–603; see also R. G. Lounsbury (British Fishery at Newfoundland, p. 296, note 34) for a discussion of the slight differences between the Watson instructions and those given to Rodney. The first sixty articles are identical. Articles 63 to 69 are changed.

[43] The "Western Charter" of 1633/4 provided that any one who killed another on the island should be brought to England so that the Earl Marshal might take cognizance of the case. This order of the Privy Council also regulated the disposition of ballast, protected the conveniences used in fishing and the trees growing on the island, forbad the selling of intoxicating beverages and tobacco, and gave authority over a harbour to the first shipmaster arriving in the spring. Papers Relating to Newfoundland (1793), pp. 3–4.

[44] For the persecution of Roman Catholics in Newfoundland in the middle of the eighteenth century see M. F. Howley: Ecclesiastical History of Newfoundland (Boston, 1888), Chap. 12.

buildings close to the shores; whether the flakes for drying the fish extended properly from the beach up onto the land, rather than along the shore to become a hindrance to building other facilities; and whether the old laudable custom was followed of allowing ships' crews a share of the total catch for the season rather than wages. Further, he was to determine the strength of the Irish Catholics in Newfoundland,[45] the methods employed by the New England merchants in carrying trade there, and the manner of conducting the taverns, so as to judge whether or not poor seamen were tempted or permitted to go so deeply into debt as to be forced to remain behind as servants or even to betake themselves to New England. In this connection he was to study the practices of the New England traders to discover if they were continuing to entice handicraftsmen, seamen, and fishermen away from the island, and was even to compel them, before returning home, to enter into obligations not to engage in this practice. Finally, he was to watch over the movements of the French, who, under the thirteenth and fourteenth clauses of the Treaty of Utrecht, were privileged, as has been made clear, to land on prescribed areas of the island to erect temporary huts for the fishing season and stages for the drying of fish, but not for the purposes of settlement or for exploiting the island's resources.

In spite of the multiplicity of duties assigned to the Governor, it appears that he performed very few of them and that, with all his powers, he was ineffective.[46] This is not surprising, since he was generally absent from his post for nine or ten months of the year. Moreover, in carrying out most of his instructions he was obliged to rely upon subordinate officials, and there was constant friction between the justices of the peace and the harbour admirals, representing respectively the traditionally hostile interests of inhabitants and Bankers.

Although the justices of the peace, appointed by the Governor from among the permanent residents, were expected to be "Men of

---

[45] In addition to the instructions given to the earlier governors, Governor Charles Watson in 1748 was directed to give an account of Irish Roman Catholics in the towns of Newfoundland. *Acts of the Privy Council, Col. Ser., 1745–1766,* p. 777.

[46] For example, the commanding officers at Placentia asserted in letters to the Duke of Bedford that many inconveniences had arisen "from his Majesty's ships not having visited that harbour for several years." These letters were placed before the Board of Trade at its meeting of April 14, 1748. See Board of Trade *Journal, 1741–1749,* p. 279.

Property and good Character," as a rule they were weak in the exercise of their office, and their authority was frequently ignored even by their fellow inhabitants. Some were accused in 1749 of great irregularities and oppressions. The same thing may be said of the harbour admirals, most of whom appear to have grossly neglected their official duties, so absorbed were they in their fishing activities.

The problem of maintaining order in Newfoundland was made especially difficult by the presence of many unruly characters who had been attracted to the fisheries. It appears from a report made by Rodney to the Admiralty in 1749 that by far the greater part of the inhabitants of Newfoundland were Irish Catholics who were hostile to the King's authority. Among more than three hundred of them living in St. John's, apparently only six would take the oath of allegiance.[47] According to the Governor, the great purpose of the Newfoundland fisheries was being defeated because of the "Notorious Practices of the Fishing Ships . . . of bringing nothing but Irish Papists. . . . I think it my duty," he declared, "to acquaint your lordships that Numbers of the Merchants of this place agree with me, that the Trade of Newfoundland, as it is at present carried on, is far from being a Nursery for British seamen. The great Numbers of Papists Employed in it being Notoriously disaffected to his Majesty and the present happy Establishment."[48]

There can be but little doubt as to the turbulent nature of the population. The commanding officers at Placentia in writing home stressed the failure of justice there.[49] A surviving description of conditions at this period is probably not far from the truth. It shows how little effective exertion of the governmental authority there was.

"That as few of the Fishing Admirals from the nature of their Employ'm[ts] can Act during their Short Occasional Residence in Newfoundland in the Adm'[tion] of Justice . . . the Country is for the Space of 9 or 10 months in the Year Destitute of any form of Governm[t.] the Military Authority & that of a few Justices of Peace only Excepted & which is Exercised in so Imperfect & Unsatisfactory

[47] Rodney to John Cleveland, September 1749, Rodney Papers, P.R.O., G.D. 20:6.
[48] *Ibid.*
[49] Board of Trade *Journal, 1741–1749*, p. 279.

a manner as to Answer to no wholesome End or purpose & during this long Interval of Anarchy & Confusion the common Method of Recovering Debts & Adjusting many other Disputes is by the Strongest hand[,] the Creditors Using no other Ceremony with their Supposed D$^{rs.}$ than by Calling a Suff$^{t.}$ Number of People to their Assistance & with open force Carrying off from the D$^{rs.}$ Plan$^{tn.}$ a Suff$^{t.}$ Quantity of Fish to pay the pretended Debt[;] nor is it less frequent for the Admiralty Judge[,] though without the least Authority being Invested only with his Admiralty Common., to Issue his Warr$^{ts..}$ to Attach the Persons of his Matys. Subjects on Land upon a bare Surmise or Complaint without any Oath made to the Pretended Debt & even to Seize their Goods & Effects in the first Instance & afterwards to Compell the Paym^{t} of such pretended Debts & even Impose & levy such Fines upon his Ma'tys. Subjects as he thinks proper."[50]

One thing that hindered the maintenance of law and order on the island was the requirement that those accused of serious offences be sent to England for trial. This presented so many inconveniences and was so repugnant to the inhabitants that the Governors were reluctant to carry out the instruction. The year following his appointment, Rodney represented to the Duke of Bedford, Secretary of State for the Southern Department, the difficulties confronting him because of his lack of authority to appoint persons competent to take cognizance of capital crimes.[51] The question of increasing the powers of the Governor to this extent was submitted to both the Attorney General and the Solicitor General, with the result that Francis Drake in 1751 was empowered in his commission to appoint commissioners of oyer and terminer for the trial of capital offences on the spot, treason excepted, with the proviso that no one should be executed until the pleasure of His Majesty were known.[52] The following year this proviso was omitted from the new commission he received. It was therefore at last possible for the judges to order

---

[50] For this report see the "Case of Lord Baltimore" (1754), Calvert Papers, No. 522, p. 4.

[51] Board of Trade *Journal, 1749–1753*, p. 48; see also C.O. 195:8, pp. 179–81, and *Acts of the Privy Council, Col. Ser., 1745–1766*, p. 55.

[52] For the new powers embodied in Drake's commission of 1751 see C.O. 5:200, pp. 669–75. For Drake's instructions on this point for the year 1751 see the order in Council of June 4, 1751, C.O. 5:21, and *Acts of the Privy Council, Col. Ser., 1745–1766*, pp. 117–19, 777–8.

the execution of criminals, but with the important limitation that no officer of a ship of war or of any British trading ship should be deprived of life and limb by any sentence of such court, but, upon conviction, should be reprieved until the pleasure of the King were known.[53]

Slight and salutary as was the provision made to prevent anarchy, it appears that there were those who became alarmed at the tendency to erect a stable government for the inhabitants of Newfoundland — something that the cod-fishing ports of England had consistently opposed for a century and a half. For example, a memorial drawn up by the merchants of Dartmouth trading to Newfoundland and presented to the Board of Trade in 1752 expressed the hope that the form of government already established would subsist without any alterations.[54] Although from this period one may date the beginnings of a somewhat more effective political control of the island, the amenities of civilized life appeared but slowly. The Board of Trade, in a representation to His Majesty of April 29, 1765, stressed the fact that the population, then consisting of about 15,000 souls, mostly Roman Catholic Irish, were still living in the most savage state, giving themselves over to every species of debauchery, violence, and wickedness.[55]

Despite the turbulence of its coast-dwelling population and its rather forbidding climate, Newfoundland remained an extraordinarily valuable British possession in the middle of the eighteenth century. Therefore, it is not surprising that the island should have attracted the attention of the heir to the Baltimore family interests.

[53] Acts of the Privy Council, Col. Ser., 1745–1766, p. 778.

[54] Board of Trade Journal, 1749–1753, p. 374.

[55] For this representation see Papers Relating to Newfoundland (1793), p. 5. Captain Griffith Williams declared that after the withdrawal of the troops following the Peace of Aix-la-Chapelle, the traders and inhabitants were left to shift for themselves, without troops to support the magistrates in the execution of justice. "At this time great Numbers of Irish Roman Catholics were in the Island as servants; but no sooner had the Troops been sent away, than they became the most outrageous Set of People that ever lived; Robberies were committed almost every Day in one Place or other, the Magistrates insulted in the Execution of their Office, and the Chief Justice murdered; many hundred of West of England People were afraid of going over, many of the Newfoundland men left the Island, and the Roman Catholics transported themselves by Hundreds from Ireland: so that at the Time the French took the country [1762], the Irish were above six times the number of the West Country and Newfoundlers. In short, they were in Possession of above three-quarters of the fish rooms and Harbours of the Island, who consequently received the French with open Arms" (Account of the Island of Newfoundland [1765], pp. 9–10).

Among these interests were the claims to the Peninsula of Avalon secured in 1623 by royal letters patent to Sir George Calvert, later the first Lord Baltimore. In the early 1750's, when Frederick, the sixth and the last Lord Baltimore, had attained his majority, he made a serious attempt to gain recognition of the so-called family rights. This episode is important to an understanding of the effects of the earlier proprietorial Crown grants upon the functioning of the imperial system in the 1750's when it was faced by growing opposition to proprietorial claims.

In the year 1753 Baltimore presented an ably drawn petition to the Crown[56] asserting that his ancestor, Sir George Calvert, principal Secretary of State to James I, having at his own great expense purchased a large tract of barren, uncultivated land in Newfoundland and having made great preparations for settling an English colony there, was granted by royal letters patent, dated April 7, 1623, the Province of Avalon.[57] This patent confirmed to him and his heirs those lands, from fifty to sixty miles in depth, lying south of a line extending westward from Petit Harbour to the Bay of Placentia, together with all the islands within ten leagues of the eastern shore, to be held *in capite* by knight's service. The sole obligation of Calvert and his heirs in return was to render a white horse as often as the King or his heirs should come into the said province, together with a fifth part of all gold and silver ore found there. According to this instrument, they were to have power, with the consent of the majority of the freeholders of Avalon, not only to make laws that would be binding upon all persons within the limits of the province, whether resident there or sailing to or from it, but also to enforce the laws by fine, imprisonment, or any other punishment, even to life and limb. They were also empowered to appoint ministers, officers, judges, justices, and other magistrates. They might, in emergencies, make ordinances for the regulation of the people and establish ports for the loading and unloading of ships, confer-

---

[56] For reference to the Committee on July 19, 1753, of the petition of Frederick, Lord Baltimore, see *Acts of the Privy Council, Col. Ser., 1745–1766*, p. 223.

[57] The patent to Calvert is among the Sloane Mss., No. 170, in the British Museum; for a printed copy of it see J. T. Scharf: *History of Maryland* (2 vols., Baltimore, 1879), I, 34–40. For the background of the Calvert grant see A. P. Newton: "Newfoundland to 1783," which constitutes Chap. 5 of *The Cambridge History of the British Empire*, Vol. VI, *Canada and Newfoundland*, pp. 119–27, and R. G. Lounsbury: *British Fishery at Newfoundland*, pp. 37–47.

ring such rights and privileges as they should think proper, provided that they reserved to all English subjects the liberty of fishing in the sea and in the ports and creeks of the province and of salting and drying the fish on the shore as had been customary. Finally, they might enjoy all subsidies, customs, and impositions payable for the lading and unlading of goods in Avalon.

Soon after receipt of the charter the Baltimore family took steps to plant a settlement on the peninsula. Sir George first of all provided for the construction of a house and a fort at a place that he called Ferryland. Subsequently, resigning his post with the King, and now created Baron Baltimore of Baltimore in Ireland, he departed in 1627 to inspect his possession, and after returning the year following, again left for the island, this time with his family. During the French war he assisted in its defence[58] and, upon his final departure, committed Avalon to the care of a deputy, Captain William Hill. After his death in 1632, his heir, Cecilius, Lord Baltimore, in a somewhat vague fashion continued to hold possession of the settlement, with Hill still acting as Governor until 1638. In 1651 it appears that Cecilius sent another deputy to manage his interest, who lived for some years in the lord proprietary's house and who was succeeded by John Littlebury and Walter Sikes, acting jointly.[59] This precaution for maintaining title did not, however, prevent the Marquess of Hamilton and others, under cover of a grant from the Crown apparently first made in 1628 and confirmed in 1637,[60] from dispossessing Cecilius of his mansion house at Ferryland and other rights, and from holding Avalon by force during the period from the Great Rebellion until the Restoration.[61] In 1660, upon petition, King Charles referred the dispute to the Lord Chief Baron of the Excheq-

---

[58] *Ibid.*, p. 48.

[59] "Case of Lord Baltimore" (1754), Calvert Papers, No. 522, pp. 1–2.

[60] For the grant of 1628 see John Reeves: *History of . . . Newfoundland* (1793), p. 7. The patent of 1637 granted proprietary rights over Newfoundland. For the background of the grant to the Marquess of Hamilton, the Earl of Pembroke, the Earl of Holland, and Sir David Kirke see *Acts of the Privy Council, Col. Ser., 1613–1680*, pp. 214–20.

[61] During the Commonwealth Baltimore attempted to recover his possession, but without success. See L. D. Scisco; "Notes and Documents: Calvert's Proceedings against Kirke," *Canadian Historical Review*, VIII, 132–6. At the time that the patent to all of Newfoundland was being pressed by Hamilton and his associates, the King had agreed never to issue a *quo warranto* against the Baltimore grant of Avalon. See R. G. Lounsbury: *British Fishery at Newfoundland*, p. 79.

uer, Sir Orlando Bridgeman, and others. These commissioners, after some deliberation, certified that they conceived the patent given to Sir George Calvert to be still in force and therefore not voided by any subsequent grant. As a result, on the twentieth of March the King ordered that the province be reconfirmed to Baltimore; he also enjoined Sir Lewis Kirke, who had a military force on the island, and all others, not to interfere with Cecilius's possession of it. Thereupon, in 1661 Lord Baltimore appointed Robert Swanley as his lieutenant for the province (which was approved by His Majesty's royal proclamation), but soon afterwards sent out Captain Pease to take over Avalon, with Captain John Raynor as Deputy Governor.[62] Although Baltimore's representatives apparently made little headway in establishing control, it seems that in 1668 he commissioned as his deputy William Hutton; in 1674 Swanley was reappointed for a second term, after which there is no evidence that other commissions were given. The death of Cecilius in 1676 ended the active interest of the Baltimore family in Avalon until the middle of the eighteenth century.

In 1699, Parliament at last intervened in the affairs of the island with the "Act to Encourage the Trade to Newfoundland,"[63] granting free trade and fishing, with the right of curing fish on shore and of cutting wood for building stages, to all who went to the island. This statute took no notice of the Baltimore grant, nor was the family consulted when it was passed. Meanwhile, Cecilius, Lord Baltimore, had been succeeded by his son, Charles; the latter survived until 1715 and was followed by Benedict, who died in the same year, leaving his son Charles as heir. Upon his death in 1751, Avalon legally descended to Frederick; so, at least, affirmed the petition of 1753.[64]

To make clear why the Baltimore family had not continuously prosecuted their claims, Frederick's petition stressed the point that, as Catholics, they had come under suspicion during the Revolution. The government of the Province of Maryland, which, with full proprietorial rights, had been patented to Cecilius about ten years after

---

[62] See "Case of Lord Baltimore" (1754), Calvert Papers, No. 522, p. 2; see also R. G. Lounsbury: British Fishery at Newfoundland, pp. 104–7.

[63] 10 and 11 William III, c. 25.

[64] In the annotated copy of the petition among the Calvert Papers its date is given as 1753.

the grant of the Province of Avalon to the family, had been taken into the hands of the Crown. There it had remained till 1720, when Charles, who had been educated in the persuasion of the Church of England and had attained the age of twenty-one, was allowed to resume the proprietorship. The family, it was claimed, suffered much distress by the temporary loss of its powers in Maryland, especially since the profits received from that province during the period that it remained in the hands of the Crown were inconsiderable. Therefore, it had been impossible — at least, so it was alleged — to prosecute the further settlement of Avalon. Moreover, in the course of the War of the Spanish Succession, the whole island came under the subjection of France and was retained until the Peace of Utrecht.

Frederick now sought permission of the Crown "to settle an established and regulated form of government" for Avalon with its numerous population. Pursuant to the several powers allotted to and the authority vested in his ancestor by the patent of 1623, he offered in his petition to appoint as the permanent resident Governor, John Bradstreet, Esq., described as a gentleman of great ability who was well acquainted with the circumstances of the province, having been for several years past entrusted by His Majesty with the administration of its affairs.[65] He also made clear that in suing for his rights he did so without any intention of overturning or infringing upon the regulations already made by the Act of King William.[66]

This petition was referred by His Majesty in Council to the Lords of the Committee of the Council for Plantation Affairs, who sent it to the Board of Trade, by whom in turn it was referred, as a matter of "great importance," to the Attorney General and the Solicitor General on November 20, 1753.[67] It involved, of course, practically the entire portion of Newfoundland which had been settled and de-

---

[65] In the petition the name is spelled Broadstreet. In 1750 Bradstreet was acting as Lieutenant Governor of St. John's, Newfoundland, where he was commanding the local garrison and remained until the following year. Stanley Pargellis in his life of Bradstreet in the *Dictionary of American Biography* has indicated that it was he who inspired Baltimore to attempt to re-establish the family claim to Avalon. Bradstreet's military services in connection with the Great War for the Empire are dealt with in Volumes VI and VII of this series.

[66] "Case of Lord Baltimore," (1754), Calvert Papers, No. 522, p. 7.

[67] Board of Trade *Journal, 1749–1753*, p. 434, *Journal, 1754–1758*, pp. 37–8, 41; D. Ryder and W. Murray to the Board of Trade, April 5, 1754, Calvert Papers, Maryland Historical Society.

veloped to any degree and included most of the English fishing villages.

While the petition was being considered by these two eminent counsellors, an elaborate series of objections and answers was prepared by Baltimore's legal adviser, which, among other points, urged that by no act either of the courts by writ of *scire facias* or that of *quo warranto*, or of the legislature, had the validity of the patent ever been called into question. As to the statute of the year 1699 for encouraging the fisheries, neither the grant nor the Proprietor's rights, it was true, were once mentioned; but the object of the law, it was contended, had to do with the entire island, while the Province of Avalon was but a district, so that the act would still be satisfied while allowing the heir to the patent the enjoyment of his rights. This, it was argued, was possible, since under the law in question no new constitution or civil government was prescribed for the province — as the statute provided only temporary regulations for the fisheries, which had, indeed, been expressly reserved to all English subjects in the patent of 1623. It was further urged that the Crown up to the present had never assumed the exercise of any of the regalities or powers given to the Baltimore family by the charter other than the limited privileges prescribed by the act with reference to the fisheries, which even in 1699 were ancient usages.

To the objections that no traces of the Baltimore family had been found in Newfoundland for sixty or seventy years and that every grant of land in America carried an implied condition of cultivation and improvement within a reasonable time and that a patentee's neglect to pursue and to accomplish these ends had always been considered as a desertion and forfeiture of his patent, it was urged that this was a grant of seigniory, an *imperium in imperio,* a type of grant quite distinct from a mere grant of the soil and a kind that had never been set aside for a non-exercise of the powers of government. Therefore, should the Crown resume tenure of the soil, it was contended that the dominion must still remain in the patentee. And as to the rights over the soil, it was believed that no instance could be found of a grant being set aside for non-cultivation where the original grantee had cultivated and improved, which, in the case of Avalon, had been done. For, they claimed, the first two of the patentees had gone over in person with their families, had built houses and cultivated the country, and for over fifty years had continued in possession of these improvements through legally appointed agents. In light of all this, the Baltimore interests argued, should not the religious disabilities and low estate of the family from the Revolution to the late Lord's restoration to Maryland about 1720 be received in extenuation of a supposed neglect in prosecuting this charter? Further, was it not a matter of moment that the Crown had established this grant to be good in an issue with a subsequent grantee? Should, therefore, the officers of the state be now admitted to question the royal determination? For, if it were once good, pray when had it first become vitiated? Surely not at the time when the act during the reign of King William was passed, for the family had not long left the country. It was true that, were the patentee to appoint a Governor, he must receive the royal approbation. Suppose, however, that he himself were to go over in person to exercise the power of his grant on the spot as his ancestors had done, was there any restraint upon him? Who then, it was asked, could restrain him from immediately erecting courts of judicature, granting lands, and so forth, and upon what foundation and by what means? Such was the case of the Calverts.

These objections and answers were submitted to the distinguished jurist Sir Robert Henley, soon to be appointed Attorney General in place of Ryder. Henley on March 25, 1754, submitted his opinion, which offered cold comfort to Baltimore. He declared "that it will be very difficult for my Ld Baltimore to maintain the Effect of this Grant, which upon all the Circumstances of the Case appears to me to be obtained on an untrue Suggestion & is therefore void as against the Crown. It appears by the Recital of the Grant," he went on to state, "that Sir George suggested that he was about to transport a Colony thither, to which End most of the Provisions & authorities of the Letters patent are adapted, & I take Such sort of a Suggestion in [the] L$^{d's}$ patent amounts to a Condition, which not being performed the L$^{d's}$ patent became void, & tho the Grant was confirmed in 1660 (if the Act stated would amount to a Confirmation) yet the End & Condition of the Grant, not having been . . . complied with I think that Confirmation would have no Effect."[68]

---

[68] "Case of Lord Baltimore," pp. 8–9. Henley's opinion is inscribed in his own hand on the document.

In spite of discouragement, Baltimore with counsel appeared in support of the petition before the Solicitor General and the Attorney General, who, on April 5, framed their opinion as to the merits of the case. Their position, following Henley's line of argument, was that, in spite of the determination of the year 1660, there was no evidence of any actual possession of the province claimed or of the exercise of any powers of government there by the Baltimore family, but on the contrary it seemed probable that at least from the year 1638 they had been out of possession and that from the year 1669 there had been many proceedings which appeared inconsistent with the right now set up. Therefore, they were of opinion that it was inadvisable for His Majesty to comply with the said petition.[69]

The decision of the Crown against the Baltimore petitions need not cause great surprise. Yet, to the student of today there seems to be something irreconcilable between the utter ignoring of these claims and the recognition in the eighteenth century of the proprietorial rights of Sir Robert Heath. Heath's patent, dating from the year 1629, was for the region south of Virginia, lying between the thirty-first and thirty-sixth parallels of north latitude. Although his "plans fell stillborn among colonial ventures"[70] and the same region was granted in 1663 to the Carolina Proprietors, nevertheless Daniel Coxe, who had come into possession of the Heath claims, was accorded 100,000 acres of land in provincial New York as indemnification and full satisfaction.

There were, it is clear, numerous weighty considerations of public policy that dictated the finding of a decision adverse to the claims of Frederick. He was already a beneficiary, in the possession of one of the most valuable provinces in America as the result of the generosity of the Crown to his ancestors. It must have been felt by the King's advisers in 1754 that Maryland had in a sense been given by Charles I as an equivalent, and more than an equivalent, for Avalon — although there had been no formal act of surrender when George, Lord Baltimore had decided that the northern locality was unsuited to carrying out his plans for a proprietary and "numerous

---

[69] See D. Ryder and W. Murray to the Board of Trade, April 5, 1754, Calvert Papers; see also Board of Trade *Journal, 1754–1758*, p. 37.

[70] C. M. Andrews: *Colonial Self-Government 1652–1689* (New York & London, 1904), p. 130.

colony" and, as a result, had sought out new lands within the bounds of Virginia. Again, in Great Britain both the spirit of the age and the genius of government in the middle of the eighteenth century were in opposition to the concept of vast proprietorial possessions carrying with them the exercise of governmental powers. The Board of Trade, then led by the powerful Halifax, had a record of consistent hostility to both proprietorial and corporate colonial charters and, far from aiding in the restoration of those that had lapsed, was ever seeking the means to recall the few that had survived out of the many granted in the seventeenth century. As to Newfoundland, it must have been apprehended that a recognition of the proprietorial rights of the Baltimore family to Avalon would lead to the greatest confusion. Under this old patent Frederick could have levied port duties on merchandise and made other exactions; he could have collected quit-rents on the lands of Avalon; he could have established a permanent government, appointed officials, summoned a legislature, and made laws — all of which activities held out the possibilities of infinite embarrassment and discouragement to those who came to fish each year in the Banks and the coves of the island. For a settled government would almost inevitably have meant control by the permanent inhabitants of the law-making processes, thereby placing them in a position of superiority, at least with respect to their rivals, the West Countrymen — something that at this juncture certainly would have aroused the English fishing towns and would in nowise have appealed to the Crown. Lastly, and more weighty than all other considerations, there was the fear that, should a settled form of government be introduced into the island, there would be every likelihood of the population already attached to the island absorbing the great Newfoundland fisheries, just as those of New England including the Gulf of Maine had been absorbed by the men who settled in Massachusetts Bay. This, statesmen were convinced, would mean the decline of English maritime power and the decay of numerous English seaports — a development that should be assiduously prevented.

So it was that Avalon, haven of Bankers and sackmen, remained the key outpost of Great Britain's cod fisheries.

CHAPTER XII

The British Colonial System in 1750

This volume of the series, as well as the preceding one, has stressed various local and regional aspects of the mid-eighteenth-century British colonial system. It now remains to emphasize some of the more general characteristics of this system.

First of all, the government of the British colonies in 1750 was based upon certain well-established principles — the same principles that later were to be called into question. Unlike the colonies of France, Spain, and Portugal in the New World, which were under the full personal control of the king and his appointed ministers, the British colonies were not subject to the personal rule of George II. It is true that in the seventeenth century the kings of England made grants to individuals and to companies of lands in the New World and at the same time issued letters patent to them for establishing governments within these possessions. But by 1750 the royal authority had declined to such a point that the exercise of the old prerogative powers in important matters had either quite ceased or was now very narrowly circumscribed by the combined authority of King, Lords, and Commons in the High Court of Parliament.

Colonials were fully aware of the evolution that had taken place in the constitution of England and of the Empire. For example, when leaders from a number of North American colonies assembled at Albany in a congress in 1754 and proceeded, among other things, to draw up a plan of union to include most of the continental colonies, it was quite clear to them that only by an act of Parliament could this union be achieved — just as the Union of England and Scotland was brought about earlier in the century under Queen Anne only by means of a fundamental statute. They therefore embodied this as a basic feature in the final draft of the Albany Plan of Union.

In other words, in 1750 Parliament alone was held to possess inherent power to determine great matters of state. Therefore, if the King's Great Seal was still the symbol for the authentication of colonial charters and the commissions of the colonial governors, this seal could not be used in derogation of the sovereign powers of the Parliament of Great Britain. This issue had been settled definitively in the days of William III when in 1698 he had sought without success to provide for a reorganization of the East India Company under the Great Seal in opposition to the views of the House of Commons. Furthermore, that the Privy Council was still active and powerful in colonial administration after the Revolution of 1688 was simply due to the fact that Parliament had seen advantages in permitting this body — initially brought into existence by the use of the royal prerogative — to continue to function as the government's chief administrative agency for colonial affairs. That sovereignty within the Empire was centred in Parliament after 1688 can also be illustrated by the comprehensive act of 1696 relating to colonial trade (7 and 8 Wm. III, c. 7), which still remained in the statute books in 1750. This statute provided that any colonial law repugnant to it or to any other law that Parliament should pass in the future was "illegal, null and void."

Parliament did not stop at this point in dealing with colonial matters. It proceeded to legislate in this field and by the middle of the eighteenth century had passed a series of laws that amounted in effect to a code held binding on all the colonies. To illustrate. It forbad the sale of colonial lands to aliens without the consent of the Crown (7 and 8 Wm. III, c. 22) and the export from the colonies of wool, woollen yarn and cloth (10 and 11 Wm. III, c. 10), provided that colonial governors accused of crimes might be tried in England (11 and 12 Wm. III, c. 12), prohibited the destruction in the colonies of pine trees designated as serviceable for the royal navy (3 and 4 Anne, c. 10), determined the value of lawful colonial currency in terms of the Spanish specie circulating in the colonies (6 Anne, c. 30 followed by 9 Anne, c. 17, 8 Geo. I, c. 12, and 2 Geo. II, c. 35), laid down a rule for the indenture to service of minors living in the colonies (4 Geo. I, c. 11), established the principle that land in the colonies was liable for the debts of its owner (5 Geo. II, c. 7), placed restraints on the manufacture of hats in the colonies and forbad their sale outside of the particular colony where they were made (5 Geo. II, c. 22), levied high duties on foreign-produced molasses, rum, and sugar imported into colonies (6 Geo. II, c. 13), provided a comprehensive rule for the naturalization of foreigners in the colonies (13 Geo. II, c. 7), extended to the colonies the restraints already placed on unlawful business enterprises and stock-jobbing in Great Britain (14 Geo. II, c. 37), and put under severe restrictions both the colonial iron industry (23 Geo. II, c. 29) and the governments of the New England colonies in the matter of issuing and circulating bills of credit (24 Geo. II, c. 53).

In view of the major issue that developed from 1760 to 1775 between Great Britain and the continental colonies over the question of what powers Parliament could exercise in colonial affairs, it is remarkable that at no time during a period of some sixty years subsequent to the Revolution of 1688 did any colonial assembly or any other authorized representative group of a colony openly challenge that body's competence and right thus to legislate. This is especially noteworthy in light of the rather impressive body of laws listed above covering many important colonial matters, both internal and external, which were enacted during that period.

While Parliament was the final source of authority throughout the Old British Empire and while it legislated freely on matters affecting the colonial system, it never saw fit to create by statute any rigid pattern of government to which all colonies should conform. On the contrary, the machinery of government of each colony in 1750 was based on the circumstances of its origins and the conditions under which it evolved. Each therefore had a constitution that was unique, at least in some respects. That of Newfoundland was markedly different from that of Nova Scotia — both of them royal colonies — and neither had much in common with the constitutions of the four New England colonies, New Hampshire, Massachusetts Bay, Rhode Island, and Connecticut, which in turn differed more or less strikingly from one another. This same point may be made concerning the constitutions of the Middle Atlantic Seaboard colonies of New York, New Jersey, Pennsylvania, and the Lower Counties on the Delaware. It was true as well of the constitutions of the Southern colonies of Maryland, Virginia, North Carolina, and South Carolina, and also the Trusteeship of Georgia, then on the threshold of becoming a royal colony. While the similarities were greater than the differences in the constitutions of the royal island colonies of the Bermudas, the Bahamas, the four British Leeward Islands, Barbados, and Jamaica, the general frame of government of each was shaped in light of existing local conditions and the specific needs of the inhabitants and was distinctive to this extent.

The colonial constitutions were based either on letters patent, as in the case of Massachusetts Bay, Rhode Island, Connecticut, Pennsylvania, Maryland, and Georgia (between 1732 and 1752), or on commissions and instructions issued to the governors of the royal colonies — these also applied to the semi-royal colony of Massachusetts Bay. To the above constitution-forming documents must be added all colonial laws of a fundamental nature passed by a colony that had been approved by the Privy Council, as well as all those parliamentary statutes that limited freedom of action and therefore restricted colonial legislative competence.

During the period under consideration, the powers that the provincial governments could freely exercise were quite broad, except in the cases of Newfoundland and Nova Scotia. This latitude accorded to the local governments helped to make possible the distinctiveness of the British colonial constitutions, something that was true in 1750 even of the four Leeward Islands of Antigua, St. Christopher, Nevis, and Montserrat, despite the fact that they were all under the same royal governor, who was granted only one commission and a single set of general instructions. For each island possessed its own assembly and used its powers within permissible limits to mould the structure of its own government.

Nevertheless, the commissions and instructions of the governors of all royal colonies were made as much alike as possible for the purpose of establishing a constitutional pattern for these colonies. That all of them could not — and therefore did not— conform rigidly to such a pattern is clear. There were, for example, striking differences between the commission and instructions issued, on the one hand, to the Governor of Newfoundland and, on the other, to the Governor of Jamaica; therefore notable variations existed between the constitutions of these two island provinces. But there were also extraordinary similarities. Certain common duties were assigned to all royal Governors as an inseparable part of the responsibilities of their high office.

When one thinks of a constitution as an instrument of government, one has in mind its quality of permanence — in so far as human institutions possess this quality. Since the governor's commission and instructions formed a most vital part of the constitutional framework of every royal colony, they were not altered each time a new governor was appointed. However, as good reasons for change arose, alterations of certain articles often resulted in both the commission and the instructions, To illustrate. In the middle of the eighteenth century the Governor of Newfoundland was empowered to set up courts of oyer and terminer on the island with power to punish offenders capitally, instead of sending persons accused of capital crimes to England for trial as had been the rule. At the time of this change the commission, as well as the general instructions, had to be recast to a certain degree in light of the opinion of the King's legal advisers that such power could be bestowed on a colonial governor only under the Great Seal.

Modifications of less importance in the structure of governmental powers would ordinarily be reflected simply in modifications in the instructions. For example, when William Henry Lyttelton was appointed Governor of South Carolina in 1755 in place of James Glen, nine articles of Glen's instructions were omitted from Lyttelton's as "useless and improper"; three other articles having to do with judicial appeals were also omitted and were replaced by a single article embodying the decision of the Privy Council respecting appeals. Such was the process in the evolution of the constitutions of the royal provinces.

One of the most salient and important features of British colonial government, in contrast to the systems of colonial government of other European powers established in the New World, was the existence in 1750 in every colony excepting Newfoundland and Nova Scotia of a legislature elected by the freemen or freeholders. These assemblies possessed very broad powers of law-making, even in the face of the limitations placed upon them by the mother country. They also had the power of the purse. Far from being awed by the governor, be he royal or proprietary, the provincial assembly was more apt to frustrate or even awe him. Indeed, in no other part of the New World did the inhabitants have such opportunity to shape their own destines as they had in the English colonies. Likewise, in no other part of the New World was so large a proportion of the people literate, possessed of knowledge of the conditions of other peoples and of a political awareness that reflected their experience in public service. Literally thousands of British colonials were active in such service at the town, parish, or county level in the middle of the eighteenth century. Every assembly contained men trained in the law — in some cases unquestionably more highly trained than the governor himself. These men were also adept in the art of the parliamentary manœuvre designed to bend the governor to the will of the representatives of the people. As a result, the colonial assemblies continued to increase in prestige during the course of the eighteenth century, while the executive authority was proportionately weakened. Therefore, only a governor who had arrived at an understanding with his assembly could expect to have a successful and fruitful administration. At the same time, if he submitted too far to the provincial legislature and in so doing ignored his instructions, he was in danger of recall. His role, except in the two corporate colonies of Connecticut and Rhode Island and in the non-corporate colony of the Lower Counties on the Delaware, was not an easy one.

One of the powers granted to all governors of royal colonies and to those of the proprietaries was a veto on colonial legislation. But the assemblies could bring pressure by refusing to appropriate funds and in other ways, with the result that the governors were frequently torn between two desires: that of maintaining friendly relations with the assemblymen, and that of fulfilling their chief responsibility — supporting the principles that were the foundation of British imperial policy.

Even when a local law had been agreed to by the governor, it was necessary, in every colony except Rhode Island, Connecticut, Maryland, and the Lower Counties on the Delaware, that it be submitted to the Privy Council in England for final approval or disapproval. This might have constituted a serious check, if not a stoppage, to most colonial legislation, especially if it differed from the laws of Great Britain. But this was not the case. While laws were disapproved from time to time, the total that met this fate was insignificant in comparison with the number submitted and permitted to stand. During the entire colonial period before 1775, less than six per cent of all laws sent home as required were disapproved.

Again, although the laws of every colony were subject to final review by the Privy Council on appeal from the highest court in a colony — irrespective of whether or not the colony was under obligation to submit its acts to the approval of the Privy Council — this happened only at rare intervals. Once a law had passed the scrutiny of a governor, it was likely to stand, unless modified subsequently by the originating assembly.

Of all the laws passed which were apt to run counter to a royal governor's instructions, none was more vigorously supported by the local assembly than currency legislation. It was obviously necessary for the colonies to have a medium of exchange for the conduct of business in the absence of English specie, which could not be sent out of the Kingdom by prohibition going back to the days of Edward I. The medium of exchange took the form of so-called bills of credit in most of the northern colonies in the eighteenth century. The debasing of this money and the consequent defrauding of creditors — especially on the part of a colony such as Rhode Island, where inflation reached unprecedented heights by 1750 — led the British government finally to take strong measures. These were to culminate in the New England currency act passed in 1751 placing the four colonies under great restraints. However, instructions had previously been sent to the governors of all royal colonies requiring them to refuse to sign any bill that would permit the inhabitants of a colony to liquidate debts incurred in terms of English sterling money by repayment in that colony's depreciated money. In North

Carolina and in New Jersey, in particular, this led to bitter controversies between the Governor and the Assembly over legal-tender acts. It may be added that, whereas North Carolina had been guilty of serious abuses in issuing paper money, New Jersey had taken steps to maintain the face value of its currency, so that the people of the colony, not without reason, felt they were being punished for the misdeeds of others. In substance, such problems as those of colonial currency were not to be resolved during the period under consideration.

There was in truth a quality of dynamism in the civilization of the eighteenth-century British Empire which was lacking in the culture of any other contemporary imperial system. This dynamic quality expressed itself in a challenging of older ideas and older modes of action and doubtless flowed from the degree of freedom enjoyed by people in every English colony. Thinking was not canalized. Books were not placed on an index of forbidden reading matter. Non-indentured white people shifted freely from one occupation to another and rose without great difficulty from one class level to a higher one, unhampered by the social restrictions of "status" in the European sense of the term. Although this was not true of people during the period of their indenture as part of a white labouring force, even the indentured servant was free to make his way as he could when he had fulfilled his obligation. People in the British colonies were on the move — and in a hurry.

The means of higher education were expanding as the older institutions of learning — Harvard, William and Mary, and Yale — were joined in the 1740's by the College of Philadelphia and Princeton, to be followed later by King's (Columbia), Brown, Queen's (Rutgers), and Dartmouth.

There was a variety of vocations and also avocations open to colonials of ambition and enterprise, despite the previously mentioned limitations on certain types of activity superimposed upon them by Parliament. It is small wonder, therefore, that the Old British Empire drew to its confines like a magnet thousands of non-English people seeking greater liberty of thought or a better way of life than was possible under existing circumstances either in their ancestral homes in the Old World or in the colonies of other European powers in the New World. By their coming they greatly enriched and slowly modified the seventeenth- and eighteenth-century English New World civilization. Among the contributors to this enrichment and flowering were Welshmen, Ulster Scots, Scottish Highlanders, native Irish, Germans, Swiss, and French Huguenots, together with the offspring of the Dutch, Swedish, and Finnish early settlers in the valleys and estuaries of the Hudson and Delaware rivers.

With all the change in modes of life which took place in this New World environment people were constantly faced with new situations. Yet a quality of stability in the British colonial institutions and a hard core of conservatism in the British-American people led most of them to hold fast to what their own lives and the experiences of their forefathers had persuaded them were good things and to discard other ideas and methods that had not met the test. Thus, the codes of laws, based upon the Old Testament, which had been adopted by the early Puritans in New England and had proved to be unworkable gave way in the eighteenth century not to new, untried, theoretical systems of jurisprudence but to judicial systems adhering ever more closely as time went on to English common and statutory laws. A similar development took place in Pennsylvania, where the Quakers in the seventeenth century had adopted a code of law based on the spirit of the New Testament which, in practice, had not met the needs of the situation. Moreover, the machinery for the administration of justice in the British colonies reflected the constant conservative attitudes of a dynamic American society.

Everywhere, by the decided preference of colonials who had read English law and knew English judicial practice and procedure, there were grand juries, petty juries, justices of the peace, sheriffs, judges of gaol delivery on circuit, and supreme courts or supreme courts of appeal. In other ways the colonial governments followed the basic features of the English government as closely as possible. This was evident in every colony in 1750. In each there was a single executive, a governor's council, and a bicameral assembly — each, that is, with the exception of Pennsylvania and Delaware, where, apparently as a result of an oversight in Penn's Charter of Liberties of 1701, the legislature was unicameral and was to remain so throughout the colonial period. Although it is true that certain structural constitutional features were embodied in the commissions of the governors of all royal colonies and were therefore mandatory, nevertheless, their approval and popularity among colonials was so universal that when the colonies became states independent of Great Britain, little alteration was made in these features (again, with the exception of Pennsylvania, which for a time experimented most unsuccessfully with a plural executive before falling completely in line with the more traditional structure of government of the English-speaking world).

The religious aspects of the British colonial system in the middle of the eighteenth century are also in sharp contrast to the situation within the French, Spanish, and Portuguese New World empires. In these empires only one religion was recognized and tolerated — that of the Roman Catholic Church. While two churches were so-called established British colonial churches — and therefore supported by rates in one or another of the English colonies — other Christian denominations and sects were present in all the colonies and were flourishing in a number of those with established churches. In Virginia, Maryland, the Bermudas, the Bahamas, the British Leewards, Barbados, and Jamaica, the Anglican Church was the provincial-supported church. In Massachusetts Bay, Connecticut, and New Hampshire, it was the Congregational Church. However, neither of these churches could lay claim to any other exclusive right to minister to the people in 1750. In the Puritan colonies, the Anglicans, Baptists, and Society of Friends were especially active; in Virginia it was the Presbyterians, in Maryland the Roman Catholics, and in the British West Indies the Moravians or Moravian Brethren. Although efforts were made to establish Anglicanism as the official public religion in New York, the Carolinas, Georgia, and Newfoundland, as well as in the old-new colony of Nova Scotia, they fell far short of fulfillment. Indeed, in Newfoundland and Nova Scotia an overwhelming majority of the inhabitants favoured and practised openly the tenets of Roman Catholicism in 1750. Still other colonies — Rhode Island, New Jersey, Pennsylvania, and Delaware — made no pretence of having an established church and offered the utmost freedom to all Protestant groups to worship according to the dictates of conscience.

Two religious groups alone were seriously discriminated against in the British colonies in 1750: Roman Catholics and Jews. No Roman Catholic could vote or hold office in Rhode Island, New York, Maryland, Virginia, Georgia, Antigua, or Nevis. In the three last-named colonies they were also forbidden to hold land. These disabilities came as a result of provincial laws passed earlier in the century or late in the preceding century. Beyond such disabilities Catholics do not seem to have been the particular objects of harassment. In fact, Nevis in 1750 repealed the act against them, a measure approved by the Privy Council. In St. Christopher and Montserrat they were permitted to vote in 1750, which was certainly not surprising in the case of Montserrat since most of the people were of Irish descent and Catholic faith. It is of interest to note that when the Assembly of this same island had sought in 1749 to exclude adherents to Catholicism from political life by requiring all voters to take the oaths of abjuration and supremacy, the Privy Council had refused to approve the law and had even gone so far as to order its repeal. As further testimony of the prevailing tolerance of British colonials toward Catholics in the middle of the eighteenth century, the case of Maryland can be cited. This colony had at an earlier period enacted a harsher body of laws against them than any other colony. But during the period under consideration these laws were not enforced — beyond those disqualifying Catholics from engaging in political life — with the result that people of this faith were living at their ease within the province. Some of them — members of the Carroll family, for instance — were socially prominent, large landowners, and leaders in the economic life of the province.

The Jews were unable in 1750 to exercise the right of franchise or to hold office in Rhode Island, New York, Pennsylvania, South Carolina, or Jamaica. In Pennsylvania by an act of 1682 freemanship had been limited to those who believed in "Jesus Christ the Son of God and Saviour of the World"; South Carolina in 1716 had required voters to be Christians; in 1719 Rhode Island had limited the suffrage to Protestants; in 1737 New York had excluded Jews, as it had still earlier excluded Catholics; and in 1740 Jamaica had acted to bar them from exercising the franchise. Yet it cannot be said that the followers of the Jewish faith were a persecuted group in British America. Many wealthy Jewish merchant families were established both in Kingston, Jamaica, and in Newport, Rhode Island. In Rhode

Island one can also point to cases of Jews who were naturalized and who acquired political rights thereby. Indeed, in no other British colony did Jews play a larger role in the commercial life than in Rhode Island, where at Newport they were to build in 1759 the first synagogue on the North American continent.

Despite the fact that so many aspects of the British Empire differed markedly from those of other contemporary empires in the New World, it did have one important thing in common with them: the exploitation of the labour of the African Negro through the institution of slavery. In every colony laws made possible the holding in lifetime bondage of the Negro slave and of his offspring, *ad infinitum.*

The economic importance of slavery to any colony depended upon the agricultural practices, climatic conditions, and concomitant factors in the region. The production in quantity of the export staples — sugar, molasses, rice and indigo — demanding a tropical or semi-tropical climate and requiring a labour force capable of working under the generally unfavourable conditions of the areas involved, made slave labor a necessity in the opinion of those who benefited from it. Most of the tobacco raised in non-tropical colonies specializing in that commodity likewise was produced on plantations employing slave or indentured labour, although much of it was also grown by the small planter utilizing no other labour than his own and that of the members of his family. In other words, in the tobacco-exporting colonies of Virginia and Maryland, Negro slavery was highly useful and profitable, but not so necessary as in the areas of the sugar and rice plantations. Although slavery existed to the north of the Chesapeake Bay region, it was even less essential to the exploitation of the land resources. What was true of the northern continental colonies was also true of the Bermudas in the middle of the eighteenth century, where slaves apparently were more frequently an economic liability than an asset. But the wealthy Bermudians continued to hold slaves because their possession meant social prestige, just as it appears to have done in Boston in Massachusetts Bay, Portsmouth in New Hampshire, Newport in Rhode Island, and in New York City.

The presence of tens of thousands of blacks within the Empire represented to their owners tangible wealth in the form of invested capital generally capable of producing more wealth, evidence of which frequently took the form of town or country mansions, rich home furnishings, thoroughbred horses, personal adornment, travel, and the higher education of children, perhaps in England. The Negroes, especially in the areas of the greatest density of slave population — as in South Carolina and the British West Indies — also brought a constant state of fear, whether suppressed or openly avowed, to the whites among whom they dwelt. An expression of the extent of this fear may be found in the public laws or codes passed by the various colonies designed to keep the blacks under control. None of these codes provided more extreme penalties than those that could be visited upon slave offenders under the laws of Jamaica, and none was more strictly enforced. Back of the laws and responsible for them were terrifying memories of slave insurrections involving incidents such as the slaughter of entire planter families. In contrast to laws like the "*code noir*" of Jamaica were those of the more northern colonies where Negroes were comparatively few and also not of the fierce warrior Koromantyn type that seemed best fitted to survive in Jamaica. Typical of the other kind of black code, the Massachusetts Bay code did make a distinction between justice for the white freeman and for the black slave, but in its comparative mildness it indicated only a slight degree of apprehension about the presence of the Negro.

Thus we find that in 1750 the British colonials reached out to secure the maximum degree of freedom of action for themselves, but at the same time felt impelled to deny this same freedom to the blacks they had brought from Africa against their will. At the same time, it was not an uncommon practice in the colonies to manumit faithful slaves, who by this process became free, if not freemen in the technical sense. Nowhere was this more common than in the West Indies, and nowhere else was it more likely that an attractive Negro woman would have children begotten by her master. As has been indicated in the preceding volume of this series, from time to time the Assembly of Jamaica was called upon to legitimatize the mother and her offspring and, in some instances, to grant — at least to the children — all the rights that would have been theirs had they had a white mother. So it was that in Jamaica, where the slave code was perhaps the harshest of any British colony, the favours extended to certain people born in slavery were perhaps the most generous.

Enough has been said about the British colonial system to make clear that each colony in structure and in its chief interests and objectives differed from every other colony, at least to some degree. Those with extensive bounds — as in the case of the colonies claiming sea-to-sea grants of land based on early letters patent, including Massachusetts Bay, Connecticut, Virginia, the Carolinas, and Georgia — were by the middle of the eighteenth century more or less aggressively expanding their settlements or at least preparing to expand them if possible. This trend toward westward expansion in most cases involved clashes with other colonies over territorial limits.

Historically, the most noted of these intercolonial boundary disputes was one between two colonies with no sea-to-sea grants — Maryland and Pennsylvania — and it was to plague the relationships of their inhabitants for some eighty years — until the 1760's. Similarly, the dispute between Maryland and Delaware, although officially settled by decision of the Lord High Chancellor in 1750, continued to be a source of friction until the final determination of the line in 1767.

Pennsylvania was also troubled by other boundary disputes in the middle of the eighteenth century. Virginia by the late 1740's had become deeply involved in a trans-Appalachian expansion program. Upon the basis of the assumed reach of the seventeenth-century sea-to-sea grant to the Virginia Company, Virginians at this period were seeking to appropriate lands in the southwestern part of Pennsylvania, including the forks of the Ohio where Pittsburgh would arise. Connecticut, likewise upon the basis of its early charter, cast its eyes in the 1750's on northern Pennsylvania and, with the organization of the so-called Susquehanna Company and backed by the Assembly, began to settle that area.

Apparently Connecticut, feeling that Pennsylvania was more vulnerable, chose to spare New York and did not therefore venture into the limits of that province. But New York in its turn was made to feel the impact of pressure from both New Hampshire and Massachusetts Bay along its eastern borders and from New Jersey along the southern border. In fact, the boundaries of but few colonies were not in question, at least to some degree. The final determination of these boundary disputes, however, was not by any sweeping decision emanating from an order in Council on the part of the government of Great Britain. Instead, commissions made up of prominent colonials were brought into existence as the situation demanded, which reported their findings after due deliberations — a procedure least liable to arouse the ire of a colony involved in a contest for territory when a decision was adverse to it. A typical example of this procedure was the case of fixing the boundary line between the Carolinas.

Intercolonial rivalry did not stop with individual boundary disputes. Between the British West Indies and the North American continental colonies economic sectionalism developed in the eighteenth century over two questions of trade policy: To what extent should the trade of the British colonies in the New World be confined to lands embraced within the Empire? — and, To what extent should the products of the foreign sugar islands be permitted to compete with the British sugar products in the markets of British North America?

The French in their West Indian possessions of St. Domingue, Martinique, and Guadeloupe enjoyed an extraordinarily favourable position in the year 1750. The islands were of marvellous fertility; the slave supply of the planters was purchased at a low rate as a result of royal subsidization; and the planters and the other inhabitants of these islands were eased of many of the financial burdens that rested very heavily on the shoulders of the British West Indian colonials. Nor did the British planters enjoy any subsidization of their slave supply. Furthermore, by the middle of the eighteenth century those of the British Leeward Islands and Barbados were obliged to face the fact that their lands were showing signs of soil exhaustion. It is therefore not surprising that during the first half of the century they were forced to witness the loss of the chief European sugar markets to their more advantageously placed French rivals. During this same period they also saw the disappearance of the hitherto profitable North American market for their molasses — a necessary by-product of the process of making sugar. The French King, on the one hand, prepared to provide every encouragement to his West Indies islands to send their sugar to France; at the same time he forbad the importation of molasses and rum into the home land to protect the interest of the brandy trade. Thus the French West India planters, faced with the choice of dumping their molasses as waste material or selling it to foreigners at a price that could not fail to appeal to them, adopted the latter course. By this means they helped to establish the distilling of rum as one of the great North American industries.

If it seemed impossible, under given conditions, that the British sugar-planters could win back the European sugar market, it seemed equally unlikely that they could win back the New World molasses market without the active support of the home government. As the contribution to the royal exchequer from the British Lesser Antilles, by means of the 4½-per-cent export duty, had long helped to support colonial enterprises elsewhere in the New World, their planters doubtless felt that their appeal should obtain sympathetic consideration. It did, for this reason as well as for others. However, Parliament was unwilling to grant the petitioners' request that the importation of foreign sugar, molasses, or rum into the North American colonies be prohibited. Instead, countervailing duties on these foreign-produced articles, sufficiently high to offset the advantages enjoyed by the French, were provided for in the Molasses Act of 1733. This act failed of its purpose. Fortunately, the consumption of sugar in the British Isles increased greatly and the British West Indies planters turned to producing rum out of molasses, which they also sent home.

Nevertheless, it was becoming clear by the middle of the eighteenth century that Barbados and the British Leeward Islands had seen their best days and were slowly declining. Planters, burdened with heavy taxes and private debts, began leaving these islands in numbers, many of them settling in the Dutch island possessions or those on the mainland of South America. Again an appeal for relief was made to the mother country to cut off all commerce between the foreign West Indies and the North American colonies. But again the effort did not succeed. Anxious as it was to help the islands in their plight, the British Government could not be prevailed upon to go beyond what it had already done for the islands in 1733 and also in 1739, when it permitted a restricted carrying of sugar directly to southern Europe. In reality these statutes were nothing more than a gesture, since no adequate machinery existed for the proper enforcement in North America or on the high seas of the Act of 1733 and no adequate facilities were ever developed to make effective the advantages of the Act of 1739 or the somewhat liberalized amendment of 1742 permitting a direct importation of sugar into southern Europe. In other words, the British sugar islands, opposed to the flourishing trade carried on by the continental colonies with the foreign West Indies, had been able to secure from Parliament a certain degree of protection of their vital interests by the passing of the Act of 1733. But neither this legislation nor their own efforts was able to prevent the flow of French-produced molasses to North America. When, in the middle of the century, they again sought a prohibition of this profitable commerce to the northern colonies, they failed to win the support of the government, despite the supposed great influence they were presumed to have in the proceedings of Parliament. By contrast, the influence of the continental colonies, despite their lack of representation in this body, was greater in 1750 than that of the British West Indies in this situation of commercial rivalry.

Any account of the British colonial system as it operated in the middle of the eighteenth century must place due emphasis on the rather complex body of laws placing restraints on the economic activities of all people within the Empire and known as the trade and navigation acts. A "List of Acts of Parliament Relative to Plantation Trade," drawn up in 1753 or shortly thereafter (to be found among the Shelburne Papers, Volume 49:99–116), lists 84 of these acts, beginning with "An Act for the Encouraging and Increasing of Shipping and Navigation" (12 Chas. II, c. 18), passed in 1660, and ending with "An Act for continuing several Laws . . . and for encouraging the Trade of the Sugar Colonies in America . . ." (26 Geo. II, c. 32), passed in 1753. As a group these laws had three chief objectives: to make England, and, after the Act of Union of England and Scotland in 1707, Great Britain, the centre of the commerce of the Empire; to ensure a favourable balance of trade to the mother country and to encourage the growth of the merchant marine in rivalry with the shipping of foreign nations. British statesmen in 1750 believed as strongly in the wisdom and justification of these objectives as did the members of Parliament in the days of

Charles II and William III who had passed the earlier groups of these acts.

No better illustration of this feeling can be found than in the very long — and by no means easy to read or to digest — report prepared in the early 1750's by James Abercromby, a man long identified in an official capacity with American affairs. This report was submitted to the Lord President of the Privy Council in 1752 under the title "An Examination of the Acts of Parliament Relative to the Trade and Government of the American Colonies" (and is referred to frequently throughout the body of this series as the "Abercromby Examination, 1752"). To Abercromby the problem appeared to be not that the acts had served their day, but that the welfare of both England and the colonies called for their strict enforcement. To this end he called for a single comprehensive statute to be passed by Parliament which would make the colonial system a much tighter system by eliminating irregularities in its operation.

Although Abercromby's recommendations were not acted upon — probably because they seemed too drastic in nature — it can hardly be questioned that before the outbreak of the War for American Independence and the publication in 1776 of Adam Smith's *Wealth of Nations* no British statesman in the eighteenth century advocated discarding this regulatory system — not even William Pitt, the Earl of Chatham, Edmund Burke, or Charles James Fox, all outspoken friends of the British colonials during the period of crisis in the 1760's and 1770's. They were not unaware that to protect the colonies from open enemies in time of war and from pirates in peace time demanded the annual expenditure of great sums of money in maintaining the royal navy and in other defence measures. Large sums were also required for the sinking fund, out of which payments could be made to reduce the national debt, which, standing at £1,000,000 in 1693, by 1749 had reached almost £80,000,000. To a considerable extent this debt had been incurred as a result of military operations designed to protect the Empire. It is therefore understandable that men in England, both in and out of government, took the position that the colonials should make some contribution, either directly or indirectly, to supporting this and other desirable objectives that benefited them. Under the terms of the trade acts they were required to do so.

While much of the British colonial commerce, especially that carried on in the New World, remained relatively free of restrictions in the 1750's , all vessels loaded with British colonial commodities destined for continental Europe were expected, before returning to America, to stop at some British port in order to pay duties on European products taken on board, less whatever drawbacks existed on particular items, and were required to secure certificates indicating that these duties had been paid. However, to give some relief to colonials certain articles — such as wines from the Azores and Madeira, servants, horses, and provisions from Ireland, and salt for the Newfoundland and North American fisheries — could be carried directly to America without going to England.

Again, under the trade-and-navigation system certain articles were placed on a list called the "enumerated commodities." By 1750 these included sugar, molasses, tobacco, cotton, indigo, ginger, dyewoods, rice, naval stores, copper, and beaver skins, as well as other furs. These enumerated commodities could only be carried to Great Britain or sent to another British plantation. Further, the provisions of the Woollen Act of 1698, the Hat Act of 1732, and the Molasses Act of 1733, prohibiting the export from any colony of wool or woollen goods or beaver hats and placing high duties on foreign-produced molasses, sugar, and rum imported into a British colony, were features of the system. Finally, ships engaged in trade to or from the colonies or any other British possession were expected — with some exceptions involving, for example, merchant ships captured from the enemy in war — to be British or British colonial built, registered, and officered, and manned by a crew of which three fourths were British subjects.

To what extent this system of restrictions actually impeded the growth and prosperity of the British colonies is not easy to determine. Like modern state systems of protection of industry and trade, it undoubtedly bore more heavily on some groups than on others. One mitigating feature was that, as the system functioned in the middle of the eighteenth century, it went hand in hand with a program that gave special encouragement by means of premiums for the development of specific industries in the colonies and the export of their products to Great Britain. In this category was the production in New England of masts, bowsprits, and yard-arms, and in the

Carolinas of pitch, tar, turpentine, rosin, and indigo; while in Georgia the making of silk was so subsidized.

Unquestionably among the chief beneficiaries of the navigation system were those colonies best prepared to profit from the construction and utilization of many types of vessels. With foreign ships barred by statute from the territorial waters of the British colonies and with the trade of the Empire further limited to ships built in Great Britain or in the colonies, the opportunity arose during the first half of the century, especially in the more northern colonies, to create two of the most prosperous lines of economic activity in all America — shipbuilding and the carrying trade. Thousands of people — among them lumbermen, shipwrights, sailors, wharfmen, and those who manned the rope-walks and cast anchors at the ironworks — were among those most immediately benefited. Thousands of others also gained from the concomitant activities that arose from or contributed to the rise of these two great colonial enterprises. Among the groups directly affected were those employed in drawing up partnership agreements, insurance policies, charter-parties, and cargo manifests. Then there were those seeking advantageous markets abroad for their raw products or their processed supplies — for example, in the provision trade. In short, the entire colonial economy felt the impact of the growth of shipbuilding and of the carrying trade, whether in the seaports and urban centres or in the agricultural areas and frontier lands. For the farmers, stock-raisers, and other producers, as well as the small merchants, merchant princes, and other middlemen thus engaged were all beneficiaries of these activities.

America was a busy and, by and large, prosperous America in 1750. Indeed the opportunities for legitimate financial gain opened up by the trade and navigation system seemed to have more than offset the hindrances posed by legal barriers against engaging in certain activities, industrial as well as commercial. Notwithstanding, there was clearly much violation of the laws that supported the system, and nowhere were these violations more widespread than in the northern colonies that had benefited so greatly by other features of the system. The most unabashed violators seem to have been the Rhode Island shippers and merchants. That this was possible was largely due to the fact that the machinery for enforcing the restraining acts operated in an easy-going fashion in the middle of the eighteenth century. Far from the uncompromising pattern of the police-state where orders were rigidly executed and offenders as rigidly punished, tide-waiters and collectors of customs at colonial ports were frequently venal and perhaps as frequently disinterested in the strict performance of their imperial duties. They preferred the friendship rather than the hostility of shipmasters and their sailors. Let James Abercromby cry out against the non-enforcement of the navigation acts, the government at home did not appear to be in any mood in the 1750's to bring about drastic alterations in the machinery of law-enforcement in America.

Among the objectives sought by the system of trade-protection within the British Empire was the goal of imperial economic self-containment, in so far as it was practical and desirable. The extent of the realization of this objective by the middle of the eighteenth century presents an impressive record of achievement, the equal of which had never been reached by any other imperial state.

In 1750 the looms of England were producing enormous quantities of woollen goods of quality, much of which, after satisfying domestic needs, could be distributed throughout the Empire and abroad. The same thing could be said of the ironware and steel produced by the forges and furnaces of England and the colonies. Ireland and Scotland were manufacturing large surpluses of linen, and Ireland likewise had a ready market for its abundant supplies of barrelled beef in the British West Indies — to which area the middle continental colonies also sent quantities of various provisions, as well as staves and headings for barrels, lumber, and other articles. In turn, the West Indies met the needs of the British Isles for sugar, if not the requirements of the northern colonies for molasses. The English and colonial annual catch of cod, herring, mackerel, and other fish from the far-flung fisheries was largely sold abroad and brought in return salt and articles of luxury. The masts from New England and the diverse naval stores from the Carolinas met a certain part of England's pressing needs in shipbuilding, a field in which by 1750 the colonies were themselves playing a leading role. British colonial tobacco, rice, and deerskins, each available for sale in great quantity, met the chief demands not only of the British Isles but also of northern Europe, as did the high-quality furs procured from the Hudson Bay area. These gainful pursuits, although worthy of special mention, were but a small part of the multifarious activities of trade and commerce carried on by the people living within the far reaches of the Old British Empire.

With the wealth accumulated from their varied activities, British North Americans continued to multiply, to lay out new farms, plantations, and towns in the great wilderness, to erect churches, to provide for the instruction of their children, to print newspapers and books, and to gather around themselves — especially in the older settled areas — many of the amenities of life afforded by the age in which they lived. An accumulation of evidence indicates that most of them were proud of their heritage as British subjects. In fact, so pleased were they with the degree of freedom allowed them by the home government in public and private affairs and with the protection afforded them from hostile neighbours, French, Indian, and Spanish, that it would doubtless have been difficult to find many colonials in the middle of the eighteenth century who would have complained — as they were to do so freely in 1775 — that it was their great misfortune to be living under a system of government in which a tyrannical King sought to rule them despotically by means of a compliant Parliament.

Index

Abbington Iron Works, at Iron Hill, Delaware, 201

Abeel, the Rev. John H., notes on New York by, 115 *n*, 116 *n*

Abercromby (Abercrombie), James, London agent for Virginia and North Carolina: the "Examination" (1752) of, 9; on exports from Great Britain, 116; report of 1752 by, on the trade and navigation acts, 290

Academy of Philadelphia, 170

Acadia, *see* Nova Scotia

Account of Six Years' Residence in Hudson's Bay, An (1752), by Joseph Robson, 231 *n*

Account of the Countries adjoining the Hudson's Bay in the Northwest part of America (1744), by Arthur Dobbs, 244 *n*

Account of the European Settlements in America, An (1757), reputedly by William and Edmund Burke, 3

Account of the Island of Newfoundland . . . , An (1765), by Griffith Williams, 249

"Account of the Several Provinces in North America," *Ames Almanack* (1756), on the population of New Hampshire, 51 *n*

Acrelius, the Rev. Israel: on Philadelphia exports in 1751, 166 *n;* on Philadelphia imports, 168; on Philadelphia harbor activities, 169; on tobacco in Delaware, 189 *n;* on quit-rents in Delaware, 199; on the town of New Castle, 201; efforts by, to preach in English in Delaware, 202; author of *History of New Sweden* (1759)

Acts and Laws of Connecticut (1750), 80

Adams, John, a Boston townsman, coheir of the Allen New Hampshire claim, 48

Adams, John, Massachusetts Bay statesman, on the advantages of New England, 37–8

Adams, Samuel: later revolutionary agitator, at Harvard, 25; political essay of, 27

Adjournment, the Assembly of Pennsylvania and the power of, 176

Admirals of harbours, the, of Newfoundland, 258, 259, 262

Admiralty Office, the, and the search for a northwest passage, 243

Adultery: revision of the capital law against, in Connecticut, 91, 92, 95; the capital crime of, in Pennsylvania, 165

Affirmation: the right of, accorded in Pennsylvania, 159; denied to Assemblymen in Delaware, 195

Africa: the slave trade in, and the Rhode Island traders, 62–6; supplies of slaves and gold from, 63 *n*

Agent, the London: activities of, of New Hampshire, 44 *n*, 45; of Rhode Island, 72; of Connecticut, 96–100; of New York, 121; of New Jersey, 133; of the East New Jersey Proprietors, 133–4; of Delaware, 197

Agricultural products: of Massachusetts Bay, 15; of New Hampshire, 51; of Rhode Island, 56; of Connecticut, 76; of New York, 117; of New Jersey, 127; of Pennsylvania, 166; of Delaware, 201, 203 *n*

Agriculture: in New England, 4; in Massachusetts Bay, 15; in New Hampshire, 57; in Rhode Island, 56–7, 67; in Connecticut, 76; in New York, 117–18; in New Jersey, 126; in Pennsylvania, 166; in Delaware, 200–1; absence of, in Hudson Bay, 233 *n*

Aix-la-Chapelle, the Peace of, and Louisbourg, 34, 223

Albany, and New York land disputes, 105; a great fur-trading centre, 118; a description of, 118–19; avarice of the traders at, 119–20; a resort for Indians preying upon the New England settlements, 120 *n*

Albany County, New York, and land riots, 107–8; influence exercised by Colonel William Johnson in, 110

Albany Fort, a Hudson's Bay Company post, 231

Albany Plan of Union, requirement of an Act of Parliament for implementation of, 274

Albany River, effects of French competition at, 234

Alexander, James, an East New Jersey Proprietor: the private concessions of, 139; defence of Proprietors by, 141 n; power in the New Jersey Council of, 147

Alexander, William, New York merchant, 106 n

Alexanders, the, among the New York aristocracy, 110

Aliens: Parliament forbids the sale of lands to, 175, 274; the naturalization of, in the colonies prescribed by Parliament, 275

Allen, James, prominent Massachusetts Bay merchant, 32

Allen, Samuel, Governor of New Hampshire and Proprietor: furnishes white-pine masts, 42 n; proprietorship of, 47

Allen, Thomas, heir of Colonel Samuel Allen, 47

American Husbandry (1775): the author of, unknown, 8; on New England, 8

American Traveller, or Observations on the British Colonies in America (1769), by Alexander Cluny, 117 n

Ames Almanack (1756), on the population of New Hampshire, 51 n

Anabaptists, see Baptists

Anamabo, the slave mart at, 64

Anarchy: in the affairs of New Jersey, 134, 138; in Newfoundland, 262–4

Anchors, the manufacture of, in Rhode Island, 218

Ancram ironworks, in New York, 117

Andros, Sir Edmund, Governor General of the Dominion of New England, 28; the cautious land policy of, as Governor of New York, 103

Angel, Nathan, a leading Rhode Island merchant, 58

Angerstein, the Swedish traveller, on Oregrund iron, 221 n

Anglicans: in Massachusetts Bay, 22; in New Hampshire, 51 n; in Rhode Island, 54; in Connecticut, 78, 81, 86 n;

Anglicans: (continued) in New York, 116, 119; in New Jersey, 137; in Pennsylvania, 149, 150, 158, 162, 170; in Delaware, 202, 204; and the colonial Church establishments, 282; toleration of, in the Puritan colonies, 282

Anglo-French Commission of 1750, the, tasks assigned to, 34

Ann Arundel County, Maryland, attempts of magistrate in, to legislate regarding transported convicts, 195 n

Annapolis Royal, Nova Scotia, menaced by the French in King George's war, 34

Antigua: imports of, 116; the constitution of, 276; disabilities of Roman Catholics in, 283

Apparel, see Dress

Apprentices, the number of, employed by American hatters, restricted, 240

Architecture: of Boston homes, 5; of Massachusetts Bay farmhouses, 8; of Wentworth's mansion, 52; of manor houses in New York, 114; influence of Dutch Renaissance in the, of New York City, 115 n; of Albany, New York, 118; of Philadelphia homes, 170; of the town hall of Philadelphia, 171

Aris's Birmingham Gazette, 212

Aristocratic tendencies: in Massachusetts Bay, 5; in New Hampshire 51–3; in Rhode Island, 57, 66–7; in Connecticut, 83; in New York, 109; in New Jersey, 146; in Pennsylvania, 171–2

Arminius, the doctrines of, in New England, 23

Arms, to be possessed by all Connecticut householders, 88 n

Armstrong, Charles, Surveyor General of the King's Woods, 41

Arnold, Benedict, of New Haven, Connecticut, popular military leader, 89

Arson, the crime of: in the Connecticut code of 1750, 92; in Pennsylvania, 165

Ashfield, Lewis Morris, appointed to the New Jersey Council, 148

Ashurst, Sir Henry, London agent for Massachusetts Bay: appointed for Connecticut, 97; the effective work of, 97

Asia, furs from, on the "enumerated" list, 238

Assembly, the: of Massachusetts Bay, composition and powers of, 31; attitude toward Governor Shirley, 35; de-

Assembly (*continued*)
nounces the disloyalty of the inhabitants of Nova Scotia, 36; expresses loyalty to the Crown, 36; of New Hampshire, opposes the garrisoning of Fort Dummer, 46; opposes the seating of deputies from the unprivileged towns, 48–9; of Rhode Island, appointment of deputies to, 67; and the choice of local officials, 67–8; and the issue of bills of credit by, 68, 70; dominated by inflationists, 72; opposes the regulation of colonial paper money by Parliament, 72; of Connecticut, the powers of, 74, 89; election of deputies to, 83; of New York, and the land law of 1699, 104; votes to support the claims of those moving into Livingston Manor, 107; controlled by the de Lancey faction, 110; elections to, 111; opposition to the Governor by, 120–5; and provincial defence, 121; the London agent of, 121; the attempts of, to control finances, 121 *n;* composition of, 122 *n;* censured by the Board of Trade, 124; of New Jersey, the relations of, with Governor Morris, 126, 131–2, 146–7; relations of, with Governor Belcher, 132, 147–8; demand by, for paper money, 134–5; meets alternately at Perth Amboy and at Burlington, 137–8; appeal of, to settle the New York-New Jersey boundary dispute, 141–2, 145; boundary law passed by, 143–4; of Pennsylvania, acts to limit the number of people on board an immigrant ship, 154 *n;* the distribution of members of, 165; the adoption of British criminal law by, 164–5; the aggressiveness of, and power of, 175–9; indulged by the Crown and Proprietors, 176–9; the claims of, to exemption from all royal and proprietorial instructions, 176–9; the issue of military defence laid before, 197; deputies of Pennsylvania and Delaware as a joint, 187; differences between representatives of the two areas debated in, 188; of Delaware, 189, 190, 191; harmonious relations of, with Governor, 193; meeting place of, 193; composition of, 193; unicameral nature of, 195; right of affirmation denied to members of, 195
Assemblies, colonial: the control of the public purse by, 278; influence over

Assemblies, colonial (*continued*)
the Governors exercised by, 278; continued increase in prestige of, 278; laws passed by most of the, sent to England for approval, 279
Assiniboine River, the, site of French trading post, 246
Assiniboines, the North American Indian tribe of, and Hudson's Bay Company trade, 235
Assistants, the Governor's Council of: in Massachusetts Bay, 29; the election of, in Rhode Island, 67; in Connecticut, 83
Atkinson, Theodore, member of the New Hampshire Assembly, 44 *n;* Chief Justice of the Supreme Court, 52; relationship to Benning Wentworth, 52
Atlas Maritimus et Commercialis (1728), 255 *n*
Attorney General, the, of England, unfavourable opinion of, on Penn's rights in Delaware, 190
Auction, the sale of beaver pelts by, in London, 237
Avalon Peninsula, Newfoundland: a description of, in 1750, 248, 252–4; importance of, to the English, 250–1; a revival of the Baltimore claims to, 265–71
Avery, Dr. Benjamin, Chairman of the Committee of English Dissenters, refuses the Connecticut London agency, 99
Axes: the manufacture of, in Masachusetts Bay, 217; loss of American markets by English manufacturers of, 217; manufacture of, in the colonies, 221
Axtell, William, on the English dependence upon Swedish iron, 220
Ayrault, Daniel, a leading Rhode Island merchant, 58; instructions to ship master from, 65
Ayrault, Stephen, a leading Rhode Island merchant, 58
Azores, the, freedom of colonial trade with, 291

Bachelor house, the keeping of, punished by the Connecticut code of 1650, 91, 93; and the Connecticut code of 1784, 95
Backus, the Rev. Isaac: on the Baptists in New England, 22; author of *A*

Backus, the Rev. Isaac: (*continued*)
Church History of New England . . .
(1777–96)

Bacon, export of, from Pennsylvania,
166 *n*

Badge of shame, the wearing of, a penalty listed in the Pennsylvania "Great Law" code, 163

Bahamas, the: government of, 276; the religious establishment of, 282

Balance of trade, the: between England and Massachusetts Bay, 8, 9, 10; the importance of a favourable, to Great Britain, 289

Ballast, the disposal of, regulated in Newfoundland, 260

Ballot, the: in Connecticut, 83; in Pennsylvania, 161

Baltimore, Benedict Calvert, 4th Baron, Lord, 267

Baltimore, Cecilius (Cecil) Calvert, 2nd Baron, Lord: patents of, to Delaware, 192 *n;* precautions of, to maintain title to Avalon, 266; Newfoundland patents confirmed to, 267; appointment of Governor of the island by, 267; death of, 267; Maryland patent of, 267

Baltimore, Charles Calvert, 3rd Baron, Lord, 267

Baltimore, Charles Calvert, 5th Baron, Lord: petition to the King by, concerning Delaware, 192; as an heir to the Newfoundland patent, 267; as Proprietor of Maryland, 268

Baltimore, Frederick Calvert, 6th Baron, Lord: claims of, in Delaware, 184, 188, 192 *n*, 193, 198; the petition of, for the recognition of his rights to Avalon, 265, 267–72; the reasons for the failure of the petition of, 271–2

Baltimore, George Calvert, 1st Baron, Lord: the attempt of, to settle at Ferryland, 249, 265, 267; a patent to, for lands in Newfoundland, 265; powers conferred upon, 265–6; the death of, 266; the patent to, declared in force, 267

Baltimore County, Maryland, attempts of magistrates in, to legislate regarding transported convicts, 195 *n*

Baltimore family, the: claims of, to the Three Lower Counties on the Delaware, 184, 185, 198–9; to the Avalon Peninsula, Newfoundland, 264–72; the

Baltimore family, the: (*continued*)
poverty of, after the English Revolution, 268

Baltimore ironworks, the, 216

Banister, John, Rhode Island molasses trader, 60; testimony of, on production of anchors in Rhode Island, 217–18

Banister, Captain Thomas: on the value of Massachusetts Bay exports in 1715, 14 *n;* author of the *Essay on the Trade of New England* (1715)

"Bankers," *see* West Countrymen

Banking: in Boston, 7; in Massachusetts Bay, 11–12; the Rhode Island government and, 68–72; the New Jersey government and, 128–36; the Pennsylvania government and, 173–4; the Delaware government and, 199–200

"Banks," the history of the Rhode Island, 68–73

Banks of Newfoundland, the, fishing interests upon, 248–9

Baptists, the: and the Massachusetts Bay Establishment, 22; the strength of, in Boston, 22; the leading denomination in Rhode Island, 54–5; the persecution of, in Connecticut, 56, 86; support Quakers for office in Rhode Island, 56; and the local ecclesiastical society in Connecticut, 81, 86 *n;* the progress of, in eastern Connecticut, 94; few numbers of, in Pennsylvania, 150; in the Pennsylvania Assembly, 162; in Philadelphia, 170; activity of, in the Puritan colonies, 282

Bar iron: the making of, on Livingston Manor, New York, 114, 117; export of, from Pennsylvania, 167; the process employed in 1750 in the production of, 210–11; a shortage of, in England, 211, 213; dependence upon foreign importation of, 211, 213; the total amount of, required in England, 211; importation from Ireland of, duty free, 211; the effects of the breaking off of relations between England and Sweden on the price of, 211, 214; of America, the importation free of duties of, into the port of London, 225, 228; the amount of, shipped from America to England, 226–7, 228; proposed duties on Swedish, 228

Barbados: Rhode Island slavers stop at, 65; imports of, compared with those of New York, 116; the government of,

Barbados: (continued)
276; the religious establishment of, 282; slow decline of the fertility of, 287

Barberry rust: and the growing of wheat in Massachusetts Bay, 15; the eradication of, and the Connecticut towns, 87

Barclay, David, London agent for Delaware, transmission of reimbursement funds by, 197

Barclays, the, among the New York aristocracy, 110

Barley, the production of, in Pennsylvania, 166

Barnstable County, Massachusetts: slave population of, 16; iron production in, 16; the representative from, to the Assembly, 32

Barrel staves, vast export of, from Pennsylvania, 166 n; exported from Delaware, 203 n

Barrington, New Hampshire, the fortified post of, 46

Barter goods, see Trading goods

Basel, Switzerland, an edict against the Moravian Brethren by, 152

Basque fishermen: and the Grand Banks of Newfoundland, 248; and the "wet" cod fishery, 253 n

Bayards, the, among the New York aristocracy, 109

Bear skins: brought out of Hudson Bay in 1749, 233; import and export duties on, 242; sought in Newfoundland, 255

Beaver: and the New York fur trade, 118; and Newfoundland, 252; see also Chap. 10

Beaver hats: the manufacture of, in New York, and the Act of 1732, 117; popularity of, 237; the making of, 237; the French take up the manufacture of, 238–9; the English hatters lose their markets for, to the French, 238–42; the making of, in the colonies restricted, 239–40; great wealth drawn to France through the sale of, 241–2; the English, priced out of the market, 242

Beaver House, London: a description of, 236; the activities at, 236–7; and the Northwest Passage project, 243

Beaver skins: high quality of, from Hudson Bay, 230; the number of, brought out of Hudson Bay in 1748, 233; auction price of, 237; the use of, in industry, 237; and the hat trade, 237–42; import and export duties on, 242; Hud-

Beaver skins: (continued)
son's Bay Company profits from, 242–3; on the enumerated list, 291

Beawes, Windham, applies for Massachusetts Bay lands for London merchants, 19 n

Bed feathers, brought out of Hudson Bay in 1748, 233

Bedford, John Russell, 4th Duke of, Secretary of State for the Southern Department, notified of the failure of His Majesty's ships to visit Placentia, 261 n

Beef: the export of, from Rhode Island, 56; from New Jersey, 127; from Pennsylvania, 166; from Delaware, 203 n

Beekmans, the: among the New York aristocracy, 110; the commercial activity of, 115 n

Beekman's Patent, New York, 102; the creation of, 104 n

Belcher, Jonathan, Governor of Massachusetts Bay and New Hampshire: opposition of, to land bank scheme, 1740, 11; instructed respecting import duties on Negroes and felons, 30 n; unpopularity of, 33; recall of, 33; on the growing scarcity of white-pine trees, 43; on the boundaries of New Hampshire, 44–5; seeks to unite his two governments, 45; represents Connecticut in London, 98; on the trade of New Jersey, 127; on the absence of taxation in New Jersey, 128; becomes Governor of New Jersey, 132; favours the New Jersey bills of credit bill of 1748, 133; the policies of, designed to win the support of the House of Representatives, 147; opposed by the Council, 147–8; failure of, to win over antiproprietorial group, 148; censured by the Board of Trade, 148

Belknap, Jeremy, author of The History of New Hampshire . . . (1813), 42 n

Bellomont, Richard Coote, Earl of, Governor of New York, Massachusetts Bay, and New Hampshire: on the high quality of New England codfish, 17 n; the cautious land policy in New York under, 104

Bellows, the use of, in the iron furnace, 208

Bennington, the creation of the township of, by Governor Wentworth, 105

Bergen County, New Jersey: Dutch settlements in, 137; the number of repre-

Bergen County (*continued*)
sentatives from, 138; the spread of land riots to, 140

Berkeley, George, Bishop of Cloyne: on the sectaries of Rhode Island, 54; the sojourn of, at Newport, Rhode Island, 66

Berkeley, Lord John, an original proprietor of New Jersey, 141, 143

Berks County, Pennsylvania: the creation of, and the racial complexion of, 158; the representation of, in the Assembly, 161

Berkshire County, Massachusetts, the number of towns within, 19 *n*

Bermudas, the: the government of, 276; the religious establishment of, 282

Bernard, Francis, Governor of New Jersey, permitted to assent under conditions to the issue of bills of credit, 135–6

Bestiality: the capital law of 1650 against, in Connecticut, 91; and the Connecticut code of 1784, 95

Bethlehem, Pennsylvania, the founding of, by the Moravian Brethren, 152

Bibles, encouragement for Connecticut homes to possess, 93

Bideford, England, the interests of, in the cod fisheries, 250

Billiards, the playing at, forbidden in Connecticut, 94

Bills of credit: of Massachusetts Bay, the redemption of, in 1749, 10–13; of other New England colonies, not to circulate, in Massachusetts Bay, 13, 71; a petition to the Crown by Boston merchants against the circulation of, in New England, 13; the history of, in Rhode Island, to 1750, 70–3; the distribution of, to the towns to loan out, 70–2; the depreciation of, 71–3; not to circulate in Connecticut, 71; the low value of, in Rhode Island, 71–3; 200 *n;* Parliament restricts the issue of, in New England, 72, 275; the cautious use of, in New Jersey, 129; the early attitude of the Crown toward, 129; certain colonies not involved in the issue of, by 1715, 129 *n;* the instruction of 1720 regarding, 129; the hostility of the Privy Council in 1731 toward, 129; the high standing of the New Jersey, 129–30; issue between the New Jersey Governor and Assembly over, 131–3;

Bills of credit: (*continued*)
arguments of the London agents on the further issue of, 133–4; The Board of Trade's rejection of the bill on, 134; the Assembly petitions the King for the right to issue further, 134; royal instructions of 1753 respecting, 134; bills of 1755 and 1757 for, meet with royal disapproval, 135; instructions of the Governor relative to, modified, 135; the Governors of New York and Pennsylvania violate the royal instruction regarding, 135; the loan of, in Pennsylvania, 174; in Delaware, the sinking fund provided for, 197 *n;* issuance of, 199–200; as a medium of exchange in most colonies, 279

Bills of exchange, the, utilized in the West Indies trade, 63, 76

Birmingham: the iron industry about, 207; production of gun barrels in, 208; the iron manufacturers of, desire a bounty on American iron, 222, 228

Biscuits: exportation of, from New York, 117 *n;* wheat, exported by Pennsylvania, 166 *n*

Blasphemy: the capital laws against, in Connecticut, 91; and the Connecticut code of 1784, 95; laws against, to be enforced in Newfoundland, 260

Bloomeries, in Pennsylvania, 167

Bluchers, the, among the New York aristocracy, 110

Board of Trade, the: attitude of, toward Massachusetts Bay currency plan, 12–13; protests to, from Rhode Island, 59; requests an account of bills of credit issued in Rhode Island, 71; checks financial responsibility of Rhode Island, 72; censures the New York Assembly, 124; activities of, concerning colonial paper currency, 130–1; recommends disallowance of the New Jersey bills of credit act of 1748, 134; the report of, respecting the New Jersey petition of 1753, 134–5; failure to secure royal approval of New Jersey law after hearing before, 144; reprimands Governor Belcher of New Jersey for recommending unfit men for the Council, 148; and Pennsylvania legislation, 177–8; support by, of Baltimore's claims to Delaware, 192 *n;* limits of Hudson's Bay Company's land claims in memorial placed before, 236; me-

Board of Trade (*continued*)
morials to, by English hatters, 239, 241; representation of, regarding the colonial hat industry, 240; on the predominance of Roman Catholics in Newfoundland, 251 *n*; on the sale in Europe of cod of poor quality, 256 *n*

Boars, the hiring of, by the Connecticut towns, 87

"Body of Libertys," the, of Massachusetts Bay, 90

Bolingbroke, Henry St. John, 1st Viscount, influences the Connecticut agent, Dummer, 97

Bonavista, Newfoundland, and inshore cod fishing, 250

"Book of Proceedings of the Bristol Merchant Venturers, 1745–1752," 245 *n*

Boring of the tongue, the, and the Duke of York laws, 163

Boston: its greatness as a commercial centre, 4, 6, 7, 10; as a cultural centre, 5; its homes, 5; slave population of, 6; its shipping, 6; the decline in shipbuilding at, 6 *n*, 7; the entrepôt for a vast territory, 7, 10; the evasion of the customs by merchants of, 8; disease in, 8 *n*; the merchants of, petition against New England bills of credit, 13 *n*; trade stagnation in 1750 in, 14; Peter Faneuil's munificence to, 18; religious groups in, 22 *n*; the press and religion in, 23, 26; the representation of, in the Assembly, 32; commercial and social relations of, with Connecticut, 76, 77, 78; compared to New York, 116; compared to Philadelphia, 169 *n*, 170; the interest of the merchants of, in Newfoundland trade, 251

Boston Evening Post, The, 14 *n* and *passim*

Boston Gazette, The: founded by William Booker, 27; characterized, 27

Boston News-Letter, The, founded by John Campbell, 26

Boston Weekly Advertiser, The, 27

Boston Weekly Post, The, issued by Thomas Fleet, 27

Boston Weekly Post-Boy, The, started by Ellis Huske, 27

Boundary commission: the New Hampshire-Massachusetts Bay, supports New Hampshire claims, 45; the New York-New Jersey, vindicates the New Jersey claims, 145

Boundaries: of the Maryland patent to Lord Baltimore, 192 *n*; of the Hudson's Bay Company grant, 236

Boundary dispute, the: of Massachusetts Bay and New Hampshire, 44–5; of New Hampshire and New York, 50 *n*, 105–6; of Massachusetts Bay and Rhode Island, 97; of New York and Massachusetts Bay, 106–7; of New York and New Jersey, 108–9; of Maryland and Pennsylvania over Delaware, 192, 193, 198–9

Bounties, British: on colonial ship timber, naval stores, and hemp, 42, 220, 291; the local, of Delaware, 200 *n*; a request for, upon iron, 220; granted by Parliament to promote imperial economic self-containment, 291–3

Bontin, M., master of the *Jupiter*, and the Jamaica vice-admiralty court, 60–1

Bowdoin, James, one of the key figures in shaping Massachusetts Bay legislation, 32

Bowls, the playing at, forbidden in Connecticut, 94

Bowsprits, a bounty on American, by Parliament, 42, 220

Braddock, General, letter to, from Governor Morris, 174

Bradley, Richard, New York Attorney General, on the aims of the colonial assemblies, 121 *n*

Bradstreet, John, the desire of Lord Baltimore to appoint, Governor of Newfoundland, 268

Branders: of horses and other animals in Connecticut, 87; of flour, and of beef and pork, and the Pennsylvania Assembly, 176

Branding: and the Connecticut code of 1650, 91; and the Duke of York laws, 163; and the New Castle code, 165

Brands, town, in Connecticut, for horses, 87 *n*

Brandy, the colonial excise on, collected in Connecticut, 87

Brandywine Creek, Delaware: location of Wilmington at, 201; location of saw, grist, paper, and flour mills upon, 202

Bread: the export of, by New York, 118; by Pennsylvania, 166; from Delaware, 203 *n*

Brenton, Jahleel, Surveyor General of his Majesty's Woods, 41

Breton fishermen, and the Grand Banks

Breton fishermen (*continued*)
of Newfoundland, 248; and the "wet"
cod fishery, 253 *n*

Bribe, attempts to, Governor Morris of
New Jersey, 132

Brick: the use of, in Boston, 5; export
of, from Massachusetts Bay, 9; in Philadelphia, 170; the superior quality of,
in Pennsylvania, 170 *n*

Bridgeman, Sir Orlando, Chief Baron of
the Exchequer, and other commissioners decide the dispute over Avalon,
267

Bridger, John, Surveyor General of His
Majesty's Woods, 41

Brief Account of Pennsylvania, A (1753),
by Lewis Evans, 226

*Brief Account of the Rise, Progress and
Present State of the Paper Currency of
New England . . . , A* (1749), 11 *n*

*Brief Consideration of New York with
respect to its Natural Advantages, its
superiority in several instances over the
neighboring Colonies, A* (1753), by
William Livingston, 112 *n*

*Brief State of the Province of Pennsyl-
vania, A* (1755), by William Smith,
150 *n*

Bristol, England: the purchase of New
England ships at, 6; the export of
American pig iron to, 216; petitions for
relief by the ironmasters and ironmongers of, 220; petition by the merchants of, in support of Arthur Dobbs's
attack on the Hudson's Bay Company,
245; the interest of, in the cod fisheries,
250

Bristol County, Massachusetts, slave population of, 16

Bristol Merchant Venturers, the: petition
of, for regulation of the American iron
industry, 224–5; petition in favour of
American bar iron, 224; disappointment of, over the Iron Act, 228; the
attempt by, to overthrow the Hudson's
Bay Company monopoly, 245 *n;* the
Book of Charters of (1749), 225 *n*

*Britain's Commercial Interest Explained
and Improved* (1757), 210 *n*

British Customs, The (1757), by Henry
Saxby, 213 *n*

British Empire, the: the dynamic quality
of the colonization of, 280; draws to
itself vast numbers of non-English
peoples, 280; enrichment of the civili-

British Empire (*continued*)
zation of, by non-British stocks, 281;
the conservatism of the people within,
281; economic sectionalism within,
287; general prosperity of, in 1750,
292–3; extent of economic self-containment within, 293–4

British Empire in America, The (1741),
reputedly by John Oldmixon, 203

British people, as indentured servants in
Pennsylvania, 157

British regulars: utilization of troops of,
in the Dutchess County land riots, 108;
use of, threatened in New Jersey land
riots, 142

British West Indies, *see* West Indies,
British

Broad arrow, the King's sign placed on
the reserved white pine, 41

Bromfield Mansion, Boston, 5

Brown family, the, of Providence, 58,
59 *n*

Brown University, and the beginnings of
higher education in America, 280

Brunigam, *see* Birmingham

Brunswick House, a Hudson's Bay Company post, 231

Bubble Act of 1718, the, parliamentary
interference in colonial finances through,
12

Bucks County, Pennsylvania: religious
elements within, 158; the representation of, 162; the possibilities for expansion beyond, 187

Bulkley, John, appointed London agent
for Connecticut, 99

Bulls, the hiring of, by the Connecticut
towns, 87

Burglary: the capital law of 1650 against,
in Connecticut, 91; a capital crime in
Pennsylvania, 165

Burke, Edmund: on New England, 3;
support of the British trade and navigation system by, 290; reputed co-author of *An Account of the European
Settlements in America* (1757)

Burke, William: on New England, 3; reputed co-author of *An Account of the
European Settlements in America*
(1757)

Burlington, a joint capital of New Jersey,
138

Burlington County, New Jersey, representation of, in the Assembly, 138

Burnaby, the Rev. Andrew: on the har-

Burnaby, the Rev. Andrew: (*continued*)
vesting of the white-pine trees, 40; on
the lawlessness of the people of Newport, 60 *n*, 61 *n*; on the commercial
activities of Rhode Island, 66; on Delaware, 200–1; on Wilmington, 201; author of *Travels through the Middle
Settlements of North America, 1759–
1760* (1775)

Burnet, William, Governor of New York,
New Jersey, Massachusetts Bay, and
New Hampshire: the death of, 98; the
financial policies of, and the New York
Assembly, 121

Burniston, Charles, Surveyor General of
His Majesty's Woods, 41

Butler, Captain, Rhode Island slaver, at
Anamabo, 64–5

Butter, the export of, by Rhode Island, 56

By-boatmen, of Newfoundland, 252

Cahoone, Captain John, Rhode Island
slaver, at Anamabo, 65 *n*

California, the, seeks a northwest passage, 244

Callendar family, the, of Newport, Rhode
Island, 66

Calvert, *see* Baltimore

Cambridge, Massachusetts Bay, a plan
to erect an Anglican college at, 36

Campbell, John, founder of *Boston News-
Letter*, 26

Canada: the projected invasion of, by
Connecticut and New York troops in
1709, 97; New York trade with, 123 *n*

Canadian Indians, the resorting of, to
Albany and Oswego, 119

Canary Islands, the, and Massachusetts
Bay, 7

Candles, spermaceti, produced in Rhode
Island, 66

Canso, the Straits of: and Massachusetts
Bay, 7; the amount of Massachusetts
Bay rum sent to, 16 *n*; Massachusetts
Bay appropriation of fisheries of, 17;
the fisheries of, fall into hands of the
French, 34

Canterbury, the Archbishop of, supports
de Lancey at court, 124 *n*

Canterbury, New Hampshire, the fortified
post of, 46

Cape Bonavista, Newfoundland, and
French fishing rights, 249; the salmon
fisheries of, 255

Cape Breton: the British colonial cam-

Cape Breton: (*continued*)
paign on, 34, 99; the French fisheries
of, 249, 250

Cape Henlopen: and the Duke of York's
deed of 1682, 185 *n*; situation of
Lewes, north of, 200

Cape May County, New Jersey, representation of, in the Assembly, 138

Cape Perdrix, Labrador, and the boundary of the Hudson's Bay Company territory, 236

Cape Riche, Newfoundland, and French
fishing rights, 249

Capital crimes: the punishment of, in
Connecticut, 91–2, 95; in Pennsylvania,
163–5; in Delaware, 193 *n*; in Newfoundland, 263

Capital laws, the: of Massachusetts Bay,
32–3; of Connecticut, 90–2, 95; of the
Duke of York, 163; of Pennsylvania,
164–5

Carbonear, Newfoundland, a garrison stationed at, 251

Cards, the playing of, forbidden in Connecticut, 94

Carlisle, Pennsylvania, settlement of the
Ulster Scots at, 159

Carolinas, the: cost of shipbuilding in,
7 *n*; imports to Massachusetts Bay,
from, 15; the purchase of New Hampshire commodities by the people of,
53; immigration of Germans to, 152;
importance of, in iron industry, 215;
iron manufactures of New England imported into, 217; and naval stores, 293

Carpenter, Captain, Rhode Island slaver,
at Anamabo, 64

Carr, Sir Robert, commander of British
forces occupying Delaware, 184

Carrot River, the, French trading post,
Fort Paskoyac, at juncture of, and the
Saskatchewan, 246

Carrying trade: the importance of the, to
the colonial economy, 292; the many
activities connected with, 292; *see also*
Commerce, Exports, Imports, Shipping

Carteret, Sir George, an original proprietor of New Jersey, 141, 143

Cassada Garden, the slaver running between Rhode Island and Africa, 64

"Case of the Right Honourable Frederick, Lord Baltimore, Relating to the
Province of Avalon in America, The"
(1753), 251

Cases Argued . . . in the High Court of

Cases Argued (continued)
    Chancery . . . (1788), by Francis
    Vesey on the Chancery decision in the
    Penn-Baltimore dispute, 198 *n*

Cast iron, the production of, and the con-
    version of, into wrought iron, 208

Castle, William, a defence of Boston, 4

Castration: punishment by, in Connecti-
    cut, 92 *n;* punishment by, in the New
    Castle code, 164 *n*

Catechisms, Connecticut selectment to see
    that homes were furnished with, 92

Catholics, *see* Roman Catholics

Cattle: export of, from Massachusetts
    Bay, 9; raising of, in Pennsylvania, 166;
    scarcity of, in Newfoundland, 252

Cedar Lake, the French trading post of
    Fort Bourbon on, 246

Cedar trees, great growth of, in New
    Jersey, 127; the white, of Pennsyl-
    vania, 170; durability of the shingles
    made from, 170

Cereals: the production of, in Massachu-
    setts Bay, 15; in Rhode Island, 56; ex-
    port of, from Connecticut, 76; export
    of, from New Jersey, 127; export of,
    from Pennsylvania, 166; production of,
    in Delaware, 201–2

Certificated goods, the importation into
    Pennsylvania of, 167–8

Chalmers, George, author of *Opinions of
    Eminent Lawyers, on Various Points of
    English Jurisprudence* (1814), 190 *n*

Chandler, Joshua, New Haven deputy,
    the conservative leanings of, 84 *n*

Charcoal, an essential in the smelting of
    iron ore in 1750, 209–11

Charles, R., of Leicesterfields, England,
    on the Iron Act of 1750, 229

Charles, Robert, Secretary to Sir Peter
    Warren, employed as London agent by
    the New York Assembly, 121

Charles, II, grant of Delaware to the
    Duke of York by, 185

Charming Polly, the, Rhode Island mer-
    chantman and the West Indies, 59

Charter, the: of Massachusetts Bay, of
    1691; effect of, on Church Establish-
    ment, 22; an analysis of, 29–31; the ex-
    planatory, of 1725, 30 *n;* of Rhode Is-
    land, analyzed, 67; of Connecticut, and
    the Congregational Establishment, 96;
    the preservation of, 100; of the Hud-
    son's Bay Company, 231; geographi-
    cal advantages allow Hudson's Bay

Charter *(continued)*
    Company to retain its, 247; to Sir
    George Calvert of Avalon by James I,
    265

*Charter granted by their Majesties King
    William and Queen Mary to the In-
    habitants of the Province of Massa-
    chusetts Bay, The* (1742), 29 *n*

Charter of Liberties of 1701, the: as the
    basis of Pennsylvania government, 175;
    proviso of, concerning Delaware, 188;
    and the government of Pennsylvania
    and Delaware, 281

Cheekley family, the, of Newport, Rhode
    Island, 66

Cheese, the export of, from Rhode Island,
    56

Cheesecook (Cheesecock) Patent, New
    York, 103; the creation of, 104 *n*

Cheshire, the County of, England, 208;
    hæmatite ore supplies the furnaces of,
    208

Chester, England, petitions in support of
    Arthur Dobbs's attack on the Hudson's
    Bay Company, 245

Chester, New Hampshire: the fortified
    post of, 46; deputies from, summoned
    to the Assembly by Wentworth, the
    dispute over seating of, 48–9

Chester (Upland), Pennsylvania: the
    code of laws adopted at, 163; act of
    union promulgated at, 163, 186

Chester County, Pennsylvania: religious
    elements within, 158; the representa-
    tion of, 162

Chests of drawers, the manufacture and
    export of, by the people of New Hamp-
    shire, 53

Chew, Samuel, Quaker and Chief Justice
    of Delaware, views on military defence,
    197 *n*

Children: "stubbornness" of, and cursing
    of parents by, a capital offence in Con-
    necticut, 91; smiting of parents by, a
    capital offence in Duke of York code,
    163

Choate, Colonel John, one of the key
    figures in shaping Massachusetts Bay
    legislation, 32

Christina River, Delaware: location of
    Wilmington at, 201; iron forge con-
    structed near, 201; importance of the
    tributaries of, 201–2; shipping facilities
    of, 202; mills located on, 202

Church communion, the Congregational:

Church communion (*continued*)
in Massachusetts Bay, 22; in Connecticut, 79–81

Churches: in Boston, 22 *n;* in Rhode Island, 54–6; in Connecticut, 78–81; in New York City, 116; in Albany, 119; in New Jersey, 137–8; in Philadelphia, 170

Church edifices: the number of, by denomination, in Rhode Island, 55 *n;* in Philadelphia, 170

Church History of New England; with Particular Reference to . . . Baptists, A (1777–96), by Isaac Backus, 22 *n*

Church of England, *see* Anglican, Anglicanism, and Anglican Establishment

Church services, the punishment by the Connecticut code of 1650 for absence from, 91, 95

Cider, the milling of, at a New York manor, 114

Clarke, George, Governor of New York, the financial policies of, and the Assembly, 121 *n*

Claverack, New York, riotous procedure at, 107

Clee Hill, England, iron, and the making of gun barrels, 208

Clergy: the Massachusetts Bay, in the seventeenth and eighteenth centuries, 19–26; in Pennsylvania, in 1750, 150

Clerk, the town, in Connecticut, the election of, and duties of, 86

Climate: in New England, 3; in Pennsylvania, 169 *n;* of Hudson Bay, 231; of Newfoundland, 251

Clinton, George, Governor of New York, and the New Hampshire boundary dispute, 50, 105, 107; issues a proclamation to arrest Massachusetts Bay encroachers, 107; repeatedly dissolves New York Assembly, 111–12; son of the Earl of Lincoln, comes to New York with expectations, 120; the character of, and relations with de Lancey, 120, 122–5; the relations of, with the Assembly, 120, 124; gives his confidence to Colden, 122; accused of malfeasance in office, 123; Colden's defence of, 123; problems of the salary of, 124 *n;* replacement of, as Governor, 125

Cluny, Alexander: on exportations by New York, 117 *n;* author of *American Traveller* . . . (1769)

Coal: the apparent lack of, in Pennsylvania in 1750, 167; an essential in the production of iron in 1750, 208, 209; the use of, in turning pig iron into bar iron, 210–11; great deposits of pit, in Worcestershire, increases iron manufacture, 210

Coasting trade, the: vessels from Massachusetts Bay engaged in, 6, 10; of Portsmouth, New Hampshire, 52–3; Rhode Island vessels engaged in, 58; out of New York, 116; out of Philadelphia, 168–9; *see also* Shipping

Cod fisheries, the: nations participating in, 248; the French enjoy the advantage in, 250; the value of, to England, 254–5

Code of laws, the: of Connecticut of 1650, 90; of 1750, 85, 90–5; of 1784, 95; of the Duke of York, 163; of Pennsylvania, 163–5; of Massachusetts Bay, 163; of New Haven Colony, 163; of Delaware, 193

Codfish: the quality of Massachusetts Bay, 17; commands a high price in Portugal, 17; French cured, preferred in the European markets, 250; the catching and curing of, in Newfoundland, 253–4; the exports of, from Newfoundland, 254–5; the poor quality of, carried by the British to southern markets from Newfoundland, 256

Coke: the use of, in England, before 1750, 209; in malt-making, 209 *n*

Colden, Cadwallader, Surveyor General of New York: on the vague terms of land grants, 104, 105; characterized, 122; opposition to, by the Council and the Assembly, 122–3; the support of Clinton by, 123; the appointment of, as Lieutenant Governor sought by Clinton, 123; appointment of, as Lieutenant Governor, in 1761, 125 *n*

"Cold short" iron ore, the location of, and use of, in England, 208

Cole, Captain T.: on the French rivalry in the cod fisheries, 249 *n,* 250; author of "State of the Fisheries" (1761), published by Griffith Williams

Collectors of the excise, in Pennsylvania, the control of, by the Assembly, 176

College: Harvard, 27–8, 28 *n,* 36, 280; Yale, 27–8, 88, 280; King's, 78, 280; Princeton, 137, 280; The "Log," 137; of Philadelphia, 161, 170, 280; William

College: (continued)
and Mary, Brown, Queen's (Rutgers), and Dartmouth, 280
Collieries, instructions against the opening of, in Nova Scotia, 227
Collins, Francis, furnishes New England white-pine masts, 43 n
Colman, John, and the plan for a Massachusetts Bay land bank, 11
Colonials, recognition by, of the supreme power of Parliament in 1754, 274
Colonies, the British: the principles underlying the government of, 273; laws passed by most of, sent to England for approval, 274; no rigid pattern of government for, ever created by Parliament, 275; each government of, unique in some respects, 275; placed under restraint by Parliament in establishing business enterprises, 275; the basis of the constitutions of, 276; veto power of the Governor of most of, 278; few laws passed by, disallowed, 279; the great extent of freedom in, 280; the lack of status among white people in, 280; higher education in, 280; the enrichment of the civilization in, by non-English stocks, 281; the strong conservatism of the people of, 281; the preference of, for English law and English political institutions, 281; varied religious patterns in, 282; slavery within, 284–5; boundary disputes among, 286–7; rivalry between the West Indies and the North American, 287–8; effects of the trade and navigation restrictions on, 291; general prosperity of in 1750, 291–2; violations of the trade laws in, 292; favourable living conditions in, 294; see also Antigua, Barbados, Bahamas, Bermudas, Connecticut, Delaware, Georgia, Jamaica, Maryland, Montserrat, Nevis, New Jersey, New York, Newfoundland, North Carolina, Nova Scotia, Pennsylvania, Rhode Island, St. Christopher, South Carolina, Virginia
Colonies, French: controlled by the King, 273; recognize but one church, 282; see also French West Indies
Colonies, Portuguese: controlled by the King, 273; recognize but one church, 282
Colonies, Spanish: controlled by the

Colonies, Spanish: (continued)
King, 273; recognize but one church, 282
Colony, the corporate: of Massachusetts Bay, under the charter of 1691, 4–39; of Rhode Island, under the charter of 1663, 54–73; of Connecticut, 74–101; see also Chaps. 1, 3, 4
Colony, the royal: of New Hampshire, 39–53; of New York, 102–25; of New Jersey, 126–48; see also Chaps. 2, 5, 6
Colony, the proprietary: of Pennsylvania, 149–83; of Maryland, 174; of the Lower Counties on the Delaware, 184–205; see also Chaps. 7, 8
Commerce: of Massachusetts Bay, 6–8; English public concern about, with Newfoundland, 18; of New Hampshire, 52; of Rhode Island, 58; with the West Indies, 58–66; with Africa, 63–6; of Connecticut, 76; of New York, 116–17; of New Jersey, 127; of Pennsylvania, 167–8; of Delaware, 201
Commissioners of oyer and terminer, the appointment of, for Newfoundland, 263
Commissions: to Governors, under the Great Seal, 31; the constitutions of the royal colonies and, 276; striking similarities and differences in the, issued to royal Governors, 277
Compton, Rhode Island, population and number of voters in, 69
Concord, New Hampshire, see Penacook
Congregational Church, the: establishment of, in New England, 21, 285; in Massachusetts Bay, in 1650 and 1750, 21–26; fellowship within, 21–2; the halfway covenant, 21, 22; the Great Awakening and, 23–6; Old Light and New Light congregations within, 25; in New Hampshire, 51; in Rhode Island, 54; in Connecticut, 79–81; at the end of the eighteenth century, 95 n; end of the Establishment of, in 1818, 96; in East New Jersey, superseded by Presbyterianism, 137
Connecticut: the value of imports and exports of, 10; Boston merchants petition the Crown against the bills of credit of, 13 n; the persecution of Baptists within, 56; the democratic constitutional basis of, in 1750, 74; characteristics of, as a corporate colony, in 1750, 74; the government of, 74,

Connecticut: (*continued*)
75, 276, 278; population and tax ratings in, 74–5; the leading towns of, 74 *n*, 75 *n*; the population of, 75, 76; the commercial relations of, 75, 76; the economy of, 75 *n*, 76; the exports of, 76; the shipping of, 76, 77; industries in, 77; Puritanism and, 78–9; local government in, 78–89; the land policy of, 84–5; the laws of, 85–95; preservation by, of the charter, 94; has eyes on northern Pennsylvania, 94, 286; the activities of the London agents of, 96–100; freedom from heavy taxation in, 101; New York City as the distributing centre of western, 116; New Jersey settlers appeal for annexation by, 142; an appeal of New York settlers to the government of, for lands west of the Hudson, 144; the constitution of, based on letters patent, 276; the Governors of, weak in authority, 278; not obliged to send laws to England for approval, 279; western charter limits of, 286

Connecticut Courant, the, 95

Connecticut Gazette, the, the first newspaper in the colony, 95

Connecticut Journal, the, 80 *n*, 95

Connecticut River, the: an abundance of white pine on the upper, 43; report on the lands of the upper, 49; divides Connecticut into economic and social sections, 77

Connecticut Valley, upper, exploitation of the lands of, 49

Consideration of the Advantages which would arise from Discovery of the Northwest Passage (1750), by Henry Ellis, 244 *n*

Considerations on the Bill . . . for Encouraging the Importation of Pig and Bar Iron from America (circa 1750), 217 *n*

Conspiracy against the colony, the capital law against, in the Connecticut code of 1750, 92

Constables, the town, of Connecticut: the election of, and duties of, 86; to suppress vice and enforce the law of the Sabbath, 93

Constitutions of the colonies, the bases of, 276–7

Contacook (Contoocook), New Hampshire, the fortified post of, 46

Contemptuous behaviour, the punishment for, in the Connecticut code of 1650, 91

Continuation of the History of the Province of Massachusetts Bay (1798–1803), by G. R. Minot, 9

Convict labour, ability of Delaware to legislate against importation of, 194

Convict transports: disallowance of Massachusetts Bay law imposing a duty on, 30 *n*; disallowance of a Pennsylvania law imposing a duty on, 177; Delaware erects a barrier against, 194; Maryland flooded with, 195

Cook-rooms, for the cod fisheries, protected in Newfoundland, 256

Copper, as an enumerated commodity, 291

Coppices: the distribution of, in England and Wales, 207; the problem of the preservation of, in England, 209–10; the value of, to the English landowners, 212

Coram, Thomas, English humanitarian, the plan of, for an Anglican college in Cambridge, Massachusetts Bay, 36

Corn, Indian: the dependence of Massachusetts Bay upon imported, 15; the export of, by Rhode Island, 56; a leading Pennsylvania crop, 166

Cornbury, Edward Hyde, Viscount (later becomes the 3rd Earl of Clarendon), Governor of New York and New Jersey: extravagant land grants of, in New York, 104; the New York Assembly under, seeks financial control, 121 *n*; the opposition of Lewis Morris to, 146

Cornell, Gideon, Newport merchant, owner of the *Jupiter*, 60–4; wins appeal from the vice-admiralty court of Jamaica, 61–2

Corner, John, London merchant, seeks Massachusetts Bay lands, 19 *n*

Cornwallis, Governor, replacement of, in Nova Scotia, 227

Cortlandt Manor, New York, 102; the creation of, 104 *n*

Cosby, William, Governor of New York: financial policies of, and the Assembly, 121; opposition to, by Lewis Morris, 146

Cotton, as an enumerated commodity, 291

Council of New England, lands included in royal patent of, 185 *n*, 192 *n*

Council, the colonial: of Massachusetts Bay, the method of selection of, 31; the powers of, 31; of New Hampshire, and the Wentworth family, 52; of Rhode Island, the election of, 67; of Connecticut, 83, 89; of New York, the refusal of, to accept the provisional New York-New Jersey boundary line of 1719, 143; of New Jersey, the opposition of, to the currency program of the House of Representatives, 133; of Pennsylvania, not a branch of the legislature, 175 n; the powers of, 175 n

Counterfeiting: the royal seal, a capital crime in the Connecticut code of 1750, 92; money, the punishment for, 92; the penalty for, in Pennsylvania, 165

Counties, the: of Massachusetts Bay, 15–16; ratable polls of and agricultural products of towns within, 19 n; of Connecticut, officers of, and their duties, 89–90; of New York, land riots in, east of the Hudson, 105–7; of New Jersey, riots within, 139–42; of Pennsylvania, religious and racial complexion of, 158–9; the representation of, in the Assembly, 161–2; of Delaware, 185, 195, 203

County courts, the: of Rhode Island, the election of judges of, 67; in Connecticut, the functions of, 89–90

Coureurs, the French, activities of, among Indians of Hudson Bay, 235, 247

Court of Chancery, the High: original charter of Massachusetts Bay voided by, in 1684, 28; decision of, in 1750, favourable to Delaware, 198

Court of election, of Rhode Island, 67

Court of vice-admiralty, see Vice-admiralty court

Coventry, England, petition from, in support of Arthur Dobbs's attack on the Hudson's Bay Company, 245

Coxe, Daniel, comes into possession of the heath patent to Carolina, 271

Crafts (handicrafts), the development of, in New England, 4; in New Hampshire, 53

Creditors, within Rhode Island, defrauded through the depreciation of the currency, 70–1; within New Jersey, opposed to currency expansion, 133

Cree Indians, the, and the Hudson's Bay Company trade, 235

Crèvecoeur, de, Michel Guillaume Jean, see de Crèvecoeur

Crime: legislation against, in Connecticut, 90–2; punishment of, in Pennsylvania, 163–5; the growth of, in Pennsylvania, 165; in Delaware, 194; the problem of, and the punishment of, in Newfoundland, 262–3

Crown, the: and Massachusetts Bay, the appointive powers of, 29; the control of law-making by, 30–1; the New Hampshire southern boundary fixed by, 45; the New Hampshire Governor supported by, against the Assembly, 48; the Connecticut London agency and appeals to, 96–101; the decision by, in the New York-New Hampshire boundary dispute, 106; New Jersey's futile appeals to, over the New Jersey-New York boundary, 144–5; questions involving the interference of, in the affairs of Pennsylvania, 177–8; the claims of, to Delaware, 191; Baltimore's petition to, in 1753, 251

Crows, the killing of, and the Connecticut town meetings, 87

Crugers, the family of, among the New York aristocracy, 109

Cumberland County, England: the quality of the iron ore of, 208; the development of ironworks between Lancaster and, 212

Cumberland County, Maine, the number of towns within, 19 n

Cumberland County, Pennsylvania: the creation of, and the racial complexion of, 158; the representation of, in the Assembly, 161; the amount raised by excises in, 174

Currency: in Massachusetts Bay, a hard money after 1750, 10, 13; in Rhode Island, depreciation of, 69; of New Jersey and the legal tender issue, 128–36; in Pennsylvania, the profits on the paper money, 174; in Delaware, 200; colonial, Parliament determined the lawful value of, 275; the Assemblies and laws relating to, 279; restrictions placed by Parliament on the issuing of, in New England, 279; no law to be approved in any colony to make the, a legal tender for all debts, 279; see also Bills of credit, Specie

Cursing a parent, the Connecticut capital law of 1650 against, 91

Customs, *see* Duties

Cutler, the Rev. Timothy, Rector of Yale College, dismissed for Anglican views, 99 *n*

Dannemora Mines, Sweden, the, Oregrund iron mined in, 221 *n*

Darby, Abraham, Coalbrookdale ironmaster, and the use of coke, 209

Darling, Thomas, New Haven deputy, conservative leanings of, 84 *n*

Dartmouth, England: the interest of, in the cod fisheries, in 1750, 250 *n;* the petition of the merchants of, against alterations in the government of Newfoundland, 264

Dartmouth College, and the beginnings of higher education in America, 280

Davenport, James, a revivalist of the Great Awakening, 24, 25

Death penalty, the: in the "Body of Libertys" of Massachusetts Bay, 90; in the Connecticut code of 1650, 91; in the Connecticut code of 1750, 91–2; in the Connecticut code of 1784, 95; in the Duke of York laws, 163; in the Upland code of 1682, 163; in the Pennsylvania eighteenth-century laws, 164–6; in Newfoundland, 263–4

Debt, public: Pennsylvania free from, 174; great increase of, in Great Britain, 290

Debtors: within Rhode Island, 70–3; gain through the depreciation of the currency, 72; the New Jersey legal tender acts and, 129–30

de Crèvecoeur, Michel Guillaume Jean, author of *Letters from an American Farmer* (1782), on the immigrants in Pennsylvania, 157

Deed of Surrender, the, of the Hudson's Bay Company, 245

Deerskins: export of, from Massachusetts Bay, 9; from Pennsylvania, 166 *n*

Defence of the New England Charters, The (1721), by Jeremiah Dummer, 97

Defences, the: of Boston, 4; of Massachusetts Bay on the northwest, 46; of the New Hampshire frontier, 46–7, 48; of New York City, 115; of New York, the Assembly responsible for the mili-

Defences (*continued*)
tary, 121; the lack of, for New Jersey, 128; pacifist principles against, in Pennsylvania, 159–61, 178–9, 197; of Delaware, 186, 196; of Hudson Bay, 232; of Prince of Wales Fort, described, 232 *n;* of Avalon Peninsula, 250–1

Deflation, of currency in New Jersey, favoured by the land-proprietorial group, 136

Deists, legislation against, in Connecticut, 80 *n*, 86; and the Connecticut code of 1784, 95

de Lancey, James: proclamations of, in connection with the New York-Massachusetts Bay boundary dispute, 108; control of one faction by, 110; as Chief Justice of New York, 110, 121 *n;* the relations of, with Governor George Clinton, 120–5; attacked by Colden, 123; becomes Lieutenant Governor and Chancellor, 125; New York southern boundary claims of, 143

de Lanceys, the : among the New York aristocracy, 109; and the Canada trade, 123 *n;* the interest of, in the Minisink Patent, 143

de la Vérendrye, Sieur Pierre, activities of, west of Hudson Bay, 234, 246

Delaware: as a colony, 174; the undefined position of, in 1750, 184; origins of rival claims to, by Penn and Baltimore families, 184–6; history of, prior to 1750, 184–91; curious legal status of, as a colony, 186; political separation of, from Pennsylvania, 186–9; territorial limits of, 187; Penn's efforts to promote union between Pennsylvania and, 188; unique and anomalous aspects of, in 1750, 189–93; efforts of, to become a royal colony, 190; government of, 193–8; laws of, 193–6; administrative divisions of, 195; sending of troops by, to the West Indies, 196; military support given by, in Spanish war, 196–8; defence measures of, 196–8; the Chancery decision in favour of Penn's title to, 198–9; finances in, 199–200; agricultural economy of, 200–1; growth of industry in, 201–2; the chief towns of, 201–2; national groups in settlement of, 202–3; religious affiliations of population of, 203–4; proportion of slaves

Delaware: (continued)
in population of, 204–5; the status of, in 1750, 205; the government of, 276; not obliged to send laws to England for approval, 279; possesses a unicameral legislature, 281; no religious establishment in, 282; boundary dispute involving, 286

Delaware Bay, the: threat of pirates in the waters of, 186; chart of, 200 n; Lewes pilots in waters of, 200

Delaware Company, the, organization of, 144; an Indian grant secured by, 144 n

Delaware River, the: as a boundary limit, 143, 185; the freezing over of, in winter, 169; threat of pirates in waters of, 186 n; Lewes pilots for, vessels sailing in, 200; waters of, charted, 200 n

Democracy, the middle-class type of, in Massachusetts Bay, 31; tendencies toward, in New Jersey, 142 n

Denial of the true God, and the death penalty in New York, 163

Denmark: an edict against the Moravian Brethren by the King of, 152; the loss of the market of, by English hatters in favour of the French, 241

de Pond, M., Hispaniola merchant, and the case of the Jupiter, 61

Deputies: in Massachusetts Bay, the reluctance of towns to send, to the Assembly, 29 n; the refusal to seat, in the New Hampshire Assembly from the unprivileged towns, 48; the election of, in Rhode Island, 67; in Connecticut, 83; in New York, 111; in New Jersey, 138; in Pennsylvania, 161–2; the religious complexion of the, in the Pennsylvania Assembly, 161–2, 176; in Delaware, right of affirmation denied to, 195

Deputy governor: of Massachusetts Bay, the powers of, 29; the election of, in Rhode Island, 67; in Connecticut, 83 n; in Pennsylvania and Delaware, 193

Derbyshire, England, iron-ore deposits of, 208

Desks, the manufacture and export of, by the people of New Hampshire, 53

Dice, the use of, forbidden in Connecticut, 94

Dickinson, Jonathan, on the quality of American iron, 219

Dinwiddie, Robert, Surveyor General of the Customs (later Deputy Governor of Virginia), estimates the value of the British colonial trade, 9–10; and of the Newfoundland fisheries, 254

Disallowance, the royal: of Massachusetts Bay legislation, 30; of Jersey legislation, 134; of Pennsylvania legislation, 176–7; of Delaware legislation, not practised, 194

Disease: in the American colonies, 8 n; on immigrant ships, 154

Dissenters, the, in Delaware, 204; see also Baptists, Quakers, Separatists

Dissolution of the Assembly: in Massachusetts Bay, 31; in Pennsylvania, 176 n

Distilleries: in Massachusetts Bay, in 1750, 16; the number of, in Newport, Rhode Island, 62, 66; in New York, 117

Dobbs, Arthur, later Governor of North Carolina, activities of, relating to Hudson Bay and search for a northwest passage, 243–4, author of Account of the Countries Adjoining Hudson Bay (1744)

Dobbs Galley, the, and the northwest-passage expedition, 244

Dogs, the use of, in Newfoundland, 252

Dollar, the Spanish-milled, shipped out of Massachusetts Bay, 14; the value of, in East and West Jersey, 128 n

Dominica, West Indies, and Rhode Island trade, 59

Dominion of New England, the, 28

Dongan, Thomas, Governor of New York, and the New Jersey boundary, 143

Douglas, Captain James, on the state of St. John's, Newfoundland, 250

Douglass, William: on shipbuilding at Boston, 6 n; on Boston as a commercial centre, 7 n; on the Massachusetts Bay debt, 10; on the white-pine trees, 39; on Connecticut shipping activities, 77 n; on the government of Connecticut, 78; on voting in Connecticut, 82; on the Connecticut code of 1750, 94; author of A Summary . . . of the British Settlements in America (1755)

Dover, county seat of Kent County, Delaware, 204

Dracut, New Hampshire, the dispute over the seating of deputies of, 48–9

Drake, Francis William, appointed Governor of Newfoundland, 259; commis-

Drake, Francis William (*continued*)
sioned to appoint commissioners for
the trial of capital offences, 263

Dress, in Pennsylvania, 171–2

Drinking at night: the punishment for,
in the Connecticut code of 1650, 91;
and the Connecticut code of 1784, 95

Drunkenness, the penalty for, in Connecticut, 91

Dudley, England, unemployment and
poor-rates at, 215

Dudley, Massachusetts Bay, fined for
neglect to send deputies, 29

Dudley, Joseph, a member of the New
England Council, 48

Dudley Castle, the decay of ironworks
about, 209

Dudley Furnace, the, and the smelting
of iron with coal, 209–10

Duke of York laws, the, origin of, and
description of, 163

Dukes County, Massachusetts Bay, slave
population of, 16

Dummer, Dr. Jeremiah, London agent
for Connecticut and Massachusetts
Bay: falls under Bolingbroke's influence, dismissed from his Connecticut
post, 97; author of *The Defence of the
New England Charters* (1721)

Dummer, Fort, New Hampshire: the
dispute over the garrisoning of, 46–9;
New Hampshire troops occupy, 49

Dunbar, David, Surveyor General of His
Majesty's Woods, 41; sells his post to
Benning Wentworth, 43

Dunkards, the: in Pennsylvania, 149; support the Quakers in office, 159

Dunkers, *see* Dunkards

Durham Iron Works, in Pennsylvania,
219

Durkee, John, of Bean Hill, Connecticut,
popular military leader, 89

Durlach, Germany, the unhappy lot in
Pennsylvania of immigrants from,
153–5

Dutch, the: of New York, 102–3; activities of, traders in Albany, 118–19; of
Holland, procure German emigrants,
153; purchase of indentured servants
by, landowners in Pennsylvania, 155;
activities of, in the settlement of Delaware, 184, 187, 202, 203; the success of, in curing cod, 250 *n;* the contribution of, to English colonial civilization, 281

Dutch iron ware, cost of, 217

Dutch Reformed Church, the: in New
York City, 116; in Albany, 119

Dutch West India Company, the, lands
in New York, granted by, 103

Dutchess County, New York, and land
riots, 107–8

Duties: the failure to pay, on sugar and
molasses, brought to Massachusetts
Bay, 17; to Rhode Island, 59–62; local
import, on Negroes in Pennsylvania,
173 *n;* on iron entering England, 211,
213–14, 225, 228; import, on beaver
skins into Great Britain, 238–9; British
import and export, on beaver skins, 242

Dye-woods, as an enumerated commodity, 291

Ears: the loss of, in the Connecticut code,
92; and the Pennsylvania code, 165

Earthenware, the export of, from Massachusetts Bay, 9

East Haddam, Connecticut, 75 *n*

East India, goods from, to Massachusetts
Bay, 9 *n*

East Main House, a Hudson's Bay Company post, 232

East New Jersey, characterized, 137

Ecclesiastical society, the, in Connecticut, 80–1, 85

Economic sectionalism, and the British
Empire, 287–9

Economic self-containment, and the British Empire, 293

Edes and Gill, printers of the *Boston
Gazette,* 27

Education: in New England, 27, 28; in
New York, 78; in reading for all in
Connecticut, 93; in New Jersey, 137;
in Philadelphia, 170

Edwards, Captain Richard, Governor of
Newfoundland, 259

Edwards, the Rev. Jonathan, pastor at
Northampton, Massachusetts Bay, and
the Great Awakening, 23–5; the repudiation of, by his congregation, 25

Elections: in Massachusetts Bay, 29 *n;*
in Rhode Island, 67; in Connecticut,
74, 83, 86, 87; in New York, 109; in
Pennsylvania, 161–2; in Delaware, 195

Electors, *see* Franchise

Eliot, Jared: on the failure of wheat crops
in Massachusetts Bay, 15 *n;* author of
Essays upon Field Husbandry . . .
(1748, 1760)

Élite: the influence of, in Massachusetts Bay, 32; in New Hampshire, 51; control of high offices in Connecticut by, 83; domination of political, social, and economic life by New York, 110–12; see also Aristocratic tendencies

Elizabeth Furnace, acreage covered by, 218

Elizabethtown, New Jersey: the New England background of, 137; the East New Jersey Proprietors and the lands of, 141; charges of frauds and abuses connected with the sale of lands of, 141

Elizer, Isaac, naturalization papers sought by, 56

Elk skins, brought out of Hudson Bay in 1748, 233

Ellery family, the, of Newport, 66

Ellery, William, Newport merchant, 63 n

Ellis, Henry: on the imports of York Fort on Hudson Bay, 232 n; the experiences of, and associates in attempting to discover the northwest passage, 244 n; author of A Voyage to Hudson's Bay by the Dobbs Galley and California in the Years 1746 and 1747 for Discovering a Northwest Passage (1749)

Emigrant ships, arrangements for German emigrants on board, 153–5

England: high cost of shipbuilding in, 7; exports from, to Massachusetts Bay, 9; concern of the people of, over Massachusetts Bay's activities in Newfoundland, 18, 258; religious latitudinarianism in, 23; absence of ship timber in, 40; trade between New York and, 116; exports to, and imports from Pennsylvania, 168; the iron industry in, 206–13; high level of poor-rates in some towns of, 215; exports of bar steel to New England from, 217; efforts by Parliament to protect the iron industry of, 219–24; hat-making and its decline in, 237–42; strong preference of English colonials for the institutions of, 281

English law, the decided preference of British colonials for, in the eighteenth century, 281

Engrossment, the, of fishing conveniences, by inhabitants of Newfoundland forbidden, 258

Entail of lands, the: in Massachusetts Bay, the repeal of a law involving,

Entail of lands (continued) 30 n; adoption of, by New York, in 1683, 112

Enumerated commodities: restrictions on the sale of, by the trade and navigation acts, 291; the list of, in 1750, 291

Episcopalians, see Anglicans

Eskimos, the, and Hudson Bay, 231

Essays upon Field Husbandry in New England and other Papers (1748–62), by Jared Eliot, 15 n

Essex County, Massachusetts Bay: population of, 15; standing of, in agriculture, 15; the slave population of, 16; number of towns within, 19

Essex County, New Jersey: representation of, in the Assembly, 138; land rioters in, 139, 140

Established Church, see Anglican Establishment and Congregational Establishment

Evangelical Church, popularity of, in Pennsylvania, 149

Evans, Lewis, Pennsylvania surveyor and map-maker: on the economical habits of the Pennsylvania Germans, 156 n; on the quality of the timber in the forests of Pennsylvania, 156 n; on the defects of the provincial government, 165–6 n; on the lack of durability of ships built in Pennsylvania, 167; on the Pennsylvania government, 175 n, 176 n; a description of the Pennsylvania land system by, 181–3; on the validity of the Maryland boundary claims, 192 n; on the Iron Act of 1750, 226; author of A Brief Account of Pennsylvania . . . (1753)

Ewing Mansion, Boston, 5

Excise, the: in Connecticut, 87; in Pennsylvania, amounts raised by, 174; the collectors of, appointed by the Pennsylvania Assembly, 176

Excise masters, the town, in Connecticut, the election and duties of, 87

Exports, British: to the colonies, 7, 9; decline in iron, to the North American colonies, 214; duties on iron, removed, 215; of bar steel to the New England ironmasters, 217; of stores and trade articles to Hudson Bay, 233–4; of beaver skins, wool, and hats to the continent, 242; to Newfoundland, 255

Exports, colonial: from Massachusetts Bay, 7, 8, 9–10; farm and fishery,

Exports, colonial: (continued)
compared, 14 n; of rum, 16; of cod, 18 n; from New Hampshire, 10 n; of white pine, 40–3, 52–3; from Rhode Island, 10 n; of provisions and horses, 10 n, 56–9; of rum, 59–66; from Connecticut, 10 n, 76; from New York, 10 n, 116, 117–19, 123; of provisions and timber from New Jersey, 127; from Pennsylvania, 10 n, 166–7, 173; from Delaware, 201, 203 n; of iron from Virginia, 216; of iron implements, from New England forges, 217; of iron ware, intercolonial, 219; of iron to England, 226–7; of Hudson Bay, 233, 242; of Newfoundland, 255, 256–8

Factories, the trading, on Hudson Bay, 231–2
Fairfield, Connecticut, the rating of, for taxation, 75 n
Fairfield County, Connecticut, meetings of freemen in, 83 n
Falmouth, England, early interest of, in the cod fisheries, 250 n
False testifying, capital law against, in Connecticut, 91; and the Connecticut code of 1784, 95
False witnessing, and the death penalty in New York, 163
Fane, Francis, legal adviser of the Board of Trade: comments upon the Connecticut law respecting freemen, 82 n; reports against the Pennsylvania convict law of 1742, 177
Faneuil, Peter, the activities of, 5, 18
Farmers: public aid to, in Rhode Island, 68–71; movement of small, from New York, 112, 113; in New Jersey, 127–8; in Pennsylvania, 173; in Delaware, 199
Farming: and the northern plantations, 3; in Massachusetts Bay, and wheat-raising, 15; importance of, 15–16; in New Hampshire, 51; in Rhode Island, 56; in Connecticut, 75–6; in New York, on the manors, 114; in New Jersey, 126; in Pennsylvania, 166; in Delaware, 200–1; absence of, in Hudson Bay area, 231, 233 n; absence of, on Newfoundland, 252
Farmington, Connecticut, the rating of, for taxation, 75 n
Farms: as distinguished from plantations, characteristic of the northern colonies,

Farms: (continued)
3; of Rhode Island, the varied size of, 57; desirability of small, in New York, 114; of Pennsylvania, the average size of and products of, 166
Felonies, capital: in Massachusetts Bay, 91; in Connecticut, in 1750, 92; in Pennsylvania, 165
Felons: laws imposing import duties on, in Massachusetts Bay, disallowed, 30 n; the Pennsylvania law of 1742 imposing duties on, reported for repeal, 177; Delaware legislates against importation of, 194–5; Maryland flooded with, 195
Felt-makers of London, Company of, petition for relief, 241
Fence viewers: in Connecticut, 85; the election of, and the duties of, 87
Fenchurch Street, London, Hudson's Bay Company's headquarters on, 236
Ferguson, Captain, Rhode Island slaver, 64
Fermor, Juliana, daughter of the Earl of Pomfret, marries Thomas Penn, 182
Ferryland, Newfoundland: George Calvert's efforts to settle at, 249, 266; a garrison stationed at, 251; the occupation of, by Hamilton and associates, 266
Finance, public: in Massachusetts Bay, 10–14; in New Hampshire, 46, 49; in Rhode Island, 68–72; in Connecticut, 90 n, 101; in New York, 120–1, 123; in New Jersey, 128–36; in Pennsylvania, 173–4, 176; in Delaware, 197, 199–200
Fines: the paying of, by Massachusetts Bay towns, 29 n; for cutting white pine without licence, the payment of heavy, 42; the punishment by, in Connecticut, 93
Finns, the: colonization of Delaware by, 184, 187, 202; contribution of, to colonial civilization, 281
Firelocks, to be possessed by all Connecticut householders, 88
Fish, the export value of, from Massachusetts Bay, 9; see also Cod, Mackerel, Salmon
Fisheries, the: and the northern colonies, 4; of Massachusetts Bay, 14 n, 17–18; of Newfoundland and the Grand Banks, 248–63; free trade in salt to be

Fisheries (*continued*)
used in the, of Newfoundland and North America, 291
Fish-stages, in Newfoundland, 252, 253, 258, 260
Fitch, Thomas, of Norwalk, Connecticut: refuses the London agency, 99; as Deputy Governor of Connecticut, acts as legal advisor of the Elizabethtown, New Jersey, rioters, 142 *n*
Flakes: for the cod fisheries, 253; Newfoundland, protected by law, 258
Flamborough House, a Hudson's Bay Company post at, 231
Flannel, export of, from England to Sweden, 220 *n*
Flax: exported by Connecticut, 76; the growing of, in New York, 117
Flaxseed, export of, from Pennsylvania, 166 *n*
Fleet, Thomas, a proprietor of the *Boston Weekly Rehearsal,* 27
Fletcher, Benjamin, Governor of New York: commissioned to command the Connecticut militia, 96; extravagant land grants by, 104
Flour: the production of, in the colonies, 4; in New York, 117; export trade in, injured by poor quality of, 118; the export of, from Pennsylvania, 166; from Delaware, 203 *n*
Food: surpluses of, from other colonies sent to Massachusetts Bay, 15; Massachusetts Bay and the production of, 15, 15 *n;* export of, from Rhode Island, 56; the raising of, in Connecticut, 76; in New York, 117–18; in New Jersey, 127; export of, from Pennsylvania, 166; from Delaware, 201; sent to Hudson Bay, 233 *n;* to Newfoundland, 252
Fordham Manor, New York, 102
Forest of Dean, the: qualities of the iron of, 208; the advantages of, for iron production, 210
Forests: of New England, 7; the white pine, of New Hampshire, 39–41; pine and cedar, of New Jersey, 127, 141, 167 *n;* of Pennsylvania, 166; the white cedar of Pennsylvania, 170 *n;* of England, importance of, to iron production, 208–13; the shifting of the iron industry to the, of Wales, 209
Forfeiture of goods, the, and the Upland code, 163; *see also* Felonies
Forges: a lack of, in Rhode Island, re-

Forges: (*continued*)
ported in 1750, 66 *n;* in Connecticut, 77; in Pennsylvania, 167; the number of, in England, 207 *n;* the idleness of, in England and Wales, 214; the number of, in New England in 1733, 217; in the middle Colonies, in 1750, 218
Fort à la Corne, on the Saskatchewan, a French trading post, 246
Fort Bourbon, Cedar Lake, a French trading post, 246
Fort Dauphin, Lac des Prairies, a French trading post, 246
Fort Dummer, *see* Dummer
Fort George, Goat Island, Narragansett Bay, fires upon His Majesty's cutter *St. John,* 62
Fort La Jouquière, a temporary French trading post, 246
Fort La Reine, on the Assiniboine, a French trading post, 246
Fort Maurepas, on the Winnipeg, a French trading post, 246
Fort Paskoyac (Poskoyac or Poskioac), on the Saskatchewan, a French trading post, 246
Fort Richmond, a Hudson's Bay Company post, 232
Fort St. Louis, on the Saskatchewan, a French trading post, 246
Forts: the demand for, by the people of Delaware, 186; in the Hudson Bay territory, 231–2
Foster, Thomas, one of the key men in shaping Massachusetts Bay legislation, 32
Fowey, England, the early interest of, in the cod fisheries, 250 *n*
Fox, Charles James, supports the British trade and navigation system, 290
Fox skins: brought out of Hudson Bay in 1748, 233; sought by trappers in Newfoundland, 255
"Frame," the Pennsylvania, of 1701, and the eighteenth-century provincial government, 175
Franchise, the: in Massachusetts Bay, 29 *n;* in Rhode Island, 55, 68; in Connecticut, 74, 81–3; in New York, 111–12, 116 *n;* in New Jersey, 138 *n;* in Pennsylvania, 176; in Delaware, 195–6; of freemen or freeholders in all colonies except Newfoundland and Nova Scotia, 278; and the disabilities of Catholics and Jews in some colonies, 282–3

Franklin, Benjamin, editor of the *Pennsylvania Gazette,* the experiments of, with electricity, 171

Franklin, James, editor of the *New England Courant,* 26

Fredericksburg, Virginia, ironworks at, 216

Freeholders, political control and participation of, in New York elections, 109; *see also* Franchise, Landowners

Freemasons, in Pennsylvania, 149

Freemen: in Rhode Island, the important powers of, 67; the meetings of, at Newport, 67; the qualifications for, 68, 69; voting numbers of, 69; in Connecticut, the qualifications for, and responsibilities of, 81–3; the proportion of population enjoying rights of, 82; the conservative leanings of, 83–4; voting privilege of Connecticut, 86; of Delaware, 193; qualifications for, 195

Freethinkers, in Pennsylvania, 149

French, the: capture of Canso Island by, 34; the return of Louisbourg to, 34; negotiations with, 34–5; in the West Indies, 58–62; activities of, in the Delaware Bay and River, 196–7, 203; assaults and capture of Hudson's Bay Company posts by, 232; competition with, in the Hudson Bay trade, 234–6; in temporary control of the Hudson's Bay Company posts, 237; the thriving beaver-hat industry of, 237–8, 239, 240, 241, 242; the activities of, about Lake Winnipeg, 246–7; privileges enjoyed by, in Newfoundland, 249; the advantages enjoyed by, in the cod fishery, 249–50; *see also* French sugar islands, West Indies

French sugar islands: Massachusetts Bay trade with, 17; Rhode Island trade with, 58–62; *see also* West Indies, French

French trading posts: and the Albany Indian trade, 118; the competition of, with those of the Hudson's Bay Company, 234–5; 246

Frielinghausen, the Rev. Theodorus, Albany pastor, 119

Fur trade, the: with the Indians in Massachusetts Bay, 16; in New York, 118–19; in Pennsylvania, 167; of the Hudson's Bay Company, 230–6

Furnaces: none reported for Rhode Island in 1750, 66 *n;* steel, in Connecticut, 77; in New York, 114, 117; in Pennsylvania, 167; in England, 207; the "high," in 1750, 207 *n;* in Virginia and Maryland, 216; steel, in New England, 217; in New Jersey and Pennsylvania, 218–19; the setting-up of steel, in America forbidden, 223

Furniture: the manufacture of, in New Hampshire, 53; the sale of, in Virginia and in the Carolinas, 53

Furs: the export of, from Massachusetts Bay, 9; New York trade in, with Indians, 118; the value of, at Oswego, 119; the export of, from Pennsylvania, 166 *n;* and the Pennsylvania Indian trade, 167; and the Hudson's Bay Company, 230–31, 237; placing of American, Asian, and African, on "enumerated" list, 238, 291

Gagging, and the Upland code of Pennsylvania, 163

Gaols: in Connecticut, taxes raised for upkeep of, 90 *n;* county taxes in Delaware and the building of, 200 *n*

Gardner, Captain, Rhode Island slaver, at Anamabo, 64

Garments, beaver skins used for lining of, 237; *see also* Dress

Garrisons, in Newfoundland, 250–1

Gaugers, in Connecticut, the election and duties of, 87

Gee, Joshua, Shrewsbury ironmaster and author of *The Trade and Navigation of Great Britain Considered* (1729), on the low cost of iron production in America, 222

Geese, the straying of, and the Connecticut town meetings, 81

General Assembly, *see* Assembly

General Court, *see* Assembly

George Augustus, King of Great Britain and Ireland and Elector of Hanover: the intolerant attitude of, as Elector and the tolerant attitude of, as King, toward the Moravian Brethren, 152–3

Georgia: the trusteeship of, about to lapse, 74 *n;* the Anglican Establishment and, 282; disabilities of Roman Catholics in, 283; western charter limits of, 286; the production of silk in, subsidized, 292

German Reformed Church, the: in New York City, 116; in Philadelphia, 170

Germanna, Virginia, ironworks at, 216

Germans: exodus of, from New York, due to the unfavourable conditions, 113; the numerical preponderance of, in Pennsylvania, 149, 150; the immigration of, into Pennsylvania in 1750, 150–2; into Maryland, the Carolinas, and Nova Scotia, 152; the persecution of, at home, 152; the economic distress of, at home, 152; lured by the Newlanders, 153; the difficulties of the journey of, to America, 153; the cost of passage of, 155; the sale of, to pay for passage, 155; services exacted of indentured, 156; the activities of, after the end of services, 156 n; the principal source for indentured labour in Pennsylvania in 1750, 157; the distribution of, in Pennsylvania, 158–9; the early lack of political consciousness of, 158–9; the increased importance of, among the electorate in 1750, 159; a demand for the disfranchisement of, 161; the condescending attitude of the English-speaking people toward, 172; in Delaware, 203; the contribution of, to English colonial civilization, 281

Germantown, Pennsylvania, site of the first colonial paper mill, 26 n

Germany; unfavourable conditions in, 152–3; the loss of the market of, by English hatters in favour of the French, 241

Gilbert, Sir Humphrey, the attempt of, to colonize Newfoundland, 249

Gilpin family, the, of Pennsylvania, establish paper and flour mills in Delaware, 202 n

Ginger, as an enumerated commodity, 291

Ginseed root, export of, from Pennsylvania, 166 n

Glamorgan County, Wales, waste and destruction of woods in, 210

Glassware, exports of, from England to Sweden, 220 n

Glen, James, Governor of South Carolina, the instructions to the successor of, altered, 277

Gloucester, Massachusetts Bay, the interest of, in whaling, 18

Gloucester, Rhode Island, the population of, and voters of, 69

Gloucester County, New Jersey, representatives of, in the Assembly, 138

Gloucestershire, iron from the Forest of Dean in, 208; waste and destruction of woodlands in, 210

Goat Island, in Narragansett Bay, 62

Godfrey, Caleb, master of the sloop *Hare*, 64

Goelet, Captain Francis, of New York, a description of Boston by, 5

Goffe, Major, of New Hampshire, the report of, on the lands of the upper Connecticut, 49

Gold, the New England trade in rum for, 63

Gold Coast, the, Africa, slave marts along, 64

Gordon, Lord Adam: on Boston, 6 n; on New York City, 116 n; on Philadelphia, 169 n; author of "Journal of an Officer of the 66th Regiment (1764–5)"

Gordon, John, *see* Earl of Sutherland

Gordon, Patrick, Lieutenant and Deputy Governor of Pennsylvania and Delaware: on the sources of the provincial revenue, 174; report of, on the relative importance of New Castle, Delaware, 201 n

Gorges, Sir Ferdinando, grant of lands to, by the Council of New England, 47

Gorton, Samuel, of Rhode Island, and soul liberty, 54

Gotha, Germany, an edict against the Moravian Brethren by the Duke of, 152

Government, the: of Massachusetts Bay, 28–38; of New Hampshire, 44–7; of Rhode Island, 67–73; of Connecticut, 74, 78; of New York, 110–12; of New Jersey, 131–2, 145–8; of Pennsylvania, 174–83; of Delaware, 193, 195; of Newfoundland, 258–64

Governor, the: of Massachusetts Bay, the powers of, 29–31; the activities of, 44–51; of New Hampshire, a family government while Benning Wentworth acted as, 52; of Rhode Island, the election of, 67; of Connecticut, the lack of authority of, 74; the method of choosing, 83 n; of New York, the loss of power of, 120–2; of New Jersey, the difficulties confronting, 131–2; 146–8; of Pennsylvania, the difficult position of, 176; the issue over the binding power of royal instructions to,

Governor (*continued*)

177; of Delaware, no specific commission or instructions given to, relating to the colony, 190; harmonious relations between the Assembly and, 193, 197; of Newfoundland, the royal instructions of, 258, 260; list of those holding office as, 1748–50, 259; brief period of tenure in office of, 259; extension of powers of, 263; early appointees to the office of, 267; Lord Baltimore seeks power to appoint, 268

Governors, colonial: the trial of, accused of crimes, might be held in England, 275; the commissions and instructions to, as basis of the constitutions in the royal colonies, 276; the power of the Assemblies exercised to curb the authority of, 278; the veto power of most of the, 278; pressures brought to bear on, by the Assemblies, 278

Graham, Andrew, factor at York Fort and Severn House, author of "Remarks on Hudson Bay's Trade . . . , 1769," 235 *n*

Grain, *see* Cereals

Grammar schools, in Massachusetts Bay, decline in number of, 27

Grand jurymen, of Connecticut, to suppress vice and enforce the law of the Sabbath, 93

Great Awakening, the: and Jonathan Edwards, 23–5; and New England Congregationalism, 25–6, 79–80; opposed and supported by many Harvard graduates, 28 *n*; the influence of, upon New Hampshire, 51; upon Rhode Island, 55; upon Connecticut, 79, 80

Great Britain: resemblance to and contrast with New England, 8; the value of commodities shipped from, to the colonies, 9–10, 116; the merchants of, secure ships built in Massachusetts Bay, 6; and at Philadelphia, 167; the royal navy of, and merchants of, dependent on America for masting, 40; the extension of the criminal laws of, to Pennsylvania, 165; importance of the Newfoundland fisheries to the maintenance of the naval power of, 253–8; the decline of the powers of the King in, 273; increase in the public debt of, 290; *see also* England, Wales, Scotland

Great Lakes, the, superiority of Hudson Bay fur to those from, 237

Great Law, the, and Pennsylvania, 163

Great Nine Partners' Patent, the, in New York, 102; the creation of, 104 *n*

Great Seal, the: of England, not affixed to royal patent to the Duke of York for Delaware, 185 *n;* of Delaware, defective, 191 *n*

Great War for the Empire, the participation of Delaware in, 197

Great Yarmouth, England, petition from, in support of Arthur Dobbs's attack on the Hudson's Bay Company, 245

Green men: requirement of ship masters sailing to Newfoundland to enlist, 252; and the Newfoundland fisheries, 257; the employment of, on the Island of Newfoundland, 260, 262

Greenwich, Rhode Island, shares of the "banks" allotted to, 68–73

Greyhound, the, carries Virginia iron to Bristol, 216

Gridley, Jeremiah, editor of *The Weekly Rehearsal,* 27

Griffin, Robert, testifies at a parliamentary hearing, 233

Grimington's Island, Labrador, and the boundary of the Hudson's Bay Company territory, 236

Grist mills: in Massachusetts Bay, 15; in Delaware, 202; a characteristic in the iron plantations, 218

Guadeloupe, importance of, as a French possession, 287

Guinea, Africa: and the slave trade along the coast of, 9, 63; rum the chief article sent to, from America, 16, 63–6; trade relations of New York with, 117

Gun barrels, iron of Shropshire used for production of, 208

Hæmatite ore, the mining of, in Cumberland, England, 208

Hale, Robert, on Portsmouth, New Hampshire, society, 53

Halfway covenant, the, and the Congregational Church of New England, 21, 22

Halifax, George Montagu Dunk, 2nd Earl of, the hostility of, toward corporate and proprietorial charters, 272

Halter, the wearing of a, and adultery in Connecticut, 92

Hamilton, Dr. Alexander, author of an itinerarium, on Wilmington, Delaware, 201 n

Hamilton, Andrew, Lieutenant Governor of Pennsylvania and Delaware, and the issue of union between the two areas, 188–9

Hamilton, James, Lieutenant Governor of Pennsylvania: on the freedom of the people from taxation, 174 n; resigns his post by reason of disputes with the Assembly, 183

Hamilton, James Hamilton, 3rd Marquess of, later Duke of: proprietary rights over Newfoundland granted to, and associates, 266; dispossesses Lord Baltimore of Avalon, 266; loss of Avalon rights by, 267

Hamlet, Captain, Rhode Island slaver, at Anamabo, 64

Hammond, Captain, Rhode Island slaver, at Anamabo, 65 n

Hampshire, England, source of supply of iron ore for furnaces of, 208

Hampshire County, Massachusetts Bay: comparative agricultural county statistics and, 15; slave population of, 16; the number of towns within, 19; claims lands within the Livingston Manor, 107

Hancock, Thomas, Boston merchant: general activities of, 7, 8; illegal traffic by, 8

Handicrafts, in the northern colonies, 4; see also Chests of drawers, Furniture

Hanover, the Elector of, a proclamation against the Moravian Brethren by, 152

Harbour admirals: in Newfoundland, limited to English shipmasters, 258; the friction between the justices of the peace and, 261; the neglect of duties by, 262

Harbours, the jurisdiction over, in Newfoundland, 258

Hard money, adopted as a basis by Massachusetts Bay in 1749, 10–14; see also Specie

Hardenburgh Patent, the, New York, 103; the creation of, 104 n

Hardware: the widespread distribution of Birmingham, in 1747, 207; the curtailment of England's great export trade in, 213, 214; the exportation of New England, 217; the excellent quality of American, 219; failure of the at-

Hardware: (continued) tempt to limit the production of American, 228

Hardwicke, Philip Yorke, 1st Earl of, Lord Chancellor, decision by, in the Penn-Baltimore dispute, 198–9

Hare, the, a Rhode Island slave ship, 64

Harrisons, the, among the New York aristocracy, 110

Hartford, Connecticut: a joint capital, 74; the population of, 74 n; the rating of, for taxation, 75 n

Hartford County, Connecticut, meetings of freemen in, 83 n

Harvard College: the growing liberalism of, in the eighteenth century, 27–8, 280; and the Great Awakening, 28

Hasselwood, Captain, brings Germans to Pennsylvania, 151

Hat Act, the, of 1732, 239–40; objectives of, 239; failure of, to deter colonial hat manufacture, 240; failure of, to restore the English hat industry, 240

Hats: the production of, in England, 237–42; the export of, from New England, 239; the prohibition against colonial exports of, in 1732, 239–40, 275; limitations on the colonial manufacture of, 275

Hatters: opulence of English master, 237; competition of English and French, 238–9; the Hat Act of 1732 and American, 239–40; petitions and memorials to Parliament by English, 241; compromise legislation of Parliament and the, 241–2

Haverhill, Massachusetts Bay, families from, settle at Penacook, 20–1

Haverhill, New Hampshire, the dispute, over seating deputies of, 48–9

Hayes River, the, Hudson Bay, location of York Fort on, 231; expedition in search of a northwest passage winters on, 244

Haywards: in Connecticut, the election of, 85; the duties of, 87

Health officer, the lucrative post of, in Pennsylvania, 176

Heath, Colonel Joseph, one of the key men in shaping Massachusetts Bay legislation, 32

Heath, Sir Robert, the patent to, to Carolina, 271

Heathcotes, the, among the New York aristocracy, 109

Heilbronn, Württemberg, Germany, the journey from, to America, by German emigrants described, 153

Hemp, premiums on American-made, 220

Hempstead, New York, the adoption of the Duke of York laws at, 163

Henday, Anthony, the journey of, into the country of the Blackfeet, 235

Hendry, Anthony, see Henday

Henley, Sir Robert (later Attorney General), the opinion of, adverse to the claims of Baltimore, 270

Henley House, a Hudson's Bay Company post, 231–2

Herefordshire, England, the waste and destruction of woods in, 210

Heretics, a Connecticut act for suppressing, disallowed by the Privy Council, 100

"Herrnhuters," see Moravian Brethren

High Court of Chancery, the, see Court of Chancery, the High

Hill, Lieutenant, of His Majesty's cutter St. John, in charge of the custom-house, fired upon in Narragansett Bay, 62

Hill, Thomas, a circular letter by, on the Iron Act, 226

Hill, Captain William, placed in charge of Avalon by Baltimore, 266

Hispaniola: the shipping of Spanish dollars from Boston to, 14; Rhode Island trade with, 59, 60, 61; importance of, as a French possession, 287

History of New-Hampshire . . . (1813), by Jeremy Belknap, 42

History of the Province of Massachusetts Bay (1798), by G. R. Minot

Hobby, Sir Charles, receiver of New Hampshire lands, 47

Hobby, John, receives half of Col. Allen's New Hampshire claim, 48

Holland: German emigration to America via, 154; skill in beaver-hat making brought to England from, 237; importation of beaver felt into, 238; importation of English hats to, 241

Holland, Henry Rich, 1st Earl of, proprietary rights over Newfoundland granted to, and associates, 266 n

Homes: in Boston, 5; in New York City, 115; in Albany, 118; in Philadelphia, 169

Honeyman family, the, of Newport, Rhode Island, 66

Hopewell Furnace, restoration of, 219 n

Hopkins, Stephen: a leading Rhode Island merchant (later Governor of Rhode Island), 58; and leader of a political faction, 67 n

Hopson, Colonel, Governor of Nova Scotia, instructions to, against the opening of collieries, 227

Horseneck, Essex County, New Jersey, the dispute over the lands of, 139

Horses: the export of, from Massachusetts Bay, 9; counties chiefly concerned in the raising of, in Massachusetts Bay, 15; the export of, from Rhode Island, 56, 57, 60; from Connecticut, 76; used in tillage in Pennsylvania, 156 n; the raising of, in Pennsylvania, 166; the scarcity of, in Newfoundland, 262

Hospitality, of the people of Pennsylvania, 166

House of Commons, the: influence of the Connecticut London agents upon the proceedings of, 100; resolutions of, against colonial bills of credit, 130; considers the petitions of English ironmasters, 221–2; and of English hatters, 241

House of Representatives, the: of Massachusetts Bay, 11, 31, 33, 36; of New Jersey, and the bills of credit bill of 1742, 131

House-breaking, a capital crime in Pennsylvania, 165

Hubbard, Thomas, a key figure in shaping legislation in Massachusetts Bay, 32; Speaker of House of Representatives of Massachusetts Bay, 36 n

Hudson Bay: a description of, in the eighteenth century, 231–2; trading posts in 1750 upon, 231–2; Indian groups resorting to, 234–5; superior quality of furs from, 237; effects of French temporary control of, 238; report of Parliamentary committee concerning, 245

Hudson River, the: manors in the area of, 102; land disputes east of, 108; as a boundary of New Jersey, 143

Hudson Strait: ice floes and icebergs in, 231; attempts to discover a northwest passage by way of, 244

Hudson's Bay Company, the: effect of the posts of, on the New York fur

Hudson's Bay Company (continued)
trade, 118; the charter of, 231; the activities of, in the 1740's, and value of its exports and imports, 233; the Indian trade and the vast region exploited by, 234–5; the extent of territory claimed by, 235–6; the London activities of, 236, 237; the great profits of, 242; attempts to overthrow the monopoly of, 242–5; the petition of, in defence of its conduct of affairs, 245; the powerful position of, in 1750, 245–7

Hudson's Bay House, a description of, 236

Huguenots, in New York City, 116; and the English beaver hat manufacture, 237; the contribution of, to English colonial civilization, 281

Humanism, development of the new, in Massachusetts Bay, 28

Hume, Benjamin, Jamaica Receiver General of Customs, seizes the Jupiter, in Jamaica waters, 61

Hundreds, the, as administrative divisions in Delaware, 195

Hunter, Robert, Governor of New York and New Jersey: the failure of the attempt by, to produce naval stores, 113 n; secures general appropriations for a five-year period, 121; the instructions of, as to equal import duties for the two provinces, 128 n

Hunterdon County, New Jersey, representation of, in the Assembly, 138; the spread of land riots to, 140–1; rioters in, seek protection from Connecticut, 142

Huske, Ellis, founder of the Boston Weekly Post Boy, 27

Hutchinson, Thomas, the plan by, for a currency system, 12; the education of, 28

Hutton, William, appointed Deputy Governor of Avalon, Newfoundland, 267

Idolatry, the capital law of 1650 against, in Connecticut, 91, 92

Immigration: into North America from Germany, 150–1; hardships involved in, 152, 153–4; into Pennsylvania from Ireland, 157; into Newfoundland, 249, 251

Immorality: laws governing, in Connecticut, 90–3; in the Duke of York laws,

Immorality: (continued)
163; English laws against, to be enforced by the Governor in Newfoundland, 260

Import duties, colonial: on Negroes and felons forbidden in Massachusetts Bay, 30 n; to be the same in New York and New Jersey, 128; high, on convicts entering Delaware, 194; English, lowering of, on beaver, 242

Imports, colonial: of Massachusetts Bay, in 1743, 8–9; the great value of, from England, 9; figures on, of Pennsylvania, the Jerseys, New York, Rhode Island, Connecticut, New Hampshire, and Nova Scotia, in 1743, 9; the unreliability of figures relating to, in the eighteenth century, 9 n; of Massachusetts Bay, of subsistence provisions from southern colonies, 15; of Connecticut from Boston and New York, 77–8; of New York, 116; of Pennsylvania, 167–8; of bar steel by the New England ironmasters, 217; of Hudson Bay, 233–4; of Newfoundland, 255

Imports of Great Britain: of vessels from New England, 6 n; of masts from New Hampshire, 40–4; from New York, 118–19; of timber from New Jersey, 127; of ships from Pennsylvania, 167; of American iron, 226; of iron from Sweden, Russia, and Spain, 211; of furs from Hudson Bay, 230, 233–4; of fish and other commodities from Newfoundland, 254–5

Imprisonment, in Connecticut, 91

Income taxes, in Pennsylvania, 173

Indentured servants: on the New York manors, 114; in Pennsylvania, means and cost of obtaining, 155; character of the services of, 155–6; Germans enter voluntarily into the ranks of, 156; unsatisfactory nature of Ulster Scots as, 157; problem created in Delaware by the enlistment of, in the armed forces, 196 n, 197 n; opportunities offered to, in the colonies after the period of service, 280

Independent Advertiser, the, Boston news sheet, 27

Independent Reflector, the, New York organ of the Livingston faction, 112 n

Indian deeds, secured by New Jersey squatters, 139

Indian trade, the: Albany as a chief

Indian trade (continued)
centre of, 118; New York, adversely affected by competition in, 118; importance to New York of, of Oswego, 119; profitable nature of, 119; the annual value of, 119; dishonest practices and, 119, 120; strict regulation of, by the Hudson's Bay Company, 234; a description of, 234–5; brandy and, 234; the influence of the French competition upon, 234–5; the variation in prices offered in, 234; native groups involved in, 235; regions involved in, 235–6; the difficulty of co-ordinating, 235; French and, 246

Indians: on Maine border, threatening attitude of, 34; among the population of Rhode Island towns, 69 n; in Connecticut, exempted from military service, 88; participation of the Far West, Plains and Blackfeet, in the Hudson's Bay Company trade, 235; no attempt by Hudson's Bay Company to civilize or Christianize the, 235

Indigo: importation of, into Rhode Island, 59; as an enumerated commodity, 291; the production of, promoted by bounties, 291; an export staple of South Carolina, 292

Industry: in Massachusetts Bay, 6, 14, 15, 16, 217, 239; in New Hampshire, 53; in Rhode Island, 66, 217–18; in Connecticut, 77, 218; in New York, 114, 117, 218, 239, 240; in Pennsylvania, 166–7, 206, 218; in New Jersey, 218; in England, the iron, 206–13, 220–9; the beaver hat, 237–42

Ingersoll, Jared, Connecticut lawyer: the education of, 28; accepts the London agency for Connecticut, 100

Inglis, Charles, the Reverend, on the condition of churches in Kent County, Delaware, 204 n

Inhabitant, town, the legal meaning of the term in Connecticut, 84–5

Innes, James, advocate of the Vice-Admiralty Court of Jamaica, and the case of the Jupiter, 61

Inshore fishing, of Newfoundland, a description of, 254–5

Instructions, royal: forbidding Massachusetts Bay to levy import duties on Negroes and felons, 30; to the Governor of Massachusetts Bay, 31; to the Governor of New Hampshire for

Instructions, royal: (continued)
the representation of New Hampshire towns, 48; to the Governor of New York, respecting exorbitant New York land grants, 108–9, 121 n, 124; to all royal governors, relating to bills of credit, 130–1; to the Governor of New Jersey on paper money, 130, 131, 134–5; questions involving the binding force of, to the Deputy Governor of Pennsylvania, 177; to the Governor of Newfoundland, 260–1; as bases for the constitutions of royal colonies, 276; striking similarities and differences in, issued to royal governors, 277

Insurance policies on ships, 10, 168 n, 292

Interest of Great Britain in Supplying Herself with Iron Impartially Considered (1747, 1750), 219 n

Intestacy law, the, of Connecticut: appeal against, to the Privy Council, 98; disapproved, 100

Intoxicants: the drinking of, and Connecticut law, 95; the sale of, forbidden in Newfoundland, 260 n; see also Rum

Ipswich, Essex County, represented in Massachusetts Bay Assembly, 32

Ireland: the export of provisions and timber to, from New Jersey, 127; the British government offers encouragement to, to increase its iron production, 211; freedom of trade of the colonies with, covering certain items, 291

Irishmen, native: small number of, in Pennsylvania, 149; as settlers in Delaware, 202–3; large numbers of, in Newfoundland, 251, 262, 264; the reluctance of, to take the oath of allegiance, 262; lawlessness of, in Newfoundland, 264; contribution of, to English colonial civilization, 281; see also Ulster Scots

Iron, American: the production and processing of, in the colonies, 4, 16, 77, 206, 215–19; in Rhode Island, 66 n, 217–18; in Connecticut, 77, 218; in New York, 114, 117, 218; in Delaware, 201; in Pennsylvania, 206, 218–19; the agitation in England for curbing the production of, and the bills of 1719 and 1738, 214–24; in Massachusetts Bay, 215, 217; in Virginia, 216; in Maryland, 216; in New Jersey, 218; desire for, in England, 220; Act of 1750

Iron, American: (*continued*)
encourages importation of crude, 223;
restrictions placed on the processing
and manufacture of, in the colonies,
223–4, 275; export of, to Great Britain,
226; the Act of 1750 restricting the
manufacturing of, 226–7; the Act of
1757, relating to, 228; efforts to secure
a bounty on the importation into Great
Britain of, 228

Iron, English: the production of, 206–14,
219–29; fear of the decline in Great
Britain of the processing and sale of,
206–7, 214–15; the significance of, in
British economy, 207; the history of
the working of, 207–8; essentials for
the production of, in the eighteenth
century, 208–9; growing demands of
the fabricators of, 210; the dependence of England upon foreign, 210–11;
use of coal in the production of, 210–
11; problems of supply and demand
for, 211–12; causes for the decline in
England in the production of crude,
211; duties on foreign and plantation,
211, 213–14; dangers involved in England's dependence upon foreign, 211,
213–14; the problem of adequate wood
supplies for, 212–13

Iron Act of 1750, the: as an example of
British imperial economic regulation,
206; criticism of, 206; the circumstances leading to the passing of, 206–
25; provisions of, 225; ineffectiveness
of, 226–8; amendment of, 228; reasons
for failure of, 228–9

Iron Hill, Delaware, iron works constructed at, 201

Iron ore: types of, in England, 208; treatment of crude, 210

Ironware: Massachusetts Bay production
and export of, 9, 16, 217; decreasing
demand for English, from the colonies,
214–15; excellent quality of American,
219

Ironworkers: the numbers of, in England, 207, 224; unemployment among,
214; inducements to encourage, in Virginia, 216; in Massachusetts Bay, 217

Ironworks: in Eastern Connecticut, 77;
the distribution of, in England and
Wales, 207; in Maryland and Virginia,
216; a description of, in Pennsylvania,
218

Iroquois Indians, the, and the New York
fur trade, 119

Isle of Wight, England, and the German
emigrant ships, 154

Isle Royale, *see* Cape Breton

Italy, the loss of the market of, by the
English hatters in favour of the French,
241; exportation of cod to, from Newfoundland, 250; and the demand for
Newfoundland cod, 254

Itinerants, the warning-out of, in Connecticut, 85

Jackson, Richard, member of Parliament,
takes over the Connecticut London
agency in 1760, 100

Jaffrey, George, President of the New
Hampshire Council and Treasurer, 52;
his relationship to Benning Wentworth,
52

Jails, *see* Gaols

Jamaica: action in the vice-admiralty
court of, 60–1; the great American
slave mart, 65; exports to, from Delaware, 203 *n;* the demand of, for
wrought iron, 222; the government of,
276; commissions and instructions issued to the governors of, 277; the religious establishment of, 282; political
disabilities of Jews in, 283; laws relating to Negro slaves in, 285–6

"Jamaica" fish: the importance of, in the
economy of Massachusetts Bay, 16, 17;
the West India demand for, 16, 17;
secured from Newfoundland, 16, 17,
254

James, Captain, Rhode Island slaver, at
Anamabo, 64

Jamestown, Rhode Island, a share in the
"banks" allotted to, 68–73

Jays, the, among the New York aristocracy, 110

Jefferies collection of manuscripts, the,
216

Jepson, Captain, Rhode Island slaver, at
Anamabo, 64

Jews: leading role played by, in Rhode
Island, 56; political disabilities of, in
Rhode Island, 56, 283; in New York,
116; toleration of, in Pennsylvania, 149;
acquire wealth in Jamaica and Rhode
Island, 283

Johnson, Dr. Samuel, pastor of the Stratford, Connecticut, Anglican church, becomes the first president of King's College, of New York, 78

Johnson, William Samuel, a Connecticut lawyer (later Connecticut London agent), the education of, 28

Johnston family, the, of Newport, Rhode Island, 66

Jones, Sir William, legal adviser to Charles II, 47

Joneses, the, among the New York aristocracy, 110

Judges: the appointment of, in Massachusetts Bay, 31; members of the Wentworth family as, in New Hampshire, 52; the election of, in Rhode Island, 67; justices of the peace as, in Pennsylvania, 164–5 n; of oyer and terminer appointed in Newfoundland, 263

Judicial system: of Connecticut, 89–90; of Delaware, 193, 193 n

Juncook (Jun Cook), New Hampshire, the fortified post of, 46

Jupiter, the, Rhode Island sloop, the vice-admiralty case involving, 60–1

Juries, the refusal of New Jersey, to convict rioters, 140

Justices of the peace: the election of, in Rhode Island, 67; exemption from service in the train bands of, in Connecticut, 88; the appointment of, in Connecticut, 89–90; power of, in Connecticut, 90, 90 n; the lack of qualification of, in Pennsylvania, 165 n; of Newfoundland, the duties of, 260; friction between the harbour admirals and, 261; the qualifications of, 261–2; weakness of, 262

Kakiate Patent, the, in New York, 103; the creation of, 104 n

Kalm, Peter: a description of New York City by, 115–16; on the New York fur trade, 119; on the oaks of Pennsylvania, 167; a description of Philadelphia by, 169; author of *Travels into North America* (1772)

Keeling, Richard, on unemployment at Stourbridge and Wolverhampton, 214–15

Keene, New Hampshire, troops of the province occupy the post at, 49

Keith, Sir William, Lieutenant Governor of Pennsylvania: approval by, of colonial legislation in contempt of proprietorial instructions, 176; petition of Delaware inhabitants to, 190; action

Keith, Sir William (*continued*) of, relative to Delaware legal documents, 191; an act during the administration of, respecting Delaware representatives, 195–6

Kelsey, Henry, the journey of, to the Indians of the Plains, 235

Kennedy, Archibald, a member of the New York Council and Collector of Customs: on the prohibition of colonial hat exports, 240 n; author of *Observations on the Importance of the Northern Colonies under Proper Regulations* (1750)

Kent County, Delaware: draft of grant of, to Penn, by James II, 186 n; representation of, in the Assembly, 193; religious affiliation of settlers in, 204; various churches and meeting houses in, 204 n

Kent County, England, additional ironworks forbidden within, 209

Kersies, export of, from England to Sweden, 220 n

Key keepers, the town, in Connecticut, 87

Kidnapping: revision of the capital law against, in Connecticut, 91, 95; and the death penalty in New York, 163

Killingsworth, Connecticut, steel production at, 77

King George's War: Massachusetts Bay receives reimbursement for expenses incurred in, 10; desolation of New England settlements by French Indians during, 120; the policy of neutrality in, pursued by the New York Assembly, 122; the Pennsylvania commerce harassed by privateers during, 196–7

King's attorney: the office of, in Connecticut, 90; in other colonies, 90 n

King's College, New York, Dr. Samuel Johnson, the first president of, 78

King's Province, Rhode Island, and the plantation system, 3; the dispute over, between Rhode Island and Connecticut, 57

Kingston, Jamaica, wealthy Jews in, 283

Kirke, Sir David, proprietary rights to Newfoundland granted to, and associates, 266 n

Kirke, Sir Lewis, enjoined not to interfere with the Baltimore rights to Avalon, 267

Knight, Edward, on the great emphasis

Knight, Edward (*continued*)
in the English iron industry of the making of nails, 215
Knight, Captain John, on the methods employed in the Newfoundland cod fisheries in 1749, 253
Knowles, Admiral Sir Charles, Governor of Jamaica, on the illicit trading of Rhode Island ships, 60

Labour, farm: in New England, mostly family and hired hands, 4, 57; in Pennsylvania, the use of indentured, 155–7; in England, skilled, essential to production of iron, 208; skilled, required in the beaver-hat industry, 237
Labrador Coast, the, a boundary at Cape Perdrix on, of the Hudson's Bay Company's grant, 236
Lac des Prairies, the French trading post at Fort Dauphin upon, 246
La France, Joseph, a Hudson's Bay Company employee, reports on the Far West Indian trade, 235
Lake Cumberland, a French trading post on, 246
Lake Mistassini, and the boundary of the Hudson's Bay Company territory, 236
Lake Superior, French influence on Indians north and west of, 234
Lake Winnipeg, French trading posts about, in 1750, 246
Lake Winnipegosis, the French trade in the area of, 246
Lake Winnepesaukee, the "King's Wood" on the shore of, 41 *n*
Lamp black, the production of, in New York, 117
Lancashire, England, source of supply of iron ore for furnaces of, 208; petitions by the ironmasters and ironmongers of, for relief, 219
Lancaster, England, the development of ironworks between Cumberland and, 212
Lancaster County, Pennsylvania: the creation of, and nationalistic complexion of, 158; the representation of, in the Assembly, 161
Land: agricultural units of, in New England, 3, 4; the policy of Massachusetts Bay respecting, in the seventeenth and eighteenth centuries, 19–21; speculation in, 19; the policy of Governor

Land: (*continued*)
Wentworth of New Hampshire regarding upper Connecticut, 49–50; shortage of, in Connecticut, 76; the granting of, in Connecticut, 84–5; policies regarding, in New York and New England contrasted, 102; abuses in the granting of New York, 104–5; riots over, in the 1760's, 108; the improvement of New Jersey, aided by loans from the provincial treasury, 128; proprietorial control of all ungranted, 136; difficulty of enforcing rights to, 139–42; the cost of acquiring, in Pennsylvania, 150–1; the improvement of, aided by the provincial loan office, 174; the sale of colonial, to aliens, prohibited by Parliament, 175, 274; made liable for debts of owners, 275
Land bank, abortive plan for a, in Massachusetts Bay, 11; *see also* Banks
Land office, the, of Pennsylvania, well managed, 181
Land patents: in New York, the vastness of, 102–5; the abuses by holders of, 103–4; inquiry into all New York, 109
Land riots: in eastern New York, 107; in New Jersey, 139–42
Land surveys, and New York lands, 104
Land titles, confusion of, in east New Jersey, 139
Landholders: of Massachusetts Bay, 19; of New Hampshire, disputes regarding proprietorial, 47–8; of western New Hampshire, 49; of Rhode Island, 57; of Connecticut, 75; of New York, influential position of, 109, strong opposition of, to New York taxation of undeveloped land, 113; two main groups of proprietorial, in New Jersey, 138; of Pennsylvania, 166, 174; the Penns as proprietorial, in Pennsylvania, 174, 179–80
Landholding systems, claims of Massachusetts Bay to New York lands typical of struggle between two contrasting, 107, 108
Landlords, absentee, of New York, 114
Landowners and the suffrage: in Massachusetts Bay, 29; in Rhode Island, 68; in Connecticut, 81; in New York, 109–12; in New Jersey, 138 *n*, 139; in Pennsylvania, 161 *n*
Law, Jonathan, Governor of Connecticut, refuses the London agency, 98 *n*

Law enforcement agents, the laxity of British, in North America, 292–3

Lawlessness: of the illicit traders of Rhode Island, 59–62, 292; in Connecticut, 84; of the land rioters in New York, 106–8; of the squatters in New Jersey, 141; in Pennsylvania as the result of the gentleness of criminal law, 164–5; in Newfoundland, 262; within the colonies, 292–3

Lawrie, Gawen, Deputy Governor of East New Jersey, and the New York boundary, 143

Laws, see Code of laws, Legislation (colonial and parliamentary)

Laws of the Government of New Castle, Kent and Sussex upon Delaware (1741), 193

Lawyers, the, of Massachusetts Bay, influence of, upon legislation, 32

Lebanon, Connecticut, 75 *n*

Lechmere, Thomas and Anne, and the Winthrop estate appeal, 98

Lee, Commodore Fitzroy Henry, on the poor quality of cod carried to the southern European markets, 256 *n*

Lee, Colonel Thomas, President of the Virginia Council, the report of, on the ironworks of Virginia, 216

Leeds, England, petition from the merchants of, supporting Arthur Dobbs's attack on the Hudson's Bay Company, 245

Leeward Islands, the British: the governorship of, sought by Shirley, 35; the government of, 276; the religious establishment of, 282; slow decline of the fertility of, 287–8; see also West Indies, British, and Antigua, Montserrat, Nevis, and St. Christopher

Legal tender: the issue over, bills of credit in Rhode Island, 70–2; in New Jersey, 129–32; hostility of the Board of Trade toward colonial, 130

Legislation, colonial: of Massachusetts Bay, relating to hard money and the circulation of bills of credit, 10, 11; the Crown control of, 30; the disallowance of, 30; the repeal of, 30; the history of, from 1703 to 1753, 30; key figures in shaping of, 32; undemocratic nature of some, in 1750, 32; of New Hampshire, respecting the rights of new towns, 49; of Rhode Island, respecting the rights of freemanship,

Legislation, colonial: (*continued*)
68; for the establishment of government "banks," 69–70; of Connecticut, together with that of Delaware, Maryland and Rhode Island, not sent to England for approval, 74; relating to dissenters, 80–1; relating to crime, 90–2, 95; concerning intestate estates, 98, 100; relating to heretics, 100 *n;* of New York, to restore the quality of exported flour, 118; relating to specific appropriations, 121; of New Jersey, relative to a paper currency, 131–6; for ascertaining the New Jersey-New York boundary, 144; for erecting Sussex County in the disputed area, 144; of Pennsylvania, limiting passengers on immigrant ships, 154 *n;* relating to crime, 163–5; on the disposal of all public money, 176; failure of, on the import of convicts, 177; the people of the province question the validity of, passed in Delaware, 187; of Delaware, lack of Crown control over, 189; the comprehensive nature of, 193–4; no requirement for Crown approval of, 194; providing for capital crimes, 194 *n;* against convict labour and transported criminals, 194–5; discriminatory nature of, on franchise, 195–6; for defence measures, 196–7; of Massachusetts Bay, granting bounties on ironware, 217

Legislation, parliamentary: to protect the white-pine belt of North America, 41; granting bounties on American ship timber, 43; placing duties on sugar, 59, 292–3; on the theft of live stock, 194 *n;* regulating the American iron industry, 206; regulating the American hat industry, 239–40; to realize the ideal of imperial economic self-containment, 293

Letter from a Gentleman in New York to his Friend in Brunswick, A (1750), on the size of the New York land grants, 103

Letter from a Merchant of the City of London (1757): on decrease of mast size white-pine trees, 43 *n;* on the Newfoundland fisheries, 254 *n*

Letters patent, the establishment of colonies by, 276

Lewes, Delaware: the commerce of, 168; defence measures provided for, 196;

Lewes, Delaware: (*continued*)
designation of, as a pilot's town, 200;
landing of Irish immigrants at, 202–3
Lex talionis, the principles of, applied by
the Connecticut courts, 92 *n*
Liberty, extreme ideas of personal, in
Pennsylvania, 173
Library: the Lending, of Philadelphia,
170; the private, of James Logan, 271
Lime, the excellent quality of Pennsyl-
vania, 170 *n*
Lincoln County, Maine, the number of
towns within, 19 *n*
Lindsay, David, Newport slaver, at Ana-
mabo, 64–5
Lindsay, John, commissary of the post at
Oswego, 119 *n*
Linen, German, shipped to the colonies,
9 *n*
Liquors, distilled: the excise tax on, col-
lected in Connecticut, 87; reduced in
Pennsylvania, 173 *n; see also* Rum
Lisbon: trade relations between New
Haven and, 75 *n;* exportation to, from
New Jersey, 127
"List of Acts of Massachusetts Bay,
1753," 30 *n*
Listers, the town, in Connecticut, elec-
tion of, and duties of, 87
Little George, the, slave ship, a revolt by
slaves on, 65
Little Harbor, the home of Governor
Wentworth at, 52
Little Nine Partners' Patent, the, New
York, 102; the creation of, 104 *n*
Littlebury, John, deputy for Lord Balti-
more in Avalon, 266
Liverpool: the purchase of New England
ships at, 6; the attempt by the mer-
chants of, to overthrow the Hudson's
Bay Company monopoly, 245
Live–stock: the raising of, in Rhode Island, 56; in Connecticut, 75; in Pennsylvania, 166; in Delaware, 201; the
scarcity of, in Newfoundland, 252
Livingston, Robert, the lord of Livingston Manor, the fear of a social revolution by, 106
Livingston, William, lawyer and grandson of Robert Livingston: control of
one New York faction by, 110; defends
the town of Elizabeth against the East
New Jersey Proprietors, 141 *n*
Livingston Manor, New York, 102; the
creation of, 104 *n;* the quit-rents of,

Livingston Manor (*continued*)
105 *n;* early history of, 106; riotous
proceedings upon, 107, 108; Robert
Livingston, first lord of, 110; ironworks within, 114, 117
Livingstons, the, among the New York
aristocracy, 109
Loan office, the: of New Jersey, public
burdens and, 133; of Pennsylvania, the
activities of, 173–4; profits from the
operation of, 174; the control of, by
the Assembly, 176; the county, in
Delaware, 199
Local officials: the election of, in Rhode
Island, 67; a description of, in Connecticut, 86–7; the inability of, in New
York, to protect the province from intruders, 107, 144; the unwillingness of,
in New Jersey, to proceed against rioters, 139–41; the activities of, in Pennsylvania elections, 161 *n;* inadequate
qualifications of, in Pennsylvania, 165 *n*
Logan, James, prominent Pennsylvania
official: the home of, 171; views of, on
military defence, 197
"Log College," the, of New Jersey, and
Presbyterianism, 137
London: the purchase of New England
ships in, 6; the shipment of Spanish
dollars from Boston to, 14; exporting
American pig iron to, 216; the free
importation into the port of, of American bar iron, 223; the iron manufacturers of, desire a bounty on American iron, 228; beaver hats produced
in, 237; petition supporting Arthur
Dobbs's attack on Hudson's Bay Company from, 245; the slight interest of,
in direct Newfoundland trade, 255
London agency, the: a survey of, in Connecticut, 96–100; as an equivalent to
colonial representation in Parliament,
100; *see also* Agent
London agent, *see* Agent
London Company of Virginia, the, charter of, and the Virginia boundaries,
185 *n*
Londonderry, New Hampshire, the fortified post of, 46
Lopez, Aaron: naturalization papers
sought by, 56; a leading merchant of
Rhode Island, 58
Lopez, Moses, a leading Rhode Island
merchant, 58
Lords of manors, of New York: the con-

Lords of manors (*continued*)
trol over tenants by, 109; multifarious activities of, 109–10; 114–15

Louisbourg, Cape Breton Island: the New England expedition against, and reimbursement by Parliament, 10, 34; the psychological influence of the capture of, on New England, 37

Love and Unity, the, German emigrant ship, 155 *n*

Lower Counties on the Delaware, the, *see* Delaware

Lucena, James, first Jew in Rhode Island to obtain naturalization papers, 56

Lumber: the carrying of, by Rhode Island ships, 60, 66; provisions for the preservation of, in Newfoundland, 260; *see also* Forests, Timbers, White pine

Lumbering: the importance of, in New Hampshire, 39–44; in New Jersey, 126–7; *see also* Masting trade, Timber, White pine

Lutherans: of New York, 116; of Pennsylvania, 149; strength of, in the Pennsylvania Assembly, 162; a church for, in Philadelphia, 170; of Delaware, 187

Lying in wait, the killing of a man while, a capital offence by the Duke of York code, 163

Lyme, England, the interest of, in the Newfoundland salmon fisheries, 255

Lyttelton, William Henry, Governor of South Carolina, the instructions to, changed, 277

Mackerel, Massachusetts Bay and the catching of, 17

Mackey, Robert, London merchant, seeks Massachusetts Bay lands, 19 *n*

Madeiras, the: and Massachusetts Bay trade, 7, 9 *n*; the New Jersey trade to, 127; freedom of colonial trade with, 291

Maine: the Province of, absorbed by Massachusetts Bay, 14, 19, 29; the Territory of, the number of towns within, 19 *n*; Shirley makes treaties with Indians living along the borders of, 34; an abundance of white pine in, 43; settlement of the southern boundary of, 45

Malbone, Godfrey, a leading Rhode Island merchant, 58; owner of *Little George* (or *Charming Betty*), Rhode Island slaver faced by Negro revolt, 65

Malt, the making of, with coke in Staffordshire, 209 *n*

Manchester, England, the hat-makers of, petition Parliament, 240

Manors: of New York, 102; methods of exploiting, 114–15; life on, of New York, 114

"Man-stealers," the Dutch, and the German emigrants, 153

Manufactures, *see* Commerce, Industry, Trade

Mariners: French, taken on by a Rhode Island trader, 61; of Connecticut, exempted from military service, 88; *see also* Sailors

Marten skins: the number of, brought out of Hudson Bay in 1748, 233; auction price of, 237

Martinique, importance of, as a French possession, 287

Maryland: and the production of flour and crude iron, 4; export of provisions from, to Massachusetts Bay, 15; immigration of Germans to, 152; a proprietary colony, 174; and the purchase of English wrought iron, 222; the exportation of pig iron to England from, 226–7; the constitution of, based on letters patent, 276; not obliged to send laws to England for approval, 279; the religious establishment of, in 1750, 282; activity of Roman Catholics in, 282; lack of enforcement of most legal disabilities of Roman Catholics in, in 1750, 283; boundary dispute between Pennsylvania and, 286

Mason, Captain John, an original Proprietor of New Hampshire, claims of, and the problem of unappropriated lands, 47

Mason, John Tufton, descendant of the original New Hampshire Proprietor, revives claims to unappropriated lands, 47–8

Mason, Robert Tufton, descendant of original New Hampshire Proprietor, claims of, to unappropriated lands, 47–8

Massachusetts Bay: the most dangerous rival of England in North America in commerce and industry, 4; the heart of New England, 4; the shipping of, 6; commercial relations of, with other regions, 6 *n*, 8; low-cost shipbuilding in, 7 *n*; the high standards of living in, 8,

Massachusetts Bay: (*continued*)
36; balances due the mother country from, 8, 9; the export to Spain and Portugal of codfish from, 8; the nature of the commercial relations of, 8–9; the value of imports of, in 1743, 9; the value of the exports of, 9, 10, 14 *n*, 18 *n;* receives reimbursement of expenses for the Louisbourg expedition, 10; the reorganization of the public finances of, in 1749, 10–14; the population of, 14, 15; occupations of the people of, 14–15; imports of staples from other colonies, 15; industry in, 16; rum, foundation of prosperity in, 16, 17; the appropriation of the fisheries of the Gulf of Maine and of Canso by the people of, 17; the growing interest of, in Newfoundland, 17, 18; the fine quality of codfish of, 17 *n;* the number of ships of, engaged in the fisheries, 17; rivalry of, with mother country over fisheries, 18; the number of whaling towns within, 18; the aggressive colonizing activities of, landmen, 18; the people of, press upon lands claimed by New York, 19; the sea-to-sea claims of, still preserved, 19, 286; the traditional policy of land grants modified by, 19; settlement of Penacook characteristic of colonization processes of, to 1750, 20–1; influence of Congregational Establishment of, 21–3; the witchcraft terror of 1692 in, 22; the effects of England's latitudinarianism in, 23; the Great Awakening and, 23–6, 276; the press and, 26–7; the influence of higher education in, 27–8; a corporate colony, 28, 276; an analysis of the charter of, 28; powers of the government of, 28–32, 276; powers of the General Court of Assembly of, 29; the governorship of, 29–31; submission of laws of, to the Privy Council, 30; the franchise in, 30, 31; the provincial council of, 31; the undemocratic nature of some laws of, in 1750, 32, 285; a commission for settling the boundary between Rhode Island and, 33; the Assembly of, denounces the French-speaking people of Nova Scotia and expresses loyalty to the Crown, 36; the self-sufficiency of, 37; virtues of, 37; disputes with New Hampshire over boundaries, 45–6; and over the gar-

Massachusetts Bay: (*continued*)
risoning of Fort Dummer, 46, 49; the religious refugees of, settle in Rhode Island, 54; the interior of, dependent upon intercourse with Narragansett Bay, 58; relationship of, with Connecticut, 78; boundary dispute between New York and, 106–8, 286–7; the Privy Council sends to the Governor of, a peremptory instruction in 1737 respecting bills of credit, 130; the iron industry within, 216; number of forges in, 217; bounties offered by, on iron products, 217; the exportation of ironware from, 217; the making of beaver hats by, restricted, 239–40; the constitution of, based on letters patent, 276; as a semi-royal colony, 276; the commissions and instructions for the royal Governor also a basis for the constitution of, 276

Mast ship, a, capacity of, 40

Masting trade, the, of New Hampshire, *see* Chap. 2

Masts: great demand by Great Britain for, from the New England white-pine belt, 40–1; bounties on, granted by Parliament, 42, 220; trade in, of New Hampshire, 43–4; secured by Pennsylvania shipbuilders from New Jersey, 167 *n*

Mayhem: the crime of, in the Connecticut code of 1750, 92; a felony of death offence in Pennsylvania, 165

McAuleys, the, of New Haven, Connecticut, carry on commerce with Lisbon, 75 *n*

Mechanics: as voters in New York City, 111; the prohibition against the carrying away of, from New Foundland, 258

Mennonites, the: in Pennsylvania, 149; support the Quakers in office, 159

Mercantile system, the British: and the Sugar Act of 1733, 59; and the Iron Act of 1750, 206–223; and the opening up of collieries in Nova Scotia, 227; and the Iron Act of 1757, 228; and the act of 1732 regulating the American beaver-hat industry, 239; supported by all British statesmen before 1776, 290; the purposes underlying, 290–1; compensation for restraints upon the colonies by, 291–2; the fruits of, 292

Merchant marine, demand for masts by the British, 40

Merchants, the: of Boston, 7–8; of Massachusetts Bay, influence of, upon provincial legislation, 32; of New Hampshire, the lumber interests of the Wentworth family as, 43–4, 52–3; of Rhode Island, influential families of, 58; trading activities of, 58–67; of New York, influential position of, 109; the Albany, and the Indian trade, 119–20; of Philadelphia, 168; of Pennsylvania, 173; dominant role in Newfoundland of Boston, 251

Merrimac river, the: and masting activities, 40; as a boundary, 47

Methuen, New Hampshire, the dispute over seating the deputies of, 48–9

Middlesex County, Massachusetts Bay: statistics on population and products of, 15; the number of towns within, 19 n

Middlesex County, New Jersey: the Scottish population of, 137; the representation of, in the Assembly, 138; the spread of land riots to, 140

Middleton, Christopher, sea captain, and the search for a northwest passage, 243–4

Middletown, Connecticut: the population of, 74 n; the rating of, for taxation, 75 n

Middletown, New Jersey, the New England background of, 137

Midlands, the, England, causes for shifting of iron-smelting from, 209

Military officers: the election of, in Rhode Island, 67; and in Connecticut, 88–9

Military service: in Connecticut, 88; exemptions from, 88–9; in Pennsylvania, the absence of, 173; in Delaware, provision for, 196

Militia, the: of Connecticut, powers of the sheriff to raise, 90 n; placed under the control of the Governor of New York, 96; the provincial troops of New York, 121; of Delaware, 186, 197; see also Train Bands

Mill Creek, a tributary of the Christina River, 202

"Miller Papers," the, regarding New York City, 115 n, 116 n

Mills, slitting and rolling, in England in 1750, 207, 208

Minisink Patent, the, New York, 103;

Minisink Patent (continued)
the extent of, and the interest of the de Lancey family in, 143

Minors, the indenture of, in the colonies regulated by Parliament, 275

Minot, G. R., author of the History of the Province of Massachusetts Bay (1798), 9 n

Miscosinke, Lake, and the boundary of the Hudson's Bay Company territory, 236

Misprision of treason, a felony of death offence in Pennsylvania, 165

Mistassini, Lake, see Miscosinke Lake

Mittelberger, Gottlieb, German music master: on liberties in Pennsylvania, 149–50; on the misery of some of the Germans, 153; a description of the journey to America on an emigrant ship by, 154; on the good will manifested by people of Pennsylvania, 160; on the rich dress of the people of Pennsylvania, 171–2; on the women of Pennsylvania, 172; author of Journey to Pennsylvania in the Year 1750

Mohammedans, in Pennsylvania, 149

Mohawk Valley, the Palatines in the, 113

Mohegan Indians, the Connecticut land controversy with the, 97

Molasses: the sale of "Jamaica" fish to the West Indies to secure, 16; number of distilleries of, in Massachusetts Bay, 16; purchased of the French planters, 17, 58; nonpayment of duties on, 17, 59–60; importation of, into Rhode Island, 59; the amount of, needed by Rhode Island distillers, 62; number of distilleries of, in Rhode Island, 62; importation of, by Newfoundland, 254; high duties on foreign produced, entering the colonies, 275; importation of, into France forbidden, 288; as an enumerated commodity, 291; why the British West Indies could not compete with the French in the sale of, 292

Molasses Act of 1733, the: the circumvention of, by colonial traders, 17, 60–1; the basis for, 288; fails of its purpose, 288–9, 291; see also Sugar Act

Money, see Bills of credit, Currency, Dollar, Legal tender, Pine Tree shillings, Spanish pieces of eight, Specie

Monmouth County, New Jersey: the Scottish population of, 137; representation of, in the General Assembly, 138

Monmouth Purchase, the, frauds and abuses connected with, 141

Monmouthshire, England, waste and destruction of woods in, 210

Montgomery, John, Governor of New York, the financial policies of, and the Assembly, 121

Montreal, and the Hudson Bay fur trade, 246

Montserrat: the constitution of, 276; Roman Catholics in, enjoy the franchise, 283; attempt in 1749 to discriminate against the Catholics of, 283; predominence of Irish Catholics in, 283

Moose, the hunting of, in Newfoundland, 255

Moose Fort, a trading post on Moose River, Hudson Bay, 231

Moose River: effects of French competition on bartering with Indians on, 231; the excellent grain grown at, 233 n

Morality, deep concern of Connecticut laws with, 93

Moravian Brethren: in Pennsylvania, 149, 151; the persecution of, in Europe, 152–3; the coming of, to Pennsylvania, 152; a welcome to, in England, 153; support the Quakers in office, in Pennsylvania, 159; in the Pennsylvania Assembly, 162; churches of, in Philadelphia, 170; activities of, in the West Indies, 282

Morris, Lewis, Governor of New Jersey: and the Assembly, 126; on the trade and shipping of New Jersey, 127; on the happy condition of the people of New Jersey, 128; refuses to sign the bill of 1744 for printing bills of credit, 131; attempt to bribe, fails, 132; integrity of, 132; the death of, 132; commissioned Governor of New Jersey in 1738, 146; the qualifications of, 146; his quarrel with the Assembly, 146; letter from, to General Braddock, 174; on the threat of war, 178–9

Morris, Robert Hunter, Chief Justice of New Jersey, an East New Jersey Proprietor: private land concessions secured by, 139; dominates the New Jersey Council, 147; opposes the ap-

Morris, Robert Hunter (continued) pointment of William Morris to the Council, 148; on the freedom of the people from taxation, 173; on the great powers exercised by the Pennsylvania Assembly, 176 n; appointed Deputy Governor of Pennsylvania and Delaware, 191

Morris, William, of Hunterdon County, New Jersey, recommended by Governor Belcher for a seat in the Council, 148

Morris County, New Jersey: the spread of land riots to, 140–1; the theft of timber from the Penn lands in, 141

Morrisania: the manor of, New York, 102; the creation of, 104 n; slavery upon, 119

Morrises, the, among the New York aristocracy, 110

"Morrison Papers," the, 37 n

Mortgages on land: in Rhode Island, 68; in New Jersey, 128; in Pennsylvania, amounts due on, 173–4

Muffs, beaver skins and the making of, 237

Murder: the capital law of 1650 against, in Connecticut, 91; in the Upland code of 1682 of Pennsylvania, 163

Murray, William (later Baron Mansfield of Mansfield), Solicitor General: the opinion of, sought on the New York Governor's power to appoint by commission, 121 n; the report of, upon Crown interference in Pennsylvania affairs, 178; and the Baltimore petition respecting Avalon, 271

Musters: penalties for failure to attend, in Delaware, 196; ironworkers in Virginia exempt from, 216–17

Mutilation: in the Connecticut codes of 1650 and 1750, 90–1, 95; and the Upland code, 163; and the New Castle code, 164

Nails: the manufacture of, at Newport, Rhode Island, 66; "cold short iron" excellent for, 208; the decline in the sale of, 214; the importance of, in the English iron industry, 215; the production of, in New England, 217; the colonial manufacture of, 221

Nanfan, Captain John, Acting Governor of New York, land grants under, 104

Nantucket, Massachusetts Bay, the interest of, in whaling, 18

Nantucket County, Massachusetts, the slave population of, 16

Narragansett Bay, ports of, 58

Narragansett country: dairy farming in, 57; as the plantation area of Rhode Island, 67; the aristocratic planters of, 67; the Connecticut-Rhode Island-Massachusetts Bay dispute over the, 97

Natural rights, the appeal to the theory of, by New Jersey rioters, 141

Naturalization: encouragement of, in Pennsylvania, 159; Pennsylvania Germans and, 159

Naval stores: the export of, by Massachusetts Bay, 9; the failure of Governor Hunter of New York to produce, 113 n; as enumerated commodities, 291

Navigation and trade system, the British, see Mercantile system

Navigation acts, see Trade and Navigation acts

Negroes: in Boston, 5, 6; Massachusetts Bay forbidden to impose an import duty on, 30 n; in Massachusetts Bay, discriminatory laws against, in 1750, 32; number of, in New Hampshire, 51; in Rhode Island, 57; and the Rhode Island slave trade, 64–5; in Connecticut, exempted from military service, 88; on New York manors, 114; in New York City, 116 n; in Pennsylvania, 149, 173; in Delaware, 204–5; employment of, in colonial hat industry prohibited, 240; the economic importance of the labour of, varies in the colonies, 284; the pressure of large numbers of, brings fear of slave insurrections, 285; severe penalties imposed in some colonies for misdeeds of, 285; unusual rights bestowed on, in Jamaica, 286

Neill, Hugh, the Reverend, on the number of Anglicans in Kent County, Delaware, 204

Neutrality, the policy of, in King George's War, pursued by the New York Assembly, 122–3

Nevis: the constitution of, 276; earlier disability of Roman Catholics in, removed by law, 283

New Bedford, Massachusetts Bay, the interest of, in whaling, 18

New Castle, Delaware: the code of 1701

New Castle, Delaware: (continued) adopted at, an analysis of, 164–5; the commerce of, 168; and the Duke of York's deed of 1682, 185 n; a privateer's attack upon, 186 n; commercial rivalry between Philadelphia and, 187; the capital of Delaware at, 189, 201; incorporation of, 191–2; as a major port of entry for immigrants, 201, 202–3; relative importance of, 201 n

New Castle County, Delaware: representation of, in Assembly, 193; semicircular limits of, 198; immigration into, 203; large numbers of Quakers in, 203

"New Charter," the, of 1675 for the Newfoundland fisheries, 257 n

New England: characterized, 3; and Massachusetts Bay, 4; the importance of shipbuilding in, 4, 6 n, 7; products of, forests, 7; resemblance to and contrast with Great Britain, 8; Massachusetts Bay acts against the bills of credit of other colonies of, 13; the fish industry and, 17, 18; superior quality of the codfish of, 17 n; spread of the doctrines of Arminius in, 23; Jonathan Edwards, leading theologian and preacher of, 23–5; the Great Awakening in, 23–5; the advantages of, 37–8; the white-pine belt of, 39; the production of rum in, 62–3; the currency act of 1751 restricting the issue of paper money in, 72; Puritanism of, 78; taste of, with New York City, 116; attitude of, toward the Albany merchants, 120; the state of the paper currency within, laid before the Privy Council, 130; the influence of, in East New Jersey, 139; the early interest of, in the iron industry, 215; workers of, in iron skilled in the eighteenth century, 217; the opening up of markets for the iron products of, 217; the number of furnaces and forges in, 217; the importation of English bar steel into, 217; and the purchase of English wrought iron, 222; the exportation to England of iron produced in, 227 n; the interest of the merchants of, in the Newfoundland trade, 252; prevention of ships from, bringing in prohibited commodities to Newfoundland, 258; the carrying of sailors and fishermen away from Newfoundland in the vessels of, prohibited, 258, 261

New England Courant, the, attacks on the clergy in, 26

New England Currency Act of 1751, 72, 73 *n*

New England Weekly Journal, the, 27

New Hampshire: the value of the imports and exports of, 9–10; Boston merchants petition the Crown against the bills of credit of, 13 *n;* the separate existence of, threatened by Massachusetts Bay, 19; the chief source of the wealth of, 39; description of the white-pine belt in, 39; lessening importance of, as a lumbering centre by 1750, 43, 44; the boundaries of, before 1741, 44–5 *n;* a commission to settle the boundary of, established by order in council, 45–7; and Fort Dummer, 46; disputes over the ownership of unappropriated lands of, 46–8; western expansion of, 48; the western lands of, granted upon a quit-rent basis, 49; the extent of the western claims of, 50; the boundary dispute between New York and, 50–5, 105, 286; the laying out of new townships within, on the upper Connecticut, 50; the aggressiveness of, 50–1; the population of, 51; economic activities of the people of, 51; religion in, 51; the influence of the Wentworth family in the affairs of, 52; the government of, 276; the religious establishment of, 282

New Haven, Connecticut: a joint capital, 74; the population of, 74 *n;* the rating of, for taxation, 75 *n;* the commerce of, chiefly with New York, 77; a centre of Anglican influences, 78; number of inhabitants of, qualified to vote, 82 *n;* the use of haywards in, 87 *n*

New Haven Colony, religion in, 79

New Haven County, Connecticut, meeting of freemen in, 83 *n*

New Jersey, the Province of: the value of the imports of, 9; New York City a distributing centre of, 116; the economic interests of, 126; the population of, 126; agriculture of, 126; lumbering in, 126; population distribution of, 127; the white-pine belt of, 127; the exports of, 127; sectional differences in, 127, 136–8; the commercial dependence of, upon New York and Pennsylvania, 127; advantageous living conditions within, 128; lack of foreign enemies of, 128;

New Jersey, the Province of: *(continued)* lack of taxation in, 128; the issue of paper money within, 128–36; the lack of solidarity of the population of, 136; lack of a capital in, 137–8; individualism in, 138; the anarchic state of, in 1750, 138; land riots over disputed ungranted lands in, 138–42; a decade of violence after 1745 in, 139; the contest between New York and, over the boundary, 142–5; the running of a boundary line *ex parte* by, 144; the struggle between the Governor and the Assembly of, over legal tender bills, 145–8, 280; the importance of the iron industry within, 218; the government of, 276; no religious establishment in, 282

New Light Congregationalists, and the Great Awakening, 25; in Connecticut, 80

New London, Connecticut: the population of, 74 *n;* the rating of, for taxation, 75 *n;* the principal port of Connecticut, 77; and the treatment of Separatists, 80

New London County: and iron production, 77; meeting of freemen in, 83 *n*

New London Gazette, the, 95

New Netherlands, the, vast land grants within, 103

New Shoreham, Rhode Island, the citizens of, share in the "banks", 68

New System of Geography, A (1764–5), by D. Fenning and J. Collyer, 245 *n*

New York, the City of: the shipping of Spanish dollars from Boston to, 14; the commercial relations of, with Connecticut, 76–8; as the port and entrepôt for the commerce of Connecticut, 77–8; the influence of the social ideals of, in western Connecticut, 77; the creation of King's College at, 78; the number of freeholders or freemen in, 111 *n;* the importance of, in 1740, 115–16; the defences of, 115; the appearance of, 115–16; compared with Boston and Philadelphia, 116, 169 *n;* as a seaport, 116–17; as a distributing centre of western Connecticut and eastern New Jersey, 116, 127; commercial activities of, 116, 116 *n,* 117 *n*

New York, the Province of: the evasion of customs by merchants of, 8; the value of imports and exports of, 9; the

New York, the Province of: (*continued*)
governorship of, sought by Shirley, 35; the dispute between New Hampshire and, over the boundary, 50, 105–6; land systems of, 102; aristocratic tendencies within, 102; the law of 1699 against exorbitant land grants within, 104–5; the land claims of, threatened by those of New Hampshire, Massachusetts Bay, and New Jersey, 105–7, 143, 286–7; political and social life of, 109; government of, 109–11; the population of, 112–13; the slow development of, 113–14; and iron production, 114, 117, 218, 222; industrial activities of, 117; and the Indian fur trade, 118–19; the non-English-speaking elements within, 119, 136; Clinton's administration of, 120–5; a plan to maintain the neutrality of, in the French and English hostilities, 122; the Assembly of, censured by the Privy Council and the Board of Trade, 124; Governors of, violate instructions respecting bills of credit, 135; iron production in, 218; the making of beaver hats in, restricted, 239–40; the government of, 276; Anglicanism and, 282; disabilities of Jews and Roman Catholics in, 282–3

New York Mercury, June 11 and 18, 1753, on shipping activity in New York City, 116 n

New York Weekly Post-Boy, the, 141

Newark, New Jersey: the New England background of, 137; rioters rescued from the gaol at, 139

Newborn, the, a Pennsylvania sect, 149

Newcastle, Thomas Pelham-Holles, Duke of, Secretary of State, and later Chief Minister: Governor Shirley seeks change of post from, 35; addressed by Deputy Governor Thomas, 198

Newfoundland: Massachusetts Bay interests in, 7, 10, 18; the amount of Massachusetts Bay rum sent to, 16, 17; the disposition of prize fish secured from, 16; the codfish of, less esteemed than that of New England, 17 n; the growing interest of Massachusetts Bay in, 17, 251–2; description of, 248; the slow movement to settle, 249; a prize in the duelling between England and France, 249; towns and garrisons in, 250–1; the population of, 250, 251; the shipping of, 251; civilization in, 251–3; the

Newfoundland: (*continued*)
isolation of, in winter, 252; the value of the fisheries of, 254–5; the value of the exports and imports of, 255–6; policies of the British government respecting, 256–60; restrictions upon the inhabitants of, 256–8; ships operated by the dwellers of, 257 n; the role of the Governor in, 259; the friction between the justices of the peace and the harbour admirals in, 261–2; anarchic conditions in, 262–4; the Baltimore family claims to, 264–72; proprietary rights over, granted to Hamilton, Pembroke, Holland, and Kirke, 266; the government of, limited before 1750, 275–6; the commissions and instructions issued to the Governors of, 277; the powers of the local government of, extended under the Great Seal, 277; no legislative assembly in, in 1750, 278; the Anglican establishment and, 282; Roman Catholicism the prevailing religion of the inhabitants of, 282; a free trade in salt for the fisheries of, 291

Newfoundland Banks, the: and European fishing interests, 248–9; as a school of seamanship, 256–7

Newfoundland London and Bristol Company, attempt to colonize Newfoundland by the, 249

"Newfoundland's Establishment and Output" (1741), by Captain Smith, 255 n

Newlanders, the Dutch agents, and the German emigrants, 153

Newport, Rhode Island: the evasion of customs by the merchants of, 9; the Jewish merchants of, 56, 283; the first synagogue in, 56; enterprise of the people of, 58; number of vessels of, in foreign and domestic trade, 58 n; merchants of, and the West Indies trade, 59; the non-enforcement of the Sugar Act of 1733 at, 59; lawlessness in, 61–2; vies with New York as a commercial centre, 66; the industries of, 66; the commerce of, 66; a centre of culture, 66; a summer resort, 67; commercial interests of, supported by Narragansett planters, 67; Providence the rival of, 67; as the seat of government, 67; the citizens of, share in the public "banks," 68; population of, 69; the "voters" in, 69

Newspapers: the influence of, in Massachusetts Bay, 26–8; in Connecticut, 95; in New York, 141; in Pennsylvania, 159–60, 171; see also Press

Nicolls, Colonel Richard, Governor of New York: and the Elizabeth and Monmouth, New Jersey, purchases, 141; and the expedition to occupy Delaware, 184

Nomination, the system of, for colonial office in Connecticut, 83

Non-Christians and freemanship in Rhode Island, 55

Nonconformity, religious, no disqualification for freemanship in Connecticut, 86

Normandy fishermen, and the Grand Banks of Newfoundland, 248

Norris, Captain, the testimony of, respecting the New England trade with Newfoundland, 251 n

North Carolina: the commercial relations between, and Boston, 10; export of staples from, to Massachusetts Bay, 15; the government of, 276; the passing of legal tender acts by, results in abuses, 279–80; the Anglican establishment and, 282; western charter limits of, 286

"North West Committee," the, administrators undertake to discover a northwest passage, 244

Northampton, Massachusetts Bay, the repudiation of Jonathan Edwards by, 25

Northampton County, Pennsylvania: the creation of, and the racial complexion of, 158; the representation of, in the Assembly, 161; the amount raised by excise in, 174; the small amount of quit-rents drawn from, in 1764, 180

Northern colonies, the: and farming, 3; and the development of handicrafts, 4; in the manufacture of rum and iron, 4; in shipbuilding, 4; in the fisheries, 4; arouse the apprehension of England, 4; do not fit into the mercantilistic theory of the role of colonies, 4; see also Connecticut, Delaware, Massachusetts Bay, New Hampshire, New Jersey, New York, Newfoundland, Nova Scotia, Pennsylvania, Rhode Island

Northey, Sir Edward, Attorney General, the opinion of, on the power of colonial legislatures, 178 n

Northwest passage, a: discovery of, an objective of Hudson's Bay Company,

Northwest passage (continued) 230; the attempt on the part of Arthur Dobbs to find, 243–5; Parliament offers a reward for the discovery of, 244

Norwich, Connecticut: the population of, 74 n; the rating of, for taxation, 75 n

Nottingham, New Hampshire, the fortified post of, 46

Nottinghamshire, England, iron ore deposits of, 208

Nova Scotia: the value of the imports and exports of, 9–10; commercial domination of, by Boston merchants, 10; appropriation of fish beds of, by Massachusetts Bay, 17; and the Massachusetts Bay Charter of 1691, 29; the Treaty of Utrecht and, 29 n; menaced by the French in King George's War, 33; Massachusetts Bay fishing interests off the coast of, 34; the conduct of the French-speaking inhabitants of, denounced by the Massachusetts Bay Assembly, 37; immigration of Germans to, 152; instructions against the working of collieries in, 227; limited power of the government of, 276; no legislative assembly in, in 1750, 278; the Anglican establishment and, 282, Roman Catholicism, the prevailing religion of the inhabitants of in 1750, 282

Oak, the: of Pennsylvania, compared with that of New England, 167; use of, for ship timber, 212

Oaths: the taking of, in Pennsylvania, 159; favoured by John Penn for Roman Catholics, 182; and Quakers, 182; required of all Governors, 182; required of members of Assembly in Delaware, 195

Oats, an important agricultural product in Pennsylvania, 166

Observations on the Importance of the Northern Colonies under Proper Regulations, by Archibald Kennedy (1750), 240 n

Odiorne, Jotham, a member of the New Hampshire Provincial Council, 52, 53; relationship to Benning Wentworth, 52

Officeholding: in Connecticut, 86–7; compulsory features of, 87

Officers: regimental, of the Connecticut train bands, 88; election by enrolled men of all, of company grade, 88–9

Officials, the local, of Delaware, payment of, 200 n; see also Officeholding

Ogden, David, recommended by the Board of Trade as a New Jersey Councillor, 148

Oil, fish: the Massachusetts Bay production of, 8; and export of, 9; produced in Newfoundland, 255; see also Train oil

Old Light Congregationalists, the, and the Great Awakening, 25, 79, 80, 94

Oldmixon, John: on the Irish immigrants landing at Newcastle, 203; description of Newfoundland by, 248; reputed author of The British Empire in America (1741)

Orange County, New York: great land patents within, 108, 143; a plating mill in, 117

Ordinance of 1734, the, of the Elector of Hanover, for freedom of private religious devotions, 152

Oregrund, Sweden, the high quality of the iron of, 221, 228

Orgroon iron, see Oregrund

Osborn, Captain Henry, first Governor of Newfoundland, 258–9

Osborne, Sir Danvers: instructions to, relating to exorbitant New York land grants, 103, 108–9; relating to a permanent revenue, 124; appointed Governor of New York, 124–5; the death of, 125

Oswego, New York, chief fur-trading post, 119

Otis, James, Sr., one of the key figures in shaping Massachusetts Bay legislation, 32

Otter: the number of, skins brought out of Hudson Bay in 1748, 233; auction price of, 237; the trapping of, in Newfoundland, 252, 255

Oxley, Joseph, on the activities of his fellow Quakers in Wilmington, Delaware, 203

Pacifism: in Pennsylvania, 159–60; in Delaware, 196

Packer, Thomas, High Sheriff in New Hampshire, 52

Packers, the town, in Connecticut, election and duties of, 87

Pagans, in Pennsylvania, 149

Palatines, the: in New York, 113; leave New York for Pennsylvania, 113; unhappy lot of some, in Pennsylvania,

Palatines (continued)
153–5; numbers of, in Pennsylvania, 157

Palmer, Anthony, President of the Council of Pennsylvania, dangers faced by the province during the administration of, 175 n

Palmer, Eliakim, London agent for Connecticut, 98; death of, 99

Paper making, colonial beginnings of, 26 n, 202 n

Paper money, see Bills of credit, Currency

Papers Relating to Newfoundland (1793), 251n and passim

Papists, see Roman Catholics

Paris, Ferdinand John, London agent for the East New Jersey Proprietors and Pennsylvania Proprietors; opposes the approval of the bills of credit act of 1748, 133; the comment of, upon the bill of 1738 for regulating the iron industry in America, 233 n

Parkin, William, English ironmaster, on the small demand in America for English iron, 222

Parliament: provides reimbursement to the New England colonies for the Cape Breton expedition, 10; legislates in 1741, against land banks, 11–12; and the protection of the North American white pine, 31, 42; grants a bounty on American ship timber, 41; regulates the paper money of New England in 1756, 72; the denial of the constitutional right of, to regulate colonial currency by the New Jersey Assembly, 131; the encouragement of the production of iron in Ireland by, 211; regulates the American iron industry in 1750 and 1757, 225–7; investigation in 1749 of Hudson Bay by, 233 n, 234; restricts the colonial beaver-hat industry, 239–40, 241, 242; offers a reward for the discovery of a northwest passage, 244; the act to encourage trade in Newfoundland, 267; the supreme regulatory authority of, within the Empire, 273–4; no rigid pattern of colonial government created by, 275; the effect on the colonies of the trade and navigation laws passed by, 290–2; the fostering of industries within the Empire by, 292

Parmyter, Susanna, enjoys a monopoly for

Parmyter, Susanna (*continued*)
the manufacture of lamp black in New York, 117 *n*

Partridge, Richard, London agent for Rhode Island and New Jersey: and the case of the Rhode Island sloop *Jupiter*, 61; opposes the regulation of colonial paper money by Parliament, 72; while London agent for New Jersey and Rhode Island, assumes the Connecticut agency, 99; supports the New Jersey bills of credit act of 1748, 133

Partridge, William, Lieutenant Governor of New Hampshire in 1696, and the masting trade, 42 *n*

Passenger, Captain, on the carrying of Newfoundland fishermen to New England, 258

Patapsco River, Maryland, Baltimore ironworks on the, 216

Patent, royal, the: to the Duke of York of 1664, 184 *n;* to Delaware of 1683, 185 *n;* to the Council of New England, 185 *n; see also* Charter

Patents, land, *see* Land patents

Patroons, the Dutch, aristocratic and monopolistic tendencies of, 102–3

Patroonships, the, in New Netherlands, 102 *n*, 103

Patten, Matthew, of New Hampshire, the report of, on the lands of the upper Connecticut, 49

Pawtucket Falls, and the southern New Hampshire boundary, 46

Pease, Captain, sent by Baltimore to take over Avalon, 267

Pelham Manor, New York, 102; the creation of, 104 *n*

Pelts, exported from Newfoundland, 252; *see also* Furs, Skins

Pembroke, Philip Herbert, 4th Earl of, proprietary rights over Newfoundland granted to, and associates, 266 *n*

Pembrokeshire, England, waste and destruction of woods in, 210

Penacook (also Penny Cook, Rumford and later Concord), New Hampshire: the settlement of, by Massachusetts Bay people, 20–1; a fortified post, 46

Penalties: prescribed by law, in Massachusetts Bay, 32–3; in Connecticut, 91–5; in Pennsylvania, 163–5; in Delaware, 194 *n;* in Newfoundland, 263–4

Penmure, Captain Richard, of the *Charm-*

Penmure, Captain Richard (*continued*)
ing *Polly,* trading voyage of, from Rhode Island to the West Indies, 59

Penn, Hannah, wife of William Penn, the sons of, receive the Proprietary of Pennsylvania, 179

Penn, John: receives one half of the proprietary, 179; his share goes to his brother Thomas upon his death, 179; characterized, 179–80; a "fighting Quaker," 182; favours the taking of oaths by Roman Catholics, 182

Penn, Richard, joint-Proprietor of Pennsylvania, 174; son of William Penn, 179; the early repudiation of Quakerism by, 182

Penn, Thomas, chief Proprietor in 1750, 174; son of William Penn, 179; the share of, in Pennsylvania increased by the death of John Penn, 179; characterized, 179–80; the businesslike methods of, 180; revenues drawn from the proprietary by, 180; the marriage of, 182; gives up Quakerism, 182; the unpopularity of, in Pennsylvania, 183; declaration respecting the Crown claims required from, 191; derives little income from Delaware, 199

Penn, William: his code of laws (the "Great Law") accepted at Upland, 163; the humane conceptions of, 164; issues his "Frame" of 1701, 175; the sons of, by Hannah Penn, 179; the will of, 179; suit brought by the descendants of the first wife of, 179; was more idealistic than his children, 180; lacks business methods, 180; dies a Quaker, 182; activities of, in behalf of Delaware, 184–8, 198; deeds of lease and release to Delaware from Duke of York obtained by, 185; relationship of Duke of York with, 198

Penn Family, the: New Jersey lands of, stripped of timber, 141; and Pennsylvania, 179–83; claims of, to the Three Lower counties on the Delaware, 184, 198–9; breviate filed by, in Chancery, 198 *n;* defectiveness of title to Delaware of, 198–9; small profits from proprietorial rights in Delaware of, 199; and "Collections of Papers Relating to Iron," 207 *n* and *passim*

Pennamite War, reason for outbreak of, 76

Pennsylvania, the Province of: the value

Pennsylvania, the Province of: (continued) of the imports and exports of, 9–10; population of, compared with New York, 113; the coming of the Palatines into, 113; the fur trade of, affects that of New York, 118; Connecticut expansion into, 142; its many religious sects, 149; relative strength of various religious groups within, 150; political position of the Quakers in, 150; numerical predominance of the Germans in, 150; German immigration into, 151–7; Ulster Scottish immigration into, 157–8; the peopling of the frontiers of, 158; Quaker domination of the government of, until 1756, 158–66; general spirit of goodwill in, 160–1; composition of the Assembly of, 161–2; the codes of laws of, 162–6; natural resources of, 166; the leading staples of, 166; imports of, 166–7; the shipping of, 167–8; culture and social life within, 168–72; slavery within, 172–3; government finances and the people of, 173–4; as a proprietary, 174–5; Penn's charter for, 175; early experimentation in the government of, 175; law-making processes in, 175–9; the Proprietors of, in 1740, 179–80; the land system of, 180–1; the management of the proprietary of, 180–3; the attitude of the Penns toward, 182; the boundary dispute between Maryland and, 192–3; 198–9; the issue of military defence in, 196–7; the importance of the iron industry within, 218–19; the government of, in 1750, 276; the constitution of, based on letters patent, 276; the laws of, modified to conform to British statutory law, 281; possesses a unicameral legislature, 281; later to experiment with a plural executive, 282; no religious establishment in, 282; political disabilities of Jews in, 283; various boundary disputes involving, 286

Pennsylvania Gazette, the, edited by Benjamin Franklin, 171

Pennsylvania Journal, the, 13 n; on the number of Germans arriving from Holland, 151

Pennsylvania Journal and Weekly Advertiser, the, 35

Pennsylvanische Berichte, the, edited by Christoph Saur, 160, 171; the influ-

Pennsylvanische Berichte (continued) ence of, among the Pennsylvania Germans, 1-60

Penny Cook, see Penacook

Pepperrell, William: commands the Louisbourg expedition, 34; knighted for his services, 34

Persecution: within Massachusetts Bay in the seventeenth century, 54; the absence of, within Rhode Island, 56; of Baptists within Connecticut, 56; of Separatists, 80–1; of preachers within Pennsylvania, 150

Perth Amboy, New Jersey: as a free port, 128 n; a joint capital of New Jersey, 138; meetings of General Assembly of New Jersey at, 138; the release of prisoners in the gaol of, by rioters, 140

Peters, Richard, Secretary of the Province of Pennsylvania: on land monopolization in New York, 113; on the Pennsylvania magistrates, 178

Petit Nord peninsula, Newfoundland, and French fishing rights, 249

Petit treason, a felony of death offence in Pennsylvania, 165

Petition, the: of Boston merchants to compel all of the New England colonies to redeem their bills of credit, 13 n; of the Massachusetts Bay Assembly, against the French of Nova Scotia, 36; of the West Indian planters against Rhode Island traders, 59; of Rhode Island merchants against paper money, 71; of the New Jersey House of Representatives in favour of an issue of bills of credit, 134; of the Hunterdon County rioters to the Connecticut Assembly for annexation, 142; of settlers in New York, to the Connecticut Assembly for lands, 144; of English ironmasters against the American iron industry, 225–6; of English iron manufacturers for a bounty on American iron, 228; of English hat-makers for relief, 240; of Arthur Dobbs to the Privy Council for a grant of lands on Hudson Bay, 244; of British merchants for freedom of trade to Hudson Bay, 245; of Lord Baltimore for the recognition of his claims to Avalon, and its failure, 265

Philadelphia: evasions of customs by the merchants of, 8; dimensions of, in comparison to New York City, 116; as

Philadelphia: (continued)
an entrepôt for West New Jersey, 127;
the coming of German immigrants to
the port of, 152; the representation of,
in the Assembly, 161; and shipbuilding, 167; descriptions of, 167–72; population of, 168, 169 n; importance of,
as a financial centre, 168; disadvantages of, as a port, 169; a cultural
centre, 170–1; social divisions in, 172;
as a market for Delaware produce,
201; rivalry of, with New Castle, Delaware, 201

Philadelphia County, Pennsylvania: the
religious elements within, 158; the
amount raised by excise in, 174

Philipsborough Manor, New York, 102;
the creation of, 104 n; slavery in, 114

Philipse's Patent, New York, 102; quit-
rents of, 105 n

Philipses, the, among the New York
aristocracy, 109

Philosophical Society, the, of Philadelphia, 170

Phips, Spencer, Lieutenant Governor of
Massachusetts Bay: the negligence of,
35; activities of, during Shirley's absence, 35; loyalty of the province to
the Crown expressed by, 36; a proclamation of, in connection with the
New York-Massachusetts Bay land
riots, 108

Pieces of eight, see Dollar, Spanish pieces
of eight

Pierce, Richard, Boston printer, issues
the first news sheet in Massachusetts
Bay, 26

Pietists, in Pennsylvania, 149

Pig iron: the production of, in Connecticut, 77; in New York, 114, 117; export of, from Pennsylvania, 167; the
process of the production of, 212; the
problem of securing an adequate supply of, in England, 212–13; the production of, in Virginia and Maryland,
215, 216; the importation into England, free of duties, of American, 225,
228; amount of, shipped from America
to England, 226–7, 228

Pigs: the yoking and ringing of, and
Connecticut town ordinances, 87; the
production of, in Pennsylvania, 166

Pillory: the use of the, in Connecticut,
91; and in Pennsylvania, 165

Pilots, the: of Lewes, Delaware, an em-

Pilots (continued)
bargo placed upon, 187 n; of New Jersey, not embargoed, 187 n; activities
of the men of Lewes as, 200

Pine Tree shillings, the disappearance of,
in Massachusetts Bay, 14

Pinkerton, John: on the use of coke in
malt-making, 209 n; author of Voyages
and Travels (1808–14)

Pipes, tobacco, export of, from England
to Sweden, 220 n

Pirates: dangers from, in the seventeenth
century at the mouth of the Delaware,
186; defence measures against, in Delaware, 196

Piscataqua River, the: waterways of, for
masting trade, 40; as a boundary, 47

Pitch, premiums, on American-made, 220

Pit-coal, see Coal

Pitt, William, supports the British trade
and navigation system, 290

Pittsburgh, dispute between Pennsylvania
and Virginia over, 286

Placard, the use of a, as a punishment by
the Connecticut code of 1650, 91

Placentia, Newfoundland: and inshore
cod fishing, 250; troops stationed at,
250; control of, transferred to the
Governors of Newfoundland, 259; the
garrison of, forbidden to engage in the
fisheries, 260

Planters, British West India: protest of,
against Rhode Island trade with the
French sugar islands, 59

Plating mills: at Wawayanda, New York,
117; in Pennsylvania, 219

Plural voting, in New York, 109

Plymouth, England, the early interest of,
in the cod fisheries, 250 n

Plymouth, Massachusetts Bay, the town
of, fined for neglect to send deputies,
30 n

Plymouth colony, absorbed by Massachusetts Bay, 19, 29

Plymouth County, Massachusetts Bay:
comparative statistics of, 15; slave
population of, 16; iron production of,
16; represented in the Massachusetts
Bay Assembly, 32

Poole, England: the interest of, in the
cod fisheries, 250 n; and in the Newfoundland salmon fisheries, 255

Population: the slave, of Boston and Suffolk County, 6 n; estimated, of Massachusetts Bay, 15; of New Hampshire,

Population: (continued)
51; of Portsmouth, New Hampshire, 53; of Rhode Island, the rapid increase of, 57; of Rhode Island towns, 69; of Connecticut and its towns, 74 n, 75–7; the slow increase of, in New York before 1746, 112, 113; the rapid increase of, after 1750, 113 n; of New York City, 115, 116 n; of New Jersey, 126; of Pennsylvania, 150; by national and religious groups, 158–9; of Philadelphia, compared with that of Boston, 168–9; of Delaware, 203–5; of Hudson Bay, 231, 232; of Newfoundland, 251, 251 n; turbulent nature of the, of Newfoundland, 262

Pork: the export of, by Rhode Island, 56; the abundant supplies of, in New Jersey, 127; the export of, by Pennsylvania, 166

Porpoises, the production of oil from, in Newfoundland, 255

Port duties, Lord Baltimore claims the right in Avalon to levy, 272

Port Royal, Jamaica, 61

Porter, James, London merchant, unwilling to present the Connecticut address to the Crown, 96

Portsmouth, New Hampshire: the chief centre for masting trade, 40; the export of masts from, 40; and the lumbering interests, 44; as one of the most flourishing seaports in North America, 52; the entrepôt for lumber commerce, 52; as a shipbuilding centre and exporting centre for wooden manufactures, 53; as a cultural centre, 53

Portsmouth, Rhode Island, shares in the government "banks," 68

Portugal: the high price paid in, for New England codfish, 17 n; the loss of the market of, by English hatters, in favour of the French and colonial rivals, 239–41, 242; exportation of cod to, from Newfoundland, 250, 254

Portuguese fishermen: and the Grand Banks of Newfoundland, 248; and the "wet" cod fishery, 253 n

Postlethwayt, Malachy: on the destruction of woods by English ironworks, 209–10; author of Britain's Commercial Interest Explained and Improved (1757)

Potash, exported by Connecticut, 76

Potomac River, the: as the southern

Potomac River (continued)
boundary of the Maryland patent, 192 n; ironworks around, 216

Pottstown, Pennsylvania, building of a forge at, 218

Pounds, the use of town, in Connecticut, 87 n

Power, from water, in the production of iron, in 1750, 208–9

Preachers: and the Great Awakening, 23–5; the trials of, in Pennsylvania, 150

Premiums, see Bounties

Presbyterian Church, the, the dominant denomination in East New Jersey, 137

Presbyterians: in New York City, 116; in New Jersey, 137; in Pennsylvania, 149, 158, 170; in Delaware, 187, 204; activity of, in Virginia, 282

Present State of the British and French Trade to Africa, The (1745), 238

Press, the, influence of, in Massachusetts Bay, 26–7; and in Connecticut, 95

Pretender, the Old, James Edward Stuart, the attempt of, to gain the throne, and the Rhode Island law against Roman Catholics, 55

Primogeniture, adoption of legal principles of, by New York in 1683, 112

Prince of Wales Fort: a Hudson's Bay Company post, 231; description of, 232 n; barter at, 235; and the search for a northwest passage, 243

Princeton College: and Presbyterianism, 137; and higher education in America, 280

Principio ironworks, the, in Maryland, 216

Privateers: threats from, in the Delaware Bay and River, 175 n, 186 n; defence measures against, in Delaware, 196–7

Privy Council, the: and the land bank project in Massachusetts Bay, 11; and Massachusetts Bay legislation before 1743, 30; the decision of, in the Massachusetts Bay-New Hampshire boundary dispute, 45, 106; an appeal to the Lords of the Committee on Appeals of, in the case of the Jupiter, 60–1; the Mohegan Indians' appeal before, 97; the Connecticut intestacy law disapproved by, 98, 100 n; the refusal of, to permit the repeal of the New York land law of 1699, 104; a decision in favour of New York in the New York-

Privy Council (*continued*)
New Hampshire boundary dispute by, 106; censures the New York Assembly, 124; the sound-money position of, 129–30; the attitude of, toward colonial bills of credit, 129–36; fails to terminate the New York-New Jersey boundary dispute, 145; the attitude of, toward the New Castle code, 164; an order of, repealing the convict transport law of Pennsylvania, 177; inaction by, on the Sutherland memorial, 193; a petition to, for leave to settle lands west of Hudson Bay, 244–5; the regulation of the Newfoundland fisheries by, 257 *n;* the approval of laws by, 276, 279; the power of, to act on appeals from all colonial courts, 279; supports the rights of Roman Catholics in Nevis and Montserrat, 283

Probate districts, the, in Connecticut, 89

Proclamation money: Massachusetts Bay currency and, 12–13; Rhode Island currency and, 70

Proposals Relating to the Education of Youth in Pennsylvania (1749) by Benjamin Franklin, 171 *n*

Proprietors: town, in Massachusetts Bay, 20; conflict in New Hampshire over the issue as to who were, of unoccupied lands, 47; in Connecticut, the meetings of, 84, 85, 86, 88; the privileged position of, 84, 85; rights of New York, ignored, 106; violent opposition to, in New Jersey, 139–42; of East New Jersey seek to settle the issue of the northern boundary of New Jersey, 143; the Pennsylvania, and the government of the province, 174–83; the conflict between the, over Delaware, 184–6, 191–3, 198–9; and over Avalon, 264–72

Proroguing the Assembly: the right of, in Massachusetts Bay, 31, 49; in Pennsylvania, 176

Protestants, *see* Anglicans, Baptists, Congregationalists, Dunkards, Lutherans, Mennonites, Moravian Brethren, Quakers, Presbyterians, Reformed, Sabbatarians, Seventh Day Baptists

Providence, Rhode Island: the enterprise of the merchants of, 58–9; their support of northern area agricultural population, 67; rivalry of, with Newport, 67; the proportion of the "banks"

Providence, Rhode Island: (*continued*)
awarded to, for loan, 68; small proportion of voters in, 69

Prussia: an edict against the Moravian Brethren by the King of, 152; why Würtembergers were unwilling to go to, 160 *n*

Public finance: in Massachusetts Bay, 10–14; in New Hampshire, 14 *n;* in Rhode Island, 70–3; in Connecticut, 90 *n,* 99; in New York, 120; in New Jersey, 128–36; in Pennsylvania, 174; in Delaware, 199

Public Occurrences, Both Foreign and Domestic, America's first news sheet, 26

Punishments, *see* Penalties

Puritanism: in Massachusetts Bay, 19, 21–26; in Connecticut, 78–80; effect on laws of, 90, 92–5

Puritans, the, of New England, modify their laws to harmonize with British statutory and common law, 281

Quakers, the: in Massachusetts Bay, the exemptions secured by, 22; in Rhode Island, the strength of, 54–5; supported for office by Baptists, 56; in Connecticut, 81, 86 *n;* reversal of attitude toward, by the Connecticut government, 99; in New York City, 116; in New Jersey, the predominance of, in west New Jersey, 137; the influence of the ideals of, 138; in the shaping of public law, 138, 162–3; in Pennsylvania, 149, 162–3; strength of, and the decline in the numerical strength of, 149–50; the dominance of, in the three old counties of Pennsylvania, 158–9; alliance of, with Germans, 159–60; dominance of, in the Pennsylvania Assembly to 1756, 161–3; resignation from the Pennsylvania Assembly of, from Bucks and Chester counties in 1756, 162; compromise of ideals in ruling Pennsylvania, 165; the attitude of, toward slavery in 1749, 172–3; in Delaware, political disabilities of, 195; franchise discrimination against, in Delaware, 196; lack of provisions in Delaware military defence legislation for scruples of, 196; relief from military service of, upon payment, 197; attitudes on defence measures by certain, 197 *n;* growing strength of, in

Quakers (continued)
Wilmington, 203; in Kent County, 204; seek to adopt laws in harmony with the New Testament, 281; activity of, in the Puritan colonies in 1750, 282

Quebec Act, the, of 1774, 29

Queen Anne: legislation in reign of, against cutting of pine trees, 41; disapproval of New York's land policy by, 104

Queen's College (Rutgers), and the beginnings of higher education in America, 280

Quit-rents: and New Hampshire, 49, 51; lower on New Hampshire lands than on those of New York, 50; not levied in Connecticut, 75; in New York, 50, 103, 104, 105 n, 109; in New Jersey, 136, 141; the collection of, in Pennsylvania, 158, 180–2; in Delaware, 199; confusion over, in Delaware, 199; Duke of York's demand for, from the Dutch and Swedes, 199 n; the Baltimore claims to Avalon and the right to, 272

Quoits, the playing at, forbidden in Connecticut, 94

Randolph, Edward, Surveyor General of His Majesty's Woods, 41; as Surveyor General of Customs, recommends the appointment of crown attorney generals in all the colonies, 96–7

Rape: the capital laws of 1650 against, in Connecticut, 91; a capital crime in Pennsylvania, 165

Raynor, Captain John, appointed Deputy Governor over Avalon, 267

Rea, William, Monmouth ironmaster, on the distribution of ironworks and coppices in England and Wales, 207 n

Reasons Against the Importation of Sow and Pig Iron from America into Great Britain under the Present low Duty (n.d.), 222 n

Reasons Against the Making and Manufacturing of Barr Iron in America . . . (n.d.), 222 n

Reasons for Allowing the Importation of Bar-Iron from America (post 1750), 228 n

Reasons for Encouraging the Importations of Iron in Bars from his Majesty's Plantations in America (1717 ?), 214 n

Rebellion, the capital law of 1650 against, in Connecticut, 91, 92 n

Redemptioners, see Indentured servants

Red River, the, and French trading posts west of the Hudson Bay area, 246

Redwood, Abraham, a leading Rhode Island merchant, 58

Redwood, Jonas and William, Rhode Island owners of the slaver Cassada Garden, 64

Rees, William, Massachusetts Bay man, killed during land dispute with New York, 108

Reeves, John, author of History of the Government of the Island of Newfoundland (1793), 257 n

Refineries, sugar, at Newport, Rhode Island, 66; in New York, 117

Reformed, the German, the large numbers of, in Pennsylvania, 149; see also Dutch Reformed Church, German Reformed Church

Reimbursement, parliamentary: voted to colonies participating in Cape Breton campaign, 34; the threat of not providing, used to check Rhode Island's financial irresponsibility, 72; of Delaware, for participation in Great War for the Empire, 197

Religion: in Massachusetts Bay, 21–6; in New Hampshire, 51; in Rhode Island, 54–6; in Connecticut, 78–81, 86, 94; in New York, 116; in New Jersey, 137–8; in Pennsylvania, 149–50, 158–63; in Delaware, 187, 203–4; in Newfoundland, 250, 250 n, 262; within the Empire, 282–4

Religious freedom: the guarantee of, in Massachusetts Bay, 30; in Rhode Island, 55–6; in Connecticut, 81, 86; in Pennsylvania, 149–50; within the Empire, 282–4

Remarks upon Captain Middleton's Defense (1743), by Arthur Dobbs, 244 n

Rensselaer Manor, New York, 102

Rensselaerwyck, New York, 102; quit-rents of, 105 n

"Report from the Committee Appointed to Inquire into the State and Conditions of the Countries adjoining the Hudson's Bay . . ." (1749), 233 n and passim

"Report on the Lands in the Province of New York" (1732), by Cadwallader Colden, 104 n

"Report on the State of the Province of New York" (1774), 114 n

Representation: of towns in Massachusetts Bay Assembly, 31; of towns in the Rhode Island Assembly, 67; of cities and counties in New Jersey, 122 n; of Philadelphia and the counties in the Pennsylvania Assembly, 161; in Delaware, by counties, 193

Revenues, see Public Finance, Quit-rents, Taxation

Revolution of 1689, the, 28, 29, 96

Rhine, upper, the, journey from, to America by German emigrants described, 153

Rhode Island and Providence Plantations: the value of the imports and exports of, 9–10; the Boston merchants petition the Crown against the bills of credit of, 13 n; the separate existence of, threatened by Massachusetts Bay, 18–19; a commission to settle the boundary between Massachusetts Bay and, 33; the sectaries of, 54; the founding of, 54–5; religious toleration in, 55, 56, 282; discrimination against Roman Catholics in, 55, 283; lack of a religious establishment within, 55, 282; contrasted and compared with Connecticut, 56, 74; the attitude toward the Jews in, 56, 283; the natural resources of, 56; the export of surplus food from, 56; the inhabitants of, 57; occupations in, 57; aristocratic elements within, 57; expanding foreign trade of, 58–9; the merchant princes of, engage in illicit trading, 58, 59–62, 291; the West India planters protest against traders of, 59; the rum industry of, 62; the slave trade and, 63; political and commercial sectionalism within, 67; the government of, 67–8, 276; public finance in, 68–71; the currency problems of, 68–73, 279; the regulation of paper money of, by Parliament, 72–3; not obliged to send laws to England for approval, 131, 279; the making of anchors within, 217–18; the constitution of, based on letters patent, 276; the Governors of, weak in authority, 278; great role in the commercial life of, played by Jews, 284

Rice, as an enumerated commodity, 291

Riots, land: on Livingston Manor, 106–8; in Dutchess County, New York, and the use of British regulars, 108; in New Jersey, 139–42, 145

Rittenhouse, William, constructs first paper mill in America, 26 n

Roads, in Connecticut, the repair of, and compulsory work, 87

Robbery: the punishment of, in Connecticut, 91; a capital crime in Pennsylvania, 165

Robson, Joseph, Hudson's Bay Company factor: on the Company posts, 231 n, 232 n; the examination of, by the parliamentary committee, 234 n; on Hudson's Bay Company trading operations, 242; author of An Account of Six Years' Residence in Hudson's Bay (1752)

Rochester, New Hampshire, a fortified post, 46

Rockingham, Charles Watson Wentworth, Marquess of, relationship of New Hampshire Wentworths to, 51 n

Rocky Mountains, the, a French trading post, Fort La Jouquière, within sight of, 246

Rodney, George Brydges: the appointment of, as Governor of Newfoundland, 256, 259; the general instructions of, 256 n, 260–1; protests against the carrying of Irish Catholics to Newfoundland, 262; the difficulties facing, in attempting to maintain order, 263

Roman Catholics: in Boston, 22 n; the denial of religious freedom to, permitted under the Massachusetts Bay Charter, 30; the disabilities of, in Rhode Island, 55; in New York, 116, 228; in Pennsylvania, 149; a church for, in Philadelphia, 170; the disabilities of, in Delaware, 196; in Newfoundland, the predominance of, from Ireland, 250; constitute the majority of the population in 1749 and 1765, 251 n, 262, 264; the lack of freedom of conscience for, in Newfoundland, 260; disabilities of, in Antigua, Georgia, Maryland, Nevis, and Virginia, 283; enjoy rights of franchise in Montserrat and St. Christopher, 283

Rope-walks, in the colonies for producing rope, 292

Rotterdam, Holland, place of embarka-

Rotterdam, Holland (*continued*)
tion for the German immigrants to
America, 153

Roxbury in Suffolk County, represented
in Massachusetts Bay Assembly, 32

Royal African Company, the, difficulties
faced by, 244–5

Royal colonies, the similarities in the governments of, 275–6; *see also* Antigua,
the Bahamas, Barbados, the Bermudas,
Jamaica, Massachusetts Bay, Montserrat, Nevis, New Hampshire, New Jersey, New York, Newfoundland, North
Carolina, Nova Scotia, South Carolina,
Virginia

Royal instructions, *see* Instructions

Rum: the production of, in Massachusetts
Bay, 16; part played by, in the economy of the province, 16; the triangular trade in, 16, 63–5; the production
of, in Rhode Island, 62; an excise on,
collected in Connecticut, 87; the production of, in New York, 117; the use
of, in the Albany-Oswego Indian trade,
119; the sale of, in Newfoundland in
1750, 251–2; the sale of, earlier forbidden by the Western Charter, 260 *n*

Rumbout's Patent, New York, 102; the
creation of, 104 *n*

Rumford, New Hampshire, the dispute
over the seating of deputies of, 48–9;
see also Penacook

Rupert, Prince, and the Hudson's Bay
Company, 236

Russia: early dependence of England for
ship timber upon, 41; an edict against
the Moravian Brethren by the Tzarina
of, 152; the dependence of English industry upon the iron of, 210; comparison of American iron to that from,
221; a demand for a duty upon iron
imported from, into Great Britain, 228

Rutter, Thomas, early ironmaster of
Pennsylvania, 218

Ryder, Sir Dudley, Attorney General:
Board of Trade seeks opinion of, on
Governor's powers to appoint by commission in New York, 121 *n;* the report
of, upon the Crown interference with
Pennsylvania, 178 *n;* and the Baltimore
petition respecting Avalon, 270

Rye, an important product in Pennsylvania, 166

Sabbatarians, the, of Westerly, Rhode
Island, 56

Sabbath, the, in Connecticut, the keeping of, 92–3

Sack-ships, the Newfoundland, 250–1,
252, 254, 255, 256, 259

Sagadahoc River (the Kennebec), the,
and land grants, 30, 47

Sailors, the radical tendencies of, in
Connecticut, 84 *n; see also* Mariners,
Seamen

St. Christopher: Rhode Island slavers stop
at, 65; the constitution of, 276; Roman Catholics of, enjoy the franchise,
283

St. Domingue, the fertility of, 287; *see
also* Hispaniola

St. Eustatius, Dutch West India island,
and Rhode Island trade, 59

St. John, His Majesty's cutter, fired upon
in 1764 in Narragansett Bay, 62

St. John's, Newfoundland: the town of,
as the centre of English activity on
Avalon peninsula, 250; the number of
Irish Catholics at, 262

St. Malo, France, the interest of, in the
Great Banks fisheries, 249

St. Vincent, West Indies, and Rhode Island trade, 59

Salem, Massachusetts Bay, the importance
of the fish exports of, 7 *n*

Salem County, representation from, in
the New Jersey Assembly, 138

Salmon fishing, in Newfoundland, 255

Salt, the importance of the best quality
of, in the curing of cod, 250 *n*

Salter, the, the part played by, in the
cod-curing process, 253

Saltonstall, Gurdon, Governor of Connecticut, sent to England by the Colony, 97

Saskatchewan River, the, French trading
posts on, 234, 246

Saugus River, Massachusetts Bay, promotion of ironworks on the, 217

Saur (Sauer, Sower), Christoph: the opposition of, to the proprietorial interests, 159; editor of the *Pennsylvanische
Berichte,* 159; on German oppression,
160

Saw mills: in Delaware, 202; on the iron
plantations, 218

Saxby, Henry: on duties on iron, 213;
author of *The British Customs . . .*
(1757)

Saybrook, Connecticut, the persecution
of Separatists at, 80

Scandinavia, the early dependence of England for ship timber upon, 41

Scarsdale Manor, New York, 102; the creation of, 104 n

Schoharie Valley, New York, the Palatines in, 113

Schuylers, the, among the New York aristocracy, 109

Scientific activity, growth of, in New England and America, 28 n

Scotch-Irish, see Ulster Scots

Scotland: settlers from, in East New Jersey, 137; relative success of farmers from, in Pennsylvania, 157 n; settlers from, in Delaware, 203

Scots, the: settled in East New Jersey, 137; number of, in Pennsylvania in 1729, 157; in Delaware, 203

Scott, George, master of the brig Little George, faced with slave revolt, 65

Scottish Highlanders, the contribution of, to English colonial civilization, 281

Scythes: the production of, in England, 208; decline in the British manufacture of, 214; decline in American demand for British, 219

Sea coal, see Coal

Seal, the Crown or colonial, of government, see Great Seal

Sealers, the town, in Connecticut, the election and duties of, 87

Seals, financial returns to Newfoundlanders by the catching of, 255

Seamen, the: of Massachusetts Bay, 17–18; the aggressiveness of, 18; the number of, on Rhode Island slave ships, 63; the prohibition against the carrying away of, from Newfoundland, 258

Secessionists, see Separatists

Secretary, the: of Massachusetts Bay a royal appointee, 29; election of, in Rhode Island, 67; in Connecticut, 83

Sects, see Religion

Selectmen, the town, in Connecticut: the election of, 85; the civil responsibilities of, 86; the religious responsibilities of, 93

Separatists: in Connecticut, the persecution of, in 1750, 80; the toleration of, by the code of 1784, 95; in Pennsylvania, 149

Servitude, white, see Indentured servants

"Seven pillars," the, of the Connecticut church communion, 79

Seventh Day Baptists: in Rhode Island, 56; in Pennsylvania, 149

Severn House, a Hudson's Bay Company post, 235 n

Severn River, England, the advantages of, for iron production, 210

Severn Valley, the, shifting of iron smelting to, 209

Sexual acts, unnatural: and the death penalty in Connecticut, 91, 95; in New York, 163

Shallops, the use of, in the Newfoundland cod fisheries, 251, 253

Sheep: the export of, by Rhode Island, 57; the scarcity of, in Newfoundland, 252

Sheffield, England, the iron manufacturers of: oppose the duty on Swedish iron, 228; on the poor quality of American iron, 228

Sheffield, Massachusetts Bay: the sheriff of Albany County, New York, confined at, 107; the incorporation of, 107 n

"Shelburne Papers," 7 and passim

Sherburne, Henry, a member of the New Hampshire Council, 52; relationship of, to Benning Wentworth, 52

Sheriff, the: in Rhode Island, the election of, 69; in Connecticut, the appointment of, 90; the duties and powers of, 90 n; in New York, the indignities experienced by, of Albany County, 107, 108

Ship timber: and the New England white-pine belt, 39; bounties on, granted by Parliament, 42; furnished by New Jersey, 127; and by Pennsylvania, 167

Shipbuilding: and the northern colonies, 4; in Massachusetts Bay, 6, 14, 53 n; the decline of, in Boston, 6 n, 7; various costs of, within the Empire, 7; at Portsmouth, New Hampshire, 52, 53; at Newport, Rhode Island, 66; in Connecticut, 76; in Pennsylvania, 167; in Delaware, 202, 203 n

Shipley, William: role of, in creation of Wilmington, 203 n; Quaker activities of, 203 n

Shipping, the: of Boston, 6, 7–8, 16, 17; of New Hampshire, 53 n; of Rhode Island, 58; of Connecticut, 76, 77 n; of New York, 116; of New Jersey, 127; of Pennsylvania, 167–9; of Delaware, 201–2; of Hudson Bay, 233; of the

Shipping (*continued*)
Newfoundland fisheries, 251 *n*, 252–5, 258

Ships: of Massachusetts Bay, sale of, to English merchants, 6, 6 *n;* owned by merchants of Rhode Island, 58; of Newport registry, in foreign and domestic trade, 58 *n;* slaving, of Rhode Island, 63; number of, owned by New York maritime interests, 116; of New Jersey, 127 *n;* emigrant, to Pennsylvania, 154; type and number of, used in Hudson Bay Trade, 233; the protection of, 260

Shirley, William, Governor of Massachusetts Bay: the commission of, 33; the early public career of, 33; characterized, 33; the activities of, during King George's War, 33–5; knighted, 34; a member of the Anglo-French commission, 34–5; harmonious relationship of, with the Assembly, 35; seeks a change of post, 35; frees the sheriff of Albany County from the Springfield gaol, 108

Shops, a penalty for keeping open, on the Sabbath in Connecticut, 97

Short Account of Iron, made in . . . Virginia and Maryland, A (post 1746), 216 *n*

Short Narrative and Justification of the Proceedings of the Committee appointed by the Adventurers to prosecute the Discovery of the Passage to the Western Ocean of America, A (1749), by Arthur Dobbs, 245 *n*

Short View of the Countries and Trade carried on by the Company in Hudson's Bay, A (1749), by Arthur Dobbs, 244 *n*

Shrewsbury, England: iron of, 222; petition from, in support of Arthur Dobbs's attack on the Hudson's Bay Company, 245

Shrewsbury, New Jersey, the New England background of, 137

Shropshire, England: iron of Clee Hills of, 208; waste and destruction of woods in, 210

Shuffle-boards, the playing at, forbidden in Connecticut, 94

Sierra Leone (Siraloone, Siralone), the, a Rhode Island slave ship, 63, 65 *n*

Sikes, Walter, the deputy for Lord Baltimore in Avalon, 266

Silk hats, supersede beaver hats in the nineteenth century, 237

Sioux Indians, the, hostilities between the Assiniboines and, 246 *n*

Skins: the Pennsylvania Indian trade in, 167; number and type of, from Hudson Bay, 233; on the enumerated list, 291; *see also* Deerskins, Pelts

Slave ships, American: from Rhode Island described, 63; the trade of, 63–5

Slave trade, the: and Massachusetts Bay rum, 16, 17; and the Rhode Island merchants, 63–6; and the export of New York spirits, 117

Slaver, *see* Slave ships

Slavery: in Massachusetts Bay, 5; in Rhode Island, 57; in New York, 114, 116 *n;* in Pennsylvania, the attitude of the Quakers toward in 1750, 172; economic importance of, determined by various factors, 284; *see also* Slaves, Slave trade

Slaves: numbers of, in Boston, 6; in Suffolk County, 6, 16; population in various Massachusetts Bay counties, 16; and the Rhode Island plantations about South Kingstown, 57; the cost of Negro, 64; difficulty of procuring, at Anamabo, 64; and the New York manors, 114; in New York City, 116 *n;* in Pennsylvania, the number of, 172–3; the import duty on, 173 *n;* in Delaware, the number of, 205; economic importance of, in areas of staple agricultural crops, 284; social importance of, in other colonial areas, 284; the concentration of, determines nature of slave codes, 285; *see also* Negroes, Slave trade

Slaying through guile: the capital law of 1650 against, in Connecticut, 91; penalty for, a defenceless man, in New York, 163

Slitting mills, provisions of the Iron Act concerning American, 229

Smelting, the process of, iron ore in 1750, 208

Smith, Captain, on the value of the Newfoundland fisheries, 255 *n*

Smith, Samuel, Clerk of the New Jersey House of Representatives, recommended for a place on the Council, 148

Smith, Dr. William, Provost of the College of Philadelphia: demands the dis-

Smith, Dr. William (*continued*)
enfranchisement of the Pennsylvania
Germans, 161; comment of, on the
Council of Pennsylvania, 175; author
of *Brief State of the Province of Pennsylvania* (1755)

Smith, William, acts as counsel for the
town of Elizabeth, 141 *n*

Smiths, the, among the New York aristocracy, 110

Smuggling: by Boston merchants, 17;
methods employed in, by Rhode Island traders, 59; in Connecticut, 77

Society for the Propagation of the Gospel in Foreign Parts, the: sermon by
Bishop George Berkeley before, 54; a
letter to, on the Anglicans in Delaware,
204

Society of Friends, the, *see* Quakers

Sodomy: the capital law of 1650 against,
in Connecticut, 91; and the Connecticut code of 1784, 95

Soil, the: of Rhode Island, the indiffer-
ent quality of, 56; of New York, the
quality of, superior to that of New
England, 112; of New Jersey, the rich
alluvial quality of, 127; of Pennsylvania, described, 166

Soldiers, *see* British regulars, Militia,
Train bands

Solicitor General, the, of England, unfavourable opinion of, on Penn's rights
in Delaware, 190

Solley, Samuel, a member of the New
Hampshire Council, 52; relationship to
Benning Wentworth, 52

*Some Account of the Pennsylvania Hos-
pital . . .* (1754), by Benjamin Franklin, 171 *n*

"Some Considerations on the Bill to Encourage the Importations of Pig and
Bar Iron from America" (1749), 224 *n*

*Some Considerations Showing that the
Importation of Iron from America will
Sooner put a Stop to the Making of
Iron in England than the Importation
of Iron from Sweden and Russia*
(1736 ?), 222 *n*

Somerset County, New Jersey: the Scottish population of, 137; representation
of, in the Assembly, 138; the spread of
land riots to, 140

South Carolina: people from, summer at
Newport, Rhode Island, 67; exporting
of axes to, 217; the government of,

South Carolina: (*continued*)
276; the instructions to the Governor
of, altered, 277; the Anglican establishment and, 282; political disabilities of
Jews in, 283; the slave code of, 285;
western charter limits of, 286

South County, Rhode Island: and slavery, 57; development of a modified
plantation system in, 57

South Hampton, New Hampshire, the
dispute over the seating of deputies of,
48–9

South Kingstown, Rhode Island: and the
plantation system, 57; a share in the
"banks" allotted to, 68; population
and number of freemen voters in, 69

Southampton, England: the early interest of, in the cod fisheries, 250 *n*; the
interest of, in the Newfoundland
salmon fisheries in 1750, 255

Spain: importation of iron from, into
England, 211; a demand by English
furnacemen for an extra duty on iron
imported from, 228; skill in making
English beaver hats derived from, 237;
the competition of English and French
beaver hat makers for the market of,
239, 241–2; the exportation of cod to,
from Newfoundland, 250, 254

Spanish pieces of eight: value of, in
sterling and proclamation money, 13;
the Massachusetts Bay bills of credit
redeemed in, 13–14

Specie: the receipt of, by Massachusetts
Bay from England, as reimbursement,
10; value of, in Massachusetts Bay in
terms of local currency, 13–14; of the
British West Indies carried by New
England traders to the French sugar
islands, 17, 65; New Jersey bills of
credit preferred to, 129

Spermaceti, the use of, in candles, 66

Spirituality, deep concern of Connecticut
lawmakers with, 93

Split Lake Fort, a Hudson's Bay Company post, 231

Spooner, Abraham, Birmingham ironmaster: on the number of those dependent upon iron production about
Birmingham, 207; on the lack of demand for English hardware in the
plantations, 215; warns that American
ironworks will destroy those in England, 222

Spotswood, William, former Deputy

Spotswood, William (*continued*)
Governor of Virginia, and the development of Virginia ironworks, 216

Springfield, Massachusetts Bay: early settlement of, on the Connecticut River, 107; the confining of the sheriff of Albany County in the gaol at, 108

Squatting: of the Palatines in New York, 113; of Ulster Scots in New Jersey, 139, 141; of Ulster Scots in Pennsylvania, 158

Staffordshire, England: source of supply of iron ore for the furnaces of, 208; waste and destruction of woods in, 210; and the making of nails, 215; petitions for relief by the ironmasters and ironmongers of, 220

Stages: and the drying of codfish, 256; the protection of, in Newfoundland, 260

Staple fur, from beaver skins, 237

State of the Trade and Manufactory of Iron in Great Britain, The (1750), 209 *n*, 227

Steel: the making of, in Connecticut, 77 *n*; iron from the Forest of Dean easily converted into, 208; the importation of bar, into New England, 217; the setting-up of, furnaces in New England, 217; and in Pennsylvania, 219; the making of, in America restricted in 1750, 219

"Stenton," the home of James Logan, 171

Stephens, William, President of the Colony of Georgia, 74 *n*

Stiles, Dr. Ezra, the early residence of, at Newport, Rhode Island, 66–7

Stocks, the use of the, in Connecticut, 91

Stoddard, the Rev. Solomon, Northampton pastor: and the church ordinances, 22; grandfather of Jonathan Edwards, 23

Stourbridge, England, unemployment in the ironworks at, 214

Strafford, Thomas Wentworth, Earl of, relationship of the New Hampshire Wentworth family to, 51 *n*

Strangers: in Connecticut towns, the treatment of, in 1750, 85; and in 1784, 95; in Pennsylvania, the kindly treatment of, 160, 166

Stratford, Connecticut: the rating of, for taxation, 75 *n*; site of first Anglican church in Connecticut, 78

Street lights, the use of, in Philadelphia, and the method of paying for, 173

Stubbornness of a child, the capital law of 1650 against, in Connecticut, 91

Success, the, Rhode Island slave ship, 63 *n*

Suffolk County, Massachusetts Bay: slaves within, 6, 16; number of ratable polls in, 15; houses in, in 1751, 15; rating of, in agriculture, 15; the production of iron in, 16; number of towns in, in 1751, 19

Sugar: the importation of, into Massachusetts Bay, 7; vast traffic in, by Rhode Island merchants, 58–9, 66; importation of, to Connecticut, 76; the manufacture of refined and baked, in New York, 117; importation of, to Newfoundland, 254; discriminatory tariffs against foreign produced, 291; an enumerated article, 291

Sugar Act of 1733, the: non-enforcement of, in Rhode Island, 59; involved high duties on foreign-produced molasses, sugar, and rum imported into the colonies, 291; *see also* Molasses Act

Sugar refineries, in Newport, Rhode Island, 66

Summary, Historical and Political . . . of the Present State of the British Settlements in North America, A (1755), by William Douglass, 6, 77

Sunderland, Massachusetts Bay, fined for neglect to send deputies to the Assembly, 29 *n*

Superior Court of Judicature, the, of Connecticut, the duties of, 90

Surrey, the County of, England, additional ironworks forbidden within, 209

Surveyor General of customs, the, estimates of imports into North America by, 9–10

Surveyor General of lands, the: of New York, condemns the loose way of granting provincial lands, 104; duties of, in Pennsylvania, 181

Surveyor General of the King's Woods: William Shirley appointed as, 33; duties of office of, 41; people who occupied the post of, 41, 43

Surveyors of highways, the town, in Connecticut, the election of, and duties of, 87

Susquehanna Company, the: formation of, by Connecticut men, 76; settle-

Susquehanna Company (*continued*)
ments in northern Pennsylvania by, 286

Sussex, the County of, England: additional ironworks forbidden within, 209; the denuding of woodlands within, 210

Sussex County, Delaware: grant of, to Penn, drafted by James II, 186 *n;* representation of, in the Assembly, 193; the unfertile soil of, 201; religious affiliation of settlers in, 204

Sussex County, New Jersey: erected out of Morris County, 144; the magistrates of, defend the rights of the New Jersey settlers, 144

Sutherland, John Gordon, Earl of, attempts by, and by his son to secure a royal grant to Delaware, 190, 192, 193

Swanley, Robert, appointed Governor of Newfoundland by Baltimore, 267

Sweden: the dependence of English industry upon the iron of, 210, 211, 213, 220, 221; restrictions on the importation of English goods into, by royal edict, 211; price of iron of, 214; English exportations to, 220; the demand for a duty on iron imported from, 228; the loss of the markets in, by English hatters in favour of the French, 241

Swedes, the: colonization of Delaware by, 184, 187, 202; the contribution of, to English colonial civilization, 281

Swedish iron, *see* Oregrund, Sweden

Swedish language, the decline in the use of, in Delaware, 202

Swedish Lutheran Church, the, in Delaware, 202

Swimming, in Connecticut, forbidden on the Sabbath, 93

Swiss, the, the contribution of, to English colonial civilization, 281

Swords, to be possessed by all Connecticut householders, 88 *n*

Tables, the playing at, forbidden in Connecticut, 94

Talbot, Charles, Solicitor General, gives an opinion on grievances by Anglicans against the Massachusetts Bay Church Establishment, 22 *n*

Tar, of New England, 7; premiums on American-made, 220

Taverns: in Connecticut, restrictions on proprietors of, 94; in Philadelphia, the

Taverns: (*continued*)
number of, 174 *n;* in Newfoundland, 252, 253

Tax Collectors, the town, in Connecticut, the election of, 87

Taxation: the lack of in Rhode Island in 1750, 70; the high rate of, in England, 101 *n*, 224; the low rate of, in Connecticut, 101; unimproved land in New York not subject to, 112; the absence of, in New Jersey, 128, 134; the absence of any general, in Pennsylvania, 173–4; absence of, in Delaware, 200

Taylor, Captain, master of the Rhode Island slaver *Cassada Garden*, 64

Taylor, Isaac, furnishes New England white-pine masts, 43 *n*

Teignmouth, England, the interest of, in the cod fisheries, 250 *n*

Tenants: of Livingston Manor, support Massachusetts Bay claims, 106; land worked by, in New York, 114; the riotous conduct of, in Hunterdon County, New Jersey, 140–1

Tennant, Gilbert, religious revivalist, 23

Territorial claims, *see* Boundaries

Territories, the, *see* Delaware

Thomas, George, Deputy Governor of Pennsylvania and Delaware: appeal by, for military support, 196; quarrels with the Pennsylvania Assembly over defensive measures, 197; approbation for Delaware given by, 197–8; on bills of credit in Delaware, 200 *n*

Thomlinson, John, London agent of New Hampshire: on the appointment of Wentworth to office, 44; the activities of, concerning the New Hampshire boundary dispute, 45–6

"Thomlinson Papers," 46 *n*

Thompson, Edward, testifies before Parliament on the growing of field crops in the Hudson Bay area, 233 *n*

Three Lower Counties on the Delaware, the, *see* Delaware

Thurston, Mark, Accountant General of the Court of Chancery, a member of the Hudson's Bay Company, 236

Tidewaiter, the struggle over the appointment of a New York, 121

Timber: ship, of New England, 8, 39; the protection of, and the Massachusetts Bay charter, 31; in New Hampshire, the value of, 39–41; Parliament

Timber: (*continued*)
and the preservation of American, 41–2; the exploitation of, promoted, 42; of Pennsylvania, 167

Timber-land: the plundering of, in New Jersey, 140, 141; the wastage of, in England, 209; the value of, in England, 212; in Wales, 214; *see also* Timber, White-pine trees

Tin, the export from England of, to Sweden, 220 *n*

Tippling, the punishment for, in Connecticut, 91, 95

Tithingmen, the town, of Connecticut, the election and duties of, 86, 93

Tiverton, Rhode Island: population of, 69; number of voters in, 69

Tobacco: the use of, and the Connecticut code of 1650, 91, 95; decline of trade in, of Delaware, 189 *n;* the sale of, forbidden in Newfoundland, 260 *n;* as an enumerated commodity, 291

Toleration, religious: in Rhode Island, 55–6; in Connecticut, 81; the English Act of, 81 *n;* in Pennsylvania, 149–50; in Delaware, 202–4

Topsham, England, the interest of, in the cod fisheries, 250 *n*

Tour Through Ireland by Two English Gentlemen, A (1748), describes Birmingham, 207

Tower Arsenal, gun barrels produced in Birmingham for the, 208

Town meeting house, symbol of social solidarity in Connecticut, 79

Town meetings: in Connecticut, 84–8; qualifications for participation in, 84–6; the courts of election at, 87; variety and importance of ordinances passed in, 87–8; and the training of politicians, 88

Towns: in Massachusetts Bay, the number of, 19–20, 31; regulations regarding the creation of new, 19–20; the creation of new, in New Hampshire, and issue over Assembly representation, 48–9; and frontier defence, 48–50; in Rhode Island, the distribution of the "banks" among the, 68–9; in Connecticut, the comparative size of, 74–5 *n;* the government of, 84–8; in New York, 115, 118; in New Jersey, and the provincial government, 137–8; in Pennsylvania, 168–9; in Delaware,

Towns: (*continued*)
168, 196, 201–2; English, interested in the cod fishery, 250 *n*

Townships: creation of, in Massachusetts Bay, 20; the granting of, about the Upper Connecticut River, 50–1; erection of, in Connecticut, 75; ownership of lands within, 75, 84; representation of, in the Connecticut Assembly, 89; of New Jersey, settled by New England people, 137, 139

Trade: of Massachusetts Bay, 8–9, 16; of New Hampshire, 51, 52; of Rhode Island, 58–61; of Connecticut, 76; of New York, 116–19; of New Jersey, 127; of Pennsylvania, 166–8; of Delaware, 201–2; of England involving iron and hardware, 211–4, 223–8; of the Hudson's Bay Company, 230–7, 242–3; the French of Canada compete for the fur, 230, 238; of England, in beaver hats, 237–42; in Newfoundland, 250–5; the issue over, between the northern British colonies and the foreign West Indies, 287–9; extent of freedom of, enjoyed by the colonies, 291; restrictions on colonial, 291; *see also* Commerce, Exports, Imports, Slave trade

Trade and Navigation acts, the: violations of, in Rhode Island, 60; observance of, at Hudson Bay, 230; and Newfoundland, 258; restricts the economic activities of British colonials, 289; the objectives of, 289–90; Abercromby's report on, 290; failure of the enforcement of, 290; support of, by all British statesmen, 290; the effect of, on the British colonies, 291–2

Traders, *see* Commerce, Fur trade, Indian trade, Merchants, Rum, Slave trade

Trading goods: value and list of, for Hudson Bay trade, 234; differences in prices of, at various posts, 234; French, and the Indian trade, 246

Trading posts: location of, on Hudson Bay, 231; cost of maintaining Hudson Bay, 233

Train bands: the radical tendencies of the, in Connecticut, 84 *n*, 88; requirements for service in, 88; exemptions from service in, 88; the organization of, 88–9; the election of the officers of, 89

Train oil, the value of, exported from Newfoundland, 252, 255

Tramount (Tremont, Trimontaine), Boston, 5

Transportation, of slaves from Africa to America, 63–5; of emigrants from Europe to America, 152–5; convenience of easy, an essential in iron production, 208; *see also* Shipping, Ships

Transported convicts, Delaware legislation provides against importation of, 195

Traveller's Magazine, The, 257 *n*

Travels into North America (1772), by Peter Kalm, 116 *n* and *passim*

Travels through the Middle Settlements of North America, 1759–1760 (1775), by Andrew Burnaby, 40 *n* and *passim*

Treason: the punishment of, in Connecticut, 91, 92 *n;* the crime of, and the Pennsylvania charter, 165; *see also* Rebellion

Treasurer, the colonial: the election of, in Rhode Island, 67; in Connecticut, 83; the Assembly and the control of the office of, in New York, 120–1; in Pennsylvania, 176

Treasurer, the town, of Connecticut, the election and duties of, 86

Treat, Colonel Robert, Governor of Connecticut, addresses King William, 96

Trees: the shade, of New York City streets, 115; the value of, in England, to the iron trade, 208–13; for cord wood, 212; *see also* Cedar, Forests, Lumber, Oak, Pine, Timber, White pine, Wood

Trepassey, Newfoundland, and the colonizing activities of Sir William Vaughan, 249

Triangular trade, the: of Massachusetts Bay, 16–17; of Rhode Island, 62–6; and of Newfoundland, 251, 254

Trinity, Newfoundland, a garrison stationed at, 251

Troops, the, provincial: of New Hampshire, 49; of New York, the Assembly control over, 121; of Delaware, sent to the West Indies, 196; indentured servants among, 196; and Newfoundland garrisons, 250–1; problems resulting from the withdrawal of, from Newfoundland after 1765, 264 *n*

Trumbull, Jonathan (later Governor of Connecticut), of the firm of Williams,

Trumbull, Jonathan (*continued*)
Trumbull and Pitkin, 75 *n;* refuses the Connecticut London agency, 99

Truro, England, the early interest of, in the cod fisheries, 250 *n*

Trustees of the loan office, in Pennsylvania, control of, by the Assembly, 176

Turpentine, premiums on American-made, 220

Tyng, Jonathan, the "million" land purchase of, from the Indians, 48

Ulster County, New York: land grants within, 143; and the Delaware Company Indian grant, 144

Ulster, Presbyterians, *see* Ulster Scots

Ulster Scots, the: northern New Jersey and, 138–9; the strength of, in Pennsylvania, 150; the early use of, as indentured servants in Pennsylvania, 157; quality of, as indentured servants, 157; communities founded by, within Pennsylvania and the Lower Counties, 158; the hostility of, to the Indians, 158; resist the payment of quit-rents, 158; the distribution of, in Pennsylvania, 158–9; in Pennsylvania Assembly, 162; the strength of, in Delaware, 202–3; the contribution of, to English colonial civilization, 281

Ulstermen, *see* Ulster Scots

Unappropriated lands, the, of New Hampshire, 46–8

Ungranted lands, the, of New Jersey, 138–42

Union, the act of, of 1682 between the Province of Pennsylvania and the Lower Counties on the Delaware, 186, 187–8; provisos of Delaware representatives on, 188

Unitarians, legislation against, in Connecticut, 80 *n*, 86, 95

Unitas Fratrum, see Moravian Brethren

United States Supreme Court, the, and the gold clause decision of 1935, 12 *n*

University of Pennsylvania, 170

Unmarried people, the payment of a special tax in Pennsylvania by, 173

Updike family, the, of Newport, Rhode Island, 66

Upland (Chester), Pennsylvania, *see* Chester

Utrecht, the Treaty of, and the French rights in Newfoundland, 249–51, 261

Van Cortlandt Manor, quit-rents of, 105 *n*

Van Cortlandts, the, among the New York aristocracy, 109

Van Dyck, John, Sheriff of New Castle County, Delaware, 202 *n*

Van Gesin, Essex County, New Jersey, the dispute over the, lands, 139

Van Rensselaers, the, among the New York aristocracy, 109

Vaughan, Sir William, the attempt of, to settle at Trepassey, Newfoundland, 249

Vernon, William, a leading Rhode Island merchant, 58; owner of the slaver, *Cassada Garden,* 64

Verplancks, the, among the New York aristocracy, 110

Vessels, *see* Ships

Veto, the: of legislation by the Governor, in Massachusetts Bay, 30; in Rhode Island and Connecticut, 74; in New York, 124; in New Jersey, 131; power of, possessed by most colonial Governors, 278

Vice-admiralty court: inability of the Massachusetts Bay Assembly to erect a, 30; Shirley appointed Advocate General of the, 33; the powers of the, extended to protect the white-pine belt, 42; records of cases brought before the, of Rhode Island, 60–1; the extension of the powers of the judge of, in Newfoundland, 262–3

Virginia: and the production of flour, 4; export from, of staples to Massachusetts Bay, 15; and the county office of King's attorney, 90 *n;* the early interest of, in the iron industry, 215; the promotion of iron production in, by Spotswood, 216; the importance of the pig iron of, 216; inducements offered by the government of, for opening up ironworks, 216; and the purchase of English wrought iron, 222; the exportation of pig iron to England from, 226; the government of, 276; the religious establishment of, 282; disabilities of Roman Catholics in, 283; western charter limits of, 286

Voting, *see* Elections, Franchise

Voyage to Hudson's Bay by the Dobbs Galley and California in the years 1746 and 1747 for Discovering a Northwest Passage, A (1749) by Henry Ellis, 232 *n,* 244

Voyages and Travels (1808–14), by John Pinkerton, 209 *n*

Wager, Sir Charles, First Lord of the Admiralty: Governor Morris reports to, on the ignorance of New Jersey legislators, 146 *n;* supports the Northwest Passage search, 243

Wainwright, John, of Ipswich, Massachusetts Bay, the attempt to dock lands entailed by, 30 *n*

Waldo, Samuel, Maine land speculator, applies for lands for London merchants, 19 *n*

Waldron, Major Richard: dismissed from the New Hampshire Council, 52; Speaker of the Assembly and Wentworth opponent, 52

Wales: the shifting of iron-smelting to the forests of, 209; the idleness of the forges in, 214

Walking, penalty for idle, on the Sabbath in Connecticut, 93

Wallingford, Connecticut: the population of, 74 *n;* the rating of, for taxation, 74 *n*

Walpole, Robert, Arthur Dobbs seeks the influence of, 243

Walsall, England, the iron manufacturers of, petition for a bounty on American iron, 228

Waltons, the, among the New York aristocracy, 109

Wampum, the making of, at Albany, New York, 119

Wanton, Joseph, deputy collector of customs at Newport, Rhode Island, and smuggling, 59–60

War: the, of the Austrian Succession, Delaware supports the prosecution of, 196; the Pennsylvania Assembly fails to support, 196–7; of the Spanish Succession and Avalon, 268; the Great, for the Empire, the effect of, on the New Jersey currency problem, 135; Delaware participates in, 197; of the Austrian Succession delays the regulation of the American iron industry, 223, 224; *see also* King George's War

Ward family, the, of Newport, Rhode Island, 66; as a political faction, 67 *n*

Ward, Richard, Governor of Rhode Island, defends the policy of currency inflation, 71

Ware, Captain, on the high value placed upon New Jersey bills of credit, 133

Warehouses, in Boston, 7

Warning out, the, of strangers in Connecticut, 85; penalties for disobeying, 95

Warren, Admiral Sir Peter, of the British navy: leadership of the Louisbourg expedition by, 34; supports de Lancey at court, 124 n

Warwick County, England, the waste and destruction of woodland in, 210

Warwick, Rhode Island, shares in the "banks" allotted to, 68–73

Water bailiff, the, in Connecticut, the sheriff's powers as, 90 n

Water power, an essential in the production of iron in 1750, 208

Watson, Admiral Charles, Governor of Newfoundland, 259, 261 n

Watts family, the, among the New York aristocracy, 109

Wawayanda Patent, the, New York, 103; the creation of, 104 n; a plating mill within, 117

Wealth of Great Britain in the Ocean, The, (1749), 250 n

Weekly Rehearsal, The, Boston news sheet, 27

Welles, Samuel, a key figure in shaping Massachusetts Bay legislation, 32

Welsh Baptists, the strength of the, in Pennsylvania, 158; in Delaware, 203 n

Welsh Tract, the, in Delaware, 201

Welshmen: as immigrants in Pennsylvania, 157; in Delaware, 187; of Quaker persuasion in Delaware, 202; of the Anglican and Baptist faiths in New Castle County, Delaware, 203 n; the contribution of, to English colonial civilization, 281

Wentworth, Benning, Governor of New Hampshire: purchases the post of Surveyor General of His Majesty's Woods, 43; protects the New Hampshire lumbering interests, 44; plans for the future of New Hampshire, 48; lays out new townships on the upper Connecticut, 49–50; disputes with the Assembly over the representation of the newer towns, 48–9; secures permission to grant lands upon a quit-rent basis, 49; the land policy of, in the valley of the upper Connecticut, 49–51, 105; establishes a family government, 51–2; overrides opposition, 52

Wentworth, John, Lieutenant Governor

Wentworth, John (continued)
of New Hampshire, the father of Benning and Mark Hunking Wentworth, 51

Wentworth, John, Governor of New Hampshire, and son of Mark Hunking Wentworth, on the harvesting of white-pine trees, 39–40, 51 n

Wentworth, Mark Hunking, brother of Governor Benning Wentworth, contractor for the royal navy, 42 n, 43, 51

Wentworth, William, of Exeter, New Hampshire, founder of the Wentworth family in America, 51

Wentworth family, the, and New Hampshire, 44, 51–3; the early history of, in New Hampshire, 51–2

Wentworth "Letter Books," 40 n

West, Daniel, describes Boston in 1720, 4

West Countrymen, and the Newfoundland Banks, 250, 252, 253, 272

West Indies, the British: and trade relations with Massachusetts Bay, 15–17, 251; with Rhode Island, 58–65; with Connecticut, 76–7; with New York, 116–17; with New Jersey, 127; with Pennsylvania, 173; with England in wrought iron, 222; with the northern colonies in beaver hats, 239; with Newfoundland in fish, 251; activities of the Moravians in, 282; high concentration of Negroes in, 285; severity of slave codes in, 285; economic rivalry between the French West Indies and, 287; failure of efforts of, to prohibit trade between the foreign sugar islands and the northern colonies, 288–9; see also Antigua, Barbados, Jamaica, Leeward Islands, Montserrat, Nevis, St. Christopher

West Indies, French: illicit sugar and molasses trade of New England merchants with, 16, 59–62, 77; economic rivalry between the British West Indies and, 287; fertility of, 287; sales of molasses of, to northern British colonies, 287; see also Guadeloupe, Martinique, St. Domingue (Hispaniola)

West Jersey Society, the tract of the, in Hunterdon County, New Jersey, 140

West New Jersey: characterized, 137; the Quaker influence dominant in, 137

Westbrook, Colonel, contracts for New England masts, 43

Westenhook, Massachusetts Bay, the people of, and Livingston Manor, 106

Westerly, Rhode Island: the Sabbatarian centre at, 56; a share in the "banks" allotted to, 68–73

Western Charter, the, for the regulation of the Newfoundland fisheries, 260 n

"Wet" fishing, the early practice of, on the Newfoundland Banks, 253 n

Wethersfield, Connecticut: commercial firm of Williams, Trumbull, and Pitkin established at, 75 n; Elisha Williams as deputy for, 99 n

Weymouth, England: the early interest of, in the cod fisheries, 250 n; in the Newfoundland salmon fisheries, 255

Whale fins, brought out of Hudson Bay in 1748, 233

Whales: the interest of Massachusetts Bay in fishing for, 18; financial return from, in Newfoundland, 255

Wheat: an inadequate supply of, in Massachusetts Bay, 15; the menace of the barberry rust to, 15, 87; a Connecticut export, 76; a staple in New York, 117; the abundance of, in New Jersey, 127; and in Pennsylvania, 166; the export of, from Philadelphia, 166 n

Whipping: in the Connecticut codes of 1650 and 1750, 91, 92, 93; and the Duke of York laws, 163; and the New Castle code, 164–5

Whipple, Joseph, a leading Rhode Island merchant, 58

White, Richard, Hudson's Bay Company factor, the testimony of, regarding the fur trade, 234

White cedar trees, see Cedar

White-pine trees: the protection to, under the Massachusetts Bay charter of 1691, 31; of New Hampshire, 39–44, 52–3; the ship-timber industry and the, 40–3; the protection of the, 41–4, 275; and New Jersey, 127

Whitefield, George, and the Great Awakening in Massachusetts Bay, 23; in New Hampshire, 51

Whitehaven, England, petition supporting Arthur Dobbs's attack on the Hudson's Bay Company from, 245

White-Marsh, Pennsylvania, the lime of, 170 n

Wigs, the wearing of, in Pennsylvania, 171

Wild-cat skins, the number of, brought out of Hudson Bay in 1748, 233

Wilkinson, Philip, a leading Rhode Island merchant, 58; the interest of, in slaving, 59, 63, 65

Wilkinson, Philip, and Company, owners of the Charming Polly, and other slave ships, 59, 63, 65 n

Wilks, Francis, London merchant, takes over the Connecticut London agency, 98

William III, encourages industry in Ireland, 211

William Alexander "Papers," 106 n

William and Mary, charter granted to Massachusetts Bay by, 29

William and Mary College, and higher education in America, 280

Williams, Colonel Elisha, assumes the London agency of Connecticut, 99; the early career of, 99 n

Williams, Captain Griffith: on the advantages enjoyed by the French in the cod fisheries, 249–50; on the difficulties of the "wet" cod fishery, 253 n; on the value of the Newfoundland fisheries, 254; on the lawlessness of the Irish settlers in Newfoundland, 264 n; author of An Account of the Island of Newfoundland with the Nature of its Trade (1765)

Williams, Josiah, a member of the Council of Massachusetts Bay, 36

Williams, Roger, and soul liberty, 55

Williams, Trumbull, & Pitkin, the mercantile establishments of, in Connecticut, 75 n

Wilmington, Delaware: description of, in 1750, 201; growing importance of, as a shipping centre, 201–2; shipbuilding at, 202; borough charter of, 202

Wilmington, The, first ocean-going vessel built at Wilmington, Delaware, 202, 203 n

Windham County, Connecticut: and iron production, 77; meetings of freemen in, 83 n

Windsor, Connecticut, the rating of, for taxation, 75 n

Windward Islands, West Indies, and Rhode Island trade, 59

Wine: the drinking of, regulated in Connecticut, 91, 95; the seizing of a cargo of, 60

Winnipeg River, the, French post of Fort Maurepas on, 234, 246

Winthrop, John, son of Wait Winthrop, grandson of the first Governor of Connecticut, as administrator of his father's estate, appeals to the Crown against the colony's intestacy law, 98 n

Winthrop, Major-General Fitz-John, Governor of Connecticut: goes to England to protect the charter, 96; opposes the commission of Governor Fletcher, 96-7

Winthrop, Major-General Wait, the estate of, involved in the appeal from the Connecticut intestacy law, 97, 98, 98 n

Witchcraft: in Massachusetts Bay, 22; revision of the capital law against, in Connecticut, 91

Wolf skins, the trapping for, in Newfoundland, 255

Wolverhampton, England: unemployment at the ironworks of, 214; the iron manufacturers of, desire a bounty on American iron, 228; petition from, in support of Arthur Dobbs's attack on the Hudson's Bay Company, 245

Wolverine skins, brought out of Hudson Bay in 1748, 233

Women, of Pennsylvania, Mittelberger's description of the, 172; the tax upon unmarried, 173

Wood: the importance of, to the production of iron in England, 208-13; the wastage of England's resources of, in iron production, 209; the shortage of, in England, 211; the value of, for cordage, 212; hauling of, in Newfoundland, 252; see also Cedar, Forests, Lumber, Oak, Pine, Timber

Woodbridge, New Jersey, the New England background of, 137

Woodbury, Connecticut, the rating of, for taxation, 75 n

Woodenware, see Barrel staves

Wool, the export of colonial, forbidden by Parliament, 274

Woolen goods: the production of domestic, in New York, 117; the high employment rate in the English production of, 207; hose and yarn products of, exempt from Swedish duties, 220 n; a bill to promote the exportation of, 222-3; importation from England of, by Newfoundland, 255; the export of colonial, forbidden by Parliament, 274

Woolen Act of 1698, places restrictions on colonial activities, 274, 291

Worcester County, Massachusetts Bay: population and agricultural statistics of, 15; slave population of, 16; number of towns within, 19 n

Worcestershire, England: source of iron ore supply for furnaces of, 208; the waste of the woods of, 210; the rise of the iron industry within, 210; and the making of nails, 215; petitions for relief by the ironmasters and ironmongers of, 220-1

Work-houses, the maintenance of, in Delaware by county taxes, 200 n

Workmen, the prohibition against the carrying away of, from Newfoundland, 258

Wrought iron, earlier and later methods of producing, 208; the amount of, shipped to the New World, 222

Württemberg (Würtemberg), the unhappy lot in Pennsylvania of immigrants from, 153

Wyoming Valley, the Susquehanna Company formed to colonize, 76

Yale College: a New England cultural centre, 27, 28; Ezra Stiles becomes the president of, 67; exemption from train bands of personnel connected with, 88; and higher education in America, 280

Yards (yard-arms), premiums on American-produced, by Parliament, 42, 220, 291

York, James Stuart, Duke of, later James II: the royal patent of, to Delaware of 1664, 184 n, 185 n; deeds of lease and release from, to Penn, 185; lack of legal transfer of territory to Penn by, 185-6; relationship of, to Penn, 198; early Delaware quit-rents payable to, 199 n

York County, Massachusetts Bay, slave population of, 16

York County, Maine, the number of towns within, 19 n

York County, Pennsylvania: the creation of, and the racial complexion of, 158; the representation of, in the Assembly, 161; the amount of excise raised in, 174

York Fort: the most important of the Hudson's Bay Company factories and posts, 231-2, 235 n; a description of,

York, Fort: (*continued*)
in 1750, 232; Indian barter at, 234; members of the Dobbs expedition winter at, 244 *n*

Yorke, Philip, Attorney General, gives an opinion on the grievances against the Massachusetts Bay Church Establishment, 22 *n*

Yorkshire, England, hæmatite ore used by the furnaces of, 208

Zinzendorf, Nicholaus Lewis, Count, of Herrnhut, Saxony, Moravian Bishop, the sermons of, banned in the Electorate of Hanover, 152

A NOTE ON THE AUTHOR

Lawrence Henry Gipson is Research Professor of History, Emeritus, at Lehigh University. He was born in Greeley, Colorado, and at an early age went to live in Idaho. After being graduated from the University of Idaho, he entered Oxford as the first Rhodes Scholar from the state of Idaho. Later he was called to three institutions for the purpose of bringing into existence departments of history and government: the College of Idaho, Wabash College, and Lehigh University. He received his doctorate at Yale, and his thesis, under the title Jared Ingersoll: A Study in American Loyalism in Relation to British Colonial Government, *was published in the Yale Historical Series and was thereupon awarded the Justin Winsor prize by the American Historical Association. Professor Gipson has subsequently published many books and articles on historical topics and has received many distinctions. In 1951 he was elected to the Harold Vyvyan Harmsworth Chair in American History at Oxford. Since his return to America the following year Professor Gipson has given his undivided attention to the completion of his series* The British Empire before the American Revolution, *and to the revision of its first three volumes. He is currently serving as President of the Conference on British Studies.*

A NOTE ON THE TYPE

This book is set in Linotype Caledonia. Caledonia belongs to the family of printing types called "modern face" by printers—a term used to mark the change in style of type-letters that occurred about 1800. Caledonia is in the general neighborhood of Scotch Modern in design, but is more freely drawn than that letter.

The book was designed by W. A. Dwiggins and composed by Publishers' Composition Service, Inc., Brattleboro, Vermont. Printed and bound by The Plimpton Press, Norwood, Massachusetts. Paper manufactured by S. D. Warren Co., Boston.